BREAKING THROUGH

A BUSINESS NOVEL

(based on the theory of constraints)

BREAKING THROUGH

A BUSINESS NOVEL

(based on the theory of constraints)

Subba Rao Chaganti

Pharma Med PRESS
An Imprint of BSP Books Pvt. Ltd.

™ **PharmaMed Press**

An imprint of BSP Books Pvt. Ltd.
4-4-309/316, Giriraj Lane,
Sultan Bazar, Hyderabad - 500 001,
Telangana, India.

Breaking Through: A Business Novel (based on the theory of constraints)

by Subba Rao Chaganti

Published by

™ **PharmaMed Press**

An imprint of BSP Books Pvt. Ltd.
4-4-309/316, Giriraj Lane, Sultan Bazar, Hyderabad - 500 001,
Telangana, India.
Phone: 040-23445688
E-mail: info@pharmamedpress.net
www.bspbooks.net/www.pharmamedpress.net

ISBN:978-93-47311-49-9 (Paperback)

Disclaimer

This book is a work of fiction inspired by real-world dynamics, themes, and scenarios from the pharmaceutical industry. While it aims to authentically portray challenges and innovations in pharma marketing, branding, and sales, all characters, companies, and situations are either the author's creations or used illustratively in a fictionalized context.

References to actual pharmaceutical companies, products, executives, or institutions are provided solely for context and realism. These references do not imply endorsement, criticism, or affiliation. Any comparisons drawn with existing organizations or individuals are presented in good faith to illustrate broader industry trends and practices. Statements regarding outperforming certain companies or practices are not intended as factual or defamatory assertions, but rather as fictionalized expressions of character viewpoints within the narrative.

Where real names or events appear, they are used under the principles of fair use—specifically for commentary, education, and industry analysis.

The author and publisher disclaim any liability or responsibility for actions taken or decisions made based on the contents of this work. The ideas and practices described herein are not substitutes for professional advice, regulatory guidance, or compliance consultation.

This manuscript has been developed with the aid of AI-powered tools to assist in drafting, structuring, and refining the narrative. These tools have been used under human authorship and editorial oversight, and the author remains fully accountable for the final content.

All efforts have been made to ensure factual accuracy where data, trends, or metrics are referenced. However, the book is not intended as a technical guide or definitive industry manual, and readers are encouraged to consult primary sources and professional expertise for operational decision-making.

Primary Characters

- **Dr. Arjun Malhotra**: Protagonist, scientist-entrepreneur with vision
- **Priya Sharma**: Co-founder, analytical chemist, eventual successor
- **Ravi Krishnan**: Veteran production manager, process optimization expert
- **Dr. Meera Patel**: Regulatory affairs head, compliance champion
- **Kavita Desai**: Marketing director, brand building strategist
- **Rajesh Khanna**: CFO, financial engineering expert
- **Dr. Vikram Singh**: Manufacturing head, quality systems builder
- **Dr. Sarah Williams**: M&A specialist, integration expert
- **Dr. Lisa Chen**: R&D head, innovation driver

Supporting Characters:

- **Suresh Aggarwal**: Distribution partner
- **James Mitchell**: International quality consultant
- **Rohit Malhotra**: Son, next generation leader
- **Amit Patel**: CIO, digital transformation leader

Acknowledgements

Writing *Breaking Through* has been a journey of discovery, constraint identification, and breakthrough thinking—much like the story it tells. This book would not have been possible without the support, insights, and encouragement of many remarkable individuals who helped transform an ambitious idea into the reality you hold in your hands.

First and foremost, I extend my deepest gratitude to Anil Shah, whose vision as a publisher brought this project to life. Anil's belief in the power of business storytelling and his commitment to bringing fresh insights to the pharmaceutical industry made this book possible. His guidance through the complex world of publishing proved invaluable, and his patience with an author learning to navigate new constraints was extraordinary.

I am equally grateful to Nikunjesh Shah, whose expertise in digital publishing has made this book accessible to readers worldwide. In an era where knowledge must transcend geographical boundaries, Nikunjesh's commitment to making *Breaking Through* available in digital formats ensures that its insights can reach pharmaceutical professionals, entrepreneurs, and students across the globe. His understanding of how digital transformation applies to publishing mirrors the very themes explored in this book.

Special recognition goes to Naresh Daver and the entire team at PharmaMedPress for their exceptional work in designing this book. Their attention to detail, understanding of pharmaceutical industry aesthetics, and commitment to excellence transformed a manuscript into a professional publication worthy of its ambitious subject matter.

The story of Dr. Arjun Malhotra and his journey through pharmaceutical constraints draws from countless conversations with industry leaders, entrepreneurs, scientists, and professionals who generously shared their experiences. While the characters in this book are fictional, the insights they embody come from real people who have faced real challenges in building pharmaceutical enterprises. Their willingness to share both successes and failures provided the authentic foundation upon which this story rests.

I am particularly grateful to the pharmaceutical entrepreneurs across India, the United States, Europe, and other regions who opened their doors, shared their stories, and helped me understand the nuanced challenges of building companies in this complex industry. Their experiences with regulatory hurdles, manufacturing challenges, innovation decisions, and market dynamics provided the raw material from which the Theory of Constraints framework could be meaningfully applied to pharmaceuticals.

The regulatory professionals, quality experts, manufacturing specialists, and research scientists who contributed their technical knowledge ensured that the book's pharmaceutical content remained accurate and relevant. Their insights helped bridge the gap between business strategy and technical execution, making the constraint-based approach practical and actionable for industry professionals.

Above all, I am profoundly grateful to my family, whose support and understanding made this intensive writing project possible. To my beloved spouse, Mahalakshmi, whose unwavering encouragement and patience during the long hours of research and writing kept me grounded and motivated. Her wisdom, perspective, and gentle corrections helped shape both the content and tone of this book. She understood, perhaps better than anyone, the constraints that writers face and helped me break through them.

To my children and their spouses—Srinivasa Phanindra, Geetha, Lavanya, Satya Sankara Aditya, Sowmya, and Chaitanya—who provided not only emotional support but also valuable feedback from their diverse professional perspectives. Their questions, challenges, and insights helped ensure that the book would resonate with readers across different backgrounds and industries.

Their own professional achievements in various fields provided constant inspiration and reminded me that constraint-based thinking applies far beyond pharmaceuticals.

To my grandchildren—Aditi, Eesha, Surya, and Shriya—who may not yet understand the business concepts in this book but whose curiosity, energy, and fresh perspectives reminded me daily of the importance of continuous learning and breakthrough thinking. They represent the next generation of leaders who will face their own constraints and must learn to break through them. This book is written with the hope that the systematic thinking it promotes will help create a better world for them to inherit.

Writing about family businesses and succession planning while being surrounded by multiple generations of achievers provided constant reminders that the most important constraints we face are often the ones we impose on ourselves. My family helped me understand that breakthrough thinking begins with breakthrough relationships—with colleagues, partners, and most importantly, with those who share our journey through life.

The pharmaceutical industry faces unprecedented challenges in the coming decades, from aging populations to emerging diseases, from regulatory complexity to innovation imperatives. The solutions will require not just technical expertise but systematic thinking about how to identify and eliminate the constraints that limit our collective ability to improve human health.

If this book contributes even modestly to that effort—if it helps one pharmaceutical company operate more efficiently, brings one life-saving medicine to market faster, or inspires one entrepreneur to pursue breakthrough innovation—then the efforts of everyone acknowledged here will have been worthwhile.

The constraint, as Dr. Malhotra learns, is not in our circumstances but in our thinking. I am grateful to everyone who helped me think more clearly about the pharmaceutical industry's constraints and the systematic approaches that can help us break through them.

To all who contributed to this journey—publishers, designers, industry professionals, and family members—thank you for helping transform an idea into impact. The breakthrough belongs to all of us.

Subba Rao Chaganti

Preface

Twenty-five years ago, Eliyahu Goldratt's groundbreaking novel *The Goal* revolutionized how we think about organizational improvement and systems thinking. Through the compelling story of plant manager Alex Rogo, Goldratt introduced the world to the Theory of Constraints—a management philosophy that has since transformed industries ranging from manufacturing to software development. Yet one sector remained largely unexplored through this lens: the complex, regulated, and increasingly vital world of pharmaceuticals.

Breaking Through was born from a simple observation: the pharmaceutical industry, with its intricate web of research and development, regulatory hurdles, manufacturing complexities, and global distribution challenges, represents perhaps the ultimate testing ground for constraint-based thinking. This book applies Goldratt's revolutionary framework to an industry where the stakes couldn't be higher—where breakthrough innovations can save millions of lives, and where a single constraint can delay life-saving medicines by years.

Dr. Arjun Malhotra is not a real person, but his journey is profoundly real. He is a composite character, carefully crafted from the experiences, challenges, and triumphs of dozens of pharmaceutical entrepreneurs who have built remarkable companies across the globe. From the garage laboratories of Hyderabad to the boardrooms of Mumbai, from the regulatory corridors of Washington D.C. to the manufacturing floors of São Paulo, Malhotra's story weaves together the authentic experiences of visionary leaders who have navigated the pharmaceutical industry's unique constraints.

In researching this book, I spent countless hours with entrepreneurs, scientists, regulators, and industry veterans across six continents. I sat with founders who mortgaged their homes to fund their first clinical trials, with regulatory affairs professionals who spent decades mastering the Byzantine approval processes of different countries, and with manufacturing experts who built world-class facilities from scratch. Each conversation revealed new dimensions of how constraints shape and reshape the pharmaceutical landscape.

The Indian pharmaceutical industry serves as our primary backdrop not by accident, but by design. Over the past three decades, Indian companies have evolved from small-scale generic manufacturers to global innovators, creating some of the world's most successful pharmaceutical enterprises. This transformation—from constraint-bound local players to constraint-breaking global leaders—perfectly illustrates the principles that drive all successful organizational evolution.

Yet this book is not about India alone. The constraints that Malhotra encounters—from working capital limitations to regulatory complexity, from talent acquisition to innovation investment— are universal challenges that pharmaceutical companies face whether they're based in Boston, Basel, or Bangalore. The solutions he discovers, the strategic choices he makes, and the organizational transformations he leads offer lessons applicable to any pharmaceutical enterprise, anywhere in the world.

Breaking Through follows the same narrative structure that made *The Goal* so powerful: a business novel that entertains while it educates. But where Goldratt's protagonist dealt with machines and manufacturing processes, Malhotra grapples with molecules and market access, clinical trials and competitive dynamics. The pharmaceutical industry's constraints are often more subtle, more interconnected, and certainly more regulated than those in traditional manufacturing, making the application of constraint-based thinking both more challenging and more rewarding.

Each chapter of Malhotra's journey corresponds to a different type of constraint that pharmaceutical companies typically encounter as they grow and evolve. The "Genesis Constraint" of limited capital gives way to the "Scale Constraint" of achieving critical mass, which eventually transforms into the "Growth Constraint" of sustainable expansion.

As companies mature, they face the "Complexity Constraint" of managing diverse portfolios and global operations, before ultimately confronting the "Innovation Constraint" of moving beyond imitation to genuine value creation. Finally, successful pharmaceutical entrepreneurs must navigate the "Legacy Constraint"—how to build organizations that outlast their founders. This progression is not merely theoretical. It represents the actual evolution that successful pharmaceutical companies undergo, with each phase demanding different strategic responses and organizational capabilities. By understanding these constraints and their sequential nature, pharmaceutical leaders can anticipate challenges, prepare solutions, and make more informed strategic decisions.The characters surrounding Malhotra—from Priya Sharma, the analytical chemist who becomes his co-founder and eventual successor, to the supporting cast of production managers, regulatory experts, and marketing professionals—represent the diverse talents required to build a successful pharmaceutical enterprise. Their interactions and conflicts illustrate how different functional perspectives on constraints can either align to drive breakthrough performance or clash to create organizational paralysis.

The technical aspects of pharmaceutical development, manufacturing, and commercialization have been carefully researched and authentically portrayed. However, the goal is not to provide a technical manual for pharmaceutical development, but rather to demonstrate how constraint-based thinking can be applied to even the most complex and regulated industries. Readers without pharmaceutical backgrounds will find the story accessible and engaging, while industry veterans will recognize the authenticity of the challenges and the practicality of the solutions.

As our global healthcare systems face unprecedented challenges—from aging populations to emerging diseases, from rising costs to access inequities—the need for more efficient, effective pharmaceutical companies has never been greater. The constraint-based approach offers a powerful framework for addressing these challenges, not through wishful thinking or generic best practices, but through systematic identification and elimination of the specific bottlenecks that limit organizational performance.

Breaking Through is ultimately a story about human potential—about how individuals and organizations can transcend their apparent limitations by understanding and addressing their true constraints. It's about the courage to make difficult strategic choices, the wisdom to focus resources on what matters most, and the persistence to continue improving even when success seems sufficient.

In a world where pharmaceutical innovation can literally mean the difference between life and death, the stakes of getting organizational design right could not be higher. This book offers a roadmap for pharmaceutical leaders who aspire not just to build successful companies, but to create organizations capable of delivering breakthrough innovations that genuinely improve human health.

The journey begins, as it did for so many real pharmaceutical entrepreneurs, in a modest laboratory with unlimited dreams and severely constrained resources. How those constraints are identified, understood, and systematically eliminated determines whether those dreams remain fantasies or become the foundation for enterprises that serve millions of patients worldwide.

Welcome to the story of *Breaking Through.*

Subba Rao Chaganti

TOC in Pharmaceuticals

The pharmaceutical industry, they told me, was different.

When I discussed about applying Goldratt's theory of constaints to the pharmaceutical industry in a book project with some of my colleagues, they were skeptical. They told me that the theory of constraints works beautifully in manufacturing, but pharmaceuticals? That's a whole different animal. The regulations alone would crush your systematic approach.

I should have known better than to accept such a sweeping statement. After all, how many times had I heard similar proclamations? "TOC doesn't work in service industries." "TOC doesn't work in complex projects." "TOC doesn't work when you're dealing with creative processes."

Each time, reality proved the skeptics wrong.

But I'll admit, when I first heard about Dr. Arjun Malhotra's story, I was curious. Here was a man who had apparently built a global pharmaceutical empire using constraint-based thinking, yet he had never attended one of my seminars, never hired my consultancy services, never even read "The Goal" until his company was already generating hundreds of millions in revenue.

So how did he do it?

The answer, as you'll discover in this remarkable book, is both simple and profound: he intuitively understood what most business leaders struggle to grasp. That in any system—whether it's a manufacturing plant, a software company, or a pharmaceutical enterprise—there is always exactly one constraint that limits the performance of the entire system.

Always exactly one.

Not two. Not three. Not "it's complicated." One.

The genius of Arjun's approach wasn't that he eliminated constraints—that's impossible. The genius was that he systematically identified the current constraint, exploited it fully, elevated it when necessary, and then moved on to the next constraint that emerged.

Let me give you an example that illustrates this beautifully.

In his early days, Arjun's constraint was obvious: working capital. He had ₹50,000 and dreams that required millions. Most entrepreneurs in this situation do one of two things: they either give up, or they spend all their time trying to raise money.

Arjun did neither.

Instead, he asked a different question: "Given that working capital is my constraint, how can I maximize the throughput of my system?" His answer was to focus on products with the fastest cash conversion cycles. Not the most profitable products. Not the most innovative products. The products that could generate cash fastest.

This decision drove everything else: which formulations to develop first, which regulatory approvals to pursue, which markets to enter, which partnerships to form. Every decision was subordinated to the constraint.

The result? Within eighteen months, working capital was no longer his constraint. Cash flow was strong enough to fund growth. The constraint had shifted.

Now, here's where most entrepreneurs make their first major mistake. They assume that since they've solved the "money problem," they can now pursue any opportunity that looks attractive. They lose focus. They scatter their resources. They optimize local efficiencies instead of global throughput.

Arjun didn't fall into this trap. He immediately asked: "What's constraining my system now?"

The answer was production capacity. So he focused everything on maximizing throughput through his manufacturing constraint. Not by working faster—that leads to quality problems. Not by working longer hours—that leads to burnout. But by eliminating everything that prevented the constraint from running at full capacity.

He eliminated changeover times between products. He eliminated quality defects that required rework. He eliminated machine downtime through preventive maintenance. He eliminated the need for his constraint resource to do anything that could be done elsewhere.

The result? Production capacity was no longer his constraint. The constraint had shifted again.

This pattern continued for thirty years. Each time a constraint was elevated to the point where it was no longer limiting the system, a new constraint emerged. Market access became the constraint, so he built distribution partnerships. Quality compliance became the constraint, so he built world-class quality systems. Regulatory approval became the constraint, so he built the most efficient regulatory affairs capabilities in the industry.

What you're reading is not just a business success story. It's a case study in systematic thinking applied with remarkable consistency over three decades.

But here's what makes this story particularly valuable: Arjun didn't just apply constraint thinking to operations. He applied it to strategy.

When his constraint was competing with multinational corporations that had unlimited resources, he didn't try to match their spending. He identified their constraint: they were slow to respond to market changes because of their size and bureaucracy. So he built speed and agility into everything his company did.

When his constraint was credibility in international markets, he didn't try to fake it until he made it. He identified what global credibility required: quality standards that exceeded what anyone else was achieving. So he made quality his obsession, not just his goal.

When his constraint was innovation capability, he didn't try to build a traditional R&D department. He identified what innovation really required in pharmaceuticals: the ability to see connections that others missed. So he built a culture of systematic experimentation and learning.

Each strategic decision was driven by the same logic: identify the real constraint, exploit it fully, and subordinate everything else to that exploitation.

The results speak for themselves. A company that started in a garage now employs tens of thousands of people. Products that began as simple generic formulations have evolved into breakthrough biotechnology therapies. A business model that started with cost leadership has transformed into innovation leadership.

But perhaps the most impressive result is this: Arjun created a systematic approach to building a world-class enterprise that others can learn from and apply in their own industries.

That's the real value of this book. It's not just the story of one remarkable entrepreneur. It's a methodology that can be applied by anyone willing to think systematically about constraints.

As you read Arjun's story, pay attention to the pattern:

Identify the current constraint that's limiting your system's performance.

Exploit that constraint—make sure nothing prevents it from operating at full capacity.

Subordinate everything else to the decision to exploit the constraint.

Elevate the constraint when exploitation alone isn't sufficient.

Repeat the process with the new constraint that emerges.

This five-step process, applied consistently over time, is what transformed a garage laboratory into a global pharmaceutical enterprise. It's what can transform your business, your career, your industry.

The only question is: Are you ready to see your constraints differently?

Because once you start seeing constraints as opportunities rather than obstacles, everything changes.

Everything.

Subba Rao Chaganti

A Note from Arjun Malhotra, the Protagonist

The journey that led to this book began in 1995 with a desperate phone call to my wife, informing her that our family savings of ₹50 lakhs had been invested in what seemed like an impossible dream: competing against multinational pharmaceutical giants with nothing more than a rented facility in Hyderabad and an unshakeable belief that constraints could become competitive advantages. Thirty years later, as I prepare to hand over the CEO role of what has become a $4.7 billion global biotechnology company, I realize that every seemingly insurmountable obstacle we encountered was actually a catalyst for breakthrough innovation and systematic excellence.

This book chronicles the transformation of Malhotra Pharmaceuticals from a struggling generic manufacturer to a globally recognized leader in pharmaceutical innovation, but more fundamentally, it explores how any organization can convert limitations into competitive advantages through systematic constraint resolution. The inspiration for this approach came from Eliyahu Goldratt's seminal work, "The Goal: A Process of Ongoing Improvement," which introduced me to the Theory of Constraints—a management philosophy that would fundamentally reshape how I understood business limitations and competitive positioning.

Goldratt's insight that every system is limited by its weakest link provided the conceptual framework for understanding that pharmaceutical success required identifying and systematically resolving constraints rather than optimizing individual components. However, applying constraint theory to pharmaceutical development revealed complexities that traditional manufacturing approaches could not address: regulatory constraints that demanded years of systematic compliance building, innovation constraints that required breakthrough thinking beyond incremental improvement, and competitive constraints that forced us to develop capabilities that larger, resource-rich competitors could not easily replicate.

Each chapter of this book examines a specific constraint that could have terminated our pharmaceutical ambitions, while demonstrating how systematic constraint resolution created unexpected competitive advantages. The capital constraint of our early years forced operational efficiency that enabled competing against companies with unlimited resources. The knowledge constraint in biotechnology development led to systematic learning approaches that accelerated our innovation capabilities beyond what traditional pharmaceutical companies achieved through massive R&D investments. The scale constraint when competing against multinational corporations resulted in strategic focus that created market leadership in specialized therapeutic areas.

Perhaps most importantly, this book explores what I now recognize as the ultimate constraint in any entrepreneurial journey: the limitation of our own imagination about what was possible. Every breakthrough we achieved required first abandoning conventional thinking about what a mid-sized Indian pharmaceutical company could accomplish while competing against century-old multinational corporations with seemingly unlimited resources and established market relationships.

The pharmaceutical industry provides a particularly compelling context for constraint analysis because it combines regulatory complexity, scientific uncertainty, competitive intensity, and global market dynamics that create interconnected limitations demanding sophisticated resolution approaches. However, the principles and methodologies documented in these pages apply to any organization facing systematic constraints that prevent achieving optimal performance and competitive positioning.

This book is written for entrepreneurs who find themselves constrained by resources, established companies limited by legacy approaches, and leaders seeking systematic methodologies for converting business limitations into competitive advantages. The pharmaceutical transformation story provides specific examples and practical frameworks, but the underlying constraint resolution principles transcend industry boundaries and organizational types.

The Theory of Constraints taught me that business optimization requires identifying and resolving systematic limitations rather than improving individual components or functions. Thirty years of pharmaceutical constraint resolution have proven that this approach can create sustainable competitive advantages while enabling achievements that conventional thinking considers impossible. Organizations that master systematic constraint resolution discover that their greatest limitations become their most distinctive competitive advantages.

As you read this pharmaceutical transformation story, I encourage you to identify the constraints limiting your organization's performance and competitive positioning. The methodologies documented in these chapters provide systematic approaches to constraint resolution that can convert your greatest limitations into your most sustainable competitive advantages. The goal is not just to eliminate constraints, but to build organizational capabilities that enable continued excellence through systematic constraint resolution and competitive advantage creation.

The pharmaceutical journey from ₹50 lakhs to $4.7 billion demonstrates that systematic constraint resolution can create exponential value while building sustainable competitive advantages through limitation-driven innovation and strategic excellence. Your constraint resolution journey awaits, and your greatest limitations may become your most distinctive competitive advantages through systematic application of constraint theory principles and strategic constraint resolution methodologies.

Dr. Arjun Malhotra
Chief Innovation Officer
Malhotra Pharmaceuticals
Mumbai, January 2026

Prologue: TIME Magazine Cover Story

Mumbai, March 2024

The photographer wants me to hold a pill.

"Just a simple white tablet, Dr. Malhotra," she says, adjusting her lens. "Something that represents your journey."

I'm sitting in my office overlooking the Jio Garden in Bandra Kurla Complex in Mumbai, thirty years and six thousand miles from where this story began. Through the floor-to-ceiling windows, I can see our latest biotechnology facility—a gleaming testament to what happens when you refuse to accept limitations others call permanent.

But the photographer wants me to hold a pill.

I reach into my desk drawer and pull out a small white tablet. Paracetamol. The same formulation I developed in that cramped garage laboratory in Hyderabad in 1994, when my entire company consisted of me, a borrowed mixing machine, and the unshakeable belief that there had to be a better way.

"Perfect," the photographer says. "Now, can you tell me what that represents?"

How do you explain thirty years in a single answer?

That pill represents the moment I realized the pharmaceutical industry had a fundamental problem. Not a money problem, not a technology problem, not even a competition problem. A thinking problem.

Everyone was trying to solve the wrong constraint.

The multinational corporations were throwing billions at R&D, convinced that the next blockbuster drug would solve everything. The generic manufacturers were racing to the bottom on price, convinced that being the cheapest was the only way to win. The biotechnology startups were chasing the latest scientific breakthrough, convinced that innovation alone would guarantee success.

They were all wrong.

The real constraint wasn't what they were making—it was how they were thinking about what they were making.

"Dr. Malhotra?" the photographer prompts. "The pill?"

"This pill," I say, holding it up to catch the afternoon light streaming through the windows, "represents a question I asked myself thirty years ago: What if we stopped trying to compete with the big pharmaceutical companies and started thinking about constraints differently?"

The TIME magazine editor, Sarah Chen, leans forward in her chair. She has been taking notes throughout our three-hour conversation, filling page after page with what she calls "the most systematic business story" she's ever covered.

"Can you explain what you mean by thinking about constraints differently?" she asks.

I smile. It's the same question I've been answering for three decades, in boardrooms and laboratories, at industry conferences and university lectures. The question that led to everything we've built.

Sarah, when I started this company, everyone told me the same thing: 'Arjun, the pharmaceutical industry is too complex, too regulated, too competitive for a small Indian company to succeed globally.' They listed the challenges like they were reading from a textbook: regulatory barriers, capital requirements, quality standards, patent protections, distribution networks.

I pause, turning the pill over in my fingers.

"But here's what they missed: those weren't really constraints. Those were just the current rules of the game. The real constraint was something much more fundamental."

"Which was?"

"The industry's assumption that those rules couldn't be changed."

Through the windows, I can see our research teams walking between buildings, carrying samples of our latest biotechnology innovations. Monoclonal antibodies that will help treat cancer patients in rural India. A biosimilar insulin that will make diabetes management affordable for millions. Peptide therapies that major pharmaceutical companies said were too complex for a company like ours to develop.

Each of these breakthroughs started with the same question: What if the current limitation isn't really a limitation?

"Let me give you an example," I tell Sarah. "In 1996, our constraint was clear: we couldn't afford to build a world-class quality control laboratory. The equipment alone would have cost more than our entire annual revenue."

"So what did you do?"

We asked a different question. Instead of 'How do we afford the best laboratory?' we asked 'How do we achieve the best quality results?' The answer was partnering with testing facilities that had excess capacity. We received world-class quality analysis at a fraction of the cost, and they gained additional revenue from their underutilized equipment.

Sarah scribbles notes rapidly. "And that worked?"

"It did more than work. It taught us something profound: every constraint in business is really an opportunity to think differently about resource allocation."

I stand and walk to the window, looking out at the campus that now employs over 33,000 people. In the distance, I see the construction cranes working on our new drug discovery facility—a place where we're developing molecules that could transform treatment for diseases affecting billions of people.

Sarah, the pill in my hand symbolizes more than just paracetamol. It signifies the moment I understood that constraints aren't barriers to be endured—they're puzzles to be solved.

The photographer adjusts her equipment. "Can you look directly at the camera now?"

As I turn toward the lens, I think about the letter I received last week from a doctor in Bangladesh. Her patient, a ten-year-old boy with diabetes, had been unable to afford insulin for three months. Then our biosimilar insulin became available at one-tenth the previous cost. The boy's life was saved.

That's what this pill truly symbolizes. It's not just a business success story but evidence that systematic thinking about constraints can literally save lives.

"You know what's interesting about this whole journey?" I tell Sarah as the camera clicks. "The biggest challenge we thought was—competing with multinational corporations with hundred-year head starts and billion-dollar budgets—turned out to be the challenge that taught us the most."

"How so?"

"Because it forced us to get good at something they were terrible at: moving fast and changing direction when the constraint shifted."

The pharmaceutical giants were designed for stability, not agility. They excelled at making small improvements within established systems. But when the constraints changed—such as when quality requirements shifted, new markets opened, or technology disrupted traditional methods—they found it hard to adapt.

We built our entire culture around adapting to constraint changes.

"Is that why you've been successful in so many different areas?" Sarah asks. "Generics, biotechnology, drug discovery—most companies specialize."

Most companies believe that specialization means concentrating on what they produce. We believe that specialization is about focusing on how you think about what you create.

I return to my desk and pick up a folder containing our latest pipeline report. Forty-three products in various stages of development. Everything from simple generic formulations to breakthrough gene therapies. To an outside observer, it might look scattered, unfocused.

But there's a pattern. Each product represents a solution to a specific constraint in the global healthcare system. High costs, Limited access, Inadequate efficacy, Poor patient compliance, Complex manufacturing.

"The real secret," I tell Sarah, "isn't that we learned to solve constraints better than our competitors. It's what we learned to see constraints that our competitors couldn't see."

The photographer packs up her equipment, satisfied with the shots. Sarah closes her notebook.

One last question, Dr. Malhotra. If you had to give advice to someone starting a business in a complex, regulated industry like pharmaceuticals, what would you tell them?

I look at the paracetamol tablet still resting in my palm. Such a simple thing. White, round, weighing less than a gram. Yet it changed everything for us.

"I'd tell them to start by identifying their first real constraint. Not the obvious one that everyone talks about. The real one that's actually limiting their system's performance. Then I'd tell them to fall in love with that constraint."

"Fall in love with it?"

"Because that constraint is going to teach them everything they need to know about building a systematic approach to business growth. It's going to show them how to think about resource allocation, priority setting, process optimization, and strategic planning."

I place the pill back in my desk drawer.

"Most importantly, it's going to teach them that every constraint they overcome makes them stronger for the next constraint they'll face. In thirty years, we've probably encountered and solved several hundred different constraints. Each one prepared us for the next level of complexity."

As Sarah and the photographer leave, I remain at my desk, watching the sun set over Mumbai. Tomorrow, our team will begin clinical trials for a breakthrough therapy that could transform treatment for a rare genetic disease. Next month, we'll open our new manufacturing facility in Kenya, bringing affordable medications to East Africa for the first time.

Each of these initiatives began the same way: with someone identifying a constraint that others accepted as permanent, and asking the simple question that started everything.

What if it doesn't have to be this way?

That question, asked consistently over thirty years, is how you build something that matters.

That question is how you change the world, one constraint at a time.

Contents

PART VI: THE LEGACY CONSTRAINT (2023-2024)

APPENDICES

PART I: THE GENESIS CONSTRAINT (1994-1999)

Chapter 1

The Modest Beginning

Hyderabad, 1994

The resignation letter sat on my desk for three weeks before I found the courage to submit it.

Not because I was afraid of leaving Ranbaxy—I'd already made that decision. But because once I handed over that letter, there would be no more steady paycheck, no more company car, no more comfortable predictability of working for India's second-largest pharmaceutical company.

There would just be me, ₹50,000 in savings, and an idea that my wife Meera thought was either brilliant or insane. She hadn't decided which yet.

"You want to do what exactly?" she'd asked when I first explained my plan over dinner at our small apartment in Banjara Hills.

"Start a pharmaceutical company."

"With what money?"

"Our savings."

"All of it?"

"Well, not all of it. We need to keep enough for rent and groceries for at least six months."

She set down her fork and looked at me the way she looked at our three-year-old son when he announced he was going to fly to the moon using bedsheets as wings.

"Arjun, do you know how much it costs to start a pharmaceutical company?"

I did know, actually. That was the problem. According to every industry analysis I'd read, we needed at least ₹50 lakhs for basic equipment, another ₹25 lakhs for working capital, and probably ₹30 lakhs more for regulatory approvals and marketing. We had ₹50,000.

"I've been thinking about that," I told her. "What if we don't start the way everyone else starts?"

The conventional wisdom was clear: to compete in pharmaceuticals, you needed modern facilities, the latest equipment, established distribution networks, and deep pockets for regulatory battles. You needed to look like Cipla or Dr. Reddy's from day one, just smaller.

But watching Ranbaxy's operations for five years had taught me something interesting. Most of their expensive equipment sat idle 60% of the time. Most of their regulatory expertise was applied to routine approvals that followed predictable patterns. Most of their distribution muscle was used to push products that competed on features any competent chemist could replicate.

What if the real competitive advantage wasn't having the most sophisticated setup? What if it was using whatever setup you had more efficiently than anyone else?

The idea crystallized one afternoon when I was reviewing batch records for a paracetamol production run. Ranbaxy's state-of-the-art facility had produced 50,000 tablets in an eight-hour shift. The equipment was capable of 75,000 tablets in the same time, but changeover delays, quality checks, and minor adjustments had eaten up the difference.

I started calculating. If we could eliminate those inefficiencies—not by having better equipment, but by designing our entire process around minimizing downtime—we could match their effective output with much simpler machinery.

The math was encouraging. The logistics were terrifying.

I called my college roommate Priya Sharma, who'd been working as an analytical chemist at a testing laboratory in Pune.

"I'm thinking of starting a pharmaceutical company," I told her over a crackling long-distance connection.

"Congratulations. How much capital do you have?"

"Fifty thousand."

Long pause.

"Rupees?"

"Yes."

Another pause.

"Arjun, I think you may have misplaced a zero. Or maybe two zeros."

"No, I mean fifty thousand. But I have an idea about how to make it work."

Priya had this wonderful quality of being simultaneously practical and optimistic. She could see all the reasons why something wouldn't work while remaining genuinely curious about whether it might work anyway.

"Tell me the idea," she said.

I explained my efficiency hypothesis. Instead of trying to compete with modern equipment, we'd compete with modern thinking applied to basic equipment. Instead of building comprehensive capabilities from day one, we'd start with one product and perfect every aspect of making it better and cheaper than anyone else.

"Which product?" she asked.

"Paracetamol. Everyone makes it. Everyone needs it. It's generic, so no patent issues. And the formulation is straightforward enough that we can focus on process optimization rather than product development."

"Where would you make it?"

That was the question I'd been dreading. Manufacturing space in Hyderabad's pharmaceutical district cost more per month than our entire startup capital. Clean rooms meeting regulatory standards cost even more.

"I was thinking we could start in my garage."

The silence on the other end of the line lasted so long I thought the connection had dropped.

"Priya? Are you there?"

"I'm here. I'm just trying to imagine explaining to regulatory inspectors that we're manufacturing pharmaceuticals in a residential garage."

"We wouldn't start with regulatory approvals. We'd start with perfecting the formulation and process using our own quality standards. Once we prove the concept works, we'll figure out the regulatory path."

It wasn't the most conventional business plan. But conventional business plans required conventional amounts of capital, which we didn't have.

Two weeks later, Priya called back.

"I've been thinking about your garage laboratory idea," she said. "I think it's crazy enough to work. When do we start?"

The day I finally submitted my resignation letter at Ranbaxy, my manager asked what I was planning to do next.

"Start my own pharmaceutical company," I said.

He smiled the kind of smile people reserve for harmless delusions. "Best of luck, Arjun. The market's always got room for another generic manufacturer."

I didn't tell him that we weren't planning to be another generic manufacturer. We were planning to be the most efficient generic manufacturer anyone had seen.

The difference seemed important.

My last day at Ranbaxy was a Friday in September 1994. That weekend, Meera and I cleared everything out of our single-car garage except her scooter, which we moved to the street. By Sunday evening, we had 200 square feet of empty concrete space that smelled like motor oil and monsoon dampness.

On Monday morning, I sat in the middle of that empty garage with a notebook and started making lists.

Equipment we needed. Suppliers we could approach. Regulatory requirements we'd eventually have to meet. Safety protocols we'd need to implement. Quality controls we'd need to develop.

Every item on every list cost money we didn't have.

That's when I realized that our capital constraint was going to force us to solve problems that our competitors never had to solve. They could buy their way out of efficiency problems. We'd have to think our way out.

The constraint was going to make us better.

I just didn't know it yet.

Priya arrived that Tuesday with two suitcases, a determination to prove that analytical chemistry could be done anywhere, and a practical question that would shape everything we built over the next five years.

"So," she said, looking around our garage laboratory, "what's the first thing we need to figure out?"

I looked at our empty space, our modest savings, and our complete lack of equipment, distribution, or regulatory approvals.

"Everything," I said.

She nodded. "Good. Let's start with something small."

That something small turned out to be finding a tablet press we could afford. It took us three weeks of calling pharmaceutical equipment dealers across South

India before we found one willing to sell to a company that consisted of two people and a garage.

The machine was a 1972 model that had been sitting in a warehouse in Chennai for two years. Single punch, manual operation, maximum capacity of 3,000 tablets per hour under ideal conditions. The seller offered no warranty and suggested we bring our own truck.

"How much?" I asked.

"Fifteen thousand."

We had ₹35,000 left after deposits on raw materials and basic laboratory supplies. Fifteen thousand for equipment meant ₹20,000 for everything else: utilities, transportation, packaging materials, and living expenses until we generated revenue.

"We'll take it," I said.

That decision—buying a twenty-two-year-old tablet press with no warranty from a seller who clearly thought we were amateurs—marked the official beginning of what would eventually become a global pharmaceutical company.

But on that October afternoon in 1994, as we watched our equipment being unloaded into our garage by three men who seemed personally offended by having to deliver machinery to a residential address, it felt like something much simpler.

It felt like two friends with an interesting problem to solve and just enough resources to discover whether they were smart enough to solve it.

The machine took up most of our available floor space. When it was running, the entire garage vibrated. When it jammed, which happened frequently, it made a grinding noise that brought concerned neighbors to investigate.

But it was ours.

And for the first time since leaving Ranbaxy, I felt like we might actually know what we were doing.

Hyderabad 1994:
Dr. Arjun Malhotra's Resignation from Ranbaxy

The air conditioning in Mr. Krishnamurthy's office had been broken for three days, and the September heat made everything feel slightly surreal. I sat across from my manager's desk, watching him read my resignation letter for the second time, his reading glasses sliding down his nose with perspiration.

"Effective immediately?" he asked, not looking up.

"Two weeks' notice, sir. As per company policy."

He set the letter down and leaned back in his chair, which creaked in protest. Outside his window, I could see the Ranbaxy production facility humming along—three shifts, 24-hour operations, everything running exactly as it had for the past five years I'd worked there.

"Arjun, you know I have to ask. Is this about the promotion?"

It wasn't, though I understood why he'd think so. The senior formulation scientist position had gone to Rajesh Gupta, who had six months less experience than me but an MBA from IIM Ahmedabad. These things happened in corporate India. I'd made my peace with it weeks ago.

"No sir, it's not about the promotion."

"The salary then? Because if it's a competing offer, we might be able to match—"

"I'm starting my own company."

The words hung in the humid air between us. Krishnamurthy removed his glasses and cleaned them slowly with his shirt, buying time to process what I'd just said.

"Your own... pharmaceutical company?"

"Yes sir."

"Here in Hyderabad?"

"Yes sir."

He put his glasses back on and studied my face as if he were seeing me for the first time. "Arjun, do you have any idea how much capital is required to establish a pharmaceutical manufacturing facility?"

I did have an idea, actually. That was part of the problem. According to every feasibility study I'd read, we needed somewhere between ₹1-2 crores for a minimal setup. I had ₹50,000 in my savings account and a theory about efficiency that might or might not work in practice.

"I have some ideas about that, sir."

He opened my personnel file and flipped through it, though I suspected he wasn't really reading. More buying time to figure out how to handle this conversation.

"You've been a good employee, Arjun. Punctual, thorough, no disciplinary issues. Your formulation work on the diabetes portfolio has been solid."

"Thank you, sir."

"So help me understand why you'd leave a stable position with India's second-largest pharmaceutical company to chase what sounds like..." He paused, searching for diplomatic language. "An ambitious venture."

I'd been preparing for this question for weeks, but sitting in that stifling office, all my rehearsed explanations felt inadequate. How do you tell your manager that you're leaving because you're tired of watching equipment sit idle? Because you think there's a better way to develop formulations? Because you've spent five years following procedures that made sense for a large corporation but might not be optimal for actually making better medicines?

"Sir, I've learned a lot here. About manufacturing, about quality control, about regulatory requirements. But I want to try applying what I've learned in a different way."

"What different way?"

The honest answer was that I wasn't entirely sure yet. I had theories about process efficiency, ideas about cost reduction, hypotheses about market opportunities that larger companies couldn't pursue profitably. But sitting across from Krishnamurthy, those concepts felt fragile and half-formed.

"I think there are opportunities in the generic market that require more flexibility than a large company can provide."

He nodded slowly, though I could tell he wasn't convinced. "And you think you can compete with established manufacturers? Cipla, Dr. Reddy's, even us?"

"I think I can compete by doing things they can't do."

"Such as?"

That was the question I'd been asking myself every night for the past month. What could two people in a garage do that Ranbaxy couldn't do better?

"Move faster. Make decisions quicker. Focus completely on efficiency instead of having to coordinate across departments and hierarchies."

Krishnamurthy smiled, not unkindly. It was the smile of someone who'd seen ambitious young employees before. "Arjun, running a pharmaceutical company isn't just about efficiency. There are regulatory requirements, quality standards, distribution networks, supplier relationships. These things take years to build."

"I understand that, sir."

"Do you? Because from where I sit, it looks like you're trading a secure position with clear advancement opportunities for a very uncertain gamble."

He wasn't wrong. That evening, I'd go home to Meera and our three-year-old son Rohit, and I'd have to explain why Daddy was giving up his steady job to chase an idea that might not work. I'd have to convince my wife that risking our savings on pharmaceutical equipment was responsible family planning.

But there was something Krishnamurthy couldn't see from his air-conditioned office with its view of the established production facility. He couldn't see the inefficiencies I noticed every day. The batch delays caused by rigid scheduling. The quality testing bottlenecks that could be eliminated with better coordination. The formulation decisions that took weeks to approve when they could be made in hours.

He couldn't see that the very systems that made Ranbaxy successful also made it slow.

"Sir, I appreciate your concern. I really do. But I need to find out if my ideas work."

"And if they don't work?"

I'd thought about this too. If we failed, I'd be back in the job market with a two-year gap in my employment history and a reputation as someone who'd made poor career decisions. Not exactly an appealing prospect for future employers.

"Then I'll have learned something valuable about business."

He closed my file and leaned forward. "Arjun, I can't officially advise you to reconsider this decision, but speaking personally... the pharmaceutical industry is very unforgiving to small players. The capital requirements alone will crush most startups before they can establish market presence."

"I understand."

"The regulatory environment is getting more complex every year. Quality standards are tightening. Competition is intensifying."

"Yes sir."

"And you still want to do this?"

I looked out his window at the production facility one more time. Steady, predictable, profitable. Everything a rational person would want in a career.

"Yes sir. I still want to do this."

He sighed and picked up a pen to sign my resignation acceptance letter. "Well, then. I wish you the best of luck. And Arjun?"

"Yes sir?"

"Keep in touch. If things don't work out the way you hope, there might be opportunities here for someone with your experience."

I thanked him and stood to leave. At the door, I turned back.

"Sir, one last question. If you were starting a pharmaceutical company today, what would you focus on first?"

He thought for a moment. "Cash flow. Everything else is secondary. If you can't generate positive cash flow within the first year, nothing else matters."

"Thank you, sir. That's very helpful."

Walking out of the Ranbaxy facility that afternoon, I felt lighter and more terrified than I'd felt in years. The security guard waved goodbye as I left my ID badge at the front desk. The receptionist wished me luck with my "new venture."

By the time I reached the bus stop, I was questioning everything. Maybe Krishnamurthy was right. Maybe I was trading security for uncertainty without adequate justification. Maybe the smart play was to stay, work for the promotion next year, build a comfortable career within an established system.

But when the bus arrived and I climbed aboard for my final commute home as a Ranbaxy employee, I realized something had changed. For the first time in five years, I was excited about going to work tomorrow.

Even if tomorrow's work was figuring out how to convert our garage into a pharmaceutical laboratory.

That evening, I called Priya.

"I did it," I told her. "I resigned today."

"How do you feel?"

I looked around our small apartment—Meera preparing dinner in the kitchen, Rohit playing with building blocks on the floor, our modest furniture and simple life that we'd built on steady employment and careful savings.

"Terrified," I said. "But also ready."

"Good. When do we start?"

"Monday morning."

"I'll be there."

After I hung up, Meera came and sat beside me on our small sofa.

"So it's really happening?" she asked.

"It's really happening."

She took my hand. "Then we'd better make sure it works."

That night, I couldn't sleep. Not because I was worried—though I was—but because my mind kept racing ahead to all the problems we'd need to solve. Equipment selection. Supplier relationships. Quality protocols. Regulatory pathways.

Each problem felt like a puzzle waiting to be solved. And for the first time in years, I had complete freedom to solve them in whatever way seemed best.

It was exactly the feeling I'd hoped for when I wrote that resignation letter three weeks earlier.

Tomorrow, we'd find out if hope was enough.

The Family Garage Laboratory with ₹50,000 Capital

Meera's scooter looked lonely parked on the street.

For three years, it had lived in our garage alongside paint cans, Rohit's outgrown bicycle, and boxes of things we'd moved from our previous apartment but never quite found places for. Now all of that was crammed into our bedroom closet, and the scooter sat outside under a plastic tarp, looking accusingly at our kitchen window every morning.

"I still think this is insane," Meera said, handing me a cup of tea as we stood in our newly emptied garage on that first Monday morning in October.

The space was smaller than I'd remembered. Maybe 200 square feet, with concrete walls that showed water stains from last monsoon and a ceiling that sloped down toward the back corner where the builders had cut corners thirty years ago. The floor was uneven—probably poured by workers who'd had a few drinks during lunch—and everything smelled faintly of motor oil and that peculiar dampness that Indian garages acquire during rainy season.

"It's not insane," I said, though I wasn't entirely convinced myself. "It's resourceful."

Priya arrived at nine o'clock sharp, carrying two large suitcases and wearing the kind of practical salwar kameez that meant business. She stood in the doorway for a long moment, surveying our pharmaceutical empire.

"Well," she said finally. "It's bigger than I expected."

"Really?"

"No. But it has potential."

We spread our financial situation across a folding table we'd borrowed from our neighbor. ₹50,000 in savings, divided into categories I'd written on index cards: Equipment, Raw Materials, Regulatory, Operating Expenses, Emergency Fund.

"Equipment budget is ₹15,000," I announced.

Priya picked up the card and examined it like she was reading Sanskrit. "Fifteen thousand rupees for pharmaceutical manufacturing equipment?"

"Plus whatever we can borrow or improvise."

"What exactly can we borrow?"

I pointed to the corner where my brother-in-law's old mixing equipment sat. He'd used it for making food supplements before his business failed last year. "That mixer. And I think we can modify it for tablet granulation."

"And what can we improvise?"

That was the interesting question. Over the weekend, I'd been walking through our neighborhood, looking at everyday items with new eyes. The pressure cooker in our kitchen could probably serve as a small autoclave for sterilization. The electronic scale Meera used for cooking could handle ingredient measurements up to 5 kilograms. Our bathroom mirror was large enough to use for visual tablet inspection.

"More than you'd think," I said.

The raw materials budget was ₹20,000, which sounds reasonable until you realize that pharmaceutical-grade ingredients cost significantly more than the industrial chemicals I'd been used to ordering at Ranbaxy. A 25-kilogram bag of microcrystalline cellulose—the basic filler for most tablets—would cost us ₹3,000. The same amount of starch binder would be another ₹2,000. By the time we added disintegrants, lubricants, and active pharmaceutical ingredients, our raw materials budget could produce maybe 10,000 tablets if everything went perfectly.

Everything never went perfectly.

"Regulatory budget?" Priya asked.

"₹5,000."

She looked at me over her reading glasses. "Arjun, a basic drug license application costs ₹3,000 just in government fees. That doesn't include consultant fees, testing costs, or documentation."

"I know. We'll have to phase the regulatory work."

"What does that mean?"

"It means we start without proper licenses and figure out the compliance pathway once we have products that actually work."

This was not conventional pharmaceutical business practice. Most companies spent months getting regulatory approvals before manufacturing their first tablet. But most companies had proper budgets. We had ₹5,000 and a theory that working products would be easier to license than theoretical formulations.

The operating expenses budget was ₹8,000, which had to cover electricity, water, telephone, transportation, and anything else we needed to keep our garage laboratory running for three months. After that, we'd either be generating revenue or looking for jobs.

The emergency fund was ₹2,000. Enough for maybe one serious crisis, provided it wasn't too serious.

"Questions?" I asked, looking at our financial breakdown.

"Several," Priya said. "Starting with where exactly we're planning to conduct analytical testing."

I pointed to the corner where I'd set up a folding table next to the electrical outlet. "Right there."

"With what equipment?"

"I have a basic pH meter from my college days. And we can send samples to commercial testing labs for anything we can't do ourselves."

"How much will commercial testing cost?"

"About ₹500 per sample for basic dissolution and content uniformity tests."

She calculated quickly in her head. "So if we test each batch properly, testing costs will be ₹500. But our total profit margin per batch needs to cover that ₹500 plus raw materials, plus equipment depreciation, plus operating expenses, plus our salaries."

"What salaries?"

"Good point."

We spent the rest of the morning setting up our workspace. The mixing equipment went in the center, where the concrete floor was most level. The folding table with analytical equipment went near the outlet. A borrowed desk from our living room became our office area, complete with a telephone and the notebook where we'd track everything from batch records to supplier contacts.

By noon, our garage looked like a pharmaceutical laboratory designed by people who'd never actually seen a pharmaceutical laboratory. Equipment sat on unstable surfaces. Extension cords snaked across the floor. Our quality control area consisted of a magnifying glass and good lighting from the overhead bulb.

"You know what's missing?" Priya asked, standing back to survey our setup.

"Professional equipment? Proper ventilation? Regulatory compliance?"

"A sign."

She was right. We needed something that announced this was a serious business operation, not just two people playing with chemicals in a residential garage.

That afternoon, we walked to the local sign painter and commissioned our first piece of corporate infrastructure: a small metal plate that read "Malhotra Pharmaceuticals - Research and Development Laboratory."

It cost ₹150, which felt extravagant given our budget constraints, but seemed necessary for psychological reasons if nothing else.

When we mounted the sign next to our garage door that evening, Rohit ran outside to see what we were doing.

"What's that say, Papa?"

"It says this is where Papa and Auntie Priya are going to make medicines."

He studied the sign seriously. "Like the medicines Mama gives me when I have fever?"

"Exactly like that."

"Can I help?"

I looked at our garage laboratory with its improvised equipment, borrowed furniture, and ₹50,000 budget. Then I looked at my three-year-old son, who thought making medicines in the garage sounded like the most natural thing in the world.

"You know what? Yes, you can help. You can be our quality inspector."

"What does a quality inspector do?"

"Makes sure everything looks right."

He nodded gravely, as if quality inspection was exactly the career path he'd been considering.

That night, after Rohit had gone to bed and Meera had stopped shaking her head at our garage transformation, Priya and I sat on the folding chairs we'd borrowed from our neighbor and tried to plan our first week of operations.

"Tomorrow we'll call suppliers about raw materials," I said. "Wednesday we'll test the mixing equipment. Thursday we'll attempt our first granulation batch."

"And if the granulation fails?"

"We'll figure out why and try again Friday."

"And if it fails again?"

"We'll try again the following Monday. And keep trying until we get it right."

Priya was quiet for a moment, looking around our garage laboratory. "Arjun, do you really think this is going to work?"

I followed her gaze across our improvised pharmaceutical facility. The borrowed equipment, the folding tables, the single electrical outlet powering our entire operation. It looked less like a business and more like an elaborate science fair project.

"I think it has to work," I said finally. "Because we've just committed our entire savings to finding out."

She nodded. "Good answer."

We locked up the garage and headed inside for dinner. Tomorrow we'd start trying to turn ₹50,000 and a garage full of borrowed equipment into a pharmaceutical company.

But tonight, for the first time since leaving Ranbaxy, it felt like we might actually know what we were doing.

Even if we were making it up as we went along.

Meeting Priya Sharma: The Analytical Chemist who becomes Co-Founder

I hadn't seen Priya Sharma in three years when I called her that Tuesday evening in September 1994.

We'd been roommates during our final year at Osmania University—not romantic roommates, just two chemistry students who'd been assigned adjacent lab benches and discovered we worked well together. While other students competed to see who could finish experiments fastest, Priya and I competed to see who could get the most accurate results.

She usually won.

After graduation, she'd taken a position at Shriram Testing Laboratories in Pune, analyzing pharmaceutical samples for various manufacturers. I'd gone to Ranbaxy. We'd exchanged a few letters in those first months—this was before email became common in India—but gradually lost touch the way college friends do when real life intervenes.

So when I dialed her number that evening, I wasn't entirely sure she'd even remember me.

"Priya? This is Arjun Malhotra. We were lab partners at Osmania."

"Arjun! Of course I remember. How are you? Still at Ranbaxy?"

"Actually, that's why I'm calling. I just resigned."

"Oh no. What happened? Did they downsize?"

"Nothing like that. I resigned to start my own pharmaceutical company."

The pause that followed lasted long enough for me to wonder if the connection had dropped. STD calls between Hyderabad and Pune weren't always reliable.

"Priya? Are you there?"

"I'm here. I'm just trying to process what you just said. You resigned from Ranbaxy to start your own pharmaceutical company?"

"Yes."

"With what capital?"

That was vintage Priya. Always the practical question first. In university, while other students were debating theoretical chemistry concepts, she'd be asking about experimental costs and equipment availability.

"Fifty thousand rupees."

Another pause. Shorter this time.

"Arjun, I'm going to ask this as gently as possible. Have you calculated how much it actually costs to start a pharmaceutical company?"

"I have. And I think there might be a different way to approach the problem."

"What different way?"

I'd been rehearsing this explanation for weeks, but sitting in our small living room with Rohit playing at my feet and Meera cooking dinner in the kitchen, my grand theories about efficiency and constraint optimization suddenly sounded flimsy.

"What if we started smaller than anyone has tried before? What if we focused on perfecting one product with minimal equipment instead of trying to build comprehensive capabilities from day one?"

"Go on."

"At Ranbaxy, I've spent five years watching expensive equipment sit idle because of scheduling inefficiencies, quality delays, changeover times. What if we could eliminate those inefficiencies by designing our entire process around a single product?"

"Which product?"

"Paracetamol. Basic, essential, good market demand. And simple enough formulation that we could focus on process optimization rather than product development."

I heard her breathing through the phone line, which meant she was thinking. Priya had this habit of taking audible breaths when she was processing complex information.

"Where would you manufacture this paracetamol?"

"My garage."

"Your residential garage?"

"Initially, yes. Just to prove the concept works. Once we demonstrate efficiency and quality, we'd scale up to proper facilities."

"Arjun, do you understand the regulatory implications of manufacturing pharmaceuticals in a residential garage?"

"I understand that we can't sell products manufactured in non-compliant facilities. But we can perfect formulations and processes before investing in regulatory compliance."

Another breathing pause.

"And you want me to... what exactly?"

This was the question I'd been dreading. What exactly was I asking her to do? Leave her secure job at a reputable testing laboratory to join two people and a garage in a venture that violated most conventional business wisdom?

"I want you to be my co-founder. Handle analytical testing, quality control, process optimization. Equal partnership."

"Equal partnership in a company with fifty thousand rupees in capital?"

"Equal partnership in whatever the company becomes."

The conversation was interrupted by long-distance line static, but I could hear her thinking through the silence.

"Arjun, I have a steady job here. Good salary, interesting work, career advancement opportunities. The laboratory is well-equipped, properly regulated, professionally managed."

"I know."

"So help me understand why I would leave all that to join your garage experiment."

It was a fair question. What could I offer that would compete with security and professional recognition? I looked around our modest apartment, thought about our ₹50,000 savings, considered our complete lack of equipment, facilities, or regulatory approvals.

"I can't offer you security, Priya. I can't offer you professional prestige or comfortable working conditions."

"What can you offer?"

"The chance to find out if we're smart enough to solve problems that everyone says are impossible to solve with the resources we have."

"That's it?"

"And the chance to build something that's completely ours. Every decision, every process, every innovation—we'd own it all."

She was quiet for so long I started to worry I'd overplayed my hand. Maybe the appeal of entrepreneurial freedom wasn't as compelling as steady employment and proper laboratory facilities.

"Can I ask you something?" she said finally.

"Of course."

"Why me? There are probably analytical chemists in Hyderabad who wouldn't require relocation."

I'd thought about this question for weeks before calling her. There were indeed local chemists available. Some with more experience, some with better equipment access, some who might work for lower compensation.

"Because you're the only person I know who thinks like I think."

"What do you mean?"

"Remember our quantitative analysis class? Professor Reddy would give us experimental procedures, and everyone else would follow them exactly. But you'd always ask whether there was a more accurate way to get the same result."

"I remember."

"And you'd redesign the procedure to eliminate potential error sources. Not because the original procedure was wrong, but because you could see how to make it better."

"That's just good analytical technique."

"No, it's systematic thinking. It's seeing inefficiencies that other people accept as normal. That's exactly what we need for this venture."

I heard her exhale slowly. "Arjun, even if your efficiency theories are correct, starting a pharmaceutical company requires more than analytical chemistry skills. You need regulatory expertise, marketing capabilities, distribution networks, financial management."

"You're right. We'd have to learn most of those things as we go."

"And you think we can learn them fast enough to succeed before our money runs out?"

"I think we have to find out."

She laughed, which I hadn't expected. "You know what's funny? This is the most interesting problem anyone's offered me in three years."

"Is that a yes?"

"It's not a no. But I need to think about it."

"How long do you need?"

"Give me a week. I want to research startup costs, regulatory requirements, market conditions. If I'm going to make this decision, I want to make it based on data, not just enthusiasm."

That was perfectly reasonable, and also perfectly Priya. She'd want to analyze every variable before committing to anything as significant as leaving steady employment for entrepreneurial uncertainty.

"One week. I'll call you next Tuesday."

"Arjun?"

"Yes?"

"This garage laboratory of yours. What kind of analytical equipment do you have?"

"I have a basic pH meter from college. And access to commercial testing labs for anything more sophisticated."

"Commercial testing labs charge about five hundred rupees per sample for basic pharmaceutical analysis."

"I know."

"So every batch we test will cost five hundred rupees, but our profit margin per batch needs to cover testing costs plus raw materials plus equipment depreciation plus operating expenses."

"That's the challenge, yes."

"Hmm. Interesting challenge."

After I hung up, Meera asked how the conversation had gone.

"I think she's interested. But she wants a week to research the feasibility."

"What did you tell her about salary?"

"Equal partnership."

"Equal partnership in what? We don't have a company yet."

"Equal partnership in whatever company we build."

Meera shook her head, but she was smiling. "You're asking her to bet her career on your garage experiment."

"Yes."

"And you think she'll do it?"

I thought about Priya's questions, her systematic approach to evaluating the opportunity, her comment about it being an interesting challenge.

"I think she might."

The week passed slowly. I spent the days clearing out our garage and researching equipment suppliers. Meera spent the evenings questioning whether we were making the right decision. Rohit spent his time asking when we were going to start making medicines.

Tuesday evening arrived with monsoon clouds gathering over Hyderabad. I dialed Priya's number at exactly seven o'clock.

"I've been expecting your call," she said before I could introduce myself.

"And?"

"I've spent the week researching pharmaceutical startup costs, regulatory pathways, market opportunities for generic manufacturers. I've also talked to three analytical chemists who've worked with small pharmaceutical companies."

"What did you learn?"

"I learned that everything you've told me about the challenges is accurate. Starting a pharmaceutical company with minimal capital is extremely difficult. The regulatory environment is complex. The competition is intense."

My heart sank. "So that's a no?"

"I also learned something else."

"What?"

"None of the people I talked to had considered your approach. They all assumed pharmaceutical startups need to look like miniature versions of large pharmaceutical companies from day one. Nobody had thought about starting with radical efficiency optimization."

"And?"

"And I realized I've spent three years doing routine analytical work for other people's products. I'd rather spend the next three years solving impossible problems for our own products."

"Does that mean yes?"

"That means yes. When do we start?"

Two weeks later, Priya arrived in Hyderabad with two suitcases, a determination to prove that pharmaceutical analysis could be done anywhere, and a practical question that would shape everything we built over the next five years.

"So," she said, standing in our garage and looking around at our borrowed equipment and improvised laboratory setup, "what's the first problem we need to solve?"

I looked at our empty space, our modest capital, and our complete lack of regulatory approvals, distribution networks, or market presence.

"Everything," I said.

She nodded and rolled up her sleeves. "Perfect. Let's start with something small."

That something small turned out to be figuring out whether we could actually make tablets in a residential garage that would meet our own quality standards, never mind regulatory requirements.

But for the first time since leaving Ranbaxy, I felt like we had the right team to find out.

First Constraint Identified: Limited Working Capital

The numbers didn't lie, but I kept recalculating them anyway.

It was our third week in the garage laboratory, and Priya had just finished our first successful tablet compression run. Fifty paracetamol tablets sat on our folding table, looking remarkably like actual pharmaceutical products. They were the right size, the right color, and when we tested them with our borrowed dissolution apparatus, they released their active ingredient at exactly the rate specified in the pharmacopeia.

We should have been celebrating. Instead, I was staring at a notebook full of calculations that told an uncomfortable story.

"Raw material cost per tablet: ₹0.75," I read aloud. "Labor cost per tablet: ₹0.15. Equipment depreciation per tablet: ₹0.10. Total manufacturing cost: ₹1.00."

Priya looked up from the analytical balance where she was weighing ingredients for our next batch. "That sounds reasonable. What's the problem?"

"The problem is cash flow."

I showed her my calculations. To produce 1,000 tablets, we needed ₹750 in raw materials upfront. To produce 10,000 tablets—the minimum quantity most distributors would consider purchasing—we needed ₹7,500 in raw materials before we could generate a single rupee of revenue.

"How long does it take to collect payment after we deliver tablets?' Priya asked.

"Based on what I learned at Ranbaxy, most distributors pay within sixty to ninety days of delivery."

She set down her measuring spoon and did quick mental arithmetic. "So we invest ₹7,500 in raw materials, spend two weeks manufacturing, deliver the products, and then wait ninety days to get paid?"

"Exactly."

"And during those ninety days, we need to eat, pay rent, and probably manufacture more batches to keep the business growing."

"That's the constraint."

We sat in silence for a moment, contemplating our cash flow reality. With ₹35,000 remaining from our initial ₹50,000 capital, we could afford to produce maybe four batches of 10,000 tablets each before running out of money. If everything went perfectly—no equipment failures, no rejected batches, no delayed payments—we might achieve positive cash flow by month four.

Everything never went perfectly.

"What do pharmaceutical companies typically do about working capital?" Priya asked.

"They start with enough capital to carry them through the first year of operations. Or they get bank loans secured against their equipment and inventory."

"How much would banks typically lend us?"

I laughed, though it wasn't particularly funny. "Banks don't lend money to two people operating out of a residential garage with no financial history, no regulatory licenses, and no established customer base."

"So we're back to our original ₹35,000."

"We're back to our original ₹35,000."

Priya walked to the garage door and looked out at the street, where her scooter was still parked under its plastic tarp. "Arjun, can I ask you something?"

"Of course."

"When you were planning this venture, how did you imagine we'd solve the working capital problem?"

It was a fair question. During my weeks of business planning, I'd focused primarily on technical challenges: equipment selection, formulation development, quality control procedures. I'd calculated startup costs and monthly operating expenses, but I hadn't fully grasped the cash flow dynamics of manufacturing businesses.

"I assumed that if we could produce good quality products at competitive prices, customers would pay us quickly enough to fund continued growth."

"But that's not how pharmaceutical distribution works."

"No, it's not."

She came back to our improvised desk and picked up my cash flow projections. "So what's our actual constraint? Is it production capacity? Quality capabilities? Market access?"

"It's none of those things. Our constraint is the gap between when we spend money on raw materials and when we collect money from customers."

"Working capital."

"Working capital."

This realization was both depressing and oddly liberating. Depressing because it meant our technical achievements—successfully developing formulations, achieving quality standards, optimizing manufacturing processes—were secondary to a simple financial timing problem. Liberating because it gave us a specific problem to solve rather than a vague challenge to overcome.

"So the question becomes," Priya said, "how do we maximize our business growth given that working capital is our limiting constraint?"

I pulled out a fresh notebook and started writing. "If working capital is the constraint, then every business decision should be evaluated based on how it affects cash conversion cycles."

"Meaning?"

"Meaning we need to focus on products and customers that generate cash faster, not necessarily products and customers that generate the most profit per unit."

This was counterintuitive. Most business planning focused on maximizing profit margins. But if we were constrained by working capital, a product that generated 50% margins with 120-day payment terms was less valuable than a product that generated 30% margins with 30-day payment terms.

"What kinds of customers pay faster?" Priya asked.

I thought about the payment practices I'd observed at Ranbaxy. "Hospitals pay slower than retail pharmacies. Government contracts pay slowest of all. Small distributors pay faster than large distributors, but they order smaller quantities."

"So we should target small distributors initially?"

"We should target whoever gives us the best combination of payment speed and order volume."

We spent the rest of the afternoon recalculating our business model based on cash flow optimization rather than profit maximization. Instead of targeting large distributors who might place orders for 100,000 tablets but pay in 90 days, we'd target smaller distributors who might order 25,000 tablets but pay in 30 days.

Instead of developing a diverse product portfolio that maximized market coverage, we'd focus on products with the fastest inventory turnover rates. Instead of building up inventory to improve economies of scale, we'd manufacture in smaller batches timed to customer demand.

"This changes everything," Priya observed.

"How so?"

"Our equipment needs, our production planning, our customer targeting, our inventory management. If we're optimizing for cash flow rather than efficiency, we need different strategies for everything."

She was right. Working capital constraints would force us to operate differently than we'd originally planned. But maybe that wasn't necessarily bad.

"You know what's interesting?" I said, looking at our revised calculations. "Our competitors probably don't face the same working capital constraints we do."

"Because they have access to better financing?"

"Because they have access to any financing. Which means they can afford to optimize for different variables than we can."

"Such as?"

"They can afford to pursue large customers with slow payment terms. They can afford to build inventory for economies of scale. They can afford to develop products with longer payback periods."

Priya nodded slowly. "So our constraint forces us to compete in market segments that aren't attractive to well-funded competitors."

"Exactly. Small distributors, fast-paying customers, quick-turnover products—those might not be interesting to companies with unlimited working capital, but they're perfect for us."

That evening, I called three small pharmaceutical distributors in Hyderabad and explained that we were a new manufacturer specializing in fast delivery and flexible payment terms. Two of them agreed to meet with us the following week.

The meetings went better than expected. Both distributors were frustrated with larger manufacturers who demanded minimum orders of 50,000 tablets and insisted on 90-day payment terms. They were interested in working with a manufacturer who could deliver 10,000 tablets on 30-day terms.

"The question is," said Mr. Patel from City Pharmaceuticals, "can you actually deliver what you're promising?"

"We can deliver quality products on time," I told him. "And we're small enough that every customer matters to us personally."

"What about pricing? We can't pay premium prices just for better service."

This was the crucial test. Our manufacturing costs were actually higher per unit than larger manufacturers because we couldn't achieve the same economies of scale. But our cash flow optimization meant we could accept lower margins in exchange for faster payments.

"Our prices will be competitive," I said. "And our payment terms will be better than anyone else you're working with."

He ordered 10,000 paracetamol tablets with payment due fifteen days after delivery.

Walking back to our garage that afternoon, Priya asked, "Do you realize what just happened?"

"We got our first customer?"

"We identified our competitive advantage. Every other manufacturer in this market is optimizing for scale and margins. We're optimizing for cash flow and service. That's not a constraint—that's a market position."

She was right. Our working capital limitation was forcing us to compete in ways that established manufacturers couldn't easily match. They were optimized for large orders and long payment cycles. We were optimized for responsiveness and cash flow.

"So our constraint is actually teaching us how to succeed?" I asked.

"Our constraint is teaching us how to succeed differently."

That night, I updated our business plan to reflect our new understanding. Instead of viewing working capital as a problem to be solved, I started viewing it as a focusing mechanism that would drive all our strategic decisions.

Products would be selected based on inventory turnover rates. Customers would be prioritized based on payment terms. Manufacturing schedules would be designed around cash flow optimization. Marketing would emphasize speed and service rather than scale and sophistication.

Six months later, when we'd achieved positive cash flow and were considering our first equipment upgrade, I realized something important: we hadn't eliminated our working capital constraint. We'd learned to exploit it so effectively that it had stopped limiting our growth.

The constraint had shifted to production capacity.

But by then, we understood that constraints weren't problems to be eliminated—they were teachers showing us how to build sustainable competitive advantages.

Our working capital constraint had taught us our first lesson: when you can't compete on scale, compete on speed. When you can't compete on financing, compete on service.

It wouldn't be our last lesson, but it was our most important one. It taught us that limitations could become advantages if you were willing to think differently about what business you were really in.

Chapter 2

The Formulation Challenge

The morning sun cast long shadows across the cluttered laboratory as Dr. Arjun Malhotra stared at the latest batch results for their paracetamol formulation. Six months into their venture, Malhotra Pharmaceuticals was surviving, but barely. The harsh reality of competing against pharmaceutical giants like Cipla and Dr. Reddy's was becoming painfully clear with each failed bid and lost contract.

"We're consistently 15-20% higher than the winning bids," Priya Sharma announced, setting down the latest tender results on Arjun's makeshift desk—a repurposed laboratory bench covered with regulatory documents and financial projections. "At this rate, we'll burn through our remaining capital in four months."

Arjun rubbed his temples, feeling the weight of responsibility for the small team that had joined their ambitious venture. The paracetamol market represented their best opportunity—a ₹200 crore annual market in India with steady demand and relatively straightforward manufacturing. Yet their cost structure made competitive bidding impossible.

"The problem isn't our efficiency," he muttered, reviewing their manufacturing data for the hundredth time. "We're actually producing faster than the industry average. But our costs are still too high."

The constraint was becoming obvious, though Arjun hadn't yet learned to think in those terms. Every aspect of their operation seemed optimized, yet they couldn't achieve the cost position necessary to compete effectively. Raw materials were sourced at competitive prices, their small team was working efficiently, and overhead was minimal. The limitation had to be elsewhere.

That's when Ravi Krishnan walked into their lives.

A veteran production manager with fifteen years at Ranbaxy, Ravi had grown frustrated with corporate bureaucracy and was seeking a new challenge. His reputation for process innovation preceded him—colleagues credited him with several breakthrough improvements in generic drug manufacturing that had saved millions in production costs.

"I've been watching your operation," Ravi said during his initial meeting with Arjun and Priya. "You're doing everything right according to standard industry practices. That's precisely the problem."

He spread out their process flow diagrams on the laboratory bench, his experienced eyes scanning the familiar steps of paracetamol synthesis. "Everyone in the industry follows essentially the same process route. Same intermediate compounds, same reaction conditions, same purification steps. No one questions whether it's optimal—they just follow established procedures."

Arjun leaned forward, intrigued. "What are you suggesting?"

"I'm suggesting we think differently about the entire synthesis approach," Ravi replied, pulling out a notebook filled with his preliminary analysis. "Your current process uses eight steps with a 72-hour cycle time. What if we could reduce that to five steps and 48 hours while improving yield?"

The next three weeks became a intensive period of experimentation and analysis. Ravi's approach was systematic—questioning every assumption, testing alternative reaction pathways, and optimizing each step for both cost and quality. His years of experience had taught him that breakthrough improvements came from fundamental process redesign rather than incremental optimization.

"The key insight," Ravi explained to the team as they reviewed his preliminary results, "is that we've been following a synthesis route designed for large-scale operations with different constraints. Small-scale production allows us to use approaches that wouldn't work at 5,000-kilogram batches but are perfect for our current volumes."

The breakthrough came on a Tuesday evening in March 1996. Ravi's alternative synthesis route had eliminated two expensive intermediate compounds, reduced energy consumption by 45%, and shortened the overall cycle time by 30%. More importantly, it maintained the same quality standards while dramatically reducing costs.

"Let me walk you through the numbers," Ravi said, his excitement evident as he presented the results to Arjun and Priya. "Our current manufacturing cost is ₹280 per kilogram. With the new process, we can produce at ₹188 per kilogram—a 33% reduction."

The room fell silent as the implications sank in. This wasn't just an improvement; it was a transformation of their competitive position.

"At ₹188 per kilo, we can bid at ₹300 and still achieve 37% gross margins," Priya calculated quickly. "That's competitive with anyone in the market while maintaining healthy profitability."

But Ravi wasn't finished. "There's more. The process improvements also enhance quality consistency and reduce batch-to-batch variation. We'll actually be delivering superior quality at a lower cost."

The implementation required careful validation and regulatory approval for the process changes. Every step had to be documented, tested, and verified to meet pharmaceutical quality standards. But within six months, the new process was operational and producing remarkable results.

The first major contract came from a regional distributor who had previously rejected their bids as too expensive. At ₹300 per kilogram, Malhotra Pharmaceuticals was suddenly the most competitive supplier while maintaining margins that allowed for growth and reinvestment.

"It's not just about the immediate cost savings," Arjun reflected as they reviewed their first quarterly results since implementing the new process. "We've demonstrated that we can innovate and compete on value, not just price. That changes everything about our strategic positioning."

The paracetamol breakthrough became a catalyst for the company's growth. Within eighteen months, they had captured 8% of the regional market and were fielding inquiries from national distributors. More importantly, they had developed a systematic approach to process optimization that would serve them well as they expanded their product portfolio.

"This taught us that constraints aren't always obvious," Arjun would later tell audiences at pharmaceutical industry conferences. "We thought our constraint was capital or competition or market access. But the real constraint was our acceptance of conventional thinking about how things had to be done."

Ravi's process innovation had eliminated their primary constraint—the cost structure that prevented competitive positioning. But as they would soon discover, eliminating one constraint inevitably reveals the next limitation that must be addressed. Success in the paracetamol market would create new challenges around scaling operations, building market presence, and managing growth.

The formulation challenge had been solved, but it was only the beginning of their constraint elimination journey. Each breakthrough would reveal new limitations, requiring continued systematic thinking and creative problem-solving. The key insight was learning to identify constraints accurately and address them systematically rather than treating symptoms or making assumptions about what limited their performance.

This early success established the foundation for Malhotra Pharmaceuticals' growth and demonstrated the power of questioning conventional approaches when systematic analysis reveals better alternatives.

Developing Cost-Effective Generic Formulations

The paracetamol tablets kept crumbling.

Not all of them—about thirty percent emerged from our tablet press intact and properly formed. The rest fell apart if you looked at them wrong, creating a fine powder that made our garage smell like a pharmacy explosion.

"It's the binder ratio," Priya said, examining the latest failed batch under our magnifying glass. "Too little starch and they don't hold together. Too much starch and they won't dissolve properly in the stomach."

We'd been trying to perfect our paracetamol formulation for six weeks. The active ingredient—paracetamol itself—was straightforward. You could buy pharmaceutical-grade paracetamol from any decent chemical supplier. The challenge was everything else: the fillers, binders, disintegrants, and lubricants that turned raw paracetamol powder into tablets that would survive shipping, storage, and digestion.

"What's the standard industry formulation?" I asked.

Priya pulled out the reference book we'd borrowed from the medical college library. "Microcrystalline cellulose as primary filler, potato starch as binder, sodium starch glycolate as disintegrant, magnesium stearate as lubricant."

"And what does that cost per tablet?"

She did quick calculations in her notebook. "About ₹1.15 per tablet in raw materials."

This was our problem. The standard formulation worked perfectly—tablets came out consistent, stable, and met all dissolution requirements. But at ₹1.15 per tablet in materials alone, plus labor and overhead costs, we'd need to sell each tablet for at least ₹1.50 to achieve minimal profitability.

The market price for generic paracetamol tablets was ₹1.25.

"So we're losing money on every tablet we make using the standard formulation," I said.

"Correct. But if we deviate from the standard formulation and something goes wrong, we're responsible for any quality issues."

This was the generic drug manufacturer's dilemma. You could copy existing formulations exactly and compete solely on price, accepting minimal margins.

Or you could develop your own formulations to reduce costs, accepting the risk that your innovations might not work as well as established approaches.

Most small manufacturers chose the first option. Safe, predictable, and unprofitable.

"What if we tried a different approach?" I suggested. "Instead of reducing the cost of individual ingredients, what if we reduced the total number of ingredients?"

Priya looked skeptical. "Pharmaceutical formulations aren't like cooking recipes, Arjun. You can't just leave out ingredients because they're expensive."

"I'm not talking about leaving out functional ingredients. I'm talking about finding single ingredients that can perform multiple functions."

We spent the next morning in the medical college library, researching alternative excipients—the inactive ingredients that made tablets work. Most pharmaceutical companies used specialized ingredients for each function: one chemical for binding, another for disintegration, another for lubrication.

But buried in the technical literature, we found references to multifunctional excipients that could serve several purposes simultaneously.

"Look at this," Priya said, pointing to a research paper from 1988. "Polyvinyl pyrrolidone can function as both binder and disintegrant, depending on the concentration and processing conditions."

"How much does it cost compared to using separate binder and disintegrant?"

She calculated for several minutes. "About forty percent less expensive. But there's a catch."

"What catch?"

"The processing parameters are more critical. Temperature, compression force, moisture content—everything has to be exactly right or the tablets won't work properly."

This was exactly the kind of trade-off that worked in our favor. Large pharmaceutical manufacturers optimized for consistency and predictability. They used proven formulations with wide tolerance margins because they couldn't afford to have production problems across multiple facilities and production lines.

We were optimizing for cost effectiveness and could accept tighter process controls in exchange for lower material costs.

"Let's try it," I said.

Our first attempt failed spectacularly. The tablets came out too hard—they met hardness specifications but failed dissolution tests because they wouldn't break down properly in simulated stomach acid.

Our second attempt produced tablets that dissolved beautifully but crumbled during handling.

Our third attempt yielded tablets that looked perfect but varied wildly in weight because we hadn't calibrated our mixing process properly.

"Maybe the standard formulation exists for good reasons," Priya said after our fourth failed batch.

"Or maybe we haven't figured out the right processing conditions yet."

This was the difference between having unlimited resources and having ₹30,000 left in our bank account. Large manufacturers could afford to stick with proven approaches. We had to make innovative approaches work because we couldn't afford the proven ones.

Over the next two weeks, we systematically varied every processing parameter we could control. Mixing time, compression force, granulation moisture, drying temperature. We made detailed notes of every variation and tested every batch for hardness, friability, disintegration time, and dissolution rate.

Slowly, patterns emerged.

"The compression force is more critical than I thought," Priya observed, reviewing our test results. "Too little force and the tablets are fragile. Too much force and they won't dissolve."

"But look at this," I said, pointing to our data spreadsheet. "Once we find the optimal compression force for our formulation, the tablets are actually more consistent than the standard formulation."

She was right. Our optimized process produced tablets with less weight variation and more predictable dissolution than tablets made with conventional formulations. The tighter process controls that seemed like a disadvantage were actually creating better quality.

"What's our material cost per tablet now?" she asked.

I did the calculations. "Seventy-eight paise."

"Compared to ₹1.15 for the standard formulation?"

"That's a thirty-two percent reduction in material costs."

For the first time in weeks, we sat back and smiled. We'd developed a paracetamol formulation that cost significantly less than standard approaches while meeting or exceeding quality specifications.

But the real test came when we delivered our first batch to Mr. Patel at City Pharmaceuticals.

"These look different from other paracetamol tablets," he said, examining our products.

"Different how?"

"Slightly different color. Different surface texture."

My heart sank. In pharmaceuticals, different often meant suspicious. Pharmacists and patients expected generic drugs to look exactly like branded equivalents.

"The active ingredient is identical," I assured him. "Same potency, same dissolution rate, same therapeutic effect."

"I'm sure it is. But will my customers accept tablets that look different from what they're used to?"

This was a problem we hadn't anticipated. Our cost-effective formulation worked perfectly from a technical standpoint, but it created marketing challenges because it looked different from conventional products.

"Would you be willing to try a small quantity?" I asked. "If your customers have any complaints, we'll take the products back at no charge."

He agreed to take 5,000 tablets on consignment.

Two weeks later, he called with feedback.

"Your paracetamol tablets are selling well," he said. "Better than I expected."

"Really? No complaints about the appearance?"

"Actually, several pharmacists mentioned that they seem to work faster than other brands. Patients are asking for them specifically."

It turned out that our tighter process controls had produced tablets with more consistent dissolution characteristics. Patients were experiencing faster pain relief because the paracetamol was being absorbed more predictably.

Our cost reduction had accidentally improved product performance.

Within a month, Mr. Patel increased his order to 25,000 tablets. Within three months, two other distributors had started carrying our paracetamol based on customer feedback.

"You know what we learned?" Priya asked one evening as we cleaned up the garage after our largest production run yet.

"That cost reduction and quality improvement aren't necessarily contradictory?"

"That innovation forced by constraints can produce better results than innovation driven by unlimited resources."

She was right. If we'd had enough capital to use standard formulations, we never would have discovered that multifunction excipients could improve consistency while reducing costs. If we'd had access to automated equipment with wide tolerance margins, we never would have learned how precise process control could enhance product performance.

Our resource limitations had forced us to understand tablet manufacturing at a deeper level than our competitors.

Six months later, when we started developing our second product—ibuprofen tablets—we applied the same approach. Instead of copying existing formulations, we researched ways to achieve superior performance at lower cost through innovative ingredient selection and precise process control.

The ibuprofen project succeeded even faster than paracetamol because we'd learned to think systematically about the relationship between formulation chemistry and manufacturing economics.

By our first anniversary, we'd developed cost-effective formulations for five different generic drugs. Each formulation cost 25-40% less than standard approaches while meeting or exceeding performance specifications.

More importantly, we'd discovered something that would guide our product development for the next twenty years: the most effective way to compete in generic pharmaceuticals wasn't to make the same products cheaper—it was to make better products for the same price.

Innovation driven by necessity had become innovation driven by systematic understanding.

Our constraint had taught us that technical excellence and economic efficiency weren't opposing forces—they were complementary approaches to solving the same problem.

We just had to be willing to think differently about what the problem actually was.

Competition with Established Players like Cipla and Dr. Reddy's

The Cipla representative arrived at City Pharmaceuticals the same day we were delivering our monthly order.

I was helping Mr. Patel's staff unload our 25,000 paracetamol tablets when a white Ambassador car pulled up with "Cipla Limited" emblazoned on the door. A man in a pressed shirt and tie emerged, carrying a leather briefcase that probably cost more than our entire month's raw material budget.

"Mr. Patel," he called out, walking directly past our small truck as if it were invisible. "I have some excellent news about pricing adjustments."

Priya and I continued unloading boxes, but we couldn't help overhearing the conversation in Mr. Patel's office.

"We're prepared to offer you a fifteen percent discount on paracetamol tablets," the Cipla representative announced. "Effective immediately, for orders of 100,000 tablets or more."

Through the office window, I could see Mr. Patel's face. He was doing mental calculations, probably comparing Cipla's new price with what he was paying us.

"What's the catch?" Mr. Patel asked.

"No catch. We're simply consolidating our distributor network and want to ensure our best partners receive competitive pricing."

The translation was obvious: Cipla had noticed that small distributors were buying from newer manufacturers and decided to undercut the competition. A fifteen percent discount on their already-efficient pricing would put their paracetamol tablets below our cost of production.

"I'll need to think about it," Mr. Patel said diplomatically.

After the Cipla representative left, Mr. Patel walked over to where we were finishing the delivery paperwork.

"Arjun, we need to talk."

We followed him into his office, where he poured three cups of tea and looked uncomfortable.

"Cipla just offered me paracetamol tablets at ₹1.05 each for orders over 100,000 units," he said without preamble.

Our current price was ₹1.25 per tablet. Our production cost was ₹0.95 per tablet. There was no mathematical way to match Cipla's pricing without losing money on every tablet we sold.

"How long have you been working with Cipla?" Priya asked.

"Twelve years. They're reliable, professional, and they have excellent distribution support."

"But?" I prompted, sensing there was more to the story.

"But their minimum order is now 100,000 tablets, and they want payment within thirty days of delivery. My cash flow can't handle orders that large."

This was exactly what we'd hoped to hear, but I tried not to look too relieved.

"What kind of order quantities work better for your business?" Priya asked.

"What I really need is 25,000 tablets delivered every two weeks, with payment terms of forty-five days. That matches my customer demand and cash flow."

"And Cipla can't accommodate that?"

Mr. Patel shook his head. "Their sales representative made it clear that flexible ordering is available only for very large distributors. Smaller partners like me need to adapt to their systems."

Here was our competitive reality in stark relief. Cipla could offer lower prices because of their scale advantages, but their scale also made them less flexible about customer requirements. They were optimized for large orders, standard payment terms, and predictable demand patterns.

We were optimized for exactly the opposite.

"Mr. Patel," I said carefully, "what if we could match Cipla's pricing for orders that fit your cash flow requirements?"

"How would you do that?"

I wasn't sure we could, but I knew we had to try. "Give us two weeks to work on our costs. If we can't offer competitive pricing with flexible terms, we'll help you transition to Cipla with no hard feelings."

That evening, Priya and I sat in our garage laboratory with calculators, notebooks, and a sense of impending crisis.

"We need to reduce our production costs by twenty paise per tablet," I said. "That's a twenty-one percent cost reduction."

"Without compromising quality," Priya added.

"Without compromising quality."

We started by examining every component of our cost structure. Raw materials were already optimized—we'd spent months finding the most cost-effective formulation. Labor costs were minimal since we were doing most of the work ourselves. Equipment depreciation was fixed.

"What about overhead allocation?" Priya suggested. "We're calculating costs based on 25,000 tablet batches, but what if we increased batch sizes?"

"Our tablet press can handle larger batches, but do we have enough mixing capacity?"

We spent the next morning testing whether we could double our batch size using our existing equipment. The answer was yes, but it required more careful attention to mixing uniformity and process timing.

"Bigger batches reduce the overhead cost per tablet," I calculated. "But they also increase our working capital requirements."

"How much increase?"

"About ₹8,000 per batch in additional raw material investment."

We had ₹15,000 in our bank account. Doubling our batch size would consume more than half our remaining capital.

"What if we asked Mr. Patel to prepay for larger orders?" Priya suggested. "If he pays fifty percent upfront, we could afford to manufacture bigger batches."

"And if he says no?"

"Then we find another way to reduce costs."

The conversation with Mr. Patel went better than expected.

"You want me to prepay for orders?" he asked.

"Fifty percent prepayment for orders of 50,000 tablets or more," I explained. "In exchange, we'll match Cipla's pricing and maintain flexible delivery schedules."

"So instead of ordering 25,000 tablets every two weeks, I'd order 50,000 tablets every month with half the payment upfront?"

"Exactly. Same monthly volume, same cash flow impact for you, but larger batch sizes that let us achieve better cost efficiency."

He thought for several minutes. "What guarantee do I have that your quality will remain consistent with larger batches?"

"We'll provide samples from every batch before delivery. If any batch doesn't meet your quality standards, we'll replace it at no charge."

"And what happens if Cipla reduces their prices further?"

That was the question I'd been dreading. We were already stretching to match their current pricing. If they decided to engage in serious price competition, we'd have no room to respond.

"We can't promise to match unlimited price reductions," I said honestly. "But we can promise to maintain our service levels and payment flexibility regardless of pricing pressure."

Mr. Patel agreed to try the new arrangement for three months.

Our first 50,000 tablet batch was nerve-wracking. Double the raw materials, double the production time, double the quality risk. If something went wrong, we'd lose more money than we could afford to lose.

Everything went perfectly. The tablets met all specifications, the larger batch size did reduce our unit costs, and Mr. Patel was satisfied with the quality and delivery timing.

But two weeks later, the Cipla representative was back.

"I understand you're still working with local suppliers," he told Mr. Patel during a visit we happened to witness. "We can offer additional volume discounts for exclusive partnerships."

"What kind of additional discounts?" Mr. Patel asked.

"Another ten percent reduction for distributors who commit to purchasing exclusively from Cipla for twelve months."

This would put Cipla's pricing at ₹0.95 per tablet—exactly our production cost. Matching their price would mean working for free.

After the Cipla representative left, Mr. Patel looked genuinely apologetic.

"Arjun, I appreciate everything you've done to accommodate my business needs. But I can't ignore a twenty-five percent cost difference."

"I understand completely," I said. "Business is business."

"Would you be interested in supplying other products? Maybe something where pricing competition isn't quite so intense?"

That conversation led to our development of ibuprofen tablets, where the competitive dynamics were different and our formulation innovations could create more defensible advantages.

But the paracetamol experience taught us something crucial about competing with established players: we couldn't win by playing their game better. We had to find games they weren't interested in playing.

Over the next year, instead of competing directly with Cipla and Dr. Reddy's for standard products in major markets, we focused on opportunities they were ignoring:

Smaller distributors who needed flexible ordering terms. Niche products with limited market size but good margins. Regional markets where local service mattered more than scale advantages. Custom formulations for specific customer requirements.

"You know what's interesting?" Priya observed six months later, as we reviewed our growing customer base. "We haven't lost customers to Cipla and Dr. Reddy's because we're cheaper or faster. We've kept customers because we're different."

She was right. The distributors who worked with us weren't looking for the lowest possible prices—they were looking for suppliers who understood their specific business requirements and could adapt accordingly.

The large pharmaceutical companies were optimized for efficiency and scale. We were optimized for flexibility and responsiveness. As long as we continued serving market segments that valued flexibility more than absolute cost, we could compete successfully despite their size advantages.

Three years later, when Cipla tried to acquire one of our major customers by offering even more aggressive pricing, the customer declined.

"Why?" I asked the distributor during our regular quarterly review.

"Because working with Cipla means adapting my business to their systems," he explained. "Working with you means you adapt your systems to my business. That flexibility is worth more than the price difference."

That's when I realized we'd found our sustainable competitive advantage: not being the cheapest, but being the most adaptable.

The giants could outspend us, but they couldn't out-think us about individual customer needs.

And in a market with thousands of small and medium distributors, that advantage was enough to build a business that complemented rather than competed directly with the industry leaders.

Learning from Ravi Krishnan, The Veteran Production Manager

Ravi Krishnan found us through our tablet press supplier.

We'd been struggling with machine breakdowns for three weeks—our twenty-two-year-old tablet press had developed an alarming tendency to jam during longer production runs, creating a grinding noise that made our neighbors file noise complaints with the local housing society.

"You need someone who understands old equipment," the equipment dealer told me over the phone. "There's a fellow named Ravi who used to maintain these machines at Lupin Pharmaceuticals before he retired. Very experienced, but very particular about how things should be done."

Particular seemed like exactly what we needed.

Ravi arrived on a Tuesday morning wearing a spotless white shirt, pressed trousers, and the kind of leather shoes that suggested he took maintenance seriously. He was probably sixty years old, with silver hair and hands that showed forty years of working with machinery.

"So," he said, looking around our garage laboratory, "this is where you're trying to manufacture pharmaceuticals."

It wasn't exactly a question, but it wasn't exactly a statement either. There was something in his tone that made me defensive.

"We're producing quality tablets that meet all specifications," I said. "We just need help with equipment reliability."

He nodded politely and walked to our tablet press. For ten minutes, he examined the machine without saying a word, running his fingers along surfaces, checking bolt tensions, listening to sounds I couldn't even hear.

"When did you last lubricate the cam assembly?" he asked finally.

"Last week. We follow the maintenance schedule from the operating manual."

"Which lubricant did you use?"

I showed him the industrial grease we'd bought from a local supplier. He examined the container label and shook his head.

"This is automotive grease. It's too thick for pharmaceutical equipment. In humid conditions like Hyderabad, thick grease attracts dust and creates binding problems."

"The equipment dealer said any high-quality grease would work."

"The equipment dealer probably never operated a tablet press for eight-hour shifts in a monsoon climate."

He opened his toolbox and pulled out a different lubricant. "This is pharmaceutical-grade machinery oil. Costs twice as much as automotive grease, but it won't create the problems you're experiencing."

"How do you know that's the cause of our jamming problems?"

Instead of answering, he started disassembling part of our tablet press. Within minutes, he'd exposed the cam assembly that controlled tablet compression timing.

"Look here," he said, pointing to a buildup of thick, dust-laden grease around the moving parts. "Your lubricant is creating friction instead of reducing it. Every time humidity increases, this gets worse."

He spent the next hour cleaning the cam assembly with solvents and cotton rags, explaining what he was doing as he worked.

"Pharmaceutical equipment maintenance isn't like maintaining cars or industrial machinery," he said, carefully applying the proper lubricant. "Pharmaceutical equipment has to run consistently for hours without variation. Any friction, any binding, any irregular movement shows up as tablet weight variation or hardness problems."

"We haven't noticed quality problems," Priya said, watching from across the garage.

"You haven't measured them yet. But I guarantee that if you check tablet weights from the beginning and end of your production runs, you'll find differences."

He was right. When we tested tablets from our most recent batch, the first 500 tablets averaged 485 milligrams each, while the last 500 tablets averaged 492 milligrams each. The variation was still within specification limits, but it was larger than we'd realized.

"Why does this matter if we're meeting specifications?" I asked.

Ravi looked at me with the patience of someone who'd answered this question many times before. "Because consistent quality is what separates professional manufacturers from garage experimenters. Anyone can make tablets that barely meet specifications. Only competent manufacturers make tablets that consistently exceed specifications."

He reassembled the tablet press and ran a test batch. The machine operated more smoothly than it had since we'd bought it, with less vibration and virtually no noise.

"How much would it cost to hire you as a consultant?" I asked.

"I don't work as a consultant. I work as a production manager or I don't work at all."

"We can't afford a full-time production manager. We're barely covering our own salaries."

"Then you can't afford to manufacture pharmaceuticals properly."

The conversation stalled there. Ravi clearly knew things we needed to learn, but we couldn't afford his services and he wasn't interested in part-time consulting arrangements.

"Could we work out a different arrangement?" Priya suggested. "What if you helped us establish proper production procedures in exchange for equity in the company?"

Ravi considered this for a long moment. "What percentage equity?"

"Five percent," I said, hoping that sounded reasonable.

"Twenty percent."

"That's too much for consulting work."

"I wouldn't be consulting. I'd be building your production capabilities from the ground up. Training you to think like professional manufacturers instead of like chemists playing with equipment."

The equity negotiation took three weeks. Ravi wanted 20%, we offered 5%, and we eventually settled on 12% equity in exchange for six months of full-time production management followed by ongoing part-time oversight.

It was the best business decision we made in our first year.

Ravi's first week with us was humbling. He identified seventeen different aspects of our production process that were creating unnecessary quality variation, equipment wear, or safety risks.

Our mixing times were too short for proper ingredient uniformity. Our compression forces were inconsistent because we weren't calibrating the tablet press properly. Our environmental controls were inadequate—humidity and temperature variations were affecting tablet hardness in ways we hadn't noticed.

"You've been lucky more than skillful," he told us after completing his initial assessment. "Your formulation is good enough to compensate for process inconsistencies, but that luck won't last as you scale up production."

He spent the next month teaching us what he called "production discipline."

Everything had to be measured and recorded. Mixing times, compression forces, environmental conditions, raw material temperatures. Everything had to be done the same way every time, not just approximately the same way.

"Pharmaceuticals aren't like cooking," he explained as we watched him calibrate our mixing equipment for the third time that week. "In cooking, you can adjust seasonings to taste and still get good results. In pharmaceuticals, every variation creates quality risks that could affect patient health."

The discipline was exhausting. Recording every parameter, following procedures exactly, double-checking every measurement. Our production rate slowed by 30% as we learned to do everything correctly instead of just quickly.

But our quality consistency improved dramatically. Tablet weight variation dropped from ±8 milligrams to ±2 milligrams. Hardness variation dropped by 60%. Dissolution rate variation practically disappeared.

"Now you're manufacturing pharmaceuticals instead of just making tablets," Ravi said after reviewing our improved quality data.

More importantly, he taught us to think systematically about process optimization.

"Every manufacturing problem has three possible causes," he would say. "Equipment problems, procedure problems, or people problems. Equipment problems show up as equipment failures. Procedure problems show up as quality variation. People problems show up as inconsistent results from the same procedures."

When our tablet press started producing tablets with surface defects, Ravi walked us through his diagnostic approach. First, check the equipment—compression forces, punch and die condition, lubrication status. Second, check the procedures—are we following standard operating procedures exactly? Third, check the people—are we rushing, getting distracted, or making assumptions about process steps?

The surface defects turned out to be caused by inadequate die cleaning between batches. We'd been cleaning the dies, but not removing all traces of lubricant residue that built up over multiple production runs.

"The equipment was fine, the procedure was incomplete," Ravi explained. "Now you know how to prevent this problem in the future."

By his fourth month with us, Ravi had transformed our garage laboratory from an experimental setup into what he called "a small but professional pharmaceutical manufacturing facility."

We had standard operating procedures for every process step. We had preventive maintenance schedules for all equipment. We had quality control checkpoints throughout production. We had documentation systems that would support regulatory inspections.

"What happens when you leave?" I asked him near the end of his six-month commitment.

"You'll continue doing things the way I've taught you to do them. And when you encounter new problems, you'll solve them using the systematic approach you've learned."

"What if we encounter problems we can't solve?"

"Then you'll call me. That's what the ongoing consulting arrangement is for."

Ravi's last week was spent documenting everything he'd taught us in detailed written procedures. Equipment maintenance schedules, quality control protocols, troubleshooting guides, supplier evaluation criteria.

"These procedures represent forty years of pharmaceutical manufacturing experience," he said, handing over the completed documentation. "Follow them exactly and you'll avoid most of the problems that destroy small manufacturers."

Six months later, when we moved from our garage to our first proper manufacturing facility, we used Ravi's procedures as the foundation for our new operation. A year later, when we hired our first production employees, we trained them using Ravi's systematic approach.

Three years later, when we achieved our first WHO-GMP certification, the regulatory inspectors commented on the quality of our production procedures and documentation systems.

"Your procedures are more thorough than companies five times your size," the lead inspector observed. "Who developed your quality systems?"

"A production manager who taught us the difference between making tablets and manufacturing pharmaceuticals," I told him.

That difference, as it turned out, was what separated companies that survived their first regulatory inspection from companies that didn't.

Ravi had given us more than technical knowledge. He'd given us the professional discipline that would allow us to scale from garage operation to global manufacturer while maintaining the quality standards that pharmaceutical manufacturing requires.

Twenty years later, when our company employed thousands of people across multiple continents, we still used modified versions of the procedures Ravi had developed in our garage laboratory.

Because some lessons, once learned correctly, never need to be relearned.

Constraint Breakthrough: Achieving 40% Cost Reduction through Process Innovation

The breakthrough came from watching Ravi clean our tablet press for the fifteenth time that month.

It was late February 1995, and we'd been manufacturing consistently for four months. Our quality was excellent, our customers were satisfied, but our profit margins were still razor-thin. Every paisa of cost reduction we'd achieved through formulation optimization had been eaten up by rising raw material prices and increased competition.

"Ravi," I said, watching him disassemble the compression chamber for what seemed like the hundredth time, "how much time do we spend on equipment cleaning every week?"

He paused, considering. "About six hours per week for thorough cleaning. Plus another four hours for routine maintenance."

"And how much production time do we lose during cleaning?"

"Complete shutdown for two hours every other day. Plus setup time to get back to consistent operation."

I started calculating in my head. Ten hours of direct labor for cleaning and maintenance, plus twelve hours of production downtime per week. On our single tablet press producing 3,000 tablets per hour, that represented 36,000 tablets in lost production capacity.

"What if we could reduce cleaning time?" Priya asked, overhearing our conversation.

"Not possible," Ravi said firmly. "Pharmaceutical equipment requires thorough cleaning between products to prevent cross-contamination. There are no shortcuts for proper hygiene."

"I'm not talking about shortcuts," she said. "I'm talking about better methods."

That afternoon, Priya started researching pharmaceutical cleaning procedures at the medical college library. What she found was interesting: most cleaning protocols had been developed for large-scale production equipment handling multiple products daily. Our situation was different—we were running single products for extended periods on simple equipment.

"Look at this," she said, showing me research papers from European pharmaceutical manufacturers. "Clean-in-place systems that reduce cleaning time by 60% while improving contamination control."

"Those are for million-dollar production lines," I pointed out. "We can't afford automated cleaning systems."

"But maybe we can adapt the principles to our equipment."

She'd found references to pharmaceutical manufacturers who'd modified their cleaning procedures based on actual contamination risk assessment rather than generic industry protocols. Instead of complete disassembly after every batch, they used validated cleaning procedures that maintained quality while reducing downtime.

"Ravi, what if we tested different cleaning approaches to see which ones actually prevent contamination?" I suggested.

He looked skeptical. "Cleaning procedures exist for good reasons. Changing them without proper validation is dangerous."

"I'm not suggesting we change them blindly. I'm suggesting we validate which steps are actually necessary for our specific equipment and products."

The conversation that followed revealed something interesting about Ravi's background. At Lupin Pharmaceuticals, he'd followed standard cleaning procedures because they were manufacturing dozens of different products on shared equipment. Cross-contamination between different active ingredients could create serious safety problems.

But we were manufacturing single products for weeks at a time on dedicated equipment. Our contamination risks were completely different.

"What would proper validation involve?" I asked.

"Testing residue levels after different cleaning procedures to determine which methods actually achieve adequate contamination control," Ravi explained. "It's not complicated, just thorough."

We spent the next month developing what we called our "cleaning optimization project." Using simple analytical methods, we tested residue levels after various cleaning procedures to see which steps were truly necessary for our operating conditions.

The results surprised all of us.

Complete disassembly and solvent cleaning—our standard procedure—reduced contamination to undetectable levels. But so did simplified cleaning using hot water and approved detergents, followed by alcohol rinse and air drying.

More importantly, the simplified procedure took 45 minutes instead of 2 hours, and required only 30 minutes of production downtime instead of 2 hours.

"Are you sure this provides adequate contamination control?" Ravi asked, reviewing our test results.

"The residue levels are identical," Priya confirmed. "And actually more consistent because there's less opportunity for recontamination during lengthy cleaning procedures."

We implemented the optimized cleaning procedure gradually, testing contamination levels weekly to ensure quality wasn't compromised. After six weeks of validation, we were confident that our new approach maintained product quality while reducing cleaning time by 75%.

The production impact was immediate. Instead of losing 12 hours per week to cleaning downtime, we lost 3 hours. Instead of dedicating 10 hours per week to cleaning labor, we needed 4 hours.

"That's 19 additional hours of production capacity per week," I calculated. "At 3,000 tablets per hour, that's 57,000 additional tablets without any additional equipment investment."

But the real breakthrough came when we applied the same analytical approach to other aspects of our production process.

"If we can optimize cleaning procedures, what other procedures might be optimizable?" Priya asked.

We started examining every time-consuming step in our operation: raw material preparation, equipment setup, in-process testing, packaging operations. Each process step had been designed based on industry standard practices, but many industry standards were developed for different operating conditions than ours.

Raw material preparation was our next target. Standard procedure called for individual weighing and verification of each ingredient, followed by documented double-checks by a second person. For our 50,000 tablet batches, this required nearly 2 hours of labor.

"What if we pre-weighed ingredients for multiple batches?" I suggested. "Bulk preparation with individual verification might be faster than individual preparation with bulk verification."

We tested different preparation methods and found that bulk weighing of dry ingredients, followed by individual portion verification, reduced preparation time by 60% while maintaining accuracy.

Equipment setup optimization came next. We'd been following manufacturer recommendations for tablet press configuration, but those recommendations assumed frequent product changes and multiple operators. We were running single products with consistent operators.

"Once we achieve optimal settings for a specific product, do we really need to recalibrate everything for each batch?" Ravi wondered.

After extensive testing, we developed product-specific setup procedures that reduced configuration time from 45 minutes to 15 minutes per batch.

In-process testing offered the biggest opportunity. We'd been testing every parameter specified in industry guidelines, but many tests were designed to catch problems that our process controls prevented from occurring.

"We're testing tablet hardness every 30 minutes," Priya observed. "But our hardness variation is so low that we could probably test every 2 hours without missing any quality problems."

We validated reduced testing frequencies for parameters that showed consistent results, freeing up analytical time for more thorough testing of critical quality attributes.

By June 1995, six months after starting our process optimization project, we'd achieved something remarkable: 40% reduction in total production costs with no compromise in product quality.

The cost reduction came from multiple sources:

- 19 additional hours of production capacity per week eliminated overtime labor costs

- Optimized raw material preparation reduced batch preparation time by 60%
- Streamlined equipment setup procedures reduced changeover time by 65%
- Validated testing frequency reductions freed up analytical resources for process improvement
- Reduced cleaning material consumption saved ₹2,000 per month in supplies

"We're producing the same tablets with the same quality using 40% less time and money," I announced to our small team. "Without purchasing any new equipment or changing any formulations."

The impact on our competitive position was dramatic. Our production costs dropped from ₹0.95 per tablet to ₹0.57 per tablet, giving us margin flexibility that transformed our pricing strategy.

More importantly, we'd discovered something that would guide our operations for the next twenty years: standard industry practices weren't necessarily optimal practices for our specific circumstances.

"You know what we learned?" Priya said, reviewing our optimization results. "Most manufacturing inefficiencies exist because people follow procedures designed for different situations than the ones they're actually facing."

Ravi, who'd initially been skeptical of changing established procedures, became our strongest advocate for systematic process analysis.

"Forty years in pharmaceutical manufacturing, and I never thought to question whether standard cleaning procedures were optimal for specific equipment and products," he admitted. "I was following procedures instead of thinking about what the procedures were supposed to accomplish."

The process optimization project taught us our first systematic approach to continuous improvement: identify the actual objective, measure current performance, test alternative methods, validate what works, and implement changes systematically.

Six months later, when we moved from our garage to our first proper manufacturing facility, we didn't just install equipment according to industry standards. We designed every process step based on our specific products, quality requirements, and operating conditions.

The result was a manufacturing facility that operated 35% more efficiently than industry benchmarks from day one, because we'd learned to think about efficiency systematically rather than just copying what everyone else was doing.

Our working capital constraint had forced us to get creative about cost reduction. That creativity had taught us that significant improvements were possible through systematic analysis of existing processes.

The constraint had become our teacher, and the lesson was more valuable than the immediate cost savings: the biggest opportunities for improvement often hide inside the procedures everyone takes for granted.

Chapter 3

The Regulatory Maze

Dancing with the Drug Controller

The rejection letter arrived on a Tuesday morning in April 1995, delivered by a postman who seemed personally offended by having to carry bad news.

"Drug License Application No. DL/HYD/1995/247 has been found deficient in the following areas," the letter began, followed by seventeen numbered paragraphs detailing everything we'd done wrong in our application to legally manufacture paracetamol tablets.

I read through the list twice, trying to understand what we'd missed. Inadequate floor space documentation. Insufficient quality control procedures. Missing environmental impact assessment. Incomplete pharmacist employment verification. The list went on for two pages.

"How long did this application take to process?" Priya asked, reading over my shoulder.

I checked the dates. "Four months. And now they want us to resubmit with corrections."

"How long will resubmission take?"

"Another four months, assuming we address all their concerns correctly."

We'd been manufacturing and selling paracetamol tablets for six months, building a customer base and generating revenue that kept our business alive. But we'd been doing it without proper drug manufacturing licenses, operating in a regulatory gray area that wouldn't survive serious scrutiny.

The rejection letter made clear that our gray area was about to become black and white.

"We need help," Priya said, stating the obvious. "This is beyond what we can figure out ourselves."

That afternoon, I called Dr. K.V. Ramana, a regulatory consultant who'd been recommended by our equipment supplier. Dr. Ramana had spent fifteen years in various drug control departments before starting his own consulting practice, helping small manufacturers navigate India's pharmaceutical licensing requirements.

"I'll need to visit your facility before I can advise you," he said over the phone. "Drug licensing isn't just about paperwork—it's about demonstrating actual compliance with manufacturing standards."

Dr. Ramana arrived the following Thursday, carrying a briefcase full of regulatory documents and wearing the expression of someone who'd seen many garage laboratories pretending to be pharmaceutical facilities.

He spent twenty minutes walking around our garage, making notes in a small notebook and asking questions that revealed gaps in our understanding of pharmaceutical regulations.

"Where do you store raw materials?" he asked.

I pointed to the metal shelving unit we'd installed against one wall. "Right there. Everything's properly labeled and inventory-controlled."

"In the same room where you manufacture tablets?"

"Well, yes. We don't have separate storage space."

He wrote something in his notebook. "Raw material storage must be segregated from manufacturing areas to prevent cross-contamination. That's a basic GMP requirement."

"What's GMP?"

"Good Manufacturing Practices. The foundation of pharmaceutical licensing in India. Without GMP compliance, you'll never get regulatory approval."

The conversation continued for two hours, with Dr. Ramana identifying problems we hadn't known were problems. Our ventilation was inadequate for pharmaceutical manufacturing. Our cleaning procedures weren't documented properly. Our quality control area didn't meet contamination prevention standards.

"The good news," he said finally, "is that your manufacturing quality is actually quite good. The tablets you've shown me meet all relevant specifications."

"What's the bad news?"

"The bad news is that regulatory compliance isn't about product quality. It's about documented systems, controlled environments, and demonstrable procedures. You're making good products using methods that don't comply with regulatory requirements."

Dr. Ramana explained that drug licensing in India followed a two-stage process. First, we needed to demonstrate that our facility, procedures, and personnel met GMP standards. Second, we needed to prove that our specific products met safety and efficacy requirements for generic drugs.

"How much would it cost to achieve GMP compliance?" I asked.

He considered for a moment. "For a facility this size, probably ₹3-4 lakhs in infrastructure improvements, plus ₹50,000 in consultant fees for documentation and preparation."

We had ₹85,000 in our bank account. GMP compliance would consume most of our working capital at exactly the time we needed cash flow to grow the business.

"What happens if we continue operating without proper licenses?" Priya asked.

"Eventually, someone will file a complaint or an inspector will visit your facility. At that point, you'll be shut down immediately and face potential criminal charges for manufacturing drugs without proper authorization."

This was not the regulatory environment I'd anticipated when we started the business. I'd assumed that small-scale pharmaceutical manufacturing would be regulated differently than large-scale industrial operations. The reality was that regulatory standards applied equally to garage laboratories and multinational facilities.

"Is there any way to phase regulatory compliance?" I asked. "Maybe get basic approvals first and add compliance requirements gradually?"

Dr. Ramana shook his head. "Indian drug regulations don't allow phased compliance. You either meet all requirements or you don't get licensed. There's no intermediate status for small manufacturers."

That evening, Priya and I sat in our small kitchen, eating dinner and contemplating the regulatory crisis that threatened to end our business before it had properly begun.

"We have three choices," I said. "Invest everything in GMP compliance and hope we can survive the cash flow impact. Continue operating without licenses and hope we don't get caught. Or shut down the business and find jobs."

"There might be a fourth choice," Priya said.

"Which is?"

"What if we found someone who's already GMP-compliant and willing to manufacture our products under contract?"

This was an interesting idea. Instead of building our own compliant facility, we could develop formulations and manage customer relationships while outsourcing actual manufacturing to licensed facilities.

"Contract manufacturing," I said, thinking through the implications. "It would solve our regulatory problems, but it would also eliminate our manufacturing cost advantages."

"Maybe, or maybe not. If we can find someone with excess capacity, they might offer competitive pricing in exchange for steady business."

The next morning, I started calling GMP-certified manufacturers in the Hyderabad area, explaining that we were a marketing company looking for contract manufacturing services.

Most weren't interested in small volumes. Their minimum batch sizes were 100,000 tablets, and their setup costs made small orders uneconomical. But a few expressed interest in discussing arrangements.

"We have capacity available on our second shift," explained Mr. Suresh Reddy, owner of a small but properly licensed pharmaceutical facility in Medchal. "If you can guarantee regular orders of 50,000 tablets or more, we might work out pricing that makes sense for both of us."

His facility was everything ours wasn't: proper raw material storage areas, controlled air handling systems, documented cleaning procedures, qualified quality control laboratory. It had taken him two years and ₹15 lakhs to achieve GMP certification.

"What would you charge for manufacturing our paracetamol formulation?" I asked.

"₹0.35 per tablet for batches of 50,000 or more, including all raw materials and quality testing."

This was actually competitive with our own manufacturing costs, especially when we factored in the regulatory compliance investments we'd need to make.

"What about product development?" Priya asked. "If we have ideas for new formulations, could we develop them using your facility?"

"Absolutely. We have excess laboratory capacity and would welcome the additional business."

The contract manufacturing arrangement solved our immediate regulatory crisis, but it also changed our business model fundamentally. Instead of being a pharmaceutical manufacturer, we became a pharmaceutical development and marketing company that happened to use external manufacturing.

"Is that necessarily bad?" Priya wondered as we drove back from Medchal.

"I don't know. It's different from what we planned, but it might actually be better suited to our capabilities."

Over the next three months, we transitioned our production to Mr. Reddy's facility while maintaining our customer relationships and continuing product development in our garage laboratory. The arrangement worked better than expected.

Our customers didn't care where the tablets were manufactured as long as quality and delivery remained consistent. Our cash flow improved because we no longer tied up working capital in manufacturing equipment and inventory. Our product development accelerated because we had access to better analytical equipment.

Most importantly, we learned something valuable about regulatory strategy: sometimes the best way to overcome regulatory constraints isn't to comply with regulations, but to restructure your business model so that compliance becomes someone else's responsibility.

"You know what's interesting?" Dr. Ramana observed during a follow-up consultation. "You've accidentally discovered one of the most effective strategies for small pharmaceutical companies. Many successful companies started as development and marketing organizations before building their own manufacturing capabilities."

"So we're not giving up on manufacturing permanently?"

"You're deferring manufacturing until you have the scale and capital to do it properly. That's smart strategic thinking, not business failure."

Two years later, when our revenues had grown to ₹2 crores annually and we had ₹20 lakhs in working capital, we revisited the question of building our own GMP-compliant facility.

By then, we understood regulatory requirements much better. We'd learned what "good manufacturing practices" actually meant by working closely with a compliant facility. We'd developed relationships with regulatory consultants and understood the approval process.

Building our own facility became a strategic choice rather than a desperate necessity.

But perhaps more importantly, we'd learned that regulatory constraints could be navigated through business model innovation as well as direct compliance. The pharmaceutical industry had multiple ways to operate successfully, and finding the right approach for our specific situation was more important than following the most obvious path.

The regulatory maze hadn't blocked our progress—it had forced us to find a better route to our destination.

Navigating India's Complex Regulatory Environment

The Drug Controller's office in Hyderabad occupied the ground floor of a colonial-era building that seemed designed to discourage visitors.

I arrived at 10 AM for what Dr. Ramana had described as a "routine pre-submission consultation" about our drug license application. The waiting room contained twenty plastic chairs, three ceiling fans that moved air without cooling anything, and a hand-painted sign that read "SILENCE IS GOLDEN."

By 2 PM, I was still waiting.

"First time here?" asked the man sitting next to me, who'd been reading the same newspaper page for the past hour.

"Yes. I was told the Drug Controller wanted to discuss our manufacturing license application."

He laughed, not unkindly. "The Drug Controller wants to discuss everyone's application. The question is when he'll have time to do it."

The man introduced himself as Mohan, owner of a small pharmaceutical company that had been trying to get approval for a new product formulation for eight months.

"Eight months?" I asked. "Dr. Ramana told us the standard processing time was four months."

"Four months is the minimum time required by regulation. Actual processing time depends on many factors."

"Such as?"

Mohan glanced around the waiting room and lowered his voice. "The completeness of your application. The workload of the reviewing officer. The complexity of your product. The phase of the moon."

I wasn't sure if he was joking about the moon.

"How do you expedite the process?" I asked.

"You don't expedite government processes. You adapt your business to government timelines."

At 3:30 PM, a clerk emerged from the inner office and called my name. I followed him through a corridor lined with filing cabinets that reached the ceiling, past offices where officials shuffled through stacks of applications that looked like they'd been accumulating for years.

The Drug Controller's office was larger than I'd expected, with a massive wooden desk covered in neat piles of documents. Dr. M.S. Krishnamurthy looked up from a file he was reviewing and gestured for me to sit in the chair across from his desk.

"So," he said, opening a folder with my name on it, "you want to manufacture pharmaceutical products."

"Yes sir. Paracetamol tablets initially, with plans to develop additional generic formulations."

"In a residential garage."

This wasn't a question, but I felt compelled to respond. "We've transitioned to contract manufacturing with a GMP-certified facility. The garage was just for product development."

"Hmm." He made a note in my file. "Tell me about your pharmaceutical background."

I explained my education and experience at Ranbaxy, my formulation development work, and our quality achievements with paracetamol production.

"And your business partner?"

"Priya Sharma. Analytical chemistry background, responsible for quality control and process optimization."

"Is she your wife?"

"No sir, business partner and co-founder."

Another note in the file. "What is your manufacturing capacity?"

"Currently 50,000 tablets per batch through our contract manufacturer. We plan to scale up based on market demand."

"What quality control testing do you perform?"

"Complete dissolution testing, hardness and friability testing, content uniformity analysis, and microbial contamination testing for every batch."

He asked detailed questions about our testing procedures, analytical methods, and quality specifications. It became clear that Dr. Krishnamurthy knew pharmaceutical manufacturing very well and wasn't interested in superficial answers.

"Your technical approach seems sound," he said after thirty minutes of questioning. "But I have concerns about your business model."

"What concerns?"

"You're a two-person company trying to compete in a market dominated by established manufacturers with decades of experience and hundreds of crores in annual revenue. What makes you think you can succeed?"

This was not the kind of question I'd expected from a regulatory official. I'd assumed the Drug Controller's interest would focus on compliance and safety, not business strategy.

"We're not trying to compete directly with large manufacturers," I explained. "We're focusing on market segments that require flexibility and responsiveness rather than scale."

"Such as?"

"Small distributors who need frequent deliveries in manageable quantities. Custom formulations for specific therapeutic requirements. Regional markets where local service matters more than national branding."

Dr. Krishnamurthy leaned back in his chair. "In twenty years of pharmaceutical regulation, I've seen hundreds of small companies with similar strategies. Most fail within three years."

"Why do they fail?"

"Because they underestimate the complexity of pharmaceutical business. Manufacturing is only one aspect. You also need regulatory expertise, quality assurance, supply chain management, customer relationships, financial management. Two people cannot master all these functions."

"That's why we're building partnerships with specialists in each area."

"Partners cost money. Small companies typically can't afford the partnerships they need to succeed."

The conversation continued for another twenty minutes, with Dr. Krishnamurthy probing our understanding of regulatory requirements, quality standards, and business sustainability. It felt more like a business school examination than a regulatory consultation.

"I'm going to approve your license application," he said finally, "but with conditions."

"What conditions?"

"First, you must submit quarterly reports on production volumes, quality test results, and any customer complaints. Second, your facility will be subject to unannounced inspections every six months for the first two years. Third, any changes to your formulations or manufacturing processes must be pre-approved through amendment applications."

"Those conditions seem reasonable."

"Fourth, you must engage a qualified regulatory consultant to ensure ongoing compliance. I recommend Dr. Meera Patel, who recently left the Central Drug Standards Control Organization to start her own practice."

Dr. Krishnamurthy wrote Dr. Patel's contact information on a piece of paper and handed it to me. "She understands both regulatory requirements and small business realities. You'll need that combination."

Walking out of the Drug Controller's office that afternoon, I felt both relieved and overwhelmed. Relieved because we'd achieved regulatory approval that legitimized our business. Overwhelmed because the approval came with oversight requirements that would add complexity and cost to our operations.

I called Dr. Meera Patel that evening.

"Dr. Krishnamurthy referred me to you," I explained. "We're a small pharmaceutical company that needs regulatory consulting support."

"How small?" she asked.

"Two founders, one product, ₹2 lakh monthly revenue."

"Most regulatory consultants won't work with companies that small. The fees don't justify the effort."

"What would justify the effort?"

"A retainer arrangement that gives me ongoing involvement in your regulatory strategy as you grow. I'd rather work with one company for five years than five companies for one year each."

We negotiated a consulting arrangement that would cost us ₹5,000 per month initially, scaling up as our business grew. In exchange, Dr. Patel would handle all our regulatory submissions, maintain compliance documentation, and provide strategic advice on product development and market expansion.

"The most important thing you need to understand about Indian pharmaceutical regulation," she told me during our first meeting, "is that it's designed for large, established manufacturers. Everything from application procedures to inspection protocols assumes you have dedicated regulatory staff and sophisticated quality systems."

"So small companies are disadvantaged?"

"Small companies have to work harder to demonstrate the same level of compliance. But they also have advantages that large companies don't have."

"Such as?"

"Flexibility to implement new requirements quickly. Direct communication between decision-makers and regulatory officials. Ability to focus resources on specific compliance issues."

Dr. Patel's guidance proved invaluable over the next eighteen months. When the Central Drug Standards Control Organization issued new guidelines for dissolution testing, she helped us implement the changes within weeks instead of months. When we wanted to add ibuprofen tablets to our product line, she managed the supplementary application process that would have taken us months to navigate alone.

Most importantly, she taught us to think proactively about regulatory compliance instead of reactively responding to requirements.

"Regulatory compliance isn't just about following rules," she explained. "It's about building systems that make compliance automatic rather than effortful."

By 1997, when we finally built our own GMP-certified manufacturing facility, we'd learned to view regulatory requirements as design specifications rather than bureaucratic obstacles. Our facility wasn't just compliant—it exceeded requirements in areas where excellence provided competitive advantages.

"You know what's interesting about your regulatory journey?" Dr. Patel observed during a facility inspection that year. "You started by seeing regulations as barriers to overcome. Now you use regulations as frameworks for building superior capabilities."

She was right. We'd discovered that regulatory compliance, properly understood and implemented, created operational excellence that our competitors found difficult to match.

The Drug Controller's warning about small company failure rates had forced us to build partnerships and systems that made us more resilient than we would have been operating independently.

Three years later, when Dr. Krishnamurthy visited our new facility for a routine inspection, he seemed genuinely pleased with what we'd accomplished.

"This is how small companies should approach pharmaceutical manufacturing," he told his inspection team. "Professional compliance, conservative growth, and systematic capability building."

Walking through our facility that day, I realized that navigating India's complex regulatory environment had taught us something more valuable than just compliance procedures. It had taught us to build business capabilities systematically rather than haphazardly.

The regulatory maze hadn't slowed our progress—it had forced us to develop the organizational discipline that would support sustainable growth for decades to come.

Building Relationships with Regulatory Consultants

Dr. Meera Patel's office was everything our garage laboratory wasn't.

Located on the third floor of a glass-fronted building in Banjara Hills, it had proper air conditioning, filing cabinets that actually closed, and a receptionist who offered visitors coffee in ceramic cups instead of plastic. The walls were covered with framed certificates from regulatory authorities I'd never heard of.

"Most pharmaceutical consultants work with established companies," Dr. Patel said, gesturing for me to sit across from her imposing mahogany desk. "Companies with dedicated regulatory departments, annual compliance budgets, and multi-product portfolios. You don't fit that profile."

I'd called her three times before she agreed to meet with me. Each conversation had been polite but brief, with Dr. Patel explaining that her practice focused on clients who could afford comprehensive regulatory services.

"What would it take for us to fit your profile?" I asked.

"A realistic understanding of what regulatory compliance actually costs," she said, opening a folder labeled "Fee Structure." "Most small companies think they can handle regulatory work part-time or outsource it cheaply. They're wrong on both counts."

She showed me a price list that made my heart sink. Basic drug license applications: ₹25,000. Product registration fees: ₹15,000 per product. Ongoing compliance monitoring: ₹10,000 per month. For a company generating ₹2 lakh monthly revenue, these fees would consume 25% of our gross income.

"We can't afford those rates," I said honestly.

"Then you can't afford to be in the pharmaceutical business."

The conversation seemed to be ending before it had properly begun. I'd expected some negotiation, maybe a discussion of reduced fees for small companies. Instead, Dr. Patel was politely explaining why we weren't suitable clients.

"Can I ask you something?" I said, gathering my papers to leave. "If small companies can't afford proper regulatory consulting, how do they ever grow large enough to afford it?"

She paused, considering the question. "Most don't. The failure rate for small pharmaceutical companies is over 80% within five years. Regulatory non-compliance is one of the primary causes."

"But some do succeed?"

"A few. Usually because they find creative ways to access regulatory expertise during their early growth phases."

I leaned forward. "What kind of creative ways?"

"Equity arrangements. Deferred fee structures. Partnership models where regulatory costs are shared across multiple small companies."

"Would any of those approaches work for our situation?"

Dr. Patel studied my business plan for several minutes, occasionally making notes in the margins. "Tell me about your growth projections," she said finally.

I explained our customer acquisition plans, product development timeline, and revenue forecasts. Nothing spectacular—we hoped to reach ₹10 lakh monthly revenue within two years and ₹25 lakh monthly revenue within five years.

"Those projections assume regulatory compliance," she observed. "Without proper licensing and ongoing compliance support, you won't achieve any of these targets."

"Which is why we need to find a way to work together."

She was quiet for a long time, reviewing our financial projections and comparing them with her fee structure. I could see her calculating whether our projected growth would eventually justify reduced initial fees.

"I have an unusual proposal," she said finally. "Instead of my standard fee structure, I'd consider an equity-plus-retainer arrangement."

"What would that involve?"

"Two percent equity in your company, plus a monthly retainer starting at ₹3,000 and scaling up as your revenue grows. In exchange, I'd handle all your regulatory work for the first three years and provide strategic guidance on compliance-related business decisions."

The equity component was larger than I'd hoped, but the reduced monthly fees would save us ₹7,000 per month initially. More importantly, tying her compensation to our success would align her interests with ours.

"Why would you consider this arrangement?" I asked.

"Because I'm tired of working with large companies that treat regulatory compliance as a necessary evil. I'd rather work with one company that sees compliance as a competitive advantage."

"Is that how we see it?"

"It's how you'll need to see it if you want to succeed."

We negotiated the arrangement for two weeks, with several phone calls to clarify expectations on both sides. Dr. Patel wanted quarterly business reviews, monthly compliance reports, and advance notice of any product development plans. We wanted response time guarantees, cost controls on external expenses, and clear communication about regulatory changes that might affect our business.

The final agreement was more comprehensive than I'd expected. Dr. Patel would serve as our outsourced regulatory department, handling everything from license applications to inspection preparations to ongoing compliance monitoring.

"One condition," she said before we signed the agreement. "You need to understand that regulatory consulting isn't just about filling out forms correctly. It's about building business processes that make compliance automatic."

"What does that mean practically?"

"It means changing how you think about documentation, quality control, supplier relationships, and product development. Regulatory compliance has to be integrated into every business decision, not treated as a separate function."

Our first project was retrofitting our existing operations to meet regulatory standards. Dr. Patel spent a week reviewing our manufacturing procedures, quality control protocols, and documentation systems.

"You're making good products using informal processes," she concluded. "But informal processes don't satisfy regulatory requirements, even when they produce acceptable results."

She helped us develop what she called "compliant business practices"—ways of operating that met regulatory standards while improving our operational efficiency.

Our quality control testing, for example, had been thorough but poorly documented. Dr. Patel showed us how to create testing records that not only satisfied inspectors but also helped us identify process improvements.

"Good documentation isn't just about regulatory compliance," she explained while reviewing our revised quality procedures. "It's about capturing institutional knowledge so you can replicate successes and avoid repeating mistakes."

Our supplier qualification process had been casual—we evaluated suppliers based on price and delivery reliability. Dr. Patel taught us to evaluate suppliers based on quality systems, regulatory compliance, and documentation capabilities.

"Your suppliers' regulatory problems become your regulatory problems," she said. "Qualifying suppliers properly prevents most quality issues before they occur."

Six months into our working relationship, Dr. Patel had transformed our approach to business operations. We weren't just complying with regulations—we were using regulatory frameworks to build more systematic and effective business processes.

"You know what's interesting about your development?" she observed during one of our quarterly reviews. "You started by seeing regulatory compliance as a cost center. Now you're seeing it as a capability driver."

She was right. The documentation systems required for regulatory compliance had improved our process consistency. The supplier qualification requirements had strengthened our supply chain reliability. The quality control protocols had enhanced our product development capabilities.

"When will we be ready for our first regulatory inspection?" I asked.

"You're ready now. But more importantly, you're ready to scale your operations without losing compliance capabilities."

Two years later, when we achieved ₹15 lakh monthly revenue and started planning our own manufacturing facility, Dr. Patel's role evolved from compliance support to strategic advisory.

"Building your own facility changes everything from a regulatory perspective," she explained. "You'll need manufacturing licenses, environmental clearances, factory inspections, and ongoing compliance monitoring."

"How much additional regulatory cost?"

"About ₹3 lakh in initial fees and approvals, plus ₹15,000 monthly for ongoing compliance management."

These costs would have seemed overwhelming when we first met. By then, they represented less than 5% of our monthly revenue and felt like reasonable investments in business capability.

"The relationship has worked well for both of us," Dr. Patel said as we planned our facility development. "You've grown faster than most small pharmaceutical companies, and I've learned more about building regulatory capabilities than I would have working with established companies."

"What made the difference?"

"Alignment of interests. When my success depends on your success, I'm motivated to find solutions that work for your specific situation rather than applying standard approaches that might not fit."

Five years after our first meeting, when Dr. Patel attended our facility inauguration ceremony, I realized something important about professional relationships in complex industries.

The most valuable partnerships aren't transactional—they're developmental. Dr. Patel hadn't just provided regulatory services. She'd taught us to think systematically about compliance, quality, and business process improvement.

"You don't need me as much anymore," she said, watching our internal regulatory team manage an inspection that would have terrified us years earlier.

"We'll always need regulatory expertise," I replied. "But now we have internal capabilities to handle routine compliance and external partnerships for strategic guidance."

"That's exactly how it should work."

By then, our monthly retainer had grown to ₹25,000, reflecting both our increased revenue and the complexity of our operations. But the 2% equity she'd received was worth significantly more than the fees she'd forgone during our early years.

More importantly, we'd learned to view regulatory relationships as investments in long-term capability building rather than expenses to be minimized.

That perspective would prove crucial as we expanded internationally and encountered regulatory environments far more complex than anything we'd faced in India.

First Major Setback: Product Recall due to Stability Issues

The phone call from Mr. Patel came at 6 AM on a Thursday morning in August 1995.

"Arjun, we have a problem with your paracetamol tablets," he said without preamble. "Several pharmacists are reporting that tablets from your July batch are crumbling in their bottles."

I was still half-asleep, trying to process what he was telling me. "Crumbling how?"

"Disintegrating into powder. Customers are opening bottles and finding tablet fragments instead of intact tablets."

"How many reports?"

"Six pharmacists so far, all from the same batch. Batch number ML-0795-PCT."

I knew that batch number by heart. It was our largest production run to date—75,000 tablets manufactured during the third week of July. We'd been proud of achieving such consistent quality across a larger batch size.

"I'll investigate immediately," I told Mr. Patel. "Can you stop selling tablets from that batch until we figure out what's happening?"

"Already done. But Arjun, I have about 15,000 tablets from that batch in my warehouse, and my pharmacists have probably sold another 20,000 to customers."

After hanging up, I sat in my kitchen for several minutes, trying to understand how tablets that had passed all our quality tests could be failing in the field. We'd tested batch ML-0795-PCT thoroughly before delivery—hardness, friability, dissolution, content uniformity. Everything had met specifications.

I called Priya, who lived twenty minutes away. "We have a stability problem with the July batch," I explained. "Can you meet me at the garage in an hour?"

"How bad?"

"Bad enough that we need to figure out what went wrong before more customers discover the problem."

The garage felt different that morning. Instead of being our proud pharmaceutical laboratory, it felt like a crime scene where we needed to reconstruct what had gone wrong.

Priya arrived with her notebook and a grim expression. "I brought samples from the July batch," she said, holding up a bottle of tablets. "These were stored in my apartment under normal conditions."

She opened the bottle and poured a few tablets into her palm. They looked perfect—smooth, white, properly formed. But when she applied gentle pressure with her thumb, one of them cracked.

"That shouldn't happen," I said. "Our hardness testing showed these tablets could withstand 8-10 kilograms of force."

"Hardness testing measures resistance to crushing force," Priya replied. "This looks more like a friability problem—the tablets are becoming fragile over time."

We spent the morning conducting accelerated aging tests on tablets from the July batch, storing samples under different temperature and humidity conditions to simulate extended storage. By afternoon, we understood the problem.

At normal room temperature and humidity, our tablets maintained their integrity for weeks. But under conditions of high humidity—like the monsoon weather Hyderabad had experienced in July and August—the tablets gradually absorbed moisture and became structurally weak.

"It's the formulation," Priya concluded after reviewing our ingredient specifications. "We optimized for cost and dissolution, but we didn't account for long-term stability under varying environmental conditions."

"What specifically is causing the problem?"

"The starch binder we're using is hygroscopic—it absorbs moisture from the air. Over time, absorbed moisture weakens the tablet matrix and causes structural failure."

This was a fundamental formulation error. We'd focused so intensively on achieving consistent quality during manufacturing that we'd neglected to test how our tablets performed during extended storage under real-world conditions.

"How do we fix this?" I asked.

"We need to reformulate using a less hygroscopic binder. But that will change our cost structure and probably require revalidation of our entire manufacturing process."

The immediate problem was more urgent than the long-term solution. We had potentially 35,000 defective tablets in the market that could continue deteriorating and create safety concerns for patients.

I called Dr. Meera Patel to understand our regulatory obligations.

"You need to initiate a voluntary recall immediately," she said after I explained the situation. "Product recalls are serious regulatory events, but voluntary recalls demonstrate responsible behavior and minimize liability."

"How does a recall work?"

"You notify all distributors and ask them to return unsold inventory. You notify relevant regulatory authorities. You investigate the root cause and implement corrective actions. And you cover all costs associated with the recall."

"What will this cost us?"

"Direct costs include refunding distributors for returned products, covering logistics for product retrieval, and laboratory costs for investigating the failure. Indirect costs include lost sales, damaged reputation, and potential customer defection."

Dr. Patel estimated our direct recall costs at ₹40,000-50,000, plus whatever revenue we'd lose from interrupted business operations. Given our monthly revenue of ₹3 lakh, this represented a significant financial impact.

But the alternative—waiting for more field failures and potential regulatory action—could be much worse.

I called Mr. Patel and three other distributors carrying our products to explain the recall.

"We've identified a stability issue with our July paracetamol batch," I told each of them. "We're voluntarily recalling all tablets from that batch and will refund your full purchase price plus logistics costs."

The conversations were uncomfortable but professional. All four distributors appreciated our proactive approach and agreed to cooperate with the recall process.

"These things happen in pharmaceuticals," Mr. Patel said. "What matters is how you handle them."

The recall process took three weeks. We retrieved 23,000 tablets from distributor inventory and estimated that another 20,000 had been sold to end customers. The financial cost was ₹48,000 in direct expenses, plus lost revenue from production downtime while we reformulated our product.

But the real cost was learning how much we didn't know about pharmaceutical manufacturing.

"We've been thinking like chemists instead of like pharmaceutical manufacturers," Priya observed as we analyzed our formulation failure.

"Chemists focus on making reactions work. Pharmaceutical manufacturers focus on making products that work consistently over their entire lifecycle."

The reformulation project took six weeks. We replaced our hygroscopic starch binder with a more stable alternative, adjusted our compression parameters to maintain tablet integrity, and conducted extensive stability testing under accelerated aging conditions.

The new formulation cost 12% more in raw materials but performed consistently under all environmental conditions we could simulate.

"Are we confident this formulation won't have the same stability problems?" I asked as we prepared to resume production.

"We're confident that we've tested this formulation more thoroughly than we tested anything before," Priya replied. "But pharmaceutical manufacturing involves risks that can't be completely eliminated, only managed intelligently."

When we resumed production in October 1995, our approach to quality control had changed fundamentally. Instead of just testing products at the time of manufacture, we implemented ongoing stability monitoring for all products in the field.

Instead of optimizing formulations solely for cost and performance, we optimized for robustness under real-world storage and handling conditions.

Instead of viewing quality control as a manufacturing function, we started viewing it as a business-wide responsibility that extended through the entire product lifecycle.

"You know what this recall taught us?" I said to Priya six months later, reviewing our improved quality systems.

"That pharmaceutical manufacturing is more complex than we thought?"

"That failures are inevitable, but how you respond to failures determines whether you build a sustainable business or become another small company casualty."

The recall had cost us ₹75,000 in direct and indirect expenses, but it had taught us quality control practices that prevented much more expensive failures as we scaled up operations.

More importantly, our distributors' reaction to the recall had taught us something valuable about customer relationships. Companies that handled problems responsibly earned more loyalty than companies that never had problems.

"Mr. Patel actually increased his orders after the recall," Priya observed. "He said working with manufacturers who took responsibility for quality issues was better than working with manufacturers who denied problems existed."

Two years later, when we encountered a minor packaging issue that could have become a major quality problem, we implemented another voluntary recall without hesitation. By then, recalls felt like standard business tools rather than catastrophic failures.

The July 1995 recall had taught us that in pharmaceutical manufacturing, the difference between professional companies and amateur companies wasn't avoiding all problems—it was solving problems quickly and learning from them systematically.

That lesson would prove crucial as we expanded into more complex products and larger markets where the stakes for quality failures would be much higher.

Dr. Meera Patel Joins as Head of Regulatory Affairs

The equity arrangement with Dr. Meera Patel was working well until it wasn't.

By early 1996, eighteen months after our consulting agreement began, we were generating ₹8 lakh in monthly revenue and had expanded to three products: paracetamol, ibuprofen, and diclofenac tablets. Our regulatory compliance was excellent, our customer relationships were strong, and our growth trajectory looked sustainable.

But Dr. Patel was spending 30 hours per week on our regulatory work while maintaining her independent consulting practice for other clients. Something had to give.

"I'm turning away new clients because of the time I'm dedicating to your company," she told me during our quarterly review meeting. "That's not sustainable for my practice."

"What would make it sustainable?"

"Either reducing my involvement in your day-to-day regulatory work, or making your company my primary focus."

The first option would leave us without adequate regulatory support just as we were planning significant expansion. The second option would mean converting Dr. Patel from external consultant to internal employee—a change that would fundamentally alter our business structure.

"If you joined us full-time, what would that look like?" I asked.

"I'd want equity compensation in addition to salary, given the opportunity cost of closing my consulting practice. And I'd want to build a proper regulatory affairs department, not just handle compliance reactively."

"What would a proper regulatory affairs department involve?"

"Systematic regulatory planning, proactive compliance monitoring, strategic guidance on product development, and eventually support for international market expansion."

Dr. Patel had been thinking about this transition for months and had developed detailed proposals for restructuring our regulatory approach.

"Right now, you call me when you need regulatory help," she explained. "That works for basic compliance, but it doesn't work for strategic growth. You need regulatory thinking integrated into business planning, not treated as a separate function."

The conversation revealed something important about our business development. We'd grown from startup to small company, but we were still operating with startup thinking about key business functions.

"Show me your regulatory department proposal," I said.

Dr. Patel opened a folder containing organization charts, job descriptions, and budget projections. Her vision was more comprehensive than I'd expected.

"Head of Regulatory Affairs—that would be me—responsible for strategic regulatory planning and external relationships. Regulatory Affairs Specialist for day-to-day compliance work and documentation. Clinical Research Associate for product development support. Regulatory Writer for preparing submissions and maintaining documentation."

"That's four people. We currently have seven employees total."

"Regulatory affairs will become more important as you expand, not less important. The cost of regulatory failures increases exponentially with company size."

Her budget projections showed regulatory department costs of ₹15 lakh annually, compared to the ₹6 lakh we were currently paying her as a consultant. But she argued that proper regulatory capabilities would enable faster product launches, fewer compliance problems, and more efficient international expansion.

"What equity compensation would you want?" I asked.

"Eight percent of the company, vesting over four years. Plus a salary of ₹25,000 per month to start, increasing with company performance."

This was a significant equity dilution for Priya and me, but it reflected the value Dr. Patel had already created and her potential contribution to future growth.

"I need to discuss this with Priya," I said. "But I'm interested in the concept."

That evening, Priya and I evaluated Dr. Patel's proposal against our growth plans. We were considering expansion into generic antibiotics, which required more complex regulatory approval processes. We were exploring export opportunities, which meant navigating international regulatory frameworks. We were planning our own manufacturing facility, which would require comprehensive regulatory compliance capabilities.

"We could probably find someone cheaper than Dr. Patel to handle basic regulatory work," Priya said. "But we couldn't find someone with her combination of technical expertise and strategic thinking."

"And we definitely couldn't find someone who already understands our business as well as she does."

The equity dilution was substantial, but the alternative—trying to build regulatory capabilities from scratch with less experienced people—seemed riskier and potentially more expensive.

We made Dr. Patel a counteroffer: 6% equity vesting over four years, ₹20,000 monthly salary with performance bonuses, and budget approval for building her regulatory affairs department gradually based on business growth.

She accepted.

Dr. Patel's transition from external consultant to internal executive took three months. She closed her independent consulting practice, transferred her other clients to colleagues, and began building our regulatory affairs department.

Her first hire was Rajesh Kumar, a young regulatory affairs specialist with experience at Dr. Reddy's Laboratories who was interested in working for a growing company where he could take on broader responsibilities.

"At Dr. Reddy's, I was responsible for one small piece of regulatory compliance," Rajesh explained during his interview. "Here, I'd be involved in building regulatory capabilities from the ground up."

Dr. Patel's approach to building the regulatory affairs department was systematic and strategic. Instead of trying to hire all positions immediately, she prioritized capabilities based on our most urgent business needs.

"Our first priority is product registration efficiency," she explained. "Every month of delay in getting new products approved costs us revenue that we can't recover later."

She implemented new procedures for managing regulatory submissions that reduced approval timelines by 40%. Instead of preparing applications reactively when we were ready to launch products, she started regulatory planning during early product development.

"Regulatory approval should be the bottleneck that determines product launch timing," she said. "Product development should be coordinated with regulatory timelines, not surprised by them."

The second priority was compliance automation. Dr. Patel developed systems for tracking regulatory obligations, monitoring deadline compliance, and maintaining documentation that reduced our regulatory preparation time for inspections and audits.

"Regulatory compliance should be automatic, not heroic," she explained. "If we're scrambling to prepare for every inspection, we're not properly managing our regulatory obligations."

Six months after joining full-time, Dr. Patel had transformed our regulatory approach from reactive compliance to proactive planning. Our product approval timelines had shortened significantly, our inspection preparation had become routine, and our regulatory costs per product had actually decreased despite increased staffing.

"You know what's interesting about having proper regulatory affairs capabilities?" she observed during a business review meeting. "It changes how you think about growth opportunities."

"How so?"

"When regulatory compliance is uncertain and expensive, you avoid complex opportunities because you can't assess the regulatory risks. When regulatory compliance is systematic and predictable, you can pursue opportunities that less well-organized competitors can't handle."

This insight proved crucial when we started evaluating international expansion opportunities. Countries like Brazil, Mexico, and South Africa had attractive market opportunities but complex regulatory requirements that would have overwhelmed our previous consulting-based approach.

"With proper regulatory affairs capabilities, international expansion becomes a project management challenge rather than an insurmountable barrier," Dr. Patel explained. "We can evaluate regulatory requirements systematically and build compliance strategies that make international markets accessible."

Two years after Dr. Patel joined full-time, our regulatory affairs department had grown to three people and was supporting product registrations in five countries. Our regulatory costs had increased in absolute terms but decreased as a percentage of revenue, and our regulatory capabilities had become a competitive advantage rather than just a compliance requirement.

"The best decision we made wasn't hiring Dr. Patel as a consultant," Priya observed. "It was converting her from consultant to partner when our business reached the point where regulatory affairs needed to be a core capability."

By 1999, when we were generating ₹25 lakh in monthly revenue and had twelve products in our portfolio, Dr. Patel's regulatory affairs department was handling complexities that would have been impossible to manage through external consulting relationships.

"What made the transition successful?" I asked Dr. Patel during her four-year anniversary with the company.

"Alignment of interests," she replied. "When I was a consultant, my success was measured by client satisfaction and fee collection. When I became an executive, my success became tied to company growth and long-term value creation."

"Any regrets about giving up your independent consulting practice?"

"None. Building regulatory capabilities for one company over several years is more interesting than providing standard regulatory services for multiple companies. I've learned more about the intersection of regulatory affairs and business strategy than I would have learned maintaining a traditional consulting practice."

The equity Dr. Patel had received for joining the company was worth significantly more than the consulting fees she'd forgone. But more importantly, she'd built regulatory affairs capabilities that would support our growth for decades.

By then, regulatory compliance had evolved from a constraint on our business to an enabler of our business—exactly what Dr. Patel had promised when she first proposed building a proper regulatory affairs department.

"You know what the real value of internal regulatory capabilities is?" she said, watching our team prepare for a complex product registration in a new international market. "It's not just managing compliance efficiently. It's thinking about regulatory requirements early enough in business planning that they shape opportunities rather than limiting them."

That perspective would prove crucial as we expanded into biotechnology products and international markets where regulatory complexity made the difference between companies that could compete globally and companies that remained regional players.

Chapter 4

The Distribution Dilemma?

Reaching the Last Mile

The distributor's warehouse in Kothagudem smelled like a combination of cardboard, disinfectant, and something that might have been expired cough syrup.

I'd driven three hours from Hyderabad to meet Ramesh Gupta, who owned what he described as "the largest pharmaceutical distribution business in Khammam district." His warehouse turned out to be a converted rice godown with makeshift shelving and a single overhead fan that moved warm air around without cooling anything.

"You want me to carry your products?" Ramesh asked, examining the samples I'd brought. "How many other distributors are you working with?"

"Four in Hyderabad, two in Warangal, one in Karimnagar."

"So you already have Telangana covered. Why do you need me?"

This was the question I'd been asked by every distributor I'd met over the past month. Each one wanted to know why they should invest shelf space and working capital in products from a small manufacturer when they already had relationships with larger companies offering similar products.

"We offer better payment terms and more flexible ordering quantities," I explained, using what had become my standard pitch.

"How much better?"

"Forty-five day payment terms instead of the industry standard sixty days. Minimum orders of 10,000 tablets instead of 50,000."

Ramesh calculated in his head for a moment. "What's your pricing compared to Cipla and Dr. Reddy's?"

"Competitive for similar quantities, but more flexible for smaller orders."

"Define competitive."

I showed him our price list, which offered paracetamol tablets at ₹1.20 each for orders over 10,000 units, compared to ₹1.15 from larger manufacturers for orders over 50,000 units.

"So your tablets cost more unless I order in smaller quantities?"

"Correct. But smaller, more frequent orders improve your cash flow and reduce your inventory risk."

Ramesh walked to his filing cabinet and pulled out what appeared to be a handwritten ledger. "Let me show you my ordering pattern for paracetamol tablets," he said, flipping through pages of entries. "I order 25,000 tablets every six weeks from Dr. Reddy's. That's about 4,000 tablets per week in actual sales."

"So you're carrying five weeks of inventory?"

"I have to. Dr. Reddy's minimum order is 50,000 tablets, so I order every twelve weeks and carry an average of six weeks inventory."

This was exactly the distribution inefficiency we'd hoped to exploit. Large manufacturers optimized for production efficiency, which meant large minimum orders that forced distributors to carry excess inventory. Small distributors like Ramesh were caught between needing frequent deliveries and being required to order in large quantities.

"What if you could order 15,000 tablets every four weeks?" I suggested. "Same annual volume, but half the average inventory."

"That would improve my working capital significantly," he admitted. "But I'd need reliable delivery. If you can't meet delivery commitments, I'd rather carry extra inventory than risk stockouts."

"What constitutes reliable delivery?"

"Orders delivered within one week of placement, no quality problems, consistent pricing for at least six months."

These requirements seemed reasonable until I started calculating the logistics. Ramesh was 180 kilometers from our contract manufacturer in Medchal. Delivering 15,000 tablets every four weeks would require either weekly truck runs or finding other distributors in the same region to justify transportation costs.

"How many distributors would I need in this area to make weekly deliveries economical?" I asked.

"Probably six or seven distributors within a fifty-kilometer radius," Ramesh replied. "That would give you enough volume to justify regular truck routes."

This conversation revealed the fundamental challenge of pharmaceutical distribution in India. The market was fragmented into thousands of small distributors serving local markets, but efficient distribution required aggregating enough volume to justify regular delivery routes.

Large pharmaceutical companies solved this problem by working with major distributors who had extensive sub-distribution networks. But major distributors weren't interested in small manufacturers who couldn't guarantee large volumes.

"Do you know other distributors in this region who might be interested in similar arrangements?" I asked.

"Maybe. But you'd have to offer them something they can't get from their current suppliers."

Over the next six weeks, I visited twelve distributors across Khammam, Warangal, and Mahbubnagar districts, trying to build a distribution network that could support weekly delivery routes. The pattern was consistent: distributors were interested in more flexible ordering terms, but skeptical about our ability to provide reliable service.

"Small manufacturers make big promises," explained Srinivas Reddy, a distributor in Mahbubnagar. "But when their production runs late or their truck breaks down, we're the ones who face angry customers."

"What would convince you that we're reliable?"

"Consistency over six months. If you can deliver on schedule for six months without quality problems or supply interruptions, I'll consider expanding our business relationship."

This created a classic chicken-and-egg problem. Distributors wanted proof of reliability before committing to regular orders, but we needed regular orders to justify the infrastructure investments that would enable reliability.

The breakthrough came from an unexpected source: Suresh Aggarwal.

I met Suresh at a pharmaceutical trade association meeting in Hyderabad, where he was complaining about the inflexibility of large manufacturers during a coffee break conversation.

"I run distribution routes covering fifteen districts in Andhra Pradesh and Telangana," he explained. "But I'm constantly dealing with minimum order requirements that don't match my customers' actual needs."

"What do you mean?"

"I have 200 small distributors on my routes. They need frequent deliveries of moderate quantities, but manufacturers want to sell in large batches to minimize their transaction costs."

Suresh had built a business model around solving exactly the distribution efficiency problem we were facing. Instead of selling directly to small distributors, he bought large quantities from manufacturers and redistributed them in smaller quantities to local distributors who needed more frequent deliveries.

"Would you consider carrying our products?" I asked.

"What's your minimum order quantity?"

"We're flexible. What quantities would work for your business model?"

"I'd want to order 100,000 tablets monthly across three or four products, delivered in weekly shipments of 25,000 tablets each."

This was larger than we'd been planning for individual distributors, but more manageable than trying to coordinate multiple small distributors across a wide geographic area.

"What payment terms would you need?"

"Thirty days from delivery, assuming consistent quality and delivery performance."

The arrangement with Suresh transformed our distribution strategy. Instead of trying to build direct relationships with dozens of small distributors, we could work with established distribution partners who already had the infrastructure and relationships to reach small retailers efficiently.

"You know what's interesting about this distribution model?" Priya observed after our first month working with Suresh. "We're not competing with large manufacturers for the same distribution channels. We're serving distribution needs that large manufacturers can't address profitably."

She was right. Cipla and Dr. Reddy's optimized their distribution for large orders to major distributors. Suresh's business model relied on serving small distributors who required flexible ordering terms that large manufacturers couldn't offer economically.

Within six months, we'd established relationships with four regional distributors like Suresh, each covering different geographic areas and serving 150-300 small retailers. Our distribution coverage had expanded to twelve states without requiring us to manage hundreds of individual distributor relationships.

"The distribution maze taught us something important about market strategy," I said to Dr. Patel during a business review meeting. "We assumed our constraint was reaching customers directly. But our real constraint was finding distribution partners whose business models aligned with our capabilities."

"How so?"

"Large distributors want to buy large quantities from large manufacturers. Small distributors want to buy small quantities from flexible suppliers. We found partners who specialized in connecting small manufacturers with small distributors."

By 1997, when our monthly revenue reached ₹15 lakhs, distribution had evolved from our biggest constraint to one of our competitive advantages. Our distribution partners understood regional markets better than national competitors, provided more responsive service than large distribution networks, and helped us identify market opportunities that larger manufacturers overlooked.

The distribution maze hadn't blocked our growth—it had taught us to find partners who could navigate local markets more effectively than we could navigate them ourselves.

Building Distribution Networks Across India

The train to Mumbai Central left Hyderabad at 11:30 PM and arrived sixteen hours later, giving me plenty of time to review my distributor prospect list and worry about whether I was making a fundamental mistake.

It was March 1996, and we'd been successfully working with regional distributors in Andhra Pradesh and Telangana for eight months. Our monthly revenue had grown to ₹12 lakhs, we had six products in the market, and our cash flow was finally positive. The logical next step was expanding beyond our home region into other Indian states.

The illogical part was that I was traveling to Mumbai with no confirmed appointments, a hotel reservation for three nights, and a list of pharmaceutical distributors I'd compiled from trade directories and industry contacts.

"You realize this could be a complete waste of time and money?" Priya had asked as I packed for the trip.

"It could be. But staying in Andhra Pradesh definitely limits our growth potential."

"Why Mumbai first? Why not expand gradually into Karnataka or Tamil Nadu?"

"Because Mumbai distributors serve retailers across Maharashtra, Gujarat, and Rajasthan. If we can establish relationships in Mumbai, we can access three states simultaneously."

This logic seemed sound until I actually arrived in Mumbai and discovered that pharmaceutical distribution was significantly more complex than I'd understood.

My first appointment was with Jayesh Mehta, who owned a distribution company in Andheri that claimed to serve 500 retail pharmacies across Western India. His office was on the fourth floor of a commercial building that required navigating around handcarts, street vendors, and traffic that seemed personally hostile to pedestrians.

"South Indian manufacturer," Jayesh said, reviewing the product samples I'd brought. "What makes your products different from the fifty other generic manufacturers trying to enter Mumbai market?"

"Better payment terms, more flexible ordering quantities, and consistent quality," I replied, using what had become my standard response.

"Every manufacturer promises better terms and consistent quality. What do you actually deliver that's different?"

This was a more pointed question than I'd encountered in Andhra Pradesh, where distributors had been willing to try new suppliers based on relationships and local connections. Mumbai distributors seemed more focused on concrete business advantages.

"We offer genuine flexibility on order quantities," I explained. "Our minimum order is 10,000 tablets per product, and we can deliver weekly instead of forcing you to order monthly."

"What's your pricing compared to established manufacturers?"

I showed him our price list, which offered competitive pricing for smaller quantities but couldn't match the volume discounts available from larger manufacturers.

Jayesh studied the numbers carefully. "Your pricing is reasonable for small orders, but most of my customers want to order 50,000-100,000 tablets at a time to get the best prices. For those quantities, you're more expensive than Cipla or Lupin."

"Do all your customers order in large quantities?"

"The profitable ones do. Small orders create more work for the same margin."

This conversation revealed something important about regional differences in pharmaceutical distribution. In Andhra Pradesh, we'd found distributors who appreciated flexibility because their customer base consisted primarily of small retailers ordering moderate quantities. In Mumbai, distributors seemed to prefer larger, less frequent orders that maximized their operational efficiency.

"What if I could offer volume pricing for smaller aggregate orders?" I suggested. "If you order 50,000 tablets across multiple products, we could offer the same pricing as single-product orders of 50,000 tablets."

"That's more interesting. But I'd need proof that you can deliver consistently before I commit inventory space to your products."

Over the next two days, I met with six Mumbai distributors and heard variations of the same message: they were interested in working with new suppliers, but only if those suppliers could offer clear advantages over existing relationships.

"Mumbai distributors are more sophisticated than regional distributors," explained Rakesh Gupta, the third distributor I met. "We have more supplier options, so we can afford to be selective about new relationships."

"What would make a new supplier relationship attractive?"

"Exclusive territory rights, marketing support, or products that fill gaps in our current portfolio."

"What kind of gaps?"

"Products in therapeutic areas where we don't have strong supplier relationships. Or products with unique features that help us compete with other distributors."

This conversation shifted my thinking about market expansion. Instead of trying to replicate our Andhra Pradesh success with generic commodity products, I needed to understand what opportunities existed in markets where competition was more intense.

"Which therapeutic areas are underserved in your market?" I asked.

"Anti-inflammatory drugs for orthopedic conditions. Most suppliers focus on basic pain relievers, but there's growing demand for specialized formulations."

"Such as?"

"Topical diclofenac gels, sustained-release tablet formulations, combination products that reduce dosing frequency."

I didn't have any of these products in development, but the conversation suggested that successful market expansion might require product innovation rather than just geographic expansion.

My fourth distributor meeting was with Sunil Agarwal, whose company had been operating in Mumbai for twenty-five years and served retailers across Maharashtra and Gujarat.

"I'll be direct with you," Sunil said after reviewing our product portfolio. "Your basic generic tablets aren't interesting to me. Every manufacturer makes paracetamol and ibuprofen. But if you could develop products that address specific market needs, I might be interested."

"What specific needs?"

"Pediatric formulations that taste good. Geriatric formulations that are easier to swallow. Products for chronic conditions that improve patient compliance."

"Are these large markets?"

"Large enough to support profitable distribution relationships, and specialized enough that you wouldn't face intense price competition from every generic manufacturer in India."

The Mumbai trip didn't result in any immediate distribution agreements, but it taught me something important about market expansion strategy. Replicating existing success in new markets worked when those markets had similar characteristics to proven markets. But entering more competitive markets required offering something that incumbent suppliers weren't providing.

I returned to Hyderabad with a different perspective on growth strategy. Instead of trying to expand geographically with existing products, we needed to expand our product capabilities to serve markets that valued innovation over commodity pricing.

"How did the Mumbai meetings go?" Priya asked.

"They went well, but not the way I expected. Mumbai distributors aren't interested in our current products, but they're very interested in products we don't make yet."

"Such as?"

"Specialized formulations, combination products, delivery systems that improve patient compliance."

Over the next six months, instead of pursuing immediate geographic expansion, we focused on developing products that would be attractive to distributors in competitive markets. We developed a sustained-release ibuprofen formulation for twice-daily dosing, rather than the traditional three-times-daily dosing. We created a pediatric paracetamol suspension that actually tasted good. We formulated combination products that reduced pill burden for patients with multiple conditions.

When I returned to Mumbai eight months later, I had products that solved specific market problems rather than just competing on price and terms.

"This sustained-release ibuprofen is interesting," Jayesh Mehta said, examining our new formulation. "How does it compare to existing options?"

"Same efficacy with better patient compliance. Patients prefer taking medication twice daily instead of three times daily."

"What's your pricing?"

"Twenty percent premium over standard ibuprofen, but better patient outcomes and higher margins for retailers."

This time, three Mumbai distributors agreed to trial our products, and within six months we had established distribution in Maharashtra, Gujarat, and Rajasthan.

"You know what we learned about market expansion?" I said to Dr. Patel during a business review meeting. "Geographic expansion works when you have products that serve unmet needs. It doesn't work when you're just trying to compete with existing suppliers using existing products."

"So market expansion requires product innovation?"

"Market expansion requires understanding what each market values most, then developing capabilities that deliver that value better than incumbent suppliers."

By 1997, we were selling in eight states and had learned that successful expansion meant adapting our capabilities to serve different market requirements rather than trying to replicate the same approach in different locations.

The distribution network we eventually built wasn't uniform across India—it was customized to match the competitive dynamics and customer needs in each regional market.

Partnership with Suresh Aggarwal's Distribution Company

Suresh Aggarwal's distribution center in Secunderabad looked like controlled chaos.

Trucks were being loaded and unloaded simultaneously in a concrete yard where workers moved between towering stacks of pharmaceutical cartons with the practiced efficiency of people who'd been doing the same job for years. Inside the warehouse, shelving stretched from floor to ceiling, labeled with product codes that meant nothing to me but apparently made perfect sense to the staff.

"This is organized?" I asked, watching workers pull orders from what appeared to be random locations throughout the facility.

"More organized than it looks," Suresh replied, leading me through aisles that seemed designed to maximize walking distance between any two points. "Every product has a designated location based on turnover rate and delivery route optimization."

It was my second visit to Suresh's operation, three weeks after our initial conversation at the pharmaceutical trade association meeting. Our first discussion had been encouraging—he'd expressed interest in carrying our products and suggested order quantities that could work for both companies. But I'd wanted to see his actual operation before committing to what would be our largest distribution partnership.

"Walk me through how this works," I said, gesturing toward the activity around us.

"We receive products from manufacturers twice weekly and ship to retailers daily. Each truck covers a specific route serving 15-20 retailers, with delivery schedules coordinated to minimize inventory at both ends."

"How many retailers do you serve total?"

"247 active accounts across Andhra Pradesh, Telangana, and parts of Karnataka. Plus about 50 occasional customers who order irregularly."

These numbers were larger than our current total customer base across all distribution partners. Working with Suresh could triple our market reach, but it would also make us dependent on a single distributor for the majority of our sales volume.

"What happens if we have production delays or quality problems?" I asked.

"Same thing that happens with my other suppliers. We notify affected customers, arrange temporary substitutions if possible, and adjust future orders based on reliability performance."

"How do you measure reliability performance?"

Suresh led me to a small office area where a clerk was updating what appeared to be a handwritten ledger. "Order fulfillment rate, delivery timing, quality complaint frequency, billing accuracy. We track everything and review supplier performance quarterly."

He showed me performance records for his current suppliers, with detailed notes about delivery delays, product returns, and customer complaints. The documentation was more thorough than our own internal tracking systems.

"What performance levels do you expect from new suppliers?" I asked.

"Ninety-five percent order fulfillment, delivery within committed timeframes, less than 0.5% customer complaints. If you can't meet those standards consistently, the partnership won't work for either of us."

These requirements were more stringent than anything our current distributors had specified, but they seemed reasonable for a business model that depended on consistent service to hundreds of retail customers.

"What would our ordering and payment arrangements look like?"

"Initial orders of 50,000 tablets monthly across your product portfolio, delivered weekly in 12,500 tablet shipments. Payment thirty days from delivery, assuming no quality issues or delivery problems."

"What products are you most interested in carrying?"

"Your paracetamol and ibuprofen formulations definitely. Maybe diclofenac tablets if you can offer competitive pricing. I'm less interested in products where I already have strong supplier relationships."

The conversation revealed something important about distributor decision-making. Suresh wasn't looking for comprehensive product portfolios from individual manufacturers. He was looking for specific products that filled gaps in his current supplier network or offered advantages over existing relationships.

"What advantages would our products need to offer?"

"Better pricing, more reliable delivery, or superior quality. Ideally, some combination of all three."

"How do you define superior quality for generic products?"

"Consistent tablet appearance, reliable dissolution characteristics, minimal customer complaints. Generic products should perform identically to branded equivalents, not just meet minimum specifications."

This quality discussion highlighted a gap in our thinking about generic drug manufacturing. We'd focused on meeting pharmacopoeial specifications, but distributors and customers apparently had additional quality expectations based on practical usage experience.

"Would you be willing to start with a trial arrangement?" I suggested. "Three months of small orders to test our reliability and quality, then scale up if performance meets your standards?"

"That makes sense. Let's try 20,000 tablets monthly for three months, delivered in weekly shipments of 5,000 tablets each."

The trial arrangement began in April 1996 with our paracetamol tablets. Suresh's first order was smaller than we'd hoped, but his delivery and documentation requirements were more sophisticated than anything we'd encountered with other distributors.

"This is like working with a larger company," Priya observed as we prepared our first shipment. "Detailed product specifications, precise delivery scheduling, formal documentation requirements."

"Is that good or bad?"

"It's different. It forces us to operate more professionally, but it also reveals gaps in our systems that we didn't know existed."

The first month went smoothly. Our tablets met Suresh's quality standards, deliveries arrived on schedule, and customer feedback was positive. But the second month presented challenges that revealed the complexity of serving demanding distribution partners.

"We have a problem with your latest batch," Suresh called on a Tuesday morning in May. "Three retailers are reporting that tablets from batch ML-0496-PCT have slight color variations."

"Color variations?"

"Some tablets are slightly more yellow than others. Same batch, but inconsistent appearance."

We'd tested that batch thoroughly and everything met specifications. Hardness, friability, dissolution, content uniformity—all within acceptable ranges. But we hadn't noticed the color variation that customers were apparently finding objectionable.

"The tablets are chemically identical," I explained. "Slight color variation doesn't affect therapeutic performance."

"Therapeutic performance isn't the only concern," Suresh replied. "Customers expect generic products to have consistent appearance. Color variation suggests quality control problems, even when it doesn't actually indicate quality problems."

This feedback taught us something important about the relationship between technical quality and market quality. Our manufacturing processes produced tablets that met all regulatory specifications, but they apparently had cosmetic inconsistencies that affected customer confidence.

"What do you want us to do about the current batch?" I asked.

"Replace the tablets that customers have returned and improve your color consistency for future batches. This is exactly the kind of quality issue that affects distributor relationships."

We replaced 2,000 tablets at a cost of ₹2,500 and modified our manufacturing procedures to improve color consistency. The incident was expensive but educational—it showed us quality expectations that weren't captured in standard testing protocols.

"You know what this partnership is teaching us?" Priya said after we resolved the color variation issue. "Distributor relationships are more demanding than we thought, but they're also more valuable."

"How so?"

"Suresh has quality standards and customer feedback systems that help us improve our products. His other suppliers have to meet the same standards, so working with him forces us to compete at a higher level."

By the end of our three-month trial, we were delivering 20,000 tablets monthly with consistently positive customer feedback. Suresh expanded our arrangement to 40,000 tablets monthly and added our ibuprofen formulation to his product line.

"This partnership is working well for both companies," he said during our quarterly performance review. "Your delivery reliability is excellent, your quality has improved significantly since April, and your pricing remains competitive."

"What areas need improvement?"

"Product packaging could be more professional, and you might consider developing additional formulations that complement your existing products."

Six months after beginning our partnership, Suresh was distributing 75,000 tablets monthly across four of our products and serving as our primary channel for reaching retail customers in three states.

"The relationship with Suresh changed how we think about distribution partnerships," I told Dr. Patel during a business review. "Instead of just finding distributors who will carry our products, we're finding distributors who help us improve our products."

"How do you mean?"

"Suresh's quality standards and customer feedback systems force us to think about market requirements that go beyond regulatory compliance. That makes us better manufacturers, not just larger manufacturers."

By 1997, when our partnership had grown to ₹8 lakh in monthly sales through Suresh's network, we realized that finding the right distribution partner was more valuable than finding multiple adequate partners.

The partnership had taught us that distribution relationships could be strategic assets that improved our capabilities rather than just sales channels that moved our products.

Competing against Multinational Corporations

The Glaxo sales representative arrived at City Pharmaceuticals in a white sedan that probably cost more than our entire annual marketing budget.

I was delivering our monthly order when he walked into Mr. Patel's office carrying a leather briefcase and wearing the kind of confidence that comes from representing a company with unlimited resources. Through the glass partition, I could see him laying out glossy product brochures and what appeared to be a detailed market analysis.

"Glaxo is launching a new paracetamol formulation," Mr. Patel told me after the representative left. "Extended-release tablets for twice-daily dosing instead of four-times-daily."

"What's their pricing?" I asked, though I suspected I already knew the answer.

"₹2.25 per tablet. Premium pricing for premium features."

Our standard paracetamol tablets sold for ₹1.25 each. Glaxo's new formulation cost almost twice as much, but it offered genuine patient benefits that our products couldn't match.

"Are you planning to carry their new product?" I asked.

"I'm considering it. Extended-release formulations are popular with doctors because they improve patient compliance. Patients prefer taking medication twice daily instead of four times daily."

This conversation revealed something uncomfortable about our competitive position. We'd been competing successfully against other Indian generic manufacturers by offering better service and competitive pricing. But multinational corporations competed with innovation that created new market categories rather than just competing within existing categories.

"Would you still carry our standard paracetamol if you add Glaxo's extended-release version?" I asked.

"Probably. They serve different market segments. Glaxo's product for patients who can afford premium pricing, yours for price-sensitive customers."

Walking back to our office that afternoon, I realized we were facing a different type of competitive challenge than anything we'd encountered before.

Indian competitors fought over price and service within established product categories. Multinational competitors created new product categories that commanded higher prices and margins.

"How do we compete with companies that can afford to develop extended-release formulations?" I asked Priya during our weekly planning meeting.

"Maybe we don't compete directly. Maybe we find ways to serve markets they're not interested in serving."

"Such as?"

"Markets too small for their business model, customers who value flexibility over innovation, applications where standard formulations work better than sophisticated alternatives."

This conversation started us thinking systematically about competitive strategy against much larger companies. Instead of trying to match their capabilities, we needed to understand their limitations and find opportunities they couldn't pursue profitably.

"What are the limitations of multinational pharmaceutical companies?" I asked Dr. Patel during one of our regulatory consultations.

"Scale requirements, bureaucratic decision-making, standardized approaches that don't accommodate local variations," she replied. "They're optimized for large markets and long product lifecycles."

"What opportunities does that create for smaller companies?"

"Quick response to market changes, customized solutions for specific customer needs, willingness to serve smaller market segments that don't justify large infrastructure investments."

We spent the next month studying multinational competitors' strategies in the Indian market. Glaxo, Pfizer, and Novartis focused on high-value therapeutic areas where they could charge premium prices. They worked with major distributors who could handle large volumes. They invested heavily in marketing to doctors and hospitals.

"They're playing a completely different game than we're playing," Priya observed. "They compete on innovation and brand recognition. We compete on flexibility and cost efficiency."

"Is there room for both approaches in the same market?"

"There might be, if we can serve customer needs that their business model doesn't address effectively."

The opportunity came from an unexpected source: rural healthcare centers.

Dr. Raghava Reddy, who managed a primary healthcare center in Mahabubnagar district, visited our office in September 1996 with a procurement challenge that multinational companies weren't equipped to handle.

"We need basic medications in small quantities delivered monthly," he explained. "Our patient volume is too low to justify the minimum orders that large manufacturers require."

"What quantities do you need?"

"Maybe 5,000 paracetamol tablets, 3,000 ibuprofen tablets, 2,000 diclofenac tablets per month. Total order value around ₹15,000."

"What are the challenges with current suppliers?"

"Minimum orders of 25,000-50,000 tablets per product. We can't afford to carry that much inventory, and most medications expire before we use them."

This was exactly the type of market opportunity that favored our business model over multinational approaches. Rural healthcare centers needed frequent deliveries of small quantities—exactly what we'd learned to provide efficiently through our distribution partnerships.

"We can deliver those quantities monthly with payment terms that match your budget cycles," I told Dr. Reddy.

"What about pricing compared to larger suppliers?"

"Competitive for the quantities you need. Probably more expensive per tablet than bulk purchases, but lower total cost due to reduced waste from expired inventory."

Dr. Reddy became our first institutional customer, and within six months we were serving twelve primary healthcare centers across three districts. The business model worked because we could aggregate small orders across multiple healthcare centers to achieve efficient delivery routes.

"You know what's interesting about this market segment?" Priya said, reviewing our healthcare center sales after our first quarter. "Multinational companies can't serve these customers profitably because the order sizes are too small for their distribution model."

"And local competitors don't serve them because they lack the delivery infrastructure to reach rural areas efficiently."

"So we found a market space that's too small for large companies and too complex for small companies."

The healthcare center business taught us something important about competing with multinational corporations: sustainable competitive advantage came from serving markets they couldn't address profitably rather than trying to compete in markets where they had natural advantages.

Over the next year, we developed similar strategies for other underserved market segments. Small hospitals that needed flexible ordering terms. Regional distributors who wanted customized product portfolios. Export customers who needed small quantities for market testing.

"We're not really competing against Glaxo and Pfizer," I realized during a strategy discussion with our growing team. "We're competing for market opportunities that don't interest them."

"Is that sustainable?" Dr. Patel asked. "What happens when these market segments grow large enough to attract multinational attention?"

"Then we'll need to have developed capabilities that are difficult for larger companies to replicate quickly," Priya replied. "Service flexibility, customer relationships, distribution efficiency in specialized markets."

By 1997, when our annual revenue reached ₹2.5 crores, we'd learned that competing against multinational corporations was less about matching their strengths and more about exploiting their structural limitations.

"The multinationals taught us something valuable," I told Suresh during one of our quarterly distributor reviews. "They showed us that there are many ways to succeed in pharmaceuticals besides trying to be the biggest or most innovative company in the market."

"How so?"

"They succeed by creating premium products for large markets. We succeed by providing flexible service for specialized markets. As long as we focus on markets where flexibility matters more than innovation, we can compete successfully."

The key insight was that pharmaceutical markets were large enough and diverse enough to support multiple successful business models. We didn't need to beat multinational competitors—we needed to serve customers and market segments that they couldn't serve as effectively as we could.

"You know what the real competition taught us?" Priya observed as we planned our expansion into new therapeutic areas. "It's not about being better than larger competitors at everything. It's about being better at the specific things that matter most to the customers you choose to serve."

That perspective would guide our competitive strategy for the next decade as we encountered increasingly sophisticated competitors in every market we entered.

Constraint Identified: Limited Market Reach

The spreadsheet numbers told a story I didn't want to believe.

It was December 1996, and I was reviewing our sales data for the year, trying to understand why our growth rate had slowed despite excellent product quality, satisfied customers, and competitive pricing. The pattern was clear but troubling: we were reaching maximum penetration in our existing markets without successfully expanding into new ones.

"Look at this," I said to Priya, pointing to our monthly sales figures. "Andhra Pradesh and Telangana account for 78% of our revenue. Karnataka and Maharashtra together are only 15%. The remaining seven states where we have distributors generate just 7% of total sales."

"Maybe that's normal for a company our size," she suggested. "Regional concentration might be more efficient than trying to serve too many markets thinly."

"But look at our growth trajectory. We grew 180% in our first year, 95% in our second year, and only 35% this year. We're hitting constraints in our established markets."

The data revealed something uncomfortable: we'd saturated our core geographic markets without successfully replicating our success in new regions. Our distributors in Andhra Pradesh and Telangana were ordering at maximum capacity, but our distributors in other states were placing modest orders that barely justified our delivery and support costs.

"What's different about our successful markets versus our struggling markets?" Priya asked.

I pulled out our distributor performance reports and started comparing regions. In Andhra Pradesh and Telangana, we had strong relationships with distributors like Suresh Aggarwal who understood our business model and actively promoted our products. In other states, we had transactional relationships with distributors who carried our products but didn't actively push them.

"It's not just about having distributors," I realized. "It's about having distributors who are invested in our success."

"What makes distributors invested in our success?"

"Profitable business relationships, exclusive territory rights, marketing support, products that help them differentiate from competitors."

This analysis revealed our market reach constraint: we could expand geographically by finding distributors willing to carry our products, but we couldn't achieve significant sales growth without building the kind of deep distributor relationships that took months or years to develop.

"So our constraint isn't access to markets—it's the time and resources required to build meaningful distributor partnerships," Priya concluded.

"And we've been trying to solve a relationship problem with a logistics problem."

I called three of our underperforming distributors to understand their perspective on our business relationship. The conversations were illuminating.

"Your products are fine," explained Rajesh Sharma, our distributor in Pune. "But they don't offer me any advantages over the twenty other generic manufacturers I work with. Why would I push your products instead of focusing on suppliers who provide marketing support or exclusive territories?"

"What kind of marketing support do other suppliers provide?" I asked.

"Sample programs for doctors, promotional materials for retailers, volume incentives that improve my margins."

"What would it take for you to actively promote our products?"

"Either better margins, exclusive territory rights, or marketing tools that help me compete more effectively."

This conversation revealed the fundamental difference between distribution coverage and market penetration. We had distributors in multiple states, which gave us geographic coverage. But we didn't have distributor commitment, which limited our market penetration.

"We need to choose between broad geographic coverage with minimal market penetration, or concentrated geographic focus with deep market penetration," I told Dr. Patel during our monthly business review.

"What are the trade-offs?" she asked.

"Broad coverage looks impressive and provides diversification, but generates limited revenue growth. Concentrated focus provides better revenue growth but creates dependency on specific markets."

"Which approach is more sustainable for a company your size?"

"Probably concentrated focus until we develop the resources to support deep relationships across multiple markets."

This strategic discussion led to a difficult decision: instead of trying to maintain distribution relationships in ten states, we would focus intensively on building dominant positions in four states where we already had established presence.

"You're talking about withdrawing from markets where we've invested time and money to establish relationships," Priya observed.

"I'm talking about redeploying resources from markets where we're marginal players to markets where we can become significant players."

The market consolidation process took four months. We terminated relationships with distributors in six states where our sales volumes were too low to justify continued investment. We redirected our sales and marketing resources to Andhra Pradesh, Telangana, Karnataka, and Maharashtra.

"This feels like moving backward," I admitted as we notified distributors about ending relationships.

"It feels like focus," Dr. Patel replied. "You're choosing sustainable growth over unsustainable expansion."

The market focus strategy worked better than expected. By concentrating our sales efforts on four states instead of ten, we could provide more intensive support to our key distributors. We developed exclusive territory arrangements, provided marketing materials, and offered volume incentives that made our products more attractive than competing generic brands.

"Our revenue per state has increased 60% since we consolidated our market focus," Priya reported six months after our strategic shift. "We're generating more total revenue from four states than we were generating from ten states."

"Why didn't we figure this out earlier?"

"Because growing the number of markets feels like progress even when it doesn't actually improve business results."

The market reach constraint taught us something important about resource allocation: limited resources could be deployed broadly for minimal impact or concentrated for significant impact, but not both simultaneously.

"What's our constraint now?" I asked, reviewing our improved sales performance.

"Production capacity. Our key distributors want to increase orders, but we're approaching the limits of what our contract manufacturer can produce reliably."

"So by solving our market reach constraint, we've elevated our production constraint?"

"Exactly. Which means we're making progress."

This progression from market reach constraint to production capacity constraint demonstrated something fundamental about business growth: constraints don't disappear when you solve them—they transform into different constraints that require different solutions.

"The market reach constraint taught us about the difference between coverage and penetration," I told Suresh during one of our distributor meetings. "We thought our problem was reaching enough markets. Our real problem was reaching markets deeply enough to generate significant business."

"How do you know when you've achieved sufficient market penetration?" he asked.

"When your constraint shifts from market reach to something else—production capacity, product development, working capital, talent acquisition."

By 1997, when we were generating ₹35 lakh in monthly revenue from our four focused markets, market reach was no longer our primary constraint. We had established strong distribution relationships that could support continued growth, and our challenge had shifted to building capabilities that could serve larger sales volumes efficiently.

"You know what the market reach constraint really taught us?" Priya said, looking at our consolidated sales territory map. "It taught us that business growth requires choosing what not to do as much as choosing what to do."

"And that sustainable competitive advantages come from building deep capabilities in selected areas rather than thin capabilities across many areas."

The lesson would prove crucial as we faced decisions about product development, manufacturing investments, and international expansion over the next several years. Each opportunity would require choosing between breadth and depth, and the market reach constraint had taught us to choose depth first.

Chapter 5

The Quality Revolution

From Garage to GMP

The pharmaceutical inspector's car had government plates and looked like it meant business.

I watched through our office window as a middle-aged man in a white shirt and dark trousers emerged from the vehicle, carrying a clipboard and the kind of purposeful expression that suggested this wouldn't be a social visit. It was February 1997, and we'd been notified that the state drug control department would be conducting "routine inspections of pharmaceutical establishments" in our area.

"Mr. Arjun Malhotra?" the inspector asked when I met him at our facility entrance.

"Yes sir. I'm expecting your visit."

"I am Drug Inspector K. Venkatesh. I need to examine your manufacturing facility and quality control procedures."

We'd been preparing for this inspection for three months, ever since Dr. Patel had warned us that our growing sales volume would eventually attract regulatory attention. But nothing had prepared me for the systematic thoroughness of Inspector Venkatesh's examination.

"Show me your manufacturing area," he said, pulling out a detailed checklist.

I led him to our production facility, which we'd upgraded significantly from our original garage laboratory. Clean, organized, and properly equipped—or so I thought until Inspector Venkatesh started pointing out deficiencies I hadn't noticed.

"Your raw material storage area is not adequately segregated from finished product storage," he observed, making notes on his clipboard. "Cross-contamination risk."

"We maintain separate shelving and clear labeling," I replied.

"Separation requires physical barriers, not just organizational systems. And where are your environmental monitoring records?"

"Environmental monitoring?"

"Temperature and humidity documentation for all storage areas. Pharmaceutical products require controlled environmental conditions throughout their lifecycle."

This was the first of seventeen deficiencies Inspector Venkatesh identified during his four-hour inspection. Most were issues I'd never considered: inadequate documentation systems, missing standard operating procedures, insufficient personnel training records, improper waste disposal protocols.

"Your products appear to meet quality specifications," he said as we reviewed his findings in our office. "But your quality systems do not meet Good Manufacturing Practice requirements."

"What does that mean practically?"

"It means you're making good products using inadequate systems. As your business grows, inadequate systems will eventually cause quality problems that could harm patients and destroy your company."

Inspector Venkatesh's report listed specific corrective actions required within ninety days: implement environmental monitoring systems, develop comprehensive standard operating procedures, establish personnel training programs, upgrade facility infrastructure to meet GMP standards.

"How much will these improvements cost?" I asked Dr. Patel after reviewing the inspection report.

"Probably ₹8-10 lakhs for infrastructure upgrades, plus ongoing costs for documentation systems and training programs."

This represented nearly 40% of our current annual revenue. But the alternative—failing to meet regulatory requirements—could result in license suspension that would end our business entirely.

"We don't have ₹10 lakhs available for facility upgrades," Priya said, reviewing our cash flow projections. "And we can't afford to shut down operations while implementing improvements."

"So we need to find a way to upgrade quality systems without disrupting current business operations," I concluded.

The solution came from an unexpected source: James Mitchell, a British quality consultant who'd been working with Indian pharmaceutical companies to implement international quality standards.

"I understand you need to achieve GMP compliance quickly and cost-effectively," James said during our first meeting. His accent made everything sound more authoritative than it probably was.

"We need to meet regulatory requirements without bankrupting the company," I replied.

"The good news is that GMP compliance is more about systematic thinking than expensive equipment. Most quality improvements can be achieved through better procedures and documentation, not just facility upgrades."

James proposed a phased implementation approach that would address the most critical deficiencies first while spreading costs over twelve months. Instead of trying to achieve perfect GMP compliance immediately, we'd build quality systems incrementally while maintaining production operations.

"Quality isn't about having the most sophisticated facility," he explained as we toured our production areas. "Quality is about having systems that ensure consistent results regardless of equipment limitations."

The first phase focused on documentation systems. James helped us develop standard operating procedures for every aspect of our operations: raw material receipt, production processes, quality testing, storage conditions, distribution procedures.

"Every activity that affects product quality must be documented, and every documented procedure must be followed exactly," he said as we drafted our first SOP manual.

"This seems like excessive paperwork," Priya observed.

"Documentation isn't paperwork—it's institutional memory. When procedures are documented, quality becomes independent of individual knowledge and experience."

The documentation process was more enlightening than I'd expected. Writing detailed procedures for activities we'd been doing informally revealed inconsistencies and gaps that could affect product quality.

"We've been mixing ingredients for five minutes because that's what worked initially," I realized as we documented our tablet granulation process. "But we never verified that five minutes is optimal for different batch sizes or environmental conditions."

"Exactly. Informal procedures work until conditions change. Documented procedures include specifications that ensure consistent results under varying conditions."

The second phase involved implementing environmental monitoring systems. Instead of expensive automated monitoring equipment, James showed us how to use manual monitoring procedures that achieved the same quality objectives at a fraction of the cost.

"Temperature and humidity logs don't require sophisticated sensors," he explained. "They require systematic measurement and recording procedures that create historical data for quality trend analysis."

The third phase focused on personnel training and quality culture development. James conducted training sessions for our entire team on GMP principles, quality procedures, and documentation requirements.

"Quality isn't just the responsibility of quality control staff," he told our production team. "Everyone involved in manufacturing affects product quality, so everyone needs to understand quality requirements."

The training revealed something important about quality culture: most quality problems resulted from people not understanding why procedures were important, not from people deliberately ignoring procedures.

"When people understand that documentation protects patients and preserves the business, they take quality procedures seriously," James observed. "When they think documentation is bureaucratic nonsense, they find ways to avoid it."

Six months after Inspector Venkatesh's initial visit, our facility had been transformed. Not just physically—though we'd made significant infrastructure improvements—but systematically. We had comprehensive quality procedures, environmental monitoring systems, and a team that understood their role in maintaining product quality.

"The transformation is remarkable," Inspector Venkatesh said during his follow-up inspection. "You've addressed all previous deficiencies and implemented quality systems that exceed minimum requirements."

"What changed most significantly?"

"Your approach to quality. Previously, you were reactive—fixing problems after they occurred. Now you're proactive—preventing problems through systematic quality management."

The quality revolution had cost us ₹12 lakhs over eight months, but it had generated unexpected benefits beyond regulatory compliance. Our production efficiency had improved because documented procedures eliminated trial-and-error approaches. Our customer complaints had dropped to near zero because systematic quality controls prevented defective products from reaching the market.

"You know what the quality revolution really taught us?" I said to James during his final consulting visit. "Quality isn't an additional cost—it's a better way of operating that actually reduces costs while improving results."

"How do you mean?"

"When quality is built into every process, you eliminate the costs of fixing problems, replacing defective products, and managing customer complaints. Prevention is less expensive than correction."

By 1998, when we achieved our first international quality certification, our quality systems had become a competitive advantage rather than just a regulatory requirement. Customers trusted our products more than competing generic brands because our quality reputation was based on systematic excellence rather than occasional good results.

The garage laboratory was a distant memory, but the lessons we'd learned about building quality systematically would guide our operations for decades as we expanded into biotechnology products and international markets where quality requirements were even more demanding.

Investing in Good Manufacturing Practices

The bank loan officer looked at our GMP implementation proposal like I'd asked to borrow money for a space mission.

"You want ₹15 lakhs to upgrade manufacturing procedures?" Ramesh Gupta asked, flipping through our detailed project plan. "Can't you just continue making tablets the way you've been making them for the past three years?"

"We could, but we'd eventually face regulatory problems that could shut down our business," I explained. "GMP compliance isn't optional for pharmaceutical manufacturers—it's a legal requirement."

"But you're already selling products successfully. Your customers seem satisfied. Why spend money fixing something that isn't broken?"

This was the fundamental challenge of investing in GMP improvements: the benefits were largely preventative rather than immediately visible. We weren't fixing broken processes—we were implementing systems to prevent future problems that might never occur without systematic quality management.

"GMP compliance is like insurance," I said, trying a different approach. "You hope you never need it, but the cost of not having it can destroy your business."

Mr. Gupta remained skeptical, but agreed to process our loan application after we provided additional documentation about regulatory requirements and potential business consequences of non-compliance.

The financing challenge revealed something important about GMP investments: they were difficult to justify using conventional cost-benefit analysis because most benefits involved avoiding problems that hadn't happened yet.

"How do we calculate return on investment for preventing hypothetical quality failures?" Priya asked as we prepared our loan application.

"We estimate the cost of regulatory shutdowns, product recalls, and customer defections," I replied. "Then we compare those potential costs to the guaranteed costs of GMP implementation."

James Mitchell helped us develop a more sophisticated business case for GMP investment by analyzing the experiences of other pharmaceutical companies that had implemented similar quality improvements.

"GMP compliance provides quantifiable benefits beyond regulatory compliance," he explained during one of our planning meetings. "Reduced production variability, lower defect rates, improved operational efficiency, enhanced customer confidence."

"Can you show us specific examples?"

"One client reduced their batch rejection rate from 8% to less than 1% within six months of implementing GMP procedures. Another client shortened their production cycle time by 20% because documented procedures eliminated trial-and-error approaches."

These concrete examples helped us understand that GMP investment wasn't just about regulatory compliance—it was about building manufacturing capabilities that could improve business performance while meeting regulatory requirements.

Our GMP implementation plan addressed five major areas: facility infrastructure, documentation systems, personnel training, quality control procedures, and management systems.

The facility infrastructure upgrades were the most expensive component. We needed to install air filtration systems, upgrade lighting to pharmaceutical standards, implement environmental monitoring equipment, and create proper segregation between different manufacturing areas.

"The air handling system alone will cost ₹4 lakhs," our facilities contractor explained. "But pharmaceutical manufacturing requires controlled air quality to prevent contamination."

"What happens if we use less expensive alternatives?"

"You'll fail regulatory inspections and potentially create quality problems that cost more than proper equipment."

This conversation illustrated a recurring theme in GMP implementation: trying to save money on infrastructure often created larger expenses later when regulatory problems or quality failures occurred.

The documentation systems required developing comprehensive standard operating procedures for every aspect of our operations. James estimated this would require 200 hours of professional time to create initial procedures, plus ongoing effort to maintain and update documentation.

"Documentation seems like overhead that doesn't improve actual manufacturing," Ravi observed during one of our planning sessions.

"Documentation captures institutional knowledge," James replied. "When procedures are properly documented, quality becomes independent of individual expertise and experience."

"What does that mean practically?"

"It means that if your most experienced operator is sick or leaves the company, production quality doesn't suffer because all critical procedures are documented and can be followed by any trained person."

The personnel training component involved educating our entire team about GMP principles, quality procedures, and their individual responsibilities for maintaining product quality.

"Everyone who works in pharmaceutical manufacturing affects product quality," James explained during our first training session. "Understanding why procedures exist helps people follow procedures consistently."

The training revealed gaps in our team's understanding of quality requirements. Most people knew how to perform their jobs, but few understood how their work connected to overall product quality or regulatory compliance.

"I never realized that cleaning procedures affected tablet dissolution rates," said Kumar, one of our production operators. "I thought cleaning was just about appearance."

"Residue from inadequate cleaning can affect tablet compression and dissolution characteristics," James explained. "That's why cleaning procedures specify exact methods and verification requirements."

The quality control procedures involved implementing systematic testing protocols, environmental monitoring systems, and batch documentation requirements that would create comprehensive quality records for every product lot.

"This seems like excessive testing," Priya said, reviewing our proposed quality control procedures. "We're already testing every batch for required specifications."

"GMP testing goes beyond minimum specifications to include trend analysis and preventive monitoring," James replied. "The goal is detecting potential problems before they become actual problems."

"Can you give an example?"

"If tablet hardness gradually increases over several batches, that suggests equipment wear or process drift that should be corrected before tablets fail specifications."

The management systems component involved creating quality oversight procedures, establishing corrective action protocols, and implementing regular management review processes that would ensure continuous improvement of our quality capabilities.

Six months into our GMP implementation, the costs were exactly what we'd projected but the benefits were larger than anticipated. Our production efficiency had improved 15% because documented procedures eliminated guesswork and variability. Our customer complaint rate had dropped to virtually zero because systematic quality controls prevented defective products from leaving our facility.

"The GMP investment is paying for itself through operational improvements," I told Mr. Gupta during our quarterly loan review meeting. "We're not just meeting regulatory requirements—we're manufacturing more efficiently."

"How do you measure the return on investment?"

"Reduced waste, fewer production delays, lower customer service costs, improved capacity utilization. Plus the prevention of regulatory problems that could have been catastrophic."

One year after completing our GMP implementation, we achieved our first WHO-GMP certification, which opened export opportunities that wouldn't have been available without internationally recognized quality systems.

"The GMP investment taught us something important about business development," I said to Dr. Patel during our annual business review. "Investing in capabilities that prevent problems is more valuable than investing in capabilities that solve problems after they occur."

"Why is prevention more valuable?"

"Because prevention costs are predictable and controllable, while problem-solving costs are unpredictable and potentially unlimited."

By 1999, when we were generating ₹50 lakh in annual revenue, our GMP-compliant manufacturing capabilities had become a key differentiator that allowed us to compete for business that required demonstrated quality systems rather than just competitive pricing.

"You know what the GMP investment really taught us?" Priya said, watching our team conduct a routine quality audit that would have been impossible three years earlier. "It taught us that building systematic capabilities creates more sustainable competitive advantages than optimizing individual processes."

The lesson would prove crucial as we expanded into biotechnology products and international markets where quality requirements were even more stringent and the costs of quality failures were exponentially higher.

Hiring International Consultant James Mitchell

The consultant's fee quote arrived by fax on a Wednesday morning and made me question whether I'd accidentally inquired about purchasing a small aircraft.

"$2,500 per week plus expenses for GMP implementation consulting," I read aloud to Priya. "That's ₹1 lakh per week at current exchange rates."

"For how many weeks?" she asked, though her expression suggested she already suspected the answer wouldn't be encouraging.

"He estimates 12-16 weeks for complete GMP implementation. So we're looking at ₹12-16 lakhs in consulting fees alone."

This was James Mitchell's response to our inquiry about hiring international quality consulting support. We'd contacted him based on a recommendation from Dr. Patel, who'd mentioned that several Indian pharmaceutical companies had used his services to achieve WHO-GMP certification.

"Why do we need an international consultant?" Priya asked. "Can't we find Indian consultants who understand GMP requirements?"

"We can find Indian consultants who understand Indian GMP requirements," I replied. "But if we want to export products eventually, we need someone who understands international quality standards."

The conversation revealed a fundamental decision point about our quality improvement strategy. We could implement basic GMP compliance using local expertise, which would satisfy Indian regulatory requirements at lower cost. Or we could implement international-standard GMP systems using expensive foreign expertise, which would position us for export opportunities but strain our current finances.

"Let's meet with him before making any decisions," Priya suggested. "Maybe his approach is worth the premium pricing."

James Mitchell arrived in Hyderabad on a Thursday afternoon, wearing khakis and a button-down shirt that somehow managed to look more professional than the business suits worn by most consultants we'd met. He was probably forty-five years old, with graying hair and the kind of understated confidence that suggested extensive experience without arrogance.

"I understand you want to implement GMP systems that will support international expansion," he said as we toured our production facility.

"Eventually, yes. But our immediate need is achieving compliance with Indian regulatory requirements."

"Those aren't necessarily different objectives," he replied, examining our tablet compression equipment. "Properly implemented GMP systems satisfy Indian requirements while creating capabilities for international market access."

"What's your background with Indian pharmaceutical companies?" I asked.

"I've worked with twelve companies over the past five years, ranging from startup manufacturers to established exporters. Each implementation was different because GMP requirements must be adapted to specific manufacturing circumstances."

"Can you give us examples of successful implementations?"

James pulled out a folder containing case studies from previous clients. The examples were encouraging: companies that had achieved WHO-GMP certification, FDA approval for US exports, and European regulatory approval using quality systems he'd helped implement.

"This company in Bangalore achieved WHO-GMP certification in eight months," he said, showing us documentation photos. "They started with manufacturing capabilities similar to yours and built international-standard quality systems incrementally."

"What did their implementation cost?"

"About ₹18 lakhs total, including infrastructure upgrades and my consulting fees. But they recovered that investment within eighteen months through export sales that wouldn't have been possible without international quality certification."

The business case was compelling, but the upfront costs remained challenging for our cash flow situation.

"Could you structure your consulting in phases?" I asked. "Maybe start with essential compliance requirements and add international standards later as our revenue grows?"

"That approach usually costs more than comprehensive implementation," James replied. "Building basic systems and then upgrading them later requires more total effort than building proper systems initially."

"Why is that?"

"Because changing established procedures is more difficult than implementing correct procedures from the beginning. People resist changing methods they're already using."

This conversation taught us something important about capability building: the most economical approach wasn't always the least expensive approach. Trying to save money through partial implementation could create larger expenses later when systems needed to be rebuilt rather than just upgraded.

"What would your implementation methodology involve?" Priya asked.

"Three phases over twelve weeks," James explained. "Phase one: assessment and planning, identifying specific gaps between current practices and GMP requirements. Phase two: system implementation, developing procedures and training personnel. Phase three: validation and certification, demonstrating that new systems actually work as intended."

"How much of your time would be on-site versus remote consulting?"

"Two days per week on-site, three days remote support and documentation development. Most GMP implementation involves creating systems and procedures that your team can maintain independently."

The consulting arrangement we eventually negotiated was more affordable than James's initial quote but more comprehensive than we'd originally planned. Instead of ₹1 lakh per week, we agreed to ₹60,000 per week for sixteen weeks, with payment spread over six months to manage our cash flow.

"Why did you reduce your fees?" I asked during contract discussions.

"Because working with smaller companies is more interesting than working with large corporations," James replied. "Large companies have established procedures that constrain innovation. Small companies let me implement optimal solutions without bureaucratic limitations."

"What do you mean by optimal solutions?"

"GMP systems designed specifically for your products, processes, and business objectives rather than generic systems adapted from other companies' implementations."

James's first week involved detailed assessment of our current manufacturing practices, quality procedures, and documentation systems. His findings were more positive than we'd expected.

"Your manufacturing quality is actually quite good," he told us during his initial assessment presentation. "The gaps are primarily in documentation and systematic controls, not in actual product quality."

"Is that easier or harder to fix?"

"Much easier. Changing documentation systems doesn't require expensive equipment or lengthy revalidation. It requires systematic thinking and disciplined implementation."

The assessment revealed specific areas where our practices differed from GMP requirements: environmental monitoring, batch documentation, cleaning validation, personnel training records, and management review procedures.

"Most of these gaps can be addressed through procedure development and training rather than facility upgrades," James explained. "That's why your GMP implementation should cost significantly less than typical industry benchmarks."

Over the following weeks, James worked with our team to develop comprehensive quality systems that exceeded Indian regulatory requirements while positioning us for international certification.

"The difference between working with James and working with local consultants," Ravi observed after our third week of implementation, "is that James explains why procedures work instead of just telling us what procedures to follow."

"How does that help?"

"When you understand why procedures exist, you can implement them more effectively and adapt them when circumstances change."

Four months after James completed his consulting engagement, we achieved WHO-GMP certification on our first inspection attempt. Six months later, we received our first export inquiry from a distributor in Bangladesh who'd found us through an international pharmaceutical directory that listed WHO-GMP certified manufacturers.

"The investment in international consulting paid for itself faster than we projected," I told Dr. Patel during our annual business review. "Export opportunities became available much sooner than we'd anticipated."

"What made the difference?"

"James didn't just help us meet minimum regulatory requirements. He helped us build quality capabilities that exceeded requirements and created competitive advantages."

"Such as?"

"Documentation systems that support rapid product development, quality procedures that prevent problems instead of just detecting them, and international credibility that opens markets we couldn't access before."

Two years after hiring James Mitchell, when we were generating ₹25 lakh in annual export revenue, I realized that investing in expensive international expertise had been more economical than trying to save money through local alternatives.

The lesson would prove crucial as we encountered increasingly complex technical challenges that required specialized knowledge unavailable through conventional consulting relationships.

First WHO-GMP Certification

The WHO inspection team arrived in two white Ambassador cars at exactly 9 AM, looking like they meant serious business.

I'd been awake since 5 AM, walking through our facility one final time, checking that every piece of equipment was clean, every document was in place, and every team member knew their role in what would be the most important three days in our company's history.

"Dr. Malhotra?" The lead inspector was a serious-looking woman in her fifties who introduced herself as Dr. Sunitha Reddy from the WHO prequalification program. "I'm here with my colleagues Dr. Patel and Mr. Kumar to conduct your GMP inspection."

"Welcome to our facility," I replied, trying to sound more confident than I felt. "We're ready for your review."

This was the culmination of eight months of preparation following James Mitchell's GMP implementation program. We'd invested ₹18 lakhs in facility upgrades, documentation systems, and quality procedures. Our entire business strategy for the next five years depended on achieving WHO-GMP certification that would allow us to export products and compete for international business.

"We'll begin with a documentation review," Dr. Reddy said, settling into our conference room with a stack of forms and checklists. "Please provide your quality manual, standard operating procedures, batch records, and training documentation."

Priya had organized our documentation with the precision of a librarian preparing for the most important exam of her career. Every procedure was indexed, every record was chronologically filed, and every training certificate was properly signed and dated.

"Your documentation appears comprehensive," Dr. Reddy observed after two hours of review. "Now we'll examine your manufacturing facility to verify that actual practices match documented procedures."

This was the moment we'd been dreading and preparing for in equal measure. Documentation was one thing—we could control paperwork. But the facility inspection would reveal whether our team actually followed the procedures we'd documented, and whether our equipment and processes could consistently produce pharmaceutical products that met international quality standards.

"Show us your raw material receiving area," Dr. Patel requested.

Kumar, our materials manager, walked the inspectors through our raw material procedures while I watched nervously from the background. Every question they asked, every note they made in their inspection notebooks, could potentially affect our certification outcome.

"How do you verify the identity of incoming raw materials?" Dr. Reddy asked.

"We conduct identification testing for every batch using infrared spectroscopy and chemical tests," Kumar replied, demonstrating our testing procedures. "All results are documented and approved before materials are released for production."

"What happens if materials fail identification tests?"

"Rejected materials are quarantined in this segregated area and returned to suppliers with detailed non-conformance reports."

The inspectors seemed satisfied with our raw material controls, but I knew the manufacturing area inspection would be more challenging. This was where all our GMP improvements would be tested under the scrutiny of international quality experts.

"Walk us through a typical production batch," Dr. Reddy said as we entered our tablet compression area.

Ravi explained our production procedures while demonstrating actual tablet compression, with the inspectors observing every detail and asking questions that revealed their deep understanding of pharmaceutical manufacturing.

"How do you ensure tablet weight uniformity?" Mr. Kumar asked.

"We test tablet weights every thirty minutes during production and adjust compression force if weights drift outside specifications," Ravi replied. "All adjustments and test results are documented in our batch records."

"Show us yesterday's batch records."

This was a critical moment. The batch records would reveal whether our documented procedures were actually being followed, or whether our team was just performing for the inspection.

Ravi pulled out the previous day's production records, which showed consistent tablet weights, proper documentation of all process adjustments, and complete signatures from production and quality control personnel.

"Your batch documentation is excellent," Dr. Reddy commented. "This demonstrates good compliance with GMP requirements."

The quality control laboratory inspection was led by Dr. Patel, who had twenty years of experience in pharmaceutical quality testing. She examined our analytical equipment, testing procedures, and laboratory records with the thoroughness of someone who'd seen every possible way that quality control could go wrong.

"Demonstrate your dissolution testing procedure," she requested.

Priya conducted a complete dissolution test while explaining our methodology, calibration procedures, and acceptance criteria. The inspectors observed every step and asked detailed questions about our analytical validation data.

"Your laboratory capabilities are impressive for a company your size," Dr. Patel said after reviewing our analytical methods. "You're conducting more comprehensive testing than many larger manufacturers."

On the second day, the inspectors examined our cleaning validation data, environmental monitoring records, and personnel training documentation. These were areas where James Mitchell's guidance had been particularly valuable, as he'd helped us develop systems that exceeded minimum requirements.

"Your environmental monitoring data shows excellent control," Dr. Reddy observed, reviewing six months of temperature and humidity records. "This demonstrates consistent adherence to storage and manufacturing conditions."

The final day involved management interviews where the inspectors questioned our quality policies, corrective action procedures, and continuous improvement processes.

"How do you handle customer complaints?" Dr. Reddy asked during my interview.

"We investigate all complaints within 48 hours, implement corrective actions if product defects are confirmed, and document findings in our quality database for trend analysis," I replied.

"Can you show us examples of complaint investigations?"

I provided documentation from three recent complaint investigations, including one where we'd identified a minor packaging issue and implemented preventive actions across our entire product line.

"This demonstrates proactive quality management," Dr. Reddy commented. "You're not just resolving individual complaints—you're using complaint data to improve your overall quality systems."

On the third afternoon, the inspection team conducted their final facility walkthrough and held a closing meeting to discuss their findings.

"We identified several minor observations during our inspection," Dr. Reddy announced, "but no major deficiencies that would prevent WHO-GMP certification."

The minor observations included recommendations for improved documentation in two procedures and suggestions for enhanced environmental monitoring in our packaging area. Nothing that would require significant time or expense to address.

"Your facility demonstrates excellent compliance with WHO-GMP requirements," Dr. Reddy continued. "We'll be recommending your company for WHO prequalification approval."

The relief I felt was overwhelming. Eight months of preparation, ₹18 lakhs in investments, and countless hours of team effort had culminated in successful certification that would transform our business opportunities.

"When will we receive official certification?" I asked.

"Typically within six weeks of our report submission. You should receive notification by the end of next month."

Six weeks later, the WHO-GMP certificate arrived by courier, along with inclusion in the WHO prequalification database that international buyers used to identify qualified pharmaceutical suppliers.

"You know what this certification really represents?" Priya said, holding our framed WHO-GMP certificate. "It represents proof that a small Indian company can build world-class quality capabilities when they're willing to invest systematically in the right systems."

"And it represents access to markets that weren't available to us before."

Within three months of receiving WHO-GMP certification, we received our first international inquiry from a distributor in Kenya who was looking for qualified suppliers of generic antibiotics. Within six months, we had export customers in four countries and international sales representing 25% of our total revenue.

"The WHO-GMP certification taught us something important about capability building," I told James Mitchell during his follow-up visit. "International recognition isn't just about meeting higher standards—it's about accessing opportunities that transform your entire business trajectory."

"What opportunities specifically?"

"Export markets, partnership discussions with international companies, credibility with sophisticated customers who require demonstrated quality capabilities."

The certification had cost us ₹18 lakhs to achieve, but it generated ₹35 lakhs in additional revenue during our first year of international sales.

More importantly, it had taught us that investing in systematic quality capabilities created value far beyond regulatory compliance—it created access to markets and opportunities that simply weren't available to companies without internationally recognized quality systems.

Cultural Transformation of the Organization

The argument started over a cleaning cloth.

Suresh, one of our production operators, had used the same cloth to clean both our tablet compression machine and the weighing balance, which violated our new cleaning procedures that required separate cloths for different equipment to prevent cross-contamination.

"It's just a cleaning cloth," Suresh said when Ravi pointed out the procedure violation. "I've been cleaning equipment the same way for two years without any problems."

"The new procedures exist for good reasons," Ravi replied. "Cross-contamination between equipment can affect product quality."

"These procedures are just paperwork. They don't change whether our tablets are actually good or bad."

This conversation, which I overheard from across the production floor, perfectly captured the cultural challenge we faced during our GMP implementation. We'd developed excellent procedures and documentation systems, but changing how people thought about their work was proving more difficult than changing what they did.

"We have a culture problem," I told Priya after witnessing several similar incidents over the past week. "People are following procedures because they have to, not because they understand why procedures matter."

"Is that necessarily bad? As long as procedures are being followed correctly, does motivation matter?"

"It matters when people encounter situations that aren't covered by specific procedures. If they don't understand the principles behind procedures, they can't make good decisions when procedures don't provide clear guidance."

The cultural transformation challenge had emerged gradually during our GMP implementation. Training sessions had successfully taught people what procedures to follow, but hadn't necessarily convinced them that new procedures were improvements over previous practices.

"Most of our team has been working in pharmaceutical manufacturing for years," observed James Mitchell during one of his consulting visits. "They've developed informal practices that worked adequately for your previous quality requirements. Now you're asking them to change established work habits for reasons that aren't immediately obvious."

"How do we convince them that new procedures are actually better?"

"By demonstrating measurable improvements that result from following new procedures, and by helping people understand how their individual work contributes to overall product quality."

James suggested implementing what he called "quality metrics visibility"—posting daily measurements of production efficiency, quality test results, and customer feedback where everyone could see how procedure changes affected actual business outcomes.

"When people can see that following new procedures produces better results, cultural change becomes easier because it's based on evidence rather than just management directives," he explained.

We installed a whiteboard in our production area where we posted daily metrics: tablet weight variation, hardness consistency, dissolution test results, batch cycle times, and customer complaint counts.

"Why are you showing us these numbers?" asked Kamala, our quality control technician, during the first week of metrics posting.

"Because these numbers show whether our quality improvements are actually working," I replied. "If new procedures don't improve these metrics, we should reconsider whether they're worth following."

"What if the numbers get worse?"

"Then we'll investigate why and adjust our procedures accordingly. The goal is better results, not just better paperwork."

The metrics visibility approach worked better than expected. Within two weeks, people started asking questions about how their individual work affected the posted numbers.

"My tablet compression settings affect weight variation?" Suresh asked, studying the daily metrics.

"Absolutely. Compression force directly influences tablet weight consistency," Ravi explained. "When you follow the calibration procedures exactly, weight variation decreases."

"Can you show me the numbers?"

Ravi pulled out batch records from before and after GMP implementation, demonstrating that tablet weight variation had decreased from ±8 milligrams to ±3 milligrams when compression procedures were followed precisely.

"I didn't realize my work had that much impact on product quality," Suresh admitted. "I thought quality control testing was what determined whether products were good or bad."

This conversation represented a breakthrough in cultural transformation. Suresh had discovered that his individual work directly affected measurable quality outcomes, which made following procedures feel personally meaningful rather than just bureaucratically required.

"You know what's happening?" Priya observed after several similar conversations. "People are starting to take ownership of quality outcomes instead of just following instructions."

"What's the difference?"

"When people follow instructions, they do exactly what they're told and nothing more. When people take ownership, they think about how to do their work better and suggest improvements to procedures."

The ownership mentality started generating unexpected improvements. Kamala suggested modifications to our dissolution testing sequence that reduced testing time by 20% without compromising accuracy. Kumar identified a raw material storage issue that could have caused quality problems before it actually affected production.

"These suggestions wouldn't have happened under our old culture," I told James during his final consulting visit. "People would have noticed the same issues but wouldn't have felt responsible for suggesting solutions."

"What changed?"

"People understand how their work connects to business outcomes, so they're motivated to identify improvements rather than just avoid problems."

The cultural transformation accelerated when we started involving the entire team in quality improvement discussions. Instead of making procedure changes based solely on management decisions, we held monthly meetings where anyone could suggest improvements to existing procedures.

"The cleaning cloth procedures are unnecessarily complicated," Suresh said during one of these meetings. "We could achieve the same contamination prevention with color-coded cloths instead of keeping separate cloths in different locations."

"That's a good suggestion," Ravi replied. "Let's test your approach and see if it works as well as current procedures."

The color-coded cloth system worked better than our original approach because it was easier to implement correctly, which reduced procedure violations while maintaining contamination prevention effectiveness.

"This is what cultural transformation looks like," James observed. "People aren't just following procedures—they're improving procedures based on their practical experience."

Six months after completing GMP implementation, our culture had evolved from "following procedures to avoid problems" to "improving procedures to achieve better outcomes."

"The cultural change is visible in our quality metrics," Priya noted, reviewing our six-month performance data. "Customer complaints have dropped to zero, production efficiency has improved 15%, and our team is suggesting an average of three process improvements per month."

"What drives the improvement suggestions?"

"People feel responsible for quality outcomes rather than just responsible for following rules. When you feel responsible for outcomes, you're motivated to find better ways to achieve those outcomes."

The cultural transformation had unexpected benefits beyond quality improvement. Employee satisfaction increased because people felt their suggestions were valued and implemented. Training new employees became easier because existing team members explained not just what procedures to follow, but why procedures existed and how to do them effectively.

"You know what the cultural transformation really achieved?" I said to Dr. Patel during our annual business review. "It converted procedure compliance from a management challenge into a team capability."

"What do you mean?"

"Previously, we had to monitor whether people followed procedures correctly. Now people monitor themselves and suggest improvements when procedures could work better."

Two years after our cultural transformation, when we had grown to 25 employees across multiple shifts, new team members were trained not just by management but by experienced employees who had internalized quality thinking and could explain both procedures and principles.

"The culture change taught us something important about organizational development," I told our expanded management team. "Sustainable improvement comes from people understanding why they're doing things differently, not just knowing what to do differently."

"And understanding why leads to continuous improvement rather than just compliance."

The lesson would prove crucial as we expanded into biotechnology products and international markets where quality requirements were even more complex and the need for systematic quality thinking was even more critical to business success.

PART II: THE SCALE CONSTRAINT (2000-2005)

Part II

The Scale Constraint (2000-2005)

The Limits of Small-Scale Success

The export order from Kenya was exactly what we'd hoped for when we achieved WHO-GMP certification, until we tried to fulfill it.

"They want 500,000 tablets of each product," I told Priya, reading the purchase order for the third time. "Delivered in two equal shipments over six months."

"That's wonderful. What's the problem?"

"The problem is that 500,000 tablets represents five months of our current production capacity. If we accept this order, we'll have to stop serving our domestic customers for half a year."

It was March 1999, and we'd been celebrating our international breakthrough for exactly one week. Our Kenyan distributor had found us through the WHO prequalification database and was offering to purchase three of our generic products at prices 40% higher than our domestic sales. The profitability was excellent, the payment terms were favorable, and the opportunity validated our investment in international quality systems.

But fulfilling the order would require production capacity we simply didn't have.

"Can we increase production by running additional shifts?" Priya suggested.

"We're already running two shifts on our tablet press. The equipment needs maintenance time, and our facility isn't set up for three-shift operations."

"What about weekends?"

"Weekend production would require additional staffing, overtime payments, and probably compromise our quality consistency. James warned us about trying to solve capacity constraints by working harder rather than working systematically."

This conversation revealed something important about our business development. We'd successfully solved our early constraints around working capital, product quality, and market access. But growth had created a new constraint that was more complex than anything we'd encountered before: the limitations of small-scale manufacturing in an industry that increasingly rewarded economies of scale.

"So what are our options?" Priya asked.

"Accept the Kenya order and disappoint our domestic customers. Reject the Kenya order and miss international growth opportunities. Or find a way to dramatically increase our production capacity."

"How dramatically?"

I did quick calculations based on our current export inquiries and domestic growth projections. "We probably need to triple our production capacity within the next two years to serve both domestic and international markets effectively."

"Triple our capacity means what exactly?"

"Multiple production lines, larger facility, significantly more equipment, probably 40-50 employees instead of our current 15."

The scale constraint wasn't just about manufacturing capacity. It affected every aspect of our business operations: quality control capabilities, regulatory compliance resources, supply chain management, customer service capacity, and financial management systems.

"We've been thinking like a small company because we are a small company," I said, reviewing our organizational structure. "But the opportunities we're pursuing require capabilities that small companies can't provide efficiently."

"So we need to stop being a small company?"

"We need to build systematic capabilities that can support larger-scale operations without losing the flexibility and quality focus that made us successful."

This transition period—1999 to 2005—would test everything we'd learned about constraint management during our startup years. The solutions that had worked for establishing market presence wouldn't necessarily work for scaling operations. The relationships that had supported small-volume business might not support large-volume requirements.

Most importantly, we'd need to develop new types of thinking about business operations. Instead of optimizing individual processes, we'd need to optimize integrated systems. Instead of managing personal relationships, we'd need to manage organizational capabilities.

"The scale constraint is different from our previous constraints," I told Dr. Patel during a strategic planning session. "Working capital constraints could be solved with better cash flow management. Quality constraints could be solved with better procedures. But scale constraints require fundamental changes to how we operate."

"What kind of fundamental changes?"

"Manufacturing systems instead of individual equipment. Management processes instead of personal oversight. Standardized procedures instead of customized approaches."

The irony was that our success had created the constraint that now limited our growth. Domestic customers who appreciated our flexibility and responsiveness wanted larger, more frequent orders. International customers who valued our quality wanted volumes that exceeded our production capacity. Distributors who trusted our reliability wanted broader product portfolios that we couldn't manufacture efficiently.

"Success creates its own problems," Priya observed as we planned our capacity expansion. "When you're small, the challenge is proving you can deliver quality and service. When you're growing, the challenge is delivering quality and service at larger volumes."

"And the solutions that work for small-volume operations often don't work for large-volume operations."

The stories in the following chapters chronicle our systematic approach to solving scale constraints without compromising the operational excellence that had enabled our growth. We'd need to build manufacturing capabilities that could produce millions of tablets monthly instead of hundreds of thousands. We'd need to develop supply chain relationships that could support predictable large-volume requirements instead of flexible small-volume orders.

Most importantly, we'd need to create organizational systems that could maintain our quality standards and customer responsiveness as we grew from 15 employees to 150 employees.

"The scale constraint taught us something important about business development," I would reflect years later. "Growth isn't just about doing more of what you're already doing well. Growth requires developing new capabilities that preserve your core strengths while enabling larger-scale operations."

The solutions we developed during this period—systematic manufacturing planning, integrated quality management, structured customer relationship management—would become the foundation for our eventual expansion into biotechnology products and global markets.

But first, we had to learn how to manufacture pharmaceutical products at volumes ten times larger than anything we'd attempted before, while maintaining the quality standards that had earned us international recognition and the customer relationships that had sustained our growth.

The scale constraint would teach us that sustainable business growth requires constant evolution of operational capabilities, and that the methods that establish competitive advantages must themselves evolve to preserve those advantages as businesses grow larger and more complex.

"You know what's interesting about the scale constraint?" Priya said as we finalized our expansion plans. "It's the first constraint that can't be solved by working harder or being more efficient with existing resources."

"What do you mean?"

"Our previous constraints could be solved by optimizing what we already had. The scale constraint requires building capabilities we've never had before."

That realization would guide our approach to business development for the next six years as we learned to think systematically about operations that were orders of magnitude larger than anything we'd previously managed.

Chapter 6

The Critical Mass Quest

When Small is No Longer Beautiful

The meeting room at Standard Chartered Bank felt like a courtroom where we were on trial for the crime of being too small.

"Your company has excellent quality credentials and impressive growth trajectory," said Rajesh Agarwal, the relationship manager reviewing our loan application. "But your current scale doesn't justify the infrastructure investment you're proposing."

I'd been explaining our expansion plans for the past hour: building a 10,000 square foot manufacturing facility, installing three production lines, hiring 40 additional employees, and increasing our monthly capacity from 2 million tablets to 15 million tablets.

"What do you mean by scale justification?" I asked.

"Banks evaluate pharmaceutical expansion loans based on revenue multiples and asset utilization ratios," he replied, consulting a spreadsheet. "Your current annual revenue of ₹3.5 crores supports a maximum facility investment of ₹2 crores. You're requesting ₹4.5 crores."

"But our projected revenue growth will reach ₹12 crores within three years based on confirmed export orders and domestic expansion plans."

"Projected growth is less reliable than demonstrated performance. Can you provide contracts or purchase orders that guarantee the revenue increases you're forecasting?"

This was our catch-22 situation: we needed larger production capacity to fulfill the orders that would justify larger production capacity. Export customers wanted suppliers who could guarantee large-volume deliveries, but we couldn't guarantee large-volume deliveries without expanded manufacturing capabilities that required financing we couldn't obtain without guaranteed large-volume orders.

"Our Kenya distributor has committed to purchasing 2 million tablets quarterly," I explained, showing him the letter of intent we'd received.

"Letters of intent aren't purchase contracts. What happens if market conditions change and your Kenya distributor reduces orders?"

"We have domestic customers who can absorb additional capacity if export orders don't materialize."

"Your domestic customers currently purchase about 1.8 million tablets monthly. Even if domestic demand doubled, that wouldn't justify tripling your production capacity."

The conversation continued for another thirty minutes, with Rajesh systematically questioning every assumption in our expansion plan. His concerns weren't unreasonable—banks had to manage risks, and pharmaceutical expansion projects had high failure rates when companies couldn't achieve the scale economies that made large facilities profitable.

"What would convince you to approve our loan application?" I asked finally.

"Confirmed purchase contracts totaling at least ₹8 crores annually, or equity partners who can provide part of the required capital to reduce our lending risk."

Walking out of the bank that afternoon, I realized we were facing a constraint that couldn't be solved through operational improvements or creative business models. We'd reached the limits of organic growth and needed to find ways to achieve critical mass quickly enough to justify the infrastructure investments that would enable further growth.

"We have a fundamental scaling problem," I told Priya over dinner that evening. "We're too small to access the financing we need to grow large enough to serve the customers who want to work with us."

"So what are our options?"

"Find equity investors, find strategic partners, or find customers willing to provide advance payments for guaranteed capacity."

"Which option is most realistic?"

"Probably strategic partnerships. Equity investors want pharmaceutical companies with proven large-scale operations. Customers want suppliers with demonstrated large-scale capacity. But strategic partners might value our capabilities enough to help us achieve the scale we need."

The strategic partnership exploration began with Biocon, India's largest biotechnology company, which had expressed interest in our tablet manufacturing capabilities for their generic drug portfolio.

"You have excellent quality systems and international certifications," said Biocon's manufacturing head during our initial meeting at Biocon's headquarters in Bangalore. "But your current capacity is too small for most of our requirements."

"What capacity levels would be interesting for Biocon?"

"We need partners who can manufacture 50-100 million tablets annually across multiple products. Your current capacity of 25 million tablets annually is below our minimum partnership threshold."

"What if we could scale to 100 million tablets annually within eighteen months?"

"That would be very interesting, but it would require demonstrated execution capability rather than just expansion plans."

The Biocon conversation revealed another aspect of the critical mass constraint: potential partners evaluated companies based on current capabilities rather than future potential. Everyone wanted to work with manufacturers who already had the scale they needed, not manufacturers who might achieve that scale eventually.

"It's like trying to get hired for a job that requires five years of experience when you only have two years of experience," Priya observed. "The only way to get the experience is to get the job, but you can't get the job without the experience."

"Except in business, the stakes are higher because expansion requires capital investments that could bankrupt the company if they don't generate expected returns."

The breakthrough came from an unexpected source: our contract manufacturer in Medchal, who was facing capacity utilization problems with their second production line.

"We're operating our primary production line at 80% capacity," explained Mr. Suresh Reddy during one of our regular meetings. "But our secondary line is only operating at 30% capacity because we don't have enough customers who need large-volume production."

"What would it take to utilize that capacity more effectively?"

"Long-term agreements with customers who can commit to steady volume requirements. The challenge is that most small pharmaceutical companies need flexible scheduling, while efficient capacity utilization requires predictable scheduling."

"What if we could guarantee predictable scheduling in exchange for favorable pricing and priority access?"

"That would be very attractive. Predictable capacity utilization would let us offer better pricing than we can provide for irregular orders."

The arrangement we developed with Mr. Reddy solved multiple constraints simultaneously: we gained access to large-scale production capacity without upfront capital investment, he gained predictable capacity utilization that improved his facility economics, and we could pursue larger orders without building our own manufacturing facility.

"This is better than building our own facility," I realized after negotiating the details. "We get immediate access to large-scale capacity without the financial risks and management complexities of facility ownership."

"And we can test our ability to manage large-volume operations before committing to permanent infrastructure investments."

The partnership with Mr. Reddy's facility allowed us to accept the Kenya order and pursue additional export opportunities that had been beyond our capacity limitations. Within six months, we were manufacturing 8 million tablets monthly and had confirmed orders that would require 12 million tablets monthly by the end of the year.

"You know what's interesting about solving the critical mass constraint?" I said to Dr. Patel during a business review meeting. "The solution wasn't building larger capabilities ourselves—it was accessing larger capabilities through strategic partnerships."

"What's the difference?"

"Building capabilities requires capital and time that small companies often can't afford. Accessing capabilities through partnerships provides immediate scale while preserving capital for growth investments."

"But doesn't partnership mean less control over operations?"

"Less direct control, but more strategic flexibility. If our volume requirements change, we can adjust partnership terms more easily than we could modify owned facilities."

The critical mass quest taught us something important about scaling constraints: they don't always require building larger internal capabilities. Sometimes they require finding creative ways to access the capabilities you need while preserving the financial flexibility that enables continued growth.

Two years later, when our monthly volume had grown to 20 million tablets and we finally built our own manufacturing facility, we maintained our partnership with Mr. Reddy's facility as a strategic backup that provided capacity flexibility during peak demand periods.

"The critical mass constraint forced us to think strategically about capability development," Priya observed as we planned our next phase of expansion. "Instead of trying to build everything ourselves, we learned to build core capabilities internally while accessing complementary capabilities through partnerships."

That strategic approach to capability development would prove crucial as we expanded into more complex therapeutic areas where the capital requirements for complete vertical integration would have been prohibitive for a company our size.

Revenue Crossing ₹100 Crores Milestone

The accountant's phone call came at 6:30 PM on a Tuesday in March 2004, just as I was reviewing production schedules for the following week.

"Mr. Malhotra, I've finished the annual revenue calculations," said Krishnan, our chartered accountant for the past three years. "The final number for fiscal year 2003-04 is ₹102.7 crores."

I set down my pen and asked him to repeat the figure, though I'd heard him clearly the first time.

"One hundred and two point seven crores," he confirmed. "You've crossed the ₹100 crore milestone."

After hanging up, I sat in my office for several minutes, trying to process what that number actually meant. Ten years earlier, we'd started with ₹50,000 in savings and a garage laboratory. Five years earlier, we'd been celebrating our first ₹1 crore revenue year. Now we were generating more than ₹100 crores annually.

"Priya," I called across the office. "Can you come here for a moment?"

"What's wrong?" she asked, probably noticing something unusual in my voice.

"Nothing's wrong. Krishnan just called with our final revenue numbers. We hit ₹102.7 crores this year."

She stared at me for a moment, then sat down heavily in the chair across from my desk.

"₹100 crores," she said quietly. "I remember when we thought ₹10 crores seemed impossibly large."

"I remember when we thought ₹1 crore seemed impossibly large."

The milestone felt simultaneously momentous and anticlimactic. Momentous because ₹100 crores represented a scale of business that we'd never imagined when we started. Anticlimactic because it had arrived through gradual growth rather than dramatic breakthrough, making it feel like a natural progression rather than a fundamental transformation.

"Should we celebrate?" Priya asked.

"Probably. But I'm not sure how to celebrate something that feels both huge and inevitable."

"What feels inevitable about it?"

"The growth trajectory. Once we solved our critical mass constraints and established international partnerships, ₹100 crores became a mathematical progression rather than an ambitious target."

This was true but incomplete. The mathematics had been predictable, but the execution had required solving dozens of operational challenges that could have derailed our growth if we hadn't addressed them systematically.

"Let's look at where the revenue actually came from," I suggested, pulling out our detailed financial reports.

The breakdown revealed how significantly our business had evolved: domestic sales contributed ₹61 crores, international sales contributed ₹41 crores. Generic tablets still represented our largest category at ₹78 crores, but specialty formulations had grown to ₹24 crores.

"International sales are 40% of our total revenue," Priya observed. "That's a complete transformation from five years ago when we had zero international sales."

"And specialty formulations are almost 25% of revenue, compared to zero three years ago."

The revenue composition told the story of systematic capability building that had enabled scale without sacrificing profitability. Instead of just growing our original generic tablet business, we'd developed new products and entered new markets that commanded higher margins and created more sustainable competitive positions.

"You know what's interesting about hitting ₹100 crores?" I said, studying our customer distribution data. "We're not dependent on any single customer or market for more than 15% of our revenue."

"Is that good or bad?"

"It's good for business stability, but it means our growth has come from breadth rather than depth. We're serving more markets instead of dominating specific markets."

This diversification had been intentional—we'd learned from other pharmaceutical companies that over-dependence on single customers or markets created vulnerabilities that could destroy businesses when those relationships changed.

"What's our largest single customer?" Priya asked.

"Biocon, at ₹14 crores annually. But that's spread across twelve different products, so we're not dependent on any single product relationship."

The customer diversification reflected something important about our scaling strategy: we'd grown by developing capabilities that served multiple customers rather than by becoming indispensable to individual customers.

"Should we announce the ₹100 crore milestone publicly?" Priya asked.

"What would be the purpose?"

"Industry recognition, customer confidence, employee pride, potential investor interest."

"And potential competitive attention, regulatory scrutiny, customer expectations for better pricing."

This conversation revealed something complicated about business milestones: they provided validation and motivation, but they also created new pressures and expectations that could affect business relationships.

"Let's celebrate internally first and think about external announcements later," I suggested.

We organized a company meeting for the following Friday, gathering all 127 employees in our main conference hall to share the milestone achievement.

"Ten years ago, this company consisted of two people in a garage laboratory," I told the assembled team. "Today, we're generating over ₹100 crores in annual revenue through the collective efforts of everyone in this room."

The response was enthusiastic but also revealed interesting perspectives on what the milestone meant to different people.

"Does this mean we'll get salary increases?" asked Ramesh, one of our production supervisors.

"It means the company is financially strong enough to invest in growth opportunities that create advancement potential for everyone," I replied.

"Does this mean we'll be acquired by a larger company?" asked Meera, from our quality control team.

"It means we have strategic options that didn't exist when we were smaller, but acquisition isn't our objective."

"Does this mean we'll go public?" asked Sunil, from our regulatory affairs department.

"It means we could consider public listing eventually, but we're focused on building capabilities rather than financial restructuring."

These questions reflected something important about organizational growth: reaching significant milestones changes how people think about their careers and the company's future trajectory.

"The ₹100 crore milestone represents proof that systematic capability building creates sustainable business growth," I said, concluding the meeting. "But it's not an endpoint—it's evidence that our approach to business development can support continued expansion into more complex products and markets."

After the meeting, Priya and I walked through our manufacturing facility, which had grown from our original garage laboratory to 25,000 square feet of WHO-GMP certified production space serving customers across fifteen countries.

"You know what the ₹100 crore milestone really represents?" she said, watching our team manage production operations that would have seemed impossibly complex during our startup years.

"What?"

"It represents the transformation from entrepreneurs learning to run a business to business leaders managing systematic growth."

"What's the difference?"

"Entrepreneurs solve problems as they arise. Business leaders build capabilities that prevent problems from arising."

"And which are we now?"

"Both. We're still solving new problems constantly, but we're solving them using systematic approaches rather than just improvising solutions."

That evening, after most employees had left for the day, I remained in my office reviewing our strategic plans for the next five years. Crossing ₹100 crores felt like completing one phase of business development and beginning another.

The next phase would involve more complex challenges: biotechnology product development, international manufacturing partnerships, potential acquisitions of complementary companies, and the organizational systems needed to manage operations approaching ₹500 crores in annual revenue.

"The ₹100 crore milestone taught us something important about business growth," I told Dr. Patel during our monthly review meeting. "Significant milestones feel inevitable in retrospect, but they require hundreds of daily decisions that could have led to different outcomes."

"Such as?"

"Choosing quality over cost savings, choosing sustainable growth over rapid expansion, choosing capability building over financial optimization."

"And now that you've reached ₹100 crores, what's the next milestone?"

"The next milestone isn't a revenue number—it's developing capabilities that can support whatever opportunities emerge from having reached this scale."

Because the most important lesson from crossing ₹100 crores was that business milestones don't represent destinations—they represent evidence of capabilities that enable access to larger opportunities.

Identifying the Minimum Viable Scale in Pharmaceuticals

The conversation with our German potential partner started well until they asked about our production volumes.

"Your quality certifications are impressive," said Dr. Klaus Weber during our video conference call from Munich. "WHO-GMP, ISO certification, excellent regulatory compliance record. But what are your current manufacturing volumes?"

"We're producing approximately 150 million tablets annually across our product portfolio," I replied.

There was a pause that lasted long enough to make me wonder if our internet connection had failed.

"150 million tablets annually?" Dr. Weber repeated. "That's roughly what we produce in six weeks."

"Yes, but our volumes are growing rapidly. We've doubled production every eighteen months for the past four years."

"That's encouraging growth, but pharmaceutical partnerships require suppliers who can guarantee volumes of at least one billion tablets annually. Below that threshold, the administrative costs of managing supplier relationships exceed the economic benefits."

After the call ended, I sat in our conference room trying to process what Dr. Weber had told us. We'd spent five years building what felt like significant scale—150 million tablets annually, ₹120 crores in revenue, facilities serving customers across twenty countries. But to serious international partners, we were apparently still below the minimum threshold for meaningful business relationships.

"We have a scale perception problem," I told Priya during our weekly planning meeting. "What feels large to us is considered small by the companies we want to partner with."

"Maybe we're targeting the wrong types of partnerships," she suggested. "Maybe there are international opportunities that don't require billion-tablet production volumes."

"Or maybe we need to understand what minimum viable scale actually means in pharmaceuticals and figure out how to achieve it systematically."

The minimum viable scale question had been lurking beneath our growth strategy for months. We'd expanded capacity, improved quality systems, and diversified into new markets, but we were still encountering situations where potential partners dismissed us based purely on volume considerations.

"Let's research what scale thresholds actually matter in pharmaceutical business," I suggested.

The research was illuminating and depressing in equal measure. For meaningful partnerships with major pharmaceutical companies, minimum annual volumes started at 500 million tablets. For private label manufacturing relationships, the threshold was typically 200-300 million tablets annually. For export to regulated markets like Europe and the US, distributors preferred suppliers who could guarantee 100 million tablets annually for individual products.

"So we're above the threshold for some opportunities but below the threshold for others," Priya observed, reviewing our findings.

"And the highest-value opportunities generally require the largest scale commitments."

"Which means we need to choose between remaining diversified across many smaller opportunities or concentrating resources to achieve scale in fewer, larger opportunities."

This analysis revealed something important about pharmaceutical business strategy: growth beyond a certain point required making trade-offs between breadth and depth that could fundamentally change the nature of your business.

"What would it take to reach 500 million tablets annually?" I asked, pulling out our production planning spreadsheets.

"Either tripling our current capacity across existing products, or focusing intensively on 3-4 high-volume products instead of our current portfolio of 15 products."

"What are the implications of each approach?"

"Tripling capacity means massive capital investment and finding customers for 350 million additional tablets annually. Focusing on fewer products means abandoning profitable market segments that don't scale to required volumes."

Both approaches involved risks that could destroy our business if market conditions changed unexpectedly. Massive capacity expansion could create fixed costs that would bankrupt us during market downturns. Product concentration could make us vulnerable to competitive threats or regulatory changes affecting our core products.

"Maybe minimum viable scale isn't just about production volumes," I suggested. "Maybe it's about building capabilities that enable scale when opportunities justify it."

"What do you mean?"

"Instead of building permanent capacity for 500 million tablets, maybe we build flexible systems that can scale to 500 million tablets when specific opportunities require that volume."

This perspective led us to investigate contract manufacturing partnerships that could provide scale flexibility without permanent capacity commitments. Instead of building larger facilities, we could develop relationships with manufacturers who had excess capacity and could accommodate our overflow requirements.

"The minimum viable scale problem might be solvable through network strategies rather than just internal capacity building," I realized after speaking with three contract manufacturers.

"How would that work?"

"We could guarantee volumes of 500 million tablets annually by aggregating our own production capacity with guaranteed access to partner capacity. Customers get the scale assurance they require, we get access to large opportunities without proportional capital investment."

The network approach required developing more sophisticated supply chain management capabilities. Instead of just managing our own production scheduling, we'd need to coordinate production across multiple facilities while maintaining quality consistency and delivery reliability.

"This changes our business model significantly," Priya observed. "Instead of being a manufacturer, we'd become more like a manufacturing coordinator."

"Is that necessarily bad?"

"It's different. It requires different capabilities and creates different risks than owning all production capacity."

We tested the network approach with a large order from our Bangladesh distributor who wanted 200 million tablets annually but needed delivery flexibility that our single facility couldn't provide efficiently.

"We can guarantee 200 million tablets annually," I told them, "with 60% produced in our facility and 40% produced through our quality-certified partner network."

"How do you ensure consistent quality across multiple manufacturing sites?"

"Common quality standards, shared raw material suppliers, standardized testing protocols, and regular audits of all partner facilities."

The Bangladesh arrangement worked better than expected. By coordinating production across three facilities, we could provide delivery flexibility and volume guarantees that none of the individual facilities could offer independently.

"You know what we learned about minimum viable scale?" I said to Dr. Patel during our quarterly business review. "The scale threshold isn't really about how much you can produce—it's about how reliably you can deliver large volumes when customers need them."

"What's the difference?"

"Production capacity is about what you own. Delivery capability is about what you can access through systematic partnerships and supply chain coordination."

"So minimum viable scale is more about logistics and coordination than just manufacturing?"

"In pharmaceuticals, customers care about supply security more than manufacturing ownership. They want assurance that orders will be fulfilled reliably, regardless of how you organize the production."

Six months after implementing our network strategy, we were able to accept orders that required 400 million tablets annually while operating our own facility at optimal capacity levels.

"The minimum viable scale constraint taught us something important about business development," Priya observed as we reviewed our expanded customer portfolio. "Sometimes the best way to achieve scale isn't to build larger capabilities yourself—it's to build systems that can access scale when you need it."

"And flexible access to scale can be more valuable than permanent ownership of scale, especially when markets are unpredictable."

The network approach enabled us to compete for opportunities that would have been impossible with our owned capacity alone, while preserving the financial flexibility that had enabled our growth throughout our company's development.

More importantly, it taught us that minimum viable scale in pharmaceuticals wasn't a fixed threshold to cross once—it was an ongoing capability to access whatever scale current opportunities required.

Strategic Decision to Focus on Therapeutic Areas

The portfolio review meeting lasted four hours and left me with a headache that perfectly matched the complexity of our product strategy.

"We currently manufacture 23 different formulations across 8 therapeutic areas," Dr. Patel announced, pointing to the whiteboard where she'd mapped our entire product portfolio. "From basic analgesics to cardiovascular drugs to antibiotics to antidiabetic medications."

"That sounds diversified and comprehensive," said Ramesh, our new business development manager.

"It sounds scattered and unfocused," replied Priya, studying the sales data for each product category. "Look at our revenue distribution. Six products generate 70% of our revenue. The remaining 17 products generate 30% of revenue but consume 60% of our management attention."

It was September 2003, and we'd reached a point where our product diversity was becoming a strategic liability rather than an asset. Each therapeutic area required different regulatory knowledge, distinct marketing approaches, separate distributor relationships, and specialized technical expertise.

"What's the problem with diversity?" Ramesh asked. "Doesn't product variety reduce business risk by avoiding dependence on single market segments?"

"Diversity reduces market risk but increases operational complexity," I explained. "Every additional therapeutic area multiplies the number of things we need to be excellent at."

The conversation revealed something important about our growth trajectory. During our startup years, product diversity had been beneficial because we could pursue any opportunity that generated cash flow and built customer relationships. But as we approached larger scale, diversity was preventing us from achieving the depth of expertise that serious customers expected.

"Let's analyze the economics of each therapeutic area," I suggested, pulling out detailed profitability reports.

The analysis was revealing. Our cardiovascular products generated ₹35 crores in annual revenue with 28% gross margins. Our pain management products generated ₹42 crores with 32% margins. Our antibiotic products generated ₹18 crores with 15% margins due to intense price competition.

"The antibiotic business is barely profitable," Priya observed. "We're investing significant regulatory and quality resources for products that generate minimal returns."

"But antibiotics represent growth opportunities in export markets," Ramesh countered. "International demand for generic antibiotics is increasing."

"International antibiotic markets are dominated by manufacturers who can produce at massive scale with very low costs," Dr. Patel replied. "Competing effectively requires either breakthrough innovations or cost structures we can't achieve with our current scale."

This debate continued for weeks as we evaluated the strategic implications of focusing versus diversifying our therapeutic portfolio. The arguments for focus were compelling: deeper expertise, stronger customer relationships, more efficient resource allocation, clearer competitive positioning.

But the arguments for diversity were also valid: reduced dependence on single markets, protection against regulatory changes affecting specific therapeutic areas, multiple revenue streams that provided financial stability.

"Maybe the question isn't whether to focus or diversify," I said during one of our strategy sessions. "Maybe the question is how to sequence our development so we can build strong positions in selected areas before expanding into new areas."

"What would that look like practically?" Priya asked.

"Choose 2-3 therapeutic areas where we already have strong positions and competitive advantages. Invest aggressively in becoming dominant players in those areas. Then use the profits and expertise from those areas to fund expansion into new therapeutic areas."

The therapeutic area evaluation process took two months and involved detailed analysis of market dynamics, competitive landscapes, regulatory requirements, and our existing capabilities in each area.

"Cardiovascular and pain management are our strongest positions," Dr. Patel concluded after reviewing all the data. "We have established customer relationships, proven product quality, and the regulatory expertise needed to develop new products in these areas."

"What about our other therapeutic areas?"

"Maintain existing products that generate positive cash flow, but don't invest in new product development outside cardiovascular and pain management unless exceptional opportunities arise."

The strategic focus decision meant discontinuing several product development projects that had consumed significant resources. We stopped developing new antibiotic formulations, postponed expansion into dermatology products, and declined opportunities in therapeutic areas that didn't align with our chosen focus.

"This feels like we're deliberately limiting our growth opportunities," Ramesh observed.

"We're trading breadth for depth," I replied. "Instead of being adequate suppliers across many therapeutic areas, we're choosing to become preferred suppliers in fewer therapeutic areas."

The focus strategy began with intensive investment in cardiovascular product development. Instead of trying to develop generic versions of every cardiac medication, we concentrated on sustained-release formulations and combination products that offered patient compliance advantages.

"By focusing on cardiovascular products, we can develop expertise in sustained-release technology that applies across multiple products in this therapeutic area," explained our new formulation scientist, Dr. Sharma, who had specialized experience in cardiovascular drug development.

"What advantages does therapeutic specialization provide?" I asked.

"Regulatory authorities recognize companies with deep expertise in specific therapeutic areas. Doctors trust suppliers who understand the clinical requirements of their specialty. Distributors prefer working with companies who can provide comprehensive product portfolios within therapeutic categories."

The pain management focus involved developing innovative delivery systems for existing analgesic molecules. Instead of competing solely on price for standard formulations, we developed topical gels, extended-release tablets, and combination products that commanded premium pricing.

"Pain management products have excellent export potential," Dr. Patel noted, reviewing international market opportunities. "Regulatory approval requirements are manageable, market demand is growing globally, and our quality certifications provide competitive advantages."

Eighteen months after implementing our therapeutic focus strategy, the results exceeded our projections. Cardiovascular revenue had grown 85% through new product launches and expanded customer relationships. Pain management revenue had grown 60% through premium product development and international expansion.

"The focus strategy is working better than diversification," Priya observed, reviewing our improved financial performance. "Revenue growth has accelerated despite abandoning several product categories."

"Why is focus more effective than diversification for our business?"

"Because customers prefer suppliers who understand their specific requirements deeply rather than suppliers who offer broad but shallow capabilities."

The therapeutic focus decision also simplified our operations significantly. Instead of managing regulatory requirements across eight therapeutic areas, we concentrated regulatory expertise on two areas and achieved much more efficient approval processes.

"Specialization allows us to build systematic advantages," I told our expanded management team during a strategy review. "When you understand one therapeutic area deeply, you can anticipate market trends, identify development opportunities, and serve customer needs that generalist competitors miss."

"Does specialization limit our growth potential?" asked our CFO.

"Specialization increases our growth potential within chosen areas while reducing our growth potential in other areas. The net effect is faster growth because we can capture larger market shares in areas where we focus."

Three years after implementing therapeutic focus, we had achieved market leadership positions in both cardiovascular and pain management segments within our geographic markets. Our customer relationships were stronger, our product development was more efficient, and our competitive position was more defensible.

"You know what the therapeutic focus strategy taught us?" I said to Dr. Patel during our annual planning session. "Strategic constraints can be more valuable than strategic options when they force you to build deep capabilities rather than broad capabilities."

"And deep capabilities in focused areas create more sustainable competitive advantages than broad capabilities across many areas."

The lesson would prove crucial as we planned our expansion into biotechnology products, where therapeutic specialization would be even more critical for achieving the technical expertise and regulatory credibility required for complex product development.

Building the Cardiovascular Portfolio

Dr. Rajesh Gupta looked at our atenolol tablets like they'd personally offended him.

"The formulation is adequate," he said, setting down our sample package after examining the tablets under his desk magnifying glass. "But adequate isn't sufficient for cardiovascular medications."

Dr. Gupta was a cardiologist at Apollo Hospital in Hyderabad and had agreed to evaluate our generic cardiovascular products as potential alternatives to the branded medications he typically prescribed. The meeting wasn't going as well as I'd hoped.

"What would make a cardiovascular formulation more than adequate?" I asked.

"Consistency that patients can rely on," he replied. "Cardiovascular medications require precise dosing because small variations can affect heart rhythm, blood pressure control, and treatment outcomes."

"Our tablets meet all pharmacopoeial specifications for content uniformity and dissolution."

"Meeting minimum specifications isn't the same as optimizing for clinical performance. Branded cardiovascular drugs are formulated to provide predictable bioavailability that doctors can depend on when making dosing decisions."

This conversation was my introduction to the cardiovascular market's unique quality requirements. Unlike pain medications where slight formulation variations rarely affected patient outcomes, cardiovascular drugs required precision that went beyond standard generic manufacturing approaches.

"What would it take to develop cardiovascular formulations that meet your clinical requirements?" I asked.

"Bioequivalence studies that demonstrate your products perform identically to branded references. Stability data showing consistent performance over extended storage periods. Manufacturing processes that minimize batch-to-batch variation."

"How much would bioequivalence studies cost?"

"Probably ₹8-12 lakhs per product, depending on the complexity of the formulation and the number of subjects required."

I did quick mental calculations. We were considering developing five cardiovascular products, which meant ₹40-60 lakhs in bioequivalence studies alone, plus the costs of enhanced manufacturing processes and extended stability testing.

"This is significantly more expensive than developing standard generic products," I told Priya after the meeting with Dr. Gupta.

"But cardiovascular products command higher margins than standard generics," she replied, reviewing market pricing data. "If we can develop products that doctors trust, we can charge premium prices that justify the additional development costs."

"What premium are we talking about?"

"Branded cardiovascular drugs sell for ₹4-6 per tablet. Standard generics sell for ₹1.50-2 per tablet. High-quality generics with bioequivalence data sell for ₹2.50-3.50 per tablet."

The economics were compelling, but the technical challenges were more complex than anything we'd attempted. Cardiovascular drug development required expertise in controlled-release technology, bioavailability optimization, and clinical testing protocols.

"We need to hire someone with specific cardiovascular formulation experience," I decided after reviewing the technical requirements for our planned products.

Dr. Meera Sharma joined us three months later with fifteen years of experience in cardiovascular drug development at Dr. Reddy's Laboratories. Her first assessment of our capabilities was encouraging but realistic.

"You have excellent basic formulation skills and quality systems," she told me during her second week. "But cardiovascular products require additional capabilities that you'll need to build systematically."

"Such as?"

"Controlled-release technology for sustained-action formulations. Bioanalytical testing capabilities for pharmacokinetic studies. Stability testing protocols that simulate real-world storage conditions."

"Can we develop these capabilities internally, or do we need external partnerships?"

"A combination. You can build controlled-release formulation capabilities internally, but bioequivalence studies require specialized clinical research organizations, and some analytical testing requires equipment that wouldn't be cost-effective for your current volume."

Our first cardiovascular product development project was atenolol sustained-release tablets, designed to provide 24-hour blood pressure control with once-daily dosing instead of the twice-daily dosing required for immediate-release formulations.

"Sustained-release atenolol is technically challenging," Dr. Sharma explained as we began formulation development. "The release rate must be precisely controlled to maintain therapeutic blood levels throughout the dosing interval."

"What happens if the release rate is incorrect?"

"Too fast and you get dose dumping that can cause dangerous blood pressure drops. Too slow and you get inadequate blood pressure control toward the end of the dosing interval."

The formulation development process took eight months and required testing dozens of different polymer combinations, compression parameters, and coating formulations. Each iteration needed dissolution testing under multiple pH conditions to simulate different locations in the gastrointestinal tract.

"This is much more complex than immediate-release formulations," I observed, watching Dr. Sharma analyze dissolution data from our latest prototype.

"Cardiovascular drugs require formulation optimization rather than just formulation adequacy," she replied. "The difference between adequate and optimal can be clinically significant for patients."

The bioequivalence study for our atenolol sustained-release tablets cost ₹11 lakhs and required 24 healthy volunteers who received both our formulation and the branded reference product in a crossover design that measured drug absorption over 48 hours.

"The bioequivalence results are excellent," announced Dr. Kumar from the clinical research organization that conducted our study. "Your formulation demonstrates bioequivalence to the reference product with 90% confidence intervals well within regulatory requirements."

"What does that mean practically?" I asked.

"It means your sustained-release atenolol tablets provide the same blood levels as the branded product, so doctors can prescribe them with confidence that patients will receive equivalent therapeutic benefits."

The regulatory approval process for bioequivalent cardiovascular products was more stringent than standard generic approvals. We needed to provide comprehensive manufacturing documentation, stability data, and bioequivalence reports that demonstrated our products met international quality standards.

"Cardiovascular product approvals require different regulatory strategy," explained Dr. Patel during our submission preparation. "Regulators scrutinize cardiovascular generics more carefully because medication errors can have serious clinical consequences."

"How does that affect our approval timeline?"

"Probably 8-12 months instead of the 4-6 months typical for standard generic approvals. But approved cardiovascular products have longer patent-protected market opportunities."

Our atenolol sustained-release tablets received regulatory approval fourteen months after we initiated development. The commercial launch exceeded our projections, with first-year sales reaching ₹8 crores and gross margins of 45%.

"The cardiovascular market responds differently to quality differentiation," I observed, reviewing our sales performance. "Doctors are willing to pay premium prices for products they trust, and patients value the convenience of once-daily dosing."

"Which creates sustainable competitive advantages that price-focused generic manufacturers can't easily replicate," Priya added.

The success of our atenolol product enabled investment in four additional cardiovascular products over the next two years: metoprolol extended-release tablets, amlodipine-hydrochlorothiazide combination tablets, ramipril sustained-release capsules, and atorvastatin high-bioavailability tablets.

"Each cardiovascular product we develop strengthens our position in this therapeutic area," Dr. Sharma noted as we planned our third-generation cardiovascular portfolio. "Doctors prefer working with suppliers who understand cardiovascular medicine comprehensively rather than suppliers who offer individual products."

"How does comprehensive understanding benefit our business?"

"Doctors prescribe multiple cardiovascular medications for individual patients. When they trust your atenolol, they're more likely to prescribe your metoprolol and amlodipine. Portfolio synergy creates customer loyalty that individual products can't achieve."

Three years after entering the cardiovascular market, we had achieved 12% market share in sustained-release cardiovascular formulations and were generating ₹45 crores annually from cardiovascular products with average gross margins of 42%.

"You know what building the cardiovascular portfolio taught us?" I said to Dr. Sharma during our annual planning session. "Therapeutic specialization requires different capabilities than general generic manufacturing, but it creates more sustainable competitive advantages."

"What capabilities specifically?"

"Clinical understanding of therapeutic requirements, formulation expertise in specialized technologies, regulatory knowledge of therapeutic-specific requirements, and customer relationships based on clinical trust rather than just commercial convenience."

"And those capabilities become harder for competitors to replicate as you develop deeper expertise."

The cardiovascular portfolio had become our most profitable business segment and provided the foundation for our expansion into other specialized therapeutic areas where technical expertise created defensible competitive positions.

More importantly, it had taught us that successful product development in specialized markets required understanding customer needs from clinical rather than just commercial perspectives.

Chapter 7

The Brand Building Paradox

Creating Identity in a Commodity Business

The marketing agency's presentation lasted forty-five minutes and left me more confused than enlightened about what our brand should actually represent.

"Malhotra Pharmaceuticals needs a distinctive brand identity that differentiates your products in an increasingly competitive generic marketplace," announced Kavitha Reddy, the creative director from Brand Dynamics, as she clicked through slides filled with color schemes, logo concepts, and messaging frameworks.

"But we manufacture generic drugs," I said, studying a proposed logo that looked suspiciously similar to every other pharmaceutical company logo I'd seen. "By definition, our products are supposed to be identical to branded originals. How do we build a distinctive brand around commodity products?"

"That's exactly the challenge," Kavitha replied. "Generic pharmaceutical companies need to establish brand recognition without claiming therapeutic differentiation. Your brand must represent quality, reliability, and trust rather than unique medical benefits."

This was my introduction to what I'd later understand as the fundamental paradox of branding in the generic pharmaceutical industry: you need brand recognition to achieve premium pricing and customer loyalty, but you can't claim the product advantages that typically drive brand preference.

"What are we actually trying to accomplish with brand building?" Priya asked, reviewing the agency's strategic recommendations.

"Customer preference over competing generic products, premium pricing versus unbranded generics, and distributor loyalty that reduces price competition," I replied, reading from the proposal.

"And how do we achieve customer preference for products that are supposed to be therapeutically identical to competitors' products?"

"Good question. Kavitha, how do successful generic pharmaceutical companies build meaningful brand differentiation?"

Kavitha showed us case studies from Dr. Reddy's, Cipla, and Lupin, each of which had developed distinctive brand positioning despite manufacturing primarily generic products.

"Dr. Reddy's positions itself as a global innovation leader. Cipla emphasizes accessibility and affordability. Lupin focuses on specialty formulations and quality excellence. Each company has found ways to create brand meaning beyond just manufacturing generic drugs."

"What would be authentic brand positioning for our company?" I asked.

"Based on our research into your business history and capabilities, we recommend positioning Malhotra Pharmaceuticals as 'The Systematic Excellence Company'—a manufacturer that combines small-company responsiveness with international-quality standards."

The proposed brand positioning sounded reasonable, but I wasn't convinced it would create meaningful differentiation in a market where every generic manufacturer claimed superior quality and customer service.

"Let's step back," I said, interrupting Kavitha's explanation of brand messaging architecture. "Before we decide what our brand should represent, maybe we should understand what customers actually value when choosing between generic suppliers."

This research project took three months and involved surveys with 47 doctors, interviews with 23 distributors, and focus groups with 15 hospital procurement managers. The findings were illuminating and somewhat depressing.

"Price is the primary decision factor for 78% of generic drug purchases," reported Dr. Suresh, the market research consultant we'd hired to conduct the customer preference study. "Quality is important, but most customers assume all WHO-GMP certified manufacturers provide adequate quality."

"So quality certification is a threshold requirement rather than a differentiator?" Priya asked.

"Correct. Customers expect WHO-GMP certification, but they don't pay premium prices for it. Quality becomes a differentiator only when problems occur—customers remember suppliers who have quality failures more than suppliers who have consistent quality."

"What factors do influence supplier preference beyond price?"

"Reliability of supply, flexibility in order quantities, responsiveness to special requests, and personal relationships with sales representatives."

This research revealed something important about generic pharmaceutical branding: customer preferences were driven more by service experiences than by product attributes or marketing messages.

"Maybe our brand building should focus on service excellence rather than product excellence," I suggested during our post-research planning session.

"What would service excellence branding look like?" Kavitha asked.

"Instead of claiming superior products, we'd demonstrate superior customer relationships. Instead of advertising quality standards, we'd showcase delivery reliability and order flexibility."

"How do you measure and communicate service excellence?"

"Customer testimonials, delivery performance data, response time metrics, customization examples—evidence of service performance rather than claims about product quality."

The service-focused branding approach required changing how we thought about marketing investments. Instead of spending money on traditional pharmaceutical advertising, we invested in customer relationship management systems, order tracking capabilities, and technical support resources.

"This doesn't look like typical pharmaceutical marketing," observed Ramesh, our business development manager, reviewing our revised marketing budget.

"Because typical pharmaceutical marketing focuses on doctors and patients, while generic pharmaceutical marketing should focus on distributors and procurement managers," I replied.

"What's the difference?"

"Doctors care about therapeutic efficacy and patient outcomes. Distributors care about inventory management and profit margins. Our marketing messages should address distributor concerns rather than medical concerns."

The service excellence branding strategy began with improving our customer communication systems. Instead of just processing orders, we started providing delivery confirmations, shipment tracking, and proactive notifications about potential delays.

"Customer service isn't just about solving problems," explained Meera, our new customer relationship manager. "It's about preventing problems and keeping customers informed when problems are unavoidable."

"How do we measure service excellence?" I asked.

"Order fulfillment rates, delivery timing accuracy, complaint resolution speed, and customer satisfaction surveys. The metrics should be specific and measurable rather than subjective."

Six months after implementing our service excellence branding, we had quantifiable evidence of improved customer relationships: 98% on-time delivery rate, 24-hour average response time to customer inquiries, and 95% customer satisfaction rating based on quarterly surveys.

"The service metrics are impressive," said Mr. Agarwal, our largest distributor, during a quarterly business review. "But what I value most is predictability. When I place an order with your company, I know exactly what to expect and when to expect it."

"How does predictability affect your business?" I asked.

"Predictable suppliers let me manage inventory more efficiently and serve my customers more reliably. Unpredictable suppliers force me to carry safety stock that ties up working capital."

This conversation revealed something important about generic pharmaceutical branding: customer loyalty was driven more by operational reliability than by marketing communication.

"You know what we learned about brand building in generic pharmaceuticals?" I told Kavitha during our final brand strategy review. "Effective branding requires delivering superior customer experiences rather than just communicating superior brand messages."

"How do superior customer experiences become brand advantages?"

"When customers associate your company name with predictable service excellence, they prefer working with you even when competitors offer lower prices. That preference is brand equity based on performance rather than perception."

"And performance-based brand equity is more sustainable than communication-based brand equity because it's harder for competitors to replicate."

Two years after implementing our service excellence branding strategy, we were charging prices 8-12% higher than competing generic manufacturers and maintaining customer loyalty despite competitive pressure.

"The brand building paradox taught us something important about marketing in commodity businesses," Priya observed, reviewing our improved pricing power. "You can't differentiate commodity products, but you can differentiate the experience of buying and using those products."

"And differentiated experiences create customer preferences that enable premium pricing even for commodity products."

The lesson proved crucial as we expanded into more competitive therapeutic areas where product differentiation was minimal but service differentiation could create sustainable competitive advantages.

More importantly, it taught us that authentic brand building required systematic operational excellence rather than just creative marketing communication.

Hiring Kavita Desai, Former Unilever Marketing Director

The salary negotiation with Kavita Desai lasted three weeks and forced me to question everything I thought I knew about hiring marketing talent.

"Your offer is competitive for pharmaceutical industry standards," Kavita said during our final discussion, "but it's 40% below what I earned at Unilever. I need to understand whether this opportunity provides non-monetary compensation that justifies the financial adjustment."

I'd been expecting this conversation ever since Kavita expressed interest in our marketing director position. She had fifteen years of experience at Unilever, had launched consumer brands across Southeast Asia, and understood marketing strategy at a level that none of our current team possessed. She was also accustomed to budgets and resources that our company couldn't match.

"What kind of non-monetary compensation would make this opportunity attractive?" I asked.

"Equity participation, leadership autonomy, and the chance to build marketing capabilities from scratch rather than managing established systems."

"Can you be more specific about equity participation?"

"Two percent equity vesting over four years, plus performance bonuses tied to revenue growth that marketing initiatives directly influence."

This was significantly more equity than we'd ever offered to a single hire, but Kavita's background suggested she could transform our approach to customer relationships and brand development in ways that would justify the investment.

"Why are you interested in leaving Unilever for a pharmaceutical company one-tenth the size?" I asked.

"Because Unilever marketing roles involve optimizing established brand strategies rather than creating new ones. I want to build marketing capabilities that have measurable business impact."

"What do you mean by measurable business impact?"

"At Unilever, successful marketing campaigns increase brand awareness and customer preference, but the connection between marketing activities and business results is often indirect. In a company your size, marketing decisions directly influence revenue, profitability, and competitive positioning."

This conversation revealed something important about hiring senior talent from larger companies: the most capable people were often attracted to smaller companies not despite their resource limitations, but because of the strategic influence those limitations made possible.

"What marketing capabilities do you think our company needs most urgently?" I asked.

"Customer segmentation strategy, value proposition development, and systematic brand building that differentiates you from generic commodity suppliers."

"We've been successful without sophisticated marketing. Our growth has come from product quality and customer service."

"Which works until competitors match your quality and service levels," Kavita replied. "Sustainable competitive advantages require systematic marketing that creates customer preference beyond just functional performance."

"Can you give examples of marketing strategies that would work for generic pharmaceutical companies?"

"Relationship marketing that emphasizes reliability and partnership. Educational marketing that helps customers optimize their operations. Service marketing that demonstrates superior customer experience. Brand marketing that associates your company name with specific value propositions."

Kavita's approach to pharmaceutical marketing was more sophisticated than anything we'd considered. Instead of traditional product advertising, she envisioned marketing systems that would strengthen customer relationships and create barriers to competitive displacement.

"What resources would you need to implement these marketing strategies?" I asked.

"A marketing budget of ₹25 lakhs annually, a marketing coordinator who can manage execution details, and access to customer data that enables segmentation analysis."

"Our current marketing budget is ₹8 lakhs annually."

"Then we'll start with ₹15 lakhs and demonstrate results that justify budget increases."

The equity negotiation required board approval, since 2% equity for a marketing hire was unprecedented in our company's history. But Kavita's track record and strategic perspective convinced the board that investing in systematic marketing capabilities could accelerate our growth trajectory.

"What convinced you to accept our offer?" I asked after Kavita agreed to join us.

"The opportunity to prove that sophisticated marketing strategies can create sustainable competitive advantages in commodity businesses. Most marketing professionals work with differentiated products. I want to test whether superior marketing can differentiate undifferentiated products."

Kavita's first month involved comprehensive analysis of our customer base, competitive landscape, and current marketing approach. Her findings were illuminating and somewhat embarrassing.

"You have excellent customer relationships but no systematic understanding of why customers choose your products over alternatives," she reported during her initial assessment presentation.

"What do you mean by systematic understanding?"

"You know that customers appreciate your service quality, but you don't know which specific service attributes drive loyalty, which customer segments value different benefits, or how competitors position themselves relative to your strengths."

"Does that matter if our customer relationships are strong?"

"Strong relationships can deteriorate quickly when competitors offer better value propositions. Systematic marketing creates deeper customer loyalty that's harder for competitors to disrupt."

Kavita's first project involved segmenting our customer base according to purchasing behavior, service preferences, and competitive vulnerabilities. The analysis revealed patterns that surprised our entire sales team.

"Large hospital customers care most about delivery reliability and technical support," she explained, presenting her segmentation findings. "Small distributors care most about inventory management and payment flexibility.

Export customers care most about regulatory compliance and documentation quality."

"How does customer segmentation affect our marketing strategy?" asked Ramesh, our business development manager.

"Instead of using the same sales approach for all customers, we can customize our value propositions for different customer segments. Large hospitals get reliability messaging, small distributors get flexibility messaging, export customers get compliance messaging."

"Does customized messaging require different marketing materials?"

"Different messaging frameworks, but often the same underlying content organized differently. It's more about emphasis than completely different information."

The segmented marketing approach produced measurable results within six months. Customer satisfaction scores increased 15% across all segments, and our customer retention rate improved from 87% to 94%.

"The segmentation strategy works because customers feel understood rather than just serviced," Kavita observed, reviewing our improved customer metrics.

"What's the difference between feeling understood and feeling serviced?"

"When customers feel serviced, they appreciate what you do for them. When customers feel understood, they believe you know what they need before they ask for it."

Kavita's second major project involved developing systematic brand positioning that differentiated us from commodity generic suppliers without making therapeutic claims that would violate regulatory requirements.

"Generic pharmaceutical companies can't differentiate their products, but they can differentiate their customer experience," she explained during a brand strategy presentation. "Superior customer experience becomes a competitive advantage that's harder to replicate than superior pricing."

"How do we communicate superior customer experience without just making claims about service quality?"

"Customer testimonials, performance metrics, case studies, and service innovations that demonstrate rather than assert our advantages."

Eighteen months after hiring Kavita, our revenue per customer had increased 22% and our average order size had grown 18%. More importantly, our customer acquisition costs had decreased because existing customers were referring new prospects more frequently.

"You know what hiring Kavita taught us about talent acquisition?" I told our board during an annual review. "The best hires aren't necessarily people who want the jobs you're offering—they're people who want to achieve something specific that your company makes possible."

"What did Kavita want to achieve?"

"Proof that sophisticated marketing could create competitive advantages in commodity businesses. We provided the opportunity to test that hypothesis."

"And now that she's proven the hypothesis?"

"Now she's building marketing capabilities that our competitors will find difficult to replicate, which creates sustainable advantages for our business growth."

The investment in Kavita's expertise had cost us ₹35 lakhs in salary and equity over two years, but had generated additional revenue of over ₹2 crores through improved customer relationships and higher pricing power.

More importantly, it had taught us that investing in world-class capabilities often requires accepting higher compensation costs in exchange for business results that justify those investments.

Creating Brand Identity for Generic Products

The brand identity workshop felt like trying to solve a puzzle where half the pieces were missing and the other half looked identical.

"Generic pharmaceutical products present unique branding challenges," Kavita explained to our assembled team, standing in front of a whiteboard covered with competitor logos that all seemed to feature variations of the same blue cross, green leaf, or medical symbol. "You can't claim therapeutic superiority because your products are required to be bioequivalent to branded originals."

"So what can we claim?" asked Ramesh, our business development manager.

"Experience, reliability, service quality, innovation in delivery or formulation, and emotional connection with customer values."

I looked around the conference room at our production manager, quality director, regulatory affairs head, and marketing coordinator. None of us had experience creating brand identity for products that were deliberately designed to be indistinguishable from competitors' products.

"Maybe we should start with what our customers actually value about working with us," suggested Priya. "Instead of trying to invent brand positioning, let's discover what brand we already represent in customers' minds."

This approach led to three weeks of customer interviews that revealed surprising insights about how our company was already perceived in the market.

"Your company feels more responsive than larger pharmaceutical manufacturers," said Dr. Krishnan, a distributor in Chennai. "When I have problems or special requests, I can call and speak with decision-makers directly rather than navigating through customer service departments."

"What value does responsiveness provide for your business?" Kavita asked during the interview.

"Speed and flexibility. If I need emergency inventory or custom packaging for specific customers, you can accommodate requests that larger companies would decline or take weeks to evaluate."

"Your quality consistency is excellent, but what I appreciate most is predictability," said Mr. Sharma, a hospital procurement manager. "Your delivery schedules are reliable, your product specifications never vary, and your pricing doesn't fluctuate based on market conditions."

"How does predictability affect your operations?" I asked.

"Predictable suppliers let me manage inventory more efficiently and budget more accurately. Unpredictable suppliers create operational headaches that affect patient care."

After fifteen customer interviews, patterns emerged that surprised our entire team. Customers weren't choosing us primarily because of product quality—they assumed all WHO-GMP certified manufacturers provided adequate quality. They were choosing us because of operational characteristics that made their businesses run more smoothly.

"Our brand identity is already established," Kavita concluded after analyzing the interview data. "Customers associate Malhotra Pharmaceuticals with 'Dependable Partnership' rather than just product supply."

"What does Dependable Partnership mean practically?" I asked.

"Responsive communication, reliable delivery, consistent quality, flexible service, and long-term relationship focus rather than transactional interactions."

This insight shifted our brand development strategy from trying to create new brand positioning to systematically strengthening the brand identity that customers already recognized.

"Instead of inventing brand attributes, we should amplify the attributes customers already value," Kavita suggested. "Make our responsiveness even more responsive, our reliability even more reliable, our flexibility even more flexible."

The brand amplification approach began with documenting specific service capabilities that differentiated us from larger competitors. We created case studies showcasing emergency deliveries, customized packaging solutions, and special formulation modifications that demonstrated our partnership approach.

"These aren't marketing claims—they're documented examples of superior customer experience," Kavita explained as we developed our brand communication materials.

"What's the difference?" asked Meera, our customer relationship manager.

"Marketing claims tell customers what you want them to believe. Documented examples show customers what you actually deliver."

The visual identity development process was more challenging than the positioning strategy. How do you create distinctive visual branding for products that must look pharmaceutical and professional but not make medical claims?

"Our packaging needs to communicate partnership and reliability without suggesting therapeutic advantages," Kavita said, reviewing initial design concepts from our graphic designer.

"Maybe the differentiation comes from information design rather than visual design," suggested Dr. Patel. "Instead of distinctive colors or graphics, we could provide more useful product information than competitors provide."

This insight led to packaging innovation that enhanced customer experience without violating regulatory requirements. Our product labels included batch-specific stability data, storage optimization recommendations, and QR codes linking to technical support resources.

"Enhanced product information demonstrates expertise and service commitment," Kavita observed. "Customers appreciate suppliers who help them use products more effectively."

The brand identity implementation required training our entire customer-facing team to understand and communicate our Dependable Partnership positioning consistently.

"Everyone who interacts with customers represents our brand," Kavita explained during training sessions. "Brand identity isn't just marketing communications—it's every customer touchpoint from order processing to technical support."

"How do we ensure consistent brand experience across all customer interactions?" asked our sales coordinator.

"Standard operating procedures for customer communication, response time commitments, and service level agreements that guarantee the partnership experience we're promising."

Six months after implementing our Dependable Partnership brand identity, customer feedback indicated significant improvement in brand perception.

"Working with your company feels different from working with other generic suppliers," said Ms. Reddy, a large distributor in Bangalore. "Other suppliers provide products and basic service. You provide solutions and genuine partnership."

"What makes the partnership feel genuine?" Kavita asked during a follow-up interview.

"Proactive communication about potential issues, suggestions for optimizing our inventory management, and willingness to accommodate special requests that help us serve our customers better."

The brand identity program also affected our internal culture in unexpected ways. Employees started taking more ownership of customer relationships because they understood how their individual performance contributed to overall brand experience.

"The Dependable Partnership positioning changed how we think about our jobs," observed Kumar, one of our production supervisors. "Instead of just manufacturing tablets according to specifications, we're creating products that enable customer success."

"How does that change your daily work?" I asked.

"We pay more attention to details that affect customer operations, like packaging integrity, labeling accuracy, and delivery preparation. We're not just making products—we're delivering reliability."

Eighteen months after launching our Dependable Partnership brand identity, we were achieving 12% higher average selling prices than competing generic manufacturers and maintaining 96% customer retention rates.

"You know what creating brand identity for generic products taught us?" I said to Kavita during our annual marketing review. "Successful branding in commodity businesses requires authentic differentiation in customer experience rather than artificial differentiation in product positioning."

"And authentic differentiation must be based on operational capabilities that customers actually value rather than marketing messages that sound appealing."

"The brand identity becomes sustainable when it's supported by systematic operational excellence rather than just creative communication."

The Dependable Partnership brand had become more than marketing positioning—it had become our operational philosophy that guided decision-making across all aspects of our business.

More importantly, it had taught us that effective brand building in generic pharmaceuticals required discovering and amplifying existing strengths rather than inventing new brand attributes that couldn't be supported by actual capabilities.

The 'HeartCare' Campaign Success Story

The campaign name came from an argument about what to call our cardiovascular product portfolio.

"We can't just call them 'Malhotra Cardiovascular Products,'" Kavita said, reviewing our initial marketing materials. "That's a product category description, not a brand name that creates emotional connection."

"What about 'CardioMax' or 'HeartShield'?" suggested Ramesh. "Something that sounds strong and protective."

"Those names sound like branded pharmaceuticals trying to suggest therapeutic superiority," replied Dr. Patel. "Generic drug marketing can't imply enhanced medical benefits."

We'd been debating cardiovascular portfolio branding for two weeks, trying to find a name that would create market recognition without violating regulatory restrictions on generic drug promotion.

"What if we focused on care rather than performance?" I suggested. "Something like 'HeartCare' that emphasizes our commitment to cardiovascular patients rather than claiming superior therapeutic effects."

"HeartCare," Kavita repeated, testing how the name sounded. "It's simple, memorable, and suggests dedication without making medical claims."

"Can we use 'HeartCare' legally for generic cardiovascular products?" I asked Dr. Patel.

"As long as the marketing materials focus on company commitment and service quality rather than drug efficacy, it should be acceptable to regulatory authorities."

The HeartCare campaign began as a modest experiment in therapeutic area branding. Instead of promoting individual cardiovascular products, we would promote our comprehensive approach to serving cardiovascular patients and healthcare providers.

"HeartCare isn't about our drugs being different," Kavita explained to our sales team during the campaign launch meeting. "It's about our service being different. We provide cardiovascular products with the reliability and support that cardiac patients deserve."

"What makes our cardiovascular service different from competitors?" asked our lead sales representative.

"Comprehensive product portfolio, bioequivalence documentation, technical support for prescribing physicians, and supply chain reliability that ensures continuous availability."

The campaign's first component involved developing educational materials for cardiologists that demonstrated our understanding of cardiovascular treatment challenges beyond just drug manufacturing.

"Most generic manufacturers provide product information," Kavita said, showing our new physician education brochures. "We're providing treatment support information that helps doctors optimize cardiovascular therapy for their patients."

"What kind of treatment support information?" asked Dr. Sharma, our cardiovascular formulation specialist.

"Drug interaction guides, dosing optimization recommendations, patient compliance improvement strategies, and therapeutic monitoring protocols."

"How is this different from pharmaceutical marketing that brands typically provide?"

"Branded pharmaceutical marketing focuses on promoting specific drugs. Our educational materials focus on optimizing treatment outcomes regardless of which specific products doctors prescribe."

The physician education component succeeded beyond our expectations. Within three months, cardiologists were requesting our educational materials and using them in patient consultations.

"Your HeartCare materials are more practical than most branded pharmaceutical resources," said Dr. Raghunath, a cardiologist at AIIMS. "They focus on clinical management rather than just drug promotion."

"How do the materials help your practice?" Kavita asked during a follow-up interview.

"They provide comprehensive cardiovascular treatment guidance that I can share with patients. Most pharmaceutical materials are product-specific, but your materials address the full spectrum of cardiovascular care."

The campaign's second component involved developing patient education resources that hospitals could provide to cardiovascular patients taking any generic medications, not just our products.

"Patient education about cardiovascular medications improves compliance and treatment outcomes," explained Dr. Sharma. "When patients understand their therapy better, they're more likely to take medications correctly and achieve therapeutic goals."

"But we're providing education that benefits all generic cardiovascular manufacturers, not just our company," Ramesh observed.

"That's exactly why it works," Kavita replied. "When we help the entire cardiovascular treatment process, healthcare providers associate our company with improved patient outcomes rather than just product sales."

The patient education materials included medication compliance tracking cards, dietary guidance for cardiovascular health, and warning signs information that patients could use regardless of which specific drugs they were taking.

"This approach to marketing feels more professional than typical pharmaceutical promotion," said Ms. Lakshmi, a hospital pharmacist. "You're contributing to cardiovascular care rather than just competing for prescription market share."

The campaign's third component involved supply chain innovations that demonstrated our commitment to cardiovascular patients' treatment continuity.

"Cardiovascular medications require consistent availability because treatment interruptions can have serious medical consequences," I explained during a hospital administrator meeting. "Our HeartCare program guarantees 30-day inventory buffers for all cardiovascular products."

"What does that mean practically?" asked the hospital's chief pharmacist.

"If you're running low on any cardiovascular medication, we'll provide emergency supply within 24 hours to prevent treatment interruptions for your patients."

"Even if the medication isn't manufactured by your company?"

"Even if it's manufactured by competitors. Cardiovascular patient care is more important than competitive considerations."

This commitment to treatment continuity, regardless of manufacturer, created unexpected competitive advantages. Hospitals started viewing us as cardiovascular care partners rather than just drug suppliers.

"The HeartCare emergency supply guarantee influenced our supplier decisions," admitted Dr. Kumar, director of pharmacy at a major cardiac hospital. "When we know a supplier prioritizes patient care over commercial interests, we prefer working with them for all our cardiovascular product needs."

Six months after launching the HeartCare campaign, our cardiovascular revenue had increased 43% and our market share in hospital cardiovascular procurement had grown from 8% to 18%.

"The campaign success surprised everyone, including me," Kavita said, reviewing our performance metrics. "Educational marketing and service innovations generated better business results than traditional product promotion."

"Why was educational marketing more effective than product marketing?" I asked.

"Because healthcare providers trust companies that demonstrate clinical expertise more than companies that just claim product advantages."

"And clinical expertise differentiated us in ways that product features couldn't?"

"Exactly. Any generic manufacturer can claim quality and reliability. But clinical expertise requires demonstrated understanding of cardiovascular treatment that takes time and investment to develop."

The HeartCare campaign also changed how we thought about product development. Instead of just developing cardiovascular formulations, we started developing comprehensive cardiovascular solutions that addressed treatment challenges beyond drug manufacturing.

"HeartCare evolved from marketing campaign to business strategy," I observed during our annual planning session. "It changed what kind of company we are, not just how we promote our products."

"And that transformation created competitive advantages that pure marketing campaigns couldn't achieve," Priya added.

Eighteen months after launching HeartCare, competitors had attempted to copy our educational materials and supply chain guarantees, but they couldn't replicate the clinical relationships and treatment expertise we'd developed through systematic investment in cardiovascular care understanding.

"You know what the HeartCare campaign taught us about marketing?" I said to Kavita during our campaign evaluation meeting. "Successful marketing in healthcare requires genuine expertise rather than just creative messaging."

"And genuine expertise creates sustainable competitive advantages because it can't be copied through marketing tactics alone."

The HeartCare campaign had become our template for therapeutic area marketing—combining clinical education, patient support, and supply chain innovation to create comprehensive solutions that differentiated us from commodity generic suppliers.

More importantly, it had taught us that effective pharmaceutical marketing required contributing to treatment outcomes rather than just competing for market share.

Learning to Think Beyond Price Competition

The price war started over five paise per tablet.

"Aurobindo is offering paracetamol at ₹1.15 per tablet," our sales representative Sunil informed me during his weekly market update. "Our current price is ₹1.20. We're losing orders because customers can save ₹500 per 10,000 tablet order."

"So we should match their pricing?" I asked.

"That's what our distributors are asking for. They're saying good relationships don't justify paying premium prices for identical products."

This conversation was becoming depressingly familiar. Every month, we'd hear about competitors offering lower prices for products that were supposed to be therapeutically equivalent to ours. Every month, we'd face pressure to reduce our prices to maintain market share.

"We're trapped in a pricing spiral," I told Kavita during our weekly marketing review. "If we match competitor prices, our margins disappear. If we don't match them, our volumes disappear."

"Maybe the problem isn't competitor pricing," she replied. "Maybe the problem is that we're competing in a market where price is the only differentiation customers recognize."

"But generic pharmaceuticals are commodities. By definition, our products are supposed to be identical to competitors' products."

"Products might be identical, but companies aren't identical. Customer experiences aren't identical. Value propositions aren't identical."

This conversation forced me to question assumptions I'd held since starting our company. I'd always believed that generic drug manufacturing was inherently a price-driven business where the lowest-cost producer would eventually dominate. But our experience with the HeartCare campaign suggested that healthcare customers valued more than just low prices.

"What would competing beyond price look like practically?" I asked.

"It would mean creating customer value that competitors can't easily replicate, then communicating that value so customers understand why paying slightly higher prices actually benefits their business."

"Such as?"

"Supply chain reliability, technical support, regulatory compliance assistance, inventory management optimization, custom packaging solutions—services that reduce customers' total cost of doing business even if our product prices are higher."

The idea was appealing but challenging to implement. How do you convince price-sensitive customers to pay premiums for services they might not initially recognize as valuable?

"Let's test the concept with our most price-sensitive customers," Kavita suggested. "If we can create non-price value for customers who only care about price, we'll prove the approach works universally."

The test began with Mr. Agarwal, a distributor in Pune who had recently threatened to switch to lower-cost suppliers if we didn't match competitor pricing.

"I understand you're evaluating alternative suppliers based on pricing," I said during a visit to his facility. "Before you make changes, can we analyze whether lower prices actually reduce your total costs?"

"What do you mean by total costs?" he asked.

"Product price is only one component of your total cost. There's also inventory carrying costs, stockout costs when suppliers can't deliver on time, quality problem costs when you have to replace defective products, and administrative costs for managing supplier relationships."

"I never calculated those costs separately."

"Would you be willing to review six months of actual cost data to see how different suppliers affect your total business costs?"

The cost analysis revealed patterns that surprised both of us. While our product prices were 8% higher than his lowest-cost supplier, our delivery reliability and quality consistency had saved him approximately ₹45,000 over six months in reduced inventory requirements and eliminated stockout incidents.

"Your higher prices are more than offset by lower operational costs," I explained, showing him the detailed analysis. "You're actually saving money by working with us despite paying higher product prices."

"I never looked at supplier relationships this way," Mr. Agarwal admitted. "I focused on price per tablet without considering the impact on my overall business efficiency."

"Which approach would you prefer—lowest product prices with higher operational costs, or slightly higher product prices with lower total costs?"

"Lower total costs, obviously. But how do I know your operational advantages will continue?"

"We can formalize them through service level agreements that guarantee delivery performance, quality standards, and response times. If we don't meet guaranteed service levels, you get automatic price reductions."

The service level agreement approach worked so well with Mr. Agarwal that we implemented it across our entire customer base. Instead of competing solely on price, we started competing on total value propositions that included guaranteed service performance.

"This changes how we think about pricing strategy," Priya observed after six months of total cost selling. "Instead of reducing prices to match competitors, we're quantifying value that justifies price premiums."

"And customers appreciate the analytical approach because it helps them optimize their own operations."

The beyond-price competition strategy required developing new capabilities throughout our organization. Our sales team needed training in cost analysis and value quantification. Our operations team needed systems for tracking and guaranteeing service performance. Our customer service team needed protocols for resolving issues that could affect total cost calculations.

"Competing beyond price is more complex than competing on price," observed Ramesh, our business development manager. "Price competition just requires being cheaper. Value competition requires being systematically better across multiple dimensions."

"But value competition also creates more sustainable competitive advantages," Kavita replied. "Competitors can match your prices immediately, but they can't match your operational capabilities without significant investment and time."

The transition from price competition to value competition wasn't immediately successful with all customers. Some distributors continued prioritizing product price over total cost analysis, especially when their own customers focused primarily on price.

"About 30% of the market will always choose the lowest price regardless of total cost considerations," I admitted during a strategy review meeting. "But 70% of customers appreciate value propositions that optimize their business operations."

"So we're deliberately choosing not to compete for 30% of the market?" asked our CFO.

"We're choosing to focus on 70% of the market where we can create sustainable competitive advantages rather than fighting for 30% of the market where we can only compete through margin destruction."

Eighteen months after shifting to value-based competition, our average selling prices were 12% higher than industry averages, but our customer retention rate had improved to 94% and our profit margins had increased despite higher sales and service costs.

"You know what learning to think beyond price competition taught us?" I said to our management team during an annual planning session. "Price competition forces you to reduce costs and margins. Value competition forces you to improve capabilities and customer relationships."

"And improved capabilities create competitive advantages that enable premium pricing rather than commodity pricing."

"The key insight was that customers don't actually want lower prices—they want lower total costs. When you help customers reduce their total costs, they're willing to pay higher prices for your products."

The beyond-price competition strategy had become our standard approach for all therapeutic areas and customer segments. Instead of trying to be the cheapest supplier, we focused on being the most valuable supplier by optimizing customers' total business costs.

More importantly, it had taught us that sustainable competitive advantages in commodity businesses come from systematic operational excellence rather than just cost leadership.

Chapter 8

The Technology Upgrade

When Manual Systems Hit their Limits

The inventory discrepancy report showed that we were simultaneously overstocked and understocked, which seemed mathematically impossible until I understood what was actually happening.

"We have 120,000 atenolol tablets in physical inventory," explained Suresh, our warehouse manager, pointing to the hand-counted numbers on his clipboard. "But our manual records show 89,000 tablets, and our customers are complaining about stockouts."

"How can we have more inventory than our records show but still be unable to fulfill customer orders?" I asked.

"Because 45,000 tablets are from a batch that's approaching expiration, 28,000 tablets are in the wrong packaging size for current orders, and 47,000 tablets are committed to export shipments that haven't left our facility yet."

This conversation took place in October 2004, and it perfectly illustrated the chaos that our manual inventory management system had created. As our business had grown from millions of tablets to tens of millions of tablets annually, our paper-based tracking systems had become inadequate for managing the complexity of multiple products, batch expiration dates, customer allocations, and packaging configurations.

"We need to implement computer-based inventory management," I told Priya after reviewing Suresh's analysis. "Manual systems worked when we had five products and ten customers. They don't work with fifteen products and fifty customers."

"How much would computerized inventory management cost?" she asked.

"I have no idea. But I know continuing with manual systems will eventually cost us more in inventory errors, customer service problems, and operational inefficiency."

The technology upgrade decision forced us to confront something we'd been avoiding: our entire business operations were still organized like a small company despite generating revenues that required large-company systems.

"Our manual processes are constraining our growth," I realized during a management team meeting. "We're spending more time managing information than we're spending managing business operations."

"What specific problems are manual systems creating?" asked Dr. Patel.

"Inventory discrepancies, production scheduling errors, customer service delays, quality documentation inefficiencies, and financial reporting that takes weeks instead of days."

"So the technology upgrade isn't just about inventory management—it's about operational efficiency across all business functions?"

"Exactly. We need integrated systems that manage inventory, production, quality control, customer relationships, and financial reporting through connected databases rather than separate manual records."

The search for appropriate business software led us into a world of enterprise resource planning (ERP) systems, customer relationship management (CRM) platforms, and manufacturing execution systems (MES) that seemed designed for companies much larger than ours.

"Most pharmaceutical ERP systems are built for companies generating ₹500 crores or more in annual revenue," explained Rajesh Kumar, a software consultant who specialized in pharmaceutical business systems. "Your revenue scale of ₹120 crores puts you in an awkward middle ground."

"What's awkward about our scale?" I asked.

"Too large for simple accounting software, too small for enterprise pharmaceutical systems. You need customized solutions that provide enterprise functionality at mid-market pricing."

"What would customized solutions cost?"

"Probably ₹25-35 lakhs for software licensing, customization, and implementation. Plus ongoing support costs of ₹3-4 lakhs annually."

This represented nearly 30% of our annual profit, but the alternative—continuing with manual systems that were becoming increasingly unreliable—seemed even more expensive in terms of operational problems and missed growth opportunities.

"Let's start with the most critical system upgrade and implement additional modules as we prove the value," Priya suggested. "What business process causes the most problems currently?"

"Inventory management," I replied without hesitation. "Inventory errors affect customer service, production planning, and financial reporting. Solving inventory management would eliminate dozens of daily operational problems."

The inventory management system implementation took four months and required entering historical data for every product batch in our facility. The process revealed gaps in our manual record-keeping that were more extensive than we'd realized.

"We have batches of ibuprofen tablets that aren't recorded anywhere," discovered Meera, our data entry coordinator, during the initial system setup. "And we have records for atenolol batches that don't exist in physical inventory."

"How is that possible?" I asked.

"Manual record-keeping errors that accumulated over time. Someone recorded production that wasn't actually completed, or recorded shipments that weren't actually sent, or forgot to record consumption for internal quality testing."

The data cleanup process required three weeks and forced us to write off ₹2.8 lakhs in inventory discrepancies that couldn't be resolved through physical investigation.

"The inventory write-offs are painful," I told our board of directors, "but they represent historical errors that were affecting our operations anyway. The computerized system will prevent similar problems in the future."

"How can you guarantee that computer systems will be more accurate than manual systems?" asked one of our board members.

"Computer systems enforce data integrity that manual systems can't provide. Every transaction requires complete information, every change leaves an audit trail, and system reports automatically identify discrepancies that would be invisible in manual records."

The computerized inventory management system produced immediate benefits that exceeded our expectations. Real-time inventory visibility allowed more accurate customer service, automated reorder calculations prevented stockouts, and batch tracking capabilities improved our quality control documentation.

"The system pays for itself through improved inventory turnover," observed our CFO after six months of operation. "We're carrying 15% less inventory while providing better customer service."

"How is that possible?" I asked.

"Better visibility into actual inventory levels eliminates safety stock that we were carrying to compensate for manual tracking uncertainty. When you know exactly what inventory you have, you can operate closer to optimal inventory levels."

The success of inventory management computerization led to rapid implementation of additional system modules. Production planning software eliminated scheduling conflicts and optimized equipment utilization. Quality management software automated batch documentation and compliance reporting. Customer relationship management software tracked order history and service issues.

"The integrated systems are transforming how we operate," Priya observed after eighteen months of technology implementation. "Instead of managing information, we're using information to manage business operations."

"What's the difference?" asked Ramesh.

"Managing information means collecting, organizing, and reporting data manually. Using information means analyzing data automatically to optimize decision-making and operational performance."

The technology upgrade also changed our competitive capabilities in unexpected ways. Automated reporting allowed us to provide customers with delivery tracking, inventory forecasting, and usage analysis that smaller competitors couldn't match.

"Your order tracking and inventory planning support is more sophisticated than what we get from larger pharmaceutical suppliers," said Mr. Agarwal, our distributor in Pune. "It helps us manage our business more efficiently."

"How does automated reporting help your business?" Kavita asked during a customer interview.

"Real-time inventory visibility lets us optimize ordering patterns, usage forecasting helps us plan cash flow, and delivery tracking eliminates uncertainty about order status."

Two years after completing our technology upgrade, our operational efficiency had improved 25% while our customer service capabilities had expanded significantly. More importantly, computerized systems had created scalability that would support continued growth without proportional increases in administrative overhead.

"You know what the technology upgrade taught us about business development?" I said to our management team during an annual review. "Manual systems that work adequately at small scale become major constraints at larger scale."

"And technology investments that seem expensive initially often pay for themselves through operational improvements that wouldn't be possible with manual systems."

"The key insight was that technology upgrades aren't just about efficiency—they're about creating capabilities that enable growth strategies that manual systems couldn't support."

The computerized business systems had become the foundation for our expansion into more complex products and markets where operational sophistication would be required for competitive success.

Modernizing Manufacturing with Automated Systems

The tablet press breakdown happened at the worst possible time, which is to say it happened exactly when we needed it most.

"The main compression roller is showing metal fatigue," Ravi explained, pointing to hairline cracks in the equipment that had been our primary production workhorse for six years. "We can probably repair it, but this is the third major breakdown in four months."

"How long would repairs take?" I asked, mentally calculating the impact on our production schedule.

"Two weeks minimum, assuming we can get replacement parts from Germany. But honestly, this machine is approaching the end of its useful life."

It was February 2005, and our tablet press—which had seemed sophisticated when we bought it in 1999—was struggling to meet the demands of producing 40 million tablets monthly with the consistency that our international customers required.

"Maybe the breakdown is telling us something we've been avoiding," Priya suggested during our emergency planning meeting. "Our manufacturing equipment hasn't kept pace with our quality requirements or production volumes."

"What would keeping pace look like?" I asked.

"Automated tablet presses with real-time quality monitoring, computerized compression force control, and integrated data logging that eliminates manual batch record keeping."

"How much would automated manufacturing equipment cost?"

"Probably ₹1.5-2 crores for a complete production line upgrade. But manual equipment repairs and lost production time are costing us ₹15-20 lakhs annually."

The manufacturing modernization decision forced us to confront something uncomfortable: we'd been thinking about equipment purchases as expenses rather than investments in production capabilities.

"Our current tablet press was adequate for our requirements five years ago," I told our board during an emergency meeting. "But our requirements have changed faster than our equipment capabilities."

"What requirements have changed specifically?" asked Dr. Sharma, one of our board members.

"Production volumes increased 300%, quality documentation requirements became more complex, international customers demand statistical process control data, and our product portfolio requires more frequent changeovers between different formulations."

"Can't these requirements be met with upgraded versions of existing equipment?"

"The technology gap is too large. Modern pharmaceutical manufacturing requires integrated automation that our current equipment can't provide even with modifications."

The search for automated manufacturing systems introduced us to production technologies that seemed designed for companies much larger than ours. Most pharmaceutical automation suppliers focused on multinational corporations installing complete manufacturing facilities rather than mid-sized companies upgrading individual production lines.

"Your production volumes are substantial but not massive," explained Klaus Weber, a technical specialist from Fette Compacting, during their system evaluation visit. "You need automation capabilities typically found in large facilities but sized appropriately for your current scale."

"What automation capabilities would optimize our production requirements?" Ravi asked.

"Real-time tablet weight monitoring with automatic compression adjustment, integrated hardness testing with statistical trend analysis, automated batch documentation, and predictive maintenance monitoring that prevents unexpected breakdowns."

"How would these capabilities change our manufacturing operations?"

"Reduced manual oversight requirements, improved product consistency, faster changeover times between products, and comprehensive quality data that satisfies international regulatory requirements."

The automated tablet press installation took six weeks and required training our entire production team on computer-controlled manufacturing processes. The learning curve was steeper than anyone had anticipated.

"The automated system requires more technical understanding than manual equipment," observed Kumar, our senior tablet press operator. "Instead of just following mechanical procedures, we need to understand software parameters and statistical quality control."

"Is the additional complexity worth the operational benefits?" I asked.

"Definitely. The automated system produces more consistent tablets with less manual intervention. But it requires different skills than traditional pharmaceutical manufacturing."

The automated production line's first month of operation revealed both the benefits and challenges of modern manufacturing technology. Tablet quality consistency improved dramatically—weight variation decreased from ±3% to ±0.8%, and compression force variability virtually disappeared.

"The quality improvements are remarkable," Dr. Patel observed, reviewing our first month of automated production data. "These statistics would have been impossible to achieve with manual equipment."

"How do improved statistics affect our business practically?" I asked.

"Better quality consistency reduces customer complaints, improves regulatory compliance documentation, and enables premium pricing for products that exceed standard generic specifications."

However, the automated system also created new operational challenges. Equipment changeovers between different products required more time and technical expertise than our manual processes. Software troubleshooting demanded specialized knowledge that our traditional production team was still developing.

"Automation traded operational simplicity for operational consistency," Ravi noted after three months of experience with the new system. "The equipment is more complex to operate, but it produces more predictable results."

"And predictable results enable better production planning and customer service," added our production coordinator.

The integrated quality monitoring capabilities proved particularly valuable for our international customers. Instead of providing manual test results, we could now provide real-time statistical process control data that demonstrated consistent quality throughout entire production runs.

"Your automated quality documentation is more comprehensive than what we receive from larger pharmaceutical suppliers," said our distributor in Kenya during a facility audit. "This level of process control gives us confidence in recommending your products to regulatory authorities."

"How does process control documentation benefit your business?" I asked.

"Regulatory authorities prefer suppliers who can demonstrate statistical process control because it provides evidence of systematic quality management rather than just batch-by-batch testing."

The automated manufacturing investment also improved our production economics in unexpected ways. Higher production speeds increased our effective capacity by 35% without requiring additional floor space or proportional increases in labor costs.

"The automated system produces more tablets per hour with fewer operators," our CFO noted during a quarterly review. "Labor cost per tablet decreased 22% despite higher equipment depreciation."

"So automation improved both quality and efficiency simultaneously?"

"Quality improved through better process control, efficiency improved through higher production speeds and reduced manual oversight requirements."

Eighteen months after installing automated manufacturing systems, our production capabilities had transformed from manual craft operations to computer-controlled industrial processes. Customer satisfaction with product consistency had improved significantly, and our ability to respond to large-volume international orders had increased dramatically.

"You know what modernizing manufacturing taught us about technology investments?" I said to Ravi during our annual equipment planning session. "Automation isn't just about replacing manual operations—it's about enabling production capabilities that manual operations can't achieve."

"Such as?"

"Statistical process control that ensures consistent quality, real-time monitoring that prevents quality problems before they occur, and production speeds that enable larger-scale operations without proportional increases in labor requirements."

"And those capabilities create competitive advantages that companies with manual manufacturing can't match."

The automated manufacturing systems had become essential for serving international markets where customers expected pharmaceutical suppliers to demonstrate systematic quality control through comprehensive process documentation.

More importantly, the modernization had taught us that sustained competitive advantages in manufacturing required continuous investment in production technologies that enabled capabilities beyond what traditional methods could provide.

Partnership with German Equipment Manufacturer

The first meeting with Fette Compacting felt like a job interview where I wasn't sure whether we were applying to be their customer or their business partner.

"Your production requirements are interesting," said Klaus Weber, their technical director, reviewing the specifications we'd submitted for automated tablet press equipment. "But your order size is below our typical minimum for international customers."

We were sitting in a sterile conference room at their Mumbai office, surrounded by glossy brochures featuring pharmaceutical manufacturing equipment that looked more sophisticated than anything I'd seen outside of textbooks.

"What's your typical minimum order size?" I asked.

"Usually ₹5-8 crores for complete production line installations. Your requirement of ₹1.8 crores represents a single tablet press with basic automation."

"Is that too small for Fette to consider?"

"Not too small, but it requires different business arrangements than our standard equipment sales model."

This conversation was my introduction to the complexities of purchasing advanced manufacturing equipment from German suppliers who were accustomed to working with multinational pharmaceutical companies rather than mid-sized Indian manufacturers.

"What different business arrangements would make our order size workable?" I asked.

"Technology transfer partnerships where we provide equipment, training, and ongoing technical support in exchange for longer-term commitments that justify our investment in supporting smaller-scale customers."

"What would longer-term commitments involve?"

"Exclusive purchasing agreements for future equipment expansions, participation in our Asian market development programs, and potentially serving as a reference customer for other Indian pharmaceutical companies."

The partnership approach was more complex than a simple equipment purchase, but it offered advantages that traditional supplier relationships couldn't provide: access to cutting-edge technology, comprehensive training programs, and ongoing technical support that would help us optimize our manufacturing capabilities.

"We're interested in exploring partnership arrangements," I told Klaus. "But we need to understand what obligations that would create for our company."

"Primarily marketing obligations. We'd want to showcase your facility to potential customers in India and Southeast Asia, include your company in case studies for emerging market pharmaceutical manufacturing, and potentially collaborate on equipment customization for mid-scale producers."

"What benefits would we receive in exchange for marketing participation?"

"Preferential pricing on current and future equipment purchases, priority access to new technology developments, comprehensive training programs for your technical staff, and ongoing technical support that most customers don't receive."

The partnership negotiation took four months and required legal reviews of technology transfer agreements, intellectual property protections, and marketing commitment specifications. The complexity was far beyond anything we'd encountered in previous equipment purchases.

"This feels more like a joint venture than an equipment purchase," Priya observed during one of our internal planning meetings.

"Because it is more like a joint venture. Fette wants Indian market access and reference customers. We want German technology and technical support. The equipment purchase is just the foundation for broader collaboration."

"Are we prepared for the obligations that partnership creates?"

"We're prepared to learn. The alternative is buying less sophisticated equipment from suppliers who can't provide the technical support we need for advanced manufacturing."

The partnership agreement we finally signed included the ₹1.8 crore tablet press purchase plus a three-year technology support contract, marketing collaboration commitments, and options for future equipment purchases at preferential pricing.

"What convinced Fette to accept a partnership arrangement with a company our size?" I asked Klaus during the contract signing.

"Growing Indian pharmaceutical market, need for reference customers who understand both German technology and Indian business practices, and your company's track record of successfully implementing complex technical improvements."

The equipment installation process revealed the value of partnering with world-class technology suppliers. Instead of just delivering equipment and basic training, Fette provided six weeks of on-site technical support that transformed our understanding of modern pharmaceutical manufacturing.

"German engineering requires German precision," explained Hans Mueller, the installation supervisor, during our first week of equipment setup. "Every parameter must be calibrated exactly, every procedure must be followed systematically, every operator must understand the technology principles rather than just following mechanical instructions."

"How is this different from other equipment we've operated?" asked Ravi.

"Previous equipment tolerated operational variations because it was mechanically controlled. This equipment optimizes performance through computer control that requires precise calibration and systematic operation."

The training program was more comprehensive than any equipment supplier had previously provided. Our entire production team received 40 hours of classroom instruction followed by 80 hours of supervised operation before being certified to operate the automated tablet press independently.

"The training investment is substantial," I told Klaus during his monitoring visit. "But our operators understand the technology much better than they would with standard equipment training."

"Understanding technology enables optimization rather than just operation," he replied. "When operators understand why parameters matter, they can optimize performance rather than just following procedures."

The partnership's marketing obligations initially felt like administrative burdens, but they provided unexpected benefits for our business development. Fette arranged facility tours for potential customers who became interested in our manufacturing services, and their case study publications increased our visibility in international pharmaceutical markets.

"Your facility has become a showcase for mid-scale pharmaceutical manufacturing in India," Klaus observed during a quarterly review meeting. "Other Indian companies are visiting to evaluate similar technology implementations."

"How does showcase status benefit our business?" I asked.

"Industry recognition as a technology leader, networking opportunities with potential customers and partners, and credibility with international buyers who prefer suppliers using advanced manufacturing systems."

Two years after implementing our partnership with Fette, the benefits extended far beyond the automated tablet press itself. We had preferential access to new equipment technologies, ongoing technical support that optimized our manufacturing efficiency, and industry recognition that enhanced our competitive positioning.

"The German partnership taught us something important about supplier relationships," I told our management team during an annual review. "The most valuable suppliers aren't necessarily those offering the lowest prices—they're those providing the greatest capability enhancement."

"How do we measure capability enhancement versus price advantages?" asked our CFO.

"Capability enhancement creates competitive advantages that enable premium pricing and market access. Price advantages provide temporary cost savings that competitors can eliminate through their own cost reduction efforts."

"So investing in premium supplier relationships creates more sustainable advantages than just optimizing purchasing costs?"

"When premium suppliers provide technology, training, and ongoing support that enables capabilities your competitors can't match."

The Fette partnership had become our template for technology supplier relationships—focusing on long-term capability development rather than short-term cost optimization.

Three years later, when we expanded into biotechnology manufacturing, we applied the same partnership approach with specialized equipment suppliers, seeking relationships that would provide technology access, technical support, and capability development beyond what standard vendor relationships could offer.

"You know what the German equipment partnership really taught us?" Priya said during a strategy planning session. "The most successful technology investments involve not just purchasing equipment, but partnering with suppliers who can help you optimize the capabilities that equipment enables."

The lesson would prove crucial as we encountered increasingly complex manufacturing requirements where equipment performance depended as much on technical expertise as on machinery specifications.

Implementing Statistical Process Control

The quality control meeting lasted three hours and left everyone more confused than when we started.

"Our new automated tablet press generates 47 different measurements every minute," explained Dr. Sharma, our quality control manager, pointing to pages of printouts covering our conference table. "Weight, hardness, thickness, diameter, disintegration time, dissolution rate, plus environmental conditions like temperature and humidity."

"That's a lot of data," I said, studying numbers that seemed to fluctuate constantly despite our tablets meeting all specifications.

"Too much data. Our previous manual testing measured five parameters per batch. Now we're measuring over 2,000 parameters per batch, but we don't know which measurements actually matter for quality."

This was my introduction to the challenge of implementing statistical process control (SPC) in pharmaceutical manufacturing. Our German automation equipment generated comprehensive data that was supposed to improve quality management, but the volume of information was overwhelming our traditional approach to quality control.

"Maybe the problem isn't too much data," suggested Hans Mueller, Fette's technical support engineer, during his monthly visit. "Maybe the problem is analyzing data individually instead of understanding patterns across all measurements."

"What do you mean by understanding patterns?" I asked.

"Statistical process control uses mathematical techniques to identify trends, correlations, and variations that indicate process improvements or potential problems before they affect product quality."

"Can you show us how statistical analysis would work with our production data?"

Hans spent the next two hours demonstrating SPC software that transformed our overwhelming data printouts into control charts, trend analyses, and correlation matrices that revealed relationships we'd never noticed.

"Look at this pattern," he said, pointing to a control chart showing tablet weight variation over time. "Every Tuesday morning, weight variation increases 15% above normal levels, then returns to baseline by afternoon."

"What causes Tuesday morning weight variations?" asked Ravi.

"Probably weekend equipment shutdown affecting compression force calibration. The variation isn't large enough to fail specifications, but it's systematic enough to indicate process optimization opportunities."

This analysis revealed something important about quality management: meeting specifications didn't necessarily mean operating optimally. Statistical process control could identify improvement opportunities that traditional pass/fail testing couldn't detect.

"How would we implement SPC throughout our manufacturing operations?" I asked.

"Start with critical quality parameters for your highest-volume products," Hans replied. "Establish baseline performance statistics, set control limits based on process capability, then monitor for trends that indicate process changes."

The SPC implementation process required training our quality control team on statistical methods that none of us had used in pharmaceutical manufacturing. Control charts, process capability studies, and correlation analysis were foreign concepts that seemed more appropriate for engineering than quality control.

"This feels like learning a new language," admitted Kumar, our senior quality technician, during SPC training sessions. "I understand tablet testing, but I don't understand statistical significance and process capability indices."

"Statistical methods are tools for understanding what tablet testing results actually mean," Hans explained. "Individual test results tell you whether specific tablets meet specifications. Statistical analysis tells you whether your process is stable, improving, or developing problems."

"What's the difference between meeting specifications and having a stable process?" I asked.

"Meeting specifications means your products are acceptable. Having a stable process means your products are predictable and improvable."

The SPC training took six weeks and required our quality team to think differently about their role in manufacturing operations. Instead of just detecting quality problems after they occurred, statistical process control enabled predicting and preventing quality problems before they affected production.

"SPC changes quality control from reactive to proactive," Dr. Sharma observed after completing training. "Instead of testing whether products meet specifications, we're monitoring whether processes are optimized for consistent quality."

The first SPC implementation focused on our atenolol sustained-release tablets, which represented our highest-volume cardiovascular product and generated the most comprehensive automated data.

"Control charts for atenolol show that our process is statistically 'in control' but not optimized," Dr. Sharma reported after analyzing two months of production data. "All tablets meet specifications, but process variability is 40% higher than achievable with proper parameter optimization."

"What would process optimization involve?" I asked.

"Adjusting compression force, tablet coating parameters, and environmental controls to minimize variability rather than just staying within specification limits."

The optimization project took three months and required systematic testing of different parameter combinations while monitoring their effects on quality variability. The statistical approach was more methodical than our previous trial-and-error optimization methods.

"Process optimization reduced weight variation from ±2.1% to ±0.8% and hardness variation from ±12% to ±4%," Dr. Sharma announced during our quarterly review. "Quality consistency improved dramatically without changing formulation or raw materials."

"How does improved consistency affect our business?" asked our CFO.

"Better consistency reduces customer complaints, enables premium pricing for superior quality products, and provides competitive advantages that purely specification-based quality can't achieve."

The SPC implementation also revealed process relationships that manual testing had never detected. Statistical correlation analysis showed that humidity variations affected tablet hardness more than temperature variations, and that compression force optimization differed between morning and evening production shifts.

"SPC taught us that our process understanding was incomplete," I told Hans during one of his monitoring visits. "We were managing individual parameters without understanding how they interacted to affect overall quality."

"Most pharmaceutical manufacturers optimize parameters individually," he replied. "Statistical process control optimizes parameter interactions systematically."

"And systematic optimization produces better results than individual parameter optimization?"

"Systematic optimization produces more predictable results. When you understand how parameters interact, you can maintain consistent quality even when individual conditions vary."

Six months after implementing SPC, our quality consistency had improved enough to attract attention from international customers who required statistical documentation of process control capabilities.

"Your SPC documentation is more comprehensive than we receive from larger pharmaceutical suppliers," said our distributor in Germany during a facility audit. "Statistical process control demonstrates systematic quality management that regulatory authorities prefer."

"How does SPC documentation benefit regulatory compliance?" I asked.

"Regulatory authorities recognize that companies using statistical process control are more likely to maintain consistent quality than companies relying only on batch testing."

Eighteen months after implementation, SPC had become integral to our manufacturing operations rather than just quality control documentation. Production operators used control charts to optimize equipment performance, and our management team used process capability studies to evaluate improvement investments.

"You know what implementing SPC taught us about quality management?" I said to Dr. Sharma during our annual quality review. "Quality isn't just about meeting specifications—it's about understanding and optimizing the processes that create consistent results."

"And statistical methods provide insights into process performance that traditional testing methods can't reveal."

"The key insight was that data analysis enables process improvement while data collection only enables problem detection."

The statistical process control capabilities had become essential for competing in international markets where customers expected pharmaceutical suppliers to demonstrate systematic quality management through comprehensive process documentation.

More importantly, SPC had taught us that sustainable quality advantages required understanding the statistical relationships between process parameters and product outcomes rather than just monitoring individual quality measurements.

Dr. Vikram Singh Joins as Head of Manufacturing

The interview with Dr. Vikram Singh lasted four hours and ended with him questioning whether we were ready for the kind of manufacturing transformation he could provide.

"Your facility has excellent equipment and quality systems," he said, reviewing notes from his facility tour, "but your manufacturing approach is still organized like a large laboratory rather than an industrial production operation."

"What's the difference?" I asked, though I suspected his answer would be uncomfortable.

"Laboratory thinking focuses on making perfect products one batch at a time. Industrial thinking focuses on designing systems that consistently produce excellent products across thousands of batches with minimal variation."

Dr. Singh had spent twelve years at Ranbaxy before joining Nicholas Piramal, where he'd built manufacturing operations that supplied generic pharmaceuticals to regulated markets across Europe and North America. His resume was exactly what we needed for scaling our production capabilities, but his assessment suggested we weren't ready for his level of operational sophistication.

"What would industrial manufacturing transformation involve for our company?" Priya asked.

"Systematic production planning, integrated supply chain management, statistical process optimization, and organizational systems that can maintain consistent performance as you scale from 50 million tablets annually to 500 million tablets annually."

"Are we prepared to scale to 500 million tablets annually?" I asked.

"Your current systems could probably handle 100-150 million tablets annually with modifications. Beyond that, you need fundamentally different approaches to manufacturing management."

The conversation revealed something important about our business development stage: we'd successfully evolved from startup manufacturing to small-scale commercial production, but we were approaching limits that would require systematic operational thinking rather than just capacity expansion.

"Why are you interested in joining a company that generates ₹140 crores annually when you've worked for companies generating ₹2,000 crores annually?" I asked.

"Because building manufacturing capabilities from 140 crores to 1,000 crores is more interesting than optimizing established systems at large corporations," he replied. "I want to design manufacturing operations rather than just manage them."

"What would you design differently if you joined our company?"

"Integrated production planning that coordinates raw material procurement, manufacturing scheduling, and finished goods distribution. Quality management systems that prevent problems rather than just detect them. Organizational structures that can support 200-300 employees rather than your current 45 employees."

The salary negotiation with Dr. Singh required board approval because his compensation expectations exceeded our current pay scales by significant margins. But his experience suggested he could accelerate our manufacturing development by years rather than just improving existing operations incrementally.

"What convinced you to offer Dr. Singh such a substantial compensation package?" our board chairman asked during the approval meeting.

"The alternative to hiring him is trying to develop equivalent manufacturing expertise internally, which would take 3-5 years and might not succeed," I replied. "His experience provides immediate access to manufacturing capabilities that would be very difficult to build organically."

"And you're confident he can transform our manufacturing operations?"

"I'm confident we need the transformation he can provide. Whether we can successfully implement his recommendations is something we'll discover together."

Dr. Singh joined us in March 2005 and spent his first month conducting detailed analysis of our manufacturing processes, organizational structure, and production economics. His findings were comprehensive and sobering.

"Your manufacturing efficiency is good for a company your size, but inadequate for the scale you're planning to achieve," he reported during his initial assessment presentation. "Labor productivity, equipment utilization, and inventory management all need systematic improvement."

"What specific improvements would have the greatest impact?" I asked.

"Production planning systems that optimize equipment scheduling across multiple products, inventory management that minimizes working capital requirements, and quality systems that reduce production cycle times through better process control."

"How long would implementing these improvements take?"

"Eighteen months for complete implementation, but you'll see benefits within the first quarter as we optimize current operations while building new capabilities."

Dr. Singh's first project involved redesigning our production scheduling from reactive order fulfillment to proactive capacity planning. Instead of manufacturing products when orders arrived, we started forecasting demand and optimizing production sequences to maximize equipment efficiency.

"The new scheduling system increased our effective capacity by 28% without purchasing additional equipment," Ravi observed after three months of implementation. "We're producing more tablets using the same resources."

"How is that possible?" I asked.

"Better coordination between different production steps, optimized changeover sequences between products, and elimination of idle time caused by poor planning," Dr. Singh explained.

"And improved planning creates capacity increases that equipment purchases couldn't provide?"

"Equipment purchases increase maximum theoretical capacity. Planning optimization increases actual achievable capacity, which is usually more cost-effective than buying more equipment."

The production planning improvements enabled Dr. Singh to tackle more complex manufacturing challenges: supply chain integration, statistical quality control, and organizational development for larger-scale operations.

"Manufacturing transformation isn't just about technical improvements," he told our management team during a quarterly review. "It's about developing systematic thinking that can support continued growth without proportional increases in complexity and costs."

"What do you mean by systematic thinking?" asked our CFO.

"Designing processes that work consistently regardless of individual expertise, creating measurement systems that enable continuous improvement, and building organizational capabilities that can adapt to changing requirements."

Six months after Dr. Singh joined, our manufacturing economics had improved significantly: production costs per tablet decreased 18%, inventory turnover increased 35%, and customer service levels improved despite handling larger order volumes.

"The manufacturing improvements are generating better financial results than we projected," our CFO noted during a board meeting. "Dr. Singh's compensation investment is paying for itself through operational improvements."

"What surprised you most about the manufacturing transformation?" I asked Dr. Singh during his six-month review.

"How quickly your team adapted to systematic manufacturing methods," he replied. "Most companies resist operational changes, but your team embraced process improvements that required learning new approaches."

"Why did our team adapt quickly?"

"Because they understood that manufacturing transformation was necessary for business growth rather than just theoretical optimization. When people understand why changes matter, they implement changes more effectively."

Dr. Singh's impact extended beyond just manufacturing efficiency. His systematic approach to operations influenced our thinking about other business functions: systematic customer relationship management, systematic product development, and systematic financial planning.

"You know what hiring Dr. Singh taught us about organizational development?" I told Priya during our annual planning session. "The most valuable hires aren't just experts in their functional areas—they're people who can teach systematic thinking that improves overall business capabilities."

"And systematic thinking creates competitive advantages that individual expertise can't provide."

Twelve months after Dr. Singh joined, our manufacturing operations had transformed from craft production to industrial systems that could support the 300-500 million tablet annual volumes we were planning for international market expansion.

"The manufacturing transformation provided the foundation for everything we're planning over the next five years," I told our board during an annual review. "Without systematic manufacturing capabilities, we couldn't compete for the larger opportunities we're pursuing."

More importantly, Dr. Singh had taught us that sustainable business growth required building systematic operational capabilities rather than just scaling existing methods to handle larger volumes.

Chapter 9

The Talent Constraint

When Good People Aren't Good Enough

The resignation letter from our quality control manager arrived on a Monday morning and created a crisis that revealed how vulnerable we'd become to individual expertise.

"Dr. Sharma is accepting a position at Biocon," Priya told me, reading the formal notice that would take effect in thirty days. "He's citing career growth opportunities and significantly higher compensation."

"How significantly higher?" I asked, though I suspected the answer would be painful.

"About 60% above what we're paying him, plus equity participation and international project exposure."

This was exactly the scenario we'd been dreading but avoiding: losing key personnel to larger companies that could offer compensation and opportunities we couldn't match. Dr. Sharma wasn't just our quality control manager—he was the institutional memory for our cardiovascular product development and the relationship manager for our German equipment partnership.

"Can we counter-offer to retain him?" I asked.

"We could match Biocon's salary, but we can't match their equity program or international project opportunities. Dr. Sharma wants career advancement that our company scale can't provide."

The conversation forced us to confront something uncomfortable about our business development: we'd reached a size where we needed senior expertise to continue growing, but we weren't large enough to provide career progression that would retain senior talent long-term.

"This is the talent constraint," I realized during our emergency management meeting. "We need experienced professionals to scale our operations, but experienced professionals want career opportunities that only larger companies can provide."

"So we're caught between needing talent we can't afford and losing talent we can't replace," Priya observed.

"And the problem will get worse as we grow, because growth requires more senior expertise that will be increasingly expensive to acquire and retain."

Dr. Sharma's departure exposed gaps in our organizational development that went beyond just quality control management. He'd been involved in product development decisions, regulatory strategy, customer relationship management, and technical problem-solving across multiple departments.

"We've been depending on individual expertise rather than building systematic capabilities," Dr. Vikram Singh pointed out during our talent assessment meeting. "When key people leave, they take institutional knowledge that can't be easily replaced."

"How do we build systematic capabilities instead of depending on individual expertise?" I asked.

"Documentation systems that capture knowledge, cross-training programs that distribute expertise, and organizational processes that work consistently regardless of individual personnel."

"But systematic capabilities still require talented people to design and implement them."

"Yes, but they require fewer irreplaceable people and more well-trained people following excellent systems."

The talent constraint analysis revealed multiple vulnerabilities in our organization: single points of failure where individual departures would disrupt operations, compensation structures that couldn't compete with larger companies, and career development limitations that made us a training ground for talent that eventually moved to better opportunities.

"We need a different approach to talent management," I told our board during an emergency session. "Traditional hiring and retention strategies aren't working for the expertise levels we need."

"What would a different approach look like?" asked our board chairman.

"Strategic partnerships with senior professionals, consultant relationships that provide expertise without full-time employment obligations, and systematic knowledge capture that reduces dependency on individual expertise."

The consultant relationship model began with Dr. James Mitchell, our former GMP implementation consultant, who agreed to provide ongoing quality system support without requiring full-time employment.

"Consultant relationships let me work with multiple companies while providing you access to senior expertise," James explained during our arrangement discussion. "You get quality leadership without full-time compensation costs, and I get project variety without employment constraints."

"How do we ensure consultant availability when we need critical support?" I asked.

"Retainer agreements that guarantee priority access, structured engagement schedules that provide predictable availability, and emergency support protocols for urgent situations."

The consultant model worked well for specialized technical expertise, but we still needed full-time management capabilities for daily operations. This led to exploring creative employment arrangements that could attract senior talent without requiring compensation packages we couldn't afford.

"What about equity participation combined with moderate salary increases?" Priya suggested. "Senior professionals might accept lower cash compensation in exchange for ownership stakes that could become valuable if the company grows successfully."

"How much equity would be attractive to senior talent?" I asked.

"Probably 1-2% for senior managers, 0.5-1% for specialized professionals, vesting over 3-4 years to encourage retention."

The equity compensation approach required legal and accounting consultation to ensure compliance with tax regulations and employment law. The complexity was far beyond anything we'd encountered with previous hiring, but the alternative—losing critical expertise—seemed more expensive than administrative complications.

"Equity compensation creates alignment between individual career success and company growth," our legal advisor explained. "Senior professionals become partners in business development rather than just employees performing specific functions."

The hybrid compensation model—moderate salary increases plus equity participation—succeeded in attracting talent that pure salary approaches couldn't access. We hired Dr. Anita Rao as our new quality control manager with pharmaceutical development experience at Dr. Reddy's, and recruited Suresh Kumar as business development director with international sales experience at Lupin.

"The equity participation model attracts people who want to build something rather than just managing established operations," Dr. Rao observed during her first month. "That creates different motivation than traditional employment relationships."

"How is the motivation different?" I asked.

"When you own part of the business, you think about long-term optimization rather than just short-term performance. Equity participation encourages systematic thinking that benefits overall company development."

Six months after implementing our new talent strategy, we had successfully replaced Dr. Sharma's expertise while building more resilient organizational capabilities. Documentation systems captured critical knowledge, cross-training programs distributed expertise across team members, and consultant relationships provided access to senior capabilities without full-time employment costs.

"The talent constraint forced us to think strategically about organizational development," I told Dr. Singh during our quarterly review. "Instead of just hiring people to fill positions, we're building talent systems that can support continued growth."

"And talent systems create competitive advantages that individual expertise alone can't provide," he replied.

"How so?"

"Individual expertise leaves when people leave. Systematic talent development creates institutional capabilities that improve over time regardless of personnel changes."

Eighteen months after confronting the talent constraint, our organizational capabilities had evolved from dependency on irreplaceable individuals to systematic expertise that could adapt to personnel changes while maintaining operational excellence.

"You know what the talent constraint taught us about business development?" Priya said during our annual planning session. "Sustainable growth requires building organizational capabilities rather than just acquiring individual talents."

"And building organizational capabilities means creating systems that enable good people to do excellent work rather than depending on excellent people to overcome inadequate systems."

The lesson would prove crucial as we expanded into biotechnology products and international markets where talent requirements would be even more specialized and competition for expertise would be even more intense.

Recruiting from Indian Institutes of Technology

The campus recruitment presentation at IIT Delhi lasted twenty minutes and attracted exactly four students to our information session.

"Malhotra Pharmaceuticals is a growing generic drug manufacturer based in Hyderabad," I explained to the sparse audience in a classroom designed for fifty people. "We're looking for chemical engineers interested in pharmaceutical process development and manufacturing optimization."

One student raised his hand. "What's your starting salary compared to Infosys and TCS?"

"Our starting salary is ₹4.5 lakhs annually," I replied, knowing this was about half what major IT companies were offering IIT graduates.

"What about career advancement opportunities?" asked another student.

"Rapid advancement based on performance, direct exposure to senior management, and ownership of significant projects from day one."

"But how does pharmaceutical manufacturing compare to software development for long-term career prospects?" the first student pressed.

This question revealed the fundamental challenge of recruiting top engineering talent for pharmaceutical manufacturing: we were competing against India's software industry, which offered higher starting salaries, better brand recognition, and career opportunities that IIT students found more attractive than pharmaceutical process engineering.

"Maybe we're targeting the wrong students," Priya suggested after our disappointing campus visit. "IIT students might be too focused on IT careers to consider pharmaceutical opportunities seriously."

"Or maybe we need to present pharmaceutical careers differently," I replied. "Instead of competing with IT companies on salary and prestige, maybe we should emphasize unique learning opportunities that pharmaceuticals provide."

"What unique learning opportunities?"

"International regulatory exposure, advanced manufacturing technology, product development from laboratory to commercial scale, and business impact that affects human health rather than just information processing."

The refined recruitment approach began with identifying IIT students who had specifically chosen chemical engineering because they were interested in process industries rather than students who were planning to switch to IT careers after graduation.

"We need to find students who actually want to work in chemical engineering," I told Dr. Singh during our recruitment planning session. "Students who chose pharmaceutical engineering electives, participated in chemical process design competitions, or expressed interest in manufacturing rather than software development."

"How do we identify those students?" he asked.

"Faculty recommendations, student project portfolios, and targeted outreach through pharmaceutical engineering societies rather than general campus recruitment."

Professor Raghavan at IIT Delhi's chemical engineering department became our key contact for identifying students with genuine interest in pharmaceutical manufacturing.

"Most chemical engineering students are pressured toward IT careers because of salary differences," he explained during our faculty meeting. "But some students are specifically interested in process engineering and would consider pharmaceutical opportunities if they understood the career development potential."

"What would make pharmaceutical careers attractive to process-oriented students?" I asked.

"Exposure to advanced manufacturing technology, international quality standards, regulatory science, and rapid career progression in growing companies where individual contributions have significant impact."

"How different is career progression in pharmaceuticals versus IT companies?"

"IT companies hire hundreds of engineers who work on incremental improvements to established systems. Pharmaceutical companies hire fewer engineers who work on complete process development from research to commercial manufacturing."

This insight led us to focus recruitment messaging on project ownership and technical learning rather than just compensation and career advancement.

"Our recruitment pitch should emphasize what chemical engineers can accomplish in pharmaceuticals that they can't accomplish in IT," I decided. "Complete process responsibility, international technology exposure, and product development that creates tangible value."

The targeted recruitment approach produced better results. We identified twelve IIT students across Delhi, Mumbai, and Chennai who had demonstrated specific interest in pharmaceutical process engineering through coursework, projects, or research experience.

"The students we're interviewing this time have much better understanding of pharmaceutical engineering," observed Dr. Rao during our selection process. "They're asking technical questions about process optimization and quality control rather than just salary and advancement questions."

"What technical questions are they asking?" I asked.

"Statistical process control implementation, scale-up challenges from laboratory to commercial manufacturing, international regulatory compliance, and continuous improvement methodologies."

The quality of technical questions indicated that we'd found students who understood pharmaceutical engineering and were genuinely interested in process development careers.

Rajesh Gupta from IIT Delhi became our first successful IIT recruit. He had completed his final year project on tablet coating optimization and was specifically interested in pharmaceutical process engineering.

"What attracted you to pharmaceutical manufacturing over IT career opportunities?" I asked during his final interview.

"IT careers involve writing code that processes information," he replied. "Pharmaceutical manufacturing involves optimizing processes that create products affecting human health. The technical challenges seem more meaningful and the learning opportunities more diverse."

"What learning opportunities are you most interested in?"

"Advanced manufacturing technology, international quality standards, and process optimization using statistical methods. Pharmaceutical engineering combines chemistry, engineering, and quality science in ways that IT doesn't provide."

Rajesh's first project involved optimizing our tablet coating process using statistical design of experiments methodology he'd learned at IIT. His technical approach was more systematic than anything our experienced operators had attempted.

"The statistical optimization reduced coating variability by 35% and identified parameter interactions that we hadn't recognized," Dr. Singh reported after Rajesh's first quarter. "His academic training provided fresh perspectives on process improvement."

"How does academic training differ from experience-based knowledge?" I asked.

"Academic training emphasizes systematic analysis and experimentation. Experience-based knowledge emphasizes practical solutions and trouble-shooting. Combining both approaches produces better results than either approach alone."

The success with Rajesh encouraged expansion of our IIT recruitment program. Over the next two years, we hired six IIT graduates who contributed process improvements, technology implementations, and analytical capabilities that significantly enhanced our manufacturing operations.

"The IIT engineers bring different thinking to pharmaceutical manufacturing," Dr. Rao observed during a team review. "They approach problems analytically rather than just experientially, which leads to more systematic solutions."

"And systematic solutions create competitive advantages that experiential solutions don't provide," added Dr. Singh.

"How so?"

"Systematic solutions can be documented, replicated, and improved continuously. Experiential solutions depend on individual knowledge that's difficult to transfer or optimize."

The IIT recruitment program also created unexpected benefits for our existing team. Young engineers with strong analytical training motivated experienced operators to think more systematically about process optimization.

"Working with IIT engineers has changed how I approach manufacturing problems," admitted Ravi, our senior tablet press operator. "Instead of just solving immediate problems, I'm learning to analyze root causes and prevent future problems."

"The combination of academic training and practical experience is more powerful than either approach individually," I told Professor Raghavan during a follow-up visit. "Your students learn from our experienced operators, and our operators learn from your students' analytical methods."

Three years after beginning IIT recruitment, our engineering capabilities had evolved significantly. Process optimization projects that previously required external consultants were now handled internally, and our manufacturing efficiency improvements accelerated through systematic analytical approaches.

"You know what recruiting from IITs taught us about talent development?" I said to Dr. Singh during our annual planning session. "The most valuable hires aren't necessarily the most experienced people—they're people whose capabilities complement and enhance your existing team strengths."

"And fresh analytical thinking often produces breakthrough improvements that experience alone can't achieve."

The IIT recruitment program had become an essential component of our talent strategy, providing analytical capabilities that enabled continuous improvement of our manufacturing operations while creating career opportunities that attracted top engineering talent to pharmaceutical manufacturing.

Creating Employee Stock Ownership Programs

The idea for employee stock ownership came from a conversation I never intended to have.

"Why should I stay here when Cipla is offering me ₹2 lakhs more annually?" asked Suresh, our production manager, during what I'd thought would be a routine performance review meeting.

"Because you have growth opportunities here that you wouldn't have at a larger company," I replied, using the standard retention argument we'd developed for situations like this.

"Growth opportunities don't pay my children's school fees," he said. "I've been here four years and helped build this production operation from 10 million tablets annually to 80 million tablets annually. But my salary has only increased 35% while the company revenue has increased 400%."

The math was uncomfortable but accurate. Our revenue growth had far exceeded our salary increases, which meant our team had created significantly more value than they'd been compensated for.

"What would make staying here financially attractive compared to joining Cipla?" I asked.

"Some way to benefit from the company growth I've helped create," Suresh replied. "At Cipla, I'll be just another employee doing a job. Here, I've built something that's become valuable. I want to share in that value somehow."

This conversation happened in November 2005, six months after we'd started our talent retention crisis with Dr. Sharma's departure. Despite hiring Dr. Rao and implementing consultant relationships, we were still losing experienced employees to larger companies that could offer higher cash compensation.

"Maybe the solution isn't matching competitors' salaries," I told Priya after the meeting with Suresh. "Maybe the solution is sharing company ownership with employees who've contributed to company growth."

"You mean equity compensation like we offered to Dr. Rao?" she asked.

"Something broader. Instead of just offering equity to senior managers, maybe we should offer ownership participation to everyone who's contributed to building the company."

"How would that work practically?"

"Employee stock ownership program where long-term employees receive company shares based on their tenure and performance, creating financial incentives to stay with the company as it grows."

The employee stock ownership concept was appealing, but the implementation complexity was daunting. We needed legal advice about share allocation methods, tax implications, vesting schedules, and valuation procedures for a privately-held company.

"Employee stock ownership programs require careful legal structuring," explained Mr. Krishnan, our corporate attorney. "Share allocation, vesting terms, and liquidity provisions must be designed to incentivize retention while protecting existing shareholders' interests."

"What's the typical equity allocation for employee stock ownership programs?" I asked.

"Usually 10-15% of total company equity, distributed among employees based on seniority, performance, and strategic importance to business operations."

"How do employees realize value from stock ownership in privately-held companies?"

"Through buyback provisions, dividend distributions, or liquidity events like acquisition or public offerings. The key is providing realistic paths to financial benefit rather than just theoretical ownership."

The ESOP design process took four months and required evaluating different approaches to equity distribution. We could allocate shares equally among all employees, distribute shares based on salary levels, or use performance-based criteria to reward exceptional contributors.

"Equal distribution seems fairest, but performance-based distribution provides better incentives," observed our CFO during the program design discussions.

"What about hybrid approaches that combine base allocation with performance bonuses?" I suggested.

"Hybrid approaches are more complex to administer but create both inclusion and incentive effects," Mr. Krishnan replied.

The ESOP structure we eventually implemented allocated 12% of company equity among employees with more than two years of tenure. Base allocation was proportional to salary levels, with performance bonuses adding up to 50% additional shares for exceptional contributors.

"The program creates ownership mentality rather than just employment mentality," I explained during the ESOP announcement meeting with our entire team. "When you own part of the company, company success becomes personal success."

"How do we know what our shares are worth?" asked Kumar, our quality control technician.

"Independent valuation annually, with buyback options after five years of vesting and dividend distributions based on company profitability."

"What happens to our shares if we leave the company before five years?"

"Vesting schedule provides partial ownership after two years, increasing to full ownership after five years. Unvested shares return to the company pool."

The employee response to ESOP announcement exceeded our expectations. Instead of just appreciating the financial opportunity, employees started thinking about business improvements that would increase company value.

"The ESOP changed how people approach their daily work," Dr. Singh observed after three months of program implementation. "Instead of just completing assigned tasks, people are suggesting process improvements that could increase profitability."

"How are process improvement suggestions different from before?" I asked.

"Before ESOP, suggestions focused on making work easier or more efficient. Now suggestions focus on reducing costs and improving quality in ways that affect company financial performance."

"Because people understand that company financial performance affects their personal wealth?"

"Exactly. Ownership creates financial incentives for business optimization rather than just operational efficiency."

The ESOP implementation also solved our talent retention problems more effectively than salary increases would have achieved. Suresh decided to remain with our company rather than joining Cipla, and several other employees declined external opportunities.

"The equity participation makes staying here financially attractive even when competitors offer higher salaries," Suresh explained during his retention discussion. "My ESOP shares could become worth more than salary differences over the next 3-5 years."

"How do you evaluate ESOP value versus guaranteed salary increases?" I asked.

"ESOP provides upside potential that salary never provides. If the company continues growing successfully, my ownership stake becomes very valuable. Salary increases provide security but no wealth-building opportunity."

Six months after ESOP implementation, our employee retention rate had improved to 94%, and our productivity metrics showed continuous improvement as employees took ownership responsibility for business performance.

"The ownership mentality is visible in daily operations," Dr. Rao noted during a management review. "People are more careful about material waste, more focused on quality consistency, and more interested in customer satisfaction because they understand how these factors affect company value."

The ESOP program also created unexpected benefits for business development. Employees became ambassadors for the company when recruiting friends and family members, and their ownership pride enhanced our reputation with customers and suppliers.

"Your employees seem more engaged than typical pharmaceutical company staff," observed our German equipment partner during a facility visit. "They discuss company performance like owners rather than just workers."

"Because they are owners," I replied. "Employee stock ownership aligns individual success with company success."

Two years after implementing ESOP, company performance had improved significantly: productivity increased 25%, employee turnover decreased 60%, and our ability to attract talented employees improved despite continued salary competition from larger companies.

"You know what creating employee stock ownership taught us about incentive systems?" I said to Priya during our annual ESOP review. "The most effective incentives align individual interests with company interests rather than just providing individual rewards."

"And aligned interests create sustainable motivation because employee success depends on company success."

"The key insight was that ownership mentality changes how people think about their work, not just how much they're compensated for their work."

The ESOP program had become integral to our talent strategy, providing retention incentives and performance motivation that traditional compensation couldn't achieve.

More importantly, it had taught us that sustainable competitive advantages often come from aligning stakeholder interests rather than just optimizing individual compensation packages.

The Exodus to US Firms and Retention Strategies

The resignation letter from Rajesh arrived on the same day as our first ₹100 crore quarterly revenue report, which seemed like cosmic irony.

"Rajesh is joining Mylan's New Jersey facility as a senior process engineer," Priya told me, reading the letter that would take effect in six weeks. "They're offering him permanent US residency sponsorship plus a salary that's three times what we're paying him."

"Three times?" I asked, though I shouldn't have been surprised given what we'd been hearing about US pharmaceutical companies aggressively recruiting Indian talent.

"₹18 lakhs annually here versus $65,000 annually there, which is about ₹30 lakhs at current exchange rates. Plus housing assistance, healthcare benefits, and eventually green card sponsorship."

Rajesh had been our star IIT recruit from three years earlier, the process optimization specialist who'd reduced our tablet coating variability and implemented statistical quality control systems. Losing him would eliminate capabilities we'd spent years developing.

"This is becoming a pattern," I said, reviewing our personnel files. "In the past six months, we've lost Dr. Patel to Teva, Suresh to Pfizer's Mumbai office, and now Rajesh to Mylan. US pharmaceutical companies are systematically recruiting our best talent."

"And we can't compete with their compensation packages or immigration opportunities," Priya replied.

"So what's our retention strategy when competitors can offer three times our salaries plus permanent US residency?"

This conversation happened in March 2006, during what the pharmaceutical industry was calling the "great talent migration" from Indian companies to US operations. American pharmaceutical companies were establishing Indian subsidiaries and recruiting experienced Indian professionals to staff both domestic operations and US facilities.

"The talent exodus isn't just about money," observed Dr. Singh during our emergency retention strategy meeting. "It's about career opportunities that Indian pharmaceutical companies can't provide."

"What career opportunities specifically?" I asked.

"Exposure to FDA-regulated manufacturing, international project management, advanced R&D capabilities, and professional networks that enable global career mobility."

"Can we provide any of those opportunities at our scale?"

"Not the same scale or sophistication that multinational companies provide. But we can provide some experiences that large companies can't offer."

The retention analysis revealed something uncomfortable: we were competing against opportunities that went far beyond just compensation differences. US pharmaceutical companies offered career experiences, professional development, and long-term prospects that our company couldn't match.

"Maybe we can't prevent the talent exodus, but we can influence who leaves and when they leave," I suggested. "Instead of losing people unexpectedly, we could plan transitions that benefit both employees and our company."

"What would planned transitions look like?" Priya asked.

"Alumni relationships with employees who join international companies, knowledge transfer programs before departures, and partnerships with US companies that hire our people."

The alumni relationship concept emerged from recognizing that employees who left for US opportunities could become valuable business contacts rather than just lost talent.

"Dr. Patel now works at Teva's quality control division," I noted during our strategy discussion. "Instead of viewing his departure as pure loss, maybe we can maintain professional relationships that benefit both parties."

"How would alumni relationships benefit our business?" asked Dr. Singh.

"Former employees understand our capabilities and could recommend us for contract manufacturing opportunities, technical partnerships, or vendor relationships."

"And maintaining contact with former employees could help us understand industry trends and competitive developments."

The knowledge transfer program required systematic documentation of departing employees' expertise before their transition to new companies.

Instead of just accepting resignations, we started conducting comprehensive knowledge capture sessions.

"Before you leave for Mylan, we'd like to document your process optimization methodologies," I told Rajesh during his transition planning. "Not just the specific improvements you've implemented, but the analytical approaches you used to identify improvement opportunities."

"How would that documentation benefit the company?" he asked.

"Future process improvement projects could build on your analytical methods rather than starting from basic principles. Your intellectual contributions would continue benefiting the company even after your departure."

"And documenting my methods might help me organize my knowledge for my new position at Mylan."

The knowledge transfer sessions revealed how much institutional capability was walking out the door with each departure. Rajesh's optimization methods, Dr. Patel's quality control insights, and Suresh's production management approaches represented years of learning that couldn't be easily replaced.

"We need to systematize knowledge capture as standard practice rather than emergency response to departures," Dr. Singh observed. "Every experienced employee should document their expertise regularly rather than just during resignation transitions."

The systematic knowledge documentation program began requiring all senior personnel to maintain detailed records of their methodologies, decision-making frameworks, and problem-solving approaches.

"This feels like extra work," complained Kumar, our quality control supervisor. "Why should I document everything I do?"

"Because documentation protects the company from knowledge loss and protects you from being irreplaceable in ways that limit your career mobility," I explained.

"How does being irreplaceable limit career mobility?"

"If your knowledge isn't documented, the company can't afford to promote you or support your external opportunities because your departure would create operational problems."

The US company partnership approach involved developing relationships with pharmaceutical companies that hired our employees, converting talent acquisition from competitive threat to collaborative opportunity.

"Instead of losing employees to Mylan, maybe we can develop vendor relationships with Mylan that benefit from our former employees' understanding of our capabilities," Priya suggested.

"Would Mylan be interested in vendor relationships with companies their employees came from?" I asked.

"Former employees would be natural advocates for working with their previous companies, especially if those relationships were managed professionally rather than resentfully."

The partnership approach succeeded beyond our expectations. Dr. Patel recommended us for a quality control consulting project with Teva, and Rajesh arranged introductions for potential contract manufacturing discussions with Mylan.

"The alumni relationships are generating business opportunities we never would have accessed otherwise," I told our board during a quarterly review. "Former employees have become business development resources rather than just lost assets."

Six months after implementing our retention strategy, we'd accepted that some talent exodus was inevitable but had transformed departures from business losses into strategic relationships.

"The retention strategy taught us something important about talent management," Dr. Singh observed during our annual review. "You can't always prevent good people from leaving, but you can influence how they leave and what relationships continue after they leave."

"And maintaining professional relationships with former employees often provides more long-term value than desperate retention efforts that postpone inevitable departures."

"The key insight was that alumni networks can become business assets when departures are managed strategically rather than just emotionally."

Two years after beginning our alumni relationship program, former employees had generated ₹8 crores in new business opportunities through introductions, recommendations, and collaborative projects.

"You know what the talent exodus taught us about competitive advantage?" I said to Priya during our planning session. "Sustainable competitive advantages come from developing capabilities faster than you lose them, not from preventing all talent departures."

"And alumni relationships can amplify your capabilities by extending your professional network into companies and markets you couldn't access independently."

The talent retention strategy had evolved from damage control to strategic relationship management, creating value from transitions that initially seemed purely destructive.

More importantly, it had taught us that in global industries, talent mobility could become a competitive advantage rather than just a competitive threat when managed systematically.

Building Leadership Pipeline

The succession planning meeting lasted six hours and ended with the uncomfortable realization that our entire company depended on three people who could all be recruited away tomorrow.

"If Arjun, Priya, and I were to leave simultaneously, the company would face operational crisis within two weeks," Dr. Singh said, pointing to our hastily drawn organizational chart. "We have excellent technical specialists, but no one prepared to assume senior management responsibilities."

"What about our department heads?" I asked, reviewing the list of experienced employees who'd been with us for 3-5 years.

"Excellent at managing their functional areas, but not prepared for cross-functional leadership or strategic decision-making," he replied. "The transition from specialist to general manager requires different capabilities than most people develop through functional experience alone."

This conversation happened in August 2006, triggered by our CFO's departure to join Biocon as their finance director. His resignation had forced us to confront something we'd been avoiding: we'd built operational expertise without developing leadership depth.

"The leadership pipeline problem is that we've promoted people based on technical competence rather than management potential," Priya observed. "Our department heads are subject matter experts who've been given administrative responsibilities."

"What's the difference between subject matter expertise and management capability?" I asked.

"Subject matter experts optimize processes within their domains. Managers optimize coordination between domains while developing strategic thinking about business direction."

"So we need to develop management capabilities among our technical experts, or hire managers with proven leadership experience."

"Both. Technical experts who develop management skills understand our business deeply. Experienced managers who learn our business bring proven leadership approaches."

The leadership development analysis revealed gaps that extended beyond just management training. Most of our senior staff had never managed budgets exceeding ₹10 lakhs, led cross-functional projects, or made decisions affecting overall business strategy.

"We need systematic leadership development rather than just promoting good performers into management roles," I told our board during an emergency succession planning session.

"What would systematic leadership development involve?" asked our board chairman.

"Management training programs, cross-functional project assignments, budget responsibility, strategic planning participation, and mentorship relationships with experienced leaders."

"How long would developing internal leadership capabilities take?"

"Probably 2-3 years to develop department heads who could assume senior management responsibilities. But we need interim solutions in case current leadership becomes unavailable."

The interim solution involved establishing advisory relationships with experienced pharmaceutical executives who could provide strategic guidance and temporary leadership if needed.

"We need a senior pharmaceutical executive who understands our industry and could step in during leadership transitions," I explained to Dr. James Mitchell during one of our consulting sessions.

"Are you talking about interim CEO arrangements or board advisory positions?" he asked.

"Both options. Strategic advisor normally, interim executive leadership during emergencies or transitions."

"What compensation structure would attract experienced pharmaceutical executives to advisory relationships with mid-sized companies?"

"Probably equity participation plus consulting fees for active involvement. Advisory relationships need to provide meaningful financial incentives without requiring full-time commitment."

The advisory board development led to recruiting Dr. Ramesh Kumar, former head of manufacturing at Dr. Reddy's, as strategic advisor with 1% equity participation and ₹2 lakh quarterly retainer.

"Advisory relationships provide access to senior expertise without the cost and commitment of executive hiring," Dr. Kumar explained during his first strategic review. "You get experienced perspective on major decisions while maintaining operational autonomy."

"How do advisory relationships differ from consulting relationships?" I asked.

"Consultants solve specific problems. Advisors provide ongoing strategic guidance and can assume temporary operational responsibility if needed."

The internal leadership development program began with identifying high-potential employees who demonstrated cross-functional thinking rather than just technical expertise.

"Leadership potential is different from technical performance," Dr. Singh observed during our talent evaluation process. "Some excellent technical specialists have no interest in management responsibility, while some good performers show natural leadership instincts."

"How do we identify natural leadership instincts?" Priya asked.

"People who take initiative beyond their assigned responsibilities, coordinate effectively with other departments, and think about business impact rather than just functional efficiency."

The leadership development program included monthly strategic planning participation for department heads, quarterly budget management responsibility, and cross-functional project leadership assignments.

"Instead of just managing quality control, I'm learning to coordinate quality requirements with production planning and customer service," observed Dr. Rao after six months in the leadership program. "Management requires understanding how different functions affect each other."

"What's been most challenging about developing management skills?" I asked.

"Thinking about trade-offs between functional optimization and overall business performance. Sometimes what's best for quality control isn't best for production efficiency or customer service."

"And learning to make those trade-offs is essential for senior management responsibility."

The cross-functional project assignments proved particularly valuable for developing management capabilities. Department heads who successfully led projects involving multiple departments demonstrated readiness for broader leadership roles.

"The new product launch project taught me more about management than five years of functional experience," said Suresh, our production manager, after leading our cardiovascular portfolio expansion. "Managing across departments requires different skills than managing within departments."

"What different skills specifically?" Dr. Singh asked.

"Negotiation, communication, strategic thinking, and decision-making with incomplete information. Functional management involves optimizing known variables. Cross-functional management involves balancing unknown variables."

Eighteen months after implementing our leadership development program, we had identified three department heads ready for senior management responsibility and two additional employees showing strong leadership potential.

"The leadership pipeline is developing faster than expected," I told Dr. Kumar during our quarterly advisory review. "Several people have demonstrated management capabilities that we didn't recognize when they were only working in functional roles."

"That's typical for leadership development programs," he replied. "Many people have management potential that becomes visible only when they're given management responsibilities."

"And providing management experience is more effective than just management training?"

"Management experience with coaching and feedback. Training provides concepts, but experience with guidance develops actual capabilities."

The leadership development program also created unexpected benefits for employee retention. People who might have left for management opportunities elsewhere chose to remain because of advancement potential within our company.

"The leadership program gives me career progression without requiring me to leave," explained Dr. Rao during her annual review. "I can develop management capabilities while building on the technical expertise I've developed here."

Two years after beginning leadership pipeline development, we had successfully transitioned three department heads into senior management roles and established advisory relationships that provided strategic guidance and succession backup.

"You know what building leadership pipeline taught us about organizational development?" I said to Priya during our annual planning session. "Leadership capabilities can be developed systematically, but they require different experiences than technical capabilities."

"And developing internal leadership is more effective than hiring external leadership because internal leaders understand the business culture and operational realities."

"The key insight was that leadership development requires providing management responsibility rather than just management training."

The leadership pipeline had become essential for supporting our continued growth while reducing dependency on individual executives whose departure could create organizational crisis.

More importantly, it had taught us that sustainable business growth required systematic capability development at all organizational levels, not just technical and operational expertise.

Chapter 10

The Financial Engineering

When Cash Flow Becomes Currency

The acquisition opportunity appeared in our inbox disguised as a routine business inquiry.

"We're interested in discussing potential collaboration regarding manufacturing capacity for generic cardiovascular products," read the email from Dr. Sanjay Patel, managing director of Cardio Generics Ltd. "Our company has strong regulatory approvals but limited manufacturing capabilities."

What began as a straightforward contract manufacturing discussion evolved into something much more complex when we discovered that Cardio Generics had ₹45 crores in annual revenue, excellent customer relationships, but was struggling with production inefficiencies that were destroying their profitability.

"They have everything we want—established customers, regulatory approvals, proven market demand—but they can't manufacture profitably," I told Priya after our initial meeting with Dr. Patel.

"And we have everything they want—efficient manufacturing, quality systems, production capacity—but we're looking for ways to expand market access quickly."

"So instead of a manufacturing services relationship, maybe we should consider an acquisition that combines our capabilities with their market position."

This conversation marked my introduction to financial engineering: using creative transaction structures to achieve business objectives that couldn't be accomplished through organic growth or traditional financing.

"What would acquiring Cardio Generics actually involve?" I asked our CFO during our initial evaluation.

"Due diligence to understand their financial condition, valuation analysis to determine fair acquisition price, and structuring an acquisition that we can afford without disrupting our cash flow."

"How much would a company generating ₹45 crores annually cost to acquire?"

"Depends on their profitability and growth potential. Profitable pharmaceutical companies typically sell for 3-5 times annual revenue. Unprofitable companies with good assets might sell for 1-2 times revenue."

"And Cardio Generics is profitable or unprofitable?"

"Marginally profitable with significant improvement potential if manufacturing efficiency problems can be solved."

The due diligence process revealed that Cardio Generics was exactly the type of acquisition opportunity that could accelerate our growth trajectory while providing immediate return on investment.

"They're generating ₹45 crores in revenue with 8% net margins," our CFO reported after reviewing their financial statements. "But their manufacturing costs are 40% higher than industry benchmarks because of production inefficiencies."

"What would happen to their profitability if we could reduce their manufacturing costs to our efficiency levels?" I asked.

"Net margins would increase from 8% to approximately 18%, which would add ₹4.5 crores annually to their profits."

"So the acquisition could pay for itself through operational improvements alone?"

"If we can successfully integrate their operations with our manufacturing systems."

The acquisition financing required creative structuring because we couldn't afford to pay ₹90 crores cash for a company that size. This led to exploring leveraged buyout techniques, earnout arrangements, and seller financing options.

"We're proposing ₹30 crores cash at closing, ₹20 crores in seller financing over three years, and ₹15 crores in earnout payments based on revenue growth targets," our investment banker explained during financing negotiations.

"What's seller financing?" I asked.

"The current owners provide part of the acquisition financing, essentially accepting payment over time rather than requiring full cash payment immediately."

"Why would sellers accept delayed payment instead of cash?"

"Because delayed payment often produces higher total consideration than immediate cash, and sellers retain upside participation if the combined company performs better than projected."

The earnout structure was even more complex: we'd pay additional amounts if the acquired company achieved specific revenue and profitability targets within three years of acquisition.

"Earnout arrangements align acquisition pricing with actual performance," Dr. Patel explained during our final negotiations. "If the acquisition succeeds, we receive higher total consideration. If integration challenges prevent success, you don't overpay for underperforming assets."

"How do earnout payments get calculated?" Priya asked.

"Revenue growth targets, profitability improvement benchmarks, and customer retention metrics. The specific targets are negotiated based on realistic projections for the combined company."

The acquisition closed in February 2007 after six months of negotiations, due diligence, and financing arrangements. The transaction structure was more sophisticated than anything we'd previously attempted: cash payment, seller notes, earnout provisions, and integration milestones.

"This feels like learning financial engineering while implementing it," I told our CFO after signing the final documents.

"Most mid-sized company acquisitions involve learning advanced financial techniques during transaction execution," he replied. "The complexity grows with company size and transaction sophistication."

The integration process revealed both the benefits and challenges of acquisition-based growth. Cardio Generics' customer relationships provided immediate access to market segments that would have taken years to develop organically.

"The acquired customers trust our quality systems more than Cardio Generics' previous manufacturing," observed Dr. Singh after our first quarter of combined operations. "Customer retention has been excellent, and several customers have increased their order volumes."

"How much revenue synergy are we achieving?" I asked.

"About ₹8 crores in additional orders from acquired customers who are now confident in our manufacturing capabilities. Plus cross-selling opportunities for our cardiovascular products to their existing distributors."

However, the operational integration was more challenging than financial projections had indicated. Consolidating two different manufacturing approaches, quality systems, and customer service processes required extensive coordination and some temporary inefficiencies.

"Integration is consuming more management attention than we anticipated," Priya observed during our quarterly review. "The financial benefits are materializing, but the operational complexity has increased significantly."

"Is the complexity temporary or permanent?" I asked.

"Probably temporary for 12-18 months until systems integration is complete. But it's requiring senior management involvement that limits our ability to pursue other growth opportunities simultaneously."

The acquisition's financial performance exceeded projections: combined revenue increased 35% and combined profitability increased 42% within the first year. More importantly, the transaction had taught us financial engineering techniques that could support additional growth strategies.

"The Cardio Generics acquisition proved that creative financing can enable transactions that pure cash purchases couldn't support," our CFO noted during our annual review.

"And acquisition integration capabilities could support additional transactions if attractive opportunities emerge."

"What other acquisition opportunities are we considering?" asked our board chairman.

"Export-focused companies with international market access but limited product portfolios, or technology companies with specialized capabilities that complement our manufacturing strengths."

The financial engineering experience also influenced our thinking about capital structure optimization. Instead of relying solely on retained earnings and bank debt, we started exploring private equity partnerships, revenue-based financing, and strategic investor relationships.

"Financial engineering enables growth strategies that operational performance alone can't support," I told Dr. Kumar during one of our advisory sessions. "Access to creative financing expands the range of opportunities we can pursue."

"And understanding financial engineering becomes essential for competing with larger companies that have sophisticated financial capabilities," he replied.

Two years after the Cardio Generics acquisition, we had identified three additional acquisition targets and were exploring private equity partnerships that could provide capital for larger transactions.

"You know what financial engineering taught us about business development?" I said to Priya during our strategic planning session. "Growth constraints are often financial rather than operational, and creative financing can eliminate constraints that traditional funding approaches can't solve."

"And financial sophistication becomes a competitive advantage that enables opportunities unavailable to companies with simpler capital structures."

The lesson would prove crucial as we planned our expansion into biotechnology products and international markets where capital requirements exceeded what organic growth could support.

First Venture Capital Round with Sequoia India

The pitch meeting with Sequoia India lasted ninety minutes and ended with a question that I hadn't prepared to answer.

"Your financial projections are impressive," said Mohit Bhatnagar, the managing director, reviewing our presentation materials. "But why do you need venture capital when your business is already profitable and generating positive cash flow?"

"Because organic growth is too slow for the opportunities we're seeing," I replied. "International expansion, biotechnology product development, and strategic acquisitions require capital that our cash flow can't support."

"How much capital do you need, and what returns can you guarantee to justify venture investment?"

"We're seeking ₹25 crores for 20% equity. We project 300% growth over three years through international expansion and product portfolio development."

"And if you don't achieve 300% growth?"

"Then you've invested in a profitable pharmaceutical company that will continue generating steady returns, albeit at lower multiples than venture capital typically targets."

This conversation represented our first serious engagement with institutional venture capital, six months after completing the Cardio Generics acquisition. The acquisition had demonstrated that external capital could accelerate growth, but it had also revealed that our expansion ambitions exceeded what traditional financing could support.

"Why are we considering venture capital instead of bank loans or private equity?" Priya asked during our fundraising strategy meetings.

"Because venture capital provides more than just money," I replied. "VCs provide strategic guidance, industry connections, and operational expertise that could be more valuable than the capital itself."

"But venture capital also requires giving up equity and accepting external oversight of business decisions."

"Which might be beneficial if the external oversight comes from people who've helped other companies navigate similar growth challenges."

The due diligence process with Sequoia was more comprehensive than anything we'd experienced with banks or private investors. Financial audits, customer interviews, competitive analysis, and management assessments that revealed aspects of our business that we hadn't examined systematically.

"Sequoia's due diligence is basically free management consulting," observed our CFO after their team completed their analysis. "They're evaluating our business more thoroughly than we've ever evaluated it ourselves."

"What are they discovering that we didn't know?" I asked.

"Market opportunities we hadn't quantified, competitive advantages we hadn't articulated clearly, and operational risks we hadn't addressed systematically."

The due diligence revealed that our business was more valuable than we'd understood, but also more complex than venture investors typically preferred.

"Your company occupies an interesting position in the pharmaceutical industry," Mohit explained during our follow-up meeting. "Too large for early-stage venture capital, too small for growth equity, but with growth potential that traditional pharmaceutical investors might not appreciate."

"Is that good or bad for fundraising?" I asked.

"It's challenging for fundraising because you don't fit standard investment categories. But it's potentially good for valuation because unique positioning often creates pricing advantages for investors who understand the opportunity."

The term sheet negotiations revealed the complexity of venture capital deal structures. Liquidation preferences, anti-dilution provisions, board composition, and management incentive alignments that seemed designed by lawyers rather than business operators.

"The term sheet is eight pages of legal language that basically determines who controls what under different scenarios," our attorney explained during the contract review process.

"What scenarios specifically?" Priya asked.

"Successful exit scenarios where everyone benefits, moderate success scenarios where investors get preferential treatment, and failure scenarios where control mechanisms determine who makes decisions about company direction."

"So venture capital terms are essentially insurance policies that protect investors while providing entrepreneurs with growth capital?"

"Exactly. The complexity reflects the different risk profiles and return expectations of entrepreneurs versus institutional investors."

The investment negotiation took four months, longer than any transaction we'd previously attempted. Valuation discussions, board seat allocations, management incentive pools, and milestone-based funding tranches that required legal and financial expertise we'd never needed before.

"This feels like learning corporate finance while negotiating it," I told Mohit during one of our term sheet discussions.

"Most venture capital transactions involve entrepreneurs learning institutional investment practices during deal execution," he replied. "The learning curve is steep, but the knowledge becomes valuable for future fundraising and strategic decision-making."

The final investment structure provided ₹25 crores for 18% equity (slightly better than our initial proposal), with Sequoia receiving two board seats and various protective provisions that limited our operational autonomy in exchange for their financial and strategic support.

"The investment terms are more restrictive than I expected," Priya observed after signing the final documents. "But the strategic support could be worth more than the restrictions cost us."

"How do we measure the value of strategic support versus the cost of operational restrictions?" I asked.

"By tracking whether Sequoia's guidance and connections generate business opportunities that exceed what we could achieve independently."

The post-investment experience was more intensive than traditional financing relationships. Monthly board meetings, quarterly strategic reviews, and ongoing operational guidance that felt like having experienced business partners rather than just financial investors.

"Sequoia's involvement is different from other financing relationships," Dr. Singh observed after our first quarterly board meeting. "They're asking strategic questions that force us to think more systematically about long-term business development."

"What strategic questions specifically?" I asked.

"Market expansion priorities, competitive positioning, technology investment decisions, and organizational development plans. Questions that require us to articulate business strategy rather than just operational execution."

Six months after closing the Sequoia investment, the benefits were becoming measurable. Introductions to potential international partners, strategic advice on biotechnology market entry, and operational guidance that accelerated our decision-making processes.

"The Sequoia relationship provides access to expertise and networks that we couldn't develop independently," I told our management team during a review meeting. "Their portfolio companies' experiences help us avoid mistakes and identify opportunities."

"And the board involvement forces more disciplined strategic planning than we maintained when all decisions were internal," added Priya.

"Is the external oversight helpful or constraining?" asked Dr. Singh.

"Both. Helpful because it forces systematic thinking about major decisions. Constraining because some decisions require board approval that previously required only management consensus."

Twelve months after the Sequoia investment, our international expansion had accelerated significantly: export revenue increased 180%, biotechnology product development was progressing ahead of schedule, and we'd identified two additional acquisition opportunities.

"You know what venture capital taught us about institutional relationships?" I said to Mohit during our annual investor review. "The most valuable investors provide strategic capabilities rather than just financial capital."

"And accessing institutional capabilities often requires accepting institutional constraints that change how companies operate."

"The key insight was that venture capital success depends on alignment between investor capabilities and company needs rather than just valuation optimization."

Two years after the Sequoia investment, we were planning our next funding round to support biotechnology manufacturing facility development and international market expansion that would position us for eventual public offering.

The venture capital experience had transformed our understanding of growth financing from simple capital access to strategic partnership development that enabled opportunities unavailable through traditional funding sources.

IPO Preparations and Market Dynamics

The investment banker's valuation estimate made me question whether I'd heard him correctly.

"Based on comparable pharmaceutical companies and your financial performance, we're projecting an IPO valuation of ₹800-1,200 crores," said Rajesh Khanna from Kotak Investment Banking, reviewing the preliminary market analysis. "That would make this one of the larger pharmaceutical IPOs this year."

"₹800 crores?" I repeated, trying to process numbers that seemed disconnected from the ₹50,000 garage laboratory we'd started with fifteen years earlier.

"Your revenue growth trajectory, international market presence, and biotechnology capabilities justify premium valuations compared to traditional generic manufacturers," he explained. "Public market investors are paying premiums for pharmaceutical companies with diversified portfolios and growth potential."

This conversation took place in March 2008, eighteen months after our Sequoia investment, when we'd begun exploring public offering opportunities to fund our biotechnology manufacturing facility and international expansion plans.

"Why are pharmaceutical companies receiving premium valuations?" Priya asked during our IPO planning meeting.

"Global demand for generic pharmaceuticals, Indian companies' success in international markets, and investor interest in healthcare sector growth stories," Rajesh replied. "Plus your company's positioning in cardiovascular and biotechnology markets that investors consider high-growth categories."

"And public market valuations are higher than private market valuations?"

"Significantly higher for companies with your growth profile. Private investors focus on current cash flow, while public investors pay for future growth potential."

The IPO preparation process revealed the complexity of transforming a private company into a public company. Financial audits, legal compliance reviews, corporate governance restructuring, and operational documentation that required capabilities we'd never developed.

"Going public isn't just about raising capital," explained our new corporate attorney, who specialized in IPO transactions. "It's about restructuring your entire organization to meet public company regulatory requirements and investor expectations."

"What regulatory requirements specifically?" I asked.

"Quarterly financial reporting, audit committee governance, insider trading policies, investor relations capabilities, and operational transparency that private companies aren't required to maintain."

"How much time and expense does IPO preparation require?"

"Typically 12-18 months and ₹3-5 crores in professional fees for companies your size. The preparation costs are significant, but public company status provides access to capital markets that justify the investment."

The financial audit process was more intensive than anything we'd experienced with private investors. Three years of historical financial statements reviewed by Big Four accounting firms, with adjustments required to meet public company accounting standards.

"The accounting standards for public companies are more stringent than private company requirements," our audit manager explained during the process. "Revenue recognition, inventory valuation, and expense allocation must comply with strict regulatory guidelines."

"Are we currently compliant with public company accounting standards?" our CFO asked.

"Mostly compliant, but some adjustments needed for inventory accounting methods and revenue timing recognition. Nothing that affects your fundamental financial performance, but changes required for regulatory compliance."

The corporate governance restructuring required establishing independent board members, audit committees, and management compensation policies that met public company standards.

"Public companies must have majority independent boards and separate audit committees," our governance consultant explained. "This means recruiting experienced directors who aren't affiliated with management or major shareholders."

"How do we recruit independent directors?" I asked.

"Usually experienced executives from similar industries, retired executives from larger companies, or professional directors who serve on multiple boards."

"What compensation do independent directors expect?"

"Typically ₹2-5 lakhs annually plus equity compensation. Independent directors provide strategic guidance and regulatory compliance oversight that justifies their compensation."

The market timing analysis revealed that pharmaceutical IPOs were experiencing favorable conditions, but that window could close quickly if market sentiment changed.

"Indian pharmaceutical companies have performed well in public markets over the past two years," Rajesh noted during our timing discussion. "But IPO markets are cyclical, and current favorable conditions might not continue indefinitely."

"What factors could affect IPO market conditions?" Priya asked.

"Overall stock market performance, pharmaceutical sector sentiment, regulatory changes affecting generic drug markets, and global economic conditions."

"So IPO timing is partly strategic and partly opportunistic?"

"Exactly. You need to be prepared to move quickly when market conditions are favorable, which means completing all preparation before optimal timing windows open."

The roadshow preparation required developing investor presentation materials that could communicate our business strategy, competitive advantages, and growth potential to institutional investors in major financial centers.

"The roadshow involves presenting to 40-50 institutional investors across Mumbai, Delhi, Bangalore, and international locations," Rajesh explained. "Each presentation is 45-60 minutes followed by detailed Q&A sessions."

"What questions do institutional investors typically ask pharmaceutical companies?" I asked.

"Competitive positioning, regulatory risk management, product pipeline development, international expansion strategies, and financial projections for key growth initiatives."

"And we need to answer these questions convincingly enough to justify our valuation expectations?"

"Your answers need to demonstrate that management has systematic strategies for achieving projected growth rather than just optimistic projections."

The IPO market conditions changed unexpectedly in September 2008 when global financial markets experienced significant volatility that affected all public offering activity.

"The IPO window has essentially closed due to market conditions," Rajesh informed us during an emergency planning call. "No pharmaceutical companies are going public until market stability returns."

"How long might market instability continue?" I asked.

"Impossible to predict accurately. Could be 6-12 months, could be longer. IPO timing depends on factors beyond individual company control."

"So we continue IPO preparation while waiting for favorable market conditions?"

"Exactly. Maintain IPO readiness while exploring alternative financing options for growth capital needs."

The IPO delay led to exploring private funding alternatives: additional venture capital rounds, private equity partnerships, and strategic investor relationships that could provide capital without requiring public market conditions.

"The IPO preparation wasn't wasted even though we didn't complete the offering," our CFO observed during our strategic review. "The financial audits, governance improvements, and operational documentation strengthened our company regardless of financing source."

"And IPO readiness provides flexibility to access public markets quickly when conditions improve," added Priya.

"The key insight was that IPO preparation creates value beyond just accessing public capital markets."

Eighteen months later, when global market conditions stabilized, we were able to complete our public offering within six months because the preparation work had been completed during unfavorable market periods.

"You know what IPO preparation taught us about capital markets?" I said to Rajesh during our eventual offering celebration. "Public market access requires systematic preparation that can't be rushed when market timing becomes favorable."

"And preparation during unfavorable conditions often enables success when favorable conditions return."

The IPO experience had taught us that accessing public capital markets required transforming not just our financial reporting but our entire approach to corporate governance, operational transparency, and strategic communication.

More importantly, it had shown us that public company status provided access to growth capital and strategic flexibility that private company structures couldn't support, but at the cost of regulatory complexity and operational oversight that fundamentally changed how we managed our business.

Using Debt Strategically for Expansion

The loan officer's reaction to our borrowing request was exactly what I'd expected, which didn't make it any less frustrating.

"You want to borrow ₹50 crores when your company is already carrying ₹15 crores in existing debt?" asked Sunil Sharma from HDFC Corporate Banking, reviewing our credit application. "That would increase your debt-to-equity ratio to levels that exceed our standard lending guidelines."

"But our debt service coverage ratio is excellent, our cash flow is predictable, and we're using the loan proceeds for revenue-generating assets," I replied, pointing to our financial projections.

"Revenue-generating assets that haven't generated revenue yet," he countered. "Your biotechnology manufacturing facility is still under construction, and your international expansion plans are projections rather than confirmed contracts."

This conversation took place in January 2009, during the global financial crisis when banks had become significantly more conservative about business lending. We needed ₹50 crores to complete our biotechnology facility and fund working capital for international expansion, but traditional lending criteria weren't designed for companies using debt strategically rather than just operationally.

"Maybe we're approaching debt financing incorrectly," I told our CFO after the HDFC meeting. "Instead of asking for general expansion capital, maybe we should structure specific asset-backed loans that reduce lender risk."

"What would asset-backed loans look like for our business?" he asked.

"Equipment financing for biotechnology manufacturing equipment, export credit facilities secured by confirmed international orders, and working capital lines secured by accounts receivable."

"So we'd replace one large loan with multiple smaller loans, each secured by specific assets?"

"Multiple smaller loans that collectively provide the capital we need while reducing individual lender risk through asset-specific collateral."

The strategic debt approach required understanding different types of commercial lending and matching each financing need with appropriate loan structures.

"Equipment financing typically provides 70-80% of equipment value at favorable interest rates," explained our new banking relationship manager at Yes Bank. "Because the equipment serves as collateral, lenders can offer better terms than unsecured business loans."

"What about export credit facilities?" I asked.

"Export financing can provide up to 85% of confirmed export order value with interest rates 2-3% below standard business loan rates. The export receivables provide security that reduces lender risk."

"And working capital lines secured by accounts receivable?"

"Typically 60-70% of qualifying receivables at variable rates tied to prime lending rates. As receivables are collected, credit availability adjusts automatically."

The structured debt approach succeeded where traditional business lending had failed. Instead of seeking ₹50 crores in general expansion capital, we secured ₹35 crores through equipment financing, ₹10 crores through export credit facilities, and ₹8 crores through receivables financing.

"The total borrowing capacity is actually higher than our original loan request," our CFO observed after finalizing the financing arrangements. "And the weighted average interest rate is lower than what HDFC was offering for unsecured business lending."

"Why is structured debt financing more favorable than traditional business loans?" I asked.

"Because lenders prefer loans secured by specific assets rather than general corporate guarantees. Asset-backed lending provides recovery options if borrowers default."

The biotechnology equipment financing proved particularly advantageous because pharmaceutical manufacturing equipment maintains resale value that makes it attractive collateral for lenders.

"Biotechnology manufacturing equipment has international resale markets that provide liquidity for lenders," our equipment financing specialist explained.

"Unlike specialized machinery that's only valuable to specific industries, pharmaceutical equipment has broad market appeal."

"So equipment financing rates reflect the collateral value rather than just our creditworthiness?" Priya asked.

"Both factors matter, but collateral value reduces lender risk enough to justify favorable pricing compared to unsecured lending."

The export credit facility required developing relationships with specialized export financing institutions that understood international pharmaceutical markets better than traditional commercial banks.

"Export-Import Bank provides financing specifically designed for Indian companies expanding into international markets," explained their relationship manager. "Our lending criteria emphasize export potential rather than just current financial performance."

"How do export financing terms compare to traditional business lending?" I asked.

"Interest rates 200-300 basis points lower than commercial loans, longer repayment terms, and credit evaluation based on export market opportunities rather than just domestic business performance."

"What documentation do export credit facilities require?"

"Confirmed export orders, international customer creditworthiness analysis, foreign exchange risk management plans, and compliance with export regulations."

The working capital financing arrangement provided operational flexibility that fixed-term loans couldn't match. As our international sales grew, available credit increased automatically without requiring additional loan applications.

"The receivables financing line adjusts to our business growth," our CFO noted after six months of operation. "When export sales increase, working capital availability increases proportionally."

"And when sales decline?" I asked.

"Available credit decreases, but so does our working capital requirement. The financing structure matches our actual capital needs rather than providing fixed amounts regardless of business conditions."

The strategic debt utilization enabled expansion investments that equity financing alone couldn't have supported. Equipment financing accelerated our biotechnology facility completion, export financing enabled larger international orders, and working capital financing supported rapid sales growth.

"The debt financing strategy provided ₹53 crores in total capital at lower cost than equity financing would have required," our CFO reported during our annual board review.

"And debt financing preserved equity ownership that venture capital expansion would have diluted," added Priya.

"But debt financing also increased our financial leverage and repayment obligations regardless of business performance," I noted.

"True. Debt amplifies both returns and risks compared to equity financing."

Twelve months after implementing strategic debt financing, our expansion had proceeded ahead of schedule: biotechnology facility operational, international sales increased 240%, and working capital management optimized through receivables financing.

"The strategic debt approach taught us that different financing needs require different capital structures," I told our board during the annual review. "Equipment needs, working capital needs, and expansion capital needs each have optimal financing solutions."

"And optimal financing minimizes capital costs while preserving operational flexibility," our CFO added.

"The key insight was that debt becomes strategic when it's structured to match specific business requirements rather than just providing general capital."

The debt financing experience also influenced our long-term capital structure planning. Instead of minimizing debt to reduce financial risk, we started optimizing debt levels to maximize return on equity while maintaining manageable repayment obligations.

"You know what strategic debt financing taught us about capital management?" I said to Priya during our planning session. "Debt isn't just a source of capital—it's a tool for optimizing returns when used appropriately."

"And appropriate use means matching debt structures with asset types and cash flow patterns rather than just borrowing whatever banks will lend."

Two years after implementing strategic debt financing, we had established credit relationships that could support continued expansion while maintaining debt service coverage ratios that provided financial flexibility during challenging market conditions.

The lesson had become essential for competing with larger pharmaceutical companies that used sophisticated capital structures to optimize growth financing while preserving shareholder returns.

CFO Rajesh Khanna's Financial Innovations

The cash flow analysis that Rajesh presented during his first week made me realize how little I understood about our own financial operations.

"Your working capital cycle is 127 days," he announced, pointing to a spreadsheet that tracked money flow through our entire business process. "You're essentially providing free financing to customers for four months while paying suppliers within 30 days."

"Is 127 days good or bad?" I asked, though his expression suggested I already knew the answer.

"Pharmaceutical industry average is 85 days. Best-in-class companies achieve 60-65 days. Your working capital cycle is consuming ₹18 crores in unnecessary financing costs annually."

Rajesh had joined us as CFO in April 2009, recruited from Biocon where he'd implemented financial management systems that had supported their rapid international expansion. His background in pharmaceutical finance was exactly what we needed for our growth trajectory, but his assessment revealed inefficiencies that had been invisible to our previous financial management.

"How do we reduce the working capital cycle from 127 days to industry benchmarks?" Priya asked.

"Optimize accounts receivable collection, negotiate better payment terms with suppliers, and improve inventory turnover through better demand forecasting," Rajesh replied. "Each component requires different approaches, but the combined impact could free up ₹12-15 crores in working capital."

"And freed working capital can fund expansion without requiring additional borrowing?"

"Exactly. Working capital optimization generates internal financing that doesn't require interest payments or equity dilution."

The accounts receivable optimization began with analyzing customer payment patterns that revealed surprising variations in collection periods across different customer segments.

"Export customers pay within 45 days on average, domestic distributors pay within 65 days, but hospital customers average 95 days," Rajesh reported after his analysis. "The payment variations suggest different credit management approaches for different customer types."

"What causes hospital customers to pay so slowly?" I asked.

"Government procurement processes, budget approval delays, and administrative inefficiencies that are built into their payment systems rather than reflecting creditworthiness problems."

"So we can't speed up hospital payments through better collection procedures?"

"We can't change their payment processes, but we can adjust our pricing and credit terms to compensate for extended payment periods."

The hospital customer repricing involved implementing early payment discounts and extending payment terms with interest charges that reflected the true cost of extended credit.

"Instead of offering standard 60-day payment terms to all customers, we're offering 2% discounts for 30-day payments and 1.5% monthly interest for payments beyond 60 days," Rajesh explained to our sales team.

"Won't interest charges on late payments upset customers?" asked our sales manager.

"Interest charges that reflect our cost of capital are business standard rather than punitive measures. Most sophisticated customers understand that extended credit has financial costs."

The supplier payment optimization required negotiating extended payment terms that matched our customer collection cycles without damaging supplier relationships.

"We're requesting 60-day payment terms from major suppliers in exchange for volume commitments and prompt payment within agreed periods," Rajesh told our procurement team.

"Will suppliers accept extended payment terms?" I asked.

"Large suppliers often prefer predictable payment schedules over faster payments with uncertain timing. Extended terms with guaranteed payment dates can be more valuable than shorter terms with variable payment timing."

The inventory optimization proved more complex because pharmaceutical inventory management involves regulatory compliance, expiration dates, and quality control requirements that pure financial optimization couldn't address.

"Pharmaceutical inventory optimization requires balancing financial efficiency with regulatory compliance," Rajesh observed during our inventory analysis. "We can't just minimize inventory levels without considering quality control and customer service requirements."

"What inventory optimization approaches work for pharmaceutical companies?" Dr. Singh asked.

"Better demand forecasting, supplier consolidation, automated reorder systems, and inventory categorization based on turnover rates and margin contributions."

The demand forecasting system that Rajesh implemented reduced inventory levels by 22% while improving customer service through better stock availability of high-turnover products.

"Statistical forecasting based on historical sales patterns and seasonal trends enables more accurate inventory planning than intuitive ordering," he explained during our quarterly review.

"How does better forecasting reduce inventory levels while improving customer service?" I asked.

"By carrying optimal quantities of fast-moving products while reducing slow-moving inventory that ties up working capital without generating sales."

The financial innovations extended beyond working capital optimization to more sophisticated cash management techniques that maximized returns on temporary surplus funds.

"We're implementing treasury management systems that optimize interest income on cash balances while maintaining operational liquidity," Rajesh announced during a management meeting.

"What does treasury management involve?" Priya asked.

"Automated cash sweeping to high-yield accounts, short-term investment vehicles for temporary surpluses, and foreign exchange hedging for international transactions."

The foreign exchange hedging proved particularly valuable as our export revenue grew, protecting us from currency fluctuations that could affect profitability unpredictably.

"Currency hedging reduces volatility in our international revenue," Rajesh explained after implementing the program. "We're locking in exchange rates for confirmed export orders to eliminate foreign exchange risk from our profit projections."

"Does hedging cost money?" I asked.

"Hedging costs are typically 0.5-1% of transaction value, but they eliminate potential losses of 5-10% from adverse currency movements."

Rajesh also implemented performance measurement systems that provided insights into business unit profitability, customer profitability, and product line economics that had been invisible under our previous financial reporting.

"Product-level profitability analysis shows that cardiovascular products generate 34% gross margins while basic generics generate only 18% margins," he reported during our strategic planning session.

"Should we discontinue low-margin products?" I asked.

"Not necessarily. Low-margin products might provide strategic value through customer relationships, market presence, or production capacity utilization that justifies their continuation despite lower profitability."

"How do we evaluate strategic value versus financial returns?"

"Through integrated analysis that considers customer lifetime value, competitive positioning, and operational efficiency rather than just individual product margins."

Eighteen months after Rajesh joined, our financial management had transformed from basic accounting to sophisticated business analytics that informed strategic decision-making across all aspects of our operations.

"The financial innovations have generated measurable business improvements," I told our board during the annual review. "Working capital cycle reduced to 89 days, treasury income increased 180%, and business unit profitability visibility enables better resource allocation decisions."

"And the financial sophistication supports more complex business strategies like international expansion and acquisition financing," added Priya.

"The key insight was that financial management innovations create competitive advantages beyond just cost savings."

Two years after implementing Rajesh's financial innovations, we had established financial capabilities that enabled growth strategies and transaction execution that would have been impossible with our previous financial management approaches.

"You know what financial innovations taught us about business development?" I said to Rajesh during his performance review. "Sophisticated financial management creates strategic options rather than just improving operational efficiency."

"And strategic options become competitive advantages when companies can pursue opportunities that less financially sophisticated competitors can't access or afford."

The lesson had become essential for competing with larger pharmaceutical companies that used advanced financial management as a tool for optimizing growth while maintaining operational flexibility.

PART III: THE GROWTH CONSTRAINT (2006-2010)

Chapter 11: The First Acquisition

Chapter 12: The Export Imperative

Chapter 13: The API Backward Integration

Chapter 14: The Innovation Inflection

Chapter 15: The Biosimilar Bet

Part III

The Growth Constraint (2006-2010)

When Success Creates its Own Ceiling

The board meeting in December 2008 lasted four hours and ended with a question that none of us could answer satisfactorily.

"We've achieved everything we set out to accomplish," said Dr. Kumar, our advisory board member, reviewing our performance metrics. "Revenue of ₹285 crores, international presence in twelve countries, WHO-GMP certified facilities, strong market positions in cardiovascular and pain management segments. So why does growth feel more difficult now than it did five years ago?"

The numbers supported his observation. Our revenue growth rate had declined from 80% annually in 2003-2005 to 35% annually in 2006-2008, despite having more resources, better systems, and larger market opportunities than ever before.

"Maybe 35% annual growth is actually excellent performance for a company our size," suggested Priya, though her tone indicated she wasn't convinced by her own argument.

"Or maybe we've reached the limits of our current business model and need to evolve our approach to growth," I replied, studying charts that showed our growth trajectory flattening despite continued market expansion.

This conversation marked our introduction to what would become the defining challenge of 2006-2010: the growth constraint that emerges when companies become too large for entrepreneurial methods but too small for corporate methods.

"The growth constraint is different from previous constraints we've encountered," I told our management team during our strategic planning session. "Working capital constraints could be solved with better financing.

Scale constraints could be solved with operational improvements. But growth constraints require fundamental changes to how we think about business development."

"What's fundamentally different about growth constraints?" asked Dr. Singh.

"Previous constraints were external limitations that prevented us from executing strategies we knew how to implement. Growth constraints are internal limitations created by our own success that require capabilities we haven't developed yet."

The analysis revealed multiple factors contributing to our growth deceleration: market share saturation in our core segments, increased competition from larger pharmaceutical companies, regulatory complexity that slowed new product development, and organizational challenges that emerged at larger scale.

"We're encountering the law of large numbers," observed Rajesh during our financial review. "When your base revenue is ₹50 crores, adding ₹40 crores represents 80% growth. When your base revenue is ₹285 crores, adding ₹40 crores represents only 14% growth."

"So maintaining high growth rates requires finding larger opportunities or achieving higher success rates with existing opportunities," Priya noted.

"Both of which become more difficult as companies grow larger and markets become more competitive."

The market saturation analysis showed that we'd achieved dominant positions in several therapeutic segments, but that further growth within those segments required competing directly against multinational corporations with substantially larger resources.

"In cardiovascular generics, we have 18% market share in sustained-release formulations," reported our business development team. "Additional market share would require displacing Pfizer, Novartis, or Dr. Reddy's, all of whom have larger sales forces and marketing budgets."

"What about expanding into new therapeutic areas?" I asked.

"New therapeutic areas require 2-3 years for product development, regulatory approval, and market establishment. Growth from new segments won't materialize until 2011-2012."

"And maintaining current growth rates requires immediate growth opportunities rather than medium-term development projects."

The competitive intensity analysis revealed that our early market advantages—flexibility, quality, service—had been matched or exceeded by larger competitors who'd adopted similar strategies while maintaining their scale advantages.

"Cipla now offers delivery flexibility comparable to ours," noted our sales manager. "Lupin has implemented quality systems that match our standards. Dr. Reddy's provides customer service that equals our responsiveness."

"So our differentiation advantages have been commoditized by competitive responses?" Dr. Singh asked.

"Not commoditized, but neutralized. We still provide excellent service, but excellent service is no longer a sustainable competitive advantage when everyone provides excellent service."

The organizational complexity challenge had emerged gradually as we'd grown from 45 employees to 180 employees. Decision-making processes that had worked efficiently at smaller scale had become bottlenecks at larger scale.

"Simple decisions now require coordination across multiple departments and approval from several managers," observed our production coordinator. "What used to take days now takes weeks."

"And slower decision-making reduces our responsiveness advantage that historically enabled us to compete against larger companies," I realized.

"So growth has created organizational constraints that limit the very capabilities that enabled our growth."

The regulatory complexity had also increased substantially as we'd expanded into international markets and biotechnology products. Compliance requirements that had been manageable for a domestic generic manufacturer had become resource-intensive for an international pharmaceutical company.

"We now maintain regulatory compliance in twelve countries, each with different requirements for product registration, quality standards, and ongoing reporting," reported Dr. Patel. "Regulatory affairs has grown from one person to eight people, but regulatory complexity continues growing faster than our compliance capabilities."

"And regulatory delays are extending product development timelines from 12 months to 24-30 months, which affects our ability to respond quickly to market opportunities."

The financial complexity had multiplied with our expansion into venture capital, debt financing, international operations, and acquisition activities. Financial management that had once required basic accounting now demanded sophisticated treasury management, foreign exchange hedging, and capital structure optimization.

"Managing working capital across twelve countries with six different currencies requires financial capabilities that didn't exist when we operated domestically," Rajesh noted. "Financial complexity grows exponentially with international expansion."

The stories in the following chapters chronicle our systematic approach to overcoming growth constraints through business model evolution, organizational transformation, and strategic capability development that enabled continued expansion despite increasing complexity.

"The growth constraint taught us something fundamental about business development," I would reflect years later. "Companies don't fail because they can't grow—they fail because they can't manage the complexity that growth creates."

The solutions we developed during this period—systematic innovation processes, organizational scalability systems, and strategic partnership models—would become the foundation for our eventual expansion into biotechnology manufacturing and global market leadership.

But first, we had to learn how to grow systematically rather than just opportunistically, and how to build organizational capabilities that could support complexity rather than being overwhelmed by it.

"You know what's ironic about the growth constraint?" Priya observed during one of our planning sessions. "The capabilities that enable initial growth often become obstacles to continued growth."

"And overcoming growth constraints requires changing successful methods rather than just improving them."

"Which is psychologically more difficult than solving external constraints because it requires admitting that approaches that worked previously might be inadequate for current challenges."

The growth constraint would force us to evolve from successful entrepreneurs managing a growing company to business leaders building sustainable competitive advantages in complex global markets.

The transition would prove more challenging than anything we'd encountered during our startup and scaling phases, but also more valuable for creating long-term business success.

Chapter 11

The First Acquisition

Learning to Buy Growth

The phone call from Dr. Sanjay Mehta came at 7 AM on a Wednesday, which should have warned me that his business proposal wouldn't be routine.

"My board has decided to sell Apex Pharmaceuticals," he said without preamble. "We're looking for a buyer who can maintain our employee base and customer relationships while providing the capital we need for facility upgrades."

"Why are you selling?" I asked, reaching for coffee and trying to process the implications of his call.

"Cash flow problems. We've grown revenue from ₹15 crores to ₹55 crores over the past three years, but working capital requirements have grown faster than our ability to finance them."

"What products do you manufacture?"

"Primarily dermatology and anti-infective generics. Twelve products with established market presence, but we're operating at 45% capacity because we can't afford raw materials for full production."

This conversation happened in March 2007, eighteen months after we'd begun exploring acquisition opportunities as alternatives to organic growth. Apex Pharmaceuticals represented exactly the type of target we'd been seeking: established products, proven customers, operational challenges that we could solve through better management.

"What price are you seeking for the company?" I asked.

"₹35 crores for 100% ownership, including all assets, customer relationships, and regulatory approvals."

"And you're confident that working capital problems are the only issues affecting profitability?"

"Working capital is the primary constraint. We have purchase orders for ₹18 crores that we can't fulfill because we lack financing for raw material procurement."

The initial assessment suggested that Apex represented a compelling acquisition opportunity: revenue of ₹55 crores at a purchase price of ₹35 crores, established market presence in therapeutic areas we didn't currently serve, and operational problems that appeared solvable through better financial management.

"This could be our first acquisition," I told Priya after the call with Dr. Mehta. "The financial structure seems favorable, and the strategic fit could accelerate our growth in new therapeutic segments."

"What do we actually know about executing acquisitions?" she asked. "We've discussed acquisition strategy, but we've never actually bought a company."

"We know enough to recognize that we need professional help for due diligence, legal documentation, and integration planning."

"How much would professional acquisition support cost?"

"Probably ₹3-5 lakhs for legal and financial due diligence. But the cost of making acquisition mistakes would be much higher than the cost of professional guidance."

The due diligence process introduced us to the complexity of evaluating another company's business operations, financial condition, and strategic value. Financial audits, legal compliance reviews, customer interviews, and operational assessments that revealed aspects of pharmaceutical business that we'd never examined systematically.

"Due diligence is essentially risk assessment disguised as business analysis," observed our attorney during the process. "We're identifying potential problems that could affect acquisition value or integration success."

"What types of problems should we be most concerned about?" I asked.

"Customer concentration risk, regulatory compliance issues, hidden liabilities, key employee dependencies, and operational inefficiencies that can't be easily corrected."

The Apex due diligence revealed both opportunities and concerns. Their customer base was more diversified than ours, their regulatory compliance was excellent, and their operational inefficiencies appeared correctable through better inventory management and supplier relationships.

However, due diligence also revealed that 40% of their revenue came from three large customers, their manufacturing equipment needed significant maintenance, and two key employees were considering leaving due to company financial instability.

"The customer concentration creates risk if major customers reduce orders," our CFO noted during the evaluation review. "But it also creates opportunity if we can strengthen relationships with those customers through improved service."

"What about the equipment maintenance requirements?" Dr. Singh asked.

"Approximately ₹8 lakhs in immediate maintenance plus ₹15 lakhs in equipment upgrades over the next eighteen months. The capital requirements are manageable if the revenue projections are accurate."

"And the key employee retention issues?"

"Probably solvable through improved compensation and career development opportunities. Employee departures are often reactions to company instability rather than fundamental job dissatisfaction."

The acquisition negotiation required learning transaction structuring techniques that we'd never used: earnout provisions, working capital adjustments, indemnification clauses, and closing conditions that protected both buyer and seller interests.

"Acquisition agreements are essentially risk allocation contracts," our attorney explained during the negotiation process. "Every provision determines who bears responsibility for different types of post-closing problems."

"What risks are we most concerned about?" I asked.

"Unknown liabilities, customer defections, regulatory problems, and integration challenges that could affect the acquired company's performance."

"How do earnout provisions protect against these risks?"

"Earnout payments are contingent on achieving specific performance targets, so sellers share the risk if acquisition benefits don't materialize as projected."

The final acquisition structure included ₹25 crores cash at closing, ₹5 crores in seller financing over two years, and ₹5 crores in earnout payments based on revenue retention and profitability improvement targets.

"The structure reduces our cash requirement while aligning seller incentives with integration success," our CFO explained to our board. "If Apex performs as projected, Dr. Mehta receives full consideration. If integration problems emerge, our financial exposure is limited."

The acquisition closed in August 2007 after five months of due diligence, negotiation, and regulatory approval. The transaction was more complex than any business deal we'd previously completed, but also more strategic than incremental growth opportunities.

"The acquisition immediately added ₹55 crores to our revenue base and provided entry into dermatology markets that would have taken 2-3 years to develop organically," I told our board during the post-closing review.

"What integration challenges are we encountering?" asked Dr. Kumar.

"Mainly systems integration and cultural alignment. Apex employees are adjusting to our quality procedures, and we're learning to manage a more geographically distributed operation."

"Are the integration challenges affecting business performance?"

"Some temporary inefficiencies, but customer retention has been excellent and production efficiency is improving as systems integration progresses."

Six months after the acquisition, the results exceeded our projections. Apex revenue increased 12% through improved customer service, manufacturing costs decreased 18% through better supplier relationships, and combined company revenues reached ₹340 crores annually.

"The first acquisition taught us that buying growth can be more efficient than building growth when targets have established market positions that would be expensive to replicate," I told our management team during the integration review.

"And successful acquisitions require systematic integration rather than just ownership transfer," added Dr. Singh.

"The key insight was that acquisition success depends on post-closing execution rather than just transaction structure."

Twelve months after the Apex acquisition, we had identified two additional acquisition targets and were developing systematic approaches to acquisition evaluation, integration planning, and performance monitoring.

"You know what the first acquisition taught us about growth strategy?" I said to Priya during our annual planning session. "Acquisitions enable growth acceleration when organic expansion would be too slow or expensive."

"And acquisition capabilities become competitive advantages when companies can systematically identify, evaluate, and integrate target companies."

The lesson would prove crucial as we expanded our acquisition program to include biotechnology companies and international market access opportunities that organic growth couldn't provide within acceptable timeframes.

More importantly, the first acquisition had taught us that buying growth required different capabilities than building growth, but could create value that justified the complexity when executed systematically.

Acquiring Smaller Biotech Firm BioGenesis

The biotechnology company looked nothing like a pharmaceutical manufacturer should look.

"This is our fermentation facility," said Dr. Neeraj Sharma, guiding us through BioGenesis Labs' production area, which resembled a cross between a brewery and a chemistry laboratory. "We culture genetically modified bacteria to produce recombinant insulin precursors."

"How is this different from traditional pharmaceutical manufacturing?" I asked, studying equipment that seemed designed for growing living organisms rather than synthesizing chemical compounds.

"Traditional pharmaceuticals are manufactured through chemical synthesis. Biotechnology products are manufactured through biological processes using living cells as production factories."

This facility tour took place in September 2008, six months after we'd begun exploring biotechnology acquisition opportunities. BioGenesis represented our potential entry into biological drug manufacturing, a market segment that commanded premium pricing but required completely different technical capabilities than generic drug production.

"What's your current production capacity?" Dr. Singh asked, examining fermentation tanks that looked more sophisticated than anything in our tablet manufacturing facility.

"We can produce 2,000 liters of fermentation broth monthly, which yields approximately 150 kilograms of purified insulin precursor," Dr. Sharma replied.

"And what's the market value of 150 kilograms of insulin precursor?"

"About ₹45 lakhs monthly, depending on purity specifications and customer contracts."

The economics were compelling but unfamiliar. BioGenesis generated ₹5.4 crores annually from a single product, compared to our ₹340 crores from dozens of products. Their gross margins exceeded 60%, compared to our 35% margins on generic pharmaceuticals.

"Why are biotechnology margins so much higher than traditional pharmaceutical margins?" Priya asked during our evaluation meeting.

"Technical barriers to entry," Dr. Sharma explained. "Biotechnology manufacturing requires specialized knowledge, expensive equipment, and regulatory approvals that few companies can obtain cost-effectively."

"So biotechnology represents premium market positioning rather than commodity competition?"

"Exactly. Biotechnology companies compete on technical capabilities rather than just pricing."

The due diligence process for BioGenesis was more complex than our previous acquisition because biotechnology operations involved intellectual property, regulatory requirements, and technical risks that didn't exist in traditional pharmaceutical manufacturing.

"Biotechnology due diligence requires evaluating scientific validity, patent protection, regulatory compliance, and technology transfer capabilities," our attorney explained during the process. "The technical risks are different from traditional pharmaceutical acquisitions."

"What technical risks specifically?" I asked.

"Production process failures, contamination problems, regulatory changes affecting biotechnology approvals, and intellectual property disputes with larger biotechnology companies."

"How do we evaluate technical risks that we don't have expertise to assess independently?"

"Through technical consultants who specialize in biotechnology operations and intellectual property attorneys who understand biotechnology patent issues."

The technical due diligence revealed that BioGenesis had developed proprietary fermentation processes for insulin precursor production, but they were operating at laboratory scale rather than commercial scale.

"Their fermentation technology works reliably for current production volumes," reported our biotechnology consultant. "But scaling to commercial volumes would require process optimization and additional equipment that could cost ₹8-12 crores."

"Are the scaling challenges solvable with available technology?" Dr. Singh asked.

"Probably, but scaling biotechnology processes involves more uncertainty than scaling traditional pharmaceutical processes. Living organisms don't always behave predictably when production conditions change."

"So biotechnology acquisitions involve technical risks that traditional pharmaceutical acquisitions don't have?"

"Yes, but they also provide market opportunities that traditional pharmaceuticals can't access."

The intellectual property evaluation revealed that BioGenesis owned patents for specific fermentation processes, but those patents didn't prevent competitors from developing alternative production methods.

"Patent protection in biotechnology is often narrower than in traditional pharmaceuticals," our IP attorney explained. "Patents protect specific processes rather than final products, so competitors can potentially circumvent patents through alternative production methods."

"Does limited patent protection reduce the acquisition value?" I asked.

"It reduces the duration of competitive advantages, but first-mover advantages and technical expertise can provide market protection even after patents expire."

The acquisition negotiation was complicated by BioGenesis's founder wanting to retain involvement in the company rather than complete exit.

"Dr. Sharma wants to continue as technical director while selling majority ownership," our attorney noted during the negotiation. "This creates governance complexities that traditional acquisitions don't involve."

"What governance complexities?" Priya asked.

"Decision-making authority, compensation structures, non-compete agreements, and succession planning for technical leadership."

"Why does Dr. Sharma want to remain involved instead of selling completely?"

"Because biotechnology companies depend heavily on founder expertise that's difficult to transfer quickly. Maintaining founder involvement often increases acquisition success probability."

The final acquisition structure provided ₹18 crores for 75% ownership of BioGenesis, with Dr. Sharma retaining 25% ownership and continuing as technical director under a five-year employment agreement.

"The structure provides us with majority control while preserving the technical expertise that creates BioGenesis's value," our CFO explained to our board.

"And Dr. Sharma's continued ownership aligns his interests with our growth objectives for the biotechnology business."

The BioGenesis integration proved more challenging than our previous acquisition because biotechnology operations required regulatory approvals, quality systems, and technical knowledge that our existing team didn't possess.

"Biotechnology manufacturing regulations are different from traditional pharmaceutical regulations," Dr. Patel discovered during the integration process. "We need separate quality systems, different analytical testing, and additional regulatory compliance capabilities."

"How long will developing biotechnology compliance capabilities take?" I asked.

"Probably 12-18 months for complete integration, plus ongoing investment in technical training and specialized equipment."

"And the integration costs?"

"Approximately ₹15 crores for facility upgrades, equipment purchases, and systems integration over the next two years."

Six months after the BioGenesis acquisition, the challenges were substantial but the opportunities were becoming clearer. Biotechnology customers valued technical capabilities and quality consistency more than price competition.

"Biotechnology customers are willing to pay premium prices for suppliers who can guarantee product quality and delivery reliability," Dr. Sharma observed during our quarterly review.

"How different are biotechnology customer relationships from traditional pharmaceutical relationships?" I asked.

"Biotechnology customers often prefer long-term partnerships with trusted suppliers rather than competitive bidding for individual orders. Technical relationships become more important than commercial relationships."

Twelve months after the acquisition, BioGenesis had achieved production scale improvements that increased output 40% while maintaining quality standards that enabled premium pricing.

"The biotechnology acquisition taught us that technical acquisitions require different integration approaches than commercial acquisitions," I told our management team during the annual review.

"And biotechnology markets reward technical excellence rather than operational efficiency," added Dr. Singh.

"The key insight was that biotechnology acquisitions provide access to premium market segments that generic pharmaceutical acquisitions can't reach."

Two years after acquiring BioGenesis, we had expanded their product portfolio to include three additional biotechnology products and were generating ₹25 crores annually from biotechnology operations.

"You know what the biotechnology acquisition taught us about portfolio diversification?" I said to Priya during our strategic planning session. "Premium market segments require different capabilities than volume market segments, but they provide better financial returns that justify the additional complexity."

"And biotechnology capabilities become competitive advantages that traditional pharmaceutical competitors can't easily replicate."

The BioGenesis acquisition had provided our entry into biotechnology markets that would become increasingly important as healthcare systems worldwide shifted toward biological therapies for complex medical conditions.

Integration Challenges and Cultural Conflicts

The email from Dr. Neeraj Sharma arrived at 11 PM on a Friday, which should have warned me that our BioGenesis integration wasn't proceeding as smoothly as our quarterly reports suggested.

"Our fermentation batch failed quality control for the third time this month," he wrote. "The contamination occurred during shift changeover when your production team didn't follow our sterile transfer protocols. We need to discuss fundamental differences in quality culture before we lose our largest customer."

This message came six months after acquiring BioGenesis, when integration problems that had seemed manageable during due diligence were revealing themselves as fundamental conflicts between different approaches to pharmaceutical manufacturing.

"What specific quality culture differences are causing the contamination problems?" I asked Dr. Sharma during our emergency meeting the following Monday.

"Traditional pharmaceutical manufacturing focuses on chemical consistency," he explained. "Biotechnology manufacturing requires biological sterility. Your team approaches quality control as testing finished products. Our process requires maintaining sterile conditions throughout entire production cycles."

"Can't we train our production team to follow biotechnology quality procedures?" Dr. Singh asked.

"Training addresses knowledge gaps, but this is a culture gap. Your team views quality control as inspection activity. Biotechnology requires quality control as continuous prevention activity."

The contamination crisis exposed something uncomfortable about our acquisition strategy: we'd assumed that good manufacturing practices were transferable between different types of pharmaceutical production, but biotechnology manufacturing required fundamentally different thinking about quality management.

"The integration problems aren't just technical," I told Priya after reviewing the situation. "They're cultural conflicts between different ways of understanding pharmaceutical manufacturing."

"What do you mean by cultural conflicts?" she asked.

"BioGenesis employees think about living organisms that require careful nurturing. Our employees think about chemical processes that require precise control. Both approaches work for their respective applications, but they're incompatible when applied to the wrong manufacturing processes."

The quality control conflict was just the beginning. Over the following weeks, we discovered cultural differences in decision-making, customer relationships, regulatory compliance, and employee expectations that created friction throughout the integration process.

"BioGenesis operates with consensus decision-making where technical teams debate optimal approaches," observed our HR manager. "Your management style emphasizes efficient decision-making where managers make quick choices based on available information."

"Both approaches have advantages," I noted. "Consensus decision-making produces better technical solutions. Efficient decision-making enables faster responses to market opportunities."

"But mixing the approaches creates confusion about who makes decisions and what criteria they use."

The customer relationship conflicts emerged when our sales team applied traditional pharmaceutical sales approaches to biotechnology customers who expected different types of technical support.

"Biotechnology customers want detailed technical discussions about production processes, quality control procedures, and regulatory compliance," explained Dr. Sharma during a sales training session. "Your sales team focuses on pricing, delivery schedules, and order quantities."

"What's wrong with focusing on commercial terms?" asked our sales manager.

"Nothing's wrong for traditional pharmaceutical customers. But biotechnology customers buy technical capabilities rather than just products. They need to understand our production expertise before they're comfortable placing orders."

"So biotechnology sales requires technical knowledge that commercial sales doesn't require?"

"Biotechnology sales requires convincing customers that we understand their technical requirements better than alternative suppliers."

The regulatory compliance differences created even more complex integration challenges. BioGenesis operated under biotechnology regulations that required different documentation, testing procedures, and inspection preparations than traditional pharmaceutical regulations.

"We need separate quality management systems for biotechnology operations," Dr. Patel discovered during her regulatory compliance review. "Biotechnology regulations require batch documentation that traditional pharmaceutical systems don't capture."

"Can't we adapt our existing quality systems to include biotechnology requirements?" I asked.

"We could, but it would create unnecessary complexity for traditional pharmaceutical operations. Separate systems would be more efficient for both business segments."

"So successful integration requires maintaining operational separation rather than achieving operational integration?"

"For technical operations, yes. For administrative functions like finance and human resources, integration provides efficiency benefits."

The compensation structure conflicts proved particularly challenging because BioGenesis employees were accustomed to research-oriented reward systems while our employees operated under manufacturing-oriented incentive programs.

"BioGenesis employees expect recognition for technical innovation and problem-solving," our HR manager reported. "Your incentive systems reward production efficiency and cost reduction."

"Can't we implement both types of reward systems?" Priya asked.

"We can, but employees compare compensation across the organization. If biotechnology employees receive innovation bonuses that production employees don't get, it creates equity concerns."

"And if we extend innovation bonuses to production employees who aren't engaged in innovation activities?"

"Then we're paying for innovation that doesn't occur, which reduces the incentive effectiveness."

The timeline expectations created additional friction because biotechnology development operated on research timelines while our business operated on commercial timelines.

"BioGenesis projects require 18-24 months for process optimization and regulatory approval," Dr. Sharma explained during our project planning session. "Your business planning assumes 6-12 month development cycles for new products."

"Why do biotechnology projects take longer than traditional pharmaceutical projects?" I asked.

"Because biotechnology involves optimizing living organisms that don't always respond predictably to process changes. Traditional pharmaceutical projects involve optimizing chemical reactions that follow predictable patterns."

"So biotechnology requires different project management approaches than traditional pharmaceutical development?"

"Different approaches and different success metrics. Biotechnology success requires technical breakthroughs that can't be scheduled precisely."

Nine months after the BioGenesis acquisition, we'd learned to manage integration challenges by maintaining operational separation while achieving administrative integration.

"The integration taught us that cultural compatibility is more important than operational synergy for acquisition success," I told our board during the annual review.

"What do you mean by cultural compatibility?" asked Dr. Kumar.

"Shared values about quality, customer service, and employee development. When cultural values align, operational differences can be managed. When cultural values conflict, operational integration creates ongoing problems."

"And BioGenesis has cultural compatibility despite operational differences?"

"Yes. Both organizations prioritize quality excellence, customer satisfaction, and technical competence. The operational differences reflect industry requirements rather than cultural conflicts."

Twelve months after the acquisition, BioGenesis was generating 25% higher revenue while maintaining the technical culture that created its market value.

"You know what the integration challenges taught us about acquisition management?" I said to Dr. Singh during our quarterly review. "Successful integration requires preserving the cultural attributes that make acquired companies valuable while eliminating operational inefficiencies that reduce their performance."

"And preservation sometimes requires separation rather than integration."

"The key insight was that integration success depends on understanding which differences should be eliminated and which differences should be maintained."

The lesson would prove crucial for our subsequent acquisitions, where we learned to evaluate cultural fit as carefully as financial fit when assessing potential targets.

More importantly, the integration experience had taught us that acquisition value often comes from preserving what makes acquired companies unique rather than making them identical to the acquiring company.

Lessons from Failed Synergies

The cost reduction analysis that our CFO presented in March 2009 made acquisition synergies look like accounting fiction.

"We projected ₹8 crores in annual cost savings from combining Apex and BioGenesis operations," Rajesh announced during our post-acquisition review meeting. "Actual savings after eighteen months: ₹1.2 crores."

"What happened to the other ₹6.8 crores in projected savings?" I asked, studying charts that showed our synergy estimates had been optimistic by a factor of seven.

"Implementation costs were higher than projected, integration timelines were longer than expected, and several synergy assumptions proved incorrect when we attempted to execute them."

This conversation marked my introduction to one of the most expensive lessons in business development: synergies that look compelling in acquisition models often prove elusive in operational reality.

"Maybe we miscalculated the synergy potential," Priya suggested, reviewing our original acquisition justifications.

"Or maybe we misunderstood what synergy implementation actually requires," I replied, realizing that our acquisition planning had focused more on identifying synergies than on executing them.

The failed synergy analysis revealed multiple gaps between theoretical opportunity and practical execution. Shared services that seemed obviously beneficial in spreadsheets created operational complexity that reduced efficiency rather than improving it.

"We assumed that combining purchasing would reduce raw material costs through volume discounts," Rajesh explained, pointing to our largest projected synergy. "But Apex and BioGenesis use completely different suppliers for completely different materials."

"Why didn't due diligence identify this incompatibility?" Dr. Singh asked.

"Due diligence confirmed that both companies purchase raw materials and that volume purchasing typically reduces costs. But we didn't analyze whether their specific supply chains could actually be combined effectively."

"So the synergy assumption was theoretically valid but practically impossible?"

"Theoretically valid if both companies manufactured similar products using similar suppliers. Practically impossible given their actual supply chain structures."

The manufacturing consolidation synergy had failed even more spectacularly. We'd projected ₹2.5 crores in annual savings from consolidating production facilities, but consolidation attempts had increased costs rather than reducing them.

"Consolidating biotechnology production with traditional pharmaceutical production required duplicate quality systems, separate production scheduling, and specialized equipment that eliminated most efficiency gains," Dr. Singh reported.

"Why did consolidation increase costs instead of reducing them?" I asked.

"Because biotechnology manufacturing requires contamination prevention that traditional pharmaceutical manufacturing doesn't need. Maintaining adequate separation within shared facilities cost more than operating separate facilities."

"So manufacturing synergies depend on product compatibility rather than just facility optimization?"

"Manufacturing synergies work when products can share equipment, quality systems, and production processes. When products require different manufacturing approaches, consolidation creates inefficiency rather than synergy."

The administrative consolidation had produced modest savings, but less than projected because acquired companies' administrative systems weren't compatible with our existing systems.

"We saved ₹80 lakhs annually by consolidating accounting, human resources, and regulatory affairs," our HR manager reported. "But systems integration required ₹45 lakhs in one-time costs and 8 months of reduced efficiency during transition."

"So administrative synergies are achievable but expensive to implement?" Priya asked.

"Administrative synergies provide real savings once integration is complete, but integration costs and timeline disruptions reduce net benefits significantly."

The sales force consolidation had failed completely because Apex's dermatology customers and BioGenesis's biotechnology customers required completely different sales approaches.

"We projected ₹1.5 crores in sales force savings by cross-training representatives to sell all company products," our sales manager explained. "But dermatology customers want pricing and availability information while biotechnology customers want technical specifications and regulatory documentation."

"Can't sales representatives be trained to handle both types of customer requirements?" I asked.

"Training can provide product knowledge, but customer relationship building requires specialized expertise that takes years to develop. Cross-training reduced sales effectiveness rather than improving operational efficiency."

The marketing synergy had produced negative results because combining marketing budgets for different therapeutic areas confused market positioning rather than improving it.

"Marketing synergies assumed that brand recognition benefits would outweigh message dilution costs," Kavita reported during her integration assessment. "But customers in different therapeutic areas don't value the same company attributes."

"What do you mean by message dilution?" I asked.

"Dermatology customers value cost-effectiveness and product availability. Biotechnology customers value technical expertise and quality consistency. Marketing messages that try to address both audiences don't resonate strongly with either audience."

"So marketing synergies require customer similarity rather than just budget consolidation?"

"Marketing synergies work when acquired companies serve the same customers with complementary products. When acquired companies serve different customers, separate marketing approaches are more effective."

The R&D synergy had failed because research and development approaches for traditional pharmaceuticals and biotechnology were fundamentally incompatible.

"We projected R&D savings through shared development costs and cross-fertilization of technical knowledge," Dr. Sharma explained. "But traditional pharmaceutical development focuses on chemical optimization while biotechnology development focuses on biological process optimization."

"Can't R&D teams benefit from exposure to different technical approaches?" Dr. Singh asked.

"Technical knowledge sharing provides educational value, but it doesn't reduce development costs or accelerate development timelines. Different types of pharmaceutical development require different expertise and different equipment."

Eighteen months after our acquisitions, we'd learned that most projected synergies had been based on superficial similarities rather than operational compatibility.

"The synergy failures taught us that acquisition value comes from what acquired companies do well independently rather than what they can do better in combination," I told our board during the annual review.

"What do you mean by independent value versus combination value?" asked Dr. Kumar.

"Independent value comes from acquiring companies that are already profitable and growing. Combination value comes from operational improvements that integration enables."

"And combination value is harder to achieve than independent value?"

"Much harder, and much less predictable. Independent value is proven by historical performance. Combination value depends on successful execution of complex integration projects."

The failed synergy experience changed our approach to acquisition evaluation. Instead of projecting synergies that might be achievable, we started focusing on standalone value that was already demonstrated.

"Our revised acquisition criteria emphasize companies that are valuable without synergies rather than companies that could become valuable through synergies," I told our management team during strategic planning.

"And if synergies materialize during integration, they're beneficial but not required for acquisition success."

Two years after our synergy failures, we had developed more realistic approaches to acquisition evaluation and integration planning that focused on preserving acquired companies' existing strengths rather than creating new operational efficiencies.

"You know what failed synergies taught us about acquisition strategy?" I said to Rajesh during our annual planning session. "The most successful acquisitions are companies that don't need fixing rather than companies that could be improved through integration."

"And integration should enhance what acquired companies already do well rather than changing what they do fundamentally."

The lesson had become essential for evaluating future acquisition opportunities: pay for demonstrated value rather than theoretical synergies, and focus integration efforts on administrative efficiency rather than operational transformation.

More importantly, failed synergies had taught us that acquisition success depends more on buying good businesses than on improving mediocre businesses through integration.

Dr. Sarah Williams, M&A Specialist, Joins the Team

The interview with Dr. Sarah Williams lasted three hours and ended with her questioning whether we were ready for the kind of acquisition program she could implement.

"Your acquisition track record shows enthusiasm but limited systematic approach," she said, reviewing our Apex and BioGenesis transactions. "You've learned valuable lessons from integration challenges, but you're still approaching acquisitions reactively rather than strategically."

"What's the difference between reactive and strategic acquisition approaches?" I asked, though I suspected her answer would reveal gaps in our current methods.

"Reactive acquisitions respond to opportunities that become available. Strategic acquisitions create opportunities by systematically identifying targets that advance specific business objectives."

Dr. Williams had spent eight years in investment banking at Goldman Sachs before joining McKinsey's pharmaceutical practice, where she'd advised Fortune 500 companies on merger and acquisition strategies. Her resume represented exactly the expertise we needed for scaling our acquisition program, but her assessment suggested we weren't operating at the sophistication level that serious M&A required.

"Why are you interested in joining a mid-sized pharmaceutical company when you've worked with multinational corporations?" Priya asked during the interview.

"Because mid-sized companies can implement acquisition strategies more quickly than large corporations, and I want to build M&A capabilities rather than just advise on individual transactions," she replied.

"What M&A capabilities would you build for our company?"

"Target identification processes, valuation methodologies, due diligence frameworks, negotiation strategies, and integration planning that enables systematic acquisition execution rather than ad hoc deal-making."

"And systematic acquisition execution provides advantages over ad hoc approaches?"

"Systematic approaches reduce transaction costs, improve due diligence accuracy, accelerate integration timelines, and increase the probability of achieving projected acquisition benefits."

The salary negotiation with Dr. Williams required significant budget adjustments because M&A specialists command compensation packages that reflect their impact on large-scale transactions.

"Her base salary requirement is ₹35 lakhs annually plus performance bonuses tied to acquisition success," our CFO noted during the hiring approval meeting. "That's higher than any non-executive compensation in our company."

"But her expertise could enable acquisitions that generate hundreds of crores in additional revenue," I replied. "M&A specialist compensation should be evaluated based on transaction value creation rather than just salary comparisons."

"How do we measure transaction value creation?" asked our board chairman.

"Acquisition ROI, integration timeline acceleration, synergy realization rates, and strategic objective achievement. If Dr. Williams improves our acquisition success rate significantly, her compensation becomes a minor component of total transaction value."

Dr. Williams joined us in June 2009 and spent her first month conducting comprehensive analysis of our acquisition history, competitive landscape, and strategic growth objectives.

"Your previous acquisitions demonstrate deal execution capability but limited strategic framework," she reported during her initial assessment. "Apex provided geographic expansion, BioGenesis provided product diversification, but neither acquisition advanced a coherent market positioning strategy."

"What would a coherent market positioning strategy look like?" I asked.

"Systematic target identification based on specific criteria: therapeutic areas where you can achieve market leadership, geographic markets where you can establish dominant presence, or technology capabilities that create sustainable competitive advantages."

"So instead of evaluating individual acquisition opportunities, we should develop acquisition criteria that guide target selection?"

"Acquisition criteria that reflect strategic priorities rather than just financial opportunities. Financial opportunities exist constantly, but strategic opportunities that advance long-term competitive positioning are much rarer."

The target identification process that Dr. Williams implemented was more sophisticated than anything we'd attempted. Instead of waiting for companies to become available for sale, she started proactively identifying companies that matched our strategic criteria.

"We've identified 47 potential acquisition targets across three categories," she announced during our first strategic review. "Market expansion targets that provide geographic reach, product portfolio targets that complement existing capabilities, and technology targets that enable entry into high-growth segments."

"How did you identify these targets?" Dr. Singh asked.

"Industry databases, financial performance analysis, competitive intelligence, and relationship mapping with investment bankers who represent pharmaceutical companies."

"And these companies are all available for acquisition?"

"Not currently, but acquisition availability changes based on market conditions, ownership transitions, and strategic pressures. Maintaining target awareness enables quick response when acquisition windows open."

The valuation methodology that Dr. Williams introduced eliminated much of the guesswork that had characterized our previous acquisition pricing.

"Pharmaceutical company valuations depend on revenue multiples, EBITDA multiples, and asset-based valuations adjusted for therapeutic area, growth trajectory, and competitive positioning," she explained during our valuation training.

"How do these factors affect acquisition pricing?" I asked.

"High-growth therapeutic areas command premium multiples, established market positions justify higher valuations, and international presence adds valuation premiums for domestic buyers seeking geographic expansion."

"So acquisition pricing reflects strategic value rather than just financial performance?"

"Strategic value determines what buyers are willing to pay above financial value. Understanding strategic value enables better negotiation positioning and more accurate bid structuring."

The due diligence framework that Dr. Williams developed was more comprehensive than our previous approaches and specifically designed to identify integration risks before transactions closed.

"Due diligence should answer three questions," she explained to our acquisition team. "Does the target company perform as advertised? Can integration be accomplished within projected timelines and budgets? Will the combined company achieve strategic objectives that justify acquisition costs?"

"How is this different from our previous due diligence approaches?" our CFO asked.

"Previous due diligence focused on confirming financial information and identifying obvious problems. Strategic due diligence evaluates cultural fit, operational compatibility, and integration complexity that affect post-closing success."

The negotiation training that Dr. Williams provided transformed our approach to acquisition discussions from simple price negotiations to complex value optimization.

"Acquisition negotiations involve multiple variables beyond just purchase price," she explained during our training session. "Payment structure, earnout provisions, management retention, integration timelines, and operational autonomy all affect total transaction value."

"And optimizing multiple variables produces better outcomes than just negotiating price?"

"Better outcomes for both buyers and sellers. Complex structures can address different risk tolerances and return expectations more effectively than simple cash transactions."

Six months after Dr. Williams joined, our acquisition pipeline had expanded significantly: 12 active target evaluations, 3 preliminary discussions, and 1 letter of intent for a dermatology company that matched our strategic criteria perfectly.

"The systematic approach is generating better acquisition opportunities than reactive opportunity evaluation," I told our board during the quarterly review.

"How do you measure 'better' acquisition opportunities?" asked Dr. Kumar.

"Strategic fit with growth objectives, financial returns that exceed cost of capital, and integration complexity that matches our execution capabilities."

"And Dr. Williams' involvement improves all three factors?"

"Her target identification finds companies that advance strategic objectives, her valuation methods ensure reasonable pricing, and her integration planning reduces execution risks."

Twelve months after Dr. Williams joined, we had completed two additional acquisitions using her systematic approach, both of which achieved integration milestones ahead of schedule and generated returns that exceeded projections.

"You know what hiring an M&A specialist taught us about acquisition capabilities?" I said to Priya during our annual planning session. "Professional acquisition expertise enables strategic growth that ad hoc deal-making cannot achieve."

"And systematic acquisition approaches create competitive advantages by identifying opportunities that less organized acquirers miss."

"The key insight was that acquisition success depends more on process discipline than individual deal evaluation."

The lesson had become essential for competing with larger pharmaceutical companies that used sophisticated M&A capabilities to achieve growth that organic expansion couldn't provide within acceptable timeframes.

More importantly, Dr. Williams had taught us that acquisition capabilities could become core competencies that enabled strategic advantages rather than just tactical growth opportunities.

Chapter 12

The Export Imperative

When Domestic Success Hits Global Walls

The email from our largest domestic customer arrived on a Monday morning and contained exactly the kind of news that forces companies to reconsider their entire strategic direction.

"We're implementing a new procurement policy that caps supplier market share at 15% of our total purchases," wrote Mr. Agarwal from Med Distributors. "Your current share is 28% of our generic drug procurement, so we'll need to reduce orders accordingly."

"Why are they implementing market share caps?" I asked our sales manager, though I suspected the answer involved risk management rather than performance issues.

"They want to avoid dependence on single suppliers," he replied. "Several large distributors have adopted similar policies after supply chain disruptions affected their operations."

This conversation took place in August 2008, when our domestic market success had created an unexpected problem: we'd achieved such large market shares with key customers that they were actively seeking to reduce their dependence on us.

"Our domestic growth is being constrained by our own success," I told Priya during our emergency planning meeting. "We can't grow beyond certain market share thresholds without triggering customer risk management policies."

"So domestic market constraints are forcing us to pursue international expansion more aggressively than we'd planned," she observed.

"International expansion isn't just growth opportunity anymore—it's business necessity for maintaining overall growth rates."

The domestic market saturation analysis revealed that we'd reached natural limits in several therapeutic segments. Our cardiovascular market share was 22%, our pain management share was 19%, and our overall generic drug market presence was approaching levels where further growth would require displacing established competitors with larger resources.

"Domestic market expansion beyond current levels would require competing directly against Cipla, Dr. Reddy's, and Lupin," our market research consultant reported. "That competition would likely reduce margins while requiring marketing investments that exceed potential returns."

"What about expanding into new therapeutic areas domestically?" I asked.

"New therapeutic area development requires 2-3 years and significant investment, but market share gains would still be limited by competitive responses from existing players."

"So domestic growth constraints aren't temporary—they're structural limitations that require geographic diversification to overcome."

The international market opportunity analysis showed that global demand for Indian generic pharmaceuticals was growing rapidly, driven by healthcare cost pressures in developed markets and expanding healthcare access in developing markets.

"Global generic drug market is projected to grow 12% annually through 2015," our business development consultant explained. "Indian manufacturers have competitive advantages in cost structure and regulatory compliance that position them well for international expansion."

"What specific advantages do Indian pharmaceutical companies have internationally?" Dr. Singh asked.

"Manufacturing cost advantages of 40-60% compared to developed market producers, English-language regulatory capabilities that facilitate approvals in English-speaking markets, and WHO-GMP compliance that meets international quality standards."

"And what obstacles do Indian companies face in international markets?"

"Regulatory approval timelines, brand recognition limitations, distribution network development costs, and currency exchange rate risks."

The regulatory complexity of international expansion was more daunting than domestic growth challenges. Each country required separate product registrations, different quality standards, and ongoing compliance monitoring that multiplied our regulatory affairs workload.

"International expansion would require registering our products in 15-20 countries initially," Dr. Patel reported during our regulatory assessment. "Each registration requires 12-18 months and costs ₹5-8 lakhs per product per country."

"So international expansion requires ₹2-3 crores in regulatory investment before generating any revenue?" I asked.

"Plus ongoing compliance costs of ₹15-20 lakhs annually per country for maintaining registrations and meeting reporting requirements."

"But international market pricing justifies higher regulatory costs?'

"International pricing is typically 40-80% higher than domestic pricing, so regulatory costs can be recovered through premium pricing if market access is successful."

The distribution network challenge was equally complex. Unlike domestic expansion where we could leverage existing distributor relationships, international expansion required building new distribution partnerships in unfamiliar markets.

"International distribution requires understanding local market dynamics, regulatory requirements, and customer preferences that vary significantly across countries," explained our international business consultant.

"Can't we use the same distribution model internationally that works domestically?" Priya asked.

"Distribution models that work in India don't necessarily work in other markets. European customers expect different service levels than Indian customers. African markets have different payment terms and logistics requirements."

"So international expansion requires developing market-specific capabilities rather than just extending domestic capabilities?"

"Each geographic market requires customized approaches to distribution, customer service, and regulatory compliance."

The currency risk management added another layer of complexity that didn't exist in domestic operations. International sales would expose us to foreign exchange fluctuations that could affect profitability unpredictably.

"Currency hedging becomes essential for international operations," our CFO explained during the financial planning session. "Export revenues in foreign currencies create risk if exchange rates move unfavorably."

"How much do currency fluctuations typically affect pharmaceutical export profitability?" I asked.

"Currency movements of 10-15% annually are common, which can eliminate profit margins if not hedged properly."

"And hedging costs money?"

"Hedging costs 1-2% of transaction value, but currency losses can exceed 10% without hedging protection."

The international market entry strategy required choosing between multiple approaches: direct export sales, licensing agreements with local companies, joint ventures with international partners, or acquiring companies with established international presence.

"Each market entry approach involves different risk profiles and return potential," our strategy consultant explained. "Direct exports provide highest margins but require largest upfront investment. Licensing provides quickest market access but lowest returns."

"Which approach matches our capabilities and risk tolerance?" I asked.

"Probably a combination. Direct exports to markets where we can achieve regulatory approval efficiently, licensing in markets with complex regulatory requirements, and strategic partnerships in markets that require local manufacturing."

The international expansion planning took eight months and required capabilities we'd never developed: international regulatory affairs, foreign exchange management, cross-cultural marketing, and global supply chain coordination.

"International expansion is essentially building a different business within our existing business," I told our board during the expansion approval meeting. "The capabilities required for international success overlap with domestic capabilities but aren't identical."

"And the investment required?" asked our board chairman.

"₹12-15 crores over three years for regulatory approvals, distribution network development, and working capital. But international revenues could reach ₹150 crores annually if execution succeeds."

"So international expansion represents our largest investment and our largest growth opportunity simultaneously?"

"And our most essential strategic initiative for overcoming domestic growth constraints."

The international expansion program launched in January 2009 with initial focus on five countries: Kenya, Bangladesh, Sri Lanka, Nigeria, and Philippines. These markets offered regulatory environments that Indian companies could navigate successfully while providing substantial market opportunities.

"The target markets represent ₹35 crores in addressable annual opportunity for our current product portfolio," our international business manager reported during the launch meeting.

Six months after beginning international expansion, early results were encouraging: regulatory approvals in three countries, distribution agreements in four markets, and first international orders totaling ₹2.8 crores.

"International expansion is proceeding faster than projected," I told our management team during the quarterly review. "Early success validates our market selection and distribution strategies."

Eighteen months after launching international operations, export revenues had reached ₹25 crores annually and were growing 15% quarterly.

"You know what the export imperative taught us about business development?" I said to Priya during our annual planning session. "Domestic success creates constraints that can only be overcome through geographic diversification."

"And international expansion requires different capabilities than domestic growth, but provides access to opportunities that domestic markets can't support."

"The key insight was that export success requires systematic international business development rather than just extended domestic operations."

The lesson had become essential for pharmaceutical companies seeking sustained growth in increasingly competitive domestic markets where market share limitations required geographic expansion for continued revenue growth.

The First FDA Approval for US Market

The FDA approval letter arrived by courier at 3:47 PM on a Tuesday in September 2009, and I read it three times before believing that we'd actually received authorization to market generic atenolol tablets in the United States.

"Application Number ANDA 78-924 is approved," the letter stated in bureaucratic language that concealed the enormity of what had just happened. "Manufacturing facility inspections have been completed satisfactorily, and bioequivalence studies meet regulatory requirements for generic drug approval."

"This is it," I told Priya, holding the document that represented three years of regulatory preparation and ₹2.5 crores in filing costs. "We're officially approved to sell pharmaceuticals in the United States."

"How big is this achievement?" she asked, though her expression suggested she understood the significance.

"FDA approval means we can compete in the world's largest pharmaceutical market. US generic drug sales are $80 billion annually. Our approval opens access to opportunities that simply don't exist in other markets."

The FDA approval process had been more complex than any regulatory challenge we'd previously encountered. US drug regulations required bioequivalence studies, facility inspections, manufacturing compliance documentation, and ongoing reporting obligations that exceeded requirements for any other market.

"FDA approval is considered the gold standard for pharmaceutical manufacturing," Dr. Patel had explained when we'd begun the application process in 2006. "Companies that achieve FDA approval gain credibility that enables access to other regulated markets worldwide."

"Why is FDA approval more difficult than other regulatory approvals?" I'd asked.

"FDA standards are more stringent, inspection processes are more thorough, and ongoing compliance requirements are more demanding than other regulatory authorities."

"But FDA approval also provides access to higher pricing and larger market opportunities?"

"US pharmaceutical pricing is typically 300-500% higher than Indian domestic pricing. FDA approval justifies the investment required for meeting US regulatory standards."

The bioequivalence study requirement had been our first major challenge. FDA regulations required demonstrating that our generic atenolol tablets produced identical blood levels compared to the branded reference product.

"Bioequivalence studies for FDA approval cost ₹15-20 lakhs and require 24-36 healthy volunteers," our clinical research consultant had explained during the planning process.

"How is FDA bioequivalence different from other bioequivalence studies we've conducted?" Dr. Singh had asked.

"FDA protocols are more rigorous, statistical requirements are more stringent, and documentation standards are more comprehensive than other regulatory authorities."

"And if bioequivalence studies fail to meet FDA requirements?"

"The application is rejected, and we'd need to reformulate the product and repeat bioequivalence testing, which could cost another ₹15-20 lakhs and delay approval by 12-18 months."

The facility inspection process had required upgrading our manufacturing operations to meet FDA Good Manufacturing Practice standards that exceeded WHO-GMP requirements.

"FDA facility inspections evaluate manufacturing controls, quality systems, documentation practices, and personnel training with much greater scrutiny than other regulatory inspections," Dr. Patel had warned during our preparation.

"What specific upgrades would our facility need for FDA compliance?" I'd asked.

"Enhanced environmental monitoring, computerized batch documentation, validated analytical methods, and quality control procedures that exceed our current standards."

"How much would FDA compliance upgrades cost?"

"Approximately ₹8-10 lakhs for equipment and system modifications, plus ongoing costs for maintaining FDA documentation standards."

The FDA facility inspection had taken place over three days in March 2009, with two FDA investigators examining every aspect of our manufacturing operations with intensity that exceeded any previous regulatory inspection.

"The FDA inspectors are evaluating whether our manufacturing systems can consistently produce pharmaceuticals that meet US quality standards," Hans Mueller, our German equipment partner, had observed during the inspection. "They're not just checking current compliance—they're assessing systematic capability for ongoing compliance."

"What specific areas are they focusing on?" I'd asked.

"Batch documentation accuracy, equipment calibration procedures, personnel training records, and quality control data integrity."

"And if they identify compliance deficiencies?"

"FDA issues Form 483 observations that must be corrected before approval, or Warning Letters that can delay approval indefinitely."

The FDA inspection had resulted in three minor observations about documentation procedures that we'd corrected within 30 days, followed by six months of additional document review before final approval.

"The FDA approval timeline was exactly what we'd projected," Dr. Patel noted during our celebration meeting. "Thirty-six months from initial application to final approval, which is typical for first-time FDA applicants."

"Was the investment justified by the approval results?" our CFO asked.

"US market pricing for generic atenolol is $0.15 per tablet compared to ₹1.20 per tablet domestically. Even small US market share could generate substantial revenue."

The US market entry strategy required capabilities we'd never developed: US pharmaceutical distribution networks, FDA-compliant labeling and packaging, US customer relationship management, and ongoing FDA compliance monitoring.

"Entering the US market requires understanding distribution channels, pricing strategies, and competitive dynamics that are completely different from other markets," our international business consultant explained.

"Can't we use the same distribution approach in the US that works in other international markets?" I asked.

"US pharmaceutical distribution is dominated by three major companies: McKesson, AmerisourceBergen, and Cardinal Health. These distributors require different service levels, documentation, and relationship management than distributors in other markets."

"And US customers have different expectations than international customers?"

"US customers expect sophisticated supply chain management, comprehensive regulatory support, and premium customer service that reflects US market pricing levels."

The first US customer inquiry came two weeks after our FDA approval announcement, from a generic drug distributor in Texas interested in purchasing 100,000 tablets monthly.

"We can offer $0.12 per tablet for guaranteed monthly volumes of 100,000 tablets," the inquiry stated. "Payment terms are 30 days from delivery, with quality specifications that meet USP standards."

"This single customer order would generate ₹36 lakhs monthly," I calculated during our response planning. "That's equivalent to our entire domestic cardiovascular revenue from one US customer."

"And we're confident we can meet their quality and delivery requirements?" Priya asked.

"Quality requirements are identical to FDA approval specifications. Delivery requirements involve shipping logistics that we'll need to develop, but the volumes are manageable with our current production capacity."

The first US shipment took place in November 2009: 150,000 atenolol tablets packed according to FDA labeling requirements and shipped via international courier to Dallas, Texas.

"Our first US pharmaceutical shipment represents entry into the world's most competitive and most profitable pharmaceutical market," I told our team during the shipment ceremony.

Three months after our first US sales, we were shipping 400,000 tablets monthly to four US customers and generating ₹1.8 crores in quarterly US revenue.

"The US market entry exceeded our projections," I told our board during the quarterly review. "US revenues are growing 25% monthly, and we've received inquiries for three additional products."

"And US market success is enabling access to other regulated markets?"

"European regulatory authorities are more receptive to applications from FDA-approved manufacturers. Our FDA approval is accelerating regulatory approvals in UK, Germany, and Netherlands."

Twelve months after our FDA approval, US revenues had reached ₹15 crores annually and represented our highest-margin business segment.

"You know what FDA approval taught us about market access?" I said to Dr. Patel during our annual regulatory review. "Premium market access requires premium regulatory compliance, but premium markets justify premium investment."

"And FDA approval creates competitive advantages that extend beyond just US market access."

"The key insight was that regulatory excellence becomes a strategic differentiator that enables access to opportunities unavailable to less compliant competitors."

The FDA approval had become the foundation for our international expansion strategy, providing credibility and market access that transformed our competitive positioning in global pharmaceutical markets.

More importantly, it had taught us that systematic regulatory excellence could create sustainable competitive advantages in markets where regulatory barriers limit competition to companies willing to invest in compliance capabilities.

Establishing Manufacturing Facility in Brazil

The feasibility study for our Brazilian manufacturing facility contained a single statistic that made the investment decision obvious: import duties on pharmaceutical products were 18%, while locally manufactured products faced no tariffs.

"Brazilian pharmaceutical imports are essentially taxed at rates that make local manufacturing economically compelling," explained Carlos Mendoza, our Brazilian business consultant, during our São Paulo market assessment meeting. "Companies that manufacture locally can underprice imports by 15-20% while maintaining better margins."

"How large is the Brazilian pharmaceutical market?" I asked, reviewing economic data that showed consistent healthcare spending growth.

"₹150,000 crores annually and growing 8% per year. Brazil is the eighth-largest pharmaceutical market globally, with strong demand for generic drugs due to government healthcare programs."

This conversation took place in March 2010, eighteen months after our FDA approval had validated our international manufacturing capabilities. Brazil represented our most ambitious international expansion: establishing local manufacturing rather than just export sales.

"Why local manufacturing instead of expanding our export strategy?" Priya asked during our initial Brazil planning session.

"Export limitations include 18% import duties, 45-day shipping timelines, and currency exchange risks that make exports less competitive than local production," Carlos replied.

"And local manufacturing eliminates these competitive disadvantages?"

"Local manufacturing provides cost advantages, delivery flexibility, and currency stability that exports can't match. Plus Brazilian regulations increasingly favor locally manufactured pharmaceuticals for government procurement."

The regulatory complexity of establishing pharmaceutical manufacturing in Brazil exceeded anything we'd encountered in previous international expansion. Brazilian health authority ANVISA required separate facility approvals, product registrations, and ongoing compliance monitoring that involved Portuguese-language documentation and local regulatory representation.

"ANVISA pharmaceutical manufacturing approval requires 18-24 months and costs approximately $200,000 in fees and compliance preparation," our Brazilian regulatory consultant explained during the planning process.

"How do ANVISA requirements compare to FDA requirements?" Dr. Patel asked.

"Similar technical standards but different documentation procedures. ANVISA requires local quality control testing, Brazilian-trained quality managers, and Portuguese-language batch records."

"So we can't just transfer our FDA-approved processes directly to Brazil?"

"FDA approval provides credibility and technical framework, but Brazilian manufacturing requires adapting processes to meet ANVISA-specific requirements."

The facility location evaluation revealed that pharmaceutical manufacturing in Brazil required proximity to major markets, access to qualified personnel, and transportation infrastructure that could support national distribution.

"São Paulo state offers the best combination of market access, workforce availability, and logistics infrastructure," our site selection consultant reported after evaluating twelve potential locations.

"What specific advantages does São Paulo provide?" Dr. Singh asked.

"Forty percent of Brazilian pharmaceutical consumption, established pharmaceutical industry workforce, international airport for raw material imports, and highway access to all major Brazilian cities."

"And the costs of establishing operations in São Paulo?"

"Higher than other Brazilian locations but justified by market access and operational efficiency advantages."

The facility design required adapting our Indian manufacturing approaches to Brazilian regulatory requirements, labor practices, and local construction standards.

"Brazilian pharmaceutical facilities must meet ANVISA Good Manufacturing Practice standards plus local environmental, safety, and labor regulations," our Brazilian engineering consultant explained.

"How do Brazilian construction and operational requirements differ from Indian standards?" I asked.

"More stringent environmental controls, different electrical and plumbing specifications, and labor regulations that require specific employee facilities and safety procedures."

"And the total facility construction cost?"

"Approximately $2.5 million for a 15,000 square foot facility capable of producing 150 million tablets annually."

The staffing challenge involved recruiting qualified pharmaceutical personnel in a competitive Brazilian job market where established companies offered attractive compensation packages.

"Pharmaceutical manufacturing talent in São Paulo is limited and expensive," our Brazilian HR consultant reported during workforce planning. "Experienced quality control managers command salaries of $60,000-80,000 annually."

"How does Brazilian pharmaceutical workforce availability compare to India?" I asked.

"Smaller talent pool but higher average skill levels. Brazilian pharmaceutical employees typically have university education and industry experience that reduces training requirements."

"And we can recruit sufficient qualified personnel for our facility?"

"With competitive compensation packages and career development opportunities, yes. Brazilian pharmaceutical professionals are interested in working for growing international companies."

The local partnership strategy required identifying Brazilian partners who could provide market knowledge, regulatory expertise, and distribution network access that would accelerate our market entry.

"Local partnerships are essential for navigating Brazilian business culture, regulatory procedures, and customer relationships," Carlos advised during our partnership evaluation.

"What type of local partner would be most valuable?" I asked.

"Established pharmaceutical distributor with national reach, strong regulatory compliance record, and interest in representing international manufacturers."

"And partnership arrangements typically involve what commitments?"

"Exclusive distribution rights for specific products, minimum purchase commitments, and shared marketing investments."

The Brazilian facility construction began in August 2010 and required 14 months of permitting, construction, equipment installation, and regulatory approval before production could commence.

"Brazilian construction timelines are longer than Indian timelines due to more complex permitting procedures," our project manager reported during monthly progress reviews.

"What specific permitting challenges are causing delays?" Dr. Singh asked.

"Environmental impact assessments, municipal construction permits, utility connections, and ANVISA pre-approval inspections that require sequential completion."

"And we can't accelerate permitting through expedited procedures?"

"Brazilian regulatory processes don't offer expedited options for pharmaceutical facility approval. Thorough compliance review is mandatory regardless of timeline pressures."

The first Brazilian production run took place in October 2011: 50,000 atenolol tablets manufactured according to ANVISA specifications and Brazilian labeling requirements.

"Our first Brazilian-manufactured pharmaceuticals represent successful international manufacturing capability," I announced during the inaugural production ceremony attended by local government officials and business partners.

Six months after beginning Brazilian production, we were manufacturing 5 million tablets monthly and supplying three major Brazilian distributors with consistent delivery performance.

"Brazilian manufacturing operations exceeded startup projections," our Brazilian facility manager reported during the six-month review. "Production efficiency reached 85% of capacity, quality compliance is excellent, and customer satisfaction is very positive."

"How do Brazilian manufacturing economics compare to export economics?" our CFO asked.

"Manufacturing costs are 20% higher than India, but elimination of import duties and shipping costs makes locally manufactured products 12% more profitable than exports."

"And market acceptance of locally manufactured products?"

"Brazilian customers prefer locally manufactured pharmaceuticals due to faster delivery, lower inventory requirements, and elimination of import documentation."

Twelve months after beginning Brazilian operations, revenues had reached ₹18 crores annually and were growing 15% quarterly as we expanded our product portfolio and distribution network.

"The Brazilian manufacturing facility proved that international manufacturing can create competitive advantages that exports cannot provide," I told our board during the annual review.

"And successful international manufacturing requires systematic adaptation to local requirements rather than direct transfer of Indian operations."

Two years after establishing Brazilian operations, we were manufacturing twelve products locally and had achieved 3% market share in generic cardiovascular drugs in Brazil.

"You know what the Brazilian facility taught us about international expansion?" I said to Carlos during our annual planning session. "Local manufacturing creates market advantages that justify the investment complexity when markets are large enough to support dedicated facilities."

"And international manufacturing capabilities become platforms for regional expansion rather than just single-country operations."

The lesson had become essential for competing in large international markets where local presence provided competitive advantages that export strategies couldn't match, despite the significantly higher investment and operational complexity required for international manufacturing.

Partnership with European Distributor

The first meeting with EuroPharma Distribution lasted six hours and ended with a handshake agreement that would transform our European market strategy from impossible to inevitable.

"Indian pharmaceutical companies face significant barriers to European market access," said Klaus Hoffman, EuroPharma's managing director, during our London meeting. "Regulatory complexity, distribution network requirements, and customer relationship development typically require 3-5 years and €2-3 million investment."

"What makes European market access so expensive and time-consuming?" I asked, reviewing market data that showed European generic drug sales of €25 billion annually.

"European Medicines Agency approval processes, country-specific product registrations, distribution network development, and customer relationship building that Indian manufacturers cannot accomplish efficiently through direct market entry."

This conversation took place in November 2010, six months after our Brazilian facility had proven our international manufacturing capabilities. Europe represented our largest potential market opportunity, but also our most complex regulatory and commercial challenge.

"Why would EuroPharma be interested in partnering with an Indian manufacturer?" Priya asked during our partnership evaluation.

"European customers increasingly demand lower-cost generic alternatives to expensive branded pharmaceuticals," Klaus explained. "Indian manufacturers provide cost advantages that European manufacturers cannot match, but Indian companies need European partners for market access."

"So the partnership provides cost advantages for EuroPharma and market access for us?"

"Mutual benefit. We gain access to competitively priced, high-quality generic products. You gain access to established European distribution networks and customer relationships."

The partnership structure that Klaus proposed was more complex than traditional distributor relationships. Instead of simple buy-sell arrangements,

EuroPharma wanted joint product development, shared regulatory investments, and coordinated market entry strategies.

"We're proposing a strategic partnership rather than a standard distribution agreement," Klaus explained during our negotiation sessions. "Strategic partnerships align both companies' interests in European market success."

"What would strategic partnership involve specifically?" I asked.

"Joint investment in European regulatory approvals, coordinated product development for European market requirements, shared marketing costs, and revenue sharing based on market performance rather than just product sales."

"And this approach provides advantages over traditional distribution arrangements?"

"Traditional distribution creates short-term transactional relationships. Strategic partnerships create long-term mutual investment in market development."

The regulatory collaboration required coordinating Indian manufacturing compliance with European approval requirements across 27 different country markets.

"European pharmaceutical registration involves EMA centralized procedures plus individual country approvals," our European regulatory consultant explained during the planning process. "Total regulatory costs for five products across major European markets could reach €800,000."

"And EuroPharma would share these regulatory costs?" Dr. Patel asked.

"EuroPharma would fund European regulatory submissions while we fund Indian manufacturing compliance. Shared investment reduces individual company risk while accelerating market entry."

"How long would European regulatory approval take?"

"Centralized EMA approval requires 12-18 months. Individual country approvals add another 6-12 months. But parallel processing can achieve market access within 24 months for most European markets."

The product development collaboration involved adapting our existing formulations to meet European packaging, labeling, and stability requirements that differed from Indian and US specifications.

"European pharmaceutical packaging requires child-resistant containers, multi-language labeling, and stability testing under European climate conditions," our product development team discovered during the collaboration.

"How do European requirements differ from FDA requirements?" I asked.

"Similar quality standards but different packaging regulations, labeling languages, and environmental testing conditions. Products approved for US markets need reformulation for European compliance."

"And reformulation costs?"

"Approximately €50,000 per product for packaging adaptation, stability testing, and regulatory documentation preparation."

The distribution network integration required understanding European pharmaceutical supply chain dynamics that were substantially different from other international markets.

"European pharmaceutical distribution involves hospital procurement systems, pharmacy chains, and government healthcare programs with different purchasing procedures," Klaus explained during our market education sessions.

"How do European customers differ from US or Brazilian customers?" our international sales manager asked.

"European customers prioritize supply chain reliability, comprehensive regulatory documentation, and long-term partnership relationships over price competition."

"So European market success requires service excellence rather than just competitive pricing?"

"European customers will pay premium prices for suppliers who provide superior service, but they'll eliminate suppliers who can't meet service commitments."

The pricing strategy required balancing competitive pricing with premium service costs that European market demands justified.

"European generic drug pricing allows 40-60% margins compared to 20-30% margins in other international markets," Klaus noted during our financial planning. "Higher margins justify investment in superior service capabilities."

"Why do European markets support higher margins?" our CFO asked.

"European healthcare systems value supply chain reliability and product quality more than pure cost minimization. They're willing to pay premiums for suppliers who reduce operational risks."

The partnership launch began in March 2011 with regulatory submissions for three cardiovascular products and distribution agreements covering Germany, UK, Netherlands, and France.

"European market entry represents our most ambitious international expansion," I told our management team during the launch meeting. "Success requires capabilities we've never developed, but provides access to our largest potential market opportunity."

Six months after partnership launch, EuroPharma had submitted regulatory applications in four countries and received preliminary approval feedback that indicated successful registration probability.

"European regulatory submissions are progressing ahead of schedule," Dr. Patel reported during our quarterly review. "EMA centralized approval is expected within 12 months."

"And European customer response to our partnership announcement?"

"Very positive. Three major hospital procurement systems have expressed interest in evaluating our products once regulatory approvals are complete."

The first European sales occurred in February 2012: €150,000 in atenolol tablets delivered to German hospital pharmacies through EuroPharma's established distribution network.

"Our first European pharmaceutical sales represent entry into the world's second-largest pharmaceutical market," I announced during our European partnership celebration.

Twelve months after first European sales, revenues had reached €2.1 million annually and EuroPharma was distributing four of our products across six European countries.

"The European partnership exceeded revenue projections while providing market access that direct entry couldn't have achieved," I told our board during the annual review.

"And partnership economics justify revenue sharing arrangements?"

"European partnership generates higher net profits than direct sales would provide, even after revenue sharing, because partnership eliminates infrastructure investments and accelerates market penetration."

Two years after the EuroPharma partnership launch, European revenues represented 18% of our total international sales and had become our highest-margin business segment.

"You know what the European partnership taught us about international expansion?" I said to Klaus during our annual partnership review. "Strategic partnerships can provide market access that direct investment cannot achieve efficiently when regulatory and commercial barriers are substantial."

"And partnership success depends on aligned interests rather than just contractual agreements."

"The key insight was that complex international markets often require partnership approaches that share both risks and returns rather than traditional buyer-seller relationships."

The EuroPharma partnership had become our template for entering regulated markets where local expertise was essential for navigating regulatory complexity and customer relationship development.

More importantly, it had taught us that strategic partnerships could create competitive advantages that individual companies couldn't achieve independently, when partnership structures aligned interests and shared investments appropriately.

Currency Hedging and International Finance

The foreign exchange loss report that Rajesh presented during our quarterly review made international expansion seem like an expensive lesson in currency volatility.

"Our unhedged exposure to USD and EUR resulted in ₹2.8 crores in foreign exchange losses during Q3," he announced, pointing to charts that showed how currency movements had eliminated most of our international profit margins.

"How is that possible when our international sales are growing successfully?" I asked, studying numbers that showed 35% revenue growth but negative net contribution from international operations.

"Revenue growth in foreign currencies becomes profit decline in rupees when exchange rates move unfavorably," he explained. "USD weakened 12% against INR during the quarter, which converted profitable sales into marginal operations."

This conversation took place in October 2011, eighteen months after we'd begun serious international expansion through Brazil, Europe, and US market development. Our international revenues had grown from ₹5 crores to ₹45 crores annually, but currency fluctuations were creating financial volatility that threatened the economic viability of our global operations.

"We're essentially gambling on currency movements instead of managing pharmaceutical business," I told Priya after reviewing the foreign exchange impact analysis.

"So we need systematic currency risk management rather than just accepting exchange rate fluctuations as unavoidable?" she asked.

"Currency hedging transforms unpredictable foreign exchange exposure into predictable transaction costs. Hedging costs money, but currency losses can eliminate entire profit margins."

The currency risk assessment revealed that our international operations faced multiple types of foreign exchange exposure: transaction exposure from sales in foreign currencies, translation exposure from international assets, and economic exposure from competitive positioning changes due to currency movements.

"Transaction exposure affects cash flows from international sales," our treasury consultant explained during our risk management education session. "When we sell products in USD or EUR, rupee strengthening reduces the rupee value of foreign currency receipts."

"How much do typical currency movements affect international profitability?" I asked.

"Currency movements of 10-15% annually are normal. For companies with significant international exposure, currency volatility can affect profits more than operational performance."

"And hedging eliminates currency volatility?"

"Hedging converts currency volatility into hedging costs. Instead of unpredictable gains or losses, you pay predictable fees for currency protection."

The hedging strategy development required understanding multiple financial instruments: forward contracts, currency options, currency swaps, and natural hedging techniques that could protect our international revenues.

"Forward contracts lock in specific exchange rates for future transactions," our forex consultant explained during our hedging education. "If you have confirmed USD sales in six months, forward contracts guarantee the rupee conversion rate regardless of market movements."

"What do forward contracts cost?" our CFO asked.

"Forward contract pricing reflects interest rate differences between currencies. Current USD/INR forward contracts cost approximately 0.5-1% of transaction value annually."

"And currency options provide different protection?"

"Options provide currency protection with upside participation. If currency moves favorably, you benefit. If currency moves unfavorably, options limit losses. But options cost more than forward contracts."

The natural hedging analysis revealed that we could reduce currency exposure by matching foreign currency costs with foreign currency revenues.

"Natural hedging involves sourcing raw materials in the same currencies as sales revenues," Rajesh explained during our hedging strategy development. "If we purchase equipment and materials in USD for US sales, currency movements affect both costs and revenues similarly."

"How much natural hedging can we achieve with our current operations?" I asked.

"About 30-40% of our international exposure. We can purchase some raw materials and equipment internationally, but most manufacturing costs remain in rupees."

"So natural hedging provides partial protection, but financial hedging is still necessary for complete coverage?"

"Natural hedging reduces exposure, financial hedging manages remaining exposure. Combined approaches provide comprehensive currency risk management."

The hedging implementation began with forward contracts covering 80% of our confirmed international receivables for the next twelve months.

"We're hedging USD receivables at 48.5 rupees per dollar and EUR receivables at 67.2 rupees per euro," Rajesh reported during our first hedging implementation. "These rates lock in profitable margins regardless of currency market movements."

"And if currencies move in our favor?" Priya asked.

"We don't benefit from favorable movements, but we're protected from unfavorable movements. Hedging provides certainty rather than maximizing returns."

The hedging cost analysis showed that currency protection consumed 1.2% of international revenues but eliminated foreign exchange volatility that had previously created losses exceeding 8% of revenues.

"Hedging costs are predictable and manageable," our CFO noted after six months of implementation. "Foreign exchange losses were unpredictable and sometimes catastrophic."

The international financing complexity extended beyond currency hedging to include export credit facilities, international working capital management, and multi-currency cash flow optimization.

"International operations require maintaining cash balances in multiple currencies for operational efficiency," our treasury manager explained during our international finance planning.

"Why can't we just convert all foreign currency receipts to rupees immediately?" I asked.

"Immediate conversion eliminates currency exposure but increases transaction costs and reduces operational flexibility. Maintaining foreign currency balances reduces conversion costs when we have foreign currency expenses."

"And foreign currency working capital management?"

"International customers often require extended payment terms that tie up working capital for 60-90 days. Export credit facilities provide financing specifically designed for international receivables."

The multi-currency accounting and reporting required upgrading our financial systems to handle foreign exchange translation, hedging accounting, and consolidated reporting across multiple currencies.

"Multi-currency operations require accounting systems that can handle foreign exchange translation for financial reporting," our accounting manager noted during the systems upgrade planning.

"How does multi-currency accounting affect our financial statements?" our board chairman asked.

"International revenues and expenses are translated to rupees for consolidated reporting, but translation rates affect reported results even when underlying operations are profitable."

"So currency movements can make profitable international operations appear unprofitable in rupee terms?"

"Currency translation affects reported results, but cash flow hedging protects actual economic value. Proper hedging separates operational performance from currency market performance."

Twelve months after implementing comprehensive currency hedging, our international operations had achieved consistent profitability despite continued currency market volatility.

"Currency hedging converted unpredictable international operations into predictable profit centers," I told our board during the annual review. "Hedging costs are manageable, and profit certainty enables better business planning."

"And international finance capabilities support continued international expansion?"

"Currency risk management, export financing, and multi-currency operations provide financial infrastructure for international growth without exposing the company to foreign exchange speculation."

Two years after implementing systematic international finance management, our international revenues had grown to ₹85 crores annually with consistent margins despite significant currency market volatility during the period.

"You know what currency hedging taught us about international business?" I said to Rajesh during our annual treasury review. "International expansion requires financial sophistication that domestic operations don't need, but financial tools exist to manage international complexity systematically."

"And international finance becomes a competitive advantage when companies can operate globally without accepting currency speculation as unavoidable business risk."

The lesson had become essential for any company with significant international exposure: currency hedging and international finance management were necessary capabilities for sustainable global operations, not optional enhancements to domestic business models.

Chapter 13

The API Backward Integration

Making the Ingredients Instead of Just the Pills

The supplier notification arrived on a Friday afternoon and contained exactly the type of message that pharmaceutical manufacturers dread receiving.

"Due to manufacturing capacity constraints and increased global demand, we are implementing a 35% price increase for atenolol API effective January 1st," read the letter from Chemsyn Industries, our primary active pharmaceutical ingredient supplier. "Additionally, minimum order quantities will increase from 500kg to 2,000kg per order."

"A 35% price increase will eliminate our profit margins on cardiovascular products," I told our procurement team during our emergency supplier meeting. "Atenolol tablets are our highest-volume product, and API costs represent 60% of our total manufacturing costs."

"Can we find alternative suppliers at current pricing?" asked our procurement manager.

"We've contacted six other API suppliers. All are implementing similar price increases due to what they describe as supply-demand imbalance in global pharmaceutical ingredient markets."

This conversation took place in November 2011, when Active Pharmaceutical Ingredient supply chains were experiencing consolidation that gave suppliers significant pricing power over generic drug manufacturers like us.

"Maybe this supply chain pressure is telling us something we've been avoiding," Priya suggested during our strategic planning meeting. "We're completely dependent on external suppliers for the most critical component of our business."

"API backward integration would require capabilities we've never developed," I replied, though I was beginning to realize that external dependence had become a strategic vulnerability.

"But API manufacturing could provide cost advantages and supply security that purchasing can't deliver."

The API market analysis revealed that pharmaceutical ingredient manufacturing was dominated by Chinese and Indian companies that had achieved economies of scale through serving global markets.

"Global API manufacturing is concentrated among 20-30 major suppliers who serve hundreds of generic drug manufacturers," our market research consultant explained during our backward integration feasibility study.

"What barriers prevent generic manufacturers from producing their own APIs?" Dr. Singh asked.

"Technical complexity, regulatory approval requirements, capital investment needs, and minimum scale requirements that make API manufacturing economical only for large volumes."

"And our API volume requirements would justify internal manufacturing?"

"Your annual consumption of 15 tons across five APIs could justify internal manufacturing if production facilities serve multiple API products rather than single ingredients."

The technical complexity assessment revealed that API manufacturing required chemical synthesis capabilities that were fundamentally different from tablet formulation and compression.

"API manufacturing involves multi-step chemical reactions, purification processes, and analytical testing that require different expertise than pharmaceutical formulation," explained Dr. Pradeep Kumar, our chemical engineering consultant.

"How different are the technical requirements?" I asked.

"Pharmaceutical formulation focuses on mixing and processing pre-manufactured ingredients. API manufacturing focuses on creating those ingredients through chemical synthesis."

"And we could develop chemical synthesis capabilities internally?"

"With appropriate expertise, equipment, and facility design. But API manufacturing requires significant investment in specialized reactors, purification systems, and analytical laboratories."

The regulatory complexity of API manufacturing exceeded pharmaceutical formulation requirements because APIs required Drug Master File approvals that documented complete manufacturing processes for regulatory authorities.

"API manufacturing requires FDA Drug Master File submission that provides complete process documentation, impurity analysis, and stability data," Dr. Patel explained during our regulatory assessment.

"How do DMF requirements differ from finished product approvals?" I asked.

"DMF approval covers raw material synthesis, intermediate purification, final API crystallization, and comprehensive impurity profiling. The documentation is more extensive than finished product applications."

"And DMF approval timelines?"

"Typically 12-18 months for new API manufacturing facilities, plus ongoing inspection and compliance monitoring requirements."

The capital investment analysis showed that API manufacturing required ₹25-35 crores for facility construction, equipment installation, and regulatory approval.

"API manufacturing facility costs include chemical reactors, distillation columns, crystallization equipment, analytical laboratories, and environmental control systems," our project consultant explained.

"How does API manufacturing ROI compare to alternative investments?" our CFO asked.

"API manufacturing could reduce ingredient costs 30-40% while providing supply security, but payback period is 4-5 years due to high capital requirements."

"And if API suppliers maintain current pricing trends?"

"Current pricing trends would reduce payback period to 3 years while improving our competitive positioning through cost advantages."

The technology selection required choosing between different chemical synthesis approaches: traditional batch reactors, continuous flow systems, or modular manufacturing platforms.

"Continuous flow technology offers advantages for pharmaceutical API manufacturing," our process technology consultant explained during the evaluation process.

"What advantages specifically?" Dr. Singh asked.

"Better reaction control, improved product quality, reduced waste generation, and easier scale-up from laboratory to commercial production."

"And disadvantages compared to traditional batch processing?"

"Higher initial investment, more complex process control, and requirement for specialized expertise in continuous manufacturing."

The facility design process required integrating chemical manufacturing with pharmaceutical quality standards in ways that neither chemical plants nor pharmaceutical facilities typically required.

"API manufacturing facilities must meet both chemical processing safety requirements and pharmaceutical GMP standards," our facility design consultant explained.

"How do chemical safety and pharmaceutical quality requirements interact?" I asked.

"Chemical safety focuses on preventing accidents and environmental releases. Pharmaceutical quality focuses on preventing contamination and ensuring product purity. Both requirements must be satisfied simultaneously."

The API manufacturing project launched in March 2012 with facility construction in Medchal, adjacent to our existing pharmaceutical manufacturing operations.

"API backward integration represents our most technically complex expansion," I told our management team during the project launch. "Success requires developing chemical manufacturing capabilities while maintaining pharmaceutical quality standards."

Construction and equipment installation took 18 months, followed by 6 months of process validation and regulatory approval before commercial production could begin.

"API facility commissioning requires more extensive testing than pharmaceutical formulation facilities," Dr. Kumar reported during the startup process. "Every chemical reaction step must be validated for consistency and impurity control."

The first commercial API production run took place in October 2013: 2,000 kilograms of atenolol API manufactured according to our approved synthesis process.

"Our first internally manufactured API represents transformation from pharmaceutical formulator to integrated pharmaceutical manufacturer," I announced during the inaugural production ceremony.

Six months after beginning API production, we were manufacturing 8 tons annually of three different APIs and had achieved cost reductions of 32% compared to external procurement.

"API backward integration exceeded cost reduction projections while providing supply security that external sourcing couldn't guarantee," I told our board during the annual review.

"And API manufacturing quality meets international standards?"

"API quality exceeds specifications required for our international customers. Several export customers have requested to purchase API directly rather than just finished products."

Twelve months after API facility startup, we were not only meeting our internal requirements but selling surplus API production to other generic manufacturers, generating ₹15 crores in additional annual revenue.

"API backward integration created unexpected business opportunities," Priya observed during our strategic review. "We've become API suppliers to companies that were previously just competitors."

"And API manufacturing capabilities enable product development opportunities that purchasing APIs couldn't support?"

"Custom API synthesis for specialized formulations, faster development timelines for new products, and intellectual property opportunities from process innovations."

Two years after completing API backward integration, our manufacturing costs had decreased 25% while our supply chain resilience had improved dramatically.

"You know what API backward integration taught us about vertical integration?" I said to Dr. Kumar during our annual facility review. "Backward integration provides cost advantages and strategic control when companies achieve sufficient scale to justify internal manufacturing."

"And vertical integration capabilities become competitive advantages when they enable opportunities that external sourcing cannot provide."

The API facility had become the foundation for our transition from generic drug manufacturer to integrated pharmaceutical company capable of controlling our entire value chain from chemical synthesis to finished product distribution.

More importantly, it had taught us that strategic investments in backward integration could transform cost centers into profit centers while providing supply chain security that pure purchasing approaches couldn't achieve.

Building Active Pharmaceutical Ingredient Capabilities

The pilot reactor failure happened at 2 AM on a Tuesday, which meant I received the emergency call while trying to figure out why our first attempt at atenolol synthesis had produced brown sludge instead of white crystalline powder.

"The reaction temperature spiked to 180°C during the final crystallization step," Dr. Pradeep Kumar explained over the phone from our API development laboratory. "We lost the entire 50-kilogram batch."

"What was supposed to happen during crystallization?" I asked, realizing that my understanding of chemical synthesis was embarrassingly superficial for someone investing ₹30 crores in API manufacturing.

"Controlled cooling should precipitate pure atenolol crystals from solution. Excessive temperature created thermal decomposition that produced impurities instead of product."

This conversation took place six months into our API capability development project, when we were discovering that chemical manufacturing involved complexities that pharmaceutical formulation had never prepared us for.

"Maybe we underestimated what API manufacturing actually requires," I told Dr. Singh during our post-failure analysis meeting. "Tablet compression involves mixing and pressing. Chemical synthesis involves controlling molecular reactions that can fail in ways we don't understand."

"So we need different expertise than pharmaceutical formulation expertise?" he asked.

"We need chemical engineering expertise, process chemistry knowledge, and analytical capabilities that our current team doesn't possess."

The expertise gap analysis revealed that successful API manufacturing required capabilities across organic chemistry, chemical engineering, process optimization, analytical chemistry, and regulatory compliance that exceeded anything our pharmaceutical experience provided.

"API manufacturing requires understanding reaction mechanisms, controlling impurity formation, optimizing yield efficiency, and developing analytical methods for detecting trace contaminants," Dr. Kumar explained during our capability assessment.

"Can our existing pharmaceutical team learn these chemical engineering skills?" I asked.

"Some pharmaceutical knowledge transfers to API manufacturing, but chemical synthesis requires specialized education and experience that takes years to develop."

"So we need to hire chemical engineering expertise rather than just training existing staff?"

"Hiring experienced chemical engineers while training existing staff to understand API manufacturing. Both approaches are necessary for building comprehensive capabilities."

The analytical chemistry challenge proved particularly complex because API manufacturing required detecting and quantifying impurities at parts-per-million levels that tablet manufacturing never needed to measure.

"API analytical testing requires identifying unknown impurities, quantifying trace contaminants, and developing stability-indicating analytical methods," our analytical consultant explained during the laboratory setup.

"How is API analytical testing different from pharmaceutical testing?" our quality control manager asked.

"Pharmaceutical testing confirms that finished products meet specifications. API testing identifies what impurities exist, where they come from, and how to eliminate them during manufacturing."

"And API analytical methods require different equipment than pharmaceutical testing?"

"High-resolution mass spectrometry, nuclear magnetic resonance spectroscopy, and advanced chromatography systems that cost ₹2-3 crores for comprehensive analytical capabilities."

The process development methodology required systematic optimization of chemical reactions through statistical design of experiments that pharmaceutical formulation had never needed.

"API process development involves optimizing reaction conditions, solvent selection, temperature profiles, and purification methods through controlled experimentation," Dr. Kumar explained during our process development training.

"How many experiments are typically required for API process optimization?" I asked.

"Usually 100-200 experiments for developing robust commercial processes. Each variable interaction must be tested systematically to ensure consistent results at manufacturing scale."

"And process development timelines?"

"Six to twelve months for established APIs using known chemistry. Longer for novel compounds or innovative synthesis routes."

The scale-up engineering challenge involved translating laboratory reactions that worked in 1-liter flasks into commercial reactions that worked in 2,000-liter reactors.

"Chemical reaction scale-up involves heat transfer, mass transfer, and mixing considerations that don't exist at laboratory scale," our chemical engineering consultant explained.

"What specific problems occur during scale-up?" Dr. Singh asked.

"Heat accumulation, incomplete mixing, different reaction kinetics, and impurity formation that doesn't occur in small-scale reactions."

"So laboratory success doesn't guarantee commercial success?"

"Laboratory optimization provides starting points for commercial process development. But commercial manufacturing requires additional optimization for large-scale equipment."

The regulatory documentation requirements for API manufacturing exceeded anything we'd encountered in pharmaceutical formulation because Drug Master Files required complete process disclosure for regulatory authorities.

"DMF documentation includes detailed synthesis schemes, impurity profiles, analytical methods, stability studies, and environmental impact assessments," Dr. Patel explained during our regulatory preparation.

"How detailed is 'detailed synthesis schemes'?" I asked.

"Every chemical reaction step, every intermediate compound, every purification method, and every analytical test used to confirm product quality."

"And regulatory authorities review all process details?"

"FDA and EMA review complete manufacturing processes to ensure product quality and patient safety. Process changes require regulatory approval through DMF amendments."

The environmental compliance challenge required managing chemical waste, solvent recovery, and emissions control that pharmaceutical formulation never generated.

"API manufacturing generates organic solvents, aqueous waste streams, and volatile emissions that require treatment before disposal," our environmental consultant explained.

"What treatment requirements?" I asked.

"Solvent recovery through distillation, aqueous waste treatment for chemical removal, and air emissions control through scrubbing systems."

"And environmental compliance costs?"

"Approximately 15-20% of total facility operating costs, but environmental violations can shut down manufacturing operations."

The commercial manufacturing startup required nine months of process validation, equipment qualification, and regulatory inspection before production approval.

"API manufacturing validation involves demonstrating that commercial processes produce consistent quality across multiple batches," Dr. Kumar reported during the validation phase.

"How many validation batches are required?" I asked.

"Minimum three consecutive batches meeting all quality specifications, but regulatory authorities may require additional batches if any parameters are borderline."

"And validation timeline risks?"

"Validation failures require process modification and revalidation, which can delay commercial production by 3-6 months."

The first successful commercial batch of atenolol API took place fourteen months after our initial pilot failure: 2,000 kilograms of white crystalline powder that met all quality specifications.

"Commercial API production represents successful transition from pharmaceutical formulator to chemical manufacturer," I announced during our production milestone celebration.

Six months after achieving consistent API production, we were manufacturing 200 kilograms monthly with quality that exceeded customer specifications and costs that were 35% below external procurement.

"API capability development proved that chemical manufacturing expertise can be systematically developed," I told our board during the annual review. "But chemical capabilities require different investment timelines and expertise than pharmaceutical capabilities."

"And API manufacturing provides competitive advantages beyond just cost reduction?"

"Supply chain control, product development flexibility, and business opportunities that purchasing APIs cannot provide."

Eighteen months after our first commercial API production, we were manufacturing five different APIs and had developed custom synthesis capabilities that enabled product development opportunities unavailable to companies dependent on external API suppliers.

"You know what building API capabilities taught us about technical capability development?" I said to Dr. Kumar during our annual technology review. "Complex technical capabilities require systematic expertise development rather than just equipment investment."

"And technical expertise becomes sustainable competitive advantage when it enables opportunities that less capable competitors cannot pursue."

The API capability development had transformed us from generic drug manufacturer dependent on external suppliers to integrated pharmaceutical company capable of controlling our entire value chain from molecular synthesis to finished product distribution.

More importantly, it had taught us that systematic technical capability building could create competitive advantages that pure financial resources couldn't purchase from external suppliers.

Joint Venture with Chinese Manufacturer

The factory tour in Shijiazhuang lasted eight hours and left me with the uncomfortable realization that our Indian API manufacturing capabilities were sophisticated compared to nothing except what I'd seen in China.

"This is our continuous flow reactor system for cardiovascular APIs," said Mr. Liu Wei, president of Hebei Pharmaceutical Industries, guiding us through production facilities that operated at scales I'd never imagined. "We produce 2,000 tons of atenolol annually using automated processes that require minimal human intervention."

"Two thousand tons?" I repeated, trying to process numbers that dwarfed our planned annual production of 50 tons. "How many finished tablets does that represent?"

"Approximately 400 million tablets worth of API annually. We supply generic manufacturers across Europe, North America, and Southeast Asia."

This conversation took place in April 2013, six months after we'd achieved commercial API production but were discovering that global API markets operated at scales that made our investments seem like expensive learning exercises.

"Chinese API manufacturers have achieved economies of scale that individual country producers cannot match," observed Dr. Kumar during our post-visit analysis. "Their cost structures and production volumes create competitive advantages that would be very difficult to replicate."

"So our API backward integration strategy is fundamentally flawed?" I asked, reviewing cost comparisons that showed Chinese suppliers offering prices 40% below our manufacturing costs.

"Not flawed, but limited. API manufacturing for domestic consumption and regional markets makes sense. Competing globally against Chinese scale requires different approaches."

The joint venture discussion began when Mr. Liu proposed combining our pharmaceutical formulation expertise with their API manufacturing capabilities for mutual market expansion.

"Chinese companies excel at API manufacturing but face barriers to pharmaceutical market access in regulated markets," he explained during our business development meeting. "Indian companies have regulatory credibility and market access that Chinese companies find difficult to obtain independently."

"What specific market access advantages do Indian pharmaceutical companies provide?" I asked.

"FDA approval processes, European regulatory relationships, established distribution networks in English-speaking markets, and customer relationships with international buyers who prefer Indian suppliers."

"And Chinese API manufacturers provide manufacturing advantages that Indian companies cannot achieve?"

"Cost structures, production scales, process technologies, and supply chain integration that enable global competitiveness in API markets."

The joint venture structure that Mr. Liu proposed involved creating a shared entity that would combine Chinese API manufacturing with Indian pharmaceutical development and international market access.

"We propose 60-40 ownership structure," he explained during our negotiation sessions. "Hebei Pharmaceutical provides API manufacturing facilities, process technologies, and Chinese market access. Malhotra Pharmaceuticals provides formulation capabilities, regulatory approvals, and international distribution networks."

"What would the joint venture actually manufacture?" Priya asked.

"Finished pharmaceutical products using APIs manufactured in China for sale in international markets where Indian regulatory approvals provide market access advantages."

"And the economic benefits for both partners?"

"Chinese API costs with Indian regulatory credibility should enable pricing advantages that neither partner could achieve independently."

The regulatory complexity of China-India pharmaceutical joint ventures exceeded anything we'd encountered in previous international partnerships because products manufactured in China with Indian regulatory oversight required approvals from multiple regulatory authorities.

"Joint venture products require Chinese manufacturing approvals, Indian regulatory oversight, and destination country import approvals," our international regulatory consultant explained during the compliance planning.

"How do multiple regulatory authorities coordinate oversight of joint venture operations?" Dr. Patel asked.

"They don't coordinate. Each regulatory authority evaluates joint venture products according to their individual requirements, which means satisfying the most stringent standards among all relevant authorities."

"And if Chinese manufacturing standards differ from Indian or US standards?"

"Joint venture manufacturing must meet the highest standards required by any market where products will be sold."

The quality control integration required harmonizing Chinese manufacturing practices with Indian pharmaceutical quality systems and international compliance requirements.

"Chinese pharmaceutical manufacturing emphasizes production efficiency and cost control," our quality consultant observed during the integration planning. "Indian pharmaceutical manufacturing emphasizes regulatory compliance and international quality standards."

"Are these approaches compatible?" I asked.

"Compatible but requiring integration protocols that preserve Chinese cost advantages while ensuring Indian quality standards."

"And integration protocols involve what specific changes?"

"Enhanced documentation, additional analytical testing, quality management systems that satisfy both Chinese and international requirements."

The technology transfer required adapting Chinese API manufacturing processes to produce pharmaceutical ingredients that met Indian formulation requirements and international quality specifications.

"Chinese API manufacturing processes are optimized for Chinese domestic pharmaceutical standards," Dr. Kumar explained during the technology evaluation. "International pharmaceutical applications may require process modifications or additional purification steps."

"What modifications specifically?" I asked.

"Impurity profiles that meet international specifications, particle size optimization for pharmaceutical formulation, stability characteristics that satisfy international storage requirements."

"And process modifications affect manufacturing costs?"

"Some cost increases for enhanced specifications, but Chinese scale advantages should maintain overall cost competitiveness."

The cultural integration challenge proved more complex than regulatory or technical integration because Chinese and Indian business practices differed in decision-making, communication, and relationship management approaches.

"Chinese business culture emphasizes hierarchy, consensus building, and long-term relationship development," our cross-cultural consultant explained during the partnership preparation.

"How do Chinese business practices differ from Indian practices?" I asked.

"Chinese decisions require extensive consultation and formal approval processes. Indian businesses often enable faster decision-making but may require more detailed explanation of reasoning."

"And successful joint ventures require adapting to both cultural approaches?"

"Successful partnerships develop hybrid approaches that incorporate both cultures' strengths while avoiding potential miscommunications."

The joint venture launch took place in September 2013 with initial focus on three cardiovascular products manufactured in China using APIs produced by Hebei Pharmaceutical for sale in international markets through our established distribution networks.

"China-India joint venture represents our most ambitious international partnership," I told our management team during the launch meeting. "Success requires integrating different manufacturing cultures, regulatory systems, and business practices."

Six months after joint venture launch, combined operations were producing 15 million tablets monthly with manufacturing costs 25% below our previous API procurement expenses.

"Joint venture economics exceed projections," our CFO reported during the quarterly review. "Chinese manufacturing costs with Indian market access create pricing advantages that enable premium margins in international markets."

"And quality compliance meets international standards?" I asked.

"Quality testing shows consistent compliance with FDA, EMA, and WHO specifications. Customer feedback has been very positive."

Twelve months after joint venture implementation, the partnership was generating ₹35 crores annually and had enabled market expansion into countries where our previous cost structures had been uncompetitive.

"The Chinese joint venture taught us that international partnerships can create competitive advantages that individual companies cannot achieve independently," I told our board during the annual review.

"And successful international partnerships require systematic integration of different business cultures and regulatory approaches?"

"Partnership success depends on combining complementary strengths rather than just sharing costs and risks."

Two years after the joint venture launch, we had expanded operations to include eight products and were serving customers across twelve countries through the combined Chinese-Indian manufacturing and distribution network.

"You know what the Chinese partnership taught us about global competitiveness?" I said to Mr. Liu during our annual partnership review. "Global pharmaceutical markets require capabilities that transcend individual countries' manufacturing or regulatory advantages."

"And international partnerships enable access to global markets that domestic capabilities alone cannot serve effectively."

The lesson had become essential for competing in global pharmaceutical markets where Chinese manufacturing costs, Indian regulatory capabilities, and international market access created competitive advantages that individual companies could not achieve independently.

Environmental Compliance Challenges

The pollution control board notice arrived on a Monday morning and contained exactly the kind of bureaucratic language that transforms routine business operations into expensive compliance projects.

"Facility inspection conducted on March 15th identified several areas of non-compliance with environmental regulations," read the notice from the Telangana State Pollution Control Board. "Immediate remedial action required within 30 days to address wastewater treatment deficiencies and air emissions monitoring gaps."

"What specific deficiencies did they identify?" I asked our facility manager, studying a document that seemed designed to make environmental compliance sound both urgent and incomprehensible.

"Inadequate treatment of API manufacturing wastewater, missing continuous emissions monitoring for solvent recovery systems, and insufficient documentation of hazardous waste disposal procedures."

This conversation took place in May 2014, eighteen months after our API manufacturing facility had begun commercial production, when we were discovering that chemical manufacturing created environmental obligations that pharmaceutical formulation had never required.

"We thought WHO-GMP compliance covered all regulatory requirements," I told our environmental consultant during our emergency compliance meeting. "But environmental regulations are completely separate from pharmaceutical quality standards."

"Environmental compliance focuses on protecting air, water, and soil from industrial contamination," she explained. "Pharmaceutical quality focuses on protecting patients from contaminated products. Different objectives requiring different regulatory approaches."

"And non-compliance consequences?"

"Facility closure, criminal liability for environmental damage, and civil penalties that can exceed annual profits for serious violations."

The wastewater treatment challenge proved most complex because API manufacturing generated organic solvents, chemical intermediates, and process residues that required specialized treatment before discharge.

"API manufacturing wastewater contains compounds that municipal treatment plants cannot handle," our environmental engineer explained during the assessment process. "Organic solvents, metal catalysts, and pharmaceutical intermediates require dedicated treatment systems."

"What treatment systems specifically?" Dr. Singh asked.

"Biological treatment for biodegradable organics, activated carbon adsorption for persistent compounds, and chemical precipitation for metal removal. Multi-stage treatment designed for pharmaceutical manufacturing waste streams."

"And treatment system costs?"

"Approximately ₹80 lakhs for equipment installation, plus ₹15 lakhs annually for operating costs and regulatory compliance monitoring."

The air emissions compliance required monitoring and controlling volatile organic compounds released during API synthesis and solvent recovery operations.

"Pharmaceutical manufacturing releases organic vapors during heating, distillation, and drying processes," our air quality consultant explained during the emissions assessment.

"Are these emissions dangerous?" I asked.

"Not acutely dangerous at typical concentrations, but regulatory limits are designed to prevent long-term health and environmental impacts from cumulative exposure."

"And monitoring requirements?"

"Continuous emissions monitoring for major emission sources, quarterly stack testing for regulatory compliance, and annual emissions reporting to pollution control authorities."

The hazardous waste management requirements involved classifying, storing, and disposing of chemical wastes according to regulations that pharmaceutical manufacturers rarely encountered.

"API manufacturing generates hazardous wastes including spent solvents, contaminated materials, and process residues that require specialized disposal," our waste management consultant explained.

"How is hazardous waste different from regular industrial waste?" our operations manager asked.

"Hazardous waste contains chemicals that could harm human health or the environment if not properly managed. Regulatory requirements include specialized containers, trained personnel, detailed documentation, and approved disposal facilities."

"And disposal costs?"

"Hazardous waste disposal costs ₹25-40 per kilogram compared to ₹2-3 per kilogram for non-hazardous waste. Plus transportation, documentation, and compliance monitoring costs."

The regulatory reporting requirements involved quarterly emissions reports, annual waste generation summaries, and ongoing compliance certifications that pharmaceutical formulation had never required.

"Environmental compliance requires extensive documentation and reporting to multiple regulatory authorities," our compliance manager discovered during the regulatory assessment.

"How extensive is 'extensive documentation'?" I asked.

"Daily operational logs, monthly monitoring reports, quarterly emissions summaries, annual compliance certifications, and immediate notification of any environmental incidents."

"And reporting to multiple authorities?"

"State pollution control boards, central pollution control board, municipal authorities for wastewater discharge, and potentially national-level agencies for hazardous waste management."

The compliance implementation required eighteen months and ₹1.5 crores in capital investments for treatment systems, monitoring equipment, and facility modifications.

"Environmental compliance represents our largest non-productive investment," our CFO noted during the project review. "Treatment systems and monitoring equipment don't generate revenue, but non-compliance could shut down operations."

"So environmental compliance is essentially insurance against regulatory shutdown?" Priya asked.

"Environmental compliance is operational requirement for maintaining manufacturing licenses. Compliance costs are business overhead that enables continued operation."

The environmental management system implementation required training personnel, establishing procedures, and creating documentation systems that integrated environmental compliance with manufacturing operations.

"Environmental management requires changing how we think about manufacturing processes," our environmental compliance manager explained during the training program.

"How specifically?" I asked.

"Considering environmental impact during process design, minimizing waste generation rather than just treating waste after generation, and maintaining environmental compliance as automatically as we maintain product quality."

"And environmental thinking affects manufacturing efficiency?"

"Environmental optimization often improves manufacturing efficiency by reducing waste, recovering valuable materials, and optimizing resource utilization."

The pollution prevention initiatives that emerged from compliance implementation actually reduced operating costs while improving environmental performance.

"Solvent recovery systems installed for emissions compliance enable reusing 85% of process solvents," our environmental engineer reported after six months of operation.

"How much does solvent recovery save annually?" I asked.

"Approximately ₹25 lakhs in reduced solvent purchases, which helps offset environmental compliance costs."

"So environmental compliance can generate cost savings rather than just consuming resources?"

"Well-designed environmental systems often provide economic benefits through waste reduction, material recovery, and process optimization."

Two years after completing environmental compliance implementation, our facility was operating with zero environmental violations and had achieved cost savings that offset 40% of compliance system investment.

"Environmental compliance taught us that manufacturing sustainability requires systematic environmental management rather than just end-of-pipe treatment," I told our management team during the annual review.

"And environmental excellence can create competitive advantages through operational efficiency and customer preference for environmentally responsible suppliers."

"The key insight was that environmental compliance, like quality compliance, works best when integrated into manufacturing processes rather than treated as separate regulatory requirement."

The environmental compliance experience also influenced our approach to facility design for international expansion, where environmental standards often exceeded Indian requirements.

"Environmental capabilities developed for Indian compliance often exceed requirements for international markets," our environmental consultant noted during our Brazil facility planning.

"And environmental excellence provides competitive advantages in markets where customers value environmental responsibility?"

"Environmental performance increasingly affects customer decisions, regulatory approvals, and community acceptance for pharmaceutical manufacturing operations."

Three years after achieving environmental compliance, we had developed environmental management capabilities that supported international expansion while reducing operating costs through resource efficiency and waste minimization.

"You know what environmental compliance taught us about business sustainability?" I said to our environmental manager during our annual compliance review. "Environmental excellence and operational excellence are complementary rather than competing objectives."

"And companies that integrate environmental thinking into business operations often achieve better financial performance than companies that treat environmental compliance as regulatory burden."

The lesson had become essential for pharmaceutical manufacturing in increasingly environmentally conscious markets where environmental performance affected customer relationships, regulatory approvals, and community acceptance as much as traditional business metrics.

Creating Cost Advantages Through Vertical Integration

The cost analysis that our CFO presented in September 2014 made vertical integration look like the most expensive way possible to save money.

"API backward integration has cost us ₹35 crores in facility investment, ₹8 crores in working capital, and ₹12 crores in development expenses over three years," Rajesh announced during our integration review meeting. "Total investment of ₹55 crores to replace external purchases that previously cost ₹18 crores annually."

"So we've spent three times our annual API costs to achieve internal manufacturing?" I asked, studying numbers that made our vertical integration strategy appear financially questionable.

"But internal API manufacturing now costs ₹11 crores annually compared to ₹18 crores for external procurement," he replied. "Annual savings of ₹7 crores provide payback period of 7.8 years on total investment."

This conversation forced us to confront something uncomfortable about vertical integration: the initial investment required to achieve cost advantages often exceeded the cumulative value of those advantages for many years.

"Maybe we're measuring vertical integration success incorrectly," Priya suggested during our strategic review. "Direct cost comparison doesn't capture all the benefits that internal manufacturing provides."

"What benefits beyond direct cost savings?" I asked.

"Supply chain security, quality control, product development flexibility, and strategic independence from external suppliers who can change prices or availability unpredictably."

The comprehensive cost analysis revealed that vertical integration created value through multiple mechanisms beyond simple input cost reduction.

"Internal API manufacturing eliminated ₹2.3 crores in annual purchasing overhead, reduced inventory requirements by ₹5.8 crores, and provided pricing stability that external sourcing couldn't guarantee," our operations analyst reported.

"How does internal manufacturing reduce inventory requirements?" Dr. Singh asked.

"External API procurement required maintaining 90-day safety stock due to supplier lead times and delivery uncertainty. Internal manufacturing enables just-in-time production with 30-day inventory levels."

"And pricing stability provides quantifiable value?"

"External API prices fluctuated 15-25% annually based on global supply-demand conditions. Internal manufacturing costs vary only 3-5% annually based on raw material prices."

The supply chain security analysis showed that vertical integration provided protection against disruptions that could shut down finished product manufacturing entirely.

"API supply disruptions had forced production shutdowns three times over the past five years," our supply chain manager noted during the risk assessment. "Each shutdown cost ₹3-4 crores in lost revenue plus customer relationship damage."

"And internal API manufacturing eliminates shutdown risks?" I asked.

"Internal manufacturing provides supply security that external procurement cannot guarantee, especially during market disruptions or supplier capacity constraints."

"How do we quantify the value of supply security?"

"Risk-adjusted cost analysis that accounts for probability and impact of supply disruptions under external sourcing versus internal manufacturing scenarios."

The quality control advantages of vertical integration enabled product differentiation that external API sourcing couldn't support.

"Internal API manufacturing allows customizing impurity profiles, particle size specifications, and stability characteristics for our specific formulation requirements," Dr. Kumar explained during the quality analysis.

"How does API customization affect finished product performance?" I asked.

"Optimized API specifications enable faster dissolution, improved bioavailability, and enhanced stability that provide competitive advantages over products using standard APIs."

"And competitive advantages translate to pricing premiums?"

"Quality-differentiated products typically command 8-12% pricing premiums over commodity alternatives in international markets."

The product development flexibility analysis revealed that internal API capabilities accelerated new product introduction timelines significantly.

"External API sourcing required 18-24 months for custom synthesis and regulatory approval," our product development manager reported. "Internal capabilities reduce development timelines to 8-12 months."

"How does faster development create financial value?" our CFO asked.

"Faster market entry provides first-mover advantages, earlier revenue generation, and extended patent protection periods that increase total product lifecycle value."

"And the cumulative value of faster development?"

"Approximately ₹15-20 crores in additional revenue over five years from accelerated product launches enabled by internal API capabilities."

The strategic independence analysis showed that vertical integration provided negotiating power and competitive positioning that external dependence had prevented.

"Internal API manufacturing enables pursuing opportunities that external sourcing constraints had made impossible," I noted during our strategic planning.

"What opportunities specifically?" Priya asked.

"Custom synthesis for specialized formulations, API sales to third parties, and manufacturing partnerships that require guaranteed API supply."

"So vertical integration creates business opportunities rather than just cost savings?"

"Vertical integration transforms manufacturing capabilities from operational functions into strategic assets that enable new business models."

The economies of scope analysis revealed that API manufacturing infrastructure could support multiple products more efficiently than single-product optimization.

"API manufacturing facility designed for five products achieves 65% capacity utilization," our facility manager reported. "Adding three more products would increase utilization to 85% while requiring only 15% additional investment."

"And higher capacity utilization improves unit cost economics?" I asked.

"Fixed costs distributed across larger production volumes reduce per-unit manufacturing costs by approximately 20%."

"Plus economies of scope from shared equipment, utilities, and regulatory compliance costs."

The competitive positioning analysis showed that vertical integration created barriers to entry that protected market position.

"Companies with integrated API manufacturing can respond to competitive pricing pressure more effectively than companies dependent on external suppliers," our market analyst observed.

"How specifically?" I asked.

"Integrated manufacturers can reduce prices to marginal cost levels during competitive situations. Non-integrated manufacturers cannot price below their API procurement costs."

"So vertical integration provides defensive advantages during price competition?"

"Vertical integration enables both offensive and defensive competitive strategies that purchasing-dependent companies cannot pursue."

Three years after completing API backward integration, the cumulative benefits exceeded our initial investment projections.

"Total cost advantages from vertical integration reached ₹28 crores over three years," Rajesh reported during our integration assessment. "Direct cost savings of ₹21 crores plus indirect benefits of ₹7 crores from quality improvements, development acceleration, and risk reduction."

"And return on integration investment?" I asked.

"Effective ROI of 17% annually when all quantifiable benefits are included in the analysis."

"Plus unquantified strategic benefits from supply security and competitive positioning."

The vertical integration experience also enabled additional backward integration opportunities that leveraged existing capabilities and infrastructure.

"API manufacturing capabilities provide foundation for intermediate chemical production that could reduce costs further," Dr. Kumar noted during our expansion planning.

"How much additional cost reduction?" I asked.

"Intermediate chemical integration could reduce total API costs by another 15-20% while providing additional economies of scope."

Four years after beginning vertical integration, we had achieved cost structures that enabled competitive pricing in global markets while maintaining margins that non-integrated competitors could not match.

"You know what vertical integration taught us about cost advantage creation?" I said to our management team during our annual strategic review. "Sustainable cost advantages require systematic capability building rather than just process optimization."

"And vertical integration creates multiple sources of value that cumulate over time rather than just immediate cost reduction."

"The key insight was that vertical integration success depends on viewing manufacturing capabilities as strategic assets rather than just operational functions."

The vertical integration experience had become our template for evaluating additional backward integration opportunities, where cost advantages could be achieved through systematic capability development rather than just input cost reduction.

More importantly, it had taught us that vertical integration provided competitive advantages and strategic flexibility that purchasing approaches could never deliver, when integration was approached systematically rather than just opportunistically.

Chapter 14

The Innovation Inflection

When Generic Becomes Insufficient

The patent expiry calendar that Dr. Sarah Williams presented during our October 2014 strategy meeting contained a statistic that fundamentally changed how we thought about our business future.

"Major cardiovascular patents expire between 2016-2020, representing approximately $45 billion in branded drug sales that will become available for generic competition," she announced, pointing to charts that showed unprecedented opportunities for generic manufacturers.

"That sounds like excellent news for generic drug companies," I said, studying patent expiries that included some of the world's largest pharmaceutical products.

"Excellent news if you can compete successfully against 15-20 other generic manufacturers who will target the same opportunities simultaneously," she replied. "Patent cliff opportunities are attracting more competition than the market can support profitably."

This conversation marked the beginning of our most fundamental strategic shift since founding the company: recognizing that generic drug manufacturing was becoming a commodity business where sustainable competitive advantages required capabilities beyond operational excellence.

"Generic competition is intensifying while innovation requirements are increasing," I told our management team during our strategic planning session. "We need to evolve beyond pure generic manufacturing toward innovation that provides sustainable differentiation."

"What type of innovation?" Priya asked. "We're not a research pharmaceutical company with drug discovery capabilities."

"Innovation in drug delivery, formulation technology, manufacturing processes, and therapeutic applications that create value beyond basic generic equivalence."

The innovation challenge analysis revealed that pharmaceutical innovation opportunities existed across multiple dimensions: novel drug delivery systems, improved formulation technologies, combination therapies, and therapeutic applications that enhanced patient outcomes.

"Innovation doesn't require discovering new drug molecules," explained Dr. Meera Nair, our newly hired VP of Innovation, during our capability assessment. "Innovation can involve improving how existing drugs are delivered, combined, or applied to specific patient populations."

"What specific innovation opportunities match our capabilities?" Dr. Singh asked.

"Extended-release formulations, combination products, pediatric formulations, and therapeutic applications that leverage our manufacturing expertise while providing patient benefits that justify premium pricing."

"And innovation provides competitive advantages that generic manufacturing cannot achieve?"

"Innovation creates intellectual property, regulatory exclusivity, and clinical differentiation that protect products from commodity competition."

The innovation investment analysis showed that pharmaceutical innovation required different resource allocation than generic manufacturing: R&D spending, clinical testing, intellectual property development, and regulatory strategies that emphasized differentiation rather than equivalence.

"Innovation requires investing 8-12% of revenue in R&D compared to 2-3% for generic manufacturing," Dr. Nair explained during our investment planning.

"And innovation ROI compared to generic expansion?" our CFO asked.

"Innovation projects require 3-5 years for commercial returns but can generate 40-60% gross margins compared to 25-35% for generic products."

"So innovation provides higher returns with longer development timelines and higher investment requirements?"

"Innovation risk-return profiles are different from generic manufacturing, but successful innovation provides sustainable competitive advantages that generic manufacturing cannot achieve."

The innovation capability development required recruiting different expertise: formulation scientists, clinical researchers, regulatory specialists, and intellectual property managers who understood innovation rather than just generic development.

"Innovation teams require different skills and thinking approaches than generic development teams," Dr. Nair observed during our team building process.

"How specifically?" I asked.

"Generic development focuses on replicating existing products efficiently. Innovation development focuses on creating new products that solve unmet medical needs."

"And both capabilities can coexist within the same organization?"

"Innovation and generic capabilities can be complementary when innovation provides advanced products while generic manufacturing provides operational efficiency and market access."

The first innovation project involved developing extended-release atenolol formulations that provided 24-hour blood pressure control with once-daily dosing compared to twice-daily dosing for immediate-release products.

"Extended-release atenolol addresses medication compliance problems that affect cardiovascular treatment effectiveness," Dr. Nair explained during the project launch. "Patient compliance improves significantly with once-daily versus twice-daily dosing regimens."

"And extended-release technology provides patent protection?" I asked.

"Novel extended-release mechanisms can provide composition of matter patents, process patents, and regulatory exclusivity that protect products from generic competition for 3-5 years."

"Plus premium pricing that reflects clinical advantages over immediate-release alternatives."

The innovation development process required capabilities we'd never needed for generic manufacturing: in vitro-in vivo correlation studies, bioequivalence studies with reference-listed drugs, and clinical studies demonstrating therapeutic advantages.

"Innovation development involves proving clinical benefits rather than just demonstrating bioequivalence," our clinical research manager explained during the project planning.

"How do clinical benefit studies differ from bioequivalence studies?" Dr. Patel asked.

"Bioequivalence studies show that generic products perform identically to branded products. Clinical benefit studies show that innovative products perform better than existing alternatives."

"And clinical benefit studies require different regulatory approaches?"

"Innovation products require New Drug Applications or supplemental NDAs rather than Abbreviated New Drug Applications used for generic products."

The intellectual property strategy required developing patent portfolios that protected innovative formulations, manufacturing processes, and therapeutic applications.

"Innovation success depends on intellectual property protection that prevents competitors from copying innovative products," our IP attorney explained during the patent strategy development.

"What types of patents protect pharmaceutical innovations?" I asked.

"Composition patents for novel formulations, process patents for manufacturing methods, use patents for new therapeutic applications, and design patents for drug delivery devices."

"And patent protection enables premium pricing for how long?"

"Patent protection typically provides 10-15 years of competitive exclusivity, during which innovative products can command premium pricing."

The regulatory strategy required positioning innovative products as improvements over existing therapies rather than just generic alternatives.

"Innovation products require demonstrating clinical advantages that justify approval and reimbursement by healthcare systems," our regulatory consultant explained.

"What clinical advantages specifically?" I asked.

"Improved efficacy, reduced side effects, enhanced patient compliance, or cost-effectiveness benefits that provide value to patients and healthcare providers."

The first innovation product launch took place in March 2016: extended-release atenolol tablets providing 24-hour cardiovascular protection with demonstrated compliance advantages over twice-daily immediate-release products.

"Our first innovation product represents transformation from generic manufacturer to pharmaceutical innovator," I announced during the product launch ceremony.

Six months after innovation product launch, extended-release atenolol was generating ₹8 crores in revenue with 55% gross margins compared to 32% margins for immediate-release generic products.

"Innovation economics validate our strategic shift toward differentiated products," I told our board during the quarterly review.

"And innovation capabilities support additional product development?" asked our board chairman.

"Innovation capabilities provide platform for developing extended-release formulations across our entire cardiovascular portfolio, plus expansion into combination therapies and specialty applications."

Twelve months after our first innovation product launch, we had three additional innovative products in development and had achieved innovation revenues of ₹25 crores annually.

"Innovation portfolio development is proceeding ahead of schedule," Dr. Nair reported during our annual innovation review. "Market acceptance of innovative products exceeds projections."

Two years after beginning innovation strategy implementation, innovation products represented 18% of total revenue but 31% of total gross profits.

"You know what the innovation inflection taught us about business strategy?" I said to Dr. Nair during our annual planning session. "Sustainable competitive advantages require continuous innovation rather than operational excellence alone."

"And innovation capabilities become more important as markets mature and competition intensifies."

"The key insight was that innovation and operational excellence are complementary rather than competing strategies for pharmaceutical companies."

The innovation inflection had become the foundation for our next phase of business development: transitioning from generic manufacturer to innovative pharmaceutical company that could compete on clinical value rather than just cost efficiency.

More importantly, it had taught us that sustainable business success required continuous capability evolution that enabled companies to create value in changing competitive environments rather than just optimizing performance in static markets.

Setting Up First R&D Center in Bangalore

The lease agreement for 15,000 square feet in Bangalore's Electronic City arrived with a rental cost that made me question whether we were establishing an R&D center or funding a small country's budget.

"₹45 lakhs annually for laboratory space, plus ₹25 lakhs for equipment installation and ₹8 lakhs monthly for operational expenses," our facility consultant announced during the lease review meeting. "Total first-year costs of approximately ₹1.2 crores before hiring any researchers."

"Why is Bangalore commercial real estate so expensive?" I asked, studying rental rates that exceeded our entire Hyderabad facility costs.

"Bangalore is India's pharmaceutical R&D hub," he explained. "Demand from multinational companies, biotech startups, and Indian pharmaceutical companies creates competition for qualified laboratory space that drives premium pricing."

This conversation took place in February 2015, six months after we'd decided that innovation strategy required dedicated R&D capabilities that our manufacturing-focused Hyderabad operations couldn't provide.

"Maybe we should establish R&D capabilities in Hyderabad rather than Bangalore," Priya suggested during our location planning discussions. "Hyderabad costs would be 40% lower than Bangalore."

"Hyderabad provides cost advantages, but Bangalore provides talent advantages," replied Dr. Meera Nair. "Pharmaceutical R&D talent concentration in Bangalore is unmatched anywhere in India."

"And talent advantages justify the cost premiums?"

"R&D success depends more on researcher quality than facility costs. The best pharmaceutical scientists in India are located in Bangalore."

The talent recruitment challenge proved even more expensive than facility costs because Bangalore's pharmaceutical R&D job market was dominated by multinational companies offering compensation packages we'd never encountered.

"Senior formulation scientists in Bangalore expect ₹25-35 lakhs annually plus equity participation," our HR consultant reported during the recruitment planning. "Plus signing bonuses, international conference attendance, and patent incentive programs."

"How do Bangalore R&D salaries compare to our current technical staff compensation?" I asked.

"Bangalore R&D salaries are 60-80% higher than equivalent positions in Hyderabad, but Bangalore talent often has experience with innovative product development that Hyderabad talent lacks."

"And we need innovative product development experience rather than just technical competence?"

"Innovation requires different thinking approaches than generic development. Experienced innovation researchers can accelerate R&D success significantly."

The laboratory design requirements exceeded anything we'd implemented for manufacturing operations because pharmaceutical R&D required specialized equipment, environmental controls, and analytical capabilities.

"Pharmaceutical R&D facilities require biosafety laboratories, analytical instrument rooms, stability testing chambers, and pilot-scale manufacturing capabilities," our laboratory design consultant explained during the planning process.

"How do R&D facility requirements differ from manufacturing facility requirements?" Dr. Singh asked.

"Manufacturing facilities optimize production efficiency and quality control. R&D facilities optimize experimental flexibility and analytical precision."

"And R&D equipment costs?"

"Approximately ₹3.5 crores for comprehensive analytical instrumentation, pilot manufacturing equipment, and specialized laboratory systems."

The regulatory compliance requirements for R&D operations involved different standards than manufacturing compliance because research activities required documentation and quality systems designed for experimental rather than production work.

"R&D regulatory compliance focuses on data integrity, experimental documentation, and intellectual property protection," our regulatory consultant explained during the compliance planning.

"How is R&D compliance different from manufacturing compliance?" Dr. Patel asked.

"Manufacturing compliance ensures consistent product quality. R&D compliance ensures reliable experimental data and protectable intellectual property."

"And R&D compliance requires different quality systems?"

"R&D quality systems emphasize experimental design, data recording, and result verification rather than production control and batch documentation."

The intellectual property strategy required establishing patent filing capabilities, prior art research systems, and freedom-to-operate analysis that manufacturing operations had never needed.

"R&D centers require intellectual property infrastructure for identifying patentable innovations, conducting patent searches, and filing patent applications," our IP consultant explained.

"What IP infrastructure specifically?" I asked.

"Patent databases, prior art search capabilities, patent drafting expertise, and legal support for intellectual property prosecution and defense."

"And IP infrastructure costs?"

"Approximately ₹15 lakhs annually for database subscriptions, plus ₹8-12 lakhs per patent application for legal and filing fees."

The R&D project management systems required different approaches than manufacturing project management because research projects involved uncertainty, iteration, and timeline flexibility that production projects couldn't accommodate.

"R&D project management requires stage-gate processes that allow project termination when research directions prove unviable," our R&D consultant explained during the project planning.

"How do R&D timelines differ from manufacturing project timelines?" I asked.

"Manufacturing projects have predictable timelines based on known processes. R&D projects have variable timelines depending on experimental success and development challenges."

"And R&D project budgeting?"

"R&D budgets require contingency funding for unexpected experiments, alternative approaches, and extended development timelines that manufacturing projects don't require."

The Bangalore R&D center opening took place in August 2015 with initial focus on extended-release formulation development, combination therapy research, and pediatric formulation innovation.

"Bangalore R&D center represents our transformation from manufacturing company to innovation company," I announced during the facility inauguration attended by pharmaceutical industry executives and government officials.

The first R&D project results emerged six months after center opening: successful development of extended-release metformin formulation that demonstrated improved glucose control with reduced gastrointestinal side effects.

"Extended-release metformin represents our first internally developed innovation product," Dr. Nair reported during the project review. "Clinical testing shows 25% improvement in patient compliance compared to immediate-release alternatives."

"And development costs compared to licensing similar technology externally?" our CFO asked.

"Internal development cost ₹85 lakhs compared to ₹2.5 crores for licensing equivalent technology from external sources."

"Plus intellectual property ownership and development capability building that licensing wouldn't provide."

Twelve months after R&D center establishment, we had four innovation projects in development and had filed three patent applications for novel formulation technologies.

"R&D center productivity exceeds expectations," I told our board during the annual review. "Innovation pipeline development is proceeding ahead of schedule."

"And R&D capabilities enable market opportunities that manufacturing alone couldn't access?" asked our board chairman.

"R&D capabilities provide access to innovation partnerships, licensing opportunities, and premium product development that generic manufacturing companies cannot pursue."

Two years after establishing Bangalore R&D operations, innovation products developed internally were generating ₹45 crores annually and had enabled partnership discussions with multinational pharmaceutical companies seeking Indian innovation capabilities.

"The Bangalore R&D center taught us that innovation requires systematic capability building rather than just increased spending on existing activities," I told Dr. Nair during our annual R&D review.

"And innovation capabilities create competitive advantages that extend beyond just product development to include partnership opportunities and strategic positioning."

"The key insight was that R&D centers succeed when they're designed for innovation rather than just relocated manufacturing support activities."

Three years after establishing dedicated R&D capabilities, we had developed innovation portfolio that provided sustainable competitive advantages in increasingly commoditized pharmaceutical markets.

"You know what setting up the R&D center taught us about capability development?" I said to our management team during strategic planning. "Innovation capabilities require dedicated resources, specialized talent, and systematic approaches that cannot be achieved through part-time efforts or manufacturing facility expansions."

"And innovation investments create competitive advantages that justify premium costs when they enable opportunities unavailable through operational excellence alone."

The Bangalore R&D center had become the foundation for our innovation strategy, providing capabilities that transformed us from generic manufacturer to pharmaceutical innovator capable of competing on clinical value rather than just cost efficiency.

Hiring Dr. Lisa Chen from Pfizer

The interview with Dr. Lisa Chen lasted four hours and ended with a compensation negotiation that made me question whether we were hiring a pharmaceutical researcher or acquiring a small biotechnology company.

"My current compensation at Pfizer includes base salary of $180,000, performance bonus of $45,000, stock options worth approximately $60,000 annually, plus comprehensive benefits and research budget autonomy," she explained during our discussion about joining our Bangalore R&D center.

"What would it take to convince you to leave Pfizer for a mid-sized Indian pharmaceutical company?" I asked, calculating that her total compensation exceeded ₹2 crores annually.

"Equity participation, research leadership autonomy, patent revenue sharing, and opportunity to build innovation capabilities from the ground up rather than just contributing to established programs."

This conversation took place in June 2015, three months after establishing our Bangalore R&D center, when we realized that serious pharmaceutical innovation required talent with multinational pharmaceutical experience that Indian companies rarely offered.

"Dr. Chen represents exactly the expertise we need for innovation success," Dr. Meera Nair observed during our hiring evaluation. "Twelve years at Pfizer developing novel drug delivery systems, 15 published papers, 8 patents, and leadership experience with FDA approval processes."

"But her compensation expectations exceed our entire R&D budget," our CFO noted during the evaluation meeting.

"Her expertise could accelerate our innovation timeline by 2-3 years while providing access to development approaches that we can't learn independently."

"So we're essentially buying innovation capabilities rather than just hiring individual expertise?"

"Dr. Chen brings systematic approaches to pharmaceutical innovation that could transform our R&D productivity."

The compensation package that we eventually offered required board approval because it exceeded any previous individual compensation arrangement: ₹1.8 crores base salary, 2% equity participation, patent revenue sharing, and $100,000 annual research budget.

"The compensation structure aligns Dr. Chen's success with company innovation success," I explained to our board during the approval meeting. "Equity participation and patent sharing ensure that her financial rewards depend on R&D productivity."

"And we're confident that her contributions will justify this investment?" asked our board chairman.

"Dr. Chen's track record at Pfizer includes developing three FDA-approved products that generated over $500 million in combined revenue. If she replicates even partial success here, the ROI exceeds the compensation investment significantly."

The culture integration challenge proved more complex than compensation negotiation because multinational pharmaceutical experience involved approaches to research, development, and decision-making that differed substantially from Indian pharmaceutical practices.

"Multinational pharmaceutical R&D emphasizes systematic experimentation, comprehensive documentation, and long-term development timelines," Dr. Chen explained during her integration discussions with our R&D team.

"How do multinational approaches differ from typical Indian pharmaceutical development?" Dr. Nair asked.

"Multinational companies invest more time in experimental design and documentation because they're developing products for global regulatory approval rather than just domestic market access."

"And longer development timelines provide better results?"

"More systematic approaches often produce more innovative products and higher regulatory success rates, but they require patience and resource commitment that shorter timelines can't support."

The laboratory infrastructure upgrades required to support Dr. Chen's research approaches exceeded our initial R&D center planning because multinational-standard research required analytical capabilities and experimental systems we hadn't anticipated.

"Advanced drug delivery research requires particle size analyzers, dissolution testing systems, permeation measurement equipment, and stability testing capabilities that basic pharmaceutical development doesn't need," she explained during our equipment planning.

"How much additional equipment investment would be required?" I asked.

"Approximately ₹1.5 crores for specialized instrumentation that enables development of novel drug delivery systems rather than just improved formulations."

"And specialized equipment enables research that conventional equipment cannot support?"

"Advanced instrumentation enables developing innovative products that can achieve patent protection and regulatory exclusivity rather than just incremental improvements."

The project selection strategy required balancing ambitious innovation objectives with realistic commercial timelines because Dr. Chen's multinational experience emphasized breakthrough research while our business needs emphasized marketable products.

"I recommend focusing on platform technologies that can be applied across multiple products rather than individual product improvements," she suggested during our research planning.

"What platform technologies specifically?" I asked.

"Nanoparticle drug delivery systems, extended-release matrix technologies, and combination therapy approaches that can enhance multiple products in our pipeline."

"And platform technologies provide advantages over individual product development?"

"Platform technologies create intellectual property portfolios and development capabilities that support multiple products while providing competitive advantages that are difficult for competitors to replicate."

The regulatory strategy development required adapting Dr. Chen's FDA experience to Indian regulatory requirements while maintaining international development standards that could support global market access.

"Indian regulatory approval processes are faster than FDA processes, but global market access requires meeting FDA and EMA standards regardless of initial approval location," she explained during our regulatory planning.

"So we should design development programs to meet global standards even for products initially targeting Indian markets?" Dr. Patel asked.

"Global-standard development provides maximum market access flexibility while protecting intellectual property more effectively than India-only development approaches."

The first research project under Dr. Chen's leadership involved developing nanoparticle formulations for poorly soluble cardiovascular drugs that could improve bioavailability and enable once-daily dosing.

"Nanoparticle formulations could transform several products in our cardiovascular portfolio from twice-daily to once-daily dosing while improving therapeutic effectiveness," she explained during the project launch.

"And nanoparticle technology provides patent protection?" I asked.

"Novel nanoparticle formulations can provide composition of matter patents, manufacturing process patents, and therapeutic use patents that create multiple layers of intellectual property protection."

Six months after Dr. Chen joined, the R&D center had initiated three platform technology projects and filed two provisional patent applications for novel formulation approaches.

"Dr. Chen's research leadership is transforming our innovation capabilities," Dr. Nair reported during our quarterly review. "Project sophistication and patent potential exceed anything we'd achieved previously."

"And her integration with existing R&D team?" I asked.

"Excellent. She's teaching our researchers multinational development approaches while learning about cost-effective innovation methods that Indian companies use successfully."

Twelve months after Dr. Chen's recruitment, our innovation pipeline included eight projects utilizing platform technologies that could support patent portfolios and premium product positioning.

"The platform technology approach is generating innovation opportunities across our entire product portfolio," I told our board during the annual review.

"And Dr. Chen's leadership is developing internal innovation capabilities beyond her individual contributions?"

"She's training our R&D team in systematic innovation approaches that will continue benefiting our capabilities long after specific projects are completed."

Two years after hiring Dr. Chen, our patent portfolio had grown from zero to twelve applications, and we had signed three licensing agreements with other pharmaceutical companies seeking access to our platform technologies.

"Dr. Chen's recruitment taught us that top-tier talent requires top-tier compensation but can transform organizational capabilities in ways that justify premium investment," I told our management team during strategic planning.

"And multinational pharmaceutical experience provides access to development approaches and regulatory strategies that can accelerate innovation success significantly."

Three years after Dr. Chen joined, our R&D center had achieved innovation productivity that enabled partnerships with multinational companies seeking access to cost-effective innovation capabilities.

"You know what hiring Dr. Chen taught us about talent investment?" I said to Dr. Nair during our annual R&D review. "Exceptional talent doesn't just perform better individually—exceptional talent elevates the capabilities of entire teams and organizations."

"And innovation talent investment creates competitive advantages that extend far beyond individual contributions to include systematic capability development."

The lesson had become essential for competing with larger pharmaceutical companies: accessing top-tier talent required compensation structures that aligned individual success with organizational innovation objectives, but exceptional talent could transform organizational capabilities in ways that justified premium investment.

First Modified Release Formulation Success

The dissolution test results that Dr. Lisa Chen presented during our December 2015 project review meeting contained exactly the kind of data that transforms years of theoretical research into commercial reality.

"The extended-release metformin formulation demonstrates linear drug release over 12 hours with zero-order kinetics," she announced, pointing to charts that showed steady medication delivery rather than the typical immediate-release spike followed by rapid decline.

"What does zero-order kinetics mean practically?" I asked, studying graphs that looked more like engineering drawings than pharmaceutical test results.

"Constant drug release rate that maintains therapeutic blood levels throughout the dosing interval without the peaks and valleys that cause side effects and compliance problems."

This presentation took place eighteen months after establishing our Bangalore R&D center and twelve months after Dr. Chen had joined from Pfizer, when we were finally seeing results from our investment in innovation capabilities.

"How does our extended-release performance compare to existing metformin products?" Dr. Nair asked during the results analysis.

"Our formulation provides 12-hour duration compared to 8 hours for current extended-release products, plus 40% reduction in gastrointestinal side effects due to smoother drug release profile," Dr. Chen replied.

"And smoother drug release translates to better patient outcomes?"

"Fewer side effects plus longer duration enable once-daily dosing that improves patient compliance significantly. Clinical studies show 65% better adherence with once-daily versus twice-daily regimens."

The bioequivalence study results exceeded our expectations because the formulation not only achieved therapeutic equivalence but demonstrated clinical advantages over existing products.

"Bioequivalence testing shows our extended-release metformin achieves identical therapeutic effect with 30% lower peak plasma concentration," our clinical research manager reported during the data review.

"Lower peak concentration reduces side effects?" I asked.

"Peak plasma concentrations often correlate with adverse effects. Lower peaks with sustained therapeutic levels provide better efficacy with improved tolerability."

"And regulatory authorities recognize therapeutic advantages rather than just bioequivalence?"

"Demonstrated clinical advantages enable premium pricing and market positioning that simple bioequivalence cannot support."

The manufacturing scale-up challenge required translating laboratory formulation success into commercial production capabilities that could produce consistent quality at volumes needed for market launch.

"Laboratory batches of 1,000 tablets must be scaled to commercial batches of 500,000 tablets while maintaining identical release characteristics," our manufacturing team explained during the scale-up planning.

"What technical challenges does scale-up create?" Dr. Singh asked.

"Mixing uniformity, compression force consistency, coating thickness control, and environmental conditions that affect tablet properties differently at laboratory versus commercial scale."

"And scale-up timeline?"

"Typically 6-8 months for process optimization, validation, and regulatory approval of commercial manufacturing procedures."

The intellectual property analysis revealed that our extended-release technology provided multiple patent opportunities across formulation composition, manufacturing processes, and therapeutic applications.

"The matrix technology we developed enables patent protection through composition claims, process claims, and method-of-use claims," our IP attorney explained during the patent strategy meeting.

"How many patent applications would comprehensive protection require?" I asked.

"Minimum three patent applications: core composition patents, manufacturing process patents, and therapeutic use patents. Additional patents possible for specific applications or improvements."

"And patent protection timeline?"

"Patent applications require 18-24 months for prosecution, but provisional patents provide immediate protection for commercial development."

The regulatory approval strategy required positioning our extended-release metformin as improved therapy rather than generic equivalent because clinical advantages justified premium regulatory pathway.

"Products with demonstrated clinical advantages can pursue 505(b)(2) regulatory pathway rather than generic ANDA pathway," Dr. Patel explained during regulatory planning.

"What advantages does 505(b)(2) provide over ANDA approval?" I asked.

"505(b)(2) enables premium pricing, market exclusivity, and brand positioning that generic approval cannot support."

"But 505(b)(2) requires more extensive clinical data than ANDA approval?"

"More clinical investment but higher commercial returns. 505(b)(2) products typically achieve 40-60% higher pricing than generic alternatives."

The market analysis showed that extended-release metformin addressed significant unmet medical needs in diabetes management where existing products had limitations.

"Current metformin extended-release products require twice-daily dosing and cause gastrointestinal side effects in 25-30% of patients," our market research consultant reported.

"And our formulation addresses both limitations?" I asked.

"Once-daily dosing plus reduced side effects could capture significant market share from existing products while enabling premium pricing."

"Market size for improved metformin products?"

"Metformin is prescribed to 120 million patients globally. Even 5% market share represents substantial revenue opportunity."

The commercial launch preparation required developing marketing strategies, distribution partnerships, and customer education programs that emphasized clinical advantages rather than cost competition.

"Extended-release metformin marketing must communicate therapeutic benefits to physicians and patients who are accustomed to viewing metformin as commodity product," our marketing consultant explained.

"How do we market improved versions of established generic drugs?" I asked.

"Clinical data demonstrating patient benefits, physician education about compliance advantages, and health economics showing cost-effectiveness of improved therapy."

The first commercial production run took place in March 2016: 2 million tablets manufactured according to validated procedures that replicated laboratory performance at commercial scale.

"Commercial production of extended-release metformin represents successful translation of innovation research into marketable pharmaceutical products," I announced during the production milestone ceremony.

The market launch results exceeded projections because physicians and patients recognized clinical advantages that justified premium pricing over generic alternatives.

"Extended-release metformin achieved ₹8 crores in first-year sales with average pricing 85% above generic metformin alternatives," our sales manager reported during the annual review.

"And customer acceptance of premium pricing?" I asked.

"Excellent. Physicians appreciate once-daily dosing for patient compliance, and patients prefer reduced side effects even at higher cost."

"Plus insurance reimbursement for therapeutically superior products?"

"Insurance coverage has been favorable because improved compliance reduces long-term diabetes complications that cost healthcare systems more than premium drug pricing."

Twelve months after commercial launch, extended-release metformin was generating ₹25 crores annually and had achieved 12% market share in premium metformin segment.

"The modified release success validated our innovation strategy," I told our board during the annual review. "Innovation products generate higher margins while providing genuine patient benefits."

"And modified release capabilities enable additional product development?" asked our board chairman.

"Extended-release technology platform can be applied across our entire portfolio plus custom development for licensing opportunities."

Two years after launch, extended-release metformin had generated ₹65 crores in cumulative revenue and enabled three additional licensing agreements with multinational pharmaceutical companies.

"Modified release formulation success taught us that pharmaceutical innovation succeeds when it addresses real clinical problems rather than just creating product differentiation," I told Dr. Chen during our annual R&D review.

"And innovation success requires systematic capability development that enables translating research discoveries into commercial products."

"The key insight was that innovation provides sustainable competitive advantages when it creates genuine therapeutic value rather than just marketing advantages."

Three years after our first modified release success, we had developed extended-release capabilities that enabled innovation partnerships, licensing revenue, and premium product positioning that generic manufacturing could never achieve.

"You know what the modified release success taught us about innovation strategy?" I said to our management team during strategic planning. "Innovation success depends on solving meaningful problems that customers value enough to pay premium prices."

"And innovation capabilities create competitive advantages that extend beyond individual products to include platform technologies and development expertise."

The modified release formulation success had become the foundation for our innovation program, demonstrating that systematic R&D investment could create commercial products that provided both patient benefits and sustainable competitive advantages.

Patent Filing Strategies and IP Protection

The patent attorney's bill for our first intellectual property filing contained a line item that made me question whether we were protecting innovations or funding someone's retirement.

"Patent prosecution for extended-release metformin formulation: $45,000 for US filing, $35,000 for European filing, $25,000 for Indian filing, plus $15,000 for international PCT application," read the invoice from our IP law firm. "Total initial filing costs: $120,000 for comprehensive global protection."

"Why does patent protection cost more than the research that created the innovation?" I asked our IP attorney during our quarterly review meeting.

"Patent protection requires legal expertise across multiple jurisdictions, extensive prior art searches, detailed technical documentation, and ongoing prosecution through complex approval processes," she explained.

This conversation took place in April 2016, six months after our extended-release metformin success, when we were learning that intellectual property protection was as complex and expensive as pharmaceutical research itself.

"Maybe we're overprotecting intellectual property," Priya suggested during our IP strategy discussion. "Do we really need patent protection in dozens of countries?"

"Patent protection must match market access strategy," our IP consultant replied. "Countries where you plan to manufacture, sell, or license products require patent protection to prevent competitive copying."

"And the cost of comprehensive protection versus the risk of inadequate protection?"

"Patent protection costs are predictable and manageable. Patent infringement losses can eliminate entire product revenue streams."

The patent landscape analysis revealed that pharmaceutical intellectual property involved multiple types of protection: composition patents, process patents, use patents, and design patents that created overlapping protection layers.

"Comprehensive IP protection requires multiple patent applications covering different aspects of the same innovation," our patent attorney explained during our IP education session.

"What different aspects specifically?" Dr. Chen asked.

"Composition patents protect formulation ingredients and ratios. Process patents protect manufacturing methods. Use patents protect therapeutic applications. Each type provides different protection scope and duration."

"And multiple patents provide stronger protection than single patents?"

"Multiple patents create patent thickets that make competitive circumvention more difficult and expensive for potential infringers."

The prior art search process required analyzing thousands of existing patents, publications, and regulatory filings to ensure our innovations were genuinely novel and patentable.

"Prior art searches for pharmaceutical patents typically identify 500-1,000 relevant documents that must be analyzed for novelty assessment," our patent search specialist explained.

"How do we know if our innovations are sufficiently different from existing patents?" I asked.

"Patent novelty requires demonstrating that our innovations provide unexpected advantages or solve problems that prior art doesn't address."

"And novelty assessment determines patent approval probability?"

"Novelty assessment plus invention utility plus non-obviousness determine patent eligibility. All three criteria must be satisfied for patent approval."

The patent prosecution strategy required different approaches for different geographic markets because patent laws, examination procedures, and protection scope varied significantly across countries.

"US patent prosecution emphasizes broad claims with commercial value," our US patent attorney explained during the global filing strategy meeting. "European prosecution emphasizes narrow claims with technical precision. Indian prosecution emphasizes therapeutic utility with social benefit."

"And we need different patent applications for different countries?" Dr. Patel asked.

"International PCT applications provide initial global filing, but individual country prosecution requires customized claims and arguments based on local patent law."

"So global patent protection involves managing dozens of separate legal proceedings simultaneously?"

"Global patent portfolios require coordinated prosecution strategies across multiple jurisdictions with different legal requirements and examination timelines."

The patent claim strategy required balancing broad protection scope with specific technical details that could withstand legal challenges from competitors seeking to invalidate patents.

"Patent claims must be broad enough to prevent competitive circumvention but specific enough to demonstrate novelty over prior art," our patent prosecution attorney explained.

"How do we achieve optimal claim breadth?" I asked.

"Hierarchical claiming strategies that include broad independent claims supported by narrow dependent claims covering specific embodiments and applications."

"And claim strategy affects patent value?"

"Claim scope determines commercial protection value. Broad claims provide stronger competitive barriers, but overly broad claims risk patent invalidation challenges."

The patent licensing strategy required developing business models that could generate revenue from intellectual property through licensing agreements with other pharmaceutical companies.

"Patent licensing can generate revenue streams that supplement product sales," our licensing consultant explained during the commercialization planning.

"What licensing opportunities exist for pharmaceutical patents?" I asked.

"Geographic licensing for markets where we don't operate, therapeutic licensing for applications we don't pursue, and technology licensing for companies seeking access to our platform innovations."

"And licensing economics?"

"Pharmaceutical patent licensing typically generates 3-8% royalties on licensed product sales, plus upfront payments and milestone fees."

The patent defense strategy required preparing for potential infringement challenges from competitors seeking to invalidate patents or design around patent protection.

"Patent defense involves monitoring competitive activities, identifying potential infringement, and enforcing patent rights through legal action when necessary," our IP enforcement attorney explained.

"How do we monitor competitive patent infringement?" Dr. Singh asked.

"Market surveillance, competitive intelligence, patent watch services, and freedom-to-operate analysis that identify potential infringement activities."

"And patent enforcement costs?"

"Patent litigation can cost $2-5 million per case, but successful enforcement can protect product revenues worth hundreds of millions."

The trade secret protection strategy involved identifying innovations that provided competitive advantages through confidentiality rather than patent disclosure.

"Some pharmaceutical innovations provide better protection through trade secrets than patents," our IP strategist explained during the protection planning.

"What innovations work better as trade secrets?" I asked.

"Manufacturing processes, analytical methods, formulation techniques, and quality control procedures that competitors cannot reverse-engineer from finished products."

"And trade secret protection requirements?"

"Confidentiality agreements, access controls, employee training, and documentation systems that maintain secrecy while enabling business operations."

The IP portfolio management required systematic approaches to patent maintenance, prosecution monitoring, and strategic decision-making about protection investments.

"Patent portfolios require ongoing investment in maintenance fees, prosecution costs, and enforcement activities," our IP portfolio manager explained.

"How much ongoing investment do patent portfolios require?" our CFO asked.

"Typically 15-25% of original filing costs annually for maintenance, prosecution, and portfolio management activities."

"And portfolio management includes what specific activities?"

"Patent renewal decisions, prosecution strategy adjustments, licensing opportunity evaluation, and competitive intelligence monitoring."

Two years after beginning systematic patent filing, our IP portfolio included 15 patent applications across 8 countries with projected protection value of ₹150 crores based on licensed product revenue potential.

"Patent portfolio development exceeded expectations," I told our board during the IP review. "Intellectual property assets provide competitive protection plus licensing revenue opportunities."

"And IP protection supports business strategies beyond just defensive patent protection?" asked our board chairman.

"Patent portfolios enable licensing partnerships, technology collaborations, and strategic alliances that pure product development cannot access."

Three years after implementing comprehensive IP strategy, our patent portfolio was generating ₹8 crores annually in licensing revenue while providing competitive protection for products worth ₹180 crores in annual sales.

"Patent filing strategies taught us that intellectual property protection requires systematic investment in legal expertise, global filing coordination, and ongoing portfolio management," I told our IP team during the annual review.

"And IP protection creates business value through multiple mechanisms: competitive barriers, licensing revenue, partnership opportunities, and strategic positioning."

"The key insight was that patent protection succeeds when it's integrated with business strategy rather than treated as separate legal requirement."

Four years after beginning patent filing activities, our intellectual property had become a strategic asset that enabled partnerships with multinational companies seeking access to our innovation capabilities and protected technologies.

"You know what IP protection taught us about innovation strategy?" I said to Dr. Chen during our annual R&D planning. "Innovation value depends as much on intellectual property protection as on technical innovation itself."

"And patent strategies become competitive advantages when they enable business opportunities that unprotected innovations cannot support."

The lesson had become essential for competing in global pharmaceutical markets where intellectual property protection determined the commercial value of innovation investments and enabled strategic partnerships that pure technical capabilities could not access independently.

Chapter 15

The Biosimilar Bet

When Biology Becomes Business

The market analysis that Dr. Sarah Williams presented during our March 2016 strategy meeting contained a statistic that made biosimilar drugs seem like either the greatest opportunity or the greatest risk in pharmaceutical development.

"Biological drug patents worth $200 billion annually will expire between 2016-2025," she announced, displaying charts that showed patent cliffs for some of the world's most expensive medications. "Biosimilar competition could reduce these drug costs by 30-70% while creating market opportunities worth $100-150 billion."

"That sounds like excellent news for companies that can develop biosimilars," I said, studying patent expiry dates for drugs that cost patients $50,000-100,000 annually.

"Excellent news if you can navigate regulatory requirements that are 10 times more complex than generic drug approval and development costs that exceed $100 million per product," she replied.

This conversation marked our introduction to the most ambitious expansion in our company's history: entering biotechnology drug development where products were manufactured by living organisms rather than synthesized through chemical processes.

"Biosimilars represent the intersection of our biotechnology manufacturing capabilities with our regulatory expertise," I told our management team during the strategic planning session. "We have fermentation experience from our insulin precursor work and FDA approval experience from our generic programs."

"But biosimilar development requires capabilities we've never attempted," Priya observed. "Biological drug development involves complexities that chemical drug development doesn't have."

"Which creates barriers to entry that could provide competitive advantages if we can develop the necessary capabilities systematically."

The biosimilar market opportunity analysis revealed that biological drugs represented the fastest-growing segment of pharmaceutical sales, with limited competition due to technical and regulatory barriers that prevented most generic manufacturers from entering the market.

"Biological drugs account for 8 of the 10 highest-revenue pharmaceutical products globally," our market research consultant reported during the opportunity assessment. "Patent expiries will create biosimilar opportunities worth $20-30 billion annually."

"Why haven't generic drug manufacturers entered biosimilar markets previously?" Dr. Singh asked.

"Biosimilar development requires biotechnology manufacturing, analytical testing capabilities, clinical trials, and regulatory expertise that traditional pharmaceutical manufacturers don't possess."

"And how many companies globally have demonstrated biosimilar development capabilities?"

"Fewer than 20 companies worldwide have achieved regulatory approval for biosimilar products, compared to hundreds of companies manufacturing generic drugs."

The technical complexity assessment revealed that biosimilar development involved biological processes that were fundamentally different from chemical drug manufacturing.

"Biosimilar drugs are produced by genetically modified living organisms rather than chemical synthesis," explained Dr. Ravi Shankar, our newly hired VP of Biotechnology. "Cell culture, fermentation, purification, and characterization require different expertise than traditional pharmaceutical manufacturing."

"How different specifically?" I asked.

"Chemical drugs have defined molecular structures that can be replicated exactly. Biological drugs are complex proteins with variable structures that can only be replicated approximately."

"So biosimilars are 'similar' rather than 'identical' to original biological drugs?"

"Biosimilars must demonstrate comparable efficacy and safety through clinical testing, whereas generic drugs demonstrate bioequivalence through laboratory testing."

The regulatory complexity for biosimilar approval exceeded anything we'd encountered in pharmaceutical development because biological drugs required extensive clinical data and manufacturing process validation.

"Biosimilar regulatory approval requires analytical similarity studies, non-clinical pharmacology studies, and clinical trials demonstrating comparable efficacy and safety," Dr. Patel explained during our regulatory assessment.

"How do biosimilar approval requirements compare to generic drug requirements?" I asked.

"Biosimilar approval costs $50-100 million and requires 5-8 years compared to $2-5 million and 2-3 years for generic drugs."

"But biosimilar market opportunities justify the additional investment?"

"Successful biosimilars can generate $200-500 million annually compared to $20-50 million for typical generic drugs."

The manufacturing infrastructure requirements for biosimilar production exceeded our existing biotechnology capabilities because biological drug manufacturing required specialized facilities, equipment, and quality systems.

"Biosimilar manufacturing requires mammalian cell culture capabilities, large-scale bioreactors, protein purification systems, and analytical laboratories that our existing facilities don't provide," Dr. Shankar explained during our infrastructure assessment.

"What additional investment would biosimilar manufacturing require?" our CFO asked.

"Approximately ₹150-200 crores for facility construction, equipment installation, and regulatory validation."

"And manufacturing scale compared to our current biotechnology operations?"

"Biosimilar manufacturing operates at 10,000-20,000 liter scales compared to our current 2,000 liter capacity."

The target product selection required analyzing patent expiry timelines, market size, competitive landscape, and technical feasibility for potential biosimilar development opportunities.

"We recommend targeting adalimumab biosimilar as our first development project," Dr. Shankar proposed during our product selection meeting. "Patent expiry in 2023, $20 billion annual market, limited competitive pipeline, and technical feasibility within our development timeline."

"What makes adalimumab technically feasible for our capabilities?" Dr. Chen asked.

"Adalimumab is a monoclonal antibody that can be produced using established cell culture techniques, with analytical methods that our capabilities can develop."

"And development timeline for adalimumab biosimilar?"

"Approximately 7 years from project initiation to regulatory approval, requiring sustained investment throughout the development period."

The partnership strategy required identifying biotechnology companies, contract research organizations, and regulatory consultants who could provide expertise that we couldn't develop internally within acceptable timelines.

"Biosimilar development requires partnerships with companies that have specialized capabilities in cell line development, analytical testing, and clinical trials," our business development manager explained during the partnership planning.

"What partnerships specifically would be required?" I asked.

"Cell line development partnerships for creating production cell lines, analytical partnerships for biosimilarity testing, and clinical research partnerships for conducting comparative efficacy studies."

"And partnership costs versus internal capability development?"

"Partnerships can reduce development timeline by 2-3 years while requiring lower upfront investment than building all capabilities internally."

The intellectual property landscape for biosimilars proved more complex than traditional pharmaceutical patents because biological drugs involved multiple patent layers covering manufacturing processes, formulations, and therapeutic applications.

"Adalimumab is protected by over 70 patents covering the antibody structure, manufacturing processes, formulation methods, and therapeutic uses," our IP attorney reported during the freedom-to-operate analysis.

"How do we develop biosimilars without infringing existing patents?" I asked.

"Biosimilar development requires designing around patent claims through alternative manufacturing processes, different formulations, and careful regulatory positioning."

"And patent circumvention affects development costs?"

"Patent design-around strategies can increase development complexity and costs, but they're essential for avoiding patent infringement litigation."

The biosimilar program launch took place in September 2016 with adalimumab biosimilar as the lead project and projected commercial launch in 2023-2024.

"Biosimilar development represents our most ambitious expansion into high-value pharmaceutical markets," I announced during the program launch ceremony attended by biotechnology industry executives and government officials.

The initial development milestones were achieved ahead of schedule: cell line development completed within 18 months, analytical method development completed within 12 months, and manufacturing process optimization progressing according to timeline.

"Biosimilar development is exceeding timeline expectations," Dr. Shankar reported during our first annual review. "Technical progress validates our capability development strategy."

"And development costs compared to projections?" our CFO asked.

"Development costs are tracking 15% below budget due to successful partnerships and efficient project management."

Two years after biosimilar program launch, we had achieved technical milestones that positioned us for clinical trial initiation and had identified three additional biosimilar opportunities for future development.

"The biosimilar bet validated our strategy of entering high-barrier markets where technical capabilities create sustainable competitive advantages," I told our board during the annual review.

"And biosimilar capabilities enable opportunities beyond just biosimilar product development?" asked our board chairman.

"Biotechnology capabilities support custom development services, technology licensing, and partnerships with multinational companies seeking biosimilar development expertise."

Three years after beginning biosimilar development, our biotechnology capabilities had attracted partnership inquiries from multinational pharmaceutical companies and licensing opportunities worth ₹50-100 crores annually.

"You know what the biosimilar bet taught us about market opportunity evaluation?" I said to Dr. Shankar during our annual biotechnology review. "The highest-value opportunities often have the highest barriers to entry, but overcoming those barriers creates competitive advantages that lower-barrier opportunities cannot provide."

"And biotechnology capabilities become platforms for multiple business opportunities rather than just individual product development."

The biosimilar program had become the foundation for our transition from generic pharmaceutical manufacturer to biotechnology company capable of competing in the highest-value segments of the pharmaceutical industry.

More importantly, it had taught us that systematic capability building could enable access to market opportunities that seemed impossible for companies without existing biotechnology expertise, when approached with sufficient investment timeline and strategic partnerships.

Strategic Decision to Enter Biologics

The board meeting in August 2016 lasted seven hours and ended with the most expensive strategic decision in our company's history.

"Entering biologics development will require ₹300 crores over five years with no guarantee of commercial success," I told our board during the final presentation. "But remaining exclusively in generic pharmaceuticals limits us to markets where pricing pressure and competitive intensity are destroying profit margins."

"What's the probability of biologics development success?" asked our board chairman, reviewing investment projections that exceeded our total previous capital expenditures.

"Industry success rates for biosimilar development are approximately 60-70% for companies with adequate resources and expertise. Our partnership strategy should improve our success probability."

This conversation represented the culmination of eighteen months of strategic analysis, market research, and capability assessment that had led us to conclude that biologics represented our only path to sustainable competitive advantages.

"Generic pharmaceuticals are becoming a commodity business where operational excellence provides temporary advantages rather than sustainable differentiation," I explained during our strategic rationale presentation.

"But biologics development involves risks and complexities that we've never encountered," Priya observed during the decision discussion.

"Which creates barriers to entry that protect successful biologics companies from the competitive pressure that's destroying generic drug margins."

The competitive landscape analysis had revealed that pharmaceutical markets were bifurcating into commodity segments where price competition eliminated profits and innovation segments where technical barriers enabled premium pricing.

"Generic drug markets are experiencing margin compression due to competitive intensity, regulatory pricing pressure, and procurement consolidation," our market analyst reported during the strategic assessment.

"How severe is margin compression in generic pharmaceuticals?" our CFO asked.

"Generic drug margins have declined from 35-45% five years ago to 15-25% currently, with continued downward pressure from competitive supply increases."

"And biologics markets show different competitive dynamics?"

"Biologics markets maintain 60-80% gross margins due to technical complexity, regulatory barriers, and limited competitive supply."

The technology assessment showed that our existing biotechnology capabilities provided a foundation for biologics development that many pharmaceutical companies lacked.

"Our insulin precursor manufacturing experience, fermentation capabilities, and biotechnology facility infrastructure provide advantages for biologics development," Dr. Ravi Shankar explained during the capability evaluation.

"But biologics development requires capabilities beyond our current biotechnology operations?" I asked.

"Mammalian cell culture, protein purification, analytical characterization, and clinical development capabilities that represent significant expansions of our current abilities."

"And we can develop these capabilities internally versus licensing or partnership approaches?"

"Combination of internal development for core capabilities and partnerships for specialized expertise provides optimal risk-return balance."

The market opportunity analysis revealed that biologics patent expiries would create opportunities for companies with development capabilities but that the window for market entry was limited.

"Major biologics patents expire between 2018-2025, representing $150 billion in annual sales that will become available for biosimilar competition," our business development consultant reported.

"And how many companies are positioned to capture these opportunities?" I asked.

"Fewer than 15 companies globally have demonstrated successful biosimilar development capabilities, compared to hundreds of companies competing in generic pharmaceuticals."

"So biologics development could provide access to markets with limited competition?"

"Biologics development enables participation in high-value, low-competition markets rather than low-value, high-competition markets."

The investment analysis showed that biologics development required front-loaded investments with delayed returns but provided superior long-term economics compared to generic drug expansion.

"Biologics development requires ₹60 crores annually for five years before generating revenue, compared to ₹15 crores for generic drug development that generates revenue within two years," our financial analyst reported.

"But biologics revenue potential justifies the investment timeline?" our board treasurer asked.

"Successful biosimilars generate ₹200-500 crores annually compared to ₹20-50 crores for generic drugs. Higher investment requirements but substantially higher returns."

"And investment risk compared to generic expansion alternatives?"

"Higher development risk but lower competitive risk. Generic expansion faces certain margin compression, while biologics development faces uncertain technical challenges."

The regulatory strategy required understanding approval processes that were fundamentally different from generic drug regulations because biosimilars required clinical proof of efficacy rather than just bioequivalence demonstration.

"Biosimilar approval requires comprehensive comparability studies, non-clinical testing, and clinical trials that can cost ₹50-80 crores per product," Dr. Patel explained during the regulatory assessment.

"How do biosimilar approval timelines compare to generic approvals?" I asked.

"Biosimilar approval requires 6-8 years compared to 2-3 years for generics, but biosimilar market exclusivity lasts longer due to limited competition."

"And regulatory approval probability?"

"Biosimilar approval probability is 70-80% for well-designed development programs, compared to 90-95% for generic drugs."

The talent acquisition strategy required recruiting biotechnology expertise that commanded compensation packages exceeding our current pharmaceutical professionals.

"Biologics development requires hiring protein scientists, cell culture specialists, analytical biochemists, and clinical development managers," our HR consultant explained during the staffing assessment.

"And biotechnology talent availability in India?" I asked.

"Growing biotechnology talent pool in Bangalore and Hyderabad, but experienced professionals often require international-level compensation packages."

"Compensation levels compared to our current pharmaceutical professionals?"

"Biotechnology professionals typically command 50-80% higher compensation than equivalent pharmaceutical positions."

The partnership strategy involved identifying international biotechnology companies that could provide technology access, development expertise, and regulatory guidance that would accelerate our biologics capabilities.

"Strategic partnerships with established biologics companies can reduce development timelines, share development risks, and provide technology access," our business development manager explained.

"What types of partnerships specifically?" Priya asked.

"Technology licensing for manufacturing processes, development partnerships for clinical trials, and commercial partnerships for international market access."

"And partnership economics versus internal development?"

"Partnerships require revenue sharing but provide faster market access and reduced development risk compared to pure internal development."

The board vote was unanimous but reflected recognition that biologics development represented a fundamental transformation of our business model rather than just expansion of existing capabilities.

"Biologics development will change our company from generic manufacturer to biotechnology company," I told our employees during the announcement meeting. "The investment is substantial, but the opportunity is transformational."

The biologics program implementation began in October 2016 with facility expansion, equipment procurement, team building, and partnership development proceeding simultaneously.

"Biologics development represents our most ambitious expansion since founding the company," I announced during the program launch ceremony.

Six months after the biologics decision, we had recruited 15 biotechnology professionals, initiated facility construction, and signed development partnerships with two international biotechnology companies.

"Biologics program implementation is proceeding according to timeline," Dr. Shankar reported during our first quarterly review. "Team building and partnership development are ahead of schedule."

Twelve months after the biologics decision, our biotechnology capabilities had attracted partnership inquiries from multinational pharmaceutical companies seeking Indian development capabilities.

"The biologics decision validated our strategic thesis that high-barrier markets provide better long-term opportunities than low-barrier markets," I told our board during the annual review.

Two years after entering biologics development, we had advanced three biosimilar projects to clinical development and established biotechnology capabilities that enabled consulting and partnership revenue.

"You know what the biologics decision taught us about strategic transformation?" I said to our management team during our annual planning session. "Sometimes the highest-risk decisions are actually the lowest-risk strategies when competitive alternatives involve certain decline."

"And strategic transformation requires accepting short-term costs for long-term competitive positioning."

The biologics decision had become the foundation for our evolution from generic pharmaceutical manufacturer to biotechnology company capable of competing in the highest-value segments of the pharmaceutical industry.

More importantly, it had taught us that strategic decisions often involve choosing between uncertain opportunities and certain competitive decline, and that systematic capability building could enable business transformations that seemed impossible without existing expertise.

Partnership with European Biotech Firm

The term sheet from BioDevelop AG arrived via encrypted email and contained partnership terms that made our previous business agreements look like simple purchase orders.

"We're proposing a joint development agreement for adalimumab biosimilar with shared investment, shared intellectual property, and tiered revenue distribution based on market performance," wrote Dr. Klaus Weber, BioDevelop's Chief Business Officer, in the accompanying letter.

"What does 'shared intellectual property' mean practically?" I asked our legal team during the term sheet review meeting.

"Joint ownership of all patents, trade secrets, and regulatory data generated during the collaboration, with both companies having rights to use the IP for their respective markets."

This correspondence took place in December 2016, three months after launching our biologics program, when we realized that biosimilar development required European partnerships to access regulatory expertise, analytical capabilities, and market knowledge that Indian companies couldn't develop efficiently.

"Why do we need European partnerships for biosimilar development?" Priya asked during our partnership evaluation meeting.

"European companies have 10+ years of biosimilar development experience, established relationships with European regulators, and analytical capabilities that would take us 3-5 years to develop independently," explained Dr. Ravi Shankar.

"And BioDevelop specifically offers what advantages?"

"BioDevelop has successfully developed three biosimilars, maintains state-of-the-art analytical laboratories, and has existing manufacturing agreements with European CMOs."

The partnership structure required understanding complex intellectual property arrangements, development cost sharing, and revenue distribution models that differed substantially from traditional licensing agreements.

"Joint development partnerships involve shared investment in development costs, shared ownership of resulting intellectual property, and shared revenues from successful products," our business development consultant explained during the partnership education session.

"How do shared costs and shared revenues work practically?" our CFO asked.

"Each partner contributes specific capabilities and funding according to agreed schedules, and revenues are distributed based on contribution percentages and market territories."

"And shared IP ownership provides what advantages over licensing arrangements?"

"Joint IP ownership provides both partners with commercial rights to developed products rather than licensor-licensee relationships that limit commercial flexibility."

The due diligence process for evaluating BioDevelop's capabilities was more comprehensive than any supplier assessment we'd conducted because partnership success depended on technical competence rather than just commercial reliability.

"BioDevelop due diligence requires evaluating their analytical laboratories, development team expertise, regulatory track record, and financial stability," our partnership consultant explained during the evaluation planning.

"What specific capabilities are most critical for biosimilar partnership success?" I asked.

"Analytical characterization capabilities for demonstrating biosimilarity, regulatory expertise for managing approval processes, and manufacturing knowledge for technology transfer."

"And we can validate these capabilities through facility visits and team interviews?"

"Comprehensive due diligence includes facility inspections, technical presentations, reference customer interviews, and regulatory authority feedback."

The technical evaluation revealed that BioDevelop's analytical capabilities exceeded what we could develop internally within acceptable timelines and budgets.

"BioDevelop maintains analytical laboratories with mass spectrometry, protein characterization, and immunogenicity testing capabilities worth approximately €15 million," Dr. Chen reported after our facility visit.

"How do their analytical capabilities compare to what we would need for biosimilar development?" Dr. Shankar asked.

"BioDevelop's capabilities provide comprehensive biosimilarity testing that would require ₹25-30 crores investment plus 2-3 years development time to replicate internally."

"And access to their capabilities through partnership versus internal development?"

"Partnership provides immediate access to validated analytical methods and experienced technical teams."

The regulatory expertise evaluation showed that BioDevelop's experience with European Medicines Agency approvals could accelerate our regulatory timeline significantly.

"BioDevelop has achieved EMA approval for three biosimilars with average approval timelines 18 months faster than industry averages," our regulatory consultant reported.

"How does European regulatory experience benefit our development program?" Dr. Patel asked.

"EMA approval often serves as reference for other regulatory authorities, and BioDevelop's regulatory relationships could facilitate approvals in multiple markets."

"And regulatory expertise transfer to our team?"

"Partnership includes regulatory consulting and training that develops our internal capabilities while leveraging their experience."

The financial terms required complex arrangements for sharing development costs, milestone payments, and revenue distribution across multiple markets and development phases.

"Partnership financial structure includes ₹45 crores shared development investment, milestone payments totaling ₹15 crores, and revenue sharing of 60-40 favoring the manufacturing partner," our financial analyst explained.

"And revenue sharing basis?" I asked.

"BioDevelop receives 40% of net revenues for markets where they provide regulatory and commercial support, we receive 60% for markets where we provide manufacturing and distribution."

"How do shared development costs compare to independent development costs?"

"Shared development reduces our total investment from ₹150 crores to ₹75 crores while providing access to capabilities worth ₹50 crores."

The manufacturing technology transfer required establishing procedures for transferring BioDevelop's cell culture and purification processes to our Indian biotechnology facility.

"Technology transfer involves documentation of manufacturing processes, training of technical personnel, and validation of transferred processes," our manufacturing team explained during the transfer planning.

"What specific manufacturing technologies would be transferred?" I asked.

"Cell line development methods, culture media optimization, purification protocols, and analytical testing procedures."

"And technology transfer timeline?"

"Approximately 12-18 months for complete process transfer, validation, and regulatory approval of manufacturing changes."

The partnership negotiation took six months and required legal expertise across intellectual property law, international business agreements, and biotechnology regulations.

"Joint development agreements involve more complex legal structures than traditional commercial contracts," our attorney explained during the negotiation process.

"What legal complexities specifically?" Priya asked.

"IP ownership allocation, liability distribution, dispute resolution procedures, and termination arrangements that protect both partners' interests."

"And international partnership legal requirements?"

"Cross-border agreements require compliance with European, Indian, and potentially US legal frameworks for intellectual property and commercial relationships."

The BioDevelop partnership agreement was signed in June 2017 with initial focus on adalimumab biosimilar development and options for additional biosimilar collaborations.

"European biotechnology partnership represents our most strategic international collaboration," I announced during the signing ceremony attended by BioDevelop executives and Indian government representatives.

The partnership implementation proceeded faster than anticipated because BioDevelop's established systems and experienced team accelerated our development timeline significantly.

"Partnership implementation is exceeding expectations," Dr. Shankar reported after six months of collaboration. "Technology transfer ahead of schedule, and development milestones achieved 20% faster than independent timeline projections."

"And partnership working relationship?" I asked.

"Excellent technical collaboration, effective communication, and aligned objectives. Cultural differences are minimal because both teams focus on technical excellence."

Twelve months after partnership implementation, the adalimumab biosimilar program had achieved analytical similarity demonstration and was preparing for clinical trial initiation.

"BioDevelop partnership validated our strategy of leveraging European expertise while maintaining Indian cost advantages," I told our board during the annual review.

"And partnership model enables additional biosimilar development opportunities?" asked our board chairman.

"Partnership success with adalimumab provides template for additional collaborations across our biosimilar pipeline."

Two years after the BioDevelop partnership launch, we had expanded collaboration to include three biosimilar programs and were generating consulting revenue from BioDevelop's other partnership projects.

"European biotech partnership taught us that international collaborations can accelerate capability development more efficiently than internal investment when partners have complementary strengths," I told our management team during strategic planning.

"And successful partnerships create platforms for additional collaborations rather than just individual project solutions."

Three years after establishing the BioDevelop partnership, our collaboration had produced two biosimilar candidates in clinical development and had enabled additional partnerships with other European biotechnology companies.

"You know what the European partnership taught us about global biotechnology collaboration?" I said to Dr. Shankar during our annual partnership review. "International partnerships succeed when they combine different regional advantages rather than just sharing development costs."

"And biotechnology partnerships create competitive advantages that individual companies cannot achieve through independent development efforts."

The BioDevelop partnership had become our model for international biotechnology collaboration, demonstrating that strategic partnerships could accelerate complex development programs while providing access to expertise and capabilities that pure financial investment couldn't access within acceptable timelines.

Building Biosimilar Manufacturing Capabilities

The equipment installation quote from Sartorius Biotech made our previous manufacturing investments look like laboratory experiments.

"Complete mammalian cell culture facility including 5,000-liter bioreactors, downstream processing equipment, and analytical instrumentation: €25 million," read the proposal that would transform our biotechnology capabilities from bacterial fermentation to complex protein production.

"€25 million is more than our total company valuation five years ago," I told our engineering team during the facility planning meeting. "Are we building a manufacturing facility or a small city?"

"Biosimilar manufacturing requires equipment precision and scale that bacterial fermentation doesn't need," explained Dr. Ravi Shankar. "Mammalian cells are more sensitive than bacteria and biosimilar products are more complex than simple proteins."

This conversation took place in March 2017, nine months after our BioDevelop partnership launch, when we realized that biosimilar development required manufacturing capabilities that exceeded our existing biotechnology infrastructure by orders of magnitude.

"Why can't we adapt our existing fermentation facility for biosimilar manufacturing?" our CFO asked during the investment evaluation.

"Bacterial fermentation operates in environments that would kill mammalian cells," Dr. Shankar explained. "Biosimilar manufacturing requires sterile conditions, precise environmental controls, and analytical capabilities that our bacterial systems don't provide."

"So biosimilar manufacturing is fundamentally different from our current biotechnology operations?"

"As different as tablet compression is from chemical synthesis. Similar principles but completely different equipment, procedures, and expertise requirements."

The facility design process required understanding cleanroom classifications, environmental controls, and production workflows that exceeded pharmaceutical manufacturing complexity.

"Biosimilar manufacturing requires ISO Class 5 cleanrooms for cell culture, ISO Class 7 for downstream processing, and ISO Class 8 for analytical testing," our cleanroom consultant explained during the design phase.

"How do biosimilar cleanroom requirements compare to pharmaceutical cleanrooms?" I asked.

"Biosimilar cleanrooms require 100 times fewer particles per cubic meter than pharmaceutical cleanrooms, plus temperature controls within ±1°C and humidity controls within ±2%."

"And cleanroom construction costs?"

"Biosimilar cleanroom construction costs ₹15,000-20,000 per square foot compared to ₹3,000-5,000 for pharmaceutical cleanrooms."

The equipment procurement required understanding biotechnology systems that operated on completely different principles than pharmaceutical manufacturing equipment.

"Bioreactor systems require oxygen transfer controls, pH monitoring, dissolved CO2 measurement, and cell density tracking that chemical reactors don't need," our equipment consultant explained during the specification development.

"How do bioreactor operating requirements differ from chemical reactor requirements?" Dr. Singh asked.

"Chemical reactors optimize reaction efficiency and product yield. Bioreactors optimize cell growth conditions and protein expression while maintaining cell viability."

"And bioreactor costs compared to chemical reactor costs?"

"5,000-liter bioreactor systems cost ₹8-12 crores compared to ₹2-3 crores for equivalent chemical reactors."

The downstream processing equipment required understanding protein purification techniques that differed substantially from small molecule purification.

"Protein purification requires chromatography columns, ultrafiltration systems, and virus inactivation equipment that small molecule processing doesn't use," our process engineer explained during the equipment evaluation.

"What makes protein purification more complex than small molecule purification?" I asked.

"Proteins are large, fragile molecules that can be damaged by conditions that don't affect small molecules. Purification must maintain protein structure while removing impurities."

"And downstream processing equipment costs?"

"Complete downstream processing equipment including chromatography, filtration, and formulation systems costs ₹15-18 crores."

The analytical instrumentation requirements exceeded our existing laboratory capabilities because biosimilar characterization required techniques that simple molecules didn't need.

"Biosimilar analytical testing requires mass spectrometry, protein sequencing, glycosylation analysis, and immunogenicity testing capabilities," our analytical manager explained during the laboratory planning.

"How do biosimilar analytical requirements differ from small molecule testing?" Dr. Chen asked.

"Small molecule testing confirms chemical identity and purity. Biosimilar testing characterizes protein structure, biological activity, and immunogenic potential."

"And analytical equipment investment requirements?"

"Comprehensive biosimilar analytical capabilities require ₹12-15 crores in specialized instrumentation."

The technology transfer from BioDevelop required adapting European manufacturing processes to Indian facility capabilities while maintaining product quality and regulatory compliance.

"Technology transfer involves recreating BioDevelop's manufacturing processes using our equipment and procedures," our technology transfer team explained during the implementation planning.

"What specific challenges does cross-border technology transfer create?" I asked.

"Different equipment suppliers, varying raw material sources, alternative environmental conditions, and distinct regulatory requirements that affect process performance."

"And technology transfer success measurement?"

"Successful technology transfer produces biosimilar products that match BioDevelop's analytical specifications and regulatory requirements."

The regulatory validation required demonstrating that our manufacturing processes could produce consistent quality products that met international standards for biosimilar approval.

"Manufacturing validation requires producing three consecutive commercial-scale batches that meet all quality specifications," Dr. Patel explained during the validation planning.

"How do biosimilar validation requirements compare to pharmaceutical validation?" I asked.

"Biosimilar validation is more extensive because biological products have greater variability than chemical products. Every aspect of manufacturing must be validated for consistency."

"And validation timeline?"

"Biosimilar manufacturing validation typically requires 12-18 months compared to 6-9 months for pharmaceutical validation."

The workforce development required recruiting and training personnel with biotechnology expertise that exceeded our existing technical capabilities.

"Biosimilar manufacturing requires biochemists, cell culture specialists, protein chemists, and analytical scientists," our HR manager explained during the staffing planning.

"How many additional personnel would biosimilar manufacturing require?" I asked.

"Approximately 45 specialized professionals for commercial biosimilar manufacturing operations."

"And biotechnology talent availability?"

"Growing biotechnology talent pool in India, but experienced professionals often require international-level compensation and training."

The facility construction took 24 months and required coordination between international equipment suppliers, Indian construction contractors, and regulatory authorities across multiple jurisdictions.

"Biosimilar facility construction involves more complexity than pharmaceutical facility construction," our project manager reported during the construction phase.

"What specific complexities?" Dr. Shankar asked.

"International equipment integration, specialized utility requirements, regulatory inspections during construction, and commissioning procedures that pharmaceutical facilities don't require."

The first commercial biosimilar production run took place in February 2019: 500 liters of adalimumab biosimilar manufactured according to validated procedures that replicated BioDevelop's European processes.

"Commercial biosimilar production represents successful transformation from pharmaceutical manufacturer to biotechnology company," I announced during the production milestone ceremony.

Six months after achieving commercial biosimilar production, our manufacturing capabilities were producing consistent quality products that met European and Indian regulatory requirements.

"Biosimilar manufacturing capabilities exceeded performance expectations," Dr. Shankar reported during the operational review. "Product quality matches BioDevelop specifications while achieving 85% of theoretical yield efficiency."

"And manufacturing costs compared to projections?" our CFO asked.

"Manufacturing costs are tracking 12% below budget due to process optimization and efficiency improvements."

Twelve months after beginning commercial production, we were manufacturing biosimilar products for clinical trials and had achieved analytical results that supported regulatory filing preparation.

"Building biosimilar manufacturing capabilities proved that systematic capability development can enable complex biotechnology operations," I told our board during the annual review.

"And biosimilar capabilities provide competitive advantages beyond just biosimilar manufacturing?" asked our board chairman.

"Biotechnology capabilities enable custom development services, technology licensing, and partnerships that pharmaceutical manufacturing cannot access."

Two years after completing biosimilar facility construction, our biotechnology capabilities had attracted development contracts from international pharmaceutical companies and licensing inquiries worth ₹80-150 crores annually.

"You know what building biosimilar capabilities taught us about technology infrastructure investment?" I said to Dr. Shankar during our annual facility review. "Complex manufacturing capabilities require systematic infrastructure development that cannot be achieved through incremental improvements."

"And biotechnology infrastructure becomes competitive advantage when it enables opportunities that less capable facilities cannot support."

The biosimilar manufacturing facility had become the foundation for our biotechnology business, providing capabilities that enabled high-value development services and strategic partnerships with multinational pharmaceutical companies.

More importantly, it had taught us that transformational capability building required investment scales and technical sophistication that exceeded previous experience, but created competitive advantages that justified the complexity when approached systematically.

The Insulin Project Breakthrough

The analytical test results that Dr. Lisa Chen presented during our July 2018 project review meeting contained data that transformed our insulin development from expensive experiment into commercial reality.

"Recombinant human insulin production yields have reached 2.8 grams per liter with 99.7% purity after downstream processing," she announced, pointing to charts that showed our biotechnology capabilities had achieved pharmaceutical manufacturing standards.

"How do our yields compare to commercial insulin production?" I asked, studying numbers that seemed too good to believe after eighteen months of development challenges.

"Our yields exceed industry benchmarks by 15-20%, and our purity specifications match branded insulin products from Novo Nordisk and Sanofi."

This presentation took place two years after launching our biologics program, when our insulin project had finally achieved the technical milestones that would enable commercial manufacturing and regulatory approval.

"What changed between our previous insulin attempts and this breakthrough?" Dr. Ravi Shankar asked during the results analysis.

"Optimized cell line development, improved fermentation conditions, and enhanced purification processes that we learned from our adalimumab biosimilar work," Dr. Chen replied.

"So biosimilar development capabilities transferred to insulin manufacturing?"

"Biotechnology capabilities are synergistic. Advanced protein production techniques benefit all biological drug manufacturing regardless of specific products."

The insulin market opportunity analysis showed that diabetes treatment represented one of the largest pharmaceutical markets globally, with growing demand in developing countries where branded insulin remained unaffordable for many patients.

"Global insulin market is $40 billion annually and growing 8% per year due to increasing diabetes prevalence," our market research consultant reported during the commercial assessment.

"And insulin pricing dynamics?" I asked.

"Branded insulin costs $200-300 per patient monthly in developed markets, but generic competition could reduce prices 40-60% while maintaining attractive margins."

"So insulin biosimilars could provide both patient access and commercial opportunity?"

"Insulin biosimilars enable expanding treatment access while generating substantial revenue from large patient populations."

The regulatory pathway for insulin biosimilars was more established than other biological drugs because insulin had been subject to biosimilar competition in Europe and emerging markets for several years.

"Insulin biosimilar approval requires demonstrating analytical similarity, pharmacokinetic equivalence, and clinical efficacy comparable to reference products," Dr. Patel explained during the regulatory planning.

"How do insulin approval requirements compare to other biosimilar approvals?" I asked.

"Insulin approval is generally faster and less expensive than monoclonal antibody biosimilars because insulin is smaller, simpler, and has established regulatory precedents."

"And approval timeline for insulin biosimilars?"

"Typically 3-4 years from clinical trial initiation to commercial approval, compared to 5-6 years for complex biosimilars."

The manufacturing scale-up required adapting our laboratory insulin production to commercial volumes that could supply thousands of patients rather than just clinical trials.

"Commercial insulin manufacturing requires 10,000-liter production capacity to supply meaningful patient populations," our manufacturing team explained during the scale-up planning.

"And our current facility capacity?" Dr. Shankar asked.

"Our biosimilar facility includes 5,000-liter bioreactors that could support regional insulin supply, with expansion capability to 15,000 liters for broader market access."

"Scale-up challenges for insulin manufacturing?"

"Maintaining cell culture performance, ensuring consistent product quality, and optimizing purification efficiency at larger scales."

The cost analysis showed that insulin manufacturing could achieve production costs that enabled competitive pricing while maintaining attractive profit margins.

"Insulin manufacturing costs approximately $15-20 per patient monthly compared to $200-300 retail pricing for branded products," our cost analyst reported.

"And our projected manufacturing costs?" our CFO asked.

"We project $25-30 per patient monthly including all manufacturing, quality control, and regulatory compliance costs."

"So insulin biosimilars could be priced at $80-120 per patient monthly while achieving 60-70% gross margins?"

"Insulin pricing enables both patient affordability and commercial viability when manufacturing is optimized."

The intellectual property landscape for insulin was more favorable than other biological drugs because original insulin patents had expired and manufacturing processes were well-established.

"Insulin composition patents expired in the 1990s, so biosimilar development faces minimal patent infringement risk," our IP attorney explained during the freedom-to-operate analysis.

"But insulin delivery devices and formulations remain patent-protected?" I asked.

"Device patents protect injection pens and pumps, but those don't prevent insulin drug product development and approval."

"So insulin biosimilars can achieve market access without significant patent circumvention costs?"

"Insulin patent landscape is much more favorable than newer biological drugs with extensive patent protection."

The clinical development strategy required demonstrating that our insulin produced identical glucose control compared to branded reference products in diabetic patients.

"Insulin clinical trials require pharmacokinetic studies, glucose clamp studies, and comparative efficacy trials in Type 1 and Type 2 diabetes patients," our clinical research manager explained.

"And clinical trial costs for insulin development?" I asked.

"Approximately ₹15-20 crores for comprehensive clinical development compared to ₹50-80 crores for complex biosimilars."

"Clinical trial timeline?"

"18-24 months for complete clinical development from first patient enrollment to regulatory submission."

The commercial strategy required understanding insulin distribution channels, physician relationships, and patient education programs that differed from our existing pharmaceutical markets.

"Insulin marketing requires relationships with endocrinologists, diabetes educators, and specialty pharmacies," our marketing consultant explained during the commercial planning.

"How do insulin distribution channels differ from oral pharmaceutical products?" I asked.

"Insulin requires cold chain distribution, injection device compatibility, and patient training that oral medications don't need."

"And insulin customer education requirements?"

"Patients need instruction on injection techniques, dosage adjustments, and glucose monitoring that create ongoing relationship opportunities."

The first clinical batch of recombinant human insulin was produced in September 2018: 200 vials manufactured according to Good Manufacturing Practice standards for human clinical testing.

"Clinical insulin production represents successful translation of biotechnology capabilities into therapeutic products," I announced during the clinical batch ceremony.

The clinical trial results exceeded expectations because our insulin demonstrated identical glucose control with improved consistency compared to branded reference products.

"Clinical trials show our insulin achieves identical hemoglobin A1c reduction with 20% less glucose variability than reference insulin," our clinical investigator reported.

"And glucose variability improvement provides clinical advantages?" I asked.

"Reduced glucose variability improves patient quality of life and potentially reduces long-term diabetes complications."

Six months after clinical trial completion, we received regulatory approval for our recombinant human insulin from Indian drug authorities and had initiated approval processes in five additional countries.

"Insulin regulatory approval validates our biotechnology development capabilities," I told our board during the milestone review.

"And commercial launch timeline?" asked our board chairman.

"Commercial insulin launch planned for Q2 2019, with international market expansion following additional regulatory approvals."

The insulin commercial launch achieved market penetration that exceeded projections because healthcare providers and patients valued cost-effective alternatives to expensive branded products.

"Insulin commercial sales reached ₹15 crores in the first six months with 12% market share in the affordable insulin segment," our sales manager reported.

"And insulin profitability compared to other product segments?" our CFO asked.

"Insulin generates 65% gross margins compared to 35% for generic pharmaceuticals and 55% for modified-release products."

Twelve months after insulin commercial launch, we were supplying 25,000 patients monthly and had signed distribution agreements for six international markets.

"The insulin breakthrough taught us that biotechnology capabilities enable developing products that provide both patient benefits and commercial success," I told our management team during the annual review.

"And insulin success validates our biologics strategy while providing revenue that supports additional biotechnology development."

Two years after the insulin breakthrough, our biological drug portfolio included insulin, one approved biosimilar, and three additional biosimilars in clinical development.

"You know what the insulin project taught us about biotechnology development?" I said to Dr. Chen during our annual R&D review. "Biotechnology success creates platforms for additional opportunities rather than just individual product achievements."

"And biotechnology capabilities become more valuable as they enable developing multiple products using shared infrastructure and expertise."

The insulin breakthrough had become the foundation for our biologics business, demonstrating that systematic biotechnology development could create products that combined therapeutic value with commercial success in markets where patients needed affordable alternatives to expensive branded drugs.

PART IV: THE COMPLEXITY CONSTRAINT (2011-2016)

Part IV

The Complexity Constraint (2011-2016)

When Success Becomes its Own Problem

The management meeting in October 2014 lasted six hours and ended with the uncomfortable realization that our company had become too complex for any single person to understand completely.

"We now operate across 18 countries, manufacture 45 products, employ 450 people, manage 12 regulatory jurisdictions, maintain 8 manufacturing facilities, and coordinate 25 active partnerships," I told our senior team, reviewing organizational charts that resembled engineering blueprints more than business structures.

"And somehow we're less agile now than when we were one-tenth the size," observed Priya, studying decision-making processes that required coordination across multiple departments, time zones, and regulatory frameworks.

This conversation marked our introduction to the complexity constraint: the phenomenon where business growth creates operational complexity that eventually constrains the very growth that created it.

"The complexity constraint is different from previous constraints we've encountered," I explained to our board during our strategic review session. "Scale constraints could be solved with more resources. Market constraints could be solved with better positioning. Complexity constraints require fundamental changes to how we organize and operate the business."

"What makes complexity constraints different from other business challenges?" asked our board chairman.

"Previous constraints were external limitations that prevented us from executing strategies we understood. Complexity constraints are internal limitations created by our own success that require capabilities we've never developed."

The complexity analysis revealed multiple dimensions of organizational complexity that had emerged gradually as we'd expanded geographically, technologically, and strategically.

Geographic Complexity: Operating across 18 countries required managing different regulatory requirements, cultural expectations, currency fluctuations, and competitive dynamics that multiplied decision-making variables exponentially.

Product Complexity: Manufacturing 45 products across generic drugs, modified-release formulations, APIs, and biological drugs required different technical expertise, regulatory pathways, and commercial strategies that strained our management capabilities.

Regulatory Complexity: Compliance with 12 different regulatory jurisdictions meant satisfying FDA, EMA, WHO, and national authorities with conflicting requirements that often required choosing between market access and operational efficiency.

Partnership Complexity: Coordinating 25 active partnerships across licensing agreements, joint ventures, distribution arrangements, and development collaborations required relationship management skills that traditional pharmaceutical operations hadn't demanded.

Organizational Complexity: Managing 450 employees across multiple locations, functions, and business units required leadership approaches, communication systems, and performance management that small company methods couldn't handle.

"Each dimension of complexity interacts with other dimensions to create exponential rather than linear increases in management difficulty," our organizational consultant explained during our assessment.

"How do complexity interactions affect business performance?" I asked.

"Geographic expansion multiplies regulatory complexity. Product diversification multiplies partnership complexity. Organizational growth multiplies communication complexity. The interactions create management challenges that exceed the sum of individual complexities."

The decision-making analysis showed that choices that used to require days now required weeks or months because complexity had created dependencies, stakeholders, and considerations that didn't exist at smaller scale.

"Simple decisions like product pricing now involve sales teams across multiple countries, regulatory considerations in different jurisdictions, partnership obligations with various collaborators, and manufacturing implications across several facilities," our operations manager reported.

"And complex decisions?" I asked.

"Strategic decisions like entering new markets or developing new products require coordination across dozens of stakeholders with different priorities, timelines, and success metrics."

The communication complexity had grown exponentially as geographic and organizational expansion created information flows that traditional management structures couldn't handle efficiently.

"We're generating 400+ emails daily, conducting 50+ meetings weekly, and producing 25+ reports monthly," our communications analyst reported. "Information processing has become a full-time activity for senior management."

"And information quality?" Priya asked.

"Information volume has increased faster than information quality. More data doesn't necessarily mean better decision-making when processing capacity is overwhelmed."

The innovation complexity had emerged as R&D activities expanded across multiple therapeutic areas, development stages, and partnership arrangements that required different management approaches.

"Innovation projects now span 2-8 year timelines, involve 5-15 partners, require compliance with multiple regulatory authorities, and compete for resources across different business units," Dr. Chen observed during our R&D review.

"How does innovation complexity affect development productivity?" I asked.

"Innovation productivity has decreased despite increased R&D investment because complexity creates coordination overhead that consumes resources without generating results."

The financial complexity had multiplied as international operations, multiple currencies, diverse business models, and complex partnerships created accounting, tax, and treasury management challenges.

"Financial reporting now requires consolidating results across 18 currencies, 8 tax jurisdictions, 12 legal entities, and 25 partnership agreements," our CFO reported. "Financial analysis that used to take hours now requires weeks."

"And financial decision-making?" I asked.

"Investment decisions require evaluating interactions between different business units, geographic markets, regulatory environments, and partnership obligations that make cost-benefit analysis extremely complex."

The competitive complexity had increased as we'd entered markets with different competitive dynamics, customer expectations, and success factors that required specialized approaches.

"We now compete against generic manufacturers in commodity markets, innovative companies in premium segments, multinational corporations in regulated markets, and local companies in emerging markets," our business development manager noted.

"Each competitive environment requires different strategies?" Dr. Singh asked.

"Different strategies, different capabilities, different metrics, and different management approaches. Success factors in one market can be irrelevant or counterproductive in other markets."

The stories in the following chapters chronicle our systematic approach to managing complexity through organizational design, process optimization, technology implementation, and leadership development that enabled continued growth despite increasing operational complexity.

"The complexity constraint taught us something fundamental about business development," I would reflect years later. "Companies don't fail because they can't handle complexity—they fail because they don't recognize when complexity is constraining their capabilities."

The solutions we developed during this period—distributed decision-making systems, cross-functional integration processes, and complexity management frameworks—would become essential for operating successfully in global pharmaceutical markets where complexity was inevitable but manageability was optional.

But first, we had to learn how to diagnose complexity before it became paralyzing, and how to design organizational systems that could handle complexity rather than being overwhelmed by it.

"You know what's paradoxical about the complexity constraint?" Priya observed during one of our planning sessions. "The capabilities that enable companies to create complexity often become inadequate for managing the complexity they create."

"And managing complexity requires different skills than creating complexity."

"Which means successful companies must continuously evolve their management capabilities to handle the complexity that their own success generates."

The complexity constraint would force us to evolve from successful entrepreneurs managing a growing business to business leaders building sustainable systems that could operate effectively regardless of individual involvement.

The transition would prove more challenging than any external competitive threat we'd encountered, but also more valuable for creating long-term business sustainability than any market advantage we'd previously developed.

Chapter 16

The Portfolio Paradox

When Diversification Dilutes Focus

The portfolio review meeting in January 2015 lasted eight hours and ended with the uncomfortable discovery that our product diversification strategy was destroying value instead of creating it.

"We now manufacture 52 products across seven therapeutic areas, but only 12 products generate meaningful profits," announced our new VP of Portfolio Management, Dr. Anjali Krishnan, during her first comprehensive analysis. "The remaining 40 products consume resources without providing strategic or financial benefits."

"How is that possible when each product was profitable when we launched it?" I asked, studying data that showed our diversification success had somehow become a diversification problem.

"Individual product profitability doesn't guarantee portfolio profitability when products compete for management attention, manufacturing capacity, and market development resources," she replied.

This conversation took place three years after we'd begun aggressive product diversification through internal development, acquisitions, and licensing agreements that had transformed us from a focused cardiovascular company to a multi-therapeutic pharmaceutical manufacturer.

"Maybe the problem isn't product diversification but portfolio management," Priya suggested during our strategic assessment. "We've been adding products without systematically managing the portfolio as an integrated business system."

"What does systematic portfolio management involve?" I asked.

"Strategic allocation of resources based on portfolio optimization rather than individual product optimization, plus active management of product lifecycle stages and competitive positioning."

The portfolio analysis revealed that our product diversification had created multiple problems that individual product success couldn't solve.

Resource Dilution: Managing 52 products required splitting R&D investment, manufacturing capacity, sales force attention, and management focus across too many priorities to achieve excellence in any area.

Complexity Multiplication: Each additional product created exponential increases in regulatory compliance, supply chain management, customer relationship complexity, and operational coordination requirements.

Cannibalization Effects: Products within the same therapeutic areas were competing against each other for market share rather than competing against external competitors.

Management Distraction: Product portfolio breadth was consuming senior management time on tactical product issues rather than strategic business development.

"Portfolio diversification has created a situation where we're managing too many products to manage any product well," Dr. Krishnan explained during our portfolio assessment.

"But doesn't product diversification provide risk reduction through portfolio balance?" our CFO asked.

"Diversification provides risk reduction only when products are genuinely independent. Related products often share common risks while requiring separate management attention."

The profitability analysis showed that portfolio performance was dramatically different from individual product performance because shared costs and resource constraints affected overall economics.

"Our top 12 products generate 78% of revenue and 91% of gross profits," Dr. Krishnan reported during the financial review. "The remaining 40 products generate 22% of revenue but only 9% of gross profits."

"So 75% of our products contribute 9% of our profits?" I asked.

"Worse than that. When we allocate shared costs appropriately, 28 products are actually losing money when fully loaded costs are considered."

"How do profitable products become unprofitable when shared costs are allocated?"

"Individual product margins look attractive until you include R&D support, regulatory maintenance, manufacturing complexity, sales force time, and management attention required for each product."

The competitive positioning analysis revealed that portfolio breadth was preventing us from achieving market leadership in any therapeutic area.

"We have 5-12% market share across seven therapeutic areas instead of 20-30% market share in 2-3 focused areas," our market research consultant reported.

"And market leadership provides advantages that diversified positioning cannot achieve?" I asked.

"Market leaders achieve pricing power, distribution advantages, regulatory influence, and competitive barriers that diversified competitors cannot access."

"So portfolio diversification is preventing us from achieving competitive advantages that focus would provide?"

"Portfolio breadth is trading depth for breadth, and pharmaceutical markets often reward depth more than breadth."

The innovation pipeline analysis showed that R&D resources were spread across too many projects to achieve breakthrough results in any development area.

"R&D investment is distributed across 15 active projects in 7 therapeutic areas," Dr. Chen reported during our innovation review. "No single area receives sufficient investment to achieve innovation leadership."

"How does R&D resource distribution affect innovation productivity?" I asked.

"Innovation breakthroughs require concentrated expertise and sustained investment that portfolio diversification makes difficult to achieve."

"And our innovation success rate compared to focused pharmaceutical companies?"

"Our innovation success rate is 40% compared to 60-70% for companies with concentrated R&D programs."

The operational complexity analysis revealed that manufacturing 52 products was creating inefficiencies that outweighed scale advantages.

"Manufacturing complexity increases exponentially with product count due to changeover costs, quality control requirements, and inventory management," Dr. Singh reported during the operations assessment.

"How do complexity costs affect manufacturing economics?" I asked.

"Manufacturing efficiency has decreased 15% over the past three years despite volume growth because product diversity creates operational overhead that volume increases cannot overcome."

The customer relationship analysis showed that portfolio breadth was confusing our market positioning rather than strengthening it.

"Customers are uncertain about our company focus and competitive advantages because we compete in too many areas without clear leadership in any area," our sales manager reported.

"How does market positioning confusion affect sales performance?" I asked.

"Sales effectiveness decreases when customers cannot easily categorize our company or understand our value proposition."

The portfolio optimization strategy required systematically divesting underperforming products while concentrating resources on products with leadership potential.

"Portfolio optimization involves identifying core focus areas, divesting non-strategic products, and concentrating resources on products that can achieve market leadership," Dr. Krishnan explained during the optimization planning.

"What criteria determine core focus areas?" I asked.

"Market size, competitive position, growth potential, strategic fit with our capabilities, and ability to achieve sustainable competitive advantages."

"And divestiture process for non-core products?"

"Systematic evaluation of licensing opportunities, asset sales, partnership arrangements, or discontinuation for products that cannot achieve strategic objectives."

The portfolio restructuring took 18 months and involved divesting 23 products while concentrating resources on 29 products across 4 therapeutic areas.

"Portfolio optimization reduced product count by 44% while concentrating 85% of resources on products with leadership potential," Dr. Krishnan reported during the restructuring review.

"And financial impact of portfolio concentration?" our CFO asked.

"Gross margins increased from 42% to 51% due to improved efficiency and competitive positioning in focused areas."

The focused portfolio performance exceeded expectations because concentrated resources enabled achieving market leadership that diversified positioning had prevented.

"Portfolio concentration increased our average market share from 8% to 18% in core therapeutic areas," our business development manager reported after 12 months of focused strategy.

"And competitive advantages from market leadership?" I asked.

"Pricing power, distribution advantages, regulatory influence, and barriers to entry that diversified positioning could not achieve."

Two years after portfolio optimization, we had achieved market leadership positions in three therapeutic areas and had developed innovation capabilities that supported sustainable competitive advantages.

"The portfolio paradox taught us that diversification can destroy value when it prevents achieving competitive advantages that focus enables," I told our board during the annual review.

"And portfolio management requires actively optimizing resource allocation rather than just adding products to the portfolio."

"The key insight was that portfolio value depends on strategic coherence rather than product count."

Three years after portfolio restructuring, our concentrated strategy had generated higher returns, stronger competitive positions, and clearer market recognition than our previous diversified approach.

"You know what the portfolio paradox taught us about business strategy?" I said to Dr. Krishnan during our annual portfolio review. "Diversification provides risk reduction only when it enables competitive advantages rather than just spreading risks across more areas."

"And successful portfolio management requires saying no to opportunities that don't advance strategic focus rather than saying yes to all profitable opportunities."

The lesson had become essential for managing business complexity: portfolio optimization required choosing strategic focus over diversification when concentration could create competitive advantages that breadth could not achieve.

Identifying the Resource Allocation Constraint

The realization hit me like a physical blow during our quarterly resource allocation meeting in March 2011. I was staring at a spreadsheet that should have been cause for celebration - we had seventeen active R&D projects, manufacturing capabilities across eight therapeutic areas, and sales teams covering twelve different product categories. Yet somehow, despite all this activity, our innovation pipeline was producing mediocre results.

"Dr. Malhotra, we need to discuss the resource allocation for Q2," announced our newly hired VP of Strategic Planning, Meera Agarwal, as she distributed thick folders containing budget requests from every division head.

"What's the total ask?" I asked, though I suspected I already knew the answer would be problematic.

"₹847 crores across all divisions, which is 2.3 times our available budget of ₹370 crores."

"How is that possible when we approved realistic budgets just six months ago?"

"Each division has identified compelling opportunities that require additional investment to capture market potential," she replied diplomatically.

This conversation marked the beginning of my understanding that our constraint wasn't lack of opportunities or even lack of capital - it was our inability to systematically allocate limited resources across unlimited possibilities.

"The cardiovascular team needs ₹120 crores for the new ACE inhibitor development," Dr. Priya Sharma explained during her presentation. "Market research shows we can capture 15% market share within three years."

"The oncology division requires ₹95 crores for the biosimilar monoclonal antibody project," Dr. Sarah Williams added. "This represents a ₹500 crore revenue opportunity."

"Respiratory needs ₹78 crores for the inhaler platform development," Dr. Vikram Singh contributed. "We're six months ahead of our nearest competitor."

"And diabetes requires ₹89 crores for the insulin delivery system," concluded Dr. Lisa Chen. "The technology could revolutionize patient compliance."

Each request was compelling when considered individually. Each division head had done thorough market analysis, competitive assessment, and financial projections. Each project promised attractive returns on investment and strategic competitive advantages.

"Every request is financially justified and strategically sound," I told Priya after the meeting. "So why do I feel like we're heading toward disaster?"

"Because we're trying to do everything instead of choosing what we should do exceptionally well?" she suggested.

"But how do we choose when every opportunity looks attractive?"

"Maybe that's exactly the problem - we're evaluating opportunities individually instead of systematically managing our resource allocation constraint."

The resource allocation constraint revelation came during a weekend strategy session at our Goa retreat center. I had gathered our senior leadership team to address what I was beginning to recognize as a fundamental business challenge.

"Let me ask a different question," I began. "What happens to project success rates when we try to fund seventeen projects instead of concentrating resources on eight projects?"

"Project success rates decrease because each project receives insufficient resources to achieve breakthrough results," Dr. Chen acknowledged reluctantly.

"And what happens to our competitive positioning when we spread R&D investment across eight therapeutic areas instead of concentrating on four areas?"

"We achieve mediocre positioning in multiple areas instead of leadership positioning in focused areas," Dr. Williams admitted.

"And manufacturing efficiency when we produce forty-seven different products instead of optimizing for twenty-five core products?"

"Manufacturing complexity increases exponentially while per-unit efficiency decreases," Dr. Singh replied.

"So our resource allocation is creating systematic disadvantages across every business function?"

"Resource allocation dilution is preventing us from achieving competitive advantages that concentrated investment would enable," Meera concluded.

The constraint identification process required systematically analyzing how resource allocation decisions affected our ability to achieve strategic objectives across different business dimensions.

Resource Dilution Analysis: We discovered that spreading R&D investment across seventeen projects meant no single project received sufficient funding to achieve breakthrough innovation that could create sustainable competitive advantages.

Competitive Positioning Assessment: Diversified investment was preventing us from achieving market leadership in any therapeutic area because concentrated competitors could outspend us in focused markets.

Operational Efficiency Impact: Manufacturing forty-seven products was creating complexity costs that exceeded scale advantages because changeover requirements and quality control complexity increased exponentially with product diversity.

Management Attention Allocation: Senior leadership time was being consumed by tactical resource allocation decisions rather than strategic business development because too many projects required ongoing management attention.

"The resource allocation constraint isn't lack of capital," I realized during our analysis review. "It's lack of systematic criteria for choosing among attractive opportunities."

"What would systematic resource allocation criteria involve?" Priya asked.

"Strategic alignment assessment, competitive advantage potential, resource requirement analysis, and portfolio optimization rather than individual project optimization."

The constraint identification led to developing a formal resource allocation framework that would guide our investment decisions based on strategic portfolio optimization.

Strategic Fit Evaluation: Each investment opportunity would be assessed based on alignment with our core competencies and strategic positioning objectives rather than individual project attractiveness.

Competitive Advantage Analysis: Resource allocation would prioritize investments that could create sustainable competitive advantages through market leadership or technological differentiation.

Portfolio Optimization Approach: Investment decisions would consider overall portfolio balance and resource concentration requirements rather than evaluating each project independently.

Resource Concentration Benefits: We would calculate the competitive advantages achievable through concentrated investment compared to diversified allocation across multiple opportunities.

"The breakthrough insight was recognizing that resource allocation is a strategic constraint that requires active management rather than just responding to individual opportunity requests," I explained to our board during the quarterly review.

"And successful resource allocation requires saying no to good opportunities in order to say yes to exceptional opportunities that can create sustainable competitive advantages."

The resource allocation constraint identification transformed our strategic planning process from opportunity evaluation to systematic portfolio optimization that would guide our business development for the next decade.

"You know what identifying the resource allocation constraint taught us about business strategy?" I told Meera six months later as we reviewed our streamlined portfolio performance. "The constraint isn't having too few resources - it's having too many attractive opportunities and insufficient discipline to choose strategically."

"And resource allocation becomes a competitive advantage when you systematically concentrate resources on opportunities that can create market leadership rather than spreading resources across all profitable opportunities."

The lesson had become fundamental to our strategic thinking: identifying resource allocation as a constraint enabled us to transform from an opportunistic company to a strategically focused enterprise that could achieve sustainable competitive advantages through disciplined investment choices.

Portfolio Rationalization Decisions

The portfolio rationalization decisions began with what I now call "the spreadsheet of uncomfortable truths" - a detailed analysis that Dr. Anjali Krishnan presented during our February 2015 strategic review meeting. The data was irrefutable, but accepting its implications would require dismantling parts of the business we had spent years building.

"We need to discuss some difficult realities about our product portfolio," Dr. Krishnan announced as she projected a matrix showing our fifty-two products plotted against profitability and strategic importance. "Twenty-eight products are destroying shareholder value when we account for their full cost allocation."

"How can profitable products be destroying value?" asked Rajesh Khanna, our CFO, though his expression suggested he suspected the answer wouldn't be pleasant.

"Individual product profitability doesn't reflect the opportunity cost of resources, management attention, and competitive focus required to maintain those products in our portfolio," she explained patiently.

This conversation marked the beginning of the most challenging business decisions I had made since founding the company - systematically eliminating products and business units that were profitable but strategically counterproductive.

"The veterinary division generates ₹67 crores in revenue with 18% gross margins," Dr. Krishnan continued with her analysis. "But maintaining veterinary products requires separate regulatory expertise, specialized sales force, distinct distribution channels, and unique manufacturing capabilities that dilute our focus on human pharmaceuticals."

"But the veterinary business is growing at 23% annually," protested Dr. Ramesh Gupta, our veterinary division head. "We're leaving money on the table."

"We're trading immediate revenue for long-term competitive advantage in our core therapeutic areas," I replied, though saying it felt like abandoning a promising child.

The portfolio rationalization framework required evaluating every product against multiple criteria that would determine which businesses deserved continued investment and which should be eliminated.

Strategic Coherence Assessment: Each product had to demonstrate clear alignment with our core competencies and reinforce our competitive positioning in target therapeutic areas.

Resource Optimization Analysis: Products had to justify their consumption of management attention, R&D investment, manufacturing capacity, and sales force time relative to alternatives.

Competitive Advantage Potential: Each business unit had to show realistic potential for achieving market leadership or sustainable differentiation that could create long-term value.

Portfolio Synergy Evaluation: Products had to contribute to overall portfolio strength rather than just individual profitability through shared capabilities, customer relationships, or strategic positioning.

"The respiratory products portfolio presents the most complex rationalization decision," Dr. Krishnan explained during our deep-dive analysis. "Respiratory generates ₹234 crores in revenue with attractive margins, but requires completely different expertise from our cardiovascular and diabetes focus areas."

"What makes respiratory products strategically problematic?" I asked, though I was beginning to understand the answer.

"Respiratory success requires pulmonology expertise, inhalation delivery technology, specialized clinical development capabilities, and distinct regulatory knowledge that we cannot develop sufficiently while maintaining excellence in our core areas."

"And our competitive position in respiratory markets?"

"We're ranked seventh with 4% market share, competing against companies like GSK and AstraZeneca that have forty years of respiratory specialization and dedicated R&D programs."

The rationalization decisions required confronting emotional attachments to businesses we had built from scratch, even when objective analysis showed they were preventing us from achieving excellence in more important areas.

"The oncology division represents our most painful rationalization decision," I admitted during our leadership team meeting. "We've invested ₹145 crores over four years developing cancer treatment capabilities."

"But oncology markets require different expertise, longer development timelines, more complex regulatory processes, and higher risk tolerance than our other therapeutic areas," Dr. Priya Sharma observed. "We're competing against companies with decades of oncology specialization."

"And our realistic prospects for achieving competitive advantage in oncology?"

"We might achieve modest market presence, but we cannot realistically expect to achieve the market leadership that would justify continued investment given our resource constraints."

The portfolio rationalization process involved developing systematic criteria for making divestiture decisions that would maximize long-term strategic value rather than preserving short-term revenue.

Business Unit Evaluation: Each division was assessed based on market position, competitive dynamics, required capabilities, and strategic fit with our overall business model.

Divestiture Option Analysis: We evaluated licensing agreements, asset sales, joint ventures, and strategic partnerships as alternatives to continued internal development for non-core businesses.

Resource Reallocation Planning: Divested business resources would be systematically redirected toward strengthening our competitive advantages in core therapeutic areas.

Timeline Optimization: Rationalization decisions were sequenced to minimize disruption while maximizing the strategic benefits of concentrated focus.

"The hardest part of portfolio rationalization isn't identifying which businesses to eliminate," I confided to Priya during one of our evening strategy discussions. "It's accepting that saying no to profitable opportunities is necessary for saying yes to exceptional opportunities."

"And managing the organizational emotions around eliminating businesses that people have worked years to build," she replied.

The implementation of rationalization decisions required careful management of internal stakeholders, external partners, and market perceptions while executing complex business transactions.

"We've structured the veterinary divestiture as an asset sale to VetPharma International for ₹89 crores," announced Dr. Sarah Williams during our transaction review. "The purchasing company specializes in animal health and can provide better growth opportunities for our veterinary team."

"What about the respiratory portfolio?" asked Rajesh.

"Respiratory products will be licensed to European partner Respira AG for upfront payments plus royalties on future sales. This provides ongoing revenue while eliminating operational complexity."

"And oncology assets?"

"The oncology pipeline will be sold to BioGenesis for ₹67 crores plus milestone payments if their clinical development succeeds."

The portfolio rationalization results exceeded our expectations because concentrated resources enabled achieving competitive advantages that diversified positioning had prevented.

"Portfolio rationalization increased our average market share in core therapeutic areas from 8% to 19% within eighteen months," Dr. Krishnan reported during our annual review. "Concentrated investment enabled us to achieve market leadership positions that diversified resource allocation could not support."

"And financial impact of focused strategy?" asked our board chairman.

"Operating margins improved from 23% to 31% due to elimination of complexity costs and achievement of competitive advantages in concentrated areas."

"R&D productivity increased 47% because concentrated investment enabled breakthrough innovations that diversified programs could not achieve."

Two years after portfolio rationalization, we had transformed from a diversified pharmaceutical company into a focused leader in cardiovascular and metabolic disorders with sustainable competitive advantages.

"Portfolio rationalization taught us that strategic focus requires the discipline to eliminate profitable businesses that prevent achieving excellence in more important areas," I reflected during our strategic planning retreat.

"And successful rationalization means optimizing for long-term competitive advantage rather than preserving short-term revenue from non-strategic businesses."

The lesson had become central to our strategic thinking: portfolio rationalization decisions required the courage to eliminate good businesses in order to build great businesses that could achieve sustainable market leadership.

The Focus vs. Diversification Debate

The focus versus diversification debate erupted during our April 2014 board meeting with an intensity that surprised everyone in the room. What began as a routine strategic planning discussion evolved into a fundamental philosophical argument about the future direction of our company, with passionate advocates on both sides presenting compelling but contradictory visions.

"We need to concentrate our resources on cardiovascular and diabetes where we have demonstrated competitive advantages," argued Dr. Priya Sharma, presenting her case for strategic focus with characteristic analytical precision. "Diversification is preventing us from achieving market leadership in areas where we could dominate."

"But diversification provides essential risk mitigation and growth opportunities that focus cannot deliver," countered Dr. Sarah Williams, our head of business development, with equal conviction. "Concentrating on two therapeutic areas exposes us to market volatility and competitive threats that could devastate our business."

This debate would continue for eight months, involving board members, senior executives, external consultants, and industry experts before we reached a decision that would reshape our entire business strategy.

"Let me present the case for strategic focus," Dr. Sharma began during our detailed strategy session. "We currently achieve 12% market share in cardiovascular medicines and 8% in diabetes treatments. With concentrated investment, we could realistically achieve 25% market share in cardiovascular and 18% in diabetes within three years."

"What makes you confident about achieving those market positions?" I asked.

"Market leadership provides pricing power, distribution advantages, regulatory influence, and competitive barriers that diversified positioning cannot access. Our cardiovascular expertise is already recognized by key opinion leaders, and concentrated R&D investment could accelerate our innovation pipeline significantly."

"But what about business risk concentration?" interrupted board member Kavita Desai. "Focusing on two therapeutic areas creates vulnerability to market disruption, regulatory changes, or competitive threats that could eliminate our primary revenue sources."

"Strategic focus reduces business risk by creating sustainable competitive advantages," Dr. Sharma responded. "Market leaders have lower business risk than diversified followers because they control their competitive destiny."

The diversification advocates presented equally compelling arguments based on portfolio theory and risk management principles that had guided business strategy for decades.

"Diversification provides mathematical risk reduction through portfolio balance," explained Dr. Williams during her presentation. "When cardiovascular markets decline due to generic competition, respiratory or oncology growth can offset those losses."

"How significant is the risk reduction benefit?" asked Rajesh Khanna, our CFO.

"Portfolio diversification can reduce earnings volatility by 30-40% compared to concentrated strategies, which provides more predictable financial performance and higher valuation multiples."

"And growth opportunities from diversification?"

"Each therapeutic area represents distinct growth potential. Oncology markets are growing at 15% annually, respiratory at 12%, and specialty pharmaceuticals at 18%. Diversification enables us to capture growth across multiple expanding markets."

The focus advocates challenged whether diversification actually provided the risk reduction and growth benefits that traditional business theory suggested.

"Diversification provides risk reduction only when businesses are truly independent," argued Dr. Krishnan during our risk analysis session. "Related pharmaceutical businesses often share common risks while requiring separate management capabilities."

"What common risks affect diversified pharmaceutical portfolios?" I asked.

"Regulatory changes, healthcare cost pressures, patent expiration risks, and competitive dynamics affect all pharmaceutical businesses similarly. Diversification doesn't eliminate these systematic risks."

"And growth benefits from diversification?"

"Diversified growth requires achieving competitive success in multiple markets simultaneously, which is more difficult than achieving market leadership in focused areas where we can concentrate our capabilities."

The debate intensified when we analyzed the performance of focused versus diversified pharmaceutical companies to understand which strategy produced superior long-term results.

"Focused pharmaceutical companies achieve higher returns on investment and faster growth rates than diversified companies," reported our strategy consultant during the competitive analysis presentation. "Companies like Gilead Sciences and Regeneron achieved exceptional performance through therapeutic area concentration."

"But what about diversified success stories?" asked Dr. Williams. "Johnson & Johnson and Roche have built successful businesses through diversification strategies."

"Large pharmaceutical companies can support diversification because they have resources to achieve competitive advantages in multiple areas simultaneously. Mid-sized companies like ours typically cannot sustain competitive excellence across diverse therapeutic areas."

"So diversification works for large companies but not mid-sized companies?"

"Diversification requires minimum scale in each business area to achieve competitive advantages. Below that scale, diversification creates disadvantages rather than benefits."

The internal debate reflected broader industry trends as pharmaceutical companies worldwide grappled with similar strategic choices between focus and diversification.

"The pharmaceutical industry is increasingly rewarding specialization over diversification," observed Dr. Lisa Chen during our industry analysis discussion. "Regulatory complexity, development costs, and competitive intensity require deeper expertise that generalized capabilities cannot provide."

"How do market valuations compare between focused and diversified pharmaceutical companies?" I asked.

"Focused companies typically achieve higher valuation multiples because investors reward clarity of strategic positioning and competitive advantages that focus enables."

"And acquisition premiums?"

"Strategic acquirers pay higher premiums for companies with market leadership in focused areas compared to diversified companies with modest positions across multiple markets."

The resolution of our focus versus diversification debate required synthesizing the arguments into a framework that could guide our specific strategic situation rather than applying general business principles.

"Our decision framework should consider our current market position, available resources, competitive landscape, and realistic prospects for achieving sustainable advantages," I concluded during our final strategy session.

"We currently rank third in cardiovascular with 12% market share and fifth in diabetes with 8% market share," Dr. Krishnan summarized our positioning analysis. "We have realistic prospects for achieving market leadership in both areas with concentrated investment."

"And our competitive position in other therapeutic areas?"

"We rank seventh or lower in respiratory, oncology, and specialty pharmaceuticals with insufficient resources to achieve competitive advantages in those markets while maintaining excellence in our core areas."

The strategic decision emerged from recognizing that focus versus diversification wasn't a philosophical choice but a practical decision based on our specific capabilities and competitive opportunities.

"Focus makes strategic sense for our company because we can achieve market leadership in cardiovascular and diabetes markets," I announced to our board during the final vote. "Diversification would prevent us from capitalizing on our competitive advantages in areas where we can realistically dominate."

"The debate taught us that strategic choice depends on company-specific factors rather than general business principles," Priya observed afterward.

The focus versus diversification debate had revealed that successful strategy requires choosing the approach that maximizes competitive advantages rather than following conventional business wisdom about portfolio balance.

"The key insight from our debate was that focus and diversification are both valid strategies, but only one strategy fits our specific competitive situation," I reflected during our implementation planning.

"And strategic success requires choosing the approach that leverages our strengths rather than the approach that sounds theoretically appealing."

The Painful Product Line Exits

The first product line exit meeting felt like planning a funeral for a healthy child. We gathered in the mahogany-paneled conference room on a gray Mumbai morning in September 2014 to discuss discontinuing our respiratory products division - a business that was generating ₹187 crores in annual revenue with respectable 19% gross margins and employing 127 dedicated professionals who had built their careers around our inhalation therapy expertise.

"I need everyone to understand that we're not eliminating the respiratory division because it's failing," I began, looking around the table at faces that ranged from confused to openly hostile. "We're eliminating it because its success is preventing us from achieving greatness in areas where we can truly dominate."

"Dr. Malhotra, with respect, this makes no sense," responded Dr. Anand Krishnamurthy, our respiratory division head, his voice tight with controlled emotion. "We've spent six years building world-class inhalation delivery capabilities. Our dry powder inhaler technology is eighteen months ahead of our nearest competitor."

"And our respiratory team has the deepest pulmonology expertise outside of GSK and AstraZeneca," added Dr. Meera Patel, our head of respiratory R&D. "We're abandoning a competitive advantage that took us a decade to develop."

This conversation marked the beginning of what would become the most emotionally challenging eighteen months in our company's history - systematically dismantling profitable business units that represented years of investment, innovation, and personal sacrifice from hundreds of employees.

"The decision isn't about the quality of our respiratory capabilities," I explained, though each word felt like betraying people who had trusted me with their careers. "It's about recognizing that excellence in respiratory medicine requires resources and focus that would prevent us from achieving market leadership in cardiovascular and diabetes."

"But we're profitable and growing," Dr. Krishnamurthy protested. "How does eliminating profitable growth make business sense?"

"Because profitable growth in secondary areas prevents exceptional growth in primary areas where we can create sustainable competitive advantages."

The veterinary products exit proved even more wrenching because it involved dismantling our oldest diversification effort - a business we had built from scratch starting in 2001 when we saw opportunities in the underserved animal health market.

"The veterinary division represents everything we've accomplished outside human pharmaceuticals," said Dr. Rashmi Gupta during our veterinary exit planning meeting. "We've built relationships with 2,400 veterinarians across twelve states. We're the third-largest player in companion animal therapeutics."

"And our veterinary products have saved thousands of animal lives while generating consistent profits for thirteen years," added Suresh Nair, our veterinary sales director, his voice breaking slightly.

"I understand the emotional attachment," I replied, feeling the weight of disappointing people who had believed in our veterinary vision. "But maintaining veterinary excellence requires capabilities, relationships, and expertise that dilute our focus on human therapeutics where we can achieve market leadership."

"Are we abandoning our commitment to animal health?" asked Dr. Gupta.

"We're recognizing that others can serve animal health better than we can while we focus on areas where we can make the greatest impact."

The oncology exit represented our most controversial decision because it involved abandoning what many considered the future of pharmaceutical innovation - cancer treatment development that could potentially save human lives and generate exceptional returns.

"Oncology represents the highest-growth, highest-value segment of pharmaceutical markets," argued Dr. Lisa Chen during our oncology review session. "We're walking away from ₹500 crore market opportunities to focus on mature cardiovascular markets."

"Our oncology pipeline includes three promising compounds that could achieve breakthrough therapy designation," added Dr. Vikram Sharma, our oncology research director. "We're eighteen months from Phase II trial results that could validate four years of development work."

"The oncology decision is the most difficult because it involves the highest opportunity costs," I acknowledged. "But oncology success requires specialized expertise, longer development timelines, higher risk tolerance, and different regulatory capabilities than our core therapeutic areas."

"So we're choosing certainty over potential?" asked Dr. Chen.

"We're choosing competitive advantage over diversified mediocrity."

The product line exit process required managing not just business logistics but also the emotional trauma of employees who felt their life's work was being discarded despite its success.

"The hardest part isn't the financial analysis or strategic planning," confided Dr. Priya Sharma during one of our late-night planning sessions. "It's looking people in the eye and telling them their successful work isn't important enough to continue."

"How do we maintain organizational morale while eliminating successful businesses?" I asked.

"By demonstrating that exit decisions are based on strategic optimization rather than performance failures, and by providing genuine opportunities for affected employees within our focused business areas."

The implementation of product line exits required developing fair processes for employee transitions, customer relationships, intellectual property management, and partner communications.

"We've identified internal placement opportunities for 78% of affected employees within our cardiovascular and diabetes divisions," announced our HR director during the transition planning review. "The remaining employees will receive enhanced severance packages plus job placement assistance."

"What about customer relationships and ongoing commitments?" asked our business development manager.

"Respiratory customers will be transitioned to our licensing partner who can provide continuity of supply and technical support. Veterinary customers will be served by our acquisition partner who specializes in animal health."

"And intellectual property from discontinued divisions?"

"Respiratory IP will be licensed to generate ongoing royalty income. Veterinary IP will be included in the asset sale. Oncology IP will be sold to recover development investments."

The emotional toll of product line exits affected everyone involved, requiring constant communication about strategic rationale and long-term benefits to maintain organizational cohesion.

"I know these decisions feel like betrayals of people who trusted us with their careers," I addressed our all-hands meeting after announcing the final exit decisions. "But our responsibility is to build a company that can create sustainable value and competitive advantages rather than preserving all existing activities."

"How do we know focus will produce better results than diversification?" asked one employee during the Q&A session.

"We don't know with certainty, but we know that our current diversified approach is preventing us from achieving the market leadership that our core capabilities could support."

Six months after completing the product line exits, the results began validating our painful decisions as concentrated resources enabled breakthrough performance in our focused therapeutic areas.

"Market share in cardiovascular increased from 12% to 18% within six months of concentrating resources," reported Dr. Krishnan during our performance review. "Diabetes market share improved from 8% to 14% over the same period."

"And employee morale in remaining divisions?" I asked.

"Higher than before the exits because people can see the competitive advantages that focus is enabling."

The painful product line exits had taught us that strategic success sometimes requires the courage to abandon good businesses to build great businesses.

"The most important lesson from our exit decisions was that emotional attachment to past investments cannot override strategic logic about future opportunities," I reflected during our annual planning retreat.

"And successful strategy requires choosing what not to do as carefully as choosing what to do."

Chapter 17

The Global Competition

David vs. Multiple Goliaths

The reality of global pharmaceutical competition hit me like a sledgehammer during the July 2012 industry conference in Boston when I found myself sitting across from Dr. Jeremy Levin, then CEO of Teva Pharmaceuticals, at what was supposed to be a casual networking dinner. As he casually mentioned Teva's $20 billion annual revenue and 40,000 employees, I realized our ₹1,847 crore company was about to compete against giants that could spend more on quarterly marketing campaigns than our entire annual budget.

"You're Malhotra Pharmaceuticals, right?" Dr. Levin asked with polite interest. "I've heard good things about your cardiovascular portfolio in India. Are you planning to expand internationally?"

"We're evaluating opportunities in regulated markets," I replied, trying to sound confident while internally calculating that Teva's revenue was roughly thirty-seven times larger than ours.

"Interesting timing," he smiled. "We're launching seventeen new generics in the US market this year. Competition should be quite robust."

That conversation crystallized a fundamental challenge I had been avoiding: we were entering a competitive arena where established players could outspend us, out-develop us, and outlast us in any direct confrontation.

"We cannot compete with Teva, Sandoz, Mylan, and Dr. Reddy's using their strategies," I told our senior leadership team during our emergency strategy session the following week. "They have resources, scale, and established relationships that we cannot replicate within any reasonable timeframe."

"So how do we compete?" asked Dr. Priya Sharma.

"We need to find competitive approaches that leverage our strengths rather than matching their resources."

The global competition analysis revealed the daunting scope of what we were attempting to challenge as a mid-sized Indian pharmaceutical company.

Market Leaders Assessment: Teva controlled 16% of the global generics market with $18.9 billion revenue, Sandoz held 9% with $9.2 billion, Mylan commanded 8% with $7.5 billion, and established Indian players like Dr. Reddy's and Cipla each controlled 3-4% with $2-3 billion revenues.

Resource Disparities: Our largest competitors spent more on R&D annually than our total revenue, maintained regulatory teams larger than our entire employee base, and operated manufacturing networks spanning multiple continents.

Competitive Advantages: Established players had decades-old relationships with major customers, regulatory approval portfolios covering hundreds of products, and economies of scale that enabled cost structures we could not approach.

Market Entry Barriers: Global pharmaceutical markets required massive upfront investments in regulatory approvals, manufacturing certifications, and market development that could consume years of cash flow before generating meaningful returns.

"The competitive landscape suggests we're attempting an impossible challenge," admitted Dr. Sarah Williams during our competitor analysis review. "How does a ₹1,800 crore company compete against $20 billion corporations?"

"By recognizing that size isn't the only competitive advantage," I replied, though I wasn't entirely convinced myself. "We need to identify competitive approaches that neutralize their scale advantages."

The strategic response required abandoning conventional pharmaceutical competition based on breadth, scale, and resource deployment in favor of focused differentiation that could create sustainable advantages despite our size disadvantage.

Therapeutic Area Specialization: Instead of competing across multiple therapeutic areas like larger competitors, we would concentrate expertise in cardiovascular and diabetes markets where deep knowledge could overcome resource limitations.

Regulatory Efficiency Focus: Rather than pursuing approvals in all major markets simultaneously, we would sequence market entry to maximize learning and resource efficiency while building regulatory expertise gradually.

Partnership-Leveraged Growth: Instead of building global infrastructure independently, we would develop strategic partnerships that provided market access while we concentrated on product development and manufacturing excellence.

Innovation-Based Differentiation: Rather than competing on price alone, we would focus on developing superior formulations, delivery systems, and patient compliance solutions that could command premium pricing.

"Our competitive strategy recognizes that we cannot out-resource the giants, but we might be able to out-focus and out-innovate them in selected areas," I explained to our board during the strategic planning presentation.

"The pharmaceutical industry rewards specialization and innovation more than scale alone," added Dr. Priya Sharma. "Focused companies can achieve competitive advantages that diversified giants cannot replicate."

The implementation of our David versus Goliaths strategy required systematic development of competitive capabilities that could neutralize the scale advantages of larger competitors.

"We're building the deepest cardiovascular formulation expertise outside the top five global companies," reported Dr. Lisa Chen during our R&D progress review. "Our modified-release platform has achieved bioequivalence results that exceed originator products in four different studies."

"How does superior formulation translate into competitive advantage?" I asked.

"Superior bioavailability and patient compliance enable premium pricing and physician preference that scale advantages cannot overcome."

"And our regulatory efficiency compared to larger competitors?"

"We achieve FDA approval timelines 18% faster than industry averages because focused expertise enables more efficient development processes."

The competitive positioning strategy began producing results as our specialized approach enabled achieving market recognition despite resource limitations compared to global giants.

"Our cardiovascular products have captured 4% US market share within eighteen months of launch," announced our international business manager during the quarterly review. "Market share growth exceeds projections despite competition from Teva, Sandoz, and established generics companies."

"What explains our competitive success against larger players?" asked Rajesh Khanna, our CFO.

"Physician preference for our superior formulations plus pharmacy acceptance of our reliable supply and competitive pricing creates competitive advantages that resource scale cannot easily replicate."

"And sustainability of competitive positioning against well-funded competitors?"

"Innovation-based differentiation provides more sustainable advantages than cost-based competition because technical expertise is harder to replicate than manufacturing scale."

The global competition taught us that successful strategy against larger competitors required leveraging unique strengths rather than attempting to match their resource advantages.

"Competing against giants requires asymmetric strategies that neutralize their scale advantages while exploiting their inability to achieve focused excellence," I told our leadership team during our annual strategic retreat.

"Large pharmaceutical companies excel at broad market coverage and resource deployment, but specialized companies can achieve deeper expertise and faster innovation in focused therapeutic areas."

Two years after implementing our focused competition strategy, we had achieved sustainable competitive positioning against much larger global players by concentrating on areas where expertise could overcome scale.

"The David versus Goliaths challenge taught us that competitive strategy is about leveraging relative advantages rather than matching absolute resources," I reflected during our competitor assessment review.

"Successful competition requires identifying what larger competitors cannot do rather than trying to replicate what they do exceptionally well."

The lesson had become fundamental to our strategic thinking: global competition required finding competitive approaches that turned our size into an advantage rather than accepting it as a limitation.

Competing with Teva, Sandoz, and Local Giants

The first direct confrontation with Teva came in March 2013 when we both filed Abbreviated New Drug Applications for the same cardiovascular combination product on the same day. What followed was a masterclass in how pharmaceutical giants use their overwhelming resources to crush smaller competitors - and how we learned to survive and eventually thrive despite being dramatically outgunned.

"Teva has filed for seventeen different strengths of the same compound while we've filed for three," announced Dr. Meera Patel during our regulatory strategy meeting. "They're also challenging our bioequivalence data with the FDA using arguments that will require us to conduct additional studies costing ₹23 crores."

"Can they do that?" I asked, though I suspected the answer would be unpleasant.

"It's completely legal. Large companies routinely use regulatory complexity as a competitive weapon against smaller players who cannot afford prolonged approval battles."

"How much can Teva afford to spend on regulatory warfare compared to us?"

"Their annual regulatory budget is larger than our total company revenue. They can sustain approval battles that would bankrupt us."

This encounter taught me that competing against pharmaceutical giants required understanding not just their products and pricing, but their systematic use of regulatory processes, legal challenges, and market access strategies to eliminate smaller competitors.

The Sandoz competition proved even more sophisticated when they launched a coordinated attack on our European market entry that demonstrated the global reach and strategic coordination that only massive pharmaceutical companies could deploy.

"Sandoz has simultaneously launched competitive products in Germany, France, and the UK with pricing 15% below our planned market entry prices," reported Dr. Sarah Williams during our European strategy review. "They've also secured exclusive distribution agreements with three major pharmacy chains that we had been negotiating with for eight months."

"How did they coordinate simultaneous launches across multiple European markets?" I asked.

"Global pharmaceutical companies maintain parallel regulatory and commercial teams that can execute coordinated strategies across multiple markets simultaneously. They can afford to lose money in individual markets to prevent competitors from establishing market presence."

"And our realistic options for responding to coordinated competition?"

"We cannot match their global coordination capabilities, so we need to identify markets and strategies where coordination advantages matter less than focused execution."

The local giant competition presented different but equally formidable challenges as companies like Dr. Reddy's, Cipla, and Lupin had achieved scale and market position that enabled them to compete using advantages we could not replicate.

"Dr. Reddy's has launched the same cardiovascular product in India with pricing 25% below our cost structure," announced our domestic marketing manager during our competitive assessment meeting. "They're leveraging manufacturing scale that enables cost advantages we cannot achieve."

"How significant is their scale advantage?" asked Dr. Priya Sharma.

"Dr. Reddy's produces this molecule at volumes twelve times larger than our capacity, which enables per-unit costs 35% lower than our optimized manufacturing."

"And Cipla's competitive response to our diabetes portfolio?"

"Cipla has bundled their diabetes products with physician education programs and patient support services that cost more than our total marketing budget for the therapeutic area."

The competitive reality forced us to abandon any hope of matching our larger competitors' strategies and instead develop asymmetric approaches that could neutralize their advantages while leveraging our unique capabilities.

Focused Innovation Strategy: Instead of competing across broad product portfolios like Teva and Sandoz, we concentrated R&D resources on developing superior formulations in specific therapeutic niches where innovation could overcome scale disadvantages.

Speed-to-Market Advantage: Rather than matching the global coordination of large competitors, we optimized for rapid decision-making and agile development that could enable first-mover advantages in selected opportunities.

Partnership Leverage: Instead of building global infrastructure to compete with established giants, we developed strategic alliances that provided market access while concentrating our resources on product development excellence.

Customer Intimacy Focus: Rather than competing through broad market coverage like local giants, we invested in deep relationships with key opinion leaders and specialized customer segments that valued expertise over scale.

"Our competitive approach recognizes that we cannot out-resource Teva, out-coordinate Sandoz, or out-scale Dr. Reddy's," I explained to our board during our strategy presentation. "But we can out-focus, out-innovate, and out-execute them in carefully selected competitive arenas."

"The key insight is that large pharmaceutical companies excel at strategies that require resource deployment but struggle with strategies that require focused expertise and rapid adaptation," added Dr. Lisa Chen.

The implementation of asymmetric competition required developing capabilities that turned our size into an advantage rather than accepting it as a limitation against larger competitors.

"Our cardiovascular development team has achieved FDA approval timelines significantly faster than industry averages because focused expertise enables more efficient regulatory processes," reported Dr. Patel during our performance review.

"How does faster approval translate into sustainable competitive advantage?" I asked.

"First-mover advantage in generic markets provides 6-12 months of premium pricing before competitive launches drive prices down. Speed can overcome scale when market windows are limited."

"And our innovation success compared to larger competitors?"

"Our modified-release platform has achieved bioequivalence success rates 15% higher than industry averages because concentrated R&D focus enables deeper technical expertise than diversified development programs."

The competitive breakthroughs came when we realized that pharmaceutical giants' greatest strengths could become vulnerabilities when market conditions favored agility over scale.

"Teva's global coordination becomes a disadvantage when rapid market response is required," observed Dr. Williams during our competitive analysis update. "Their decision-making processes require global consultation that delays responses to local market opportunities."

"And Sandoz's broad portfolio creates resource allocation constraints that prevent achieving innovation leadership in specific therapeutic areas," added Dr. Chen.

"Dr. Reddy's scale advantages become less relevant when physician preference is based on product superiority rather than cost competition."

The sustained competition against pharmaceutical giants taught us that asymmetric strategies could create sustainable competitive advantages despite dramatic resource disparities.

"We've achieved 8% market share in US cardiovascular generics despite Teva controlling 23% and Sandoz holding 16%," I announced during our annual competitive review. "Market share growth has exceeded projections because focused innovation creates physician preference that scale advantages cannot easily overcome."

"Our European diabetes products have captured 12% market share in Germany within two years despite aggressive competition from Sandoz and local European companies," reported our international manager.

"And domestic competition against Indian giants?"

"We've maintained 15% market share in cardiovascular despite pricing pressure from Cipla and Dr. Reddy's because superior formulations enable premium positioning."

The competition with pharmaceutical giants had transformed us from a company that feared larger competitors to one that could create sustainable competitive advantages through focused excellence.

"Competing with Teva, Sandoz, and local giants taught us that pharmaceutical competition rewards specialized expertise more than generalized resources," I reflected during our strategic planning retreat.

"Successful competition requires finding arenas where your advantages matter more than their advantages rather than attempting direct resource-based competition."

The lesson had become central to our competitive philosophy: sustainable success against larger competitors required developing asymmetric capabilities that neutralized their scale while leveraging focused expertise they could not easily replicate.

Price Erosion in US Generic Markets

The first brutal lesson in US generic market economics came in September 2013 when our Amlodipine tablets, which had launched six months earlier at $47 per bottle, suddenly faced competition from four new generic entrants that drove the market price to $12 per bottle within sixty days. I watched our projected annual revenue of $67 million evaporate to $18 million as I learned that American generic markets operated with a ruthlessness that made Indian price competition look genteel.

"How is this mathematically possible?" I asked Dr. Sarah Williams during our emergency pricing strategy meeting, staring at charts that showed our gross margins collapsing from 68% to 23% in eight weeks. "We spent eighteen months and $4.2 million obtaining FDA approval based on market research showing sustainable pricing at $40-45 per bottle."

"US generic markets follow predictable but brutal economics," she explained with the patience of someone who had witnessed this cycle dozens of times. "First generic entrants achieve premium pricing for 6-12 months until additional competitors receive FDA approval and trigger price wars that continue until only the most efficient manufacturers survive."

"But how do companies justify the development costs if prices collapse so quickly?"

"They don't. Most generic products lose money after the initial exclusivity period ends. Successful generic companies depend on portfolio management and timing strategies rather than individual product profitability."

This conversation marked my introduction to the unforgiving reality of US pharmaceutical economics, where generic drug prices could fall 85-90% from peak levels as competition intensified, making long-term planning nearly impossible and forcing constant adaptation to survive.

The Atorvastatin price erosion proved even more devastating when our entry into the cholesterol market coincided with patent expiration that triggered what industry analysts called "the generic pricing apocalypse of 2014."

"Atorvastatin prices have declined from $185 per bottle to $23 per bottle in fourteen months," reported our US commercial manager during our quarterly review. "Thirty-seven companies have received FDA approval for generic versions, and three additional approvals are expected before year-end."

"How many competitors can the market sustain at current pricing levels?" I asked.

"Economic analysis suggests only 8-10 manufacturers can remain profitable at $23 pricing. The remaining competitors will either exit the market or continue selling at losses to maintain manufacturing utilization."

"And our competitive position in this pricing environment?"

"We rank nineteenth in market share with 1.2% despite having superior bioequivalence data. Market share depends primarily on pharmacy contracting and supply chain efficiency rather than product quality once bioequivalence is established."

The systematic price erosion affected every aspect of our US strategy as products that had been profitable during development became loss-generating commodities within months of competitive entry.

"Our Metformin Extended Release tablets launched at $89 per bottle and now sell for $31 per bottle after eighteen months of competition," Dr. Williams continued her grim recitation during our pricing review. "Projected five-year NPV has declined from $47 million to $8 million."

"Is this price decline pattern inevitable for all generic products?" asked Rajesh Khanna, our CFO.

"Price erosion is systematic and predictable. First generic receives 6-month exclusivity with pricing typically 20-30% below brand. Second generic entry reduces prices to 40-50% of brand pricing. Each additional competitor drives prices down further until commodity levels are reached."

"And timeframe for reaching commodity pricing?"

"Most products reach commodity pricing within 24-36 months of first generic entry, depending on the number of approved competitors and market demand elasticity."

The pricing pressure forced us to completely restructure our US business model from one based on individual product profitability to portfolio optimization and operational efficiency.

Manufacturing Efficiency Focus: We invested $23 million in automated production systems that reduced per-unit costs by 35% to maintain competitiveness despite price erosion.

Supply Chain Optimization: We developed direct relationships with major pharmacy chains to eliminate distributor markups that consumed 12-15% of selling prices.

Portfolio Timing Strategy: We concentrated resources on products with limited competition rather than entering crowded therapeutic areas where price erosion had already reached commodity levels.

Regulatory Speed Advantage: We optimized FDA approval processes to achieve first-to-market positioning that could capture premium pricing during exclusivity periods.

"The US generic market rewards operational excellence and timing more than innovation or quality differentiation," I explained to our board during our strategy revision presentation. "Success requires treating generic pharmaceuticals as commodity manufacturing with sophisticated supply chain management."

"How does this differ from our Indian market experience?" asked board member Kavita Desai.

"Indian markets allow sustainable differentiation through physician relationships and brand building. US markets are driven purely by pharmacy economics and cost competition."

The price erosion cycle created opportunities for companies that could optimize for efficiency rather than premium positioning, though the margins were dramatically lower than we had projected.

"We've achieved 7% market share in US Lisinopril despite commodity pricing because operational efficiency enables profitability at price levels that force inefficient competitors to exit," reported our manufacturing director during our operational review.

"What operational advantages enable sustained profitability in eroded markets?" I asked.

"Automated manufacturing reduces labor costs by 45%, optimized supply chain eliminates intermediary markups, and scale purchasing reduces raw material costs by 18%."

"And sustainability of competitive positioning in commodity markets?"

"Operational advantages create barriers to entry for less efficient competitors while enabling profitable operations at price levels that eliminate marginal players."

The adaptation to price erosion required accepting fundamentally different economics where success meant achieving adequate returns from commodity products rather than premium returns from differentiated products.

"US generic markets have taught us that pharmaceutical manufacturing can be profitable even with severe price erosion if operational efficiency is optimized for commodity competition," I told our leadership team during our annual US strategy review.

"The key insight is that price erosion is predictable and manageable if business models are designed for commodity economics rather than premium pharmaceutical economics."

Two years after experiencing our first price erosion cycle, we had developed portfolio and operational strategies that enabled sustained profitability despite systematic price declines across our US product portfolio.

"Price erosion taught us that generic pharmaceutical success requires treating drug manufacturing as a commodity business with sophisticated operational management rather than a premium product business with differentiation strategies," I reflected during our strategic planning session.

"Successful adaptation requires optimizing for efficiency and scale rather than pricing power and product differentiation."

The lesson had become fundamental to our US strategy: price erosion was not a temporary market condition but a permanent feature of generic pharmaceutical economics that required business models designed specifically for commodity competition rather than traditional pharmaceutical marketing.

"The most important insight from price erosion was recognizing that different markets require fundamentally different business models," I concluded. "US generic success demands operational excellence rather than commercial differentiation."

Strategic Response through Differentiation

The differentiation breakthrough came during a frustrated late-night session in October 2013 when Dr. Lisa Chen burst into my office with what she called "the solution to our commodity pricing problem." She had spent three weeks analyzing why our bioequivalent generic products were indistinguishable from competitors despite superior manufacturing quality, and her discovery would fundamentally reshape our competitive strategy.

"We're approaching differentiation completely wrong," she announced, spreading bioequivalence studies across my desk. "Everyone focuses on matching the original brand product, but no one optimizes beyond bioequivalence to create meaningful clinical advantages."

"What do you mean by optimizing beyond bioequivalence?" I asked, though her excitement suggested she had discovered something significant.

"Our Amlodipine formulation achieves 127% bioavailability compared to competition, which only requires 80-125% for FDA approval. We're exceeding requirements by 27%, but we're not leveraging that superiority into competitive advantage."

"How does superior bioavailability translate into competitive differentiation when all approved generics meet FDA standards?"

"Physicians care about patient outcomes, not just regulatory compliance. Superior bioavailability means better blood pressure control, fewer dose adjustments, and improved patient compliance - advantages that justify premium pricing even in generic markets."

This conversation launched our systematic differentiation strategy based on creating measurable clinical superiority rather than just regulatory equivalence, transforming us from a commodity generic manufacturer into a specialized pharmaceutical company.

The formulation differentiation approach required investing significantly more in development than standard generic strategies, but the results enabled competitive positioning that price erosion could not eliminate.

"Our modified-release Metformin platform achieves 23% better glucose control compared to immediate-release generics while reducing gastrointestinal side effects by 40%," reported Dr. Chen during our differentiation progress review. "Clinical studies show physicians can reduce dosing frequency from twice daily to once daily for 67% of patients."

"How do clinical advantages translate into market access and pricing power?" I asked.

"Pharmacy benefit managers accept 15-20% premium pricing for formulations that reduce patient compliance issues and improve clinical outcomes. Superior formulations create value for the entire healthcare system, not just pharmaceutical companies."

"And physician acceptance of differentiated generics compared to standard bioequivalent products?"

"Physicians prescribe our enhanced formulations 34% more frequently than standard generics when they understand the clinical advantages. Differentiation creates prescription preference that commodity products cannot achieve."

The delivery system differentiation proved even more effective when we developed novel drug delivery technologies that solved real patient compliance problems while maintaining cost-effectiveness for healthcare systems.

"Our sublingual delivery system for cardiovascular medications eliminates swallowing difficulties for elderly patients while achieving faster onset of action than traditional oral tablets," explained Dr. Vikram Sharma during our innovation review. "Patient compliance increases from 67% to 89% with sublingual delivery."

"What development costs are required for delivery system differentiation compared to standard generic development?" asked Rajesh Khanna, our CFO.

"Delivery system development costs are 3-4 times higher than standard generic development, but successful differentiation enables pricing premiums that more than offset additional investment."

"And competitive barriers created by delivery system innovation?"

"Delivery system patents provide 5-7 years of market exclusivity compared to 6-12 months for standard generic exclusivity. Innovation creates sustainable competitive advantages that commodity manufacturing cannot replicate."

The combination product differentiation strategy enabled us to create entirely new therapeutic categories by combining existing molecules in ways that provided superior patient outcomes.

"Our fixed-dose combination of Amlodipine and Atorvastatin addresses both hypertension and hyperlipidemia in a single tablet," announced Dr. Priya Sharma during our combination product presentation. "Patient compliance for dual therapy increases from 43% to 78% with single-tablet formulations."

"How do combination products compete against established single-molecule generics?" I asked.

"Combination products create new market categories where we can achieve first-mover advantages rather than entering established commodity markets with multiple competitors."

"And physician adoption of combination therapy compared to separate medications?"

"Physicians prefer combination products because simplified dosing improves patient compliance while reducing pharmacy costs and medication management complexity."

The differentiation strategy required developing clinical evidence that demonstrated meaningful advantages over standard generic products, which involved additional studies and regulatory submissions.

"We've completed comparative effectiveness studies showing our enhanced formulations achieve superior clinical outcomes compared to standard generics in head-to-head trials," reported our clinical research manager during our evidence development update.

"What types of clinical evidence support differentiation claims?" I asked.

"Bioavailability studies showing superior absorption, patient compliance analyses demonstrating improved adherence, and clinical outcome studies proving better therapeutic results compared to standard generic formulations."

"And regulatory acceptance of differentiation claims?"

"FDA supports scientifically validated differentiation claims that provide measurable patient benefits. Regulatory agencies encourage innovation that improves therapeutic outcomes rather than just cost reduction."

The market response to our differentiation strategy exceeded expectations as healthcare providers recognized the value of superior formulations despite premium pricing compared to commodity generics.

"Our differentiated cardiovascular portfolio has achieved 23% market share in targeted physician segments despite pricing 18% above standard generic competitors," announced our commercial director during our quarterly review.

"What explains physician willingness to pay premium pricing for differentiated generics?" I asked.

"Clinical evidence demonstrating superior patient outcomes plus economic analysis showing reduced total healthcare costs through improved compliance and reduced adverse events."

"And payer acceptance of differentiated product pricing?"

"Insurance companies approve premium pricing for formulations that reduce long-term healthcare costs through better patient management and fewer complications."

The sustainable competitive advantages created by differentiation enabled us to escape commodity pricing cycles that were devastating competitors focused on cost competition alone.

"Differentiation has enabled us to maintain 12-15% price premiums compared to commodity generics across our entire US portfolio," I announced during our annual strategic review. "While competitors experience 60-80% price erosion, our differentiated products maintain stable pricing through clinical value creation."

"How sustainable are differentiation advantages as more competitors adopt similar strategies?" asked board member Kavita Desai.

"Differentiation creates intellectual property barriers and clinical evidence requirements that are difficult for competitors to replicate quickly or economically."

Two years after implementing systematic differentiation, we had transformed from a commodity generic manufacturer into a specialized pharmaceutical company with sustainable competitive advantages.

"Strategic differentiation taught us that generic pharmaceutical success requires creating measurable value for patients and healthcare systems rather than just regulatory compliance," I reflected during our innovation planning session.

"The key insight was that pharmaceutical markets reward clinical innovation even in generic segments when differentiation provides genuine therapeutic advantages."

The differentiation strategy had proven that escaping commodity competition required investing in capabilities that created clinical value rather than just cost advantages, enabling sustainable competitive positioning in increasingly competitive markets.

"Differentiation transformed our entire business philosophy from cost competition to value creation," I concluded. "Success requires solving clinical problems rather than just manufacturing equivalent products more efficiently."

Building Competitive Moats

The competitive moat concept crystallized for me during a humbling conversation with Warren Buffett at the 2014 Berkshire Hathaway annual meeting, where I had traveled specifically to understand how his investment philosophy might apply to pharmaceutical competition. When I asked him about sustainable competitive advantages in commodity-driven industries, his response fundamentally changed how I thought about building defensible business positions.

"Young man, the question isn't whether your products are better today," Buffett said with characteristic directness. "The question is whether you're building competitive advantages that will be stronger five years from now, even if your competitors know exactly what you're doing and try to copy you."

"But pharmaceuticals is a knowledge-intensive industry," I replied. "Can't competitors eventually replicate any technical advantages we develop?"

"Technical advantages are temporary. Sustainable competitive advantages come from building systems and capabilities that become stronger over time through compound effects that competitors cannot easily replicate, even when they understand your strategy."

This conversation forced me to abandon our focus on individual product advantages and instead concentrate on building systematic competitive moats that would strengthen through use rather than erode through competition.

The regulatory expertise moat emerged as our first systematic attempt to create advantages that would compound over time through accumulated knowledge and relationships that competitors could not quickly duplicate.

"We're building the deepest cardiovascular regulatory expertise outside the top five global pharmaceutical companies," announced Dr. Meera Patel during our regulatory strategy review. "Our team has successfully navigated forty-three FDA approval processes with a 94% first-submission success rate."

"How does regulatory expertise create sustainable competitive advantages?" I asked.

"Regulatory knowledge accumulates through experience and creates faster approval timelines, higher success rates, and better relationships with regulatory agencies that competitors cannot purchase or replicate quickly."

"And the sustainability of regulatory advantages as competitors develop similar capabilities?"

"Regulatory expertise strengthens through use because each successful approval generates additional knowledge and credibility that enhances future submissions. The gap between experienced and inexperienced regulatory teams actually widens over time."

The manufacturing excellence moat required developing operational capabilities that would become more efficient and effective as production volumes increased, creating cost advantages that competition would strengthen rather than erode.

"Our automated manufacturing platform achieves 99.7% quality consistency compared to industry averages of 96.8%," reported Dr. Vikram Singh during our operational review. "Higher quality enables premium pricing while lower defect rates reduce manufacturing costs by 23%."

"How does manufacturing excellence create competitive barriers?" I asked.

"Manufacturing excellence requires years of process optimization, equipment refinement, and quality system development that cannot be replicated quickly. Operational advantages strengthen through scale and experience."

"And the defensibility of manufacturing advantages against well-funded competitors?"

"Manufacturing excellence creates network effects where superior quality enables higher volumes, which enable further process improvements, which enable even better quality and lower costs. Success creates conditions for continued success."

The physician relationship moat proved most challenging to build but ultimately most valuable because medical professional relationships required years of consistent interaction and clinical evidence that competitors could not quickly establish.

"We've developed prescribing relationships with 2,847 cardiologists and 1,634 endocrinologists who preferentially prescribe our formulations based on clinical experience and patient outcomes," announced our medical affairs director during our relationship assessment.

"How do physician relationships translate into sustainable competitive advantages?" I asked.

"Physician prescribing behavior depends on clinical confidence developed through successful patient experiences over time. Established relationships create prescription loyalty that new market entrants cannot easily overcome."

"And the sustainability of physician relationships as competitors develop similar clinical evidence?"

"Medical relationships strengthen through accumulated clinical experience and professional trust that requires years to develop. Physicians prefer working with companies that have demonstrated consistent reliability and clinical support."

The intellectual property moat required systematic innovation that would create multiple layers of patent protection around our core technologies, making competitive entry increasingly difficult and expensive.

"Our modified-release platform has generated seventeen patent applications covering formulation technology, manufacturing processes, and clinical applications," reported our patent attorney during our IP review. "Patent protection extends through 2029 with continuation applications pending."

"How does intellectual property create sustainable competitive barriers?" I asked.

"Patent portfolios create multiple obstacles for competitors who must either develop alternative technologies or license our innovations. Strong IP forces competitors to choose more expensive and riskier development paths."

"And the strengthening effects of IP portfolios over time?"

"Each successful product generates additional clinical data and manufacturing innovations that support new patent applications. IP portfolios become broader and stronger through commercial success."

The customer intimacy moat emerged from developing deep understanding of healthcare system needs that enabled creating tailored solutions competitors could not easily replicate without similar customer development investments.

"We've developed specialized formulations for 127 hospital systems based on their specific patient populations and clinical protocols," explained our hospital sales manager during our customer analysis. "Customized solutions create switching costs that maintain customer loyalty."

"How does customer intimacy create competitive advantages that strengthen over time?" I asked.

"Deep customer relationships generate insights about unmet needs that enable developing solutions competitors cannot create without similar customer access and understanding."

"And the defensibility of customer relationships against aggressive competitive pricing?"

"Customer intimacy creates value beyond pricing through clinical outcomes, operational efficiency, and regulatory compliance that price competition alone cannot replace."

The compound effects of multiple competitive moats created systematic advantages that became stronger through interaction and mutual reinforcement rather than weakening through competitive pressure.

"Our regulatory expertise enables faster development of innovative formulations, which strengthens our IP portfolio, which enhances physician confidence, which increases prescribing volumes, which improves manufacturing efficiency, which enables continued innovation investment," I explained to our board during our annual competitive assessment.

"Each competitive advantage reinforces the others, creating a system of mutually strengthening capabilities that becomes more defensible over time."

Three years after systematically building competitive moats, we had created market positions that competitors acknowledged but could not easily replicate despite understanding our strategies.

"Competitive moat construction has enabled us to maintain 15-20% price premiums compared to commodity competitors while achieving market share growth in increasingly competitive markets," I reported during our strategic review.

"More importantly, our competitive advantages are stronger today than three years ago despite intensive competitive pressure from well-funded global companies."

The competitive moat philosophy had transformed our entire approach to strategy from defending current positions to building capabilities that would be stronger in the future regardless of competitive responses.

"Building competitive moats taught us that sustainable success requires creating advantages that strengthen through use rather than erode through competition," I reflected during our annual planning retreat.

"The key insight was that true competitive advantages come from building systems that benefit from competitive pressure rather than being weakened by it."

The lesson had become central to our strategic thinking: competitive moats required patient investment in capabilities that would compound over time, creating defensible positions that competition would strengthen rather than erode.

Chapter 18

The Regulatory Harmonization

Navigating the Global Maze

The regulatory harmonization revelation struck me during a particularly frustrating conference call in November 2014 with our regulatory teams across four different continents, where I realized we were conducting essentially the same clinical study five different ways to satisfy five different regulatory authorities who were supposedly following "harmonized" international guidelines. The irony was not lost on me that global regulatory harmonization had somehow created more complexity rather than less.

"We need separate bioequivalence studies for FDA, EMA, Health Canada, TGA, and PMDA because each agency has different statistical requirements despite all claiming to follow ICH guidelines," announced Dr. Meera Patel during our regulatory coordination meeting. "Total cost for 'harmonized' global registration is $8.7 million compared to $2.1 million for single-country approval."

"How is this possible when ICH harmonization was supposed to eliminate regulatory duplication?" I asked, staring at a timeline showing eighteen months of sequential submissions across different regulatory authorities. "Regulatory harmonization exists in principle but not in practice," she replied with the weary tone of someone who had spent years navigating bureaucratic inconsistencies. "Each agency interprets harmonized guidelines differently and maintains unique requirements that prevent true global regulatory efficiency."

"So harmonization has actually increased regulatory complexity rather than reducing it?"

"Harmonization created the illusion of simplified global registration while maintaining agency-specific requirements that multiply rather than minimize compliance obligations."

This conversation launched our systematic analysis of global regulatory systems that revealed the gap between harmonization promises and regulatory realities that every international pharmaceutical company faced but rarely discussed publicly.

The ICH guideline implementation proved particularly frustrating when we discovered that "harmonized" standards were interpreted differently by each major regulatory authority, creating compliance requirements that varied significantly despite supposedly uniform global guidelines.

"ICH E6 Good Clinical Practice guidelines require identical clinical data quality standards globally, but FDA requires electronic case report forms while EMA accepts paper submissions and PMDA requires specific Japanese patient data," explained Dr. Sarah Williams during our harmonization assessment.

"What additional costs result from these interpretation differences?" asked Rajesh Khanna, our CFO.

"Implementation variations require separate clinical data management systems, different statistical analysis approaches, and unique submission formats that increase regulatory costs by 340% compared to truly harmonized requirements."

"And timeline implications of sequential regulatory submissions?"

"Sequential submissions extend global approval timelines from 12 months to 36 months because each agency requires specific modifications to previously approved applications."

The bioequivalence study harmonization represented the most egregious example of how regulatory agencies maintained unique requirements despite international agreements designed to eliminate duplication.

"FDA requires fasting and fed bioequivalence studies with 80-125% acceptance criteria, EMA demands additional metabolite analysis, Health Canada requires specific dissolution testing, and PMDA insists on Japanese population studies," Dr. Patel recited during our bioequivalence planning session.

"Can't we conduct one comprehensive study that satisfies all requirements simultaneously?" I asked. "Each agency's unique requirements are mutually exclusive. FDA's fed study design conflicts with EMA's metabolite requirements, which cannot be combined with PMDA's population-specific protocols."

"So we must conduct separate studies for each agency despite harmonized bioequivalence guidelines?"

"Regulatory harmonization covers general principles but not specific implementation requirements, which forces separate studies for each major market."

The regulatory strategy adaptation required developing systematic approaches to manage global regulatory complexity while minimizing duplication and maximizing efficiency across multiple jurisdictions.

Phased Registration Strategy: We prioritized regulatory submissions based on market importance and technical feasibility rather than attempting simultaneous global registration that multiplied compliance requirements.

Reference Agency Approach: We designated FDA as our primary regulatory reference and adapted other submissions to leverage FDA-approved data while meeting local requirements.

Regional Harmonization Focus: We concentrated on truly harmonized regions like EU member states rather than attempting global harmonization across fundamentally different regulatory systems.

Regulatory Intelligence Investment: We hired agency-specific expertise rather than relying on generalized regulatory consultants who understood principles but not implementation nuances.

"Our regulatory strategy recognizes that harmonization exists primarily in regulatory rhetoric rather than practical implementation," I explained to our board during our global strategy presentation. "Success requires navigating actual regulatory requirements rather than theoretical harmonized guidelines."

"How does this affect our global expansion timeline and cost structure?" asked board member Kavita Desai.

"Realistic regulatory planning requires accepting that global registration takes 2-3 times longer and costs 3-4 times more than harmonization advocates suggest."

The regulatory relationship development proved essential for understanding how different agencies actually implemented supposedly harmonized guidelines in practice rather than theory.

"FDA emphasizes statistical rigor and systematic evidence evaluation, EMA prioritizes clinical relevance and patient benefit assessment, Health Canada focuses on safety documentation, and PMDA requires Japanese-specific population data regardless of global clinical evidence," summarized our regulatory affairs manager after eighteen months of agency interactions.

"How do these agency priorities affect our submission strategies?" I asked. "Each agency's priorities require different clinical evidence emphasis and submission organization despite identical underlying data. Success requires understanding agency culture, not just regulatory guidelines."

"And the practical implications for global pharmaceutical development?"

"Effective global registration requires agency-specific relationships and expertise rather than generic regulatory compliance capabilities."

The harmonization workaround strategies enabled us to achieve global market access while minimizing the regulatory complexity that had initially seemed overwhelming.

"We've achieved registration in twelve major markets using phased submission strategies that leverage agency precedents rather than attempting simultaneous global harmonization," reported Dr. Patel during our annual regulatory review.

"Sequential registration reduces total regulatory costs by 35% compared to simultaneous submission approaches while achieving comparable market access timelines," added Dr. Williams.

"And competitive advantages from regulatory efficiency?"

"Regulatory efficiency enables faster market entry and lower development costs that create competitive advantages over companies struggling with harmonization complexity."

Two years after adapting our regulatory strategy to harmonization realities, we had achieved more efficient global market access by accepting rather than fighting regulatory system differences.

"Regulatory harmonization taught us that international pharmaceutical success requires understanding regulatory systems as they actually function rather than as international agreements suggest they should function," I reflected during our global strategy review.

"The key insight was that harmonization is an aspiration rather than a reality, and successful companies adapt to actual regulatory requirements rather than theoretical harmonized guidelines."

The regulatory harmonization experience had transformed our approach from expecting global regulatory simplicity to developing systematic capabilities for managing regulatory complexity efficiently.

"The most important lesson from harmonization was recognizing that regulatory systems reflect national sovereignty and cultural differences that international agreements cannot eliminate," I concluded during our regulatory planning session.

"Successful global pharmaceutical development requires embracing regulatory diversity rather than expecting regulatory uniformity. "The lesson had become fundamental to our international strategy: regulatory harmonization was a useful goal but not a practical reality, and success required building capabilities to navigate regulatory complexity rather than waiting for regulatory simplification.

Achieving Regulatory Approvals Across Markets

The first international regulatory approval came after eighteen grueling months of submissions, revisions, and bureaucratic warfare that nearly bankrupted our regulatory department and taught me that achieving market access across multiple jurisdictions required the patience of a saint and the resources of a multinational corporation. Our FDA approval for Amlodipine extended-release tablets arrived on March 15, 2014, followed by what I naively expected would be straightforward approvals in Europe and Canada using the same clinical data.

"FDA approval doesn't guarantee acceptance by other regulatory agencies," Dr. Meera Patel explained during our post-approval strategy meeting, dampening my celebration with regulatory realities I hadn't anticipated. "Each agency requires specific modifications to FDA-approved submissions, additional studies, and unique documentation that can take 12-24 months per market."

"But we've already proven safety and efficacy through FDA's rigorous review process," I protested. "Why do other agencies need different evidence for the same product?"

"Regulatory agencies maintain sovereignty over their markets and require evidence that satisfies their specific scientific standards, patient populations, and healthcare systems regardless of other agencies' conclusions."

"How different can the requirements be for bioequivalent generic products?"

"Dramatically different. European Medicines Agency requires additional dissolution testing, Health Canada demands specific stability data, and Australian TGA requires unique bioequivalence study designs that weren't needed for FDA approval."

This conversation marked the beginning of our systematic global regulatory campaign that would consume three years and $12.7 million while teaching us that international pharmaceutical success required understanding each regulatory system as a distinct competitive challenge.

The European regulatory approval process proved particularly complex when we discovered that achieving centralized authorization through EMA required different clinical evidence than our successful FDA submission, despite both agencies claiming to follow identical ICH guidelines.

"EMA requires comparative dissolution studies across multiple pH conditions that FDA didn't request, plus stability data under European climatic conditions that differ from US requirements," reported Dr. Sarah Williams during our European strategy review. "Additional studies will cost $2.3 million and delay European approval by eight months."

"Can't we argue that FDA's approval demonstrates equivalent safety and efficacy?" I asked.

"EMA acknowledges FDA approval but requires European-specific evidence to ensure product performance under European healthcare conditions and patient populations."

"And timeline for European approval assuming we complete additional studies?"

"European centralized procedure requires 210 days for scientific evaluation plus additional time for national implementations, meaning 12-15 months from submission to market authorization."

The Canadian regulatory approval presented unique challenges when Health Canada requested post-market surveillance data and risk management plans that exceeded both FDA and EMA requirements, demonstrating that smaller regulatory agencies often imposed more stringent requirements than larger ones.

"Health Canada requires comprehensive post-market surveillance protocols, adverse event reporting systems, and risk evaluation programs that weren't needed for FDA or EMA approvals," announced our Canadian regulatory consultant during our market access planning.

"What additional compliance obligations does Canadian approval create?" asked Rajesh Khanna, our CFO.

"Canadian approval requires ongoing pharmacovigilance reporting, annual safety updates, and periodic benefit-risk assessments that cost approximately $340,000 annually to maintain."

"And competitive advantages from Canadian market access?"

"Canadian generic markets provide more stable pricing than US markets but require sustained regulatory investment to maintain market authorization."

The Asian regulatory approvals proved most challenging when we encountered regulatory systems that required completely different clinical evidence despite our extensive global approval portfolio.

"Japan's PMDA requires Japanese population bioequivalence studies regardless of global clinical data because genetic and dietary differences affect drug metabolism in Japanese patients," explained our Asian regulatory manager during our expansion planning.

"How significant are the differences in Japanese regulatory requirements?" I asked.

"Japanese approval requires conducting entirely new bioequivalence studies in Japanese subjects plus unique stability testing under Japanese climatic conditions. Total additional investment approaches $4.7 million."

"And regulatory timelines for Japanese approval?"

"PMDA review process requires 12 months for scientific evaluation plus 6 months for manufacturing facility inspection, meaning 18-24 months from submission to approval."

The regulatory strategy optimization required developing systematic approaches to sequence global approvals in ways that maximized efficiency while meeting each agency's unique requirements.

Reference Regulatory Authority Strategy: We designated FDA as our primary regulatory reference and structured subsequent submissions to leverage FDA precedents while meeting local requirements.

Phased Market Entry Approach: We prioritized markets based on regulatory complexity and commercial potential rather than attempting simultaneous global registration that multiplied compliance costs.

Regulatory Intelligence Investment: We hired agency-specific consultants who understood implementation nuances rather than relying on generalized regulatory expertise.

Data Package Optimization: We designed clinical studies to satisfy multiple agencies simultaneously whenever possible while accepting that some markets required unique evidence.

"Our regulatory strategy balances global efficiency with agency-specific requirements by leveraging common data while accepting that some markets require unique investments," I explained to our board during our international expansion review.

"The key insight is that regulatory approval costs and timelines vary dramatically across markets, requiring strategic prioritization based on commercial potential and regulatory complexity."

The regulatory approval achievements began validating our systematic approach as we successfully navigated increasingly complex agency requirements while maintaining reasonable timelines and costs.

"We've achieved regulatory approval in eight major markets with average timelines of 14 months per market and total costs of $1.8 million per approval," reported Dr. Patel during our annual regulatory review. "Approval success rate is 94% across all submissions."

"How do our regulatory timelines compare to industry benchmarks?" I asked.

"Our approval timelines are 23% faster than industry averages because systematic preparation and agency-specific expertise enable more efficient submissions."

"And regulatory competitive advantages from our approval portfolio?"

"Multiple market approvals create barriers for competitors who must replicate our regulatory investments while enabling us to achieve global market coverage that smaller companies cannot afford."

The sustained regulatory success enabled global market access that transformed us from a domestic pharmaceutical company into an international competitor with presence across major regulated markets.

"Regulatory approvals across twelve markets have enabled global revenue diversification with 67% of sales now generated outside India," I announced during our strategic review. "International market access provides growth opportunities and competitive positioning that domestic-only companies cannot achieve."

"More importantly, our regulatory approval portfolio creates competitive moats because replicating our global market access requires competitors to invest years and millions of dollars in regulatory submissions."

Three years after beginning our international regulatory campaign, we had achieved market authorization across major regulated markets while developing systematic capabilities for continued global expansion.

"Achieving regulatory approvals across markets taught us that international pharmaceutical success requires treating each regulatory agency as a distinct competitive challenge with unique requirements and cultural expectations," I reflected during our global strategy planning.

"The key lesson was that regulatory success requires patience, resources, and agency-specific expertise rather than expecting harmonized global approval processes."

The regulatory approval achievements had proven that systematic global market access was possible for mid-sized pharmaceutical companies willing to invest in understanding and navigating regulatory complexity across multiple jurisdictions.

"Our regulatory approval portfolio demonstrates that global pharmaceutical success is achievable through systematic preparation and sustained investment in regulatory excellence," I concluded. "Success requires building capabilities to navigate regulatory complexity rather than waiting for regulatory simplification."

Building a Global Regulatory Team

The decision to build our global regulatory team came during a catastrophic submission failure in June 2014 when our European Medicines Agency application was rejected after eight months of review because our regulatory consultant had misinterpreted fundamental EMA requirements that any experienced European regulatory professional would have identified during initial planning. The rejection cost us $3.2 million in wasted development work and eighteen months of delayed market entry.

"We cannot continue relying on external consultants who understand regulatory theory but lack practical experience with agency-specific requirements," I announced during our emergency regulatory strategy meeting, staring at EMA's devastating rejection letter that detailed fourteen fundamental deficiencies in our submission. "We need internal regulatory expertise that understands how agencies actually implement their guidelines."

"Building internal regulatory capabilities will require significant investment in specialized personnel who command premium salaries," cautioned Rajesh Khanna, our CFO. "Experienced regulatory professionals cost 40-60% more than equivalent R&D or commercial positions."

"What's the alternative cost of continued submission failures and regulatory delays?"

"Our EMA rejection represents the third major regulatory setback this year, with total costs approaching $8.7 million plus incalculable opportunity costs from delayed market entry."

This conversation marked the beginning of our systematic effort to build world-class regulatory capabilities that could navigate the complexity of global pharmaceutical approval processes with the expertise that external consultants had failed to provide.

The regulatory team recruitment proved more challenging than anticipated when we discovered that experienced regulatory professionals were scarce, expensive, and typically committed to large pharmaceutical companies that could offer career advancement opportunities we couldn't match.

"Experienced FDA regulatory managers command salaries of $180,000-220,000 annually plus equity compensation and comprehensive benefits," reported our recruitment consultant during our hiring strategy review. "EMA specialists require $160,000-190,000 euros plus relocation assistance for candidates willing to work outside major European pharmaceutical centers."

"How do we compete for regulatory talent against Novartis, Roche, and other major pharmaceutical companies?" I asked.

"Mid-sized companies typically cannot match multinational compensation packages, but we can offer broader responsibility, faster career advancement, and equity participation that large companies rarely provide."

"And availability of qualified regulatory professionals?"

"Global shortage of experienced regulatory professionals means recruitment timelines of 6-12 months for senior positions, with intense competition among pharmaceutical companies for proven talent."

The regulatory team structure required balancing global coordination with regional expertise, since successful regulatory submissions demanded both strategic oversight and detailed knowledge of specific agency requirements.

"We need a global regulatory director for strategic coordination plus regional specialists for FDA, EMA, Health Canada, and Asian markets," explained Dr. Meera Patel during our organizational planning session. "Each major regulatory agency requires dedicated expertise because submission requirements and agency relationships cannot be managed effectively from a single location."

"What organizational structure enables both global efficiency and regional expertise?" I asked.

"Matrix organization with global regulatory leadership for strategy and standards plus regional teams for agency-specific submissions and relationship management."

"And coordination mechanisms between global and regional regulatory functions?"

"Weekly global regulatory calls, quarterly strategy reviews, and annual regulatory planning sessions to ensure consistency while maintaining regional autonomy for agency-specific requirements."

The regulatory talent acquisition strategy required offering unique value propositions that could attract experienced professionals despite our inability to match multinational pharmaceutical compensation packages.

"We're targeting mid-career regulatory professionals who want broader responsibility and faster advancement than large pharmaceutical companies typically provide," announced our head of talent acquisition during our recruitment update. "Our value proposition emphasizes leadership opportunities, equity participation, and direct impact on company strategy."

"How effective is this positioning compared to traditional pharmaceutical career paths?" I asked.

"Regulatory professionals often feel constrained by bureaucratic processes and limited advancement opportunities at large companies. We can offer entrepreneurial environments and strategic influence that appeals to ambitious regulatory talent."

"And retention strategies for regulatory team members?"

"Competitive compensation plus equity participation, professional development opportunities, and clear advancement paths within our growing international organization."

The global regulatory team development required systematic investment in training, systems, and processes that would enable coordinating complex submissions across multiple jurisdictions while maintaining agency-specific expertise.

"Our regulatory team requires specialized training in electronic submission systems, agency relationship management, and global harmonization principles," reported our newly hired Global Regulatory Director, Dr. Amanda Richardson, during her first quarterly review. "Investment in regulatory infrastructure and training approaches $1.7 million annually."

"What capabilities does this investment provide compared to external regulatory consultants?" I asked.

"Internal regulatory teams develop institutional knowledge, agency relationships, and submission expertise that external consultants cannot provide. Long-term capability building creates competitive advantages that consulting relationships cannot achieve."

"And regulatory team productivity compared to outsourced regulatory services?"

"Internal regulatory teams achieve 35% faster submission timelines and 28% higher approval rates because dedicated professionals understand our products and develop ongoing agency relationships."

The regulatory team performance validation came when our newly assembled global regulatory organization successfully managed simultaneous submissions across five regulatory agencies using coordinated strategies that external consultants had been unable to execute.

"Our global regulatory team has achieved FDA approval in 11 months, EMA approval in 13 months, and Health Canada approval in 9 months for our Metformin extended-release product," Dr. Richardson reported during our annual regulatory review. "Simultaneous submissions enabled global market access 18 months faster than sequential regulatory approaches."

"How do our regulatory timelines compare to industry benchmarks with our internal team?" I asked.

"Our approval timelines are 31% faster than industry averages, with 96% first-submission success rates across all major agencies."

"And cost efficiency of internal regulatory capabilities compared to external consultants?"

"Internal regulatory team costs are 45% lower than equivalent external consulting while achieving superior results through dedicated expertise and agency relationships."

The global regulatory team expansion enabled us to pursue market opportunities that had been impossible with limited regulatory capabilities, transforming our international growth potential.

"Our expanded regulatory capabilities enable pursuing approval in fifteen additional markets that were previously inaccessible due to regulatory complexity," I announced during our strategic planning session. "Global regulatory expertise has become a competitive advantage that enables international expansion other mid-sized companies cannot achieve."

Two years after building our global regulatory team, we had achieved market access capabilities that rivaled much larger pharmaceutical companies while maintaining the agility and focus that multinational corporations could not match.

"Building our global regulatory team taught us that regulatory expertise is a strategic capability that requires systematic investment rather than tactical outsourcing," I reflected during our organizational review.

"The key insight was that regulatory success requires dedicated professionals who understand both our products and agency requirements rather than generalized consulting services."

The regulatory team development had proven that mid-sized pharmaceutical companies could build world-class regulatory capabilities through strategic talent acquisition and systematic capability development.

"Our global regulatory team demonstrates that specialized expertise can be built systematically through strategic investment in talent and infrastructure," I concluded. "Success requires treating regulatory capabilities as strategic assets rather than administrative functions."

The lesson had become fundamental to our international strategy: global pharmaceutical success required building internal regulatory expertise that could navigate complex agency requirements while maintaining the strategic focus that external consultants could not provide.

The European EMA Approval Milestone

The European Medicines Agency approval notification arrived at 3:47 AM Mumbai time on September 23, 2015, in a tersely worded email that represented the culmination of twenty-two months of bureaucratic warfare, $4.3 million in regulatory investment, and the professional reputations of everyone involved in what had become our most challenging regulatory campaign. Dr. Amanda Richardson called me from London at dawn, her voice mixing exhaustion with triumph.

"We got it," she announced simply. "EMA has granted marketing authorization for our Amlodipine/Atorvastatin fixed-dose combination across all 28 European Union member states."

"After everything we've been through, that's it?" I asked, though relief was flooding through me as I realized we had finally broken through the European regulatory fortress that had seemed impenetrable for nearly two years.

"The approval letter is remarkably brief considering the complexity of getting here," she replied. "But this authorization provides immediate market access across the entire European Union, representing 447 million potential patients and annual market potential exceeding €2.3 billion."

This moment marked not just regulatory success but strategic validation that our global pharmaceutical ambitions were achievable despite the overwhelming complexity of international market access requirements.

The EMA approval journey had begun eighteen months earlier with what we thought would be a straightforward submission leveraging our successful FDA approval, only to discover that European regulatory requirements demanded completely different clinical evidence and submission approaches.

"EMA requires comparative dissolution studies across multiple pH conditions, stability data under European climatic zones, and specific bioequivalence studies that account for European dietary patterns," Dr. Richardson had explained during our initial European strategy planning. "FDA approval provides regulatory precedent but not regulatory shortcuts for European authorization."

"How different can European patients be from American patients for the same cardiovascular medications?" I had asked.

"European regulatory philosophy emphasizes population-specific evidence and real-world clinical conditions that require separate validation despite identical active pharmaceutical ingredients."

"And additional costs for European-specific studies?"

"European regulatory requirements add $2.7 million to development costs plus 14 months to approval timelines compared to FDA-only registration."

The submission preparation consumed eight months of intensive work as our regulatory team navigated EMA's complex electronic submission requirements while coordinating with European clinical research organizations and manufacturing partners.

"European submission requires Common Technical Document format with specific modules organized according to EMA guidelines that differ substantially from FDA eCTD requirements," reported our regulatory affairs manager during submission preparation updates. "Document compilation involves 47,000 pages across multiple languages with cross-referencing systems that must satisfy both EMA and national regulatory authorities."

"What makes European submissions more complex than FDA submissions?" I asked.

"EMA operates as a coordinating authority for 28 national agencies, each with unique requirements and review processes that must be satisfied simultaneously through the centralized procedure."

"And quality control requirements for European submission documentation?"

"EMA requires trilingual summaries, country-specific labeling, and regulatory compliance certificates from each manufacturing facility involved in European supply chains."

The EMA review process proved more interactive than FDA evaluation, with ongoing scientific dialogue that required sophisticated understanding of European regulatory expectations and clinical evidence standards.

"EMA has issued Day 120 questions requesting additional bioequivalence data, clarification of manufacturing processes, and expanded stability studies," Dr. Richardson reported during our mid-review update. "European regulatory review involves collaborative scientific dialogue rather than binary approval decisions."

"How do we respond to EMA questions without triggering additional delays?" I asked.

"EMA questions represent opportunities to provide clarifying evidence rather than regulatory obstacles. Comprehensive responses can accelerate approval while inadequate responses trigger clock stops and additional review cycles."

"And timeline implications of EMA scientific dialogue?"

"Thorough preparation for EMA questions can maintain standard 210-day review timelines, while inadequate responses can extend evaluation to 12-18 months through repeated clock stops."

The manufacturing inspection represented the most stressful component of EMA approval when European inspectors conducted on-site evaluation of our Mumbai facility using standards that exceeded even FDA requirements.

"EMA manufacturing inspection team will evaluate our facility compliance with European Good Manufacturing Practice guidelines that include specific requirements for European supply chain management," announced our manufacturing director during inspection preparation. "European GMP standards require documentation systems and quality controls that go beyond FDA compliance."

"What additional manufacturing capabilities do European requirements demand?" I asked.

"European markets require batch tracking systems, recall procedures, and pharmacovigilance capabilities that enable real-time monitoring across 28 different healthcare systems."

"And inspection timeline and approval implications?"

"EMA manufacturing inspection requires 3-5 days of intensive facility evaluation plus 60 days for inspection report preparation. Manufacturing approval is prerequisite for marketing authorization."

The approval decision culminated months of anticipation as EMA's Committee for Medicinal Products for Human Use evaluated our complete submission package and recommended marketing authorization across all European Union member states.

"CHMP has adopted positive opinion recommending marketing authorization for our fixed-dose combination with approved labeling for cardiovascular risk reduction in European patients," Dr. Richardson announced during our final regulatory review. "European approval includes 28 EU markets plus Iceland, Norway, and Liechtenstein through European Economic Area agreements."

"What commercial opportunities does EMA approval provide?" asked our business development manager.

"European approval enables immediate market entry across major pharmaceutical markets including Germany, France, UK, Italy, and Spain representing combined annual generic cardiovascular markets exceeding €4.2 billion."

"And competitive positioning advantages from European regulatory approval?"

"EMA approval provides regulatory precedent for additional European products while establishing our company as credible European pharmaceutical supplier for partnership and licensing opportunities."

The European market entry strategy required coordinating launch activities across multiple countries while satisfying national implementation requirements that varied despite centralized EMA approval.

"European marketing authorization requires national implementation in each target market with country-specific pricing negotiations, reimbursement approvals, and distribution arrangements," explained our European commercial manager during launch planning. "EMA approval provides regulatory authorization but not market access."

"How long does national implementation take following EMA approval?" I asked.

"National implementation timelines vary from 2 months in Germany to 8 months in France, depending on pricing negotiations and healthcare system integration requirements."

The EMA approval milestone transformed our company from an Indian pharmaceutical manufacturer with limited international presence to a global pharmaceutical company with regulatory credibility across major developed markets.

"European approval validates our global pharmaceutical capabilities and provides platform for continued international expansion," I announced during our board presentation. "EMA authorization demonstrates that we can successfully navigate the world's most sophisticated regulatory systems."

The milestone had proven that systematic regulatory investment could enable mid-sized pharmaceutical companies to achieve global market access despite overwhelming complexity and resource requirements.

"The EMA approval taught us that European regulatory success requires understanding European pharmaceutical culture and patient care philosophy rather than just meeting technical requirements," I reflected during our achievement celebration.

"The key lesson was that regulatory approval is just the beginning of European market success, which requires continued investment in market access and commercial capabilities."

The European approval milestone had become proof that our global pharmaceutical ambitions were achievable through systematic investment in regulatory excellence and strategic persistence despite seemingly insurmountable barriers.

Japanese PMDA Partnership Strategy

The Japanese market opportunity crystallized during a Tokyo pharmaceutical conference in March 2016 when I learned that Japan's rapidly aging population was creating unprecedented demand for cardiovascular medications, while the country's complex regulatory system and cultural business practices were deterring many international pharmaceutical companies from serious market entry. The PMDA partnership strategy emerged from recognizing that Japan required a fundamentally different approach than our successful US and European regulatory campaigns.

"Japan represents the world's third-largest pharmaceutical market with ¥10.2 trillion annual revenue, but successful market entry requires understanding Japanese regulatory culture and business relationships that differ dramatically from Western approaches," explained Dr. Hiroshi Tanaka, our newly hired Japanese regulatory consultant, during our market assessment meeting.

"How different can Japanese regulatory requirements be from FDA and EMA standards?" I asked, though I suspected the answer would challenge everything we had learned about international pharmaceutical markets.

"PMDA requires Japanese population-specific clinical data regardless of global regulatory approvals because genetic and dietary differences affect drug metabolism in Japanese patients. Additionally, Japanese business culture emphasizes long-term relationships and consensus-building that cannot be replicated through standard regulatory submissions."

"And the implications for our Japanese market entry strategy?"

"Japanese success requires local partnership with established pharmaceutical companies who understand PMDA requirements and possess the cultural relationships necessary for sustainable market access."

This conversation launched our systematic analysis of Japanese pharmaceutical markets that would lead to our most complex and rewarding international partnership arrangement.

The PMDA regulatory requirements proved more challenging than anticipated when we discovered that Japanese approval demanded completely new clinical studies despite our extensive global regulatory portfolio including FDA, EMA, and Health Canada approvals.

"PMDA requires bioequivalence studies conducted in Japanese subjects because population pharmacokinetics differ significantly from Western patients," reported Dr. Tanaka during our Japanese regulatory planning session. "Japanese bioequivalence studies must demonstrate equivalent safety and efficacy in Japanese population using PMDA-specific protocols."

"What additional costs do Japanese population studies require?" asked Rajesh Khanna, our CFO.

"Japanese bioequivalence studies cost $3.8 million plus 18 months of clinical development time because PMDA requires larger patient populations and longer observation periods than Western regulatory agencies."

"And manufacturing requirements for Japanese market authorization?"

"PMDA requires on-site facility inspection plus Japanese Good Manufacturing Practice certification that involves 6-month qualification process with ongoing compliance monitoring."

The partnership strategy development required identifying Japanese pharmaceutical companies with complementary capabilities who could provide regulatory expertise, manufacturing infrastructure, and market access while benefiting from our innovative formulation technologies.

"We need Japanese partners with established PMDA relationships, domestic manufacturing capabilities, and cardiovascular market presence who can benefit from our modified-release platform technologies," I explained during our partnership planning session. "Japanese partnership must create mutual value rather than just providing market access."

"What value propositions can we offer potential Japanese partners?" asked Dr. Priya Sharma.

"Our proprietary formulation technologies enable Japanese companies to develop differentiated products for domestic and export markets while we gain access to Japanese regulatory expertise and market relationships."

"And partnership structure that protects our intellectual property while enabling Japanese market success?"

"Joint venture arrangements with shared investment in Japanese clinical development plus licensing agreements that provide ongoing royalty income from Japanese market sales."

The partner identification process involved extensive evaluation of Japanese pharmaceutical companies with cardiovascular expertise and strategic interest in international collaboration opportunities.

"Takeda, Astellas, and Daiichi Sankyo possess the capabilities we need but are too large for meaningful partnership arrangements," reported our business development manager during partner assessment updates. "Mid-sized companies like Kyowa Kirin, Sawai Pharmaceutical, and Towa Pharmaceutical offer better partnership potential with complementary capabilities."

"What criteria should guide Japanese partner selection?" I asked.

"PMDA regulatory track record, cardiovascular therapeutic focus, manufacturing capacity for our products, and cultural compatibility for sustained collaboration."

"And due diligence requirements for Japanese partnership evaluation?"

"Financial analysis, regulatory capability assessment, intellectual property evaluation, and extensive cultural compatibility discussions because Japanese partnerships require long-term relationship commitment."

The Sawai Pharmaceutical partnership emerged as our optimal Japanese market entry strategy when their cardiovascular expertise, PMDA regulatory capabilities, and strategic vision aligned with our formulation technologies and international expansion objectives.

"Sawai Pharmaceutical has achieved PMDA approval for 47 cardiovascular products with 94% first-submission success rates over the past decade," announced Dr. Tanaka during our partner evaluation presentation. "They possess the regulatory expertise and market relationships necessary for successful Japanese market entry."

"What makes Sawai an ideal partner compared to other Japanese pharmaceutical companies?" I asked.

"Sawai specializes in generic cardiovascular medications with strong PMDA relationships, modern manufacturing facilities, and strategic interest in innovative formulation technologies that complement their existing portfolio."

"And proposed partnership structure with Sawai Pharmaceutical?"

"Joint venture for Japanese clinical development and market entry plus licensing agreements for our proprietary technologies with milestone payments and ongoing royalties from Japanese sales."

The partnership implementation required extensive cultural adaptation and relationship building that exceeded typical pharmaceutical business development processes.

"Japanese partnership success requires understanding consensus-building processes, long-term relationship commitments, and cultural protocols that differ significantly from Western business practices," Dr. Tanaka explained during our cultural preparation sessions. "Partnership negotiations involve extensive relationship development that can require 6-12 months before substantive business discussions begin."

"How do we balance cultural sensitivity with business efficiency in partnership development?" I asked.

"Japanese business culture prioritizes relationship quality over transaction speed. Successful partnerships require patient investment in cultural understanding and mutual respect that Western companies often underestimate."

"And ongoing partnership management requirements?"

"Japanese partnerships require continuous relationship maintenance through regular meetings, cultural events, and collaborative decision-making that becomes integral to business operations rather than periodic business reviews."

The PMDA submission preparation through our Sawai partnership demonstrated the value of local expertise in navigating complex Japanese regulatory requirements while leveraging our global regulatory experience.

"Sawai's regulatory team has prepared PMDA submissions using our global clinical data supplemented with Japanese population studies that address PMDA-specific requirements," reported Dr. Richardson during our Japanese regulatory update. "Partnership approach reduces submission costs by 45% while improving approval probability through local expertise."

"And timeline advantages from Japanese partnership compared to independent PMDA submission?" I asked.

"Sawai partnership enables PMDA approval timelines of 14-18 months compared to 24-36 months for independent foreign companies due to established agency relationships and cultural understanding."

The Japanese partnership strategy success validated our approach of combining global pharmaceutical capabilities with local market expertise to achieve sustainable competitive advantages in complex international markets.

"Sawai partnership has enabled Japanese market entry with shared risks and costs while providing platform for additional Asian market expansion," I announced during our annual international review. "Japanese partnership demonstrates that strategic collaboration can overcome regulatory and cultural barriers that prevent independent market entry."

The PMDA partnership strategy had proven that successful international pharmaceutical expansion required cultural adaptation and local expertise rather than just regulatory compliance and product quality.

"The Japanese partnership taught us that Asian pharmaceutical markets require relationship-based strategies that differ fundamentally from Western transactional approaches," I reflected during our strategic planning session.

"The key insight was that Japanese success requires understanding business culture and building long-term relationships rather than just meeting technical requirements."

The PMDA partnership strategy had become our model for entering complex international markets through strategic collaboration that leveraged local expertise while protecting our core competitive advantages.

Chapter 19

The Digital Transformation

When Spreadsheets Became Algorithms

The digital transformation awakening came during a particularly frustrating morning in April 2016 when I discovered that our "integrated" pharmaceutical operations were actually managed through 247 different Excel spreadsheets maintained by various departments, none of which communicated with each other. The absurdity hit me when our regulatory team spent three days manually reconciling batch records with quality control data to respond to an FDA inspection request that should have taken thirty minutes with proper digital systems.

"We're operating a billion-rupee pharmaceutical company using the same data management approach as a corner grocery store," I announced during our emergency IT strategy meeting, holding printouts of seventeen different spreadsheets that supposedly tracked the same manufacturing batch. "Our competitors are using artificial intelligence for drug discovery while we're using calculators for inventory management."

"But our current systems work," protested Dr. Vikram Singh, our head of manufacturing, with the defensive tone of someone who had spent years perfecting manual processes. "We've never had significant quality issues or regulatory violations using our established procedures."

"Our systems work until they don't," I replied, remembering the previous week's near-miss when a manual data entry error almost resulted in incorrect labeling that could have triggered a product recall. "Digital transformation isn't about fixing problems - it's about creating competitive advantages that manual processes cannot achieve."

"What specific advantages would digital systems provide over our current operations?" asked Dr. Priya Sharma.

"Real-time data integration, predictive analytics, automated compliance reporting, and competitive intelligence capabilities that could transform how we develop, manufacture, and market pharmaceuticals."

This conversation launched our systematic digital transformation that would revolutionize every aspect of our pharmaceutical operations over the following three years.

The manufacturing digitalization proved most immediately valuable when we implemented integrated systems that connected production planning, quality control, inventory management, and regulatory reporting through real-time data sharing.

"Our new Manufacturing Execution System integrates batch production data with quality control results and regulatory compliance requirements in real-time," announced our newly hired Chief Technology Officer, Rahul Mehta, during our digital implementation review. "Digital integration eliminates manual data reconciliation while providing instant access to complete manufacturing histories."

"How does digital manufacturing integration affect operational efficiency?" I asked.

"Manufacturing productivity has increased 23% through automated scheduling, predictive maintenance, and real-time quality monitoring that prevents problems rather than detecting them after they occur."

"And regulatory compliance advantages from digital manufacturing systems?"

"Digital systems generate automated FDA-compliant documentation, enable instant recall traceability, and provide real-time compliance monitoring that reduces regulatory risk while simplifying inspection responses."

The regulatory digitalization transformed our global submission management from manual document compilation to automated regulatory intelligence that accelerated approval timelines while improving submission quality.

"Our Regulatory Information Management System tracks global submission status, deadline management, and regulatory intelligence across all markets simultaneously," reported Dr. Amanda Richardson during our regulatory technology update. "Digital regulatory management has reduced submission preparation time by 47% while improving approval success rates."

"What specific advantages do digital regulatory systems provide?" I asked.

"Automated compliance checking, real-time regulatory intelligence, and integrated submission management that eliminates manual errors while accelerating approval timelines."

"And competitive intelligence capabilities from digital regulatory systems?"

"Digital systems monitor competitor approvals, market trends, and regulatory changes in real-time, providing strategic intelligence that manual processes cannot deliver efficiently."

The research and development digitalization enabled sophisticated data analytics and artificial intelligence applications that transformed how we identified opportunities and optimized formulation development.

"Our R&D digital platform integrates formulation databases, clinical trial management, and predictive modeling systems that accelerate product development while improving success rates," explained Dr. Lisa Chen during our innovation technology review. "Digital R&D tools enable sophisticated analysis that manual processes cannot achieve."

"How does digital R&D compare to traditional pharmaceutical development approaches?" I asked.

"Digital formulation optimization reduces development timelines by 35% through predictive modeling and automated screening that identifies optimal formulations faster than traditional trial-and-error approaches."

"And artificial intelligence applications in pharmaceutical development?"

"AI systems analyze molecular interactions, predict bioavailability, and optimize manufacturing processes using pattern recognition that exceeds human analytical capabilities."

The commercial digitalization created customer relationship management and market intelligence capabilities that enabled sophisticated targeting and competitive positioning that manual sales processes could not support.

"Our digital commercial platform integrates physician prescribing data, market trends, and competitive intelligence to optimize sales force effectiveness and marketing strategy," announced our commercial director during our digital marketing review. "Digital commercial systems provide real-time market insights that enable rapid competitive responses."

"What commercial advantages do digital systems provide over traditional pharmaceutical sales approaches?" I asked.

"Digital systems enable personalized physician engagement, predictive market analysis, and automated competitive intelligence that increases sales effectiveness while reducing commercial costs."

"And customer relationship management capabilities from digital commercial systems?"

"Digital CRM systems track physician interactions, prescribing patterns, and market preferences to optimize sales force productivity and improve customer satisfaction."

The supply chain digitalization integrated global manufacturing, distribution, and inventory management systems that enabled real-time optimization and predictive planning across our international operations.

"Our digital supply chain platform connects manufacturing, distribution, and inventory systems across twelve countries to optimize global operations in real-time," reported our supply chain manager during our logistics technology update. "Digital integration reduces inventory costs by 28% while improving delivery reliability."

"How does digital supply chain management affect international operations?" I asked.

"Digital systems enable real-time visibility across global operations, predictive demand planning, and automated optimization that manual processes cannot achieve at international scale."

"And risk management advantages from digital supply chain systems?"

"Digital systems provide early warning for supply disruptions, automated contingency planning, and real-time risk monitoring that prevents problems rather than reacting to them."

The digital transformation results exceeded expectations as integrated systems created operational efficiencies and competitive advantages that manual processes could not deliver.

"Digital transformation has increased overall operational efficiency by 34% while reducing compliance costs by 41% through automation and real-time monitoring," I announced during our annual technology review. "More importantly, digital systems provide competitive intelligence and predictive capabilities that enable strategic advantages over competitors using manual processes."

"And return on investment from digital transformation initiatives?" asked Rajesh Khanna, our CFO.

"Digital transformation investments of ₹47 crores have generated annual savings of ₹23 crores plus competitive advantages that cannot be quantified easily but significantly improve our market positioning."

Two years after implementing comprehensive digital transformation, we had evolved from a manually operated pharmaceutical company to a technology-enabled organization with capabilities that exceeded many larger competitors.

"Digital transformation taught us that pharmaceutical success increasingly depends on data analytics and technological capabilities rather than just clinical expertise and manufacturing quality," I reflected during our strategic technology planning.

"The key insight was that digital systems create compound advantages where efficiency gains enable competitive capabilities that manual processes cannot achieve."

The digital transformation had proven that pharmaceutical companies could achieve sustainable competitive advantages through technological innovation that enhanced rather than replaced core pharmaceutical expertise.

"Digital transformation demonstrated that technology amplifies pharmaceutical capabilities rather than replacing them," I concluded. "Success requires integrating digital tools with pharmaceutical expertise to create competitive advantages that neither can achieve independently."

The lesson had become central to our competitive strategy: digital transformation was not about replacing pharmaceutical expertise but about creating technological capabilities that enhanced our ability to develop, manufacture, and market pharmaceuticals more effectively than competitors using manual processes.

Implementing ERP Systems Across Global Operations

The ERP implementation nightmare began during what was supposed to be a routine system cutover on Saturday morning, October 14, 2017, when our new SAP system crashed spectacularly, leaving our Mumbai manufacturing facility unable to process batch records, our European distribution center paralyzed without inventory data, and our US sales team locked out of customer information systems. I spent the weekend in our emergency command center watching three years of careful planning dissolve into chaos as we scrambled to restore basic operational functionality.

"We have manufacturing lines shut down because the new system cannot access batch formulations, European shipments delayed because inventory data is corrupted, and US sales representatives unable to process orders because customer records are inaccessible," reported Rahul Mehta, our Chief Technology Officer, his voice strained from thirty-six hours of crisis management. "The ERP cutover has created a complete operational breakdown."

"How long to restore basic functionality?" I asked, though I dreaded the answer as I watched our global operations grinding to a halt in real-time.

"Emergency restoration requires reverting to legacy systems for critical operations while debugging the new ERP configuration. Full system recovery could take 72-96 hours if we can resolve the data integration failures."

"And financial impact of operational shutdown?"

"Each day of system downtime costs approximately ₹2.3 crores in lost production plus incalculable damage to customer relationships and regulatory compliance obligations."

This crisis marked the lowest point of our digital transformation journey and taught me that ERP implementation across global pharmaceutical operations required understanding not just software functionality but the complex interdependencies that connected every aspect of our international business.

The ERP selection process had consumed eighteen months of vendor evaluations, system demonstrations, and consultant assessments that somehow failed to anticipate the complexity of integrating pharmaceutical operations across multiple countries with different regulatory requirements.

"SAP was selected based on pharmaceutical industry experience, global implementation capabilities, and integration with regulatory compliance systems," Dr. Priya Sharma had explained during our original vendor selection presentation. "SAP's pharmaceutical module supposedly addresses unique requirements for batch tracking, regulatory reporting, and global supply chain management."

"What made SAP preferable to Oracle, Microsoft, or specialized pharmaceutical ERP systems?" I had asked.

"SAP's global pharmaceutical client base includes Novartis, Roche, and Merck, suggesting proven capability for international pharmaceutical operations. Additionally, SAP's regulatory compliance modules address FDA, EMA, and PMDA requirements through integrated workflows."

"And implementation timeline and cost projections?"

"SAP implementation requires 24 months for global deployment with total costs of ₹34 crores including software licenses, implementation services, and internal resource allocation."

The system configuration challenges proved more complex than anticipated when we discovered that pharmaceutical ERP systems required extensive customization to accommodate our specific formulation processes, regulatory workflows, and international business requirements.

"Pharmaceutical ERP configuration requires mapping 247 different business processes across manufacturing, quality control, regulatory affairs, and commercial operations," reported our ERP project manager during implementation planning. "Each business process requires specific system configuration plus integration with existing databases and external systems."

"How does pharmaceutical ERP complexity compare to general manufacturing systems?" I asked.

"Pharmaceutical ERP systems require specialized modules for batch genealogy, regulatory compliance, pharmacovigilance, and global supply chain management that general manufacturing systems cannot support."

"And customization requirements for our specific operations?"

"Our formulation processes, regulatory workflows, and international compliance requirements demand extensive system customization that increases implementation complexity and ongoing maintenance obligations."

The data migration process revealed the horrifying reality of how fragmented our global operations had become when we attempted to consolidate information from 247 different Excel spreadsheets, sixteen separate databases, and countless manual filing systems into integrated ERP modules.

"Data migration requires cleaning and standardizing customer records, product specifications, supplier information, and financial data from fourteen different legacy systems," announced our data management consultant during migration planning. "Data quality issues affect 67% of existing records, requiring manual verification and correction."

"What specific data quality problems are we discovering?" I asked.

"Duplicate customer records, inconsistent product codes, conflicting supplier information, and incomplete financial data that accumulated over years of manual data management across multiple locations."

"And timeline implications of data cleaning requirements?"

"Data migration extends ERP implementation by 8 months due to extensive data quality issues that require manual resolution before system cutover."

The user training requirements proved more extensive than projected when we realized that ERP implementation required retraining 340 employees across twelve countries on completely different business processes and system workflows.

"ERP implementation requires comprehensive training for manufacturing operators, quality control technicians, regulatory affairs specialists, and commercial teams," reported our training manager during user preparation updates. "Training curriculum involves 127 different job functions with varying system access requirements."

"How does ERP training compare to traditional software training programs?" I asked.

"ERP training requires understanding integrated business processes rather than just software functionality. Users must learn how their activities affect other departments and global operations through system connections."

"And training delivery across international locations?"

"Global training requires coordinating sessions across different time zones, languages, and cultural contexts while ensuring consistent understanding of new business processes."

The post-implementation stabilization consumed six months of intensive troubleshooting, system optimization, and process refinement as we gradually restored operational efficiency while adapting to new ERP workflows.

"ERP stabilization requires resolving 347 system issues, optimizing performance bottlenecks, and refining business processes to achieve intended operational benefits," Rahul reported during our recovery assessment. "System performance has improved significantly, but we're still operating at 78% of pre-implementation efficiency."

"What operational improvements are we achieving through ERP implementation?" I asked.

"Real-time inventory visibility has reduced stock-outs by 34%, integrated quality control has accelerated batch release by 23%, and automated regulatory reporting has improved compliance efficiency by 41%."

"And timeline for achieving projected ERP benefits?"

"Full ERP benefits require 12-18 months of optimization and user adaptation before achieving the operational efficiency and competitive advantages that justified the implementation investment."

The ERP implementation lessons fundamentally changed our approach to technology projects as we learned that system integration required understanding business processes rather than just software capabilities.

"ERP implementation taught us that technology success depends more on business process optimization than software functionality," I reflected during our post-implementation review. "Systems integration requires changing how people work, not just changing what systems they use."

Two years after ERP implementation, we had achieved the operational integration and real-time visibility that enabled competitive advantages across our global pharmaceutical operations.

"ERP systems have created integrated global operations with real-time visibility, automated compliance, and predictive analytics that provide competitive advantages over companies using fragmented legacy systems," I announced during our annual technology assessment.

"The key lesson was that ERP implementation requires treating technology deployment as business transformation rather than software installation."

The ERP implementation had proven that global pharmaceutical operations could achieve significant competitive advantages through integrated systems, but success required patient investment in business process optimization rather than just technology deployment.

"ERP implementation demonstrated that pharmaceutical companies can achieve operational excellence through technology integration, but success requires understanding that systems enable business transformation rather than automatically creating it," I concluded.

The lesson had become fundamental to our technology strategy: ERP systems provided tools for operational excellence, but achieving competitive advantages required optimizing business processes to leverage technology capabilities rather than expecting technology to solve business problems independently.

Data Analytics for Supply Chain Optimization

The supply chain revelation struck me during a mundane inventory review meeting in February 2018 when I discovered we were simultaneously experiencing stockouts of our bestselling cardiovascular product in Germany while maintaining six months of excess inventory for the same product in our Mumbai warehouse. The absurdity became even more pronounced when I learned that our "optimized" global supply chain was actually a collection of isolated regional operations making independent decisions based on incomplete information.

"We're operating twelve separate supply chains instead of one integrated global system," announced Dr. Meera Agarwal, our newly hired VP of Supply Chain Analytics, as she projected a map showing our fragmented operations across four continents. "Each location makes inventory and production decisions based on local data while remaining blind to global demand patterns and capacity constraints."

"How is this possible when we've invested millions in supply chain management systems?" I asked, staring at charts showing that our inventory turnover rates varied from 3.2 times annually in India to 12.7 times in Germany for identical products.

"Supply chain systems capture data efficiently but lack the analytical capabilities to optimize across global operations. We're data-rich but insight-poor, collecting millions of data points without converting them into actionable intelligence."

"And the cost implications of supply chain fragmentation?"

"Fragmented operations cost us approximately ₹67 crores annually through excess inventory, expedited shipping, stockouts, and suboptimal production scheduling that integrated analytics could eliminate."

This conversation launched our systematic implementation of supply chain analytics that would transform our global operations from reactive logistics management to predictive optimization that could anticipate and prevent problems before they occurred.

The demand forecasting analytics proved most immediately valuable when we discovered that sophisticated algorithms could predict customer demand patterns with accuracy that human forecasters could never achieve using traditional planning methods.

"Our machine learning algorithms analyze physician prescribing patterns, seasonal trends, competitive dynamics, and economic indicators to predict demand with 94% accuracy compared to 67% accuracy from traditional forecasting methods," reported our data science manager during our analytics implementation review.

"How does improved demand forecasting translate into operational advantages?" I asked.

"Accurate demand prediction reduces safety stock requirements by 34% while improving service levels to 98.7% through better production planning and inventory positioning."

"And the competitive advantages from superior demand forecasting?"

"Predictive demand management enables faster response to market opportunities while reducing inventory costs that provide pricing flexibility against competitors using reactive supply chain management."

The inventory optimization analytics revealed the staggering inefficiencies in our global inventory management when algorithms identified optimal stock levels that reduced total inventory investment by 42% while improving product availability.

"Analytics identify optimal inventory levels for each product at each location based on demand variability, supply lead times, and service level requirements," explained Dr. Agarwal during our inventory optimization presentation. "Current inventory investment of ₹234 crores could be reduced to ₹136 crores while maintaining superior customer service."

"What enables such dramatic inventory reduction without affecting availability?" I asked.

"Analytics optimize inventory allocation across global network rather than local optimization at each location. Global optimization eliminates duplicate safety stocks while improving overall system performance."

"And implementation challenges for inventory optimization recommendations?"

"Inventory optimization requires coordination across multiple locations and functions that must trust algorithmic recommendations rather than relying on traditional safety stock approaches."

The production planning analytics transformed our manufacturing operations from reactive scheduling to predictive optimization that could balance production efficiency with customer service requirements across our global manufacturing network.

"Production optimization algorithms consider demand forecasts, manufacturing capacity, raw material availability, and distribution constraints to optimize global production scheduling," reported our manufacturing analytics manager during our operations review. "Optimized scheduling improves manufacturing efficiency by 28% while reducing delivery times by 19%."

"How does production optimization differ from traditional manufacturing planning?" I asked.

"Traditional planning optimizes individual facilities independently while analytics optimize entire global network simultaneously, enabling superior overall performance through coordinated decision-making."

"And flexibility advantages from analytical production planning?"

"Analytics enable rapid response to demand changes, supply disruptions, and capacity constraints through real-time optimization that manual planning cannot achieve."

The supplier performance analytics provided unprecedented visibility into global supplier reliability and quality patterns that enabled proactive supplier management and risk mitigation.

"Supplier analytics track delivery performance, quality metrics, and financial stability across 347 global suppliers to predict and prevent supply disruptions," announced our procurement analytics specialist during our supplier management review. "Predictive supplier scoring identifies high-risk suppliers 6-8 months before problems occur."

"What specific advantages do supplier analytics provide over traditional vendor management?" I asked.

"Analytics enable proactive supplier development, risk mitigation, and performance optimization rather than reactive problem-solving after disruptions occur."

"And cost savings from analytical supplier management?"

"Supplier optimization reduces procurement costs by 23% through better vendor selection, negotiation leverage, and risk prevention while improving supply reliability."

The distribution optimization analytics revealed opportunities to reduce global logistics costs while improving delivery performance through sophisticated network optimization and route planning.

"Distribution analytics optimize global shipping routes, warehouse locations, and inventory allocation to minimize total logistics costs while maximizing customer service," reported our logistics analytics manager during our distribution review. "Optimized distribution reduces logistics costs by 31% while improving average delivery times by 22%."

"How does distribution optimization handle the complexity of international shipping and customs requirements?" I asked.

"Analytics incorporate international shipping constraints, customs delays, and regulatory requirements into optimization models that balance cost efficiency with compliance obligations."

"And competitive advantages from optimized distribution networks?"

"Superior distribution efficiency enables competitive pricing while improving customer satisfaction through reliable delivery performance that competitors using manual logistics cannot match."

The supply chain analytics integration created real-time visibility and control across our global operations that enabled rapid response to disruptions and continuous optimization of performance.

"Integrated supply chain analytics provide real-time dashboard visibility across global operations with automated alerts for potential problems and recommended corrective actions," I announced during our annual operations review. "Analytics have transformed our supply chain from reactive problem-solving to proactive optimization."

"And measurable benefits from supply chain analytics implementation?" asked Rajesh Khanna, our CFO.

"Supply chain analytics have reduced total logistics costs by 37% while improving customer service levels to 99.2% through predictive optimization and real-time response capabilities."

Two years after implementing comprehensive supply chain analytics, we had achieved operational excellence that provided sustainable competitive advantages over companies using traditional supply chain management approaches.

"Supply chain analytics taught us that global operations optimization requires treating the entire supply chain as an integrated system rather than managing individual components independently," I reflected during our strategic operations planning.

"The key insight was that data analytics enable competitive advantages through superior operational efficiency and customer service that manual management cannot achieve."

The supply chain analytics implementation had proven that pharmaceutical companies could achieve significant competitive advantages through analytical optimization that enhanced operational performance while reducing costs.

"Data analytics for supply chain optimization demonstrated that technology can create sustained competitive advantages through operational excellence that becomes difficult for competitors to replicate," I concluded.

The lesson had become fundamental to our operational strategy: supply chain analytics provided capabilities for predictive optimization that transformed global operations from reactive logistics management to proactive competitive advantage creation.

Digital Marketing Strategies

The digital marketing awakening came during a mortifying presentation to our European distributors in March 2018 when a twenty-eight-year-old pharmacy chain buyer casually mentioned that our competitors were using targeted social media campaigns to influence physician prescribing behavior while we were still relying on printed brochures and face-to-face sales calls that physicians increasingly avoided. The generational divide became painfully obvious when she showed me how German cardiologists were discussing our products on professional networks we didn't even know existed.

"Your competitors are engaging physicians through LinkedIn thought leadership, targeted medical journal advertising, and interactive clinical decision tools while your sales approach feels like pharmaceutical marketing from 1995," she explained with the brutal honesty that only comes from someone young enough to view traditional marketing as quaintly obsolete. "Physicians under forty prefer digital information sources over sales representative visits."

"But pharmaceutical marketing is highly regulated," I protested. "We cannot just post advertisements on social media like consumer products companies."

"Digital pharmaceutical marketing follows strict compliance guidelines, but sophisticated companies use educational content, scientific communications, and targeted professional engagement that builds physician relationships more effectively than traditional sales calls."

"And our current marketing effectiveness compared to digital approaches?"

"Traditional pharmaceutical marketing achieves 12-15% physician engagement rates while targeted digital strategies achieve 45-67% engagement through relevant content delivered when physicians actually need clinical information."

This conversation forced me to confront the uncomfortable reality that our marketing strategies were becoming increasingly irrelevant to a generation of physicians who expected digital engagement and scientific information delivered through modern communication channels.

The physician engagement analytics revealed the shocking inadequacy of our traditional marketing when we discovered that our expensive sales force was achieving face-to-face meetings with target physicians only 23% of the time, while digital channels could provide clinical information access 24/7.

"Our sales representatives average 2.3 physician meetings per day with 47% of physicians refusing to see pharmaceutical sales representatives altogether," reported our newly hired Digital Marketing Director, Priya Malhotra, during our marketing strategy assessment. "Meanwhile, 89% of physicians actively seek clinical information online during patient consultations."

"How does physician digital behavior affect our marketing strategy?" I asked.

"Physicians prefer accessing clinical information when they need it rather than during scheduled sales presentations. Digital marketing enables providing relevant information at the point of clinical decision-making."

"And competitive advantages from digital physician engagement?"

"Digital marketing enables personalized content delivery, real-time clinical support, and ongoing relationship building that traditional sales calls cannot achieve efficiently."

The content marketing strategy required developing sophisticated educational materials that could provide genuine clinical value while building physician confidence in our products through scientific credibility rather than sales pressure.

"Digital content marketing involves creating clinical case studies, therapeutic guidelines, patient management tools, and continuing medical education programs that position our products as solutions to real clinical challenges," explained Priya during our content strategy development. "Educational marketing builds physician trust through clinical value rather than promotional messaging."

"What types of digital content resonate with physician audiences?" I asked.

"Physicians prefer interactive clinical decision tools, peer-reviewed case studies, comparative effectiveness analyses, and real-world evidence that supports clinical decision-making rather than promotional product information."

"And regulatory compliance requirements for digital medical content?"

"Medical content marketing requires legal review, scientific accuracy verification, and regulatory compliance monitoring that ensures educational value while meeting pharmaceutical advertising guidelines."

The targeted digital advertising proved more effective than anticipated when sophisticated algorithms enabled reaching specific physician specialties with relevant clinical information at precisely the moments when prescribing decisions were being made.

"Digital advertising platforms enable targeting cardiologists researching hypertension management or endocrinologists evaluating diabetes treatments with relevant clinical information about our therapeutic solutions," reported our digital advertising manager during our campaign performance review. "Targeted advertising achieves 67% higher engagement rates than broad pharmaceutical advertising."

"How does targeted digital advertising compare to traditional medical journal advertising?" I asked.

"Digital targeting enables reaching specific physician interests and specialties with relevant content while traditional journal advertising reaches broad audiences with generic messaging that may not address immediate clinical needs."

"And cost effectiveness of digital versus traditional pharmaceutical advertising?"

"Digital advertising costs 45% less than traditional medical journal advertising while achieving 3.2 times higher physician engagement through targeted relevance and interactive content."

The social media strategy required understanding how physicians use professional networks for clinical information sharing and continuing education while maintaining strict compliance with pharmaceutical marketing regulations.

"Physicians use LinkedIn for professional networking, Twitter for medical news updates, and specialized platforms like Doximity for clinical discussions," explained our social media manager during our platform strategy session. "Professional social media enables thought leadership and clinical education that builds physician relationships through valuable content."

"What regulatory constraints affect pharmaceutical social media marketing?" I asked.

"Social media pharmaceutical marketing requires monitoring all interactions, maintaining fair balance in clinical discussions, and ensuring compliance with advertising guidelines while engaging authentically in professional conversations."

"And competitive advantages from pharmaceutical social media presence?"

"Social media enables real-time clinical communication, peer-to-peer education, and thought leadership positioning that traditional marketing channels cannot achieve effectively."

The marketing automation systems enabled sophisticated physician relationship management through personalized content delivery, engagement tracking, and automated follow-up that scaled personal relationships across thousands of healthcare providers.

"Marketing automation enables tracking physician content preferences, clinical interests, and engagement patterns to deliver personalized information that supports individual clinical practice needs," announced our marketing technology manager during our automation implementation review. "Automated personalization achieves relationship depth that manual sales processes cannot scale effectively."

"How does marketing automation enhance traditional sales force effectiveness?" I asked.

"Automation provides sales representatives with detailed physician engagement data, content preferences, and clinical interests that enable more relevant and effective sales conversations."

"And competitive intelligence capabilities from digital marketing systems?"

"Digital marketing platforms monitor competitor activities, physician engagement patterns, and market trends that provide strategic intelligence for competitive positioning and market development."

The digital marketing results exceeded expectations as sophisticated targeting and content strategies enabled achieving physician engagement rates that traditional pharmaceutical marketing could never accomplish.

"Digital marketing campaigns have achieved 73% physician engagement rates with 34% of target physicians requesting additional clinical information compared to 12% engagement from traditional sales approaches," I announced during our annual marketing review. "Digital strategies have transformed physician relationships from transactional sales interactions to ongoing clinical partnership."

"And return on investment from digital marketing compared to traditional pharmaceutical promotion?" asked Rajesh Khanna, our CFO.

"Digital marketing generates 4.3 times higher ROI than traditional sales force investment while providing measurable engagement analytics that enable continuous optimization."

Two years after implementing comprehensive digital marketing strategies, we had transformed physician relationships from periodic sales interactions to continuous clinical engagement that supported prescribing decisions.

"Digital marketing taught us that pharmaceutical promotion must provide genuine clinical value rather than just product information to build meaningful physician relationships," I reflected during our marketing strategy planning.

"The key insight was that physicians want clinical partners who support patient care rather than sales representatives who promote products."

The digital marketing transformation had proven that pharmaceutical companies could achieve superior physician engagement through educational value and targeted relevance rather than traditional promotional approaches.

"Digital marketing strategies demonstrated that pharmaceutical success requires understanding how physicians actually seek and use clinical information rather than assuming traditional sales approaches remain effective," I concluded.

The lesson had become central to our commercial strategy: digital marketing enabled building physician relationships through clinical value creation that supported better patient outcomes while achieving superior commercial results.

CIO Amit Patel's Technology Roadmap

The technology roadmap presentation that would reshape our entire digital future began with Amit Patel calmly dismantling everything we thought we knew about pharmaceutical IT during a sweltering August morning in 2018. Our newly hired Chief Information Officer had spent his first ninety days conducting what he called a "digital autopsy" of our technology infrastructure, and his findings were more devastating than any FDA warning letter we had ever received.

"You're operating a global pharmaceutical company using technology architecture that wouldn't be acceptable for a mid-sized accounting firm," Amit announced as he projected a bewildering diagram showing our IT systems connected by what appeared to be digital duct tape and prayer. "Your current technology infrastructure is not just inefficient - it's actively preventing you from competing against companies that understand pharmaceutical digitalization."

"But we've invested ₹23 crores in IT systems over the past three years," protested Rajesh Khanna, our CFO, though his expression suggested he suspected our technology investments had been poorly directed.

"You've invested in individual software solutions without creating an integrated technology architecture," Amit replied with the patient tone of someone explaining basic concepts to confused students. "Pharmaceutical companies require sophisticated technology ecosystems that enable competitive advantages, not just administrative efficiency."

"And the implications for our competitive positioning?"

"Your competitors are using artificial intelligence for drug discovery, predictive analytics for supply chain optimization, and real-time data integration for regulatory compliance while you're manually reconciling Excel spreadsheets to prepare basic business reports."

This conversation marked the beginning of Amit's systematic technology transformation that would evolve our pharmaceutical operations from digital primitive to technological sophistication over the following four years.

The infrastructure assessment revealed the horrifying scope of our technology debt when Amit documented that our "integrated" systems were actually forty-seven different software applications held together by manual data transfers and email communications.

"Your current IT architecture includes legacy manufacturing systems that cannot communicate with quality control databases, regulatory software that requires manual data entry from production records, and financial systems that operate independently from operational data," Amit explained during his comprehensive technology audit presentation. "Technology fragmentation multiplies administrative work while preventing real-time decision-making."

"How does our technology infrastructure compare to industry standards?" I asked.

"Your technology maturity ranks in the bottom quartile of mid-sized pharmaceutical companies. Leading pharmaceutical companies achieve operational integration and predictive analytics that your current systems cannot support."

"And specific competitive disadvantages from technology limitations?"

"Technology constraints prevent real-time inventory optimization, predictive quality control, automated regulatory reporting, and competitive intelligence capabilities that sophisticated pharmaceutical companies consider basic operational requirements."

The cloud migration strategy represented Amit's first major infrastructure modernization initiative, requiring systematic replacement of on-premises systems with scalable cloud platforms that could support global operations.

"Cloud migration enables global accessibility, automatic scalability, and integrated data analytics while reducing IT maintenance costs by 67%," Amit reported during our cloud strategy presentation. "Cloud infrastructure provides technology capabilities that on-premises systems cannot achieve regardless of investment levels."

"What specific advantages does cloud infrastructure provide for pharmaceutical operations?" I asked.

"Cloud platforms enable real-time collaboration across global locations, automatic backup and disaster recovery, integrated security management, and scalable computing power for complex analytics applications."

"And regulatory compliance implications of cloud-based pharmaceutical systems?"

"Modern cloud platforms exceed FDA cybersecurity requirements while providing audit trails, data integrity controls, and regulatory reporting capabilities that surpass traditional on-premises systems."

The data integration roadmap required developing sophisticated analytics platforms that could convert our fragmented operational data into actionable business intelligence for strategic decision-making.

"Data integration enables creating unified views of manufacturing, quality, regulatory, and commercial operations through real-time analytics dashboards," Amit explained during our data strategy session. "Integrated analytics provide competitive intelligence and predictive capabilities that fragmented systems cannot deliver."

"How does data integration affect operational decision-making?" I asked.

"Real-time data integration enables predictive maintenance, automated quality control, optimized inventory management, and regulatory compliance monitoring that transform reactive operations into proactive competitive advantages."

"And artificial intelligence applications for pharmaceutical data analytics?"

"AI systems can predict equipment failures, optimize formulation development, identify quality trends, and automate regulatory compliance monitoring using pattern recognition that human analysis cannot achieve efficiently."

The cybersecurity enhancement represented Amit's most critical infrastructure priority when he discovered that our current security systems would not withstand sophisticated cyber attacks that increasingly targeted pharmaceutical companies.

"Pharmaceutical cybersecurity requires military-grade protection for intellectual property, regulatory data, and patient information that current systems cannot provide," Amit announced during our security assessment. "Cybersecurity breaches could destroy competitive advantages while creating regulatory violations that threaten business continuity."

"What specific cybersecurity vulnerabilities are we facing?" I asked.

"Current systems lack multi-factor authentication, encrypted data transmission, intrusion detection systems, and automated threat response capabilities that sophisticated attackers could exploit easily."

"And cybersecurity investment requirements for pharmaceutical-grade protection?"

"Cybersecurity modernization requires ₹12 crores investment in security infrastructure, monitoring systems, and staff training to achieve protection levels that regulatory agencies and business partners expect."

The innovation platform development focused on creating technology capabilities that could accelerate pharmaceutical development through computational drug design and predictive modeling systems.

"Innovation platforms enable computational formulation optimization, predictive bioavailability modeling, and automated regulatory compliance checking that accelerate product development while improving success rates," Amit explained during our innovation technology planning. "Advanced pharmaceutical companies achieve competitive advantages through technology-enabled innovation that traditional development approaches cannot match."

"How do innovation platforms affect our R&D capabilities?" I asked.

"Innovation platforms reduce formulation development timelines by 43% through predictive modeling while improving clinical success rates through computational optimization that eliminates suboptimal candidates early in development."

"And competitive differentiation from technology-enabled innovation?"

"Innovation platforms enable developing superior products faster than competitors using traditional development approaches while creating intellectual property around technological capabilities that competitors cannot easily replicate."

The technology roadmap implementation timeline required coordinating multiple simultaneous modernization projects while maintaining operational continuity across our global pharmaceutical operations.

"Technology modernization requires 36-month phased implementation with cloud migration in year one, data integration in year two, and innovation platform development in year three," Amit announced during our implementation planning. "Phased approach ensures operational continuity while achieving systematic technology advancement."

"And total investment requirements for complete technology modernization?" asked Rajesh.

"Technology roadmap requires ₹89 crores investment over three years with projected annual savings of ₹34 crores plus competitive advantages that enable revenue growth impossible with current technology limitations."

Two years into Amit's technology roadmap implementation, we had achieved operational capabilities that exceeded many larger pharmaceutical companies while positioning for continued technological advancement.

"Amit's technology roadmap has transformed our competitive positioning through operational excellence and innovation capabilities that our previous technology infrastructure could never support," I announced during our annual technology review.

"The key insight was that pharmaceutical success increasingly requires technology sophistication rather than just clinical expertise and manufacturing quality."

Amit's technology roadmap had proven that systematic digital transformation could enable mid-sized pharmaceutical companies to achieve competitive advantages through technological capabilities that enhanced every aspect of pharmaceutical operations.

"Amit's leadership taught us that technology strategy requires understanding how digital capabilities create pharmaceutical competitive advantages rather than just improving administrative efficiency," I concluded.

The lesson had become fundamental to our strategic thinking: technology roadmap development required treating digital capabilities as core competitive assets rather than supporting infrastructure for traditional pharmaceutical operations.

Chapter 20

The Leadership Transition

Passing the Torch to the Next Generation

The leadership transition conversation that would define our company's future began during an unexpectedly candid moment in December 2019 when Dr. Priya Sharma asked me a question that I had been avoiding for months: "When are you planning to step back from day-to-day operations?" Her inquiry came during what was supposed to be a routine strategic planning session, but the weight behind her words suggested she had been thinking about succession planning far longer than I had been comfortable contemplating.

"I'm fifty-seven years old and have been CEO for eighteen years," I replied, suddenly aware that my reluctance to discuss succession was becoming a strategic liability rather than personal preference. "I suppose the question isn't when I should step back, but whether our company is ready for leadership transition without losing the institutional knowledge and relationships that took decades to build."

"The company has evolved far beyond any single person's capabilities," Priya observed with characteristic directness. "Our global operations, regulatory complexity, and technological sophistication require leadership expertise that spans multiple domains rather than depending on individual experience."

"But what about continuity of vision and strategic direction?"

"Leadership transition enables continuity through institutional systems rather than individual dependency. Strong companies survive leadership changes because their competitive advantages exist in organizational capabilities rather than personal relationships."

This conversation forced me to confront the uncomfortable reality that successful leadership transition required actively preparing the organization for my eventual departure rather than hoping that succession planning could be indefinitely postponed.

The succession planning process revealed the complexity of identifying and developing next-generation pharmaceutical leadership capable of managing global operations that had grown far beyond what any single executive could oversee effectively.

"Leadership succession requires evaluating internal candidates who understand our company culture while possessing the strategic vision and operational expertise necessary for continued international expansion," announced our board chairman during our governance planning session. "Pharmaceutical leadership demands unique combinations of scientific knowledge, regulatory expertise, commercial acumen, and global management experience."

"What specific qualifications should guide our succession evaluation?" I asked.

"Next-generation pharmaceutical leadership requires understanding digital transformation, global regulatory systems, strategic partnerships, and competitive positioning in addition to traditional pharmaceutical expertise."

"And internal versus external succession considerations?"

"Internal succession provides cultural continuity and institutional knowledge while external leadership could bring fresh perspectives and industry best practices that internal development might not achieve."

The leadership development program required systematic investment in preparing high-potential executives for increased responsibilities while providing opportunities to demonstrate strategic thinking and operational excellence.

"We've identified seven internal candidates with leadership potential across different functional areas who could benefit from expanded responsibilities and strategic development opportunities," reported our head of talent development during our succession planning review. "Leadership development requires structured progression through increasing responsibilities plus external education and industry exposure."

"How do we balance leadership development with operational requirements?" I asked.

"Leadership development through stretch assignments, cross-functional projects, and strategic initiatives that contribute to business objectives while building executive capabilities."

"And timeline for developing internal leadership candidates?"

"Executive development requires 3-5 years of systematic preparation including board exposure, external education, and increasing strategic responsibilities before candidates are ready for senior leadership roles."

The organizational restructuring began preparing our company for distributed leadership that could manage global pharmaceutical operations without depending on centralized decision-making that had become increasingly inefficient as we expanded internationally.

"Global pharmaceutical operations require regional autonomy with strategic coordination rather than centralized control that cannot respond quickly to local market conditions," explained Dr. Amit Patel during our organizational development planning. "Leadership transition provides opportunities to implement organizational structures that enable faster decision-making and regional responsiveness."

"What organizational changes support effective leadership transition?" I asked.

"Distributed leadership with clear accountability, empowered regional management, and systematic communication processes that enable coordination without centralized bottlenecks."

"And maintaining strategic coherence across decentralized operations?"

"Strategic coherence through shared vision, standardized processes, and regular coordination mechanisms rather than direct control over operational decisions."

The mentorship program involved systematically transferring institutional knowledge and strategic relationships to next-generation leaders while ensuring continuity of critical business relationships and regulatory expertise.

"Leadership transition requires transferring not just operational knowledge but strategic relationships with regulatory agencies, key customers, and industry partners that took years to develop," I explained during our knowledge transfer planning. "Mentorship programs enable systematic transfer of institutional knowledge that cannot be documented in procedures manuals."

"What specific knowledge transfer priorities should guide mentorship programs?" asked our board development committee.

"Regulatory relationships, strategic partnerships, competitive intelligence, and cultural understanding that enable continued success in complex international markets."

"And maintaining external relationships during leadership transition?"

"Gradual introduction of next-generation leaders to key external stakeholders while maintaining continuity of established relationships through overlapping responsibilities and joint participation in strategic activities."

The leadership transition timeline required balancing organizational readiness with succession urgency while ensuring smooth transfer of responsibilities without disrupting business continuity.

"Leadership transition should occur when organizational capabilities exceed individual contributions rather than waiting for external pressures or emergency succession requirements," advised our governance consultant during transition planning. "Planned succession enables optimal timing and preparation rather than reactive leadership changes."

"What indicators suggest organizational readiness for leadership transition?" I asked.

"Systematic processes, distributed expertise, strong financial performance, and developed internal leadership candidates indicate organizational maturity that can sustain leadership transition successfully."

"And transition timeline that balances preparation with succession urgency?"

"Two-year transition period with gradual responsibility transfer, overlapping leadership, and systematic knowledge transfer that ensures continuity while enabling new leadership to establish strategic direction."

The succession announcement represented culmination of eighteen months of systematic preparation as we announced Dr. Priya Sharma's promotion to Chief Executive Officer while I transitioned to Executive Chairman role focused on strategic guidance and external relationships.

"Priya's promotion to CEO represents natural evolution of our leadership development while ensuring continuity of strategic vision and operational excellence," I announced during our succession press conference. "Leadership transition enables our company to benefit from fresh perspectives while maintaining institutional knowledge and established relationships."

"And my continuing role as Executive Chairman?" I continued.

"Executive Chairman responsibilities focus on strategic guidance, board governance, and external relationships while enabling CEO autonomy for operational leadership and strategic implementation."

Six months after leadership transition, our company had achieved seamless succession that enhanced rather than disrupted our competitive positioning and strategic momentum.

"Leadership transition has enabled faster decision-making, enhanced strategic focus, and continued international expansion under Priya's leadership," I reflected during our post-transition assessment. "Successful succession demonstrates organizational maturity and leadership depth that strengthens competitive positioning."

The leadership transition had proven that systematic succession planning could enhance organizational capabilities while ensuring continuity of strategic vision and competitive advantages.

"Leadership transition taught us that successful companies transcend individual leadership through systematic capabilities and institutional knowledge that enable continued excellence regardless of personnel changes," I concluded.

The lesson had become fundamental to our governance philosophy: leadership transition represented organizational evolution rather than individual replacement, enabling continued competitive advantage through systematic capabilities rather than personal dependency.

Grooming Internal Successors

The succession grooming revelation came during a particularly uncomfortable board meeting in March 2019 when our governance consultant bluntly informed me that our company had grown to $347 million in annual revenue with zero viable internal candidates prepared for senior leadership succession. The assessment was devastating because it exposed a fundamental failure in my leadership philosophy - I had been so focused on building the business that I had neglected to build the leaders who could sustain it.

"Dr. Malhotra, you've created a company that depends entirely on your personal decision-making and relationships," announced Patricia Williams, our governance advisor, as she presented succession planning assessments that ranked our leadership development as "critically inadequate." "Your senior executives are highly competent functional specialists, but none have been systematically developed for strategic leadership or CEO succession."

"But we have excellent people running every department," I protested, though I was beginning to recognize the difference between operational excellence and strategic leadership capability. "Dr. Priya Sharma has built our regulatory capabilities, Dr. Chen leads innovation, and Rajesh manages our finances exceptionally well."

"Functional excellence doesn't automatically translate into CEO readiness," she replied with the patience of someone who had witnessed countless succession failures. "Strategic leadership requires broader capabilities including vision development, stakeholder management, competitive positioning, and organizational transformation that functional expertise alone cannot provide."

"And the implications for our company's sustainability?"

"Leadership dependency creates existential risk. If something happens to you, your company lacks internal succession options and would require external CEO recruitment that could disrupt competitive advantages built over decades."

This conversation launched our systematic internal succession development program that would transform high-performing functional leaders into strategically capable executives prepared for senior leadership responsibilities.

The leadership assessment process revealed significant gaps between our executives' current capabilities and the requirements for running a global pharmaceutical company with complex regulatory, commercial, and operational challenges.

"We've evaluated twelve senior executives across strategic thinking, operational management, stakeholder relationships, and industry expertise," reported our leadership development consultant during our succession planning review. "Current assessment identifies three candidates with CEO potential who require systematic development in strategic vision, board governance, and external relationship management."

"What specific capabilities do our high-potential leaders need to develop?" I asked.

"Strategic planning beyond functional expertise, stakeholder management including regulatory agencies and partners, financial management at enterprise level, and organizational leadership during transformation and growth."

"And timeline for developing CEO-ready internal candidates?"

"Leadership development requires 3-4 years of systematic preparation including expanded responsibilities, external education, industry exposure, and board interaction to build strategic capabilities."

The rotational assignment program became our primary vehicle for broadening executives' understanding of pharmaceutical operations beyond their functional specializations while providing exposure to strategic decision-making.

"Dr. Priya Sharma will spend six months leading our European commercial operations to understand market dynamics beyond regulatory affairs," I announced during our leadership development planning. "Cross-functional assignments provide strategic perspective that functional excellence cannot achieve independently."

"How do rotational assignments balance leadership development with operational requirements?" asked our head of talent development.

"Rotational assignments in critical growth areas where leadership development contributes to business objectives while building executive capabilities through real strategic challenges."

"And assessment criteria for rotational assignment success?"

"Strategic thinking demonstration, stakeholder relationship building, operational improvement achievement, and cross-functional collaboration that indicates readiness for broader leadership responsibilities."

The external education investment required sending high-potential leaders to advanced management programs that could provide strategic frameworks and industry best practices beyond what internal development could deliver.

"We're investing in executive education at Wharton, INSEAD, and Harvard Business School for our succession candidates," announced our leadership development manager during our education planning session. "External education provides strategic frameworks, industry benchmarking, and networking opportunities that internal development cannot replicate."

"What specific programs address pharmaceutical leadership development needs?" I asked.

"Advanced strategy programs, global management education, and pharmaceutical industry leadership courses that combine strategic frameworks with industry-specific challenges."

"And integration of external education with internal leadership development?"

"Executive education followed by application projects that enable leaders to implement strategic frameworks within our company while demonstrating enhanced capabilities."

The mentorship structure involved pairing high-potential leaders with board members and external advisors who could provide strategic guidance and industry perspective beyond what internal mentoring could achieve.

"Each succession candidate will work directly with board members on strategic projects while receiving guidance from external pharmaceutical executives who can share industry leadership experience," I explained during our mentorship program launch. "External mentorship provides perspectives and relationships that internal development cannot deliver."

"How does external mentorship complement internal leadership development?" asked Dr. Priya Sharma.

"External mentors provide industry benchmarking, strategic frameworks, and relationship networks while internal mentorship focuses on company culture and operational expertise."

"And specific outcomes expected from mentorship relationships?"

"Strategic thinking enhancement, external relationship development, and leadership confidence building through exposure to senior pharmaceutical executives and board governance processes."

The succession readiness evaluation required systematic assessment of leadership candidates' strategic capabilities and readiness for CEO responsibilities through real strategic challenges and stakeholder interactions.

"Succession candidates will lead strategic initiatives including international expansion planning, competitive positioning development, and stakeholder relationship management," I announced during our succession assessment planning. "Leadership readiness requires demonstrating strategic thinking and execution under real business conditions."

"What criteria determine succession candidate evaluation?" asked our board development committee.

"Strategic vision articulation, stakeholder management effectiveness, operational improvement delivery, and organizational leadership during challenging business situations."

"And timeline for succession readiness determination?"

"Leadership assessment through eighteen months of strategic project leadership plus board interaction and external stakeholder engagement to evaluate CEO readiness."

The succession development results exceeded expectations as systematic leadership grooming created multiple internal candidates capable of senior leadership succession while strengthening our overall organizational capabilities.

"Leadership development has produced three internal candidates ready for CEO succession plus enhanced strategic capabilities across our senior management team," I reported during our annual governance review. "Succession preparation has strengthened organizational leadership while ensuring continuity options for strategic leadership transition."

"And competitive advantages from internal leadership development?" asked our board chairman.

"Strong internal leadership creates organizational stability, cultural continuity, and strategic depth that external CEO recruitment cannot provide while reducing succession risks that affect competitive positioning."

Two years after implementing systematic succession grooming, we had transformed from leadership-dependent organization to leadership-rich company with multiple internal options for strategic succession.

"Internal succession grooming taught us that leadership development is a strategic investment that strengthens competitive advantages while ensuring organizational sustainability," I reflected during our leadership planning retreat.

"The key insight was that grooming successors requires systematic development rather than hoping that functional excellence automatically creates strategic leadership capabilities."

The succession grooming program had proven that pharmaceutical companies could develop internal leadership through systematic investment in strategic development that enhanced organizational capabilities while preparing for leadership transition.

"Grooming internal successors demonstrated that leadership development creates competitive advantages through organizational depth and strategic capabilities that extend far beyond succession planning," I concluded.

The lesson had become fundamental to our organizational philosophy: internal leadership development represented strategic investment in organizational sustainability rather than just succession insurance, creating competitive advantages through enhanced leadership capabilities across the entire organization.

Board Governance Evolution

The board governance awakening came during a painfully awkward annual meeting in June 2018 when I realized that our seven-member board consisted primarily of family friends and long-time business associates who nodded approvingly at my presentations without asking a single challenging question about our strategic direction. The uncomfortable truth hit me when our largest institutional investor pointed out that our board governance resembled a social club rather than the strategic oversight body that a global pharmaceutical company required.

"Dr. Malhotra, your board lacks the pharmaceutical expertise, regulatory knowledge, and international experience necessary to provide meaningful guidance for a company operating in twelve countries with $347 million in annual revenue," observed Kavita Desai, our lead independent director, during what was supposed to be a routine governance review. "Board composition that worked for a domestic pharmaceutical startup is inadequate for global pharmaceutical operations."

"But our board members have supported the company through difficult periods and understand our business philosophy," I replied, though I was beginning to recognize that loyalty and understanding were insufficient qualifications for pharmaceutical board service.

"Board governance requires specific expertise rather than general business knowledge," she continued with diplomatic firmness. "Pharmaceutical companies need directors who understand regulatory systems, global markets, competitive dynamics, and industry transformation trends that general business experience cannot provide."

"And the implications for our competitive positioning and growth strategy?"

"Inadequate board governance limits strategic options, reduces investor confidence, and prevents accessing expertise that sophisticated pharmaceutical companies consider essential for competitive advantage."

This conversation marked the beginning of our systematic board transformation that would evolve from founder-centric governance to professional pharmaceutical board oversight over the following eighteen months.

The board assessment process revealed fundamental gaps between our current governance structure and the sophisticated oversight requirements of an international pharmaceutical company competing against multinational corporations.

"Current board composition includes three family members, two longtime business associates, and two financial investors who lack pharmaceutical industry experience," reported our governance consultant during her comprehensive board evaluation. "Pharmaceutical board governance requires regulatory expertise, international market knowledge, clinical development understanding, and competitive intelligence capabilities that current membership cannot provide."

"What specific pharmaceutical expertise should guide board recruitment?" I asked.

"Pharmaceutical boards require former FDA or EMA officials, international pharmaceutical executives, clinical development experts, and digital transformation specialists who understand industry challenges and competitive dynamics."

"And governance structure modifications necessary for pharmaceutical board effectiveness?"

"Committee structure including audit, compensation, regulatory affairs, and strategic planning committees with specialized expertise rather than general oversight responsibilities."

The board recruitment strategy required identifying pharmaceutical industry leaders with specific expertise while balancing independence requirements with industry knowledge that could provide strategic guidance.

"We're targeting former pharmaceutical executives from companies like Novartis, Roche, and Johnson & Johnson who understand global pharmaceutical operations," announced our board recruitment consultant during our director search planning. "Board candidates require pharmaceutical industry experience plus specific expertise in areas critical to our strategic development."

"How do we attract experienced pharmaceutical executives to our board?" I asked.

"Pharmaceutical board service appeals to executives seeking continued industry involvement while contributing to growing companies with competitive potential and strategic challenges."

"And compensation and commitment expectations for pharmaceutical board directors?"

"Pharmaceutical board service requires quarterly meetings, committee participation, and strategic project involvement that demands significant time commitment compensated through director fees plus equity participation."

The governance committee structure required developing specialized oversight capabilities that could provide strategic guidance on pharmaceutical-specific challenges including regulatory affairs, competitive positioning, and international expansion.

"Pharmaceutical governance requires specialized committees including Regulatory Affairs Committee, Strategic Planning Committee, and Risk Management Committee that address industry-specific challenges," explained our governance advisor during committee structure planning. "Committee specialization enables focused expertise rather than general oversight that cannot address pharmaceutical complexity effectively."

"What specific responsibilities should specialized committees assume?" I asked.

"Regulatory Affairs Committee monitors global compliance and agency relationships, Strategic Planning Committee guides competitive positioning and market expansion, and Risk Management Committee oversees pharmaceutical-specific risks including patent challenges and product liability."

"And coordination between specialized committees and overall board governance?"

"Committee recommendations inform board discussions while specialized expertise enables more sophisticated strategic guidance than general business oversight can provide."

The board education program involved systematic orientation for new pharmaceutical directors while providing ongoing industry updates that kept governance current with regulatory changes and competitive developments.

"Pharmaceutical board education requires understanding regulatory systems, competitive dynamics, clinical development processes, and international market challenges that general business knowledge cannot address," reported our director education manager during our governance development planning. "Board effectiveness requires ongoing pharmaceutical industry education rather than one-time orientation programs."

"How does pharmaceutical board education differ from general corporate governance training?" I asked.

"Pharmaceutical governance education focuses on industry-specific challenges including regulatory compliance, patent protection, clinical development risks, and international market access that general corporate education cannot cover adequately."

"And ongoing education requirements for pharmaceutical board effectiveness?"

"Quarterly regulatory updates, annual industry conferences, and specialized training programs that keep directors current with pharmaceutical industry developments and competitive trends."

The governance transformation results created board oversight capabilities that enhanced strategic decision-making while providing pharmaceutical expertise that founder-centric governance could not deliver.

"Board governance evolution has created pharmaceutical-specific oversight with regulatory expertise, international market knowledge, and competitive intelligence that enables superior strategic guidance," I announced during our annual governance assessment. "Professional pharmaceutical board governance provides strategic capabilities that general business oversight cannot achieve."

"And investor confidence improvements from enhanced board governance?" asked our institutional investor representative.

"Professional pharmaceutical governance increases investor confidence through demonstrated oversight capabilities, industry expertise, and strategic guidance that reduces investment risks while enhancing competitive positioning."

The board governance evolution enabled strategic initiatives including international partnerships, regulatory expansion, and competitive positioning that previous governance structure could not support effectively.

"Enhanced board governance has enabled regulatory expansion into Asian markets, strategic partnerships with European companies, and competitive positioning initiatives that required pharmaceutical expertise," I reported during our strategic review. "Board evolution created strategic capabilities that founder-centric governance could not provide."

Two years after implementing professional pharmaceutical board governance, we had achieved oversight capabilities that enhanced competitive advantages while providing strategic guidance that exceeded internal expertise.

"Board governance evolution taught us that pharmaceutical success requires specialized oversight rather than general business governance," I reflected during our governance planning retreat.

"The key insight was that pharmaceutical board governance creates competitive advantages through industry expertise and strategic guidance that general business oversight cannot deliver."

The board governance transformation had proven that pharmaceutical companies could enhance strategic capabilities through professional governance that provided industry expertise and oversight capabilities beyond what founder-centric governance could achieve.

"Board governance evolution demonstrated that pharmaceutical success requires treating governance as strategic capability rather than administrative requirement," I concluded.

The lesson had become fundamental to our governance philosophy: board evolution represented strategic investment in oversight capabilities that enhanced competitive advantages through pharmaceutical expertise and professional guidance that founder-centric governance could not provide.

Family Business to Professional Management

The family business transformation moment arrived during a heated argument in my home study on a Sunday evening in February 2019 when my younger brother Vikram stormed out after I questioned his marketing budget decisions, leaving my wife Meera to deliver the uncomfortable truth I had been avoiding for months: "You cannot run a global pharmaceutical company like a family grocery store where relatives make decisions based on personal relationships rather than professional competence."

"Vikram has been with the company since the beginning and understands our values better than any external hire," I protested, though even as I spoke the words, I recognized the weakness of defending family employment based on loyalty rather than performance. "Family members have emotional investment in company success that professional managers cannot match."

"Emotional investment doesn't compensate for lack of pharmaceutical marketing expertise," Meera replied with the brutal honesty that only comes from someone who loves you enough to tell difficult truths. "Your brother's marketing decisions are costing millions in missed opportunities while creating competitive disadvantages that professional marketing leadership could eliminate."

"But family involvement provides continuity and trustworthiness that professional management might not deliver."

"Family involvement becomes a liability when emotional relationships prevent objective performance evaluation and strategic decision-making that global pharmaceutical competition requires."

This conversation forced me to confront the fundamental tension between family loyalty and professional excellence that was limiting our company's competitive potential as we expanded into increasingly sophisticated international markets.

The family involvement assessment revealed the uncomfortable reality that several family members had assumed senior positions based on relationships rather than qualifications, creating management gaps that were becoming increasingly visible as our operations grew more complex.

"Current family involvement includes your brother as Marketing Director despite lacking pharmaceutical marketing experience, your cousin as Regional

Sales Manager without international sales background, and your brother-in-law as Manufacturing Supervisor lacking pharmaceutical production expertise," reported our organizational development consultant during her comprehensive management evaluation. "Family appointments have created capability gaps in critical functional areas."

"What specific performance issues result from family management appointments?" I asked, though I suspected the answer would be difficult to hear.

"Marketing effectiveness below industry benchmarks, regional sales performance lagging projections, and manufacturing efficiency gaps compared to pharmaceutical industry standards. Family loyalty cannot substitute for professional expertise in competitive markets."

"And organizational implications of mixed family-professional management?"

"Dual management standards create employee confusion, limit professional advancement opportunities, and reduce organizational credibility when family relationships override performance-based decisions."

The professionalization strategy required developing systematic approaches to transition family members from operational roles to governance or advisory positions while recruiting professional management with pharmaceutical expertise.

"Family business transformation requires separating ownership from management while maintaining family involvement through board governance and strategic guidance rather than operational control," explained our family business advisor during our transition planning. "Professional management enables competitive capabilities while preserving family legacy through ownership and strategic direction."

"How do we manage family member transitions without creating personal conflicts?" I asked.

"Family member transition through enhanced governance roles, advisory positions, and strategic project leadership that utilizes family knowledge while enabling professional operational management."

"And timeline for family-to-professional management transition?"

"Systematic transition over 18-24 months with family member development into governance roles while recruiting professional managers for operational responsibilities."

The professional recruitment process proved more challenging than anticipated when we discovered that experienced pharmaceutical executives were hesitant to join companies with significant family involvement due to concerns about decision-making authority and career advancement opportunities.

"Pharmaceutical executive recruitment faces skepticism about family business culture, reporting relationships, and advancement opportunities in organizations where family relationships might override professional performance," reported our executive search consultant during our recruitment review. "Professional managers prefer clear governance structures with merit-based advancement rather than family-influenced decision-making."

"What strategies overcome professional manager concerns about family business culture?" I asked.

"Clear organizational structure with defined professional authority, transparent performance evaluation systems, and governance policies that separate family ownership from operational management."

"And compensation strategies that attract pharmaceutical executives to family businesses?"

"Competitive compensation plus equity participation and clearly defined professional authority that demonstrates commitment to merit-based management rather than family-controlled operations."

The governance restructuring involved creating formal policies that separated family ownership interests from professional management authority while maintaining family involvement through strategic oversight rather than operational control.

"Family business governance requires formal policies defining family member roles, professional management authority, and decision-making processes that prevent personal relationships from affecting business operations," announced our governance consultant during our policy development session. "Professional management requires clear authority without family interference in operational decisions."

"What specific governance policies support family-to-professional transition?" I asked.

"Employment policies requiring professional qualifications for operational roles, performance evaluation systems based on business metrics rather than family relationships, and succession planning that prioritizes competence over family membership."

"And maintaining family legacy while enabling professional management?"

"Family involvement through board governance, strategic planning participation, and ownership oversight that preserves family values while enabling professional operational excellence."

The organizational culture transformation required addressing employee concerns about favoritism while building confidence in merit-based advancement that professional management could provide.

"Organizational culture change requires demonstrating that professional qualifications determine advancement opportunities rather than family relationships," reported our human resources director during our culture development planning. "Employee engagement improves when advancement depends on performance rather than personal relationships."

"How do we address employee skepticism about family business fairness?" I asked.

"Transparent performance evaluation, clear advancement criteria, and visible examples of merit-based promotion that demonstrate commitment to professional management principles."

"And maintaining company values during family-to-professional transition?"

"Preserving core values through governance policies and cultural initiatives while enabling professional management to implement competitive strategies without family interference."

The transformation results exceeded expectations as professional management enabled competitive capabilities while family governance provided strategic continuity and values preservation.

"Professional management transition has improved operational performance by 34% while maintaining family values through governance oversight," I announced during our annual transformation review. "Professional expertise combined with family strategic guidance creates competitive advantages that neither family management nor external ownership could achieve independently."

"And employee satisfaction improvements from professional management?" asked our board development committee.

"Employee engagement has increased 47% through merit-based advancement opportunities and transparent performance evaluation that professional management enables."

Two years after implementing professional management, we had achieved operational excellence while preserving family legacy through strategic governance rather than operational control.

"Family-to-professional management taught us that family businesses can achieve competitive advantages through professional expertise while maintaining family values through governance oversight," I reflected during our organizational planning session.

"The key insight was that family legacy is preserved through strategic ownership rather than operational control."

The transformation had proven that family businesses could achieve professional management excellence while maintaining family involvement through governance structures that separated ownership from operations.

"Family business to professional management demonstrated that competitive pharmaceutical success requires professional expertise while family values can be preserved through strategic governance rather than operational control," I concluded.

The lesson had become fundamental to our organizational philosophy: family business transformation enabled competitive advantages through professional management while preserving family legacy through strategic oversight that enhanced rather than limited operational excellence.

Son Rohit Malhotra's Role Definition

The most uncomfortable family business conversation of my life took place in my home office on a rain-soaked Tuesday evening in September 2019 when my twenty-eight-year-old son Rohit asked me directly whether he would inherit the company CEO position or earn it through professional merit. His question cut through years of unspoken expectations and forced me to confront the difference between family succession and leadership competence in ways that no business school case study could prepare you for.

"Dad, I need to understand whether you see me as your heir apparent or as a potential candidate who must prove himself worthy of leadership consideration," Rohit said with the directness that had characterized him since childhood, though the weight behind his question suggested months of internal deliberation. "Because those are fundamentally different career paths with different expectations and different outcomes."

"You're my son and you've been groomed for business leadership since you were in high school," I replied, though even as I spoke, I realized my answer avoided his actual question about merit versus inheritance. "Of course you're being considered for senior leadership positions."

"But am I being considered because I'm qualified or because I'm family?" he pressed. "Because if it's family, then I'm not really building a career - I'm just fulfilling predetermined expectations regardless of my actual capabilities or the company's needs."

"And if it's merit?"

"Then I need to earn leadership positions through professional achievement and prove that I can create value for the company beyond what external candidates could provide. Which means I might not become CEO, and that needs to be acceptable to both of us."

This conversation marked the beginning of our systematic approach to defining Rohit's role based on professional contribution rather than family entitlement, a process that would challenge both of us in ways we hadn't anticipated.

The competency assessment phase required subjecting Rohit to the same rigorous evaluation that we applied to external leadership candidates, despite the obvious discomfort of having his father's company assess his professional capabilities.

"Rohit's MBA from Wharton plus two years at McKinsey provide strong analytical and strategic frameworks, but pharmaceutical industry experience is limited to summer internships and board meeting observations," reported our leadership development consultant during Rohit's professional evaluation. "Current capabilities suggest potential for strategic roles but require significant industry development before senior operational responsibility."

"How does Rohit's leadership potential compare to external candidates?" I asked, though the question felt oddly clinical when discussing my own son's career prospects.

"Strong analytical capabilities and strategic thinking ability, but lacks pharmaceutical operations experience, regulatory knowledge, and international market understanding that senior pharmaceutical leadership requires."

"And development timeline for pharmaceutical leadership readiness?"

"Leadership development requires 5-7 years of progressive pharmaceutical experience including operational roles, regulatory exposure, and international assignment before CEO readiness evaluation."

The role definition process involved creating specific professional pathways that would enable Rohit to earn leadership positions through demonstrated performance rather than family succession expectations.

"Rohit's career development should follow pharmaceutical industry leadership progression through operational roles, functional expertise, and strategic project leadership," I announced during our family business planning session. "Professional development must demonstrate value creation rather than just competency maintenance."

"What specific roles provide pharmaceutical leadership development for family members?" asked our governance advisor.

"Progressive assignments in manufacturing operations, regulatory affairs, international markets, and strategic development that build pharmaceutical expertise while creating measurable business value."

"And performance evaluation criteria that separate family relationship from professional assessment?"

"Objective business metrics, peer evaluation, and external assessment that measure professional contribution rather than family loyalty or personal relationships."

The mentorship structure required finding external pharmaceutical executives who could provide Rohit with industry guidance and objective career feedback independent of family business relationships.

"Rohit will work with former pharmaceutical CEOs and current industry leaders who can provide objective career guidance and professional development advice," announced our mentorship program coordinator. "External mentorship ensures professional development rather than family business grooming."

"How does external mentorship complement internal pharmaceutical experience?" Rohit asked during our career planning discussion.

"External mentors provide industry benchmarking, objective performance feedback, and career guidance that family business relationships cannot deliver without bias."

"And specific outcomes expected from pharmaceutical industry mentorship?"

"Strategic thinking development, industry network building, and objective assessment of leadership readiness that internal evaluation cannot provide fairly."

The international assignment strategy involved placing Rohit in operational roles within our European and Asian operations where he could develop pharmaceutical expertise while creating measurable value independent of family oversight.

"Rohit will spend eighteen months managing our German operations followed by twelve months developing our Japanese market entry strategy," I announced during our international development planning. "International assignments provide pharmaceutical operations experience while demonstrating leadership capabilities under real business conditions."

"What success criteria determine international assignment evaluation?" asked our board development committee.

"Operational improvement metrics, market development achievements, and team leadership effectiveness that demonstrate professional capability rather than family support."

"And career advancement implications of international assignment performance?"

"Assignment success enables continued leadership development while assignment failure suggests alternative career paths that better utilize individual capabilities and company needs."

The role boundaries required establishing clear policies about family member advancement that prioritized company competitive needs over family succession expectations.

"Family member career advancement must serve company competitive interests rather than family succession planning," I explained during our governance policy development. "Professional merit determines leadership opportunities regardless of family relationships."

"How do we maintain family business values while ensuring merit-based advancement?" Rohit asked.

"Family values guide company culture and strategic direction while professional competence determines operational leadership and advancement opportunities."

"And handling potential conflicts between family expectations and professional assessment?"

"Company competitive needs override family preferences when leadership decisions affect business performance and competitive positioning."

The development results demonstrated that systematic professional development could prepare family members for meaningful leadership contribution while maintaining objective performance standards.

"Rohit's international assignment has generated 23% improvement in German operations efficiency while developing market entry strategies that contributed ₹34 crores in new revenue," I reported during our annual family business review. "Professional performance demonstrates leadership potential through business value creation rather than family succession."

"And organizational acceptance of merit-based family member advancement?" asked our governance consultant.

"Employee confidence in merit-based advancement has improved organizational culture while demonstrating that family members must earn leadership positions through professional achievement."

Three years after implementing systematic role definition, Rohit had earned respect through professional contribution while preparing for potential senior leadership based on demonstrated competence rather than family entitlement.

"Rohit's role definition taught us that family business sustainability requires professional competence rather than succession entitlement," I reflected during our leadership planning retreat.

"The key insight was that family members serve company interests best when they earn leadership positions through professional merit rather than inheriting them through family relationships."

Rohit's professional development had proven that family business members could contribute meaningfully to company success through earned leadership rather than inherited authority.

"Rohit's career development demonstrated that family business success requires treating family members as professional candidates rather than succession guarantees," I concluded.

The lesson had become fundamental to our family business philosophy: family members could enhance company competitive advantages through professional excellence, but family relationships could not substitute for leadership competence in competitive pharmaceutical markets.

PART V: THE INNOVATION CONSTRAINT (2017-2022)

Part V

The Innovation Constraint (2017-2022)

The innovation paradox revealed itself during a crushing defeat in December 2017 when our most promising R&D project - three years and ₹67 crores in development - failed Phase III clinical trials just six months before anticipated market launch. The failure wasn't due to safety issues or regulatory problems, but because a competitor had launched a superior formulation that made our innovation obsolete before it reached the market. I sat in our emergency board meeting staring at charts showing our innovation pipeline producing technically successful products that were commercially irrelevant.

"We're achieving technical innovation without creating competitive advantage," announced Dr. Lisa Chen during her post-mortem analysis, her voice reflecting the exhaustion of someone who had poured her professional reputation into a project that market forces had rendered worthless. "Our R&D processes optimize for regulatory approval rather than market differentiation, creating products that meet scientific standards but fail competitive requirements."

"But we've invested more in R&D than ever before," I protested, reviewing budget allocations that showed innovation spending had increased 340% over five years. "How can increased R&D investment produce less competitive advantage?"

"Innovation spending doesn't automatically generate innovation results," she replied with the clinical precision that had made her our head of R&D. "Pharmaceutical innovation requires systematic approaches to identifying unmet needs, developing differentiated solutions, and achieving market advantage rather than just conducting sophisticated research."

"And our competitive positioning compared to companies achieving breakthrough innovations?"

"We're becoming a fast follower rather than an innovation leader, developing technically competent products that trail market leaders by 18-24 months. Fast following provides predictable returns but prevents achieving competitive advantages that innovation leadership enables."

This conversation marked my recognition that our company had encountered the innovation constraint - the point where continued growth required breakthrough innovation capabilities rather than operational excellence and execution efficiency that had driven our success for the previous decade.

The innovation constraint manifested across every aspect of our pharmaceutical operations as we discovered that technical competence could not substitute for innovative thinking when competitive dynamics demanded differentiated solutions rather than optimized execution.

Product Development Limitation: Our formulation capabilities could improve existing products but struggled to create breakthrough therapies that could command premium pricing and market leadership positions in increasingly competitive therapeutic areas.

Regulatory Efficiency Paradox: Our regulatory expertise enabled faster approvals for conventional products while innovation leadership required navigating complex regulatory pathways for novel therapies that our conventional capabilities could not support effectively.

Manufacturing Excellence Trap: Our operational efficiency optimized production of established products but lacked the flexibility and innovation required for advanced drug delivery systems and personalized medicine applications that represented the industry's future.

Commercial Sophistication Gap: Our marketing expertise succeeded with traditional pharmaceutical promotion but failed to develop strategies for innovative products requiring different physician education and patient engagement approaches.

"The innovation constraint represents a fundamental strategic challenge that operational improvements cannot solve," I explained to our board during our strategic assessment meeting. "Continued growth requires developing innovation capabilities that can create competitive advantages rather than just improving execution of existing strategies."

"What distinguishes innovation constraints from operational challenges?" asked our lead independent director.

"Operational challenges can be solved through better execution of proven approaches. Innovation constraints require developing new capabilities that can create solutions for problems that current approaches cannot address effectively."

The innovation constraint had emerged because pharmaceutical industry dynamics were evolving faster than our capability development, creating gaps between market requirements and internal expertise that threatened our competitive positioning.

Technology Acceleration: Digital therapeutics, artificial intelligence applications, and personalized medicine were transforming pharmaceutical innovation while our R&D capabilities remained focused on traditional drug development approaches.

Regulatory Evolution: Regulatory agencies were developing approval pathways for breakthrough therapies, adaptive clinical trials, and real-world evidence that required innovation capabilities beyond our conventional regulatory expertise.

Competitive Transformation: Leading pharmaceutical companies were achieving competitive advantages through platform technologies, ecosystem partnerships, and innovative business models rather than traditional product development and marketing strategies.

Patient Expectation Changes: Healthcare providers and patients increasingly demanded personalized treatments, digital health integration, and outcome-based therapies that conventional pharmaceutical approaches could not deliver effectively.

"The pharmaceutical industry is transitioning from traditional drug development to innovation-driven competitive differentiation," observed Dr. Priya Sharma during our strategic planning session. "Companies that cannot innovate beyond conventional approaches will become commodity manufacturers rather than pharmaceutical leaders."

"How do we develop innovation capabilities while maintaining operational excellence in current businesses?" I asked.

"Innovation constraint resolution requires systematic investment in new capabilities while optimizing existing operations to fund innovation development that may not generate returns for several years."

The innovation constraint resolution would require transforming our entire approach to pharmaceutical development, moving from optimization-focused execution to innovation-centered value creation that could generate sustainable competitive advantages.

Innovation Culture Development: Building organizational capabilities that rewarded breakthrough thinking rather than incremental improvement, enabling creative problem-solving that could identify novel approaches to pharmaceutical challenges.

Technology Platform Investment: Developing advanced capabilities in artificial intelligence, digital therapeutics, and personalized medicine that could create differentiated products rather than optimized versions of existing therapies.

Partnership Ecosystem Creation: Establishing collaboration networks with biotechnology companies, academic institutions, and technology firms that could provide innovation capabilities beyond internal development capacity.

Risk Management Sophistication: Creating systematic approaches to innovation investment that could balance breakthrough potential with development risk while maintaining financial stability during extended innovation timelines.

"Innovation constraint resolution requires treating innovation as a systematic capability rather than hoping that increased R&D spending will automatically generate breakthrough results," I reflected during our capability development planning.

"The fundamental challenge is building innovation systems that can consistently create competitive advantages rather than just conducting sophisticated research that produces technically excellent but commercially irrelevant products."

The innovation constraint represented our most significant strategic challenge since founding the company, requiring capabilities that were fundamentally different from the operational excellence and execution efficiency that had enabled our previous success.

"The innovation constraint taught us that pharmaceutical success requires different capabilities at different stages of company development," I announced during our strategic review. "Continued growth requires mastering innovation-driven competitive advantage creation rather than just optimizing established business approaches."

The following chapters would document our systematic approach to developing innovation capabilities that could overcome the constraint while maintaining competitive advantages in our established business areas, demonstrating that mid-sized pharmaceutical companies could achieve breakthrough innovation through systematic capability development rather than hoping for accidental discovery.

Chapter 21

The R&D Investment Leap

Betting the Company on Innovation

The R&D investment decision that would either transform our company or bankrupt it began during a somber financial review meeting in March 2018 when I announced we would triple our research and development spending from ₹47 crores to ₹142 crores annually - representing 23% of projected revenue for what our CFO grimly called "the most expensive experiment in our company's history." The decision came after months of agonizing analysis showing that incremental R&D improvements could not create the breakthrough innovations necessary to compete against pharmaceutical giants investing billions in next-generation therapies.

"This investment level exceeds the R&D spending of companies three times our size," announced Rajesh Khanna during his financial impact presentation, his voice reflecting the anxiety of someone asked to fund what seemed like an impossibly ambitious gamble. "R&D investment of ₹142 crores annually will consume 67% of our current operating cash flow while requiring sustained commitment for 4-5 years before generating meaningful returns."

"But what's the alternative?" I asked, reviewing competitive analysis showing that our largest rivals were achieving breakthrough innovations through R&D investments we had never contemplated. "Continuing incremental R&D spending guarantees that we'll remain a fast follower while competitors establish market leadership through innovation advantages we cannot match."

"The alternative is financial stability and predictable growth rather than betting our entire company on unproven innovation capabilities," Rajesh replied with the conservative wisdom that had guided our financial management for years.

"And the competitive implications of maintaining conservative R&D investment?"

"Conservative R&D ensures short-term financial stability while potentially sacrificing long-term competitive positioning if innovation becomes essential for pharmaceutical success."

This conversation marked the beginning of our systematic transformation from a financially conservative pharmaceutical company to an innovation-driven organization willing to risk everything on developing breakthrough capabilities that could create sustainable competitive advantages.

The R&D investment justification required demonstrating that breakthrough innovation could generate returns sufficient to justify investment levels that exceeded industry benchmarks for companies our size.

"Pharmaceutical innovation leaders achieve 40-60% higher profit margins through proprietary technologies and differentiated products that command premium pricing," reported Dr. Lisa Chen during our innovation strategy presentation. "Innovation investment enables competitive advantages that operational excellence alone cannot achieve in increasingly competitive markets."

"What specific innovation capabilities could justify tripling our R&D investment?" I asked.

"Advanced drug delivery platforms, personalized medicine technologies, and artificial intelligence applications that could create proprietary competitive advantages rather than just improved versions of existing products."

"And timeline for achieving innovation returns that justify current investment levels?"

"Innovation platforms require 4-6 years of development before generating revenue, but successful platforms can create competitive advantages lasting 10-15 years through patent protection and technological barriers."

The research infrastructure development consumed the largest portion of our R&D investment as we built laboratory capabilities and analytical equipment necessary for advanced pharmaceutical innovation.

"Innovation-level R&D requires sophisticated analytical instrumentation, specialized laboratory facilities, and advanced computational capabilities that our current infrastructure cannot support," announced our head of R&D

operations during our facility planning session. "Infrastructure investment of ₹89 crores enables innovation capabilities that incremental equipment upgrades cannot achieve."

"How does advanced R&D infrastructure affect our innovation potential?" I asked.

"Sophisticated instrumentation enables molecular-level analysis, computational drug design, and advanced formulation development that conventional laboratory capabilities cannot support effectively."

"And competitive advantages from advanced R&D infrastructure?"

"Advanced infrastructure enables developing proprietary technologies and differentiated products that competitors using conventional R&D capabilities cannot replicate easily."

The talent acquisition strategy required recruiting pharmaceutical scientists with expertise in emerging technologies who commanded compensation packages that exceeded our traditional salary structures.

"Innovation R&D requires scientists with expertise in artificial intelligence, nanotechnology, and personalized medicine who typically work for biotechnology companies or major pharmaceutical corporations," reported our scientific recruitment manager during our talent acquisition planning. "Competitive recruitment requires offering compensation packages 60-80% above our current scales plus equity participation and research autonomy."

"How do we attract world-class pharmaceutical scientists to our company?" I asked.

"Innovation scientists seek research challenges, publication opportunities, and intellectual property development rather than just competitive compensation. We must offer scientific problems that showcase their expertise."

"And retention strategies for high-caliber pharmaceutical researchers?"

"Research autonomy, professional development opportunities, and meaningful equity participation that enables scientists to benefit from successful innovation commercialization."

The innovation project portfolio required balancing breakthrough potential with development risk while maintaining focus on therapeutic areas where we could achieve competitive advantages.

"Innovation portfolio includes three platform technologies: modified-release drug delivery systems, AI-driven formulation optimization, and personalized cardiovascular therapies," Dr. Chen announced during our project planning review. "Portfolio balances near-term opportunities with long-term breakthrough potential while concentrating on our therapeutic expertise areas."

"What criteria guide innovation project selection and resource allocation?" I asked.

"Commercial potential assessment, technical feasibility analysis, competitive differentiation evaluation, and patent protection opportunities that could create sustainable competitive advantages."

"And risk management approaches for innovation portfolio development?"

"Stage-gate development processes with systematic go/no-go decisions based on technical milestones and commercial validation that minimize resource commitment to unsuccessful projects."

The innovation partnership strategy involved establishing collaboration relationships with biotechnology companies and academic institutions that could accelerate our innovation development while sharing costs and risks.

"Innovation partnerships with IIT Delhi, AIIMS, and three biotechnology companies provide access to complementary expertise while sharing development costs," announced our business development manager during our partnership review. "Collaboration enables innovation capabilities that internal development alone cannot achieve efficiently."

"How do innovation partnerships enhance our internal R&D capabilities?" I asked.

"External partnerships provide specialized expertise, shared infrastructure, and risk distribution while enabling faster innovation development than purely internal approaches."

"And intellectual property protection strategies for collaborative innovation?"

"Partnership agreements define IP ownership and commercialization rights that protect our innovation investments while enabling collaborative development benefits."

The R&D investment results began validating our strategy when early-stage projects demonstrated breakthrough potential that conventional R&D approaches could not achieve.

"Our AI-driven formulation platform has identified twelve novel drug delivery configurations that conventional research would require 3-4 years to develop," Dr. Chen reported during our innovation progress review. "Advanced R&D capabilities enable innovation timelines and technical achievements that justify current investment levels."

"And competitive differentiation from innovation R&D compared to traditional approaches?" I asked.

"Innovation R&D produces proprietary technologies with patent protection and competitive barriers rather than optimized versions of existing products that competitors can replicate easily."

"What commercial potential do early innovation results suggest?"

"Platform technologies could generate ₹340-450 crores annual revenue within 5-7 years through proprietary products that command premium pricing and market leadership positions."

Two years after implementing our R&D investment leap, we had achieved innovation capabilities that exceeded many larger pharmaceutical companies while positioning for breakthrough product development.

"R&D investment leap has created innovation platforms with breakthrough potential that conventional R&D spending could never achieve," I announced during our annual innovation review. "Innovation capabilities provide competitive advantages and commercial opportunities that justify current investment levels."

The R&D investment leap had proven that mid-sized pharmaceutical companies could achieve breakthrough innovation through systematic investment in advanced capabilities rather than hoping that incremental improvements would create competitive advantages.

"The R&D investment leap taught us that pharmaceutical innovation requires betting on breakthrough capabilities rather than optimizing conventional approaches," I reflected during our strategic planning session.

"The key insight was that innovation leadership demands investment levels that seem excessive until breakthrough results demonstrate competitive advantages that conventional R&D cannot achieve."

The lesson had become fundamental to our innovation philosophy: breakthrough innovation required investment commitments that exceeded comfortable financial parameters, but successful innovation could create competitive advantages that justified seemingly excessive resource allocation.

Massive Increase in R&D Spending

The R&D spending shock waves began reverberating through our organization in April 2018 when I announced that our annual research and development budget would increase from ₹47 crores to ₹186 crores over the next eighteen months - a 295% increase that would consume nearly 30% of our projected revenue while our competitors typically allocated 12-15% to R&D activities. The magnitude of this financial commitment terrified our finance team and board members who had grown comfortable with our historically conservative approach to innovation investment.

"This spending increase represents the largest single financial commitment in our company's history," announced Rajesh Khanna during his budget impact analysis, his hands visibly trembling as he presented cash flow projections that showed our operating margins shrinking to razor-thin levels. "R&D investment of ₹186 crores annually exceeds the total revenue of many successful pharmaceutical companies and requires sustaining losses for potentially three years before any return on investment."

"How does this spending level compare to pharmaceutical industry standards?" I asked, though I suspected our commitment would dwarf typical R&D allocations for companies our size.

"Major pharmaceutical companies like Novartis and Roche spend 15-18% of revenue on R&D, while biotechnology companies might reach 25-35%. Our proposed 30% allocation exceeds spending ratios of companies ten times our size," he replied grimly.

"And the financial risks if our innovation investments fail to generate expected returns?"

"R&D failure at this investment level could force asset sales, debt restructuring, or potential bankruptcy if we cannot sustain losses while innovation projects develop over 4-6 year timelines."

This conversation crystallized the enormous financial gamble we were undertaking as we transformed from a financially prudent pharmaceutical company into an innovation-obsessed organization willing to risk our entire financial foundation on breakthrough research capabilities.

The spending allocation breakdown revealed the staggering scope of our R&D investment as we simultaneously upgraded infrastructure, expanded research teams, and launched multiple breakthrough innovation projects.

"R&D spending increase includes ₹67 crores for advanced laboratory infrastructure, ₹78 crores for scientific talent acquisition, ₹34 crores for technology platform development, and ₹47 crores for innovation project execution," reported Dr. Lisa Chen during our budget planning session. "Comprehensive innovation capability development requires simultaneous investment across multiple areas rather than gradual spending increases."

"What justifies such massive simultaneous R&D investment rather than phased spending increases?" I asked.

"Innovation breakthrough requires reaching critical mass in research capabilities. Incremental spending increases cannot achieve the infrastructure and talent density necessary for competitive innovation development."

"And operational implications of quadrupling R&D spending within eighteen months?"

"Massive spending increase requires complete organizational restructuring with R&D becoming our primary operational focus rather than supporting function for established business operations."

The infrastructure investment consumed unprecedented resources as we built pharmaceutical research capabilities that rivaled major biotechnology companies despite our mid-sized revenue base.

"Advanced R&D infrastructure requires specialized laboratory facilities, sophisticated analytical instrumentation, and computational capabilities costing ₹89 crores for equipment and facilities," announced our facilities manager during our infrastructure planning. "Laboratory infrastructure investment exceeds the capital equipment budgets of most pharmaceutical companies our size."

"How does advanced infrastructure enable innovation capabilities that justify extreme spending levels?" I asked.

"Sophisticated instrumentation enables molecular-level research, computational drug design, and advanced analytical capabilities that conventional laboratories cannot support, creating innovation potential impossible with incremental equipment upgrades."

"And maintenance costs for advanced R&D infrastructure?"

"Advanced laboratory operations require ₹23 crores annually for maintenance, calibration, and technical support that substantially increases our fixed cost structure regardless of research project success."

The talent acquisition costs proved even more shocking when we discovered that recruiting world-class pharmaceutical scientists required compensation packages that approached CEO-level salaries at traditional pharmaceutical companies.

"Innovation scientists with artificial intelligence expertise command ₹2 - 3 crores annually plus equity participation, while nanotechnology specialists require ₹1.8-3.2 crores plus research budgets and publication rights," reported our scientific recruitment manager during our hiring budget review. "Competitive scientific talent acquisition costs exceed traditional pharmaceutical salary structures by 200-300%."

"What enables justifying such extreme compensation for research personnel?" I asked.

"Innovation scientists create intellectual property and breakthrough technologies that can generate hundreds of crores in revenue through patent protection and competitive advantages that conventional research cannot achieve."

"And talent retention costs for high-caliber innovation teams?"

"Retention requires ongoing research funding, professional development opportunities, and equity participation that creates long-term financial commitments beyond initial recruitment costs."

The project funding allocation required supporting multiple high-risk innovation initiatives simultaneously while maintaining sufficient resources for each project to achieve breakthrough potential.

"Innovation project portfolio includes six breakthrough research initiatives requiring ₹12-34 crores per project over 3-5 year development timelines," Dr. Chen announced during our project funding review. "Multiple project funding enables portfolio diversification while ensuring adequate resources for technical success."

"How do we determine optimal funding levels for breakthrough innovation projects?" I asked.

"Innovation projects require sufficient funding to achieve technical milestones without resource constraints that compromise breakthrough potential. Underfunding eliminates innovation advantages while overfunding wastes resources."

"And risk management strategies for massive innovation project investments?"

"Stage-gate development with systematic project evaluation and resource reallocation based on technical progress and commercial potential assessment."

The financial discipline required managing massive R&D spending increases while maintaining operational efficiency in established business areas that would fund innovation development during extended development periods.

"R&D spending increase requires improving operational efficiency in manufacturing and commercial operations to generate cash flow supporting innovation investment," I announced during our financial planning session. "Innovation funding depends on optimizing established business performance while investing heavily in breakthrough development."

"How do we balance innovation investment with operational financial requirements?" asked our board finance committee.

"Operational excellence in established businesses provides financial foundation for innovation investment while innovation development creates competitive advantages that enhance overall business performance."

The spending results began demonstrating innovation capabilities that conventional R&D budgets could never achieve, validating our massive investment commitment through early technical breakthroughs.

"Massive R&D spending has enabled developing three proprietary technology platforms with patent applications and breakthrough potential that incremental R&D investment could not achieve," Dr. Chen reported after twelve months of increased spending. "Innovation capabilities justify current investment levels through competitive advantages and commercial potential."

"And competitive positioning improvements from massive R&D investment?" I asked.

"Advanced innovation capabilities provide technological leadership and competitive differentiation that positions us ahead of companies relying on conventional R&D spending levels."

Eighteen months after implementing massive R&D spending increases, we had achieved innovation capabilities that exceeded many larger pharmaceutical companies while creating competitive advantages that justified extreme financial commitments.

"Massive R&D spending increase taught us that breakthrough innovation requires financial commitments that exceed comfortable investment levels," I reflected during our innovation strategy review.

"The key insight was that innovation leadership demands spending levels that appear excessive until breakthrough results demonstrate competitive advantages that conventional R&D budgets cannot achieve."

The lesson had become central to our innovation philosophy: massive R&D investment enabled breakthrough capabilities that incremental spending increases could never achieve, creating competitive advantages that justified seemingly excessive financial commitments.

Building Drug Discovery Capabilities

The drug discovery awakening came during a humbling visit to a biotechnology conference in Boston in May 2018 when I realized that while we had spent fifteen years optimizing existing pharmaceutical formulations, our competitors were designing entirely new molecules using computational chemistry and artificial intelligence that made our conventional R&D approach seem quaintly obsolete. The revelation hit me when a twenty-six-year-old computational biologist casually mentioned that his company had identified seventeen novel drug candidates in six months using AI algorithms that would have required decades of traditional medicinal chemistry.

"We're still operating like a 1990s pharmaceutical company in an era when drug discovery is becoming a computational science," I confided to Dr. Lisa Chen during our flight back to Mumbai, reviewing conference materials that described breakthrough drug discovery technologies we didn't even understand. "Our competitors are designing molecules from scratch while we're optimizing formulations for drugs that other companies invented."

"Drug discovery represents the ultimate pharmaceutical competitive advantage," she replied with the excitement of a scientist who had spent years dreaming of breakthrough research opportunities. "Companies that can discover novel therapeutic targets and design original molecules control their competitive destiny rather than competing for market share with existing drugs."

"But drug discovery requires capabilities we've never developed and investments that dwarf our current R&D spending," I protested.

"Drug discovery investment is enormous, but successful discovery creates patent-protected competitive advantages that last 15-20 years rather than the 3-5 year advantages that formulation improvements can achieve."

"And our realistic prospects for achieving meaningful drug discovery capabilities?"

"Modern drug discovery combines computational approaches with targeted research that enables mid-sized companies to compete against major pharmaceutical corporations through focused innovation rather than broad discovery programs."

This conversation launched our systematic development of drug discovery capabilities that would transform us from a generic pharmaceutical manufacturer into an innovative drug company capable of creating original therapeutic solutions.

The computational drug discovery platform required investing in artificial intelligence systems and molecular modeling capabilities that could accelerate the identification of novel therapeutic targets and drug candidates.

"Computational drug discovery enables screening millions of molecular combinations, predicting drug-target interactions, and optimizing molecular properties using artificial intelligence that reduces discovery timelines from years to months," announced Dr. Raj Patel, our newly hired head of computational biology, during our discovery platform presentation. "AI-driven discovery identifies novel therapeutic opportunities that traditional medicinal chemistry approaches cannot achieve efficiently."

"How does computational discovery compare to traditional pharmaceutical research methods?" I asked.

"Traditional discovery requires synthesizing and testing thousands of compounds individually, while computational approaches can evaluate millions of molecular configurations virtually before selecting optimal candidates for synthesis and testing."

"And competitive advantages from computational discovery capabilities?"

"Computational discovery enables identifying novel therapeutic targets and designing original molecules that competitors using traditional approaches cannot replicate easily or quickly."

The medicinal chemistry team development required recruiting pharmaceutical scientists with expertise in organic synthesis, molecular design, and drug optimization who could translate computational discoveries into viable therapeutic candidates.

"Drug discovery requires medicinal chemists who can design novel molecular structures, optimize drug properties, and solve complex synthesis challenges," explained Dr. Sarah Williams during our scientific recruitment planning. "Discovery chemistry demands creativity and technical expertise that conventional pharmaceutical development cannot provide."

"What specific expertise do medicinal chemists contribute to drug discovery?" I asked.

"Molecular design creativity, synthetic methodology development, and structure-activity relationship understanding that enables converting computational predictions into actual therapeutic compounds."

"And collaboration requirements between computational and experimental discovery teams?"

"Integrated discovery requires seamless collaboration between computational scientists who identify opportunities and medicinal chemists who create viable drug candidates through iterative design and optimization."

The target identification research focused on discovering novel therapeutic mechanisms and disease pathways that could provide competitive advantages through proprietary understanding of disease biology.

"Target identification involves discovering novel protein interactions, disease mechanisms, and therapeutic pathways that competitors have not identified," reported Dr. Chen during our discovery strategy session. "Proprietary target knowledge creates first-mover advantages and patent protection opportunities that enable market leadership."

"How do we identify therapeutic targets that major pharmaceutical companies have overlooked?" I asked.

"Target discovery through specialized disease focus, novel analytical approaches, and computational biology techniques that enable identifying therapeutic opportunities in underexplored biological pathways."

"And validation requirements for novel therapeutic targets?"

"Target validation requires demonstrating biological relevance, therapeutic potential, and druggability through systematic research that proves novel targets can produce viable therapeutic interventions."

The preclinical development capabilities required establishing sophisticated biological testing systems that could evaluate drug candidates for safety, efficacy, and optimization before clinical development.

"Preclinical development requires cell culture systems, animal models, and pharmacological testing capabilities that can evaluate drug candidate potential and optimize molecular properties," announced our preclinical research manager during our facility planning. "Comprehensive preclinical capabilities enable internal evaluation of discovery compounds rather than relying on external testing that delays development and increases costs."

"What specific preclinical capabilities are essential for drug discovery success?" I asked.

"In vitro screening systems for activity evaluation, pharmacokinetic testing for drug absorption and metabolism, and toxicology assessment for safety evaluation that enable comprehensive candidate evaluation."

"And timeline advantages from internal preclinical capabilities?"

"Internal preclinical testing reduces development timelines by 12-18 months while providing proprietary evaluation data that external testing cannot deliver confidentially."

The intellectual property strategy required developing systematic approaches to patent protection that could create competitive barriers around our drug discovery innovations.

"Drug discovery intellectual property includes novel molecular structures, therapeutic targets, synthetic methodologies, and therapeutic applications that require comprehensive patent protection," explained our patent attorney during our IP strategy session. "Discovery patents provide 15-20 years of market exclusivity compared to 3-5 years for formulation patents."

"How does discovery IP create sustainable competitive advantages?" I asked.

"Novel molecule patents prevent competitors from developing identical therapeutic compounds while target patents can block entire therapeutic approaches from competitive development."

"And global patent strategy for drug discovery innovations?"

"International patent filing in major pharmaceutical markets ensures global protection for discovery innovations while preventing competitors from exploiting novel therapeutic opportunities in unprotected markets."

The discovery pipeline development required balancing multiple research projects across different therapeutic areas while maintaining sufficient resources for each project to achieve breakthrough potential.

"Drug discovery pipeline includes twelve active projects across cardiovascular, metabolic, and neurological therapeutic areas with 3-7 year development timelines," Dr. Chen reported during our pipeline review. "Portfolio diversification enables managing discovery risks while concentrating expertise in therapeutic areas where we can achieve competitive advantages."

"How do we optimize resource allocation across multiple discovery projects?" I asked.

"Stage-gate development with systematic project evaluation and resource reallocation based on scientific progress, competitive landscape, and commercial potential assessment."

Two years after implementing drug discovery capabilities, we had achieved breakthrough research potential that positioned us as an innovative pharmaceutical company rather than just a generic manufacturer.

"Drug discovery capabilities have generated four novel therapeutic candidates with patent applications and breakthrough potential that generic pharmaceutical approaches could never achieve," I announced during our annual discovery review. "Discovery capabilities create competitive advantages and commercial opportunities that justify massive R&D investment."

The drug discovery development had proven that mid-sized pharmaceutical companies could achieve breakthrough innovation through systematic investment in discovery capabilities rather than remaining limited to generic pharmaceutical optimization.

"Building drug discovery capabilities taught us that pharmaceutical innovation leadership requires creating original therapeutic solutions rather than optimizing existing drugs," I reflected during our innovation strategy planning.

"The key insight was that drug discovery enables controlling competitive destiny through proprietary therapeutic innovations rather than competing for market share with existing pharmaceutical products."

The lesson had become fundamental to our innovation philosophy: drug discovery capabilities represented the ultimate pharmaceutical competitive advantage, enabling creation of proprietary therapeutic solutions that could achieve sustainable market leadership through patent protection and innovative therapeutic approaches.

Licensing Deals with Universities

The university licensing revelation struck me during a casual conversation at the IIT Delhi alumni dinner in September 2018 when Professor Ananya Gupta mentioned that her bioengineering lab had developed a revolutionary drug delivery nanotechnology that could potentially solve medication adherence problems affecting millions of patients worldwide. What shocked me wasn't the technological breakthrough itself, but her admission that the university had no idea how to commercialize innovations that could transform pharmaceutical treatment while generating substantial revenue for academic institutions.

"We've developed nanotechnology platforms that can deliver medications directly to diseased cells while avoiding healthy tissue, potentially revolutionizing cancer therapy and cardiovascular treatment," Professor Gupta explained with the frustrated tone of a brilliant scientist watching her innovations gather dust in academic journals. "But universities excel at discovery research, not commercial development that requires pharmaceutical expertise and regulatory navigation."

"Why don't pharmaceutical companies license university technologies more aggressively?" I asked, though I suspected our industry's preference for internal development might be creating massive missed opportunities.

"Most pharmaceutical companies prefer controlling their entire innovation pipeline rather than collaborating with academic institutions that operate on different timelines and have different success metrics," she replied. "Universities measure success through publications and scientific recognition while pharmaceutical companies require commercial applications and regulatory approval."

"And the potential for university-industry collaboration in drug development?"

"Academic institutions generate breakthrough discoveries that could revolutionize pharmaceutical treatment if properly developed, but commercialization requires pharmaceutical expertise that universities cannot provide independently."

This conversation launched our systematic university licensing strategy that would transform academic discoveries into commercial pharmaceutical innovations while providing universities with revenue streams from their research investments.

The technology assessment process required developing sophisticated evaluation criteria that could identify academic innovations with commercial potential while distinguishing breakthrough discoveries from interesting but unmarketable research.

"University technology assessment requires evaluating scientific merit, commercial potential, competitive differentiation, and regulatory feasibility for academic discoveries that exist primarily in research publications," announced Dr. Lisa Chen during our licensing strategy development. "Academic technologies often require significant additional development before achieving commercial viability."

"What criteria determine which university technologies warrant licensing investment?" I asked.

"Novel therapeutic mechanisms, proprietary intellectual property, competitive advantages over existing treatments, and realistic pathways to regulatory approval that could generate sustainable commercial returns."

"And due diligence requirements for university technology licensing?"

"Scientific validation, intellectual property analysis, competitive landscape assessment, and regulatory pathway evaluation that determines commercial development feasibility and investment requirements."

The licensing negotiation strategy required understanding academic priorities and constraints while structuring agreements that provided universities with fair compensation and pharmaceutical companies with commercial development rights.

"University licensing negotiations must balance academic interests in continued research and publication with commercial requirements for proprietary development and market exclusivity," explained our business development manager during our licensing planning session. "Academic institutions prefer ongoing collaboration while pharmaceutical companies require clear commercial control."

"How do we structure licensing agreements that satisfy both university and commercial requirements?" I asked.

"Licensing agreements with upfront payments, development milestone compensation, and ongoing royalties that provide universities with immediate and long-term revenue while granting commercial development and marketing rights."

"And intellectual property considerations for university licensing agreements?"

"University licensing requires clear IP ownership definitions, publication restrictions during commercial development, and patent prosecution responsibilities that protect commercial investments while respecting academic research freedom."

The partnership development approach involved establishing long-term collaboration relationships with leading academic institutions rather than pursuing individual licensing transactions.

"Strategic university partnerships with IIT Delhi, AIIMS, and IISc Bangalore provide ongoing access to breakthrough research while supporting academic institutions through sustained collaboration and funding," I announced during our partnership strategy session. "Long-term partnerships enable deeper collaboration than transactional licensing relationships."

"What advantages do strategic partnerships provide over individual licensing deals?" I asked.

"Strategic partnerships provide early access to emerging research, collaborative development opportunities, and ongoing innovation pipelines rather than just individual technology acquisitions."

"And partnership structure that supports both academic research and commercial development?"

"Collaborative research agreements with shared funding, joint IP development, and coordinated publication and commercialization strategies that advance both academic research and commercial applications."

The commercialization development process required bridging the gap between academic proof-of-concept research and pharmaceutical products ready for clinical development and regulatory approval.

"University technologies typically exist at early research stages requiring extensive additional development before achieving pharmaceutical product status," reported our technology transfer manager during our development planning. "Commercialization requires 2-4 years of additional research plus significant investment in formulation development, manufacturing optimization, and regulatory preparation."

"What specific development activities transform university research into commercial pharmaceutical products?" I asked.

"Formulation optimization, manufacturing scale-up, stability testing, quality control development, and regulatory documentation that enables clinical development and eventual market approval."

"And cost implications of university technology commercialization?"

"Technology commercialization requires ₹8-23 crores additional investment per licensed technology depending on development complexity and regulatory requirements."

The regulatory strategy adaptation required understanding how novel university technologies fit within existing regulatory frameworks while developing approval pathways for innovations that might not match conventional pharmaceutical categories.

"University technologies often represent novel therapeutic approaches that require developing new regulatory strategies and potentially working with regulatory agencies to establish appropriate approval pathways," explained Dr. Amanda Richardson during our regulatory planning. "Academic innovations may not fit standard regulatory categories requiring creative compliance approaches."

"How do novel university technologies affect regulatory approval strategies?" I asked.

"Novel technologies may qualify for breakthrough therapy designation, orphan drug status, or expedited approval pathways that can accelerate market entry while requiring specialized regulatory expertise."

"And regulatory risk management for university technology development?"

"Early regulatory consultation, systematic documentation, and ongoing agency communication that ensures novel technologies meet regulatory requirements while maintaining innovation advantages."

The licensing portfolio results demonstrated that university partnerships could provide access to breakthrough innovations while enabling academic institutions to benefit financially from their research investments.

"University licensing has generated access to seven breakthrough technologies including nanotechnology drug delivery, AI-driven therapeutic target identification, and personalized medicine platforms," I announced during our annual licensing review. "Academic partnerships provide innovation capabilities that internal R&D could not achieve independently."

"And commercial development progress for licensed university technologies?" asked our board technology committee.

"Three licensed technologies have advanced to preclinical development with two technologies scheduled for clinical trials within eighteen months, demonstrating successful technology transfer from academic research to commercial development."

Two years after implementing systematic university licensing, we had established innovation pipelines that exceeded internal R&D capabilities while creating beneficial partnerships with leading academic institutions.

"University licensing taught us that academic institutions generate breakthrough discoveries that pharmaceutical companies can develop into commercial successes through collaborative partnerships," I reflected during our innovation strategy review.

"The key insight was that university-industry collaboration enables combining academic discovery capabilities with pharmaceutical development expertise to create innovations that neither could achieve independently."

The university licensing strategy had proven that pharmaceutical companies could enhance their innovation capabilities through strategic academic partnerships that provided access to breakthrough research while supporting academic institutions through commercialization revenue.

"Licensing deals with universities demonstrated that innovation leadership requires collaborative approaches that leverage external discovery capabilities rather than relying exclusively on internal R&D development," I concluded.

The lesson had become fundamental to our innovation philosophy: university partnerships enabled access to breakthrough discoveries while creating collaborative relationships that enhanced both academic research and pharmaceutical innovation through shared expertise and resources.

The First New Drug Application Filing

The new drug application moment that would define our transformation from generic manufacturer to innovative pharmaceutical company arrived at 4:23 AM on November 15, 2020, when Dr. Amanda Richardson hit the submit button transmitting our first-ever New Drug Application to the FDA for AMT-2847, our novel cardiovascular compound that represented four years of breakthrough research and ₹127 crores in development investment. The submission felt simultaneously like vindication of our massive R&D gamble and the beginning of an even more terrifying regulatory journey that would determine whether we could compete as pharmaceutical innovators.

"We've just submitted 347,000 pages of clinical data, manufacturing documentation, and regulatory analysis representing the most comprehensive pharmaceutical submission in our company's history," Dr. Richardson announced to our assembled team, her voice mixing exhaustion with pride after eighteen months of preparing documents that would be scrutinized by FDA scientists with the power to approve or destroy our innovation dreams. "This NDA submission transforms us from a generic pharmaceutical company into an innovative drug developer seeking approval for an original therapeutic compound."

"How does filing an NDA compare to our previous generic drug submissions?" I asked, though I suspected the complexity difference would be staggering.

"Generic submissions require proving bioequivalence to existing drugs through straightforward comparative studies. NDA submissions require demonstrating that novel compounds are safe and effective through comprehensive clinical trials, manufacturing validation, and risk assessment that can take 12-18 months for FDA review."

"And the implications if FDA approves our new drug application?"

"NDA approval provides 15-20 years of market exclusivity for our novel compound compared to the 6-month exclusivity periods that generic approvals can achieve. Innovation approval creates sustained competitive advantages that generic pharmaceuticals cannot deliver."

This submission marked our evolution from a company that optimized existing drugs to one that created original therapeutic solutions through breakthrough research and systematic innovation development.

The clinical development program that supported our NDA had consumed three years of patient studies across multiple countries while demonstrating that AMT-2847 could reduce cardiovascular events more effectively than existing standard-of-care treatments.

"Our Phase III clinical trials enrolled 2,847 patients across 67 clinical sites in India, Europe, and the United States to demonstrate that AMT-2847 reduces major cardiovascular events by 34% compared to current standard therapy," reported Dr. Priya Sharma during our clinical data presentation. "Clinical evidence shows superior efficacy with comparable safety profile that supports regulatory approval for cardiovascular risk reduction."

"What makes our clinical data compelling for FDA approval consideration?" I asked.

"Superior efficacy results combined with novel mechanism of action that addresses unmet medical needs in cardiovascular treatment while demonstrating consistent benefits across diverse patient populations."

"And competitive advantages from our clinical development program?"

"Clinical data demonstrates therapeutic superiority that enables premium pricing and physician preference while patent protection prevents competitors from developing identical therapeutic approaches."

The manufacturing documentation proved more complex than anticipated when we discovered that FDA required comprehensive validation of our novel synthesis processes and quality control systems for producing pharmaceutical-grade AMT-2847.

"NDA manufacturing documentation includes detailed synthesis procedures, quality control specifications, stability data, and facility validation for producing AMT-2847 at commercial scale," announced our manufacturing director during our submission preparation. "Manufacturing documentation demonstrates that we can consistently produce high-quality drug substance and drug product that meets pharmaceutical standards."

"How does novel drug manufacturing differ from generic production requirements?" I asked.

"Novel drug manufacturing requires developing original synthesis processes, establishing quality specifications, and validating production systems rather than replicating established manufacturing procedures for existing drugs."

"And regulatory implications of manufacturing validation for NDA approval?"

"FDA manufacturing approval requires demonstrating process control, quality assurance, and production capability that ensures consistent product quality and patient safety throughout commercial production."

The regulatory strategy required coordinating with FDA throughout the development process while addressing agency questions and concerns that could affect approval probability and timeline.

"FDA regulatory strategy included pre-IND meetings, end-of-Phase II discussions, and pre-NDA consultations that enabled aligning our development program with regulatory expectations," Dr. Richardson explained during our regulatory review. "Ongoing FDA communication reduces approval risks while ensuring our submission addresses agency priorities and scientific concerns."

"What specific regulatory advantages result from early FDA engagement?" I asked.

"Early FDA communication enables optimizing clinical trial design, addressing manufacturing concerns, and developing risk management strategies that improve approval probability while reducing development costs."

"And regulatory timeline expectations for NDA review and approval?"

"Standard NDA review requires 10-12 months for FDA evaluation with potential for expedited review if our compound qualifies for breakthrough therapy designation or priority review status."

The commercial strategy development required planning market launch activities while preparing for potential FDA approval of our novel cardiovascular compound.

"Commercial strategy for AMT-2847 includes pricing analysis, market access planning, and physician education programs that position our novel compound as superior therapy for cardiovascular risk reduction," announced our commercial director during our launch preparation. "Innovation marketing requires different strategies than generic pharmaceutical promotion because physicians must understand novel therapeutic mechanisms and clinical benefits."

"How does marketing novel drugs differ from generic pharmaceutical promotion?" I asked.

"Novel drug marketing requires educating physicians about new therapeutic mechanisms, clinical evidence, and patient selection criteria rather than just promoting cost advantages and bioequivalence that generic marketing emphasizes."

"And pricing strategy for our novel cardiovascular compound?"

"Innovation pricing based on therapeutic value and clinical superiority rather than cost competition that enables premium pricing justified by superior patient outcomes."

The intellectual property protection surrounding AMT-2847 created competitive barriers that could sustain market advantages for 15-20 years through comprehensive patent coverage.

"AMT-2847 patent portfolio includes composition of matter, synthesis methodology, therapeutic applications, and formulation patents that provide comprehensive protection against competitive development," reported our patent attorney during our IP review. "Patent protection creates sustained competitive advantages that generic pharmaceuticals cannot achieve."

"How does novel drug IP differ from generic pharmaceutical patent strategies?" I asked.

"Novel drug patents protect original innovations for decades while generic pharmaceutical patents typically provide shorter-term advantages through formulation improvements or manufacturing optimizations."

The NDA submission results positioned us among innovative pharmaceutical companies capable of developing original therapeutic solutions rather than just optimizing existing drugs.

"Our first NDA submission demonstrates innovation capabilities that transform us from generic manufacturer to pharmaceutical innovator capable of creating novel therapeutic solutions," I announced during our submission celebration. "NDA filing validates our massive R&D investment while positioning us for sustained competitive advantages through proprietary drug development."

Six months after NDA submission, we had established credibility as innovative pharmaceutical developers while awaiting FDA approval that could provide validation of our transformation strategy.

"Filing our first new drug application taught us that pharmaceutical innovation requires systematic development capabilities rather than hoping for accidental discoveries," I reflected during our innovation strategy review.

"The key insight was that NDA submission represents the culmination of systematic innovation investment and the beginning of competitive advantages that only original drug development can provide."

The new drug application filing had proven that mid-sized pharmaceutical companies could achieve innovation leadership through systematic investment in breakthrough research and comprehensive development capabilities.

"Our first NDA filing demonstrated that innovative pharmaceutical success requires sustained commitment to original research rather than just optimizing existing therapeutic approaches," I concluded.

The lesson had become central to our innovation philosophy: new drug development enabled creating competitive advantages that generic pharmaceutical approaches could never achieve, transforming companies from commodity manufacturers to innovative therapeutic leaders.

Chapter 22

The Specialty Pharma Pivot

Abandoning Volume for Value

The specialty pharmaceutical revelation came during a devastating quarterly review in January 2021 when I realized that our traditional generic pharmaceutical strategy was slowly killing us through a death spiral of price erosion and commoditization that no amount of operational efficiency could overcome. Our gross margins had collapsed from 47% to 23% over three years while specialty pharmaceutical companies were achieving 70-85% margins through focused therapeutic approaches that commanded premium pricing despite smaller patient populations.

"We're competing in pharmaceutical markets where success is measured by volume and cost efficiency while our most successful competitors focus on value creation through specialized therapeutic solutions," announced Dr. Priya Sharma during her strategic assessment presentation, projecting market data that showed specialty pharmaceutical companies achieving returns that made our volume-based approach look economically primitive. "Generic pharmaceutical competition rewards scale and efficiency while specialty markets reward innovation and clinical value."

"But specialty pharmaceuticals serve smaller patient populations with higher development risks," I protested, though I was beginning to understand that smaller markets with premium pricing might be more attractive than large markets with commodity pricing. "How can serving fewer patients generate superior returns compared to broad market generic pharmaceuticals?"

"Specialty pharmaceuticals address complex medical conditions where physicians and patients value therapeutic superiority over cost savings," she replied with the conviction of someone who had spent months analyzing pharmaceutical market dynamics. "Specialty markets enable sustained pricing power through clinical differentiation while generic markets drive prices toward manufacturing costs."

"And our realistic prospects for transitioning from generic to specialty pharmaceutical focus?"

"Our cardiovascular expertise, regulatory capabilities, and innovation investments provide foundation for specialty pharmaceutical development, but success requires fundamentally different commercial strategies than generic pharmaceutical approaches."

This conversation launched our systematic transformation from volume-driven generic manufacturer to value-focused specialty pharmaceutical company that would require abandoning established business models in pursuit of premium market positioning.

The specialty market analysis revealed that focused therapeutic approaches could generate superior returns through deep clinical expertise and differentiated product development rather than broad market coverage and cost competition.

"Specialty pharmaceutical markets achieve average gross margins of 73% compared to 31% for generic pharmaceuticals through therapeutic focus that enables premium pricing and physician loyalty," reported our market research consultant during our specialty strategy assessment. "Specialty success requires understanding complex medical conditions rather than optimizing manufacturing efficiency and distribution scale."

"What specific characteristics distinguish specialty pharmaceutical markets from generic pharmaceutical competition?" I asked.

"Specialty markets involve complex diseases, limited treatment options, specialized physician knowledge, and patient populations that prioritize therapeutic efficacy over cost considerations."

"And competitive dynamics in specialty pharmaceutical markets compared to generic competition?"

"Specialty competition emphasizes clinical differentiation and therapeutic value while generic competition focuses on cost efficiency and supply chain optimization."

The therapeutic area selection required identifying medical specialties where our existing capabilities could create competitive advantages while avoiding areas dominated by major pharmaceutical corporations with decades of specialized expertise.

"Specialty pharmaceutical focus should concentrate on cardiovascular subspecialties, metabolic disorders, and inflammatory conditions where our existing regulatory expertise and clinical knowledge provide competitive advantages," announced Dr. Lisa Chen during our therapeutic strategy planning. "Specialty success requires deep medical expertise rather than broad therapeutic coverage."

"How do we determine optimal therapeutic areas for specialty pharmaceutical development?" I asked.

"Therapeutic area evaluation based on market size, competitive intensity, regulatory complexity, and alignment with our existing capabilities and clinical expertise."

"And competitive positioning strategies for entering established specialty markets?"

"Specialty market entry through differentiated therapeutic approaches, superior clinical evidence, and focused physician relationships rather than broad market competition."

The product development transformation required abandoning generic pharmaceutical optimization in favor of innovative therapeutic solutions that could address unmet medical needs in specialty patient populations.

"Specialty pharmaceutical development requires creating differentiated therapeutic solutions rather than optimizing existing generic formulations," Dr. Chen explained during our development strategy revision. "Specialty products must demonstrate clinical superiority or address therapeutic gaps that existing treatments cannot resolve effectively."

"What specific development capabilities distinguish specialty pharmaceutical innovation from generic pharmaceutical optimization?" I asked.

"Specialty development requires understanding complex disease mechanisms, identifying unmet therapeutic needs, and developing innovative solutions rather than just improving existing drug formulations."

"And regulatory strategies for specialty pharmaceutical approval compared to generic pharmaceutical submissions?"

"Specialty regulatory strategies emphasize clinical evidence and therapeutic value while generic submissions focus on bioequivalence and manufacturing quality."

The commercial strategy restructuring involved developing specialized sales and marketing capabilities that could engage physicians through clinical education rather than cost-based promotional approaches.

"Specialty pharmaceutical marketing requires clinical expertise and therapeutic education rather than price competition and volume promotion," announced our commercial director during our marketing strategy transformation. "Specialty success depends on physician confidence in therapeutic value rather than cost advantages."

"How does specialty pharmaceutical marketing differ from generic pharmaceutical promotion?" I asked.

"Specialty marketing emphasizes clinical education, therapeutic differentiation, and patient outcome improvement while generic marketing focuses on cost savings and supply reliability."

"And sales force requirements for specialty pharmaceutical success?"

"Specialty sales requires clinical knowledge and therapeutic expertise that enables meaningful physician education rather than just promotional product information."

The pricing strategy development required understanding how specialty pharmaceutical value-based pricing could achieve premium returns through therapeutic superiority rather than cost competition.

"Specialty pharmaceutical pricing based on therapeutic value and clinical outcomes rather than cost competition enables premium pricing that reflects medical benefits," explained our pricing analyst during our commercial strategy development. "Value-based pricing rewards innovation and clinical superiority rather than manufacturing efficiency."

"What enables specialty pharmaceuticals to achieve premium pricing that generic pharmaceuticals cannot command?" I asked.

"Therapeutic differentiation, clinical evidence, and physician confidence in superior patient outcomes that justify premium pricing for specialty pharmaceutical solutions."

"And market access strategies for specialty pharmaceutical products?"

"Specialty market access requires demonstrating therapeutic value and patient outcome improvements that justify premium pricing to insurance providers and healthcare systems."

The specialty pharmaceutical pivot results began demonstrating that focused therapeutic approaches could generate superior returns while creating sustainable competitive advantages through clinical expertise.

"Specialty pharmaceutical development has achieved gross margins of 68% compared to 23% for our generic pharmaceutical products through therapeutic focus and value-based pricing," I announced during our annual specialty review. "Specialty strategy creates competitive advantages and financial returns that generic pharmaceutical approaches cannot achieve."

"And physician acceptance of our specialty pharmaceutical approach?" asked our commercial review committee.

"Physician engagement has increased 47% through clinical education and therapeutic expertise that demonstrates meaningful value rather than just cost savings."

Two years after implementing our specialty pharmaceutical pivot, we had transformed from commodity generic manufacturer to specialized therapeutic company with premium market positioning.

"The specialty pharmaceutical pivot taught us that pharmaceutical success requires choosing between volume competition and value creation," I reflected during our strategic planning retreat.

"The key insight was that specialty pharmaceutical focus enables sustained competitive advantages through therapeutic expertise rather than operational efficiency."

The specialty pharmaceutical pivot had proven that mid-sized pharmaceutical companies could achieve superior returns through focused therapeutic approaches rather than broad market generic competition.

"Specialty pharmaceutical transformation demonstrated that value creation requires abandoning volume strategies in favor of specialized therapeutic excellence," I concluded.

The lesson had become fundamental to our business philosophy: specialty pharmaceutical focus enabled creating sustainable competitive advantages through therapeutic expertise that commodity generic approaches could never achieve.

Acquiring Specialty Pharmaceutical Companies

The specialty pharmaceutical acquisition opportunity that would accelerate our transformation from generic manufacturer to focused therapeutic company emerged during a casual conversation at the Mumbai Pharmaceutical Conference in March 2021 when Dr. Rajesh Mittal mentioned that his dermatology specialty company, DermaTech Pharmaceuticals, was struggling with manufacturing scale-up while sitting on a portfolio of innovative topical treatments that commanded 73% gross margins in niche therapeutic markets.

"We've developed five proprietary dermatology formulations that dermatologists prefer over existing treatments, but manufacturing complexity and regulatory expansion requirements exceed our capital capabilities," Dr. Mittal explained with the frustrated tone of a successful entrepreneur watching growth opportunities slip away due to resource constraints. "Specialty pharmaceutical success requires operational capabilities that innovation-focused companies often cannot develop independently."

"What makes dermatology formulations achieve such attractive margins compared to traditional pharmaceutical products?" I asked, though I suspected the answer would illuminate the fundamental differences between specialty and generic pharmaceutical economics.

"Dermatology specialists value formulation elegance, patient compliance, and therapeutic outcomes over cost considerations," he replied. "Physicians prescribe superior topical treatments that patients prefer even when premium pricing exceeds generic alternatives by 200-300%."

"And your manufacturing challenges that limit growth potential?"

"Topical pharmaceutical manufacturing requires specialized equipment, complex quality control, and regulatory expertise that our company cannot afford while maintaining R&D investment in new product development."

"What would acquisition by a company with manufacturing capabilities enable for your specialty pharmaceutical portfolio?"

"Manufacturing partnership could enable market expansion, regulatory approvals in additional countries, and accelerated product development that our independent operations cannot achieve."

This conversation crystallized our acquisition strategy for building specialty pharmaceutical capabilities through targeted acquisitions that could provide therapeutic expertise, innovative products, and specialized market access that internal development could not achieve efficiently.

The acquisition screening process required developing evaluation criteria that could identify specialty pharmaceutical companies with valuable therapeutic portfolios while avoiding businesses with unsustainable competitive positions or problematic regulatory issues.

"Specialty pharmaceutical acquisition candidates should possess differentiated product portfolios, specialized therapeutic expertise, established physician relationships, and sustainable competitive advantages," announced our business development manager during our acquisition strategy planning. "Acquisition targets must provide capabilities that enhance our specialty transformation rather than just adding revenue volume."

"What specific characteristics distinguish attractive specialty pharmaceutical acquisition targets?" I asked.

"Proprietary formulations with patent protection, therapeutic focus that complements our capabilities, proven clinical differentiation, and growth potential that our operational capabilities could accelerate."

"And due diligence requirements for specialty pharmaceutical acquisitions?"

"Clinical evidence validation, intellectual property assessment, regulatory compliance evaluation, and competitive positioning analysis that determines sustainable value creation potential."

The DermaTech acquisition negotiation required understanding specialty pharmaceutical valuation methods that emphasized therapeutic differentiation and market potential rather than traditional revenue multiples used for generic pharmaceutical transactions.

"Specialty pharmaceutical valuations based on therapeutic value, patent protection duration, market exclusivity potential, and competitive barriers rather than revenue multiples or manufacturing efficiency," explained our acquisition consultant during valuation planning. "Specialty companies command premium valuations through sustained competitive advantages that generic pharmaceuticals cannot achieve."

"How do specialty pharmaceutical acquisition valuations compare to generic pharmaceutical transactions?" I asked.

"Specialty acquisitions typically command 8-12 times revenue multiples compared to 2-4 times revenue for generic pharmaceutical companies due to sustainable competitive advantages and premium pricing power."

"And specific valuation drivers for DermaTech's dermatology portfolio?"

"Patent-protected formulations, established dermatologist relationships, premium pricing sustainability, and market expansion potential that our manufacturing capabilities could accelerate."

The integration planning required understanding how to preserve specialty pharmaceutical innovation culture while leveraging operational capabilities that could accelerate market expansion and product development.

"Specialty pharmaceutical integration must preserve innovation capabilities and physician relationships while providing operational support that enables growth acceleration," I announced during our integration strategy development.

"Acquisition success requires enhancing specialty capabilities rather than imposing generic pharmaceutical approaches."

"What integration approaches preserve specialty pharmaceutical value while enabling operational synergies?" I asked.

"Autonomous operations for R&D and medical affairs while integrating manufacturing, regulatory, and commercial support functions that can accelerate specialty market expansion."

"And cultural integration challenges for specialty pharmaceutical acquisitions?"

"Specialty pharmaceutical culture emphasizes clinical innovation and therapeutic excellence while generic pharmaceutical operations focus on efficiency and cost optimization."

The regulatory coordination strategy involved leveraging our global regulatory capabilities to accelerate specialty pharmaceutical approvals in international markets while maintaining therapeutic focus and clinical expertise.

"DermaTech's dermatology portfolio provides expansion opportunities in European and Asian markets where our regulatory expertise can accelerate approval timelines," reported Dr. Amanda Richardson during our regulatory integration planning. "Specialty pharmaceutical international expansion creates market opportunities that independent operations cannot achieve efficiently."

"How do our regulatory capabilities enhance specialty pharmaceutical acquisition value?" I asked.

"Global regulatory expertise enables faster international market entry while specialty therapeutic knowledge provides differentiated market positioning that generic regulatory approaches cannot support."

"And regulatory synergies from specialty pharmaceutical integration?"

"Combined regulatory capabilities enable portfolio expansion while specialized therapeutic expertise enhances our competitive positioning in focused medical specialties."

The commercial integration required developing sophisticated marketing approaches that could leverage specialty pharmaceutical clinical expertise while accessing broader physician networks through our established commercial relationships.

"Specialty pharmaceutical commercial integration combines therapeutic expertise with expanded market access through our physician relationships and distribution capabilities," announced our commercial director during integration planning. "Commercial synergies enable broader market penetration while preserving specialty therapeutic focus."

"What commercial advantages result from specialty pharmaceutical acquisition integration?" I asked.

"Enhanced physician access, accelerated market penetration, and broader therapeutic portfolio that enables comprehensive specialty pharmaceutical positioning."

"And sales force integration strategies for specialty pharmaceutical products?"

"Specialized sales teams for complex therapeutic areas while leveraging broader commercial capabilities for market expansion and physician relationship development."

The acquisition results demonstrated that targeted specialty pharmaceutical acquisitions could accelerate transformation while providing immediate access to differentiated therapeutic portfolios.

"DermaTech acquisition has contributed ₹67 crores annual revenue with 71% gross margins while providing dermatology expertise that enhances our specialty pharmaceutical positioning," I announced during our annual acquisition review. "Specialty pharmaceutical acquisitions provide immediate therapeutic capabilities while accelerating our transformation from generic to specialty focus."

"And integration success metrics for specialty pharmaceutical acquisitions?" asked our board acquisition committee.

"Successful integration measured through sustained product differentiation, physician relationship preservation, and accelerated market expansion that justifies acquisition investment."

Two years after completing our first specialty pharmaceutical acquisition, we had accelerated our transformation while building therapeutic expertise that internal development could not achieve efficiently.

"Acquiring specialty pharmaceutical companies taught us that transformation can be accelerated through targeted acquisitions that provide immediate therapeutic capabilities," I reflected during our acquisition strategy review.

"The key insight was that specialty pharmaceutical acquisitions provide therapeutic expertise and market positioning that internal development requires years to achieve."

The specialty pharmaceutical acquisition strategy had proven that focused acquisitions could accelerate business transformation while providing access to differentiated therapeutic portfolios and specialized market expertise.

"Specialty pharmaceutical acquisitions demonstrated that strategic transactions can accelerate transformation while providing immediate access to therapeutic expertise and competitive advantages," I concluded.

The lesson had become central to our growth strategy: targeted acquisitions enabled accelerating specialty pharmaceutical transformation through immediate access to therapeutic capabilities that internal development could not achieve efficiently.

Building Hospital and Specialty Channels

The hospital channel awakening came during a humbling visit to AIIMS Delhi in April 2021 when I discovered that our traditional pharmacy-focused distribution strategy was completely inadequate for reaching the cardiologists and endocrinologists who actually prescribed our specialized cardiovascular and diabetes treatments. The reality hit me when Dr. Suresh Khanna, head of cardiology, mentioned that he rarely saw pharmaceutical representatives despite prescribing millions of rupees worth of cardiovascular medications annually, because hospital access required entirely different commercial approaches than retail pharmacy relationships.

"Hospital prescribing decisions involve clinical committees, formulary approvals, and evidence-based treatment protocols that your retail pharmaceutical sales approach cannot influence effectively," Dr. Khanna explained with the patient tone of someone educating a pharmaceutical executive about medical realities I should have understood years earlier. "Hospital physicians evaluate therapeutic evidence and clinical outcomes rather than responding to traditional pharmaceutical sales presentations."

"But we've built successful relationships with thousands of physicians through our retail-focused sales force," I protested, though I was beginning to recognize that hospital-based specialists operated in fundamentally different professional environments.

"Retail physicians make individual prescribing decisions based on patient preferences and cost considerations, while hospital specialists work within institutional guidelines that prioritize clinical evidence and therapeutic protocols," he replied. "Hospital market access requires understanding institutional decision-making rather than individual physician relationships."

"And the implications for reaching specialists who control high-value prescribing decisions?"

"Hospital and specialty channel development requires clinical evidence, institutional relationships, and therapeutic expertise that traditional pharmaceutical sales approaches cannot provide effectively."

This conversation launched our systematic development of hospital and specialty channels that would require abandoning retail-focused commercial strategies in favor of institutional relationship building and evidence-based medical affairs approaches.

The hospital market analysis revealed that institutional healthcare providers controlled 67% of specialty pharmaceutical prescribing despite representing only 23% of total physician interactions, creating concentrated opportunities for companies that could navigate complex institutional sales processes.

"Hospital pharmaceutical purchasing involves clinical committees, pharmacy formularies, and institutional contracts that require different commercial approaches than individual physician relationships," reported our newly hired Hospital Sales Director, Dr. Meera Joshi, during our channel strategy assessment. "Hospital sales cycles require 6-18 months of relationship building and clinical evidence development compared to 3-6 months for retail physician engagement."

"What specific capabilities distinguish successful hospital pharmaceutical sales from retail commercial strategies?" I asked.

"Hospital sales requires clinical evidence presentation, institutional relationship management, and formulary navigation expertise rather than individual physician promotion and relationship building."

"And competitive advantages from hospital channel development?"

"Hospital relationships create preferred supplier status and formulary inclusion that provides sustained competitive advantages while generating higher-value contracts than retail pharmaceutical sales."

The institutional relationship building required developing medical affairs capabilities that could engage hospital clinical committees through scientific evidence rather than traditional pharmaceutical promotional approaches.

"Hospital medical affairs involves clinical evidence presentation, therapeutic education, and scientific communication that builds institutional confidence in our therapeutic capabilities," announced our Medical Affairs Director during our hospital strategy development. "Medical affairs creates clinical credibility that enables commercial access to hospital decision-makers."

"How does medical affairs differ from traditional pharmaceutical sales approaches?" I asked.

"Medical affairs emphasizes scientific education and clinical evidence while traditional sales focuses on product promotion and relationship building."

"And medical affairs requirements for successful hospital channel development?"

"Clinical expertise, scientific communication capabilities, and therapeutic knowledge that enables meaningful engagement with hospital specialists and clinical committees."

The formulary management strategy required understanding hospital pharmaceutical decision-making processes while developing evidence-based presentations that could demonstrate therapeutic value and economic benefits.

"Hospital formulary inclusion requires demonstrating therapeutic superiority, cost-effectiveness, and clinical evidence that justifies preferred product status," explained our Formulary Access Manager during our institutional strategy planning. "Formulary success depends on clinical evidence and economic analysis rather than traditional pharmaceutical promotional approaches."

"What specific evidence requirements determine hospital formulary inclusion decisions?" I asked.

"Clinical trial data, real-world evidence, pharmacoeconomic analysis, and therapeutic differentiation that demonstrates superior patient outcomes and institutional value."

"And formulary maintenance requirements for sustained hospital market access?"

"Ongoing clinical evidence generation, outcome monitoring, and institutional relationship management that maintains preferred formulary status through demonstrated therapeutic value."

The specialty channel development involved building relationships with subspecialty physicians who required advanced therapeutic knowledge and clinical support beyond traditional pharmaceutical sales capabilities.

"Specialty channel development requires understanding complex medical conditions, therapeutic protocols, and clinical decision-making that general pharmaceutical sales representatives cannot provide effectively," announced our Specialty Sales Manager during our channel expansion planning. "Specialty physicians require clinical expertise and therapeutic education rather than traditional promotional approaches."

"How do specialty physician relationships differ from primary care physician engagement?" I asked.

"Specialty physicians evaluate therapeutic mechanisms, clinical evidence, and patient outcome data while primary care physicians often prioritize cost considerations and prescribing convenience."

"And competitive advantages from specialty channel relationships?"

"Specialty physician relationships create clinical advocacy and therapeutic preference that generates sustained prescribing loyalty and premium pricing acceptance."

The clinical support services development required providing hospitals and specialty practices with educational resources and patient management tools that enhanced therapeutic outcomes while building institutional relationships.

"Clinical support services include physician education programs, patient monitoring tools, and therapeutic protocols that enhance institutional capabilities while building relationships with hospital systems," reported our Clinical Services Manager during our support program development. "Clinical support creates institutional value that enables sustained commercial relationships."

"What specific clinical support services provide value for hospital and specialty customers?" I asked.

"Continuing medical education, patient management protocols, outcome monitoring systems, and therapeutic consultation that enhances institutional clinical capabilities."

"And competitive differentiation through clinical support services?"

"Clinical support creates institutional dependency and therapeutic preference that competitors without similar capabilities cannot easily replicate."

The contract negotiation strategy required understanding institutional purchasing processes while developing value-based pricing agreements that reflected therapeutic benefits rather than cost competition.

"Hospital contracts require value-based pricing that reflects therapeutic outcomes and institutional benefits rather than cost-focused negotiations," explained our Institutional Sales Director during our contracting strategy development. "Value-based contracting enables premium pricing through demonstrated therapeutic superiority and patient outcome improvements."

"How do hospital contract negotiations differ from retail pharmaceutical pricing discussions?" I asked.

"Hospital contracts emphasize therapeutic value and institutional benefits while retail pricing focuses on cost competition and pharmacy margin considerations."

"And contract structure that sustains hospital channel profitability?"

"Outcome-based pricing, volume commitments, and therapeutic partnership agreements that align institutional success with our commercial objectives."

The hospital and specialty channel results demonstrated that institutional commercial strategies could generate superior returns while creating sustainable competitive advantages through clinical relationships.

"Hospital and specialty channel development has achieved 43% higher average selling prices compared to retail pharmaceutical sales while building institutional relationships that create sustained competitive advantages," I announced during our annual channel review. "Institutional channels provide premium pricing and competitive positioning that retail pharmaceutical approaches cannot achieve."

"And physician engagement improvements through specialty channel development?" asked our commercial review committee.

"Specialty physician engagement has increased 67% through clinical expertise and therapeutic education that demonstrates meaningful value beyond traditional pharmaceutical promotion."

Two years after building hospital and specialty channels, we had transformed our commercial approach from retail-focused volume sales to institutional value-based relationships that supported premium pricing and therapeutic differentiation.

"Building hospital and specialty channels taught us that pharmaceutical success requires understanding how different physician segments make prescribing decisions," I reflected during our commercial strategy planning.

"The key insight was that institutional channels require clinical evidence and therapeutic expertise rather than traditional pharmaceutical promotional approaches."

The hospital and specialty channel development had proven that focused commercial strategies could achieve premium pricing and competitive advantages through institutional relationship building and evidence-based therapeutic positioning.

"Hospital and specialty channel development demonstrated that commercial success requires aligning sales approaches with physician decision-making processes rather than applying uniform promotional strategies," I concluded.

The lesson had become fundamental to our commercial philosophy: hospital and specialty channels enabled achieving premium pricing and competitive advantages through clinical expertise and institutional relationship building that traditional pharmaceutical sales approaches could not provide effectively.

High-Value, Low-Volume Product Strategy

The high-value, low-volume revelation struck me during a shocking financial analysis in June 2021 when I discovered that our orphan disease product for a rare cardiovascular condition - serving only 2,400 patients annually - generated more profit per employee than our bestselling generic diabetes medication that reached 340,000 patients. The mathematics were undeniable: our rare disease product achieved 78% gross margins with minimal competitive pressure while our high-volume generic faced relentless price erosion and required massive sales force investment for commodity returns.

"We're optimizing for the wrong metrics," announced our newly hired VP of Strategic Planning, Dr. Kavya Reddy, as she presented market analysis that would fundamentally challenge our volume-obsessed business philosophy. "Pharmaceutical success should be measured by value creation per patient rather than total patient numbers, because niche therapeutic markets can generate superior returns with less competitive risk than mass market generic pharmaceuticals."

"But serving 2,400 patients seems insignificant compared to reaching hundreds of thousands of patients with our mainstream products," I protested, though the profit-per-patient calculations were forcing me to question everything I believed about pharmaceutical market opportunities.

"Patient volume becomes irrelevant when therapeutic value enables premium pricing that exceeds commodity pharmaceutical margins by 200-400%," she replied with the analytical precision that had convinced me to hire her from McKinsey. "High-value, low-volume markets reward therapeutic expertise and clinical differentiation while mass markets punish companies through cost competition and margin compression."

"And our competitive positioning in niche markets compared to mass market pharmaceutical competition?"

"Niche markets enable establishing dominant market positions with limited competition while mass markets require fighting against dozens of competitors for marginal market share gains."

This conversation launched our systematic transformation from volume-driven generic manufacturer to value-focused specialty pharmaceutical company that would prioritize therapeutic impact over patient numbers in pursuit of sustainable competitive advantages.

The market opportunity analysis revealed that numerous high-value, low-volume pharmaceutical markets existed where therapeutic expertise could command premium pricing without facing the brutal competition that characterized mass market generic pharmaceuticals.

"High-value, low-volume opportunities include rare cardiovascular conditions, specialized metabolic disorders, and complex inflammatory diseases that affect 1,000-10,000 patients annually but command average treatment costs of ₹2-8 lakhs per patient," reported our market research consultant during our niche strategy assessment. "Specialty markets enable achieving dominant market positions with sustained premium pricing that mass market competition cannot deliver."

"What characteristics distinguish attractive high-value, low-volume markets from less promising niche opportunities?" I asked.

"Attractive niche markets involve complex medical conditions, limited treatment options, specialized physician expertise, and patient populations that prioritize therapeutic efficacy over cost considerations."

"And competitive dynamics in high-value, low-volume markets compared to mass market pharmaceutical competition?"

"Niche markets reward clinical expertise and therapeutic differentiation while mass markets emphasize cost efficiency and distribution scale."

The product development strategy required focusing R&D resources on creating therapeutic solutions for unmet medical needs in specialized patient populations rather than developing generic versions of existing mass market pharmaceuticals.

"High-value, low-volume product development requires understanding complex disease mechanisms and developing innovative therapeutic approaches rather than optimizing existing generic formulations," announced Dr. Lisa Chen during our R&D strategy revision. "Niche product success depends on therapeutic superiority and clinical differentiation rather than cost optimization and manufacturing efficiency."

"How does niche product development differ from traditional pharmaceutical R&D approaches?" I asked.

"Niche development requires deep medical expertise and innovative therapeutic approaches while traditional pharmaceutical R&D focuses on bioequivalence demonstration and manufacturing optimization."

"And regulatory strategies for high-value, low-volume pharmaceutical products?"

"Niche pharmaceutical regulation often involves orphan drug designation, expedited approval pathways, and specialized regulatory guidance that enables faster market entry with extended market exclusivity."

The pricing strategy development required understanding how value-based pricing could achieve premium returns through therapeutic benefits rather than competing on cost considerations that dominated mass market pharmaceutical pricing.

"High-value, low-volume pricing based on therapeutic value and patient outcomes rather than cost competition enables achieving ₹50,000-300,000 per patient annually compared to ₹2,000-8,000 for mass market generics," explained our pricing analyst during our specialty strategy development. "Value-based pricing rewards innovation and clinical superiority rather than manufacturing efficiency and distribution scale."

"What enables niche pharmaceutical products to achieve premium pricing that mass market products cannot command?" I asked.

"Therapeutic necessity, limited treatment alternatives, specialized physician relationships, and insurance coverage that prioritizes clinical outcomes over cost considerations."

"And pricing sustainability for high-value, low-volume pharmaceutical products?"

"Patent protection, regulatory exclusivity, and therapeutic differentiation create pricing sustainability that generic pharmaceutical competition cannot achieve."

The commercial strategy transformation required developing specialized sales and marketing capabilities that could engage subspecialty physicians through clinical expertise rather than traditional volume-based promotional approaches.

"High-value, low-volume commercial strategy requires clinical specialists who can provide therapeutic education and medical support rather than traditional sales representatives promoting cost advantages," announced our commercial director during our sales strategy revision. "Niche commercial success depends on clinical credibility and therapeutic expertise rather than promotional frequency and relationship building."

"How does niche pharmaceutical marketing differ from mass market promotional strategies?" I asked.

"Niche marketing emphasizes clinical education and therapeutic differentiation while mass market promotion focuses on cost advantages and prescribing convenience."

"And sales force requirements for high-value, low-volume pharmaceutical success?"

"Niche sales requires medical specialists with therapeutic expertise rather than general pharmaceutical sales representatives with relationship-building capabilities."

The distribution strategy adaptation involved developing specialized channels that could reach subspecialty physicians and rare disease treatment centers rather than pursuing broad market coverage through traditional pharmaceutical distribution.

"High-value, low-volume distribution requires accessing specialized treatment centers, academic medical institutions, and subspecialty physician networks rather than broad pharmaceutical distribution," reported our distribution manager during our channel strategy development. "Niche distribution emphasizes clinical expertise and therapeutic support rather than volume logistics and cost efficiency."

"What distribution capabilities distinguish successful niche pharmaceutical companies?" I asked.

"Specialized clinical support, therapeutic expertise, and institutional relationships that enable accessing subspecialty prescribers and rare disease treatment centers."

"And distribution advantages for high-value, low-volume pharmaceutical products?"

"Focused distribution enables building deeper clinical relationships while avoiding competitive pressure and margin compression that broad distribution channels experience."

The portfolio transformation results demonstrated that high-value, low-volume products could generate superior returns while creating sustainable competitive advantages through therapeutic expertise.

"High-value, low-volume product strategy has achieved average gross margins of 71% compared to 28% for our mass market generic products while building therapeutic expertise and competitive positioning," I announced during our annual strategy review. "Niche product focus creates sustainable competitive advantages and financial returns that mass market competition cannot deliver."

"And competitive positioning improvements from high-value, low-volume strategy?" asked our board strategy committee.

"Niche market focus has established dominant market positions in specialized therapeutic areas while reducing competitive pressure from mass market pharmaceutical companies."

Two years after implementing high-value, low-volume product strategy, we had transformed from commodity generic manufacturer to specialized therapeutic company with premium market positioning and sustainable competitive advantages.

"High-value, low-volume product strategy taught us that pharmaceutical success requires choosing therapeutic impact over patient volume," I reflected during our strategic planning retreat.

"The key insight was that niche markets enable creating sustainable competitive advantages through therapeutic expertise rather than competing for market share in commoditized mass markets."

The high-value, low-volume transformation had proven that specialty pharmaceutical companies could achieve superior returns through focused therapeutic approaches rather than pursuing broad market coverage with generic pharmaceutical competition.

"High-value, low-volume strategy demonstrated that pharmaceutical value creation requires therapeutic expertise and clinical differentiation rather than manufacturing efficiency and distribution scale," I concluded.

The lesson had become fundamental to our business philosophy: high-value, low-volume markets enabled creating sustainable competitive advantages through therapeutic specialization that mass market pharmaceutical approaches could never achieve.

The Orphan Drug Opportunity

The orphan drug revelation came during a chance encounter at the Mumbai International Airport in September 2021 when I met Dr. Ravi Shankar, whose twelve-year-old daughter suffered from a rare metabolic disorder affecting fewer than 1,800 children in India. His anguished description of searching desperately for treatment options that simply didn't exist in our pharmaceutical market forced me to confront a sobering reality: while we had spent decades optimizing treatments for common diseases, millions of patients with rare conditions remained abandoned by an industry focused exclusively on blockbuster drug opportunities.

"No Indian pharmaceutical company develops treatments for rare diseases because the patient populations seem too small to justify development costs," Dr. Shankar explained with the quiet desperation of a father watching his child suffer from a condition that had effective treatments in Europe and America but remained inaccessible in India due to regulatory and commercial barriers. "Rare disease patients become medical orphans because pharmaceutical companies cannot see profitable opportunities in small patient populations."

"But how can pharmaceutical companies justify massive R&D investments for diseases affecting only thousands of patients?" I asked, though his daughter's situation was forcing me to examine the human cost of our profit-maximizing business strategies.

"Orphan drug regulations provide market exclusivity, expedited approvals, and premium pricing that can generate substantial returns despite small patient populations," he replied with the detailed knowledge of someone who had researched every possible treatment avenue. "Pharmaceutical companies avoid orphan diseases due to misconceptions about market potential rather than actual economic limitations."

"And the regulatory environment for orphan drug development in India?"

"Indian orphan drug policies are evolving to provide incentives similar to FDA and EMA programs, creating opportunities for pharmaceutical companies willing to serve rare disease communities."

This conversation crystallized our entry into orphan drug development as both a moral imperative and a strategic business opportunity that could generate sustained competitive advantages while serving desperately underserved patient populations.

The orphan drug market analysis revealed that rare disease treatments commanded extraordinary pricing power and market exclusivity that could generate returns exceeding blockbuster drug investments despite dramatically smaller patient populations.

"Orphan drug markets involve 7,000 - 200,000 patients globally with average annual treatment costs of $100,000 - 500,000 per patient, generating $500 million-2 billion market opportunities with minimal competitive pressure," reported our newly hired Orphan Drug Development Director, Dr. Anita Malhotra, during our rare disease strategy assessment. "Orphan designation provides 7-12 years of market exclusivity plus expedited regulatory approval and premium pricing that blockbuster drugs cannot achieve."

"How do orphan drug economics compare to traditional pharmaceutical development?" I asked.

"Orphan drugs achieve 80-95% gross margins with sustained pricing power while traditional pharmaceuticals face generic competition and price erosion within 10-15 years of launch."

"And development cost implications for orphan drug compared to conventional pharmaceutical products?"

"Orphan drug development costs 60-70% less than traditional pharmaceuticals due to smaller clinical trials, expedited regulatory pathways, and specialized patient populations that enable efficient development programs."

The regulatory advantage analysis demonstrated that orphan drug designation provided unprecedented development and commercial benefits that could accelerate market entry while ensuring sustained competitive positioning.

"Orphan drug designation provides accelerated regulatory review, reduced clinical trial requirements, extended market exclusivity, and tax incentives that enable faster development with superior competitive protection," explained Dr. Amanda Richardson during our orphan regulatory strategy planning. "Regulatory advantages for orphan drugs exceed benefits available for any other pharmaceutical development pathway."

"What specific regulatory benefits distinguish orphan drug development from traditional pharmaceutical approval processes?" I asked.

"Expedited review timelines, smaller clinical trial requirements, regulatory guidance and support, plus extended market exclusivity that prevents generic competition for 7-12 years after approval."

"And global regulatory coordination opportunities for orphan drug development?"

"Orphan drug designation in major markets enables accelerated approval across multiple countries through regulatory harmonization and expedited review processes."

The unmet medical need assessment revealed numerous rare cardiovascular and metabolic conditions where existing treatments remained inadequate while patient populations desperately needed therapeutic innovations.

"Rare cardiovascular conditions including hypertrophic cardiomyopathy, pulmonary arterial hypertension, and genetic lipid disorders affect 50,000-200,000 patients in India with limited treatment options," reported our medical affairs team during our orphan indication evaluation. "Unmet medical needs in rare cardiovascular diseases provide development opportunities that align with our therapeutic expertise."

"What criteria determine attractive orphan drug development opportunities?" I asked.

"Clear unmet medical need, defined patient population, feasible clinical development pathway, and alignment with our existing therapeutic and regulatory capabilities."

"And competitive landscape analysis for rare cardiovascular conditions?"

"Most rare cardiovascular conditions have fewer than three approved treatments globally, creating opportunities for therapeutic differentiation and market leadership through innovative development approaches."

The development strategy required adapting our clinical capabilities to conduct efficient orphan drug trials while building relationships with rare disease patient organizations and specialized treatment centers.

"Orphan drug development requires specialized clinical trial design, rare disease patient recruitment, and academic medical center partnerships that differ substantially from traditional pharmaceutical development," announced

Dr. Priya Sharma during our orphan development planning. "Rare disease trials involve smaller patient populations but require specialized expertise and patient community relationships."

"How does orphan drug clinical development differ from traditional pharmaceutical trials?" I asked.

"Orphan trials involve 50-300 patients compared to 1,000-3,000 for traditional trials, but require specialized recruitment through patient organizations and treatment centers."

"And timeline advantages for orphan drug clinical development?"

"Expedited regulatory pathways enable 3-5 year development timelines compared to 7-10 years for traditional pharmaceutical development."

The commercial strategy development required understanding how to reach specialized physicians and rare disease treatment centers while building relationships with patient advocacy organizations that could support market access and adoption.

"Orphan drug commercial strategy involves specialized physician networks, academic treatment centers, and patient advocacy partnerships rather than broad pharmaceutical sales approaches," announced our orphan commercial manager during our rare disease marketing planning. "Orphan drug success requires building rare disease expertise and community relationships rather than traditional pharmaceutical promotion."

"What commercial capabilities distinguish successful orphan drug companies?" I asked.

"Medical expertise in rare diseases, relationships with patient advocacy organizations, and specialized distribution capabilities that can reach rare disease treatment centers."

"And pricing strategies for orphan drug products?"

"Value-based pricing that reflects therapeutic benefits and unmet medical need rather than cost-based competition that characterizes traditional pharmaceutical markets."

The orphan drug program results demonstrated that rare disease development could generate exceptional returns while serving critically underserved patient populations.

"Orphan drug development has generated three promising rare cardiovascular programs with breakthrough therapy potential and projected peak sales of $200-800 million annually," I announced during our annual orphan review. "Rare disease focus creates sustainable competitive advantages while addressing critical unmet medical needs."

"And patient community response to our orphan drug development efforts?" asked our board medical committee.

"Rare disease patient organizations have provided exceptional support and collaboration that accelerates development while building strong advocacy relationships."

Three years after entering orphan drug development, we had established leadership in rare cardiovascular diseases while achieving development efficiency and commercial potential that exceeded traditional pharmaceutical approaches.

"The orphan drug opportunity taught us that pharmaceutical success requires serving patient needs rather than just pursuing large market opportunities," I reflected during our rare disease strategy review.

"The key insight was that orphan drugs enable creating sustainable competitive advantages while addressing critical medical needs that large pharmaceutical companies typically ignore."

The orphan drug program had proven that specialty pharmaceutical companies could achieve exceptional returns through rare disease focus while serving desperately underserved patient communities.

"Orphan drug development demonstrated that pharmaceutical success requires balancing commercial objectives with medical responsibility to serve all patient populations regardless of market size," I concluded.

The lesson had become fundamental to our mission: orphan drug opportunities enabled creating both sustainable competitive advantages and meaningful medical impact through serving rare disease communities that traditional pharmaceutical development had abandoned.

Chapter 23

The Biotechnology Expansion

From Chemistry to Biology

The biotechnology awakening came during a devastating competitive analysis meeting in October 2021 when I realized that while we had spent years perfecting small molecule pharmaceutical development, the entire industry was rapidly transitioning toward biologics and biotechnology innovations that made our chemical synthesis expertise increasingly obsolete. The harsh reality crystallized when our market research showed that eight of the top ten pharmaceutical approvals that year were biologics - complex protein therapeutics that our traditional chemistry-based R&D capabilities could never develop.

"We're operating a 20th-century pharmaceutical company in an era dominated by 21st-century biotechnology," announced Dr. Lisa Chen during her strategic assessment presentation, projecting market data showing that biologics commanded 45% of global pharmaceutical revenue despite representing only 18% of approved products. "Traditional small molecule development cannot compete against biologics that achieve superior therapeutic outcomes with patent protection lasting decades rather than years."

"But biotechnology development requires completely different capabilities than our established pharmaceutical expertise," I protested, reviewing investment requirements that showed biologics development could cost 3-4 times more than traditional pharmaceutical R&D. "How can we justify entering biotechnology markets where we have no competitive advantages?"

"Biotechnology represents the future of pharmaceutical innovation," she replied with the conviction of a scientist who had watched traditional pharmaceuticals become commoditized while biologics achieved breakthrough therapeutic results. "Companies that cannot develop biologics will become generic manufacturers serving declining markets while biotechnology companies create innovative treatments that transform medical care."

"And our realistic prospects for achieving meaningful biotechnology capabilities?"

"Modern biotechnology platforms enable mid-sized companies to compete through focused therapeutic applications rather than requiring the broad capabilities that only major pharmaceutical corporations can sustain."

This conversation launched our systematic expansion into biotechnology development that would require building entirely new scientific capabilities while maintaining our existing pharmaceutical operations during a complex technological transition.

The biotechnology market analysis revealed that biological therapeutics were achieving clinical outcomes and commercial success that traditional pharmaceutical approaches could never match, creating competitive imperatives for continued pharmaceutical industry relevance.

"Biotechnology products achieve average gross margins of 87% compared to 34% for traditional pharmaceuticals while commanding premium pricing through superior therapeutic efficacy," reported our biotechnology consultant during our expansion strategy assessment. "Biologics enable treating previously incurable conditions while achieving sustained competitive advantages through complex manufacturing requirements that prevent generic competition."

"What specific advantages do biotechnology products provide over traditional pharmaceutical treatments?" I asked.

"Biologics offer targeted therapeutic mechanisms, superior efficacy profiles, reduced side effects, and personalized treatment approaches that small molecule pharmaceuticals cannot achieve through conventional chemical synthesis."

"And competitive barriers that biotechnology creates compared to traditional pharmaceutical development?"

"Biotechnology manufacturing requires specialized facilities, complex quality control, and regulatory expertise that create substantial barriers to competitive entry while providing sustained market exclusivity."

The biotechnology platform development required investing in cell culture systems, protein purification capabilities, and specialized analytical equipment that could support biological product development and manufacturing.

"Biotechnology platform development requires bioreactor systems, chromatography equipment, and specialized analytical instrumentation costing ₹156 crores for basic biologics development capabilities," announced our biotechnology facilities manager during our expansion planning. "Biological manufacturing demands sterile production environments and complex quality control systems that traditional pharmaceutical facilities cannot support."

"How do biotechnology infrastructure requirements compare to traditional pharmaceutical manufacturing?" I asked.

"Biotechnology production requires living cell systems, controlled environmental conditions, and specialized purification processes that exceed traditional pharmaceutical manufacturing complexity by orders of magnitude."

"And timeline for achieving functional biotechnology development capabilities?"

"Biotechnology infrastructure development requires 18-24 months for basic capabilities plus additional time for regulatory validation and process optimization before commercial production."

The scientific team recruitment proved more challenging than anticipated when we discovered that biotechnology expertise commanded premium compensation while experienced professionals typically preferred established biotechnology companies over traditional pharmaceutical manufacturers attempting biotechnology expansion.

"Biotechnology scientist recruitment requires offering ₹2 - 3 crores annually for experienced professionals plus equity participation and research autonomy," reported our biotechnology talent acquisition manager during our hiring strategy review. "Competitive biotechnology recruitment demands compensation packages that exceed traditional pharmaceutical salary structures while providing research opportunities that showcase scientific expertise."

"What attracts biotechnology scientists to pharmaceutical companies expanding into biologics development?" I asked.

"Research challenge opportunities, publication potential, intellectual property development, and equity participation in biotechnology breakthrough development that enables scientists to benefit from successful innovation commercialization."

"And retention strategies for biotechnology talent in pharmaceutical company environments?"

"Scientific autonomy, professional development opportunities, conference participation, and research funding that enables biotechnology scientists to maintain academic credibility while contributing to commercial product development."

The therapeutic area selection required identifying biotechnology applications where our existing disease expertise could provide competitive advantages while avoiding markets dominated by established biotechnology companies with decades of experience.

"Biotechnology expansion should focus on rare cardiovascular conditions and metabolic disorders where our existing therapeutic knowledge provides competitive advantages," announced Dr. Chen during our biotechnology strategy development. "Focused therapeutic applications enable leveraging existing expertise while building biotechnology capabilities rather than competing broadly against established biologics companies."

"How do we determine optimal biotechnology therapeutic areas for pharmaceutical company expansion?" I asked.

"Therapeutic area evaluation based on unmet medical need, competitive landscape, alignment with existing expertise, and realistic biotechnology development timelines that enable successful market entry."

"And competitive positioning strategies for biotechnology expansion by traditional pharmaceutical companies?"

"Biotechnology competitive positioning through therapeutic focus, innovative development approaches, and partnership strategies that enable competing against established biologics companies."

The partnership strategy involved establishing collaboration relationships with biotechnology companies and academic institutions that could accelerate our biologics development while sharing costs and technical risks.

"Biotechnology partnerships with IIT Bombay, NCL Pune, and three specialized biotechnology companies provide access to expertise and infrastructure that enables biologics development," announced our biotechnology business development manager during our partnership review.

"Collaboration relationships enable biotechnology capabilities that independent development could not achieve efficiently."

"How do biotechnology partnerships enhance pharmaceutical company expansion capabilities?" I asked.

"External partnerships provide specialized expertise, shared infrastructure, risk distribution, and accelerated development that enables biotechnology entry without massive independent investment."

"And intellectual property strategies for biotechnology partnership development?"

"Partnership agreements defining IP ownership, commercialization rights, and revenue sharing that protect biotechnology investments while enabling collaborative development benefits."

The regulatory strategy adaptation required understanding biologics approval pathways while developing specialized expertise in biotechnology regulatory requirements that differed substantially from traditional pharmaceutical submissions.

"Biotechnology regulatory strategy requires understanding biologics licensing applications, manufacturing compliance, and specialized safety assessment that exceed traditional pharmaceutical regulatory complexity," explained Dr. Amanda Richardson during our biotechnology regulatory planning. "Biologics approval demands demonstrated manufacturing consistency, complex quality control, and specialized safety monitoring that traditional pharmaceutical regulatory expertise cannot address adequately."

"How do biotechnology regulatory requirements differ from traditional pharmaceutical approval processes?" I asked.

"Biologics regulation emphasizes manufacturing process validation, facility inspection, and ongoing quality monitoring rather than just clinical efficacy and safety demonstration."

"And biotechnology regulatory timeline implications for pharmaceutical company expansion?"

"Biotechnology regulatory approval requires 12-18 months longer than traditional pharmaceuticals due to manufacturing validation and specialized safety assessment requirements."

The biotechnology expansion results began demonstrating that biological product development could achieve therapeutic differentiation and commercial potential that traditional pharmaceutical approaches could never deliver.

"Biotechnology expansion has generated two promising biologics programs with breakthrough potential and projected peak sales exceeding traditional pharmaceutical products by 200-400%," I announced during our annual biotechnology review. "Biologics development creates competitive advantages and therapeutic opportunities that traditional pharmaceutical capabilities cannot achieve."

Two years after implementing biotechnology expansion, we had achieved biological product development capabilities that positioned us for next-generation pharmaceutical innovation while maintaining traditional pharmaceutical operations.

"The biotechnology expansion taught us that pharmaceutical success requires evolving capabilities rather than optimizing existing approaches when industry transformation demands new technologies," I reflected during our innovation strategy review.

"The key insight was that biotechnology represents pharmaceutical industry evolution rather than just alternative development approaches."

The biotechnology expansion had proven that traditional pharmaceutical companies could successfully transition to biologics development through systematic capability building and strategic partnerships while maintaining competitive positioning during technological transformation.

"Biotechnology expansion demonstrated that pharmaceutical innovation requires embracing new technologies rather than perfecting traditional approaches when industry dynamics favor biological therapeutics," I concluded.

The lesson had become fundamental to our innovation philosophy: biotechnology expansion enabled participating in pharmaceutical industry evolution while creating competitive advantages through next-generation therapeutic development capabilities.

Building Peptide Synthesis Capabilities

The peptide synthesis awakening came during a frustrating technology transfer meeting in November 2021 when I discovered that our promising diabetes treatment - a novel peptide hormone analog designed to revolutionize blood glucose control - remained trapped in academic research because we lacked the specialized synthesis capabilities required to manufacture even gram quantities for clinical testing. The technological gap became embarrassingly obvious when Professor Rajesh Khare from IISc explained that peptide synthesis required entirely different chemistry than our traditional pharmaceutical manufacturing, involving complex solid-phase reactions that our conventional equipment could never support.

"Peptide therapeutics represent the fastest-growing segment of pharmaceutical development, combining the specificity of biologics with the manufacturability of traditional drugs," Professor Khare explained during his presentation on peptide hormone development, projecting market data that showed peptide drugs achieving exceptional therapeutic outcomes while avoiding the complexity of full protein manufacturing. "But peptide synthesis requires specialized chemistry, automated synthesis equipment, and purification capabilities that traditional pharmaceutical companies typically don't possess."

"How different can peptide manufacturing be from our existing pharmaceutical synthesis capabilities?" I asked, though his description of solid-phase peptide synthesis sounded more like advanced chemistry research than pharmaceutical production.

"Peptide synthesis involves sequential amino acid coupling reactions using specialized resins, protecting group chemistry, and sophisticated purification techniques that exceed traditional pharmaceutical synthetic complexity," he replied. "Conventional pharmaceutical manufacturing cannot produce peptides because the chemistry and equipment requirements are fundamentally different."

"And the commercial opportunities for pharmaceutical companies with peptide synthesis capabilities?"

"Peptide therapeutics command premium pricing with minimal generic competition because synthesis complexity creates natural barriers to competitive entry while enabling development of innovative treatments for diabetes, cardiovascular disease, and metabolic disorders."

This conversation launched our systematic development of peptide synthesis capabilities that would enable us to participate in the rapidly expanding peptide therapeutics market while creating competitive advantages through specialized manufacturing expertise.

The peptide market analysis revealed that peptide drugs achieved extraordinary commercial success while remaining protected from generic competition through synthesis complexity that prevented conventional pharmaceutical manufacturers from entering these markets.

"Peptide therapeutics generate average annual revenues of $2-8 billion per approved product with gross margins exceeding 85% while maintaining market exclusivity for 15-20 years through manufacturing barriers," reported our peptide market consultant during our capability development assessment. "Peptide drugs combine the commercial advantages of biologics with synthesis approaches that mid-sized companies can master through focused investment."

"What specific advantages do peptide therapeutics provide over traditional pharmaceutical products?" I asked.

"Peptides achieve targeted therapeutic mechanisms with superior efficacy and safety profiles while avoiding the manufacturing complexity and regulatory requirements that characterize full protein biologics."

"And competitive landscape analysis for peptide pharmaceutical development?"

"Peptide markets remain dominated by specialized biotechnology companies and major pharmaceutical corporations with dedicated peptide capabilities, creating opportunities for companies that can develop synthesis expertise."

The synthesis equipment investment required purchasing automated peptide synthesizers and specialized purification systems that could support both research-scale development and commercial-scale manufacturing.

"Peptide synthesis capabilities require automated solid-phase synthesizers, high-performance liquid chromatography systems, and mass spectrometry equipment costing ₹89 crores for comprehensive peptide development and manufacturing," announced our peptide technology manager during our equipment planning session. "Peptide synthesis demands specialized instrumentation that traditional pharmaceutical equipment cannot support effectively."

"How do peptide synthesis equipment requirements compare to traditional pharmaceutical manufacturing?" I asked.

"Peptide synthesis requires automated chemical coupling systems, sophisticated purification equipment, and analytical instrumentation that exceed traditional pharmaceutical manufacturing complexity while enabling precise control over amino acid sequence and purity."

"And facility requirements for peptide synthesis operations?"

"Peptide manufacturing requires controlled environments, specialized waste management, and quality control capabilities that traditional pharmaceutical facilities must adapt significantly to support effectively."

The chemistry team development required recruiting peptide synthesis specialists with expertise in solid-phase chemistry, protecting group strategies, and purification optimization who commanded premium compensation in competitive talent markets.

"Peptide synthesis team recruitment requires chemists with specialized training in amino acid chemistry, solid-phase synthesis, and peptide purification," explained our peptide talent acquisition manager during our hiring strategy review. "Peptide chemistry expertise commands ₹1 - 2 crores annually for experienced professionals plus research autonomy and publication opportunities."

"What specific expertise distinguishes successful peptide synthesis chemists?" I asked.

"Solid-phase chemistry mastery, protecting group strategy development, coupling reaction optimization, and purification method development that enables producing high-purity peptides at commercial scale."

"And training requirements for traditional pharmaceutical chemists transitioning to peptide synthesis?"

"Peptide chemistry training requires 12-18 months of specialized education plus hands-on experience with automated synthesis equipment and purification techniques."

The process development strategy required establishing systematic approaches to peptide synthesis optimization while developing scalable manufacturing processes that could support both clinical development and commercial production.

"Peptide process development involves optimizing synthesis efficiency, purification yields, and quality control procedures that enable reliable production of pharmaceutical-grade peptides," announced our peptide process manager during our development planning. "Process optimization requires balancing synthesis speed with product quality while achieving cost-effective manufacturing."

"How does peptide process development differ from traditional pharmaceutical manufacturing optimization?" I asked.

"Peptide process development requires optimizing hundreds of sequential chemical reactions while traditional pharmaceutical synthesis typically involves fewer than twenty reaction steps."

"And scalability considerations for peptide synthesis manufacturing?"

"Peptide synthesis scalability requires automated equipment that can handle larger reaction volumes while maintaining precise control over reaction conditions and product quality."

The quality control development required establishing specialized analytical methods for peptide characterization while implementing quality systems that could ensure consistent product specifications.

"Peptide quality control requires mass spectrometry, amino acid analysis, and peptide mapping techniques that exceed traditional pharmaceutical analytical requirements," reported our peptide quality manager during our QC system development. "Peptide characterization demands sophisticated analytical methods that can verify amino acid sequence, purity, and biological activity."

"What quality control capabilities distinguish pharmaceutical-grade peptide manufacturing?" I asked.

"Comprehensive analytical testing including sequence verification, impurity analysis, and stability assessment that ensures peptide products meet pharmaceutical quality standards."

"And regulatory compliance requirements for peptide manufacturing operations?"

"Peptide manufacturing requires FDA validation of synthesis processes, quality control methods, and facility operations that exceed traditional pharmaceutical compliance complexity."

The therapeutic application development focused on cardiovascular and metabolic peptide opportunities where our existing disease expertise could provide competitive advantages in peptide drug development.

"Peptide therapeutic development includes cardiovascular peptide hormones, metabolic enzyme inhibitors, and diabetes treatment peptides that align with our therapeutic expertise," announced Dr. Chen during our peptide pipeline planning. "Focused therapeutic applications enable leveraging existing disease knowledge while building peptide synthesis capabilities."

"How do peptide therapeutics enhance our existing cardiovascular and diabetes portfolios?" I asked.

"Peptide drugs provide superior therapeutic mechanisms and clinical outcomes compared to traditional small molecule treatments while enabling premium pricing and competitive differentiation."

"And development timeline for peptide therapeutic products?"

"Peptide drug development requires 4-6 years from synthesis optimization to regulatory approval, comparable to traditional pharmaceutical timelines but with superior commercial potential."

The peptide synthesis results demonstrated that specialized chemistry capabilities could enable participating in high-value therapeutic markets while creating competitive advantages through manufacturing expertise.

"Peptide synthesis capabilities have generated three promising therapeutic programs with breakthrough potential and projected peak sales exceeding ₹500 crores annually per product," I announced during our annual peptide review. "Peptide capabilities create competitive advantages and commercial opportunities that traditional pharmaceutical manufacturing cannot achieve."

"And competitive positioning improvements from peptide synthesis expertise?" asked our biotechnology development committee.

"Peptide synthesis expertise provides technological differentiation that enables competing in premium therapeutic markets while creating barriers to competitive entry."

Two years after building peptide synthesis capabilities, we had established specialized manufacturing expertise that positioned us in rapidly growing therapeutic markets while creating sustainable competitive advantages.

"Building peptide synthesis capabilities taught us that pharmaceutical success requires developing specialized technologies rather than just scaling traditional manufacturing approaches," I reflected during our technology strategy review.

"The key insight was that peptide synthesis enables accessing premium therapeutic markets through specialized chemistry that creates natural competitive barriers."

The peptide synthesis development had proven that pharmaceutical companies could achieve technological differentiation through specialized capabilities that opened new therapeutic opportunities while creating competitive advantages.

"Peptide synthesis capabilities demonstrated that pharmaceutical innovation requires investing in specialized technologies that enable accessing high-value therapeutic markets," I concluded.

The lesson had become fundamental to our technology philosophy: peptide synthesis capabilities enabled participating in premium pharmaceutical markets through specialized chemistry that created sustainable competitive advantages and therapeutic differentiation.

Monoclonal Antibody Development

The monoclonal antibody awakening came during a sobering visit to Biocon's Bangalore facility in December 2021 when I witnessed firsthand the sophisticated biomanufacturing capabilities required to produce therapeutic antibodies that were generating billions in revenue while our traditional pharmaceutical expertise remained completely inadequate for participating in what had become the most valuable segment of modern medicine. The technological chasm became painfully obvious when Dr. Kiran Mazumdar Shaw casually mentioned that their single monoclonal antibody facility represented more advanced biotechnology than our entire pharmaceutical manufacturing operation.

"Monoclonal antibodies have revolutionized cancer treatment, autoimmune therapy, and cardiovascular medicine while achieving commercial success that exceeds traditional pharmaceuticals by orders of magnitude," Dr. Shaw explained during our facility tour, gesturing toward bioreactors containing genetically engineered cells producing therapeutic proteins worth more per gram than gold. "But antibody development requires biological expertise, specialized manufacturing, and regulatory capabilities that traditional pharmaceutical companies cannot adapt from small molecule experience."

"How fundamentally different is antibody development from our existing pharmaceutical capabilities?" I asked, though the complexity of the biological systems surrounding us suggested the answer would be intimidating.

"Monoclonal antibodies are living therapeutic systems produced by engineered mammalian cells rather than chemical synthesis," she replied with the authority of someone who had built India's biotechnology industry. "Antibody manufacturing requires understanding cell biology, protein engineering, and biological quality control that pharmaceutical chemistry cannot address effectively."

"And the commercial potential for companies that can develop therapeutic antibodies?"

"Successful monoclonal antibodies generate $5-15 billion annual revenue with 20+ year market exclusivity through biological complexity that prevents generic competition while enabling treatment of previously incurable conditions."

This conversation crystallized our entry into monoclonal antibody development as the ultimate pharmaceutical biotechnology challenge that could transform us from a traditional drug company into a next-generation biologics innovator.

The antibody market analysis revealed that therapeutic antibodies commanded the highest valuations and most sustained competitive advantages in pharmaceutical markets while requiring capabilities that few companies could master successfully.

"Monoclonal antibody therapeutics represent 60% of new pharmaceutical approvals with average peak sales of $8.3 billion per product while maintaining market exclusivity for 15-25 years through biological manufacturing complexity," reported our antibody market consultant during our development strategy assessment. "Antibody drugs achieve therapeutic outcomes that small molecules cannot deliver while commanding premium pricing that exceeds traditional pharmaceutical margins by 300-500%."

"What specific therapeutic advantages enable antibodies to achieve such exceptional commercial success?" I asked.

"Monoclonal antibodies provide targeted therapeutic mechanisms, superior efficacy profiles, and personalized treatment approaches that traditional pharmaceuticals cannot achieve through chemical synthesis."

"And competitive barriers that protect antibody therapeutics from generic competition?"

"Antibody manufacturing requires mammalian cell culture, complex protein purification, and sophisticated quality control that create natural barriers to biosimilar competition while providing sustained market exclusivity."

The cell line development required establishing genetically engineered mammalian cell systems that could produce therapeutic antibodies with consistent quality and commercial-scale yields.

"Monoclonal antibody production requires developing stable Chinese hamster ovary cell lines that can produce therapeutic proteins with human-compatible glycosylation patterns," announced our newly hired Antibody Development Director, Dr. Ravi Krishnamurthy, during our cell line strategy planning. "Cell line development involves genetic engineering, clone selection, and stability testing that requires 12-18 months before achieving production-ready cell systems."

"How does cell line development compare to traditional pharmaceutical manufacturing processes?" I asked.

"Cell line development requires biological expertise and genetic engineering capabilities that exceed traditional pharmaceutical chemistry by requiring understanding of living cellular systems rather than chemical reactions."

"And intellectual property considerations for therapeutic antibody cell lines?"

"Cell line development generates proprietary biological systems that can be protected through trade secrets and manufacturing know-how that competitors cannot easily replicate."

The biomanufacturing infrastructure required investing in mammalian cell culture systems, protein purification equipment, and specialized quality control capabilities that could support antibody production from research scale through commercial manufacturing.

"Antibody biomanufacturing requires bioreactor systems, chromatography equipment, and viral safety testing capabilities costing ₹234 crores for integrated antibody development and production," announced our biomanufacturing director during our facility planning session. "Antibody production demands sterile manufacturing environments and complex quality systems that traditional pharmaceutical facilities cannot support without massive modification."

"What biomanufacturing capabilities distinguish successful antibody development companies?" I asked.

"Mammalian cell culture expertise, protein purification optimization, and viral safety validation that enables producing pharmaceutical-grade antibodies that meet regulatory requirements for therapeutic applications."

"And scalability requirements for commercial antibody manufacturing?"

"Antibody biomanufacturing requires 2,000-20,000 liter bioreactor systems with sophisticated process control and quality monitoring that enables reliable commercial-scale production."

The antibody engineering capabilities required developing protein design expertise that could optimize therapeutic antibodies for enhanced efficacy, reduced immunogenicity, and improved pharmacological properties.

"Antibody engineering involves optimizing protein structure, binding affinity, and pharmacokinetic properties through computational design and laboratory testing," explained Dr. Krishnamurthy during our antibody design planning. "Protein engineering enables developing superior therapeutic antibodies that achieve competitive advantages through enhanced clinical performance."

"How does antibody engineering differ from traditional pharmaceutical development?" I asked.

"Antibody engineering requires understanding protein structure and function rather than small molecule chemistry, involving biological design principles that pharmaceutical chemistry cannot address."

"And competitive advantages from proprietary antibody engineering capabilities?"

"Antibody engineering enables developing differentiated therapeutic products that achieve superior clinical outcomes while creating intellectual property that competitors cannot easily replicate."

The regulatory strategy adaptation required understanding biologics licensing applications while developing specialized expertise in antibody safety assessment and manufacturing compliance that exceeded traditional pharmaceutical regulatory complexity.

"Monoclonal antibody regulatory strategy requires biologics license applications, manufacturing facility validation, and specialized safety assessment that exceed traditional pharmaceutical regulatory requirements," explained Dr. Amanda Richardson during our antibody regulatory planning. "Antibody approval demands demonstrated manufacturing consistency, viral safety validation, and immunogenicity assessment that traditional pharmaceutical regulatory expertise cannot address adequately."

"What regulatory advantages do therapeutic antibodies provide compared to traditional pharmaceutical development?" I asked.

"Antibody therapeutics often qualify for orphan drug designation, breakthrough therapy status, and expedited approval pathways that can accelerate market entry while providing extended market exclusivity."

"And regulatory timeline implications for antibody development programs?"

"Antibody regulatory approval typically requires 10-15 years from discovery to market but provides 20+ years of market exclusivity through biological complexity and patent protection."

The therapeutic focus strategy required identifying antibody opportunities in cardiovascular and metabolic diseases where our existing expertise could provide competitive advantages while avoiding crowded oncology markets dominated by established biotechnology companies.

"Antibody therapeutic development should focus on cardiovascular applications including PCSK9 inhibitors for cholesterol management and metabolic targets for diabetes treatment," announced Dr. Chen during our antibody pipeline planning. "Focused therapeutic applications enable leveraging existing disease expertise while building antibody development capabilities."

"How do cardiovascular antibodies complement our existing therapeutic portfolio?" I asked.

"Cardiovascular antibodies provide breakthrough therapeutic mechanisms that exceed small molecule efficacy while enabling premium pricing and competitive differentiation in our core therapeutic areas."

"And development timeline for cardiovascular antibody therapeutics?"

"Antibody development requires 8-12 years from target identification to regulatory approval but provides sustained competitive advantages through biological complexity and superior therapeutic outcomes."

The monoclonal antibody development results began demonstrating that biological therapeutics could achieve therapeutic breakthroughs while creating competitive advantages that traditional pharmaceutical approaches could never deliver.

"Monoclonal antibody development has generated two promising cardiovascular programs with breakthrough potential and projected peak sales exceeding ₹2,000 crores annually per product," I announced during our annual antibody review. "Antibody capabilities create competitive advantages and therapeutic opportunities that traditional pharmaceutical development cannot achieve."

"And competitive positioning improvements from antibody development expertise?" asked our biotechnology development committee.

"Antibody development capabilities provide technological leadership that enables competing against major biotechnology companies while creating barriers to competitive entry."

Three years after implementing monoclonal antibody development, we had achieved biological therapeutic capabilities that positioned us among next-generation pharmaceutical innovators while creating sustainable competitive advantages through specialized biotechnology expertise.

"Monoclonal antibody development taught us that pharmaceutical leadership requires mastering biological therapeutics rather than just optimizing traditional chemical approaches," I reflected during our biotechnology strategy review.

"The key insight was that antibody therapeutics represent the future of pharmaceutical innovation through biological precision that small molecule drugs cannot achieve."

The monoclonal antibody development had proven that traditional pharmaceutical companies could successfully transition to biological therapeutics through systematic capability building while creating competitive advantages that exceeded traditional pharmaceutical approaches.

"Monoclonal antibody development demonstrated that pharmaceutical innovation requires embracing biological complexity rather than avoiding it when therapeutic superiority demands biological precision," I concluded.

The lesson had become fundamental to our biotechnology philosophy: monoclonal antibody development enabled creating next-generation therapeutic solutions while establishing competitive advantages through biological expertise that traditional pharmaceutical chemistry could never provide.

Partnership with Biotech Startups

The biotech startup partnership revelation came during a frustrating board meeting in January 2022 when I realized that despite our ₹340 crore biotechnology investment, we were still years away from achieving meaningful therapeutic breakthroughs while nimble biotech startups across Bangalore and Hyderabad were developing innovative biological therapeutics with fraction of our resources but exponentially faster innovation timelines. The competitive disadvantage became painfully obvious when our head of R&D mentioned that a three-person startup had achieved proof-of-concept for a novel cancer immunotherapy in eighteen months while our well-funded antibody program remained stuck in cell line optimization after two years of development.

"We're approaching biotechnology like a traditional pharmaceutical company trying to build everything internally, while successful biotech innovation happens through collaborative ecosystems that combine specialized expertise from multiple organizations," announced Dr. Lisa Chen during her quarterly innovation review, projecting a map showing 47 biotech startups within 50 kilometers of our Bangalore facility. "Biotech startups achieve breakthrough innovation through focused expertise and risk-taking that large pharmaceutical organizations cannot replicate through internal development."

"But partnering with startups seems risky when we're investing hundreds of crores in biotechnology capabilities," I protested, though I was beginning to recognize that our internal development approach might be inherently disadvantaged compared to startup innovation models.

"Startup partnerships enable accessing breakthrough innovation while sharing development risks and costs," she replied with the enthusiasm of someone who had been networking with biotech entrepreneurs for months. "Biotech innovation requires entrepreneurial speed and focused expertise that traditional pharmaceutical companies cannot achieve through conventional R&D approaches."

"And our competitive advantages in biotech startup partnerships compared to venture capital investors or major pharmaceutical companies?"

"Mid-sized pharmaceutical companies can provide regulatory expertise, manufacturing capabilities, and commercialization support that startups need while offering partnership terms that major corporations cannot match."

This conversation launched our systematic biotech startup partnership strategy that would transform us from an isolated pharmaceutical company into a collaborative innovation hub leveraging external biotechnology expertise.

The startup ecosystem analysis revealed that India's biotech startup community was generating breakthrough innovations while struggling with scale-up challenges that our pharmaceutical capabilities could address through strategic partnerships.

"Indian biotech startups have developed innovative therapeutic approaches including CAR-T cell therapies, gene editing applications, and novel drug delivery systems that exceed our internal capabilities," reported our newly hired VP of Innovation Partnerships, Dr. Kavya Menon, during her ecosystem assessment. "Startup innovation focuses on breakthrough discoveries while lacking regulatory expertise and manufacturing capabilities that pharmaceutical companies can provide."

"What specific advantages do biotech startups provide compared to internal R&D development?" I asked.

"Startup innovation enables rapid experimentation, focused expertise, and entrepreneurial risk-taking that traditional pharmaceutical R&D cannot achieve through conventional development approaches."

"And partnership opportunities that align startup innovation with pharmaceutical commercialization capabilities?"

"Startups provide breakthrough innovation while pharmaceutical partners enable regulatory development, manufacturing scale-up, and global commercialization that startups cannot achieve independently."

The partnership evaluation criteria required developing systematic approaches to assess startup technologies while identifying collaboration opportunities that could accelerate our biotechnology development without excessive risk exposure.

"Biotech startup evaluation requires assessing scientific merit, intellectual property strength, team expertise, and commercialization potential for early-stage technologies," announced Dr. Menon during our partnership strategy development. "Startup partnerships involve higher technical risks but enable accessing breakthrough innovations that internal development cannot achieve within reasonable timelines."

"What criteria distinguish attractive biotech startup partnership opportunities?" I asked.

"Novel therapeutic mechanisms, strong intellectual property, experienced scientific teams, and realistic pathways to clinical development that align with our therapeutic expertise and commercial capabilities."

"And due diligence requirements for biotech startup partnership evaluation?"

"Scientific validation, IP analysis, team assessment, and commercial feasibility evaluation that determines partnership value while managing development risks."

The collaboration structure development required creating partnership models that could provide startups with development support while enabling our company to participate in breakthrough innovation success.

"Biotech startup partnerships require flexible collaboration structures including licensing agreements, joint ventures, and equity investments that align startup innovation with pharmaceutical development capabilities," explained our business development manager during partnership planning. "Partnership structures must provide startups with development resources while enabling pharmaceutical companies to benefit from breakthrough innovation success."

"How do we structure partnerships that benefit both startups and established pharmaceutical companies?" I asked.

"Collaborative agreements with shared development costs, milestone payments, and revenue sharing that provide startups with resources while enabling pharmaceutical companies to access breakthrough innovations."

"And intellectual property considerations for biotech startup partnerships?"

"Partnership agreements defining IP ownership, development rights, and commercialization responsibilities that protect both startup innovations and pharmaceutical investments."

The portfolio development strategy involved establishing partnerships with multiple biotech startups across different therapeutic areas while maintaining focus on cardiovascular and metabolic applications that aligned with our expertise.

"Biotech partnership portfolio includes collaborations with six startups developing cardiovascular gene therapy, diabetes cell therapy, and inflammatory disease immunotherapy," announced Dr. Chen during our partnership review. "Portfolio diversification enables accessing multiple breakthrough technologies while managing development risks through partnership rather than internal investment."

"How do we manage multiple startup partnerships while maintaining strategic focus?" I asked.

"Partnership portfolio management through staged development agreements, milestone-based progression, and systematic evaluation that enables supporting multiple innovations while concentrating resources on most promising opportunities."

"And competitive advantages from biotech startup partnership portfolio?"

"Partnership portfolio provides access to breakthrough innovations across multiple therapeutic areas while enabling faster development timelines than internal R&D could achieve."

The integration support systems required developing capabilities to provide startups with regulatory guidance, manufacturing support, and commercialization expertise while preserving their innovative culture and entrepreneurial speed.

"Biotech startup integration requires providing regulatory expertise, manufacturing capabilities, and commercial support while maintaining startup innovation culture and decision-making speed," reported our partnership operations manager during integration planning. "Support systems must enhance startup capabilities without imposing pharmaceutical bureaucracy that could slow innovation development."

"What specific support capabilities distinguish successful pharmaceutical-startup partnerships?" I asked.

"Regulatory guidance, clinical development expertise, manufacturing scale-up support, and global commercialization capabilities that enable startups to advance breakthrough innovations toward market success."

"And maintaining startup innovation culture within pharmaceutical partnership frameworks?"

"Partnership structures that provide resources and expertise while preserving startup autonomy for scientific decision-making and development strategy."

The early partnership results demonstrated that biotech startup collaborations could accelerate our innovation timeline while providing access to breakthrough technologies that internal development could never achieve efficiently.

"Biotech startup partnerships have generated access to three breakthrough therapeutic platforms including gene editing for cardiovascular disease, cell therapy for diabetes, and immunotherapy for inflammatory conditions," I announced during our annual partnership review. "Startup collaborations provide innovation capabilities that exceed our internal R&D potential while sharing development risks and costs."

"And development timeline improvements from startup partnerships compared to internal biotechnology programs?" asked our innovation committee.

"Startup partnerships have accelerated breakthrough technology access by 2-3 years compared to internal development while providing access to innovations that our capabilities could never generate independently."

"What competitive advantages result from biotech startup partnership strategy?"

"Partnership strategy provides access to breakthrough innovations while enabling faster market entry and reduced development risks compared to traditional pharmaceutical R&D approaches."

Two years after implementing biotech startup partnerships, we had established innovation capabilities that exceeded major pharmaceutical companies while maintaining entrepreneurial speed and breakthrough potential.

"Partnership with biotech startups taught us that pharmaceutical innovation requires collaborative ecosystems rather than isolated internal development," I reflected during our innovation strategy review.

"The key insight was that startup partnerships enable accessing breakthrough innovations while sharing risks and accelerating development timelines that internal R&D cannot achieve."

The biotech startup partnership strategy had proven that traditional pharmaceutical companies could enhance innovation capabilities through collaborative approaches that leveraged external expertise while providing commercialization support.

"Biotech startup partnerships demonstrated that pharmaceutical success requires building innovation ecosystems rather than just internal R&D capabilities," I concluded.

The lesson had become fundamental to our innovation philosophy: biotech startup partnerships enabled accessing breakthrough technologies while sharing development risks and accelerating innovation timelines that traditional pharmaceutical approaches could never achieve independently.

The Oncology Biosimilar Portfolio

The oncology biosimilar awakening came during a heartbreaking encounter at Tata Memorial Hospital in February 2022 when I met Mrs. Sunita Sharma, a 47-year-old teacher whose breast cancer treatment was costing her family ₹4.2 lakhs monthly for imported monoclonal antibody therapy that represented her only hope for survival. The cruel irony struck me when her oncologist mentioned that identical biosimilar versions of her life-saving treatment were available in Europe for 60% less cost, but regulatory barriers and commercial priorities had prevented these affordable alternatives from reaching Indian patients who desperately needed access to breakthrough cancer therapies.

"Cancer patients in India pay premium prices for imported biologics while identical biosimilar alternatives remain unavailable due to pharmaceutical companies avoiding oncology markets they perceive as too complex or risky," explained Dr. Rajesh Gupta, her treating oncologist, with the frustration of someone watching patients suffer from financial barriers to essential medical care. "Oncology biosimilars could revolutionize cancer treatment access while generating substantial returns for companies willing to navigate regulatory complexity."

"But oncology biosimilar development must require specialized expertise that we've never possessed," I replied, though Mrs. Sharma's situation was forcing me to consider whether our biotechnology capabilities could address critical unmet medical needs in cancer therapy.

"Oncology biosimilars require biological expertise and regulatory knowledge rather than novel drug discovery," he responded. "Companies with biotechnology capabilities can develop biosimilar cancer treatments that provide identical therapeutic outcomes at significantly reduced costs."

"And the commercial potential for oncology biosimilar development?"

"Oncology biosimilars represent billion-dollar market opportunities with sustained competitive advantages through regulatory barriers while enabling access to life-saving cancer treatments that patients otherwise cannot afford."

This conversation crystallized our entry into oncology biosimilar development as both a moral imperative to improve cancer treatment access and a strategic business opportunity that could leverage our biotechnology investments while serving desperately underserved patient populations.

The oncology biosimilar market analysis revealed massive commercial opportunities combined with urgent medical needs that created compelling business and humanitarian justifications for biosimilar development.

"Oncology biosimilar markets represent ₹25,000-45,000 crores annual opportunities globally with 40-60% cost savings compared to originator biologics while achieving identical therapeutic outcomes," reported our oncology market consultant during our biosimilar strategy assessment. "Oncology biosimilars enable expanding cancer treatment access while generating substantial returns through premium pricing that remains significantly below originator product costs."

"What specific market advantages distinguish oncology biosimilars from other therapeutic areas?" I asked.

"Oncology biosimilars command premium pricing due to life-saving therapeutic value while achieving rapid market penetration through physician and patient demand for affordable cancer treatment alternatives."

"And competitive landscape analysis for oncology biosimilar development?"

"Oncology biosimilar markets remain underserved by established pharmaceutical companies due to regulatory complexity and perceived development risks, creating opportunities for companies with biological capabilities."

The regulatory strategy development required understanding oncology biosimilar approval pathways while developing specialized expertise in cancer therapy safety assessment and therapeutic equivalence demonstration.

"Oncology biosimilar regulatory approval requires demonstrating analytical similarity, pharmacokinetic equivalence, and clinical comparability to originator cancer therapies," announced Dr. Amanda Richardson during our oncology regulatory planning. "Biosimilar approval demands comprehensive analytical characterization and clinical studies that prove therapeutic equivalence while ensuring patient safety."

"How do oncology biosimilar regulatory requirements compare to traditional pharmaceutical approvals?" I asked.

"Oncology biosimilars require biological characterization, immunogenicity assessment, and clinical efficacy studies that exceed traditional pharmaceutical regulatory complexity while providing expedited approval pathways for life-saving treatments."

"And regulatory timeline advantages for oncology biosimilar development?"

"Biosimilar approval requires 5-7 years compared to 12-15 years for novel cancer drug development while providing immediate market access upon originator patent expiration."

The manufacturing adaptation required modifying our biotechnology capabilities to produce oncology-grade monoclonal antibodies while implementing specialized quality control systems for cancer therapeutic applications.

"Oncology biosimilar manufacturing requires pharmaceutical-grade protein production with enhanced purity specifications and specialized quality control for cancer therapeutic applications," announced our biosimilar manufacturing director during our production planning. "Cancer therapy manufacturing demands sterile production environments and rigorous quality systems that ensure patient safety for life-threatening conditions."

"What manufacturing capabilities distinguish oncology biosimilar production from traditional biotechnology manufacturing?" I asked.

"Oncology manufacturing requires enhanced purification, specialized stability testing, and rigorous quality control that ensures therapeutic equivalence while meeting cancer therapy safety standards."

"And scalability requirements for oncology biosimilar commercial production?"

"Oncology biosimilar production requires flexible manufacturing that can support multiple product development while achieving cost efficiencies that enable affordable cancer treatment pricing."

The therapeutic portfolio selection focused on high-impact cancer treatments including breast cancer, lung cancer, and colorectal cancer therapies where biosimilar alternatives could provide significant cost savings while maintaining therapeutic efficacy.

"Oncology biosimilar portfolio includes trastuzumab for breast cancer, bevacizumab for colorectal cancer, and rituximab for lymphoma," announced Dr. Chen during our portfolio planning. "Portfolio focuses on high-volume cancer treatments where biosimilar alternatives can provide substantial patient access improvements while generating significant commercial returns."

"How do we prioritize oncology biosimilar opportunities for maximum patient impact?" I asked.

"Portfolio prioritization based on patient population size, treatment cost reduction potential, and therapeutic importance for cancer care that enables maximizing both commercial success and patient access improvement."

"And competitive advantages from focused oncology biosimilar portfolio?"

"Therapeutic focus enables developing specialized expertise and market positioning that creates competitive advantages while building oncology commercial capabilities."

The market access strategy required developing relationships with cancer treatment centers while building oncologist confidence in biosimilar therapeutic equivalence and patient safety.

"Oncology market access requires clinical evidence communication, oncologist education, and patient support programs that build confidence in biosimilar therapeutic equivalence," announced our oncology commercial director during our market access planning. "Oncology marketing emphasizes clinical data and safety evidence rather than cost advantages alone."

"How does oncology biosimilar marketing differ from traditional pharmaceutical promotion?" I asked.

"Oncology marketing requires clinical expertise and therapeutic education that builds physician confidence in biosimilar safety and efficacy for life-threatening conditions."

"And patient access programs for oncology biosimilar products?"

"Patient support programs including financial assistance, therapy management, and clinical monitoring that ensure cancer patients can access and benefit from biosimilar treatments."

The clinical development program required conducting comparative studies that could demonstrate therapeutic equivalence while building oncologist confidence in biosimilar cancer treatment outcomes.

"Oncology biosimilar clinical development includes pharmacokinetic studies, efficacy trials, and safety monitoring that demonstrate therapeutic equivalence to originator cancer treatments," reported our clinical development manager during our study planning. "Clinical evidence provides oncologist confidence while meeting regulatory requirements for biosimilar approval."

"What clinical evidence requirements distinguish oncology biosimilar development?" I asked.

"Oncology biosimilars require comparative efficacy studies and safety monitoring that prove therapeutic equivalence for life-threatening conditions while ensuring patient outcomes remain identical to originator treatments."

"And timeline advantages from oncology biosimilar clinical development?"

"Biosimilar clinical development requires 3-4 years compared to 8-12 years for novel cancer drug development while providing equivalent therapeutic outcomes."

The oncology biosimilar results demonstrated that biological therapeutics could address critical unmet medical needs while generating sustainable competitive advantages through specialized therapeutic focus.

"Oncology biosimilar development has generated three promising cancer therapy programs with regulatory approval potential and projected revenues exceeding ₹800 crores annually," I announced during our annual oncology review. "Biosimilar capabilities enable improving cancer treatment access while creating competitive advantages in high-value therapeutic markets."

"And oncologist acceptance of our biosimilar cancer treatments?" asked our oncology development committee.

"Oncologist engagement has exceeded expectations through clinical evidence and therapeutic expertise that demonstrates biosimilar safety and efficacy for cancer treatment."

Two years after implementing oncology biosimilar development, we had established cancer therapy capabilities that addressed critical patient needs while creating competitive advantages in premium therapeutic markets.

"The oncology biosimilar portfolio taught us that biotechnology capabilities can address urgent medical needs while generating sustainable competitive advantages," I reflected during our therapeutic strategy review.

"The key insight was that oncology biosimilars enable improving patient access to life-saving treatments while creating commercial opportunities through specialized therapeutic expertise."

The oncology biosimilar development had proven that pharmaceutical companies could achieve meaningful therapeutic impact through biological capabilities while generating competitive advantages in high-value medical markets.

"Oncology biosimilar development demonstrated that biotechnology success requires balancing commercial objectives with medical responsibility to improve patient access to essential treatments," I concluded.

The lesson had become fundamental to our therapeutic mission: oncology biosimilar capabilities enabled creating both sustainable competitive advantages and meaningful medical impact through providing affordable access to breakthrough cancer treatments that could save lives while generating substantial commercial returns.

Chapter 24

The Global Manufacturing Network

From Single Site to Worldwide Production

The global manufacturing awakening came during a devastating supply chain crisis in March 2022 when a contamination incident at our Mumbai facility forced us to halt production of seventeen different products, leaving patients across twelve countries without access to essential cardiovascular medications while I watched our competitors seamlessly shift production between facilities across multiple continents. The vulnerability of our single-site manufacturing became painfully obvious when European distributors started switching to alternative suppliers who could guarantee uninterrupted supply through global production networks that made our isolated operations look dangerously primitive.

"We're operating like a pharmaceutical company from the 1980s with all production concentrated in one location while our competitors have built resilient global manufacturing networks that can withstand facility disruptions, regulatory shutdowns, and supply chain interruptions," announced our newly hired VP of Global Operations, Dr. Sarah Williams, as she presented competitive analysis showing that major pharmaceutical companies operated 8-15 manufacturing sites across different continents. "Single-site manufacturing creates existential risks that global pharmaceutical operations cannot tolerate."

"But building multiple manufacturing facilities requires enormous capital investment that could consume years of cash flow," I protested, though our recent production shutdown had cost ₹67 crores in lost revenue plus incalculable damage to customer relationships. "How can we justify the complexity and expense of global manufacturing when our current facility serves our needs?"

"Global manufacturing provides supply security, regulatory flexibility, and competitive advantages that single-site operations cannot achieve," she replied with the conviction of someone who had managed international pharmaceutical operations. "Manufacturing network effects create competitive barriers while enabling market access that isolated facilities cannot support."

"And our realistic timeline for developing global manufacturing capabilities?"

"Global manufacturing network development requires 3-5 years of systematic facility development, regulatory approvals, and operational integration that transforms manufacturing from cost center to competitive advantage."

This conversation launched our systematic development of a global manufacturing network that would transform us from a vulnerable single-site manufacturer to a resilient international pharmaceutical company with production capabilities spanning multiple continents.

The manufacturing strategy analysis revealed that global production networks enabled competitive advantages through supply security, regulatory flexibility, and market access optimization that single-site operations could never achieve.

"Global manufacturing networks provide supply chain resilience, regulatory redundancy, and market access advantages while enabling cost optimization through location-specific production strategies," reported our manufacturing consultant during our network development assessment. "Multi-site manufacturing creates competitive barriers through operational complexity that smaller companies cannot replicate while providing supply security that customers increasingly demand."

"What specific advantages do global manufacturing networks provide over single-site operations?" I asked.

"Supply chain security, regulatory backup capabilities, market access optimization, and cost efficiency through location-specific production strategies that single-site manufacturing cannot deliver."

"And competitive positioning advantages from global manufacturing capabilities?"

"Global networks enable serving international markets while providing supply security and regulatory flexibility that customers require for strategic supplier relationships."

The site selection strategy required identifying optimal locations for pharmaceutical manufacturing while balancing regulatory requirements, cost considerations, and market access advantages across different geographic regions.

"Global manufacturing site selection includes European facility for EU market access, US facility for FDA-regulated markets, and Asian facility for regional supply optimization," announced Dr. Williams during our location planning session. "Site selection balances regulatory advantages, cost efficiency, and market proximity while ensuring comprehensive global coverage."

"What criteria determine optimal pharmaceutical manufacturing locations?" I asked.

"Regulatory environment quality, skilled workforce availability, infrastructure capabilities, cost competitiveness, and market access advantages that enable efficient production while meeting pharmaceutical quality standards."

"And timeline for establishing functional manufacturing facilities in multiple locations?"

"Manufacturing facility development requires 18-36 months per site including construction, equipment installation, regulatory approval, and operational validation before achieving commercial production capability."

The regulatory coordination required developing expertise in multiple pharmaceutical regulatory systems while establishing manufacturing compliance capabilities that could satisfy FDA, EMA, and other international quality standards simultaneously.

"Global manufacturing requires maintaining FDA, EMA, WHO-GMP, and other regulatory compliance across multiple facilities while ensuring consistent quality standards and production processes," explained Dr. Amanda Richardson during our regulatory planning. "Multi-site regulatory compliance demands systematic quality management and ongoing coordination that exceeds single-facility regulatory requirements."

"How does global manufacturing affect pharmaceutical regulatory complexity?" I asked.

"Global manufacturing multiplies regulatory requirements while providing backup approval capabilities that enable continued market access if individual facilities encounter regulatory issues."

"And regulatory advantages from multi-site manufacturing capabilities?"

"Regulatory diversification enables market access continuity while providing flexibility to optimize production based on regulatory efficiency and market requirements."

The technology integration strategy required standardizing manufacturing processes across multiple facilities while implementing systems that could coordinate global production planning and quality management.

"Global manufacturing integration requires standardized equipment, unified quality systems, and coordinated production planning that enables seamless operation across multiple facilities," announced our technology integration manager during our systems planning. "Manufacturing network integration demands technology platforms that can coordinate complex global operations while maintaining pharmaceutical quality standards."

"What technology capabilities distinguish successful global pharmaceutical manufacturing?" I asked.

"Integrated production planning, real-time quality monitoring, supply chain coordination, and regulatory compliance management that enables optimizing global manufacturing efficiency while ensuring consistent product quality."

"And operational advantages from integrated global manufacturing systems?"

"Technology integration enables production optimization, supply chain efficiency, and quality assurance that maximizes global manufacturing network benefits while minimizing operational complexity."

The supply chain optimization required developing sophisticated logistics capabilities that could coordinate raw material procurement, production scheduling, and finished product distribution across a global manufacturing network.

"Global manufacturing supply chain requires coordinated raw material sourcing, production planning, and distribution logistics that optimize efficiency while ensuring supply security," reported our supply chain director during our logistics planning. "Supply chain optimization enables cost reduction while improving delivery reliability through manufacturing network flexibility."

"How does global manufacturing affect pharmaceutical supply chain management?" I asked.

"Global manufacturing enables supply chain optimization through production location flexibility while providing backup capabilities that ensure continued supply despite individual facility disruptions."

"And competitive advantages from optimized global pharmaceutical supply chains?"

"Supply chain efficiency enables cost competitiveness while supply security provides customer confidence that creates competitive advantages over single-site manufacturers."

The quality management system required implementing standardized quality controls across multiple facilities while ensuring consistent pharmaceutical quality regardless of production location.

"Global manufacturing quality management requires standardized processes, unified quality systems, and coordinated compliance monitoring that ensures consistent pharmaceutical quality across all production facilities," announced our global quality manager during our quality planning. "Quality standardization enables leveraging manufacturing network benefits while maintaining pharmaceutical quality standards that regulatory agencies require."

"What quality management capabilities distinguish successful global pharmaceutical manufacturing?" I asked.

"Standardized quality processes, integrated compliance monitoring, and coordinated quality assurance that ensures consistent pharmaceutical quality while enabling global manufacturing flexibility."

"And quality advantages from global manufacturing compared to single-site operations?"

"Quality system redundancy enables continued production and supply security while providing backup capabilities that ensure pharmaceutical quality standards during facility disruptions."

The global manufacturing network results demonstrated that multi-site production could provide competitive advantages while ensuring supply security that single-facility operations could never achieve.

"Global manufacturing network development has established production capabilities in Europe, Asia, and North America that provide supply security while enabling market access optimization," I announced during our annual manufacturing review. "Manufacturing network creates competitive advantages through operational resilience and regulatory flexibility while reducing supply chain risks."

"And cost implications of global manufacturing compared to single-site operations?" asked our operations committee.

"Global manufacturing achieves 23% cost reduction through production optimization while providing supply security and market access advantages that justify network investment."

Three years after implementing global manufacturing network development, we had achieved operational resilience and competitive advantages that transformed our market positioning while ensuring supply security.

"The global manufacturing network taught us that pharmaceutical success requires operational resilience rather than just cost efficiency," I reflected during our manufacturing strategy review.

"The key insight was that manufacturing networks create competitive advantages through supply security and operational flexibility that single-site operations cannot provide."

The global manufacturing development had proven that international pharmaceutical companies could achieve competitive advantages through manufacturing networks that provided operational resilience while enabling market access optimization.

"Global manufacturing network demonstrated that pharmaceutical success requires treating manufacturing as strategic capability rather than just production function," I concluded.

The lesson had become fundamental to our operational philosophy: global manufacturing networks enabled creating competitive advantages through operational resilience that provided supply security and market access capabilities that single-site manufacturing could never achieve.

Establishing Facilities Across Continents

The global facility establishment revelation came during a particularly stressful negotiation with European distributors in April 2022 when they bluntly informed me that our Indian manufacturing base had become a commercial liability rather than a cost advantage, because European healthcare systems increasingly demanded local production capabilities to ensure supply security and regulatory compliance. The crushing reality hit me when Klaus Weber, our largest German distributor, mentioned that three competing pharmaceutical companies had secured major hospital contracts by guaranteeing European-manufactured products while we remained dependent on complex import logistics that created unacceptable supply risks.

"European pharmaceutical markets increasingly require local manufacturing for supply security, regulatory confidence, and political considerations that Indian production cannot address regardless of cost advantages," Klaus explained with the diplomatic firmness of someone delivering uncomfortable truths about global pharmaceutical realities. "Healthcare systems prefer suppliers with regional manufacturing capabilities that can ensure uninterrupted supply during international crises or regulatory disruptions."

"But establishing manufacturing facilities across multiple continents requires massive capital investment and operational complexity that could overwhelm our resources," I protested, though our recent supply chain disruptions had demonstrated the vulnerability of single-location manufacturing. "How can we justify building pharmaceutical facilities in markets where we already have successful import operations?"

"Local manufacturing provides competitive advantages through supply security, regulatory positioning, and market access that import operations cannot achieve," he replied. "Pharmaceutical companies with global manufacturing networks command premium pricing and strategic partnerships that import-dependent suppliers cannot access."

"And our realistic prospects for developing continental manufacturing capabilities?"

"Systematic facility development across key markets enables transforming from regional pharmaceutical supplier to global pharmaceutical company with competitive advantages that transcend cost considerations."

This conversation launched our ambitious continental facility establishment program that would require the largest capital investment in our company's history while fundamentally transforming our operational complexity and competitive positioning.

The continental strategy development required identifying optimal locations for pharmaceutical manufacturing while understanding regional market dynamics, regulatory requirements, and competitive positioning advantages that local production could provide.

"Continental facility strategy includes European manufacturing hub in Ireland for EU market access, North American facility in North Carolina for US operations, and Asian expansion facility in Singapore for ASEAN market coverage," announced Dr. Sarah Williams during our global expansion planning. "Strategic facility locations enable comprehensive market coverage while optimizing regulatory advantages and operational efficiency."

"What criteria determine optimal continental manufacturing locations for pharmaceutical operations?" I asked.

"Regulatory environment quality, pharmaceutical industry infrastructure, skilled workforce availability, tax advantages, and market access benefits that enable efficient operations while meeting international pharmaceutical quality standards."

"And timeline for establishing operational pharmaceutical facilities across multiple continents?"

"Continental facility development requires 2-4 years per location including site selection, construction, equipment installation, regulatory validation, and operational qualification before achieving commercial production capabilities."

The European facility development proved most complex when we discovered that EU pharmaceutical manufacturing required understanding intricate regulatory coordination between EMA centralized approval and individual member state implementation requirements.

"European pharmaceutical manufacturing requires EMA manufacturing authorization plus individual country registrations that enable EU-wide market access while meeting member state regulatory requirements," explained Dr. Amanda Richardson during our European regulatory planning. "EU manufacturing compliance demands understanding complex regulatory coordination that exceeds single-country pharmaceutical operations."

"How does European manufacturing differ from our existing Indian pharmaceutical operations?" I asked.

"European manufacturing requires higher automation levels, enhanced quality systems, and specialized workforce training that meets EU pharmaceutical standards while enabling cost-competitive production."

"And competitive advantages from European pharmaceutical manufacturing capabilities?"

"European manufacturing provides immediate market access, supply security, and regulatory credibility that enables competing against established European pharmaceutical companies while eliminating import-related supply risks."

The North American facility establishment required navigating FDA manufacturing approval while understanding US pharmaceutical market dynamics that differed substantially from European or Asian commercial environments.

"US pharmaceutical manufacturing requires FDA facility registration, cGMP compliance validation, and specialized quality systems that meet American pharmaceutical standards," announced our US operations manager during our North American facility planning. "FDA manufacturing approval demands comprehensive validation and ongoing compliance monitoring that ensures product quality while enabling US market access."

"What operational requirements distinguish US pharmaceutical manufacturing from international operations?" I asked.

"US manufacturing requires enhanced documentation, specialized quality controls, and automated production systems that meet FDA standards while enabling efficient operations in competitive American pharmaceutical markets."

"And market access advantages from US pharmaceutical manufacturing capabilities?"

"US manufacturing enables direct hospital system access, government contract eligibility, and supply chain partnerships that import operations cannot achieve while providing competitive advantages over international suppliers."

The Asian facility development strategy required understanding regional market dynamics while establishing manufacturing capabilities that could serve diverse regulatory environments across multiple Asian countries.

"Asian manufacturing hub in Singapore enables serving ASEAN markets, Japanese distribution, and Chinese pharmaceutical opportunities through strategic location advantages," reported our Asian expansion manager during our regional facility planning. "Singapore manufacturing provides regulatory credibility and operational efficiency that enables comprehensive Asian market coverage."

"How does Asian pharmaceutical manufacturing differ from European or US facility requirements?" I asked.

"Asian manufacturing requires flexibility to meet diverse regulatory standards while maintaining cost efficiency that enables competitive positioning in price-sensitive regional markets."

"And competitive positioning advantages from Asian manufacturing capabilities?"

"Asian manufacturing enables regional market penetration while providing supply chain efficiency and cost competitiveness that supports growth in emerging pharmaceutical markets."

The technology standardization required implementing consistent manufacturing processes across continental facilities while adapting to local regulatory requirements and operational constraints.

"Global facility standardization requires unified equipment specifications, standardized production processes, and integrated quality systems that enable consistent pharmaceutical quality while meeting regional regulatory requirements," announced our global manufacturing director during our standardization planning. "Technology standardization provides operational efficiency while ensuring pharmaceutical quality consistency across continental operations."

"What technology capabilities enable successful multi-continental pharmaceutical manufacturing?" I asked.

"Standardized equipment platforms, integrated quality management, real-time production monitoring, and coordinated supply chain systems that enable optimizing global manufacturing efficiency while maintaining pharmaceutical quality standards."

"And operational advantages from standardized continental manufacturing systems?"

"Standardization enables production flexibility, quality consistency, and operational efficiency that maximizes global manufacturing network benefits while simplifying multi-continental operations management."

The regulatory coordination required developing expertise in multiple pharmaceutical regulatory systems while maintaining consistent quality standards across facilities operating under different regulatory authorities.

"Multi-continental manufacturing requires coordinating FDA, EMA, Health Canada, and Asian regulatory compliance while ensuring consistent pharmaceutical quality standards," explained Dr. Richardson during our global regulatory planning. "Regulatory coordination demands systematic compliance management and ongoing coordination that enables leveraging global manufacturing capabilities while meeting diverse regulatory requirements."

"How does multi-continental manufacturing affect pharmaceutical regulatory complexity?" I asked.

"Global manufacturing multiplies regulatory requirements while providing regulatory diversification that enables continued operations despite individual facility regulatory issues."

"And regulatory advantages from continental manufacturing capabilities?"

"Regulatory diversification enables market access optimization while providing backup capabilities that ensure continued pharmaceutical supply despite individual regulatory disruptions."

The continental facility results demonstrated that global manufacturing capabilities could provide competitive advantages while enabling market access that single-location operations could never achieve.

"Continental facility establishment has created manufacturing capabilities in Europe, North America, and Asia that provide comprehensive global market access while ensuring supply security," I announced during our annual global operations review. "Continental manufacturing creates competitive advantages through local market presence while eliminating supply chain vulnerabilities."

"And financial performance of continental manufacturing compared to single-site operations?" asked our global operations committee.

"Continental manufacturing achieves 34% higher average selling prices through local market positioning while providing supply security that enables strategic customer partnerships."

Four years after implementing continental facility establishment, we had transformed from regional pharmaceutical supplier to global manufacturing company with competitive advantages that transcended cost considerations.

"Establishing facilities across continents taught us that pharmaceutical success requires local market presence rather than just cost-competitive production," I reflected during our global strategy review.

"The key insight was that continental manufacturing creates competitive advantages through market access and supply security that import operations cannot provide."

The continental facility development had proven that international pharmaceutical expansion required local manufacturing capabilities that provided competitive advantages through market presence and operational resilience.

"Continental facility establishment demonstrated that global pharmaceutical success requires treating manufacturing as market access strategy rather than just production function," I concluded.

The lesson had become fundamental to our global strategy: continental manufacturing facilities enabled creating competitive advantages through local market presence that provided supply security and regulatory credibility that import-dependent operations could never achieve.

Supply Chain Resilience Strategies

The supply chain resilience awakening came during the terrifying weeks of March 2020 when COVID-19 lockdowns across Asia caused our raw material supplies to evaporate overnight, forcing us to halt production of critical cardiovascular medications while I watched helplessly as our single-source procurement strategy collapsed in a matter of days. The vulnerability of our lean supply chain became catastrophically obvious when our key API supplier in Hyderabad couldn't deliver essential ingredients while European competitors with diversified sourcing networks continued operating normally, highlighting the difference between cost optimization and strategic resilience.

"We've optimized our supply chain for efficiency rather than resilience, creating a system that works perfectly under normal conditions but fails catastrophically during disruptions," announced our newly hired VP of Supply Chain Resilience, Dr. Rajesh Kumar, as he presented failure analysis showing that 67% of our critical materials came from single suppliers within a 200-kilometer radius. "Supply chain efficiency becomes irrelevant when external shocks eliminate your ability to manufacture products that patients desperately need."

"But building supply chain redundancy requires maintaining excess inventory and multiple supplier relationships that increase costs significantly," I protested, though our recent production shutdown had cost ₹89 crores while competitors with resilient supply chains captured market share we might never recover. "How can we justify the expense of supply chain resilience when efficiency has driven our competitive advantages?"

"Supply chain resilience provides insurance against existential risks while enabling continued operations during crises that destroy efficiency-focused competitors," he replied with the analytical precision of someone who had managed pharmaceutical supply chains through multiple global disruptions. "Resilient supply chains cost more during normal times but provide survival advantages during crisis periods that justify long-term investment."

"And our competitive positioning implications from building supply chain resilience?"

"Supply chain resilience creates competitive advantages through operational continuity and customer confidence that efficiency-optimized competitors cannot provide during uncertain business environments."

This conversation launched our systematic transformation from efficiency-optimized supply chain to resilience-focused procurement and logistics network that would require fundamentally restructuring our operational philosophy and investment priorities.

The vulnerability assessment revealed the shocking fragility of our supposedly sophisticated supply chain when systematic analysis showed that single points of failure could shut down our entire pharmaceutical manufacturing operation.

"Supply chain vulnerability analysis identifies 47 critical materials sourced from single suppliers, 23 essential components with no backup production sources, and 12 key transportation routes with no alternative logistics options," reported Dr. Kumar during his comprehensive supply chain audit. "Current supply chain configuration creates multiple single points of failure that could halt pharmaceutical production through individual supplier disruptions."

"What specific vulnerabilities pose the greatest risks to our pharmaceutical operations?" I asked.

"API sourcing concentration, packaging material dependency, transportation route limitations, and raw material inventory policies that optimize costs while creating operational vulnerabilities during supply disruptions."

"And timeline for addressing critical supply chain vulnerabilities?"

"Supply chain resilience development requires 18-24 months of systematic supplier diversification, inventory optimization, and logistics redundancy implementation before achieving operational security."

The supplier diversification strategy required identifying and qualifying alternative sources for critical materials while building relationships with backup suppliers who could maintain pharmaceutical quality standards during primary supplier disruptions.

"Supplier diversification requires establishing qualified alternative sources for all critical materials including APIs, excipients, packaging components, and specialty chemicals," announced our procurement director during supplier strategy planning. "Diversification enables continued pharmaceutical production despite individual supplier failures while maintaining quality standards and regulatory compliance."

"How does supplier diversification affect pharmaceutical procurement costs and complexity?" I asked.

"Supplier diversification increases procurement costs by 12-18% through redundant supplier relationships while providing operational security that enables continued production during supply disruptions."

"And quality assurance requirements for alternative pharmaceutical suppliers?"

"Alternative supplier qualification requires comprehensive quality audits, regulatory compliance verification, and production capability assessment that ensures pharmaceutical quality standards while providing supply security."

The strategic inventory management required balancing carrying costs against supply security while developing sophisticated forecasting systems that could optimize stock levels for resilience rather than just efficiency.

"Strategic inventory management involves maintaining 90-180 days of critical material inventory compared to traditional 30-45 day lean inventory policies," explained our inventory optimization manager during our resilience planning. "Strategic inventory provides supply security during extended disruptions while requiring substantial working capital investment and warehouse capacity expansion."

"What inventory levels provide optimal balance between resilience and efficiency?" I asked.

"Resilience-focused inventory requires maintaining 3-6 months of critical materials while traditional efficiency optimization targets 4-6 weeks of inventory to minimize carrying costs."

"And inventory management systems that support supply chain resilience?"

"Advanced forecasting, automated reordering, and scenario planning systems that enable optimizing inventory levels while maintaining supply security during various disruption scenarios."

The logistics redundancy development required establishing alternative transportation routes and backup distribution capabilities that could maintain product delivery during transportation system disruptions.

"Logistics redundancy includes alternative shipping routes, backup transportation providers, and distributed warehouse networks that enable continued pharmaceutical distribution despite individual logistics disruptions," reported our logistics manager during redundancy planning. "Transportation diversification provides delivery security while enabling continued market access during shipping system failures."

"How does logistics redundancy affect pharmaceutical distribution costs and delivery timelines?" I asked.

"Logistics redundancy increases distribution costs by 8-15% while providing delivery security that enables continued customer service during transportation disruptions."

"And regional logistics strategies that support global pharmaceutical operations?"

"Regional logistics hubs with alternative transportation capabilities that enable continued distribution while providing backup delivery options during regional disruption events."

The crisis management planning required developing systematic response protocols that could coordinate supply chain recovery while maintaining pharmaceutical production during various disruption scenarios.

"Crisis management protocols include supplier communication systems, alternative sourcing procedures, and production adjustment strategies that enable rapid response to supply chain disruptions," announced our crisis management director during contingency planning. "Crisis response systems provide operational continuity while enabling systematic recovery from supply chain failures."

"What crisis management capabilities distinguish resilient pharmaceutical supply chains?" I asked.

"Real-time monitoring, automated alert systems, and coordinated response protocols that enable rapid identification and resolution of supply chain disruptions before they affect pharmaceutical production."

"And communication systems that support supply chain crisis management?"

"Integrated communication platforms that enable coordinating supplier relationships, transportation logistics, and production planning during crisis situations while maintaining pharmaceutical quality standards."

The technology integration required implementing sophisticated monitoring systems that could provide real-time visibility across global supply chains while enabling predictive analytics for disruption prevention.

"Supply chain technology integration includes real-time tracking, predictive analytics, and automated monitoring systems that provide comprehensive visibility while enabling proactive disruption management," announced our supply chain technology manager during system planning. "Technology integration enables optimizing supply chain resilience while maintaining operational efficiency through advanced analytics and automation."

"How does technology integration enhance supply chain resilience capabilities?" I asked.

"Technology provides real-time visibility, predictive disruption identification, and automated response capabilities that enable preventing supply chain failures while optimizing resilience investments."

"And competitive advantages from advanced supply chain technology systems?"

"Technology integration enables superior supply chain performance while providing operational advantages that create competitive differentiation through reliable pharmaceutical supply capabilities."

The supply chain resilience results demonstrated that systematic redundancy and diversification could provide operational security while enabling competitive advantages through supply reliability.

"Supply chain resilience strategies have eliminated single points of failure while reducing supply disruption risks by 78% through supplier diversification and strategic inventory management," I announced during our annual supply chain review. "Resilience investments provide operational security while enabling competitive advantages through reliable pharmaceutical supply capabilities."

"And cost implications of supply chain resilience compared to efficiency-optimized operations?" asked our operations committee.

"Supply chain resilience increases operating costs by 14% while providing operational security that prevents production shutdowns and enables continued market access during disruption periods."

Three years after implementing supply chain resilience strategies, we had achieved operational security that enabled continued pharmaceutical production while providing competitive advantages through supply reliability.

"Supply chain resilience strategies taught us that pharmaceutical success requires operational security rather than just cost optimization," I reflected during our strategic planning review.

"The key insight was that supply chain resilience creates competitive advantages through operational continuity that efficiency optimization cannot provide during crisis periods."

The supply chain resilience development had proven that pharmaceutical companies could achieve competitive advantages through operational security that provided supply reliability while enabling continued operations during global disruptions.

"Supply chain resilience demonstrated that pharmaceutical success requires treating supply chain as strategic capability rather than just cost center," I concluded.

The lesson had become fundamental to our operational philosophy: supply chain resilience enabled creating competitive advantages through operational security that provided supply reliability and customer confidence that efficiency-optimized competitors could not match during uncertain business environments.

The COVID-19 Pandemic Response

The COVID-19 pandemic collision with our pharmaceutical operations began at 2:15 AM on March 24, 2020, when a frantic phone call from our Mumbai facility manager informed me that the Indian government's sudden lockdown announcement had stranded 340 of our essential workers at home while critical cardiovascular and diabetes medications sat unfinished on production lines, creating a supply crisis that could leave thousands of patients without life-saving treatments. The magnitude of the operational catastrophe became clear over the following hours as facility shutdowns, supply chain disruptions, and transportation lockdowns created a perfect storm that threatened to paralyze global pharmaceutical operations.

"We're facing simultaneous disruptions across every aspect of pharmaceutical operations including manufacturing, supply chain, logistics, and regulatory systems while patient demand for essential medications continues unabated," announced our crisis response coordinator, Dr. Meera Patel, during our emergency management meeting as reports flooded in about border closures, supplier shutdowns, and transportation restrictions across three continents. "The pandemic has created operational challenges that no pharmaceutical company has encountered while maintaining responsibility for producing medications that patients cannot survive without."

"But surely pharmaceutical operations qualify as essential services that governments will prioritize during health emergencies," I replied, though early reports suggested that even essential healthcare supply chains were experiencing unprecedented disruptions.

"Essential service designation doesn't eliminate supply chain failures, workforce disruptions, or transportation restrictions that affect every component of pharmaceutical manufacturing," she responded with the grim reality of someone coordinating global crisis response. "Pandemic response requires systematic adaptation of pharmaceutical operations while maintaining product quality and patient supply under conditions that no operational planning had anticipated."

"And our competitive positioning compared to pharmaceutical companies with more robust crisis management capabilities?"

"Companies with diversified manufacturing, resilient supply chains, and systematic crisis response capabilities maintain operational continuity while competitors dependent on concentrated operations face extended shutdowns."

This crisis management challenge would test every operational system we had developed while forcing innovations in pharmaceutical manufacturing that would permanently transform our approach to operational resilience and crisis preparedness.

The immediate response coordination required implementing emergency protocols that could maintain essential pharmaceutical production while protecting employee safety and complying with rapidly changing government restrictions across multiple countries.

"Emergency response protocols include workforce safety measures, essential worker designation procedures, and production prioritization systems that enable continued pharmaceutical manufacturing during lockdown conditions," reported our operations director during our crisis management implementation. "Emergency protocols balance employee safety with pharmaceutical production obligations while adapting to continuously changing regulatory requirements."

"What specific measures enable maintaining pharmaceutical production during pandemic lockdowns?" I asked.

"Essential worker documentation, enhanced safety protocols, modified work schedules, and production prioritization that enables continued manufacturing while meeting health authority requirements and employee safety obligations."

"And coordination requirements for maintaining global operations during simultaneous country lockdowns?"

"Real-time communication systems, alternative logistics arrangements, and coordinated production planning that enables maintaining pharmaceutical supply despite individual facility or country disruptions."

The supply chain adaptation required developing alternative sourcing strategies while managing raw material shortages that threatened pharmaceutical production across multiple therapeutic areas.

"Supply chain adaptation includes emergency supplier qualification, alternative transportation arrangements, and strategic inventory management that enables continued pharmaceutical production despite widespread supplier disruptions," announced Dr. Rajesh Kumar during our supply chain crisis response. "Pandemic supply chain management requires flexibility and rapid decision-making that exceeds normal pharmaceutical procurement procedures."

"How do pandemic conditions affect pharmaceutical supply chain management compared to normal operations?" I asked.

"Pandemic disruptions require immediate supplier diversification, alternative logistics coordination, and emergency procurement procedures that enable maintaining pharmaceutical production despite systematic supply chain failures."

"And inventory management strategies during pandemic-related supply uncertainties?"

"Strategic inventory accumulation, alternative material sourcing, and production prioritization that ensures continued availability of essential pharmaceutical products while managing supply chain disruptions."

The workforce management challenges required implementing safety protocols while maintaining essential pharmaceutical production through modified operational procedures that could protect employee health while ensuring medicine availability.

"Workforce management during pandemic includes health screening procedures, modified work schedules, enhanced safety protocols, and essential worker transportation that enables continued pharmaceutical production while protecting employee safety," reported our human resources director during workforce planning. "Employee safety measures must balance health protection with pharmaceutical production obligations that patients depend on."

"What workforce adaptations enable maintaining pharmaceutical production during health emergencies?" I asked.

"Enhanced safety protocols, modified shift schedules, remote work capabilities for administrative functions, and essential worker support that enables continued operations while protecting employee health."

"And employee support systems during pandemic-related operational challenges?"

"Health monitoring, transportation assistance, family support services, and enhanced safety training that enables employees to continue essential pharmaceutical production while managing personal health and safety concerns."

The regulatory coordination required navigating rapidly changing regulatory environments while maintaining pharmaceutical quality standards and regulatory compliance during crisis conditions.

"Regulatory coordination during pandemic includes emergency use authorizations, modified inspection procedures, and expedited approval processes that enable continued pharmaceutical operations while meeting evolving regulatory requirements," explained Dr. Amanda Richardson during regulatory crisis management. "Pandemic regulatory management requires understanding emergency procedures while maintaining pharmaceutical quality and compliance standards."

"How do pandemic conditions affect pharmaceutical regulatory requirements and compliance obligations?" I asked.

"Emergency regulatory procedures provide operational flexibility while maintaining pharmaceutical quality standards through modified inspection processes and expedited approval mechanisms."

"And international regulatory coordination during simultaneous global health emergencies?"

"Coordinated regulatory response with international agencies enables continued pharmaceutical operations while ensuring product quality and safety during emergency conditions."

The technology acceleration required rapidly implementing digital systems that could support remote operations while maintaining pharmaceutical production coordination and quality management during distributed work arrangements.

"Technology acceleration includes remote monitoring systems, digital quality management, virtual collaboration platforms, and automated production control that enables continued pharmaceutical operations during social distancing requirements," announced our technology director during digital transformation planning. "Technology solutions enable maintaining operational coordination while adapting to pandemic-related work restrictions."

"What technology capabilities distinguish effective pandemic response in pharmaceutical operations?" I asked.

"Remote monitoring, digital collaboration, automated quality control, and virtual coordination systems that enable maintaining pharmaceutical operations while accommodating social distancing and remote work requirements."

"And long-term technology implications from pandemic-driven operational adaptations?"

"Accelerated digital transformation creates operational capabilities that provide competitive advantages while enabling enhanced operational resilience for future crisis management."

The pandemic response results demonstrated that systematic crisis management and operational adaptability could maintain pharmaceutical production while creating competitive advantages through operational resilience.

"COVID-19 pandemic response maintained 94% production capacity while protecting employee safety and ensuring continued pharmaceutical supply to patients across twelve countries," I announced during our annual crisis response review. "Pandemic response capabilities created operational resilience while demonstrating competitive advantages through crisis management and operational adaptability."

"And competitive positioning improvements from pandemic response capabilities?" asked our operations committee.

"Crisis response capabilities provided competitive advantages through operational continuity while enabling market share gains from competitors unable to maintain pharmaceutical production during pandemic disruptions."

Two years after implementing pandemic response capabilities, we had achieved operational resilience that exceeded pre-pandemic capabilities while creating competitive advantages through crisis management expertise.

"The COVID-19 pandemic response taught us that pharmaceutical success requires operational adaptability rather than just efficiency optimization," I reflected during our crisis management review.

"The key insight was that pandemic response capabilities create competitive advantages through operational resilience that enables continued pharmaceutical production during global crisis conditions."

The pandemic response had proven that pharmaceutical companies could maintain essential operations during global disruptions while creating competitive advantages through systematic crisis management and operational adaptability.

"COVID-19 pandemic response demonstrated that pharmaceutical success requires building operational resilience capabilities rather than depending on stable operating conditions," I concluded.

The lesson had become fundamental to our operational philosophy: pandemic response capabilities enabled creating competitive advantages through operational resilience that provided continued pharmaceutical production and patient service during global crisis conditions that efficiency-optimized competitors could not navigate successfully.

Manufacturing Excellence Initiatives

The manufacturing excellence awakening came during a humbling facility tour at Novartis Basel in September 2022 when I witnessed pharmaceutical manufacturing operations that made our supposedly advanced Mumbai facility look like an industrial museum from the 1990s. The technological sophistication gap became embarrassingly obvious when their production manager casually mentioned that their fully automated facility produced ten times our output with half our workforce while achieving 99.7% quality consistency that exceeded our best performance by an order of magnitude.

"Manufacturing excellence isn't just about producing pharmaceutical products - it's about creating systematic competitive advantages through operational capabilities that competitors cannot easily replicate," explained Dr. Klaus Weber, Novartis' manufacturing director, as we observed robotic systems seamlessly coordinating complex production sequences that our manual operations required days to complete. "World-class pharmaceutical manufacturing combines technological sophistication with operational discipline to achieve quality and efficiency levels that become competitive barriers."

"But our manufacturing operations meet all regulatory requirements and produce quality pharmaceutical products," I protested, though the comparison between their automated precision and our labor-intensive processes was forcing me to reconsider what constituted acceptable manufacturing performance.

"Meeting minimum standards isn't manufacturing excellence," he replied with Swiss precision. "Manufacturing excellence involves optimizing every aspect of pharmaceutical production to achieve operational superiority that enables cost advantages, quality differentiation, and supply reliability that traditional manufacturing cannot deliver."

"And the investment requirements for achieving world-class pharmaceutical manufacturing capabilities?"

"Manufacturing excellence requires systematic investment in automation, quality systems, and operational optimization that transforms manufacturing from cost center to competitive advantage through superior operational performance."

This conversation launched our comprehensive manufacturing excellence program that would require rebuilding our production philosophy from manual operations to automated precision while establishing quality standards that exceeded regulatory requirements.

The current state assessment revealed the shocking gap between our manufacturing performance and world-class pharmaceutical production standards when systematic analysis showed inefficiencies and quality variations that we had accepted as normal operations.

"Manufacturing assessment identifies 34 areas requiring improvement including production scheduling efficiency, quality control automation, waste reduction opportunities, and operational coordination that could enhance manufacturing performance," reported our newly hired Manufacturing Excellence Director, Dr. Anand Krishnamurthy, during his facility evaluation. "Current manufacturing operates at 67% of optimal efficiency while achieving quality consistency below industry benchmarks."

"What specific manufacturing improvements could provide the greatest competitive advantages?" I asked.

"Automation implementation, quality system enhancement, production optimization, and operational coordination that could improve efficiency while reducing costs and enhancing pharmaceutical quality."

"And benchmark comparisons with world-class pharmaceutical manufacturing operations?"

"Current manufacturing performance ranks in bottom quartile of pharmaceutical industry while world-class operations achieve 40-60% higher efficiency with superior quality consistency."

The automation strategy required implementing robotic systems and advanced control technologies that could eliminate manual variability while achieving precision and consistency that human operations could never maintain.

"Manufacturing automation includes robotic material handling, automated quality control, and integrated production systems that eliminate manual variability while achieving consistent pharmaceutical quality," announced Dr. Krishnamurthy during automation planning. "Automation enables precision manufacturing that exceeds human capabilities while reducing labor costs and improving production reliability."

"How does manufacturing automation affect pharmaceutical production costs and quality?" I asked.

"Automation reduces production costs by 35-45% while improving quality consistency and eliminating human error that affects pharmaceutical manufacturing reliability."

"And implementation timeline for comprehensive manufacturing automation?"

"Automation implementation requires 18-24 months of systematic equipment installation, system integration, and operational validation before achieving full automation benefits."

The quality excellence program required implementing sophisticated quality management systems that could achieve pharmaceutical quality levels that exceeded regulatory requirements while creating competitive advantages through superior product consistency.

"Quality excellence involves statistical process control, automated testing systems, and comprehensive quality management that ensures pharmaceutical quality exceeds regulatory standards while achieving competitive differentiation," reported our quality excellence manager during quality planning. "Quality excellence creates competitive advantages through product consistency and reliability that traditional quality control cannot achieve."

"What quality management capabilities distinguish world-class pharmaceutical manufacturing?" I asked.

"Real-time quality monitoring, statistical process control, predictive quality management, and comprehensive quality systems that ensure pharmaceutical quality while enabling continuous improvement."

"And competitive advantages from pharmaceutical quality excellence compared to standard quality control?"

"Quality excellence enables premium pricing, customer loyalty, and regulatory advantages through demonstrated quality superiority that creates competitive barriers."

The operational efficiency optimization required implementing lean manufacturing principles while developing systematic approaches to waste elimination and production optimization that could maximize pharmaceutical manufacturing performance.

"Operational efficiency includes lean manufacturing implementation, waste elimination programs, and production optimization that maximizes manufacturing performance while reducing costs," announced our operational efficiency manager during process improvement planning. "Efficiency optimization enables competitive cost structure while improving pharmaceutical production capability."

"How does operational efficiency optimization affect pharmaceutical manufacturing competitiveness?" I asked.

"Efficiency optimization reduces manufacturing costs while improving production capacity and operational flexibility that enables competitive advantages through superior manufacturing performance."

"And sustainable efficiency improvement strategies for pharmaceutical manufacturing?"

"Continuous improvement culture, systematic waste elimination, and operational optimization that creates sustained competitive advantages through manufacturing excellence rather than one-time efficiency gains."

The technology integration required implementing advanced manufacturing systems that could coordinate complex pharmaceutical production while providing real-time monitoring and control capabilities.

"Technology integration includes advanced process control, real-time monitoring systems, and integrated production management that enables optimizing pharmaceutical manufacturing while ensuring quality and efficiency," reported our technology integration manager during system planning. "Manufacturing technology provides operational capabilities that exceed traditional pharmaceutical production while enabling competitive advantages."

"What technology capabilities distinguish excellent pharmaceutical manufacturing operations?" I asked.

"Advanced automation, real-time monitoring, predictive maintenance, and integrated control systems that enable optimizing pharmaceutical manufacturing while ensuring consistent quality and operational efficiency."

"And return on investment from advanced pharmaceutical manufacturing technology?"

"Manufacturing technology investment generates 25-40% annual returns through efficiency improvement, quality enhancement, and operational optimization that creates sustained competitive advantages."

The workforce development required training manufacturing teams in advanced operational techniques while creating quality culture that could sustain manufacturing excellence through employee engagement and systematic improvement.

"Workforce development includes advanced training programs, quality culture development, and continuous improvement engagement that enables employees to contribute to manufacturing excellence," announced our training director during workforce planning. "Employee development creates manufacturing capabilities that technology alone cannot achieve while ensuring sustained operational improvement."

"How does workforce development contribute to pharmaceutical manufacturing excellence?" I asked.

"Employee training and engagement enables maximizing manufacturing technology benefits while creating quality culture that sustains operational excellence through systematic improvement and operational discipline."

"And employee engagement strategies that support manufacturing excellence initiatives?"

"Continuous improvement participation, quality responsibility, and operational ownership that enables employees to contribute to manufacturing excellence while creating competitive advantages through workforce capabilities."

The manufacturing excellence results demonstrated that systematic operational improvement could create competitive advantages while achieving pharmaceutical quality and efficiency levels that exceeded industry benchmarks.

"Manufacturing excellence initiatives have achieved 43% efficiency improvement while reducing quality defects by 67% through automation, quality systems, and operational optimization," I announced during our annual manufacturing review. "Manufacturing excellence creates competitive advantages through operational superiority that enables cost leadership while maintaining pharmaceutical quality standards."

"And competitive positioning improvements from manufacturing excellence compared to standard pharmaceutical operations?" asked our operations committee.

"Manufacturing excellence provides cost advantages, quality differentiation, and operational reliability that create competitive barriers while enabling premium market positioning."

Three years after implementing manufacturing excellence initiatives, we had achieved operational capabilities that are comparable to larger pharmaceutical companies while creating competitive advantages through manufacturing superiority.

"Manufacturing excellence initiatives taught us that pharmaceutical success requires operational superiority rather than just regulatory compliance," I reflected during our operational strategy review.

"The key insight was that manufacturing excellence creates sustainable competitive advantages through operational capabilities that competitors cannot easily replicate."

The manufacturing excellence program had proven that pharmaceutical companies could achieve competitive advantages through systematic operational improvement that created cost leadership while maintaining superior pharmaceutical quality.

"Manufacturing excellence demonstrated that pharmaceutical success requires treating manufacturing as strategic capability rather than just production function," I concluded.

The lesson had become fundamental to our operational philosophy: manufacturing excellence enabled creating competitive advantages through operational superiority that provided cost leadership and quality differentiation while establishing operational capabilities that became competitive barriers against less sophisticated pharmaceutical manufacturers.

Chapter 25

The ESG Integration

When Values Became Valuation

The ESG awakening came during a shocking investor presentation in November 2022 when our largest institutional investor, BlackRock's Mumbai representative, bluntly informed me that our company's environmental and social practices had become investment liabilities that were affecting our valuation despite strong financial performance. The uncomfortable reality crystallized when she mentioned that pharmaceutical companies with poor ESG ratings were trading at 20-30% discounts to ESG-compliant competitors, forcing me to confront how sustainability and social responsibility had evolved from optional corporate initiatives to mandatory competitive requirements.

"ESG compliance has become a valuation multiplier rather than just a compliance exercise," announced Priya Malhotra, BlackRock's ESG investment director, as she presented analysis showing that pharmaceutical companies with strong environmental, social, and governance practices commanded premium valuations while ESG laggards faced capital constraints and reputational risks. "Investors increasingly evaluate pharmaceutical companies based on sustainability practices and social impact rather than just financial metrics."

"But we're a pharmaceutical company that saves lives through essential medications," I protested, though I was beginning to understand that good intentions couldn't substitute for measurable ESG performance. "Shouldn't our therapeutic contributions automatically qualify as positive social impact?"

"Pharmaceutical companies receive ESG credit for therapeutic value only when combined with environmental responsibility, ethical business practices, and sustainable operations," she replied with the analytical precision that had made BlackRock the world's largest asset manager. "ESG evaluation requires systematic measurement and transparent reporting of environmental impact, social responsibility, and governance practices."

"And the competitive implications for pharmaceutical companies that ignore ESG requirements?"

"ESG non-compliance creates investment constraints, regulatory risks, and reputational damage that affect competitive positioning while ESG leadership enables access to sustainable investment capital and premium valuations."

This conversation launched our systematic ESG integration program that would require fundamentally restructuring our operational philosophy from profit maximization to stakeholder value creation while maintaining pharmaceutical excellence and competitive performance.

The ESG assessment revealed the shocking scope of environmental and social improvements required to achieve compliance with evolving sustainability standards that pharmaceutical investors increasingly demanded.

"ESG assessment identifies significant gaps in environmental management, social responsibility programs, and governance practices that affect investment attractiveness," reported our newly hired ESG Director, Dr. Kavya Reddy, during her comprehensive sustainability audit. "Current ESG performance ranks in bottom quartile of pharmaceutical companies while institutional investors require top-quartile ESG ratings for investment consideration."

"What specific ESG improvements would provide the greatest investment and competitive advantages?" I asked.

"Environmental sustainability initiatives, social impact programs, and governance transparency that demonstrate commitment to stakeholder value creation while maintaining pharmaceutical performance and competitive positioning."

"And timeline for achieving investment-grade ESG performance?"

"ESG transformation requires 2-3 years of systematic improvement across environmental, social, and governance dimensions before achieving institutional investor requirements and competitive ESG positioning."

The environmental sustainability program required implementing comprehensive environmental management systems while reducing pharmaceutical manufacturing's environmental impact through waste reduction and energy efficiency initiatives.

"Environmental sustainability includes carbon footprint reduction, waste management optimization, water conservation programs, and renewable energy implementation that reduces pharmaceutical manufacturing environmental impact," announced our environmental manager during sustainability planning. "Environmental performance creates competitive advantages while meeting investor requirements for sustainable pharmaceutical operations."

"How does environmental sustainability affect pharmaceutical manufacturing costs and competitive positioning?" I asked.

"Environmental initiatives require upfront investment but generate long-term cost savings through efficiency improvements while creating competitive advantages through sustainable operations that investors and customers increasingly demand."

"And regulatory advantages from environmental sustainability in pharmaceutical operations?"

"Environmental leadership provides regulatory advantages and government support while reducing compliance risks that affect pharmaceutical operations and competitive positioning."

The social responsibility initiatives required developing comprehensive programs that could demonstrate meaningful social impact while addressing healthcare access and community development challenges.

"Social responsibility programs include patient access initiatives, community healthcare programs, and employee development that demonstrate pharmaceutical company commitment to social impact beyond therapeutic development," reported our social impact manager during program planning. "Social initiatives create competitive advantages through stakeholder engagement while meeting investor requirements for social responsibility."

"What social responsibility programs provide the greatest competitive and investment advantages?" I asked.

"Healthcare access programs, community development initiatives, and employee welfare programs that demonstrate measurable social impact while creating competitive advantages through stakeholder loyalty and community support."

"And measurement systems for social impact that satisfy ESG investor requirements?"

"Systematic social impact measurement, transparent reporting, and independent verification that enables demonstrating social responsibility performance to institutional investors and stakeholders."

The governance excellence program required implementing transparent governance practices while establishing ethical business standards that could satisfy institutional investor requirements for corporate governance quality.

"Governance excellence includes board independence, executive compensation transparency, ethical business practices, and stakeholder engagement that meets institutional investor requirements," announced our governance consultant during corporate governance planning. "Governance practices create competitive advantages through investor confidence while reducing regulatory and reputational risks."

"How does governance excellence affect pharmaceutical company valuation and competitive positioning?" I asked.

"Governance excellence enables premium valuations through investor confidence while reducing regulatory risks and creating competitive advantages through ethical business practices and transparent operations."

"And governance practices that distinguish pharmaceutical companies in ESG investor evaluation?"

"Board diversity, executive accountability, ethical supply chain management, and stakeholder engagement that demonstrate commitment to responsible pharmaceutical business practices."

The stakeholder engagement strategy required developing systematic approaches to community relations while building partnerships that could demonstrate pharmaceutical company commitment to social responsibility and sustainable development.

"Stakeholder engagement includes community partnerships, patient advocacy collaboration, and healthcare provider relationships that demonstrate pharmaceutical company commitment to stakeholder value creation," reported our stakeholder relations manager during engagement planning. "Stakeholder engagement creates competitive advantages while satisfying ESG investor requirements for social responsibility."

"What stakeholder engagement practices provide the greatest ESG and competitive advantages?" I asked.

"Community healthcare partnerships, patient access programs, and healthcare provider collaboration that demonstrate meaningful social impact while creating competitive advantages through stakeholder loyalty."

"And measurement systems for stakeholder engagement that satisfy institutional investor ESG requirements?"

"Systematic stakeholder feedback, impact measurement, and transparent reporting that enables demonstrating stakeholder value creation to ESG investors and regulatory authorities."

The ESG reporting and transparency required implementing comprehensive disclosure systems that could provide institutional investors with measurable

ESG performance data while demonstrating pharmaceutical company commitment to sustainability and social responsibility.

"ESG reporting includes comprehensive sustainability disclosure, social impact measurement, and governance transparency that enables institutional investor evaluation while demonstrating pharmaceutical company ESG performance," announced our ESG reporting manager during disclosure planning. "ESG transparency creates competitive advantages through investor confidence while meeting regulatory requirements for sustainability reporting."

"How does ESG reporting affect pharmaceutical company investment attractiveness and competitive positioning?" I asked.

"ESG reporting enables accessing sustainable investment capital while creating competitive advantages through transparency and accountability that distinguish responsible pharmaceutical companies."

"And ESG reporting standards that satisfy institutional investor requirements?"

"Global Reporting Initiative standards, SASB pharmaceutical metrics, and CDP environmental disclosure that enable comprehensive ESG reporting while meeting institutional investor evaluation requirements."

The ESG integration results demonstrated that sustainability and social responsibility could create competitive advantages while enabling access to investment capital that ESG non-compliant companies could not access.

"ESG integration has achieved top-quartile pharmaceutical industry ESG ratings while reducing environmental impact by 34% and creating social programs that benefit 250,000 patients annually," I announced during our annual ESG review. "ESG performance creates competitive advantages through stakeholder value creation while enabling access to sustainable investment capital."

"And valuation improvements from ESG integration compared to pharmaceutical companies without ESG programs?" asked our investment committee.

"ESG integration has enabled 18% valuation premium compared to pharmaceutical industry average while providing access to ESG-focused investment capital that enables continued growth and competitive positioning."

Three years after implementing comprehensive ESG integration, we had achieved sustainability leadership that created competitive advantages while demonstrating that pharmaceutical success required stakeholder value creation rather than just shareholder returns.

"ESG integration taught us that pharmaceutical success requires creating value for all stakeholders rather than just maximizing profits," I reflected during our sustainability strategy review.

"The key insight was that ESG performance creates competitive advantages through stakeholder engagement while enabling access to sustainable investment capital that drives long-term pharmaceutical success."

The ESG integration had proven that pharmaceutical companies could achieve competitive advantages through sustainability and social responsibility while demonstrating that values-based business practices enhanced rather than compromised financial performance.

"ESG integration demonstrated that pharmaceutical success requires balancing profit creation with social responsibility and environmental stewardship," I concluded.

The lesson had become fundamental to our corporate philosophy: ESG integration enabled creating competitive advantages through stakeholder value creation while demonstrating that sustainable pharmaceutical business practices enhanced long-term performance and competitive positioning.

Environmental Sustainability Programs

The environmental sustainability awakening came during a devastating audit by our European customers in December 2022 when they discovered that our pharmaceutical manufacturing was generating 347% more carbon emissions per unit of production than industry benchmarks, forcing several major hospital systems to threaten contract cancellations unless we could demonstrate measurable environmental improvements within twelve months. The magnitude of our environmental impact became painfully obvious when the auditor mentioned that our single facility's annual carbon footprint exceeded that of entire small European cities while producing medications that were supposed to improve human health.

"We're operating pharmaceutical manufacturing like an environmental disaster while our customers increasingly require suppliers to demonstrate environmental responsibility as a condition for continued business relationships," announced Dr. Priya Nair, our newly hired Director of Environmental Sustainability, as she presented carbon footprint analysis that showed our operations ranking in the bottom 5% of pharmaceutical companies for environmental performance. "Environmental compliance has evolved from regulatory requirement to competitive necessity that affects market access and customer relationships."

"But implementing environmental programs requires massive capital investment that could compromise our pharmaceutical manufacturing efficiency," I protested, though customer contract threats were forcing me to recognize that environmental sustainability had become a business survival issue rather than optional corporate responsibility.

"Environmental sustainability programs generate long-term cost savings through efficiency improvements while creating competitive advantages through environmental leadership," she replied with the conviction of someone who had implemented sustainability programs at major pharmaceutical corporations. "Environmental excellence enables cost reduction while meeting customer requirements and regulatory expectations that traditional manufacturing cannot satisfy."

"And our realistic timeline for achieving environmental compliance that satisfies customer requirements?"

"Environmental transformation requires 18-24 months of systematic improvement across energy efficiency, waste reduction, and carbon footprint management before achieving customer and regulatory sustainability requirements."

This conversation launched our comprehensive environmental sustainability program that would require fundamental changes to pharmaceutical manufacturing operations while proving that environmental responsibility could enhance rather than compromise competitive performance.

The environmental impact assessment revealed the shocking scope of our manufacturing operations' environmental footprint when systematic analysis showed waste generation, energy consumption, and carbon emissions that exceeded pharmaceutical industry standards by substantial margins.

"Environmental impact assessment identifies carbon emissions 340% above industry averages, waste generation 280% higher than benchmark companies, and energy consumption 220% beyond efficient pharmaceutical manufacturing standards," reported Dr. Nair during her comprehensive environmental audit. "Current environmental performance creates regulatory risks while affecting customer relationships and competitive positioning."

"What environmental improvements could provide the greatest competitive and cost advantages?" I asked.

"Energy efficiency optimization, waste reduction programs, and carbon footprint management that reduce environmental impact while generating cost savings through operational efficiency improvements."

"And regulatory compliance implications of environmental sustainability improvements?"

"Environmental leadership provides regulatory advantages while reducing compliance risks that affect pharmaceutical operations and competitive positioning in environmentally conscious markets."

The carbon footprint reduction program required implementing comprehensive energy management systems while transitioning to renewable energy sources that could eliminate pharmaceutical manufacturing's contribution to climate change.

"Carbon footprint reduction includes energy efficiency improvements, renewable energy implementation, and emissions management systems that reduce pharmaceutical manufacturing environmental impact," announced our carbon management director during emissions planning. "Carbon reduction creates competitive advantages while meeting customer and regulatory requirements for environmental responsibility."

"How does carbon footprint reduction affect pharmaceutical manufacturing costs and operational efficiency?" I asked.

"Carbon reduction initiatives require upfront investment but generate substantial long-term savings through energy efficiency while creating competitive advantages through environmental leadership that customers increasingly demand."

"And timeline for achieving carbon neutral pharmaceutical manufacturing operations?"

"Carbon neutrality requires 3-5 years of systematic emissions reduction and renewable energy implementation before achieving net-zero carbon pharmaceutical manufacturing operations."

The waste reduction and circular economy initiatives required developing comprehensive waste management systems while implementing recycling and reuse programs that could eliminate pharmaceutical manufacturing waste streams.

"Waste reduction programs include material optimization, recycling implementation, and circular economy principles that eliminate pharmaceutical manufacturing waste while reducing raw material costs," reported our waste management director during sustainability planning. "Waste reduction creates cost savings while demonstrating environmental responsibility that customers and regulators require."

"What waste reduction opportunities provide the greatest environmental and cost benefits?" I asked.

"Packaging optimization, solvent recovery, and material recycling that reduce waste generation while creating cost savings through improved resource efficiency and reduced disposal costs."

"And competitive advantages from waste reduction in pharmaceutical manufacturing?"

"Waste reduction enables cost leadership while creating environmental differentiation that provides competitive advantages through operational efficiency and environmental responsibility."

The water conservation and management program required implementing sophisticated water treatment systems while developing conservation strategies that could reduce pharmaceutical manufacturing's water consumption and environmental impact.

"Water conservation includes recycling systems, treatment optimization, and consumption reduction that minimizes pharmaceutical manufacturing water usage while ensuring regulatory compliance," announced our water management specialist during conservation planning. "Water conservation creates environmental benefits while reducing operational costs through efficient resource utilization."

"How does water conservation affect pharmaceutical manufacturing operations and environmental performance?" I asked.

"Water conservation reduces environmental impact while generating cost savings through efficiency improvements that create competitive advantages through resource optimization and environmental responsibility."

"And regulatory advantages from water conservation in pharmaceutical operations?"

"Water conservation provides regulatory compliance benefits while demonstrating environmental leadership that enables competitive advantages in environmentally conscious markets."

The renewable energy transition required implementing solar power systems and energy storage capabilities while developing partnerships that could eliminate pharmaceutical manufacturing's dependence on fossil fuel energy sources.

"Renewable energy implementation includes solar installation, energy storage systems, and grid optimization that enables sustainable pharmaceutical manufacturing while reducing energy costs," reported our renewable energy manager during transition planning. "Renewable energy creates environmental benefits while providing long-term cost advantages through energy independence and price stability."

"What renewable energy solutions provide optimal environmental and economic benefits for pharmaceutical manufacturing?" I asked.

"Solar power with battery storage provides reliable renewable energy while reducing long-term energy costs and creating environmental leadership that customers and investors increasingly require."

"And timeline for achieving renewable energy independence in pharmaceutical operations?"

"Renewable energy transition requires 2-3 years of systematic implementation before achieving energy independence while generating substantial cost savings and environmental benefits."

The environmental monitoring and reporting systems required implementing comprehensive tracking capabilities while developing transparent disclosure that could demonstrate environmental performance improvements to customers and stakeholders.

"Environmental monitoring includes real-time tracking, performance measurement, and transparent reporting that demonstrates pharmaceutical manufacturing environmental improvements," announced our environmental reporting manager during monitoring system planning. "Environmental transparency creates competitive advantages through accountability while meeting customer and investor requirements for environmental performance."

"How does environmental monitoring enhance pharmaceutical company competitive positioning?" I asked.

"Environmental monitoring enables demonstrating continuous improvement while providing transparency that creates competitive advantages through environmental leadership and stakeholder confidence."

"And reporting standards that satisfy customer and investor environmental requirements?"

"Global Reporting Initiative standards, Science-Based Targets, and CDP environmental disclosure that enable comprehensive environmental reporting while meeting stakeholder evaluation requirements."

The environmental sustainability results demonstrated that systematic environmental improvements could create competitive advantages while generating cost savings through operational efficiency and resource optimization.

"Environmental sustainability programs have achieved 47% carbon footprint reduction, 56% waste reduction, and 34% energy consumption decrease while generating ₹23 crores annual cost savings," I announced during our annual sustainability review. "Environmental leadership creates competitive advantages through operational efficiency while meeting customer and regulatory requirements for environmental responsibility."

"And customer relationship improvements from environmental sustainability compared to environmentally poor-performing competitors?" asked our sustainability committee.

"Environmental leadership has secured long-term customer contracts while enabling premium pricing through environmental differentiation that creates competitive advantages."

Three years after implementing comprehensive environmental sustainability programs, we had achieved environmental leadership that created competitive advantages while demonstrating that environmental responsibility enhanced rather than compromised pharmaceutical manufacturing performance.

"Environmental sustainability programs taught us that environmental responsibility creates competitive advantages rather than imposing operational constraints," I reflected during our environmental strategy review.

"The key insight was that environmental excellence enables cost leadership while creating competitive differentiation through operational efficiency and environmental stewardship."

The environmental sustainability program had proven that pharmaceutical companies could achieve competitive advantages through environmental responsibility while demonstrating that sustainable manufacturing practices enhanced operational performance and competitive positioning.

"Environmental sustainability demonstrated that pharmaceutical success requires balancing therapeutic value creation with environmental stewardship," I concluded.

The lesson had become fundamental to our operational philosophy: environmental sustainability programs enabled creating competitive advantages through operational efficiency while demonstrating that environmental responsibility enhanced pharmaceutical manufacturing performance and competitive positioning rather than compromising business success.

Social Impact through Access Programs

The social impact awakening came during a devastating visit to a rural health clinic in Maharashtra in January 2023 when I met seven-year-old Anjali Patil, whose family had spent their entire savings of ₹47,000 attempting to purchase diabetes medications that cost more than her father's annual income as a subsistence farmer. The cruel irony struck me when I realized that our company manufactured identical medications in our facility just 200 kilometers away, but pricing structures designed for urban affluent patients had made life-saving treatments financially impossible for the rural poor who represented 60% of India's population.

"Pharmaceutical companies optimize pricing for maximum revenue extraction while millions of patients remain unable to access essential medications due to economic barriers that our industry creates," explained Dr. Sunita Krishnan, who ran the rural clinic with the dedication of someone watching preventable deaths occur daily due to medication access failures. "Social responsibility requires pharmaceutical companies to balance profit maximization with therapeutic access that serves all patient populations rather than just affluent urban markets."

"But providing medications at reduced prices could undermine our entire pricing structure and affect our ability to fund R&D investments," I protested, though Anjali's situation was forcing me to confront the moral implications of pharmaceutical pricing that prioritized shareholders over patients.

"Patient access programs enable serving underserved populations while maintaining profitable operations through tiered pricing and strategic partnerships," she replied with the practical wisdom of someone who had spent decades working within pharmaceutical industry limitations. "Social impact creates competitive advantages through community relationships and government support while demonstrating corporate responsibility that increasingly affects business reputation and regulatory relationships."

"And our competitive positioning implications from implementing comprehensive patient access programs?"

"Access programs create competitive advantages through government partnerships, community loyalty, and regulatory goodwill while demonstrating social responsibility that affects pharmaceutical company valuation and market positioning."

This conversation launched our systematic patient access program that would require fundamentally restructuring our pricing philosophy from revenue maximization to tiered access strategies that could serve all patient populations while maintaining business sustainability.

The access gap analysis revealed the shocking scope of medication inaccessibility when systematic assessment showed that 73% of patients requiring our cardiovascular and diabetes treatments could not afford standard pricing despite critical medical needs.

"Patient access assessment identifies 2.3 million patients across India who require our medications but cannot afford current pricing structures," reported our newly hired Director of Patient Access, Dr. Kavya Menon, during her comprehensive access audit. "Pricing barriers affect 73% of potential patients while creating untapped market opportunities that access programs could address through innovative pricing and distribution strategies."

"What specific access barriers prevent patients from obtaining essential pharmaceutical treatments?" I asked.

"Economic barriers including unaffordable pricing, geographic barriers through limited distribution, and information barriers where patients lack awareness of treatment options and financial assistance possibilities."

"And market opportunities from addressing pharmaceutical access barriers?"

"Access programs could serve 2.3 million additional patients while creating competitive advantages through market expansion and government partnership opportunities that traditional pricing strategies cannot achieve."

The tiered pricing strategy required developing sophisticated pricing structures that could provide affordable access to underserved populations while maintaining revenue sustainability for continued R&D investment and business operations.

"Tiered pricing includes income-based pricing, government partnership rates, and volume discounting that enables patient access while maintaining pharmaceutical business sustainability," announced our pricing strategy manager during access program planning. "Tiered pricing creates market expansion opportunities while demonstrating social responsibility that affects competitive positioning and stakeholder relationships."

"How does tiered pricing affect pharmaceutical revenue and competitive positioning?" I asked.

"Tiered pricing reduces per-unit revenue but increases volume substantially while creating competitive advantages through market access and government relationships that traditional pricing cannot achieve."

"And implementation challenges for tiered pricing in pharmaceutical markets?"

"Tiered pricing requires sophisticated distribution systems, eligibility verification, and pricing coordination that prevents arbitrage while ensuring access programs serve intended patient populations."

The rural distribution network required developing specialized logistics capabilities that could reach underserved patient populations while maintaining pharmaceutical quality and supply reliability in challenging geographic environments.

"Rural distribution includes mobile health clinics, community health worker partnerships, and specialized logistics that enable pharmaceutical access in underserved geographic areas," reported our rural access manager during distribution planning. "Rural distribution creates market opportunities while demonstrating social responsibility through geographic access expansion."

"What distribution strategies enable pharmaceutical access in rural and underserved communities?" I asked.

"Community health partnerships, mobile distribution systems, and local clinic collaboration that enable pharmaceutical access while maintaining quality and supply reliability in challenging environments."

"And competitive advantages from rural pharmaceutical distribution capabilities?"

"Rural distribution enables market expansion while creating government partnerships and community relationships that provide competitive advantages through geographic coverage and social impact demonstration."

The financial assistance programs required developing systematic approaches to income verification while providing medication subsidies that could eliminate economic barriers for eligible patient populations.

"Financial assistance programs include income-based subsidies, copayment assistance, and free medication programs that eliminate economic barriers for qualifying patients," announced our patient assistance coordinator during program development. "Financial assistance creates patient access while demonstrating social responsibility that affects competitive positioning and stakeholder relationships."

"How do financial assistance programs affect pharmaceutical company economics and social impact?" I asked.

"Financial assistance reduces short-term revenue but creates long-term market expansion and competitive advantages through patient loyalty and social responsibility demonstration that affects company valuation and market positioning."

"And eligibility criteria that balance patient access with program sustainability?"

"Income verification, medical necessity confirmation, and geographic targeting that ensures assistance reaches intended populations while maintaining program financial sustainability."

The community health partnerships required establishing collaboration relationships with NGOs and government agencies that could amplify pharmaceutical access while creating systematic approaches to underserved population outreach.

"Community partnerships include NGO collaboration, government health program integration, and community health worker training that amplifies pharmaceutical access through established healthcare networks," reported our community partnership manager during collaboration planning. "Community partnerships create access multiplication while demonstrating social responsibility through healthcare system strengthening."

"What partnership strategies provide optimal pharmaceutical access and social impact?" I asked.

"Healthcare NGO collaboration, government program integration, and community health worker partnerships that leverage existing healthcare infrastructure while expanding pharmaceutical access capabilities."

"And competitive advantages from community health partnerships in pharmaceutical markets?"

"Community partnerships create government relationships, healthcare provider loyalty, and social impact demonstration that provide competitive advantages through stakeholder engagement and market access expansion."

The digital health integration required implementing technology solutions that could improve medication adherence while providing patient education and support services that enhanced therapeutic outcomes in underserved populations.

"Digital health programs include medication adherence apps, patient education platforms, and remote monitoring systems that improve therapeutic outcomes while supporting patient access initiatives," announced our digital health manager during technology planning. "Digital health creates patient engagement while demonstrating innovation and social responsibility that affects competitive positioning."

"How does digital health integration enhance pharmaceutical access programs and patient outcomes?" I asked.

"Digital health improves medication adherence and therapeutic outcomes while enabling scalable patient support that amplifies access program impact through technology-enabled patient engagement."

"And competitive differentiation from digital health integration in pharmaceutical access programs?"

"Digital health creates competitive advantages through innovation demonstration while improving patient outcomes that strengthen access program effectiveness and social impact measurement."

The social impact measurement required implementing comprehensive tracking systems that could demonstrate program effectiveness while providing transparent reporting on pharmaceutical access improvements and community health outcomes.

"Social impact measurement includes patient access tracking, health outcome monitoring, and community impact assessment that demonstrates access program effectiveness," reported our impact measurement manager during evaluation planning. "Impact measurement creates competitive advantages through accountability while providing evidence for program optimization and stakeholder communication."

"What measurement systems enable demonstrating pharmaceutical access program social impact?" I asked.

"Patient enrollment tracking, health outcome monitoring, economic impact assessment, and community feedback systems that provide comprehensive access program evaluation and optimization capabilities."

The patient access program results demonstrated that systematic access initiatives could create competitive advantages while serving underserved populations and generating measurable social impact through pharmaceutical access expansion.

"Patient access programs have enrolled 340,000 patients with 89% reporting improved health outcomes while creating government partnerships and community relationships that enhance competitive positioning," I announced during our annual access review. "Access programs create competitive advantages through market expansion while demonstrating social responsibility that affects stakeholder relationships and company valuation."

"And business impact from patient access programs compared to traditional pharmaceutical marketing approaches?" asked our social impact committee.

"Access programs have generated new market opportunities worth ₹156 crores annually while creating competitive advantages through government partnerships and community loyalty that traditional marketing cannot achieve."

Three years after implementing comprehensive patient access programs, we had created social impact that enhanced competitive positioning while demonstrating that pharmaceutical companies could balance profitability with social responsibility.

"Social impact through access programs taught us that pharmaceutical success requires serving all patient populations rather than just affluent markets," I reflected during our social impact strategy review.

"The key insight was that patient access creates competitive advantages through market expansion while demonstrating social responsibility that enhances pharmaceutical company reputation and stakeholder relationships."

The patient access program had proven that pharmaceutical companies could achieve competitive advantages through social responsibility while demonstrating that access initiatives enhanced business performance and community health outcomes.

"Social impact through access programs demonstrated that pharmaceutical success requires balancing profit optimization with patient access responsibilities," I concluded.

The lesson had become fundamental to our social mission: patient access programs enabled creating competitive advantages through social impact while demonstrating that pharmaceutical companies could enhance business performance through serving underserved patient populations and creating meaningful community health improvements.

Governance Framework Strengthening

The governance framework awakening came during a shocking regulatory investigation in February 2023 when the Securities and Exchange Board of India discovered that our board approval processes, executive compensation decisions, and stakeholder communication procedures violated multiple corporate governance requirements that we hadn't even realized existed. The magnitude of our governance deficiencies became embarrassingly obvious when the SEBI investigator mentioned that our governance practices resembled those of a family-owned business from the 1990s rather than a publicly accountable pharmaceutical company operating in global markets.

"Your governance framework lacks the transparency, accountability, and stakeholder protection mechanisms that institutional investors require for continued investment in pharmaceutical companies," announced Advocate Priya Sharma, the SEBI compliance officer, as she presented findings that showed our governance practices ranking among the worst in the pharmaceutical industry. "Modern corporate governance requires systematic board oversight, executive accountability, and stakeholder engagement that your current practices cannot provide."

"But we've always operated with integrity and made decisions in the best interests of our shareholders," I protested, though the investigation was forcing me to recognize that good intentions couldn't substitute for systematic governance processes that protected all stakeholders.

"Governance excellence requires documented processes, independent oversight, and transparent decision-making rather than just ethical intentions," she replied with the authority of someone who had investigated countless governance failures. "Institutional investors evaluate pharmaceutical companies based on governance frameworks that demonstrate accountability and stakeholder protection through systematic processes rather than relying on management integrity alone."

"And the competitive implications for pharmaceutical companies with inadequate governance frameworks?"

"Governance deficiencies create investment constraints, regulatory risks, and reputational damage that affect competitive positioning while governance excellence enables access to capital and premium valuations that poor governance companies cannot achieve."

This regulatory investigation launched our comprehensive governance framework strengthening program that would require rebuilding our entire approach to corporate oversight, executive accountability, and stakeholder engagement while maintaining pharmaceutical performance and competitive effectiveness.

The governance assessment revealed the shocking scope of structural deficiencies when systematic analysis showed that our board composition, committee structures, and oversight processes failed to meet basic corporate governance standards that institutional investors required.

"Governance assessment identifies critical deficiencies including inadequate board independence, insufficient committee oversight, weak executive accountability, and limited stakeholder engagement," reported our newly hired Chief Governance Officer, Dr. Rajesh Khanna, during his comprehensive governance audit. "Current governance framework creates regulatory risks while affecting investment attractiveness and competitive positioning in institutional investor markets."

"What specific governance improvements could provide the greatest competitive and investment advantages?" I asked.

"Board independence enhancement, committee structure optimization, executive accountability systems, and stakeholder engagement processes that demonstrate governance excellence while meeting institutional investor requirements for corporate oversight."

"And timeline for achieving investment-grade governance that satisfies regulatory and investor requirements?"

"Governance transformation requires 12-18 months of systematic improvement across board composition, oversight processes, and accountability systems before achieving institutional investor governance standards."

The board independence and composition required recruiting qualified independent directors while restructuring board committees to provide effective oversight of pharmaceutical operations, executive performance, and strategic decision-making.

"Board independence requires recruiting qualified independent directors with pharmaceutical expertise while establishing committee structures that provide effective oversight of operations, audit, compensation, and strategic planning," announced our board development consultant during governance planning. "Board independence creates competitive advantages through improved decision-making while meeting institutional investor requirements for corporate oversight."

"How does board independence affect pharmaceutical company decision-making and competitive positioning?" I asked.

"Independent boards provide strategic guidance and risk oversight that enhances decision-making while creating competitive advantages through governance excellence that institutional investors require for investment consideration."

"And director qualification requirements for pharmaceutical industry board service?"

"Pharmaceutical board service requires industry expertise, regulatory knowledge, and governance experience that enables effective oversight while providing strategic guidance for competitive pharmaceutical operations."

The executive accountability systems required implementing performance measurement and compensation structures that could align management incentives with stakeholder interests while ensuring transparency in executive decision-making and performance evaluation.

"Executive accountability includes performance measurement systems, compensation transparency, and decision-making oversight that aligns management incentives with stakeholder interests," reported our executive compensation consultant during accountability planning. "Executive accountability creates competitive advantages through improved performance while meeting institutional investor requirements for management oversight."

"What executive accountability measures provide optimal governance and competitive advantages?" I asked.

"Performance-based compensation, transparent decision-making processes, and systematic performance evaluation that ensures executive accountability while incentivizing pharmaceutical performance and competitive positioning."

"And compensation structures that balance executive motivation with stakeholder protection?"

"Long-term incentive programs, performance-based compensation, and clawback provisions that align executive interests with pharmaceutical performance while protecting stakeholder value through accountability mechanisms."

The risk management and compliance systems required implementing comprehensive oversight capabilities that could identify and mitigate governance risks while ensuring regulatory compliance across pharmaceutical operations and strategic decision-making.

"Risk management includes systematic risk identification, compliance monitoring, and oversight processes that protect stakeholder interests while ensuring pharmaceutical operations meet regulatory and governance requirements," announced our risk management director during compliance planning. "Risk management creates competitive advantages through regulatory compliance while meeting institutional investor requirements for corporate oversight."

"How does risk management enhance pharmaceutical company governance and competitive positioning?" I asked.

"Risk management enables identifying and mitigating governance risks while ensuring regulatory compliance that creates competitive advantages through operational reliability and stakeholder confidence."

"And compliance systems that satisfy pharmaceutical industry regulatory and governance requirements?"

"Comprehensive compliance monitoring, systematic risk assessment, and oversight processes that ensure pharmaceutical operations meet regulatory standards while providing governance transparency that institutional investors require."

The stakeholder engagement and transparency required developing systematic communication processes while implementing disclosure practices that could provide stakeholders with comprehensive information about pharmaceutical performance and governance practices.

"Stakeholder engagement includes systematic communication, transparent reporting, and feedback mechanisms that demonstrate governance accountability while meeting institutional investor requirements for corporate transparency," reported our stakeholder relations manager during engagement planning. "Stakeholder engagement creates competitive advantages through relationship building while providing governance transparency that affects investment attractiveness."

"What stakeholder engagement practices provide optimal governance and competitive advantages?" I asked.

"Regular communication, transparent reporting, systematic feedback collection, and responsive stakeholder relations that demonstrate governance accountability while building competitive advantages through stakeholder loyalty."

"And disclosure requirements that satisfy institutional investor governance evaluation criteria?"

"Comprehensive governance reporting, transparent decision-making disclosure, and systematic stakeholder communication that meets institutional investor requirements while demonstrating governance excellence."

The ethics and compliance culture required implementing systematic ethics training while developing compliance monitoring that could ensure ethical business practices across pharmaceutical operations and stakeholder relationships.

"Ethics and compliance culture includes comprehensive training, systematic monitoring, and accountability mechanisms that ensure ethical business practices while meeting governance requirements," announced our ethics officer during culture development planning. "Ethics culture creates competitive advantages through stakeholder trust while providing governance accountability that institutional investors require."

"How does ethics culture enhancement affect pharmaceutical company governance and competitive positioning?" I asked.

"Ethics culture improves stakeholder relationships while reducing regulatory risks that creates competitive advantages through trust and accountability that governance excellence enables."

"And compliance monitoring systems that ensure ethical pharmaceutical business practices?"

"Systematic ethics training, compliance monitoring, whistleblower protection, and accountability mechanisms that ensure ethical business practices while meeting governance standards that institutional investors evaluate."

The governance technology and systems required implementing sophisticated monitoring capabilities while developing integrated systems that could provide real-time governance oversight and transparent reporting to stakeholders and regulators.

"Governance technology includes board portal systems, compliance monitoring platforms, and integrated reporting systems that enable effective governance oversight while meeting transparency requirements," reported our governance technology manager during system planning. "Governance technology creates competitive advantages through efficiency while providing oversight capabilities that governance excellence requires."

"What technology capabilities distinguish excellent pharmaceutical company governance frameworks?" I asked.

"Integrated governance systems, real-time monitoring capabilities, automated compliance tracking, and comprehensive reporting platforms that enable governance excellence while meeting institutional investor oversight requirements."

The governance framework results demonstrated that systematic governance improvement could create competitive advantages while enabling access to institutional investment capital that governance-deficient companies could not access.

"Governance framework strengthening has achieved top-quartile pharmaceutical industry governance ratings while reducing regulatory risks and enabling access to ESG investment capital worth ₹340 crores," I announced during our annual governance review. "Governance excellence creates competitive advantages through institutional investor confidence while providing operational oversight that enhances pharmaceutical performance."

"And valuation improvements from governance framework strengthening compared to governance-deficient pharmaceutical companies?" asked our governance committee.

"Governance excellence has enabled 22% valuation premium compared to pharmaceutical companies with poor governance while providing access to institutional investment capital that enables continued growth and competitive positioning."

Two years after implementing comprehensive governance framework strengthening, we had achieved governance excellence that created competitive advantages while demonstrating that systematic oversight enhanced rather than constrained pharmaceutical performance.

"Governance framework strengthening taught us that pharmaceutical success requires systematic accountability rather than just ethical intentions," I reflected during our governance strategy review.

"The key insight was that governance excellence creates competitive advantages through stakeholder confidence while enabling access to institutional investment capital that drives pharmaceutical success."

The governance framework strengthening had proven that pharmaceutical companies could achieve competitive advantages through governance excellence while demonstrating that systematic oversight enhanced stakeholder value creation and competitive positioning.

"Governance framework strengthening demonstrated that pharmaceutical success requires balancing management autonomy with stakeholder protection through systematic oversight and accountability," I concluded.

The lesson had become fundamental to our corporate philosophy: governance framework strengthening enabled creating competitive advantages through stakeholder confidence while demonstrating that systematic oversight enhanced pharmaceutical performance and competitive positioning rather than constraining management effectiveness.

The UN Global Compact Commitment

The UN Global Compact awakening came during a humbling presentation at the World Economic Forum in Davos in January 2024 when I realized that pharmaceutical companies worldwide were making binding commitments to the United Nations' ten principles of responsible business while we remained conspicuously absent from the world's largest corporate sustainability initiative. The competitive disadvantage became painfully obvious when Pfizer's CEO mentioned that UN Global Compact membership had become a prerequisite for partnership discussions with major pharmaceutical companies and multilateral organizations that controlled billions in healthcare contracts.

"UN Global Compact commitment represents the global standard for corporate responsibility that institutional investors, government partners, and pharmaceutical customers increasingly require for business relationships," explained Dr. Sarah Vandenberg, UN Global Compact's pharmaceutical sector leader, during a session on sustainable healthcare that highlighted how our absence from the initiative was affecting our competitive positioning. "Pharmaceutical companies cannot claim ESG leadership without demonstrating commitment to internationally recognized sustainability principles through UN Global Compact participation."

"But implementing UN Global Compact principles requires systematic changes across every aspect of pharmaceutical operations," I protested, though major contract losses due to sustainability non-compliance were forcing me to recognize that UN principles had become business requirements rather than optional initiatives.

"UN Global Compact provides framework for systematic sustainability implementation while creating competitive advantages through international recognition and stakeholder confidence," she replied with the authority of someone who had guided hundreds of companies through sustainability transformation. "Global Compact commitment enables pharmaceutical companies to demonstrate credible sustainability leadership while accessing partnership opportunities that non-participants cannot achieve."

"And our competitive implications from UN Global Compact participation compared to continued non-participation?"

"Global Compact membership creates competitive advantages through international recognition, partnership access, and stakeholder confidence while non-participation increasingly excludes pharmaceutical companies from major business opportunities and government contracts."

This conversation crystallized our decision to pursue UN Global Compact membership as both a sustainability imperative and a competitive necessity that could transform our international positioning while demonstrating commitment to responsible pharmaceutical business practices.

The UN principles assessment revealed the comprehensive scope of organizational transformation required to align pharmaceutical operations with Global Compact principles covering human rights, labor standards, environmental protection, and anti-corruption practices.

"UN Global Compact assessment identifies alignment gaps across human rights protection, labor practice standards, environmental sustainability, and anti-corruption policies that require systematic improvement before achieving Global Compact compliance," reported our newly hired UN Global Compact Director, Dr. Meera Agarwal, during her comprehensive principles audit. "Global Compact commitment requires organizational transformation across all business functions rather than just policy declarations."

"What specific improvements enable pharmaceutical companies to achieve UN Global Compact compliance?" I asked.

"Human rights due diligence, labor standard enhancement, environmental management systems, and anti-corruption program implementation that demonstrate commitment to Global Compact principles through measurable actions rather than policy statements."

"And timeline for achieving UN Global Compact membership eligibility?"

"Global Compact readiness requires 12-18 months of systematic implementation across human rights, labor, environment, and anti-corruption dimensions before achieving membership eligibility and ongoing compliance capabilities."

The human rights commitment required implementing comprehensive due diligence systems while developing policies that could protect patient rights, employee rights, and community rights across pharmaceutical operations and supply chain relationships.

"Human rights implementation includes patient access policies, employee protection programs, and community impact assessment that demonstrates pharmaceutical industry human rights commitment," announced our human rights officer during rights protection planning. "Human rights policies create competitive advantages through stakeholder confidence while meeting UN Global Compact requirements for rights protection."

"How does human rights commitment affect pharmaceutical operations and competitive positioning?" I asked.

"Human rights commitment improves stakeholder relationships while reducing regulatory risks that creates competitive advantages through trust and accountability that responsible pharmaceutical companies demonstrate."

"And human rights due diligence requirements for pharmaceutical supply chain management?"

"Supplier human rights assessment, community impact evaluation, and patient access monitoring that ensures pharmaceutical operations protect human rights while meeting UN Global Compact standards for rights protection."

The labor standards enhancement required implementing comprehensive employee protection systems while developing workplace policies that could exceed international labor standards across pharmaceutical operations and supplier relationships.

"Labor standards include employee safety programs, fair compensation policies, and workplace rights protection that exceeds international labor standards while demonstrating pharmaceutical industry commitment to employee welfare," reported our labor standards manager during workplace policy development. "Labor excellence creates competitive advantages through employee engagement while meeting UN Global Compact requirements for workplace standards."

"What labor standard improvements provide optimal employee welfare and competitive advantages?" I asked.

"Employee safety enhancement, fair compensation implementation, workplace rights protection, and professional development programs that create competitive advantages through employee engagement while exceeding international labor standards."

"And supply chain labor monitoring requirements for UN Global Compact compliance?"

"Supplier labor auditing, workplace assessment, and employee protection verification that ensures pharmaceutical supply chain meets international labor standards while demonstrating Global Compact commitment."

The environmental responsibility acceleration required implementing comprehensive environmental management while developing sustainability programs that could exceed UN environmental principles across pharmaceutical manufacturing and operations.

"Environmental responsibility includes carbon neutrality programs, waste elimination initiatives, and biodiversity protection that exceeds UN environmental principles while demonstrating pharmaceutical industry environmental leadership," announced our environmental manager during sustainability planning. "Environmental excellence creates competitive advantages while meeting UN Global Compact requirements for environmental protection."

"How does environmental responsibility enhancement affect pharmaceutical competitive positioning?" I asked.

"Environmental leadership enables competitive differentiation while meeting customer and investor requirements for environmental responsibility that creates competitive advantages through sustainability excellence."

"And environmental monitoring systems that satisfy UN Global Compact environmental principles?"

"Comprehensive environmental tracking, sustainability reporting, and improvement measurement that demonstrates environmental responsibility while meeting UN Global Compact standards for environmental protection."

The anti-corruption program required implementing sophisticated compliance systems while developing transparency mechanisms that could eliminate corruption risks across pharmaceutical operations and stakeholder relationships.

"Anti-corruption implementation includes compliance monitoring, transparency reporting, and ethical business practices that eliminate corruption risks while demonstrating pharmaceutical industry commitment to ethical operations," reported our compliance director during anti-corruption planning.

"Anti-corruption excellence creates competitive advantages through stakeholder trust while meeting UN Global Compact requirements for ethical business practices."

"What anti-corruption measures provide optimal ethical protection and competitive advantages?" I asked.

"Comprehensive compliance monitoring, transparent business practices, ethical training programs, and systematic risk assessment that eliminate corruption risks while creating competitive advantages through trust and accountability."

"And anti-corruption monitoring requirements for pharmaceutical supply chain and partner relationships?"

"Partner due diligence, transaction monitoring, and ethical assessment that ensures pharmaceutical business relationships meet anti-corruption standards while demonstrating UN Global Compact compliance."

The Global Compact reporting and communication required implementing comprehensive disclosure systems while developing stakeholder engagement that could demonstrate progress on UN principles through transparent measurement and public accountability.

"UN Global Compact reporting includes annual Communication on Progress, stakeholder engagement, and transparency disclosure that demonstrates pharmaceutical company commitment to Global Compact principles," announced our Global Compact reporting manager during communication planning. "Global Compact communication creates competitive advantages through accountability while meeting UN requirements for progress reporting."

"How does UN Global Compact reporting enhance pharmaceutical company competitive positioning?" I asked.

"Global Compact reporting enables demonstrating sustainability leadership while creating competitive advantages through international recognition and stakeholder confidence that responsible pharmaceutical companies achieve."

"And Global Compact communication standards that satisfy UN requirements and stakeholder expectations?"

"Comprehensive progress reporting, stakeholder engagement documentation, and transparent disclosure that meets UN Global Compact standards while demonstrating pharmaceutical industry sustainability leadership."

The UN Global Compact membership results demonstrated that international sustainability commitment could create competitive advantages while enabling access to partnership opportunities that non-participating companies could not achieve.

"UN Global Compact membership has provided international recognition for sustainability leadership while enabling partnership opportunities worth ₹450 crores annually through government contracts and multilateral organization relationships," I announced during our annual Global Compact review. "Global Compact commitment creates competitive advantages through international credibility while demonstrating pharmaceutical industry responsibility."

"And competitive positioning improvements from UN Global Compact membership compared to non-participating pharmaceutical companies?" asked our sustainability committee.

"Global Compact membership has enabled premium positioning in government tenders while providing access to international partnerships and investment opportunities that non-participants cannot access."

Two years after achieving UN Global Compact membership, we had established international sustainability leadership that created competitive advantages while demonstrating commitment to responsible pharmaceutical business practices.

"UN Global Compact commitment taught us that pharmaceutical success requires international accountability rather than just local compliance," I reflected during our Global Compact strategy review.

"The key insight was that Global Compact membership creates competitive advantages through international recognition while demonstrating pharmaceutical industry commitment to global sustainability principles."

The UN Global Compact commitment had proven that pharmaceutical companies could achieve competitive advantages through international sustainability leadership while demonstrating commitment to global responsibility principles.

"UN Global Compact commitment demonstrated that pharmaceutical success requires participating in global sustainability leadership rather than just meeting minimum regulatory requirements," I concluded.

The lesson had become fundamental to our global strategy: UN Global Compact commitment enabled creating competitive advantages through international sustainability leadership while demonstrating pharmaceutical industry responsibility for global health and environmental protection that enhanced competitive positioning and stakeholder relationships.

Chapter 26

The Drug Discovery Breakthrough

From Optimization to Innovation

The drug discovery breakthrough moment that would validate four years of massive R&D investment arrived at 11:47 PM on June 15, 2023, when Dr. Lisa Chen burst into my home office with preliminary results showing that our AI-driven compound AMT-3471 had achieved 94% efficacy in treating familial hypercholesterolemia - a rare genetic condition that had resisted effective treatment for decades. The magnitude of our discovery became clear over the following hours as additional testing confirmed that we had identified a completely novel therapeutic mechanism that could potentially revolutionize cardiovascular treatment while establishing our company as a legitimate pharmaceutical innovator rather than just a sophisticated generic manufacturer.

"We've achieved breakthrough efficacy against a disease target that many leading corporations have been pursuing unsuccessfully for fifteen years," Dr. Chen announced, her voice trembling with the excitement of someone who had spent her career hoping for this moment. "AMT-3471 represents genuine pharmaceutical innovation that could establish our company among the world's leading cardiovascular drug developers while providing treatment hope for 50,000 patients who currently have no effective therapeutic options."

"But how do we know this isn't just promising preclinical data that will fail in human trials like 90% of drug discovery projects?" I asked, though the sophistication of our testing results was suggesting that we had achieved something fundamentally different from typical pharmaceutical development.

"Our AI-driven discovery platform identified therapeutic mechanisms that traditional drug development approaches couldn't detect," she replied with the confidence of someone presenting game-changing scientific evidence. "Computational drug design enabled targeting biological pathways that conventional medicinal chemistry never explored while predictive modeling suggests clinical success probability exceeding 75% compared to industry averages of 12-15%."

"And the competitive implications if AMT-3471 achieves clinical success?"

"Breakthrough drug discovery transforms us from generic pharmaceutical company to innovative therapeutic leader while creating competitive advantages that generic manufacturing could never provide through proprietary intellectual property and market exclusivity lasting decades."

This discovery breakthrough marked our transformation from a company that optimized existing drugs to one that created original therapeutic solutions through cutting-edge pharmaceutical innovation capabilities that few companies could replicate.

The compound characterization revealed the sophisticated molecular properties that enabled AMT-3471 to achieve therapeutic effects through entirely novel biological mechanisms that existing cardiovascular treatments had never targeted.

"AMT-3471 targets genetic cholesterol synthesis pathways through selective enzyme inhibition that reduces LDL cholesterol by 78% while avoiding side effects that plague existing statin therapies," reported Dr. Rajesh Patel, our computational biology director, during molecular analysis presentation. "Novel mechanism enables treating genetic hypercholesterolemia that conventional therapies cannot address while providing superior efficacy and safety profiles."

"What specific molecular properties distinguish AMT-3471 from existing cardiovascular treatments?" I asked.

"Selective targeting of genetic cholesterol pathways, enhanced bioavailability through optimized molecular structure, and reduced drug interactions that enable superior therapeutic outcomes compared to conventional cardiovascular medications."

"And intellectual property protection for our novel therapeutic mechanism?"

"Composition of matter patents, method of treatment patents, and manufacturing process patents provide comprehensive intellectual property protection lasting 15-20 years while preventing competitive development of identical therapeutic approaches."

The computational discovery platform validation demonstrated that our AI-driven drug development approach could consistently identify breakthrough therapeutic opportunities that traditional pharmaceutical research methodologies could not achieve efficiently.

"Computational discovery platform has generated 47 novel compound candidates with breakthrough therapeutic potential across cardiovascular, diabetes, and rare disease applications," announced our AI platform director during discovery review. "AI-driven drug development enables identifying therapeutic mechanisms that conventional research approaches require decades to discover while reducing development timelines by 60-70%."

"How does computational drug discovery compare to traditional pharmaceutical research approaches?" I asked.

"AI-driven discovery evaluates millions of molecular combinations virtually while traditional approaches require synthesizing and testing thousands of compounds individually, enabling faster identification of optimal therapeutic candidates."

"And competitive advantages from proprietary computational discovery capabilities?"

"AI discovery platform provides sustained competitive advantages through breakthrough compound identification while creating intellectual property and therapeutic mechanisms that competitors using traditional approaches cannot replicate efficiently."

The clinical development strategy required designing sophisticated human trials that could demonstrate AMT-3471's therapeutic superiority while navigating regulatory pathways for breakthrough therapy designation and accelerated approval.

"Clinical development includes Phase I safety studies in 120 healthy volunteers followed by Phase II efficacy trials in 450 familial hypercholesterolemia patients," explained Dr. Amanda Richardson during clinical planning. "Breakthrough therapy designation enables accelerated regulatory approval while orphan drug status provides extended market exclusivity and development incentives."

"What clinical evidence requirements enable demonstrating AMT-3471's therapeutic breakthrough potential?" I asked.

"Superior efficacy compared to existing treatments, improved safety profile, and clinical benefits that address unmet medical needs while satisfying FDA requirements for breakthrough therapy approval."

"And regulatory timeline for achieving AMT-3471 market approval?"

"Breakthrough therapy pathway enables market approval within 5-7 years compared to 12-15 years for conventional drug development while providing regulatory support and guidance that accelerates clinical development."

The commercial strategy development required understanding how breakthrough drug discovery could command premium pricing while establishing market positioning that reflected AMT-3471's therapeutic innovation and competitive differentiation.

"Commercial strategy positions AMT-3471 as breakthrough cardiovascular therapy commanding premium pricing through therapeutic superiority and unmet medical need fulfillment," announced our commercial director during market planning. "Breakthrough positioning enables pricing 300-500% above conventional cardiovascular treatments while achieving rapid market penetration through therapeutic necessity."

"How does breakthrough drug pricing differ from traditional pharmaceutical commercial strategies?" I asked.

"Breakthrough therapy pricing based on therapeutic value and clinical necessity rather than cost competition enables premium pricing that reflects innovation value while achieving rapid market adoption through physician and patient demand."

"And market access strategies for breakthrough cardiovascular therapeutics?"

"Specialty pharmaceutical distribution, academic medical center partnerships, and payer value-based contracts that demonstrate therapeutic superiority while ensuring patient access to breakthrough treatment options."

The manufacturing transition required adapting our pharmaceutical production capabilities to synthesize complex molecular structures while implementing quality systems that could support breakthrough drug commercial manufacturing.

"AMT-3471 manufacturing requires advanced synthetic chemistry, specialized purification processes, and enhanced quality control that exceeds traditional pharmaceutical production complexity," reported our manufacturing director during production planning. "Breakthrough drug manufacturing creates competitive barriers through synthetic complexity while enabling premium pricing through proprietary production capabilities."

"What manufacturing capabilities distinguish breakthrough drug production from traditional pharmaceutical operations?" I asked.

"Advanced synthetic chemistry, specialized equipment, and enhanced quality systems that enable producing complex molecular structures while meeting breakthrough therapy manufacturing standards."

"And manufacturing scalability for commercial AMT-3471 production?"

"Commercial manufacturing requires specialized facilities and enhanced capabilities that create competitive advantages through production complexity while enabling supply security for breakthrough therapeutic applications."

The partnership opportunities required evaluating collaboration relationships with major pharmaceutical companies that could accelerate AMT-3471 development while providing commercialization capabilities for global market access.

"Partnership opportunities include licensing agreements with major pharmaceutical companies, joint venture arrangements for global development, and strategic collaborations that provide commercialization capabilities," announced our business development manager during partnership evaluation. "Breakthrough discovery creates partnership value that enables accessing development resources while maintaining significant commercial participation."

"How do breakthrough drug partnerships differ from traditional pharmaceutical licensing arrangements?" I asked.

"Breakthrough therapy partnerships command premium valuations and milestone payments while enabling shared development costs and global market access that independent development cannot achieve efficiently."

"And partnership structure that maximizes AMT-3471 commercial potential while preserving innovation value?"

"Licensing agreements with milestone payments, royalty participation, and development cost sharing that enable global commercialization while maintaining significant value capture from breakthrough innovation."

The drug discovery breakthrough results validated our transformation from generic manufacturer to pharmaceutical innovator while demonstrating that systematic investment in discovery capabilities could create competitive advantages that traditional approaches could never achieve.

"AMT-3471 breakthrough discovery demonstrates our evolution from generic pharmaceutical company to innovative therapeutic leader capable of creating original breakthrough treatments," I announced during our annual discovery review. "Drug discovery success validates our R&D investment while establishing competitive positioning that generic manufacturing could never provide."

One year after achieving drug discovery breakthrough, we had established innovation capabilities that positioned us among pharmaceutical industry leaders while creating intellectual property and therapeutic opportunities that could generate sustained competitive advantages.

"The drug discovery breakthrough taught us that pharmaceutical leadership requires creating original therapeutic solutions rather than just optimizing existing treatments," I reflected during our innovation strategy review.

"The key insight was that breakthrough drug discovery creates competitive advantages through proprietary innovation that transforms companies from commodity manufacturers to therapeutic innovators."

The drug discovery breakthrough had proven that mid-sized pharmaceutical companies could achieve innovation leadership through systematic investment in discovery capabilities while demonstrating that breakthrough innovation provided competitive advantages that operational excellence alone could never deliver.

"Drug discovery breakthrough demonstrated that pharmaceutical success requires innovation courage rather than just operational efficiency," I concluded.

The lesson had become fundamental to our innovation philosophy: breakthrough drug discovery enabled creating competitive advantages through proprietary therapeutic innovation that established sustainable market positioning while providing treatment solutions for previously unaddressed medical needs.

First Molecule Entering Phase II Trials

The Phase II milestone moment that would validate our transformation from generic manufacturer to innovative pharmaceutical company arrived during a nerve-wracking FDA teleconference on September 27, 2023, when Dr. Rebecca Martinez, the agency's cardiovascular division director, officially approved our Investigational New Drug application to begin Phase II efficacy trials for AMT-3471 in patients with familial hypercholesterolemia. The magnitude of this regulatory achievement became clear when she mentioned that our accelerated approval pathway represented one of only twelve breakthrough therapy designations granted that year for cardiovascular applications.

"Phase II trial approval represents a watershed moment for pharmaceutical companies attempting to transition from generic manufacturing to innovative drug development," announced Dr. Amanda Richardson during our post-FDA meeting debrief, her voice reflecting the exhaustion and elation of someone who had spent eighteen months preparing the most complex regulatory submission in our company's history. "FDA approval validates our scientific approach while establishing credibility as legitimate pharmaceutical innovators capable of advancing breakthrough therapeutics through sophisticated clinical development."

"But Phase II trials represent exponentially greater complexity and risk than the Phase I safety studies we've completed," I replied, though regulatory approval was forcing me to confront the reality that we were now committed to clinical development requiring capabilities we had never fully tested.

"Phase II efficacy trials require patient recruitment, clinical site management, regulatory compliance, and data analysis that exceed Phase I complexity while providing definitive evidence of therapeutic efficacy that determines commercial viability," she explained with the systematic precision that had guided our regulatory strategy. "Phase II success enables Phase III trials and eventual market approval while Phase II failure typically terminates drug development programs regardless of previous investment."

"And our competitive positioning implications from entering Phase II clinical development?"

"Phase II entry establishes us among serious pharmaceutical innovators while demonstrating clinical development capabilities that generic companies typically cannot achieve through proprietary compound advancement and regulatory expertise."

This Phase II approval marked our evolution from a company with promising laboratory results to one conducting human efficacy trials that could validate breakthrough therapeutic potential while establishing competitive credibility in pharmaceutical innovation markets.

The clinical trial design required developing sophisticated protocols that could demonstrate AMT-3471's therapeutic superiority while meeting FDA requirements for breakthrough therapy approval and eventual market authorization.

"Phase II trial design includes 450 patients with familial hypercholesterolemia enrolled across 35 clinical sites in randomized, placebo-controlled study measuring LDL cholesterol reduction and cardiovascular event prevention," reported Dr. Priya Sharma during clinical protocol presentation. "Trial design enables demonstrating therapeutic superiority compared to existing treatments while meeting FDA requirements for breakthrough therapy efficacy evidence."

"What specific efficacy endpoints enable demonstrating AMT-3471's breakthrough therapeutic potential?" I asked.

"Primary endpoints include LDL cholesterol reduction exceeding 60% compared to 40% for existing therapies, plus secondary endpoints measuring cardiovascular event reduction and safety profile improvements that demonstrate therapeutic advancement."

"And clinical trial timeline for achieving Phase II efficacy results?"

"Phase II trials require 18-24 months for patient enrollment and treatment evaluation before generating efficacy data that determines Phase III advancement and commercial development continuation."

The patient recruitment strategy required establishing relationships with specialized medical centers while developing sophisticated enrollment systems that could identify and engage patients with rare genetic cholesterol disorders.

"Patient recruitment includes partnerships with 35 academic medical centers specializing in genetic lipid disorders plus patient advocacy organization collaboration that enables identifying eligible participants," announced our clinical operations director during recruitment planning. "Specialized recruitment enables enrolling patients with familial hypercholesterolemia while building relationships with key opinion leaders who influence therapeutic adoption."

"How does rare disease patient recruitment differ from traditional pharmaceutical clinical trial enrollment?" I asked.

"Rare disease recruitment requires specialized medical center partnerships and patient advocacy collaboration rather than broad population screening because eligible patients concentrate in specialized treatment centers."

"And competitive advantages from rare disease clinical development expertise?"

"Rare disease clinical capabilities provide competitive advantages through specialized patient access and regulatory expertise while establishing relationships with medical communities that influence therapeutic adoption."

The clinical site management required coordinating complex multi-site operations while ensuring consistent protocol implementation and data quality across diverse medical centers and geographic regions.

"Clinical site management includes 35 medical centers across North America and Europe with centralized monitoring, standardized protocols, and coordinated data collection that ensures clinical trial quality and regulatory compliance," reported our clinical site manager during operations planning. "Multi-site coordination enables rapid patient enrollment while maintaining clinical trial integrity and regulatory standards."

"What clinical site capabilities distinguish successful Phase II trial management?" I asked.

"Experienced principal investigators, specialized patient populations, advanced clinical infrastructure, and systematic protocol compliance that ensures clinical trial quality while enabling efficient patient enrollment and data collection."

"And regulatory compliance requirements for international Phase II clinical trials?"

"Multiple regulatory authority coordination, standardized protocols, and systematic monitoring that ensures clinical trial compliance while meeting FDA, EMA, and other regulatory requirements for breakthrough therapy development."

The data management and analysis required implementing sophisticated systems that could collect and analyze clinical trial information while providing real-time monitoring of patient safety and therapeutic efficacy.

"Clinical data management includes electronic data capture systems, real-time safety monitoring, and statistical analysis platforms that enable comprehensive clinical trial oversight while ensuring regulatory compliance," announced our clinical data director during system planning. "Advanced data systems provide competitive advantages through efficient trial management while enabling rapid decision-making based on emerging clinical evidence."

"How does Phase II data management compare to Phase I clinical trial requirements?" I asked.

"Phase II data management requires more sophisticated efficacy analysis, larger patient datasets, and complex statistical evaluation that determines therapeutic advancement and commercial development decisions."

"And data quality requirements for regulatory submission and breakthrough therapy evaluation?"

"Comprehensive data verification, statistical validation, and regulatory compliance documentation that enables FDA submission while providing evidence for breakthrough therapy designation and accelerated approval consideration."

The regulatory strategy coordination required managing complex interactions with FDA while preparing for potential breakthrough therapy meetings and accelerated development pathways.

"Regulatory strategy includes quarterly FDA meetings, breakthrough therapy designation maintenance, and accelerated approval pathway preparation that enables optimized development timelines," explained Dr. Richardson during regulatory planning. "Proactive FDA engagement provides competitive advantages through regulatory guidance while ensuring clinical development aligns with approval requirements."

"What regulatory advantages result from breakthrough therapy designation during Phase II development?" I asked.

"Breakthrough designation provides FDA priority review, accelerated approval consideration, and ongoing regulatory guidance that reduces development timelines while increasing approval probability through agency support."

"And regulatory preparation for potential Phase III advancement and market approval?"

"Phase II regulatory strategy includes manufacturing planning, commercial preparation, and market access coordination that enables rapid Phase III initiation and eventual market launch if efficacy results support therapeutic advancement."

The commercial preparation required developing market access strategies while building relationships with healthcare providers and payers who would ultimately determine AMT-3471's commercial success.

"Commercial preparation includes key opinion leader engagement, payer value proposition development, and market access planning that prepares for therapeutic launch while building stakeholder relationships," announced our commercial director during market preparation. "Early commercial engagement provides competitive advantages through stakeholder education while building support for breakthrough therapy adoption."

"How does breakthrough therapy commercial preparation differ from traditional pharmaceutical marketing approaches?" I asked.

"Breakthrough therapy marketing emphasizes therapeutic value and unmet medical need fulfillment rather than cost competition while building relationships with specialized medical communities that influence adoption."

"And pricing strategy development for breakthrough cardiovascular therapeutics?"

"Value-based pricing that reflects therapeutic innovation and clinical superiority while demonstrating economic benefits through improved patient outcomes and reduced healthcare costs."

The Phase II milestone results demonstrated that systematic clinical development could advance breakthrough therapeutics while establishing competitive credibility in pharmaceutical innovation markets.

"Phase II trial initiation establishes our company among legitimate pharmaceutical innovators capable of advancing breakthrough therapeutics through sophisticated clinical development," I announced during our annual clinical review. "Phase II entry validates our transformation from generic manufacturer to innovative pharmaceutical company while demonstrating clinical development capabilities that few companies can achieve."

Six months after Phase II trial initiation, we had achieved clinical development credibility that positioned us among innovative pharmaceutical companies while demonstrating systematic advancement of breakthrough therapeutic innovation.

"Phase II trial entry taught us that pharmaceutical innovation requires systematic clinical development rather than just promising laboratory results," I reflected during our clinical strategy review.

"The key insight was that Phase II advancement establishes innovation credibility while demonstrating clinical development capabilities that transform companies from generic manufacturers to therapeutic innovators."

The Phase II milestone had proven that mid-sized pharmaceutical companies could achieve clinical development success through systematic investment in breakthrough therapeutics while establishing competitive positioning in innovative pharmaceutical markets.

"Phase II trial advancement demonstrated that pharmaceutical innovation requires clinical development excellence rather than just discovery capabilities," I concluded.

The lesson had become fundamental to our innovation philosophy: Phase II clinical development enabled establishing innovation credibility through systematic therapeutic advancement that transformed companies from generic manufacturers to legitimate pharmaceutical innovators capable of breakthrough therapy development.

Building Clinical Development Capabilities

The clinical development awakening came during a devastating Phase I trial failure in November 2022 when our promising cardiovascular compound failed safety requirements not because of inherent toxicity, but because our inexperienced clinical team had designed flawed protocols that generated inconclusive data unusable for regulatory submission. The humiliating setback became painfully obvious when the FDA reviewer mentioned that our clinical trial design resembled student research rather than professional pharmaceutical development, forcing me to confront the reality that drug discovery success meant nothing without sophisticated clinical capabilities to advance compounds through human testing.

"We've discovered breakthrough compounds that could revolutionize cardiovascular treatment, but our clinical development capabilities remain at generic pharmaceutical levels rather than innovative drug development standards," announced Dr. Amanda Richardson during our post-failure analysis, reviewing protocols that had consumed ₹34 crores while producing results that regulatory agencies couldn't evaluate. "Clinical development requires specialized expertise in protocol design, patient safety, regulatory compliance, and data analysis that generic pharmaceutical experience cannot provide."

"But we've hired experienced clinical researchers and followed industry standard protocols," I protested, though mounting evidence suggested that clinical development required systematic capabilities that individual expertise could not substitute.

"Clinical development success requires integrated capabilities across protocol design, site management, regulatory compliance, and data analysis rather than just hiring experienced professionals," she replied with the systematic analysis that had guided our regulatory strategy. "Pharmaceutical innovation demands clinical development excellence that transforms laboratory discoveries into marketable therapeutics through sophisticated human testing capabilities."

"And our competitive positioning implications from building world-class clinical development capabilities?"

"Clinical development excellence enables advancing breakthrough discoveries to market approval while creating competitive advantages through faster development timelines and higher success rates that inadequate clinical capabilities cannot achieve."

This clinical failure launched our systematic development of world-class clinical capabilities that would require building entirely new organizational competencies while learning from costly mistakes that had taught us the difference between conducting research and developing pharmaceuticals.

The clinical operations infrastructure required establishing comprehensive systems that could manage complex multi-site trials while ensuring patient safety, regulatory compliance, and data quality across diverse medical centers and patient populations.

"Clinical operations infrastructure includes centralized trial management, standardized protocols, real-time safety monitoring, and coordinated site oversight that enables managing complex pharmaceutical development programs," reported our newly hired VP of Clinical Development, Dr. Sarah Martinez, during infrastructure planning. "Clinical operations excellence provides competitive advantages through efficient trial execution while ensuring regulatory compliance and patient safety standards."

"What clinical operations capabilities distinguish successful pharmaceutical development companies?" I asked.

"Integrated trial management systems, standardized protocols, experienced site networks, and comprehensive safety monitoring that enable efficient clinical development while maintaining regulatory compliance and competitive development timelines."

"And clinical operations scalability for managing multiple simultaneous development programs?"

"Scalable clinical platforms enable managing portfolio development programs while maintaining quality standards and regulatory compliance that support multiple breakthrough compounds through clinical advancement."

The regulatory expertise development required building specialized knowledge of FDA interactions while developing sophisticated understanding of breakthrough therapy pathways and accelerated approval requirements.

"Regulatory expertise includes FDA relationship management, breakthrough therapy strategy, and accelerated approval navigation that enables optimizing development timelines while ensuring regulatory compliance," announced Dr. Richardson during regulatory capability planning. "Regulatory excellence creates competitive advantages through faster approvals and higher success rates while building agency relationships that support breakthrough therapy development."

"How does innovative pharmaceutical regulatory expertise differ from generic drug regulatory capabilities?" I asked.

"Innovative pharmaceutical regulation requires breakthrough therapy navigation, novel endpoint development, and adaptive trial design that exceed generic pharmaceutical regulatory complexity through original compound development rather than bioequivalence demonstration."

"And regulatory relationship advantages for breakthrough pharmaceutical development?"

"Strong FDA relationships provide regulatory guidance, priority review consideration, and accelerated approval access that enable competitive development advantages while reducing regulatory risks and approval uncertainties."

The clinical site network development required establishing relationships with leading medical centers while building investigator partnerships that could ensure high-quality patient enrollment and protocol execution.

"Clinical site network includes partnerships with 45 leading medical centers specializing in cardiovascular, diabetes, and rare disease research," reported our clinical site director during network planning. "Investigator relationships provide competitive advantages through quality patient recruitment while ensuring protocol compliance and data integrity that regulatory agencies require."

"What clinical site capabilities enable successful pharmaceutical development trials?" I asked.

"Experienced principal investigators, specialized patient populations, advanced clinical infrastructure, and systematic protocol compliance that ensure trial quality while enabling efficient patient recruitment and regulatory compliance."

"And competitive advantages from established clinical investigator networks?"

"Investigator partnerships enable faster patient enrollment, higher protocol compliance, and superior data quality while building relationships with key opinion leaders who influence therapeutic adoption."

The data management and biostatistics capabilities required implementing sophisticated systems that could handle complex clinical datasets while providing real-time analysis and regulatory-quality documentation.

"Clinical data management includes electronic data capture, real-time monitoring, biostatistical analysis, and regulatory reporting systems that ensure clinical trial data quality while enabling efficient analysis and regulatory submission," announced our clinical data director during system development. "Data management excellence provides competitive advantages through efficient trial oversight while ensuring regulatory compliance and submission quality."

"How do innovative pharmaceutical data requirements differ from generic drug clinical data management?" I asked.

"Innovative pharmaceutical data management requires complex efficacy analysis, safety monitoring, and regulatory documentation that exceed generic pharmaceutical clinical data complexity through original compound evaluation rather than bioequivalence demonstration."

"And data quality standards for breakthrough therapy regulatory submissions?"

"Comprehensive data verification, statistical validation, and regulatory compliance documentation that enables FDA submission while supporting breakthrough therapy designation and accelerated approval consideration."

The patient recruitment and engagement required developing sophisticated strategies that could identify and enroll appropriate patient populations while ensuring informed consent and protocol compliance.

"Patient recruitment includes disease-specific outreach, patient advocacy partnerships, and digital engagement platforms that enable efficient enrollment while ensuring informed participation," reported our patient recruitment manager during enrollment planning. "Patient recruitment excellence provides competitive advantages through faster enrollment and higher retention while building relationships with patient communities that support therapeutic development."

"What patient recruitment capabilities distinguish successful clinical development programs?" I asked.

"Disease-specific expertise, patient advocacy relationships, digital outreach capabilities, and retention programs that enable efficient enrollment while maintaining patient engagement and protocol compliance."

"And patient engagement strategies for complex clinical trial participation?"

"Comprehensive patient education, ongoing support programs, and retention incentives that ensure informed participation while maintaining protocol compliance throughout extended clinical trial periods."

The safety monitoring and pharmacovigilance required implementing comprehensive systems that could track adverse events while ensuring patient safety and regulatory compliance throughout clinical development.

"Safety monitoring includes real-time adverse event tracking, independent safety committee oversight, and comprehensive pharmacovigilance that ensures patient safety while meeting regulatory requirements," announced our safety director during monitoring system planning. "Safety excellence provides competitive advantages through regulatory confidence while ensuring patient protection and clinical trial integrity."

"How does breakthrough therapy safety monitoring differ from traditional pharmaceutical safety requirements?" I asked.

"Breakthrough therapy safety monitoring requires enhanced vigilance, expedited reporting, and comprehensive risk assessment that ensures patient safety while maintaining accelerated development timelines through regulatory confidence."

"And safety monitoring integration with regulatory strategy and clinical operations?"

"Integrated safety monitoring enables proactive risk management while providing regulatory agencies with comprehensive safety data that supports breakthrough therapy designation and accelerated approval consideration."

The clinical development capability results demonstrated that systematic clinical excellence could advance breakthrough compounds while establishing competitive advantages through superior development efficiency and regulatory success.

"Clinical development capabilities have enabled advancing three breakthrough compounds through Phase I trials with 94% success rate compared to industry averages of 67% while reducing development timelines by 35%," I announced during our annual clinical review. "Clinical excellence creates competitive advantages through faster development and higher success rates while enabling breakthrough therapy advancement that inadequate clinical capabilities cannot achieve."

"And competitive positioning improvements from clinical development excellence compared to companies with limited clinical capabilities?" asked our clinical development committee.

"Clinical excellence enables competitive development timelines while building regulatory relationships and investigator networks that create sustained competitive advantages through superior clinical execution."

Two years after building comprehensive clinical development capabilities, we had achieved development excellence that enabled advancing breakthrough therapeutics while establishing competitive advantages through systematic clinical capabilities.

"Building clinical development capabilities taught us that pharmaceutical innovation requires clinical excellence rather than just discovery capabilities," I reflected during our clinical strategy review.

"The key insight was that clinical development excellence enables transforming laboratory discoveries into marketable therapeutics through systematic capabilities that few companies can master effectively."

The clinical development capability building had proven that pharmaceutical companies could achieve innovation success through systematic investment in clinical excellence while demonstrating that development capabilities created competitive advantages that discovery alone could never provide.

"Clinical development capabilities demonstrated that pharmaceutical innovation requires systematic clinical excellence rather than just promising compound discovery," I concluded.

The lesson had become fundamental to our innovation philosophy: clinical development capabilities enabled transforming breakthrough discoveries into marketable therapeutics through systematic excellence that created competitive advantages while establishing innovation credibility in pharmaceutical markets.

The Regulatory Strategy for New Drug Approval

The regulatory strategy revelation came during a crushing FDA pre-IND meeting in December 2022 when our carefully prepared submission for AMT-3471 was systematically dismantled by Dr. Rebecca Martinez, who explained that our regulatory approach resembled generic drug strategies rather than the sophisticated new drug development pathways that breakthrough therapeutics required. The magnitude of our regulatory naivety became embarrassingly obvious when she mentioned that successful new drug approval demanded understanding complex regulatory frameworks that bore no resemblance to the bioequivalence submissions that had defined our pharmaceutical expertise for two decades.

"New drug approval requires navigating breakthrough therapy designation, adaptive clinical trial design, and accelerated approval pathways that exceed generic pharmaceutical regulatory complexity by orders of magnitude," Dr. Martinez explained with the patient authority of someone educating pharmaceutical executives about regulatory realities they should have understood years earlier. "Successful new drug development demands regulatory strategy sophistication that transforms clinical development from standard protocols to customized regulatory pathways that maximize approval probability while minimizing development timelines."

"But we've achieved hundreds of successful regulatory approvals using systematic approaches that ensure compliance," I protested, though her assessment was forcing me to recognize that new drug regulation represented entirely different challenges than generic pharmaceutical submissions.

"Generic drug regulation focuses on demonstrating bioequivalence to existing products while new drug approval requires proving safety and efficacy for novel therapeutic mechanisms," she replied. "New drug regulatory strategy demands understanding FDA priorities, breakthrough therapy criteria, and accelerated approval requirements that generic pharmaceutical regulatory experience cannot provide."

"And our competitive implications from developing world-class new drug regulatory capabilities?"

"Regulatory excellence enables faster approval timelines, higher success rates, and competitive advantages through superior FDA relationships while inadequate regulatory strategy creates development delays and approval failures that destroy innovative pharmaceutical investments."

This regulatory education launched our systematic development of new drug approval expertise that would require abandoning generic pharmaceutical regulatory approaches while building sophisticated capabilities for navigating the complex pathways that governed innovative pharmaceutical development.

The breakthrough therapy designation strategy required understanding FDA criteria while developing evidence packages that could qualify AMT-3471 for expedited development pathways and accelerated approval consideration.

"Breakthrough therapy designation requires demonstrating substantial improvement over existing treatments for serious conditions affecting unmet medical needs," announced Dr. Amanda Richardson during our breakthrough strategy planning, reviewing FDA guidance that outlined qualification criteria we had never previously considered. "Breakthrough designation provides FDA priority review, intensive guidance, and accelerated approval pathways that reduce development timelines by 2-4 years while increasing approval probability through agency support."

"What specific evidence enables qualifying for breakthrough therapy designation?" I asked.

"Clinical evidence demonstrating superior efficacy compared to existing treatments, compelling data from early-phase trials, and mechanistic rationale showing therapeutic advancement that addresses significant unmet medical needs."

"And competitive advantages from breakthrough therapy designation compared to standard development pathways?"

"Breakthrough designation enables priority FDA review, ongoing regulatory guidance, and accelerated approval consideration that create competitive advantages through faster market entry and reduced development costs."

The adaptive clinical trial design required developing sophisticated protocols that could modify trial parameters based on emerging data while maintaining regulatory compliance and statistical validity.

"Adaptive trial design includes interim analyses, protocol modifications, and enrollment adjustments that optimize clinical development efficiency while maintaining regulatory compliance," reported our clinical development director during adaptive strategy planning. "Adaptive trials enable faster decision-making and resource optimization while providing regulatory advantages through innovative development approaches that FDA increasingly supports."

"How do adaptive clinical trials differ from traditional pharmaceutical development protocols?" I asked.

"Adaptive trials enable real-time protocol optimization based on emerging data while traditional trials follow fixed protocols regardless of interim results, enabling more efficient development and faster regulatory approval."

"And regulatory acceptance of adaptive trial designs for new drug development?"

"FDA increasingly supports adaptive trials for breakthrough therapeutics because adaptive design enables faster development while maintaining regulatory standards through sophisticated statistical approaches and enhanced monitoring."

The accelerated approval pathway strategy required understanding FDA requirements while developing evidence packages that could support conditional approval based on surrogate endpoints and post-market confirmatory studies.

"Accelerated approval enables market authorization based on surrogate endpoints that predict clinical benefit while requiring post-market confirmatory studies," explained Dr. Richardson during accelerated pathway planning. "Accelerated approval provides competitive advantages through earlier market entry while requiring ongoing evidence generation that confirms therapeutic benefits."

"What evidence requirements enable accelerated approval for new cardiovascular therapeutics?" I asked.

"Surrogate endpoint data demonstrating therapeutic benefit, reasonable likelihood of clinical advantage, and commitment to post-market confirmatory studies that validate surrogate endpoint predictions."

"And post-market obligations for maintaining accelerated approval authorization?"

"Confirmatory clinical studies, ongoing safety monitoring, and additional efficacy evidence that validates initial approval while ensuring continued market authorization through demonstrated therapeutic benefits."

The FDA relationship management required developing systematic interactions with regulatory reviewers while building agency confidence in our development capabilities and therapeutic innovation.

"FDA relationship management includes pre-submission meetings, ongoing communication, and collaborative problem-solving that builds regulatory confidence while optimizing development strategy," announced our regulatory affairs director during relationship planning. "Strong FDA relationships provide competitive advantages through regulatory guidance and support while reducing approval risks through agency confidence in development capabilities."

"How do FDA relationships affect new drug approval probability and timelines?" I asked.

"Positive FDA relationships enable proactive regulatory guidance, faster review processes, and collaborative problem-solving that increase approval probability while reducing development timelines through agency support and confidence."

"And FDA communication strategies for breakthrough therapy development?"

"Regular pre-submission meetings, transparent data sharing, and collaborative protocol development that build agency confidence while ensuring regulatory alignment throughout development programs."

The regulatory submission strategy required developing comprehensive documentation packages that could demonstrate safety and efficacy while meeting FDA requirements for new drug approval and market authorization.

"Regulatory submission strategy includes comprehensive data packages, risk-benefit analysis, and manufacturing documentation that demonstrate therapeutic value while meeting FDA approval requirements," reported our regulatory submission manager during documentation planning. "Submission excellence provides competitive advantages through faster review and higher approval probability while ensuring comprehensive regulatory compliance."

"What submission components distinguish successful new drug applications?" I asked.

"Comprehensive clinical data, manufacturing quality documentation, risk assessment analysis, and benefit-risk evaluation that demonstrate therapeutic value while addressing regulatory concerns and approval criteria."

"And submission timing optimization for competitive market entry advantages?"

"Strategic submission timing that balances data completeness with competitive positioning while ensuring regulatory readiness and optimal approval probability through comprehensive evidence packages."

The post-approval regulatory strategy required planning for ongoing regulatory obligations while developing systems that could support commercial manufacturing and post-market surveillance requirements.

"Post-approval strategy includes manufacturing compliance, pharmacovigilance systems, and ongoing regulatory reporting that maintain market authorization while ensuring patient safety," announced our post-approval planning director during commercial preparation. "Post-approval excellence provides competitive advantages through regulatory compliance while ensuring sustainable commercial operations and market authorization maintenance."

"How do post-approval regulatory requirements affect commercial pharmaceutical operations?" I asked.

"Post-approval regulation requires ongoing compliance monitoring, adverse event reporting, and regulatory communication that ensure continued market authorization while maintaining pharmaceutical quality and patient safety standards."

"And post-approval regulatory advantages for establishing market leadership?"

"Regulatory compliance excellence enables market expansion, additional indication development, and competitive positioning while maintaining FDA confidence that supports continued innovation and market authorization."

The regulatory strategy results demonstrated that sophisticated new drug regulatory capabilities could accelerate approval while creating competitive advantages through superior FDA relationships and regulatory excellence.

"New drug regulatory strategy has achieved breakthrough therapy designation for AMT-3471 while establishing FDA relationships that provide competitive advantages through regulatory guidance and accelerated approval pathways," I announced during our annual regulatory review. "Regulatory excellence creates competitive advantages through faster approval and higher success rates while building agency confidence that supports breakthrough therapeutic development."

"And regulatory positioning improvements compared to pharmaceutical companies with limited new drug regulatory experience?" asked our regulatory strategy committee.

"Regulatory excellence enables competitive development timelines while building FDA relationships that create sustained competitive advantages through superior regulatory execution and agency confidence."

Two years after developing comprehensive new drug regulatory capabilities, we had achieved regulatory excellence that enabled breakthrough therapy advancement while establishing competitive advantages through sophisticated regulatory strategy.

"The regulatory strategy for new drug approval taught us that pharmaceutical innovation requires regulatory excellence rather than just clinical development capabilities," I reflected during our regulatory planning review.

"The key insight was that regulatory strategy creates competitive advantages through faster approval and higher success rates while building agency relationships that support breakthrough therapeutic development."

The new drug regulatory strategy had proven that pharmaceutical companies could achieve innovation success through systematic regulatory excellence while demonstrating that sophisticated regulatory capabilities created competitive advantages that generic pharmaceutical regulatory experience could never provide.

"New drug regulatory strategy demonstrated that pharmaceutical innovation requires regulatory sophistication rather than just compliance with standard requirements," I concluded.

The lesson had become fundamental to our regulatory philosophy: new drug regulatory strategy enabled creating competitive advantages through regulatory excellence that accelerated approval while building FDA relationships that supported breakthrough therapeutic development and sustainable pharmaceutical innovation.

The Potential Blockbuster Compound

The blockbuster realization struck me during a confidential market analysis meeting in January 2024 when our commercial forecasting team projected that AMT-3471 could achieve peak annual sales exceeding $8.2 billion globally if clinical trials confirmed the breakthrough efficacy we had demonstrated in preclinical studies. The magnitude of this opportunity became overwhelming when I realized that our single compound could generate more revenue than our entire company's current operations while transforming us from a mid-sized pharmaceutical manufacturer into one of the world's leading cardiovascular therapy companies.

"AMT-3471 represents the first truly novel mechanism for treating genetic hypercholesterolemia in over two decades, creating market opportunities that could establish our company among pharmaceutical industry leaders," announced Dr. Kavya Reddy, our newly hired VP of Strategic Planning, as she presented market analysis showing that our compound could capture 60-70% of a rapidly expanding therapeutic market. "Blockbuster pharmaceutical success requires compounds that address large patient populations with significant unmet medical needs while providing therapeutic advantages that justify premium pricing for extended periods."

"But achieving blockbuster success requires clinical validation, regulatory approval, and commercial execution capabilities that we've never demonstrated," I replied, though the revenue projections were forcing me to contemplate competitive positioning that seemed almost impossible for our company to achieve.

"Blockbuster compounds transform pharmaceutical companies from regional players to global leaders while creating competitive advantages through proprietary therapeutic mechanisms that competitors cannot easily replicate," she responded with the analytical confidence that had convinced me to hire her from McKinsey's pharmaceutical practice. "AMT-3471 possesses the therapeutic differentiation, market size, and competitive barriers that enable blockbuster pharmaceutical success through sustained market leadership."

"And our realistic prospects for achieving blockbuster commercial success if clinical trials validate therapeutic efficacy?"

"Blockbuster success requires systematic commercial capabilities, global market access, and competitive positioning that transform therapeutic innovation into sustained market leadership through superior execution across all pharmaceutical business functions."

This blockbuster opportunity crystallized our transformation from a company focused on operational excellence to one pursuing pharmaceutical innovation that could create competitive advantages lasting decades while generating returns that would justify every risk we had taken during our evolution from generic manufacturer to innovative drug developer.

The market opportunity analysis revealed the massive commercial potential when systematic assessment showed that genetic hypercholesterolemia and related cardiovascular conditions affected 34 million patients globally who required lifelong treatment with medications that current therapies could not address effectively.

"Market analysis identifies 34 million patients globally with genetic cholesterol disorders requiring lifelong treatment, representing $47 billion annual market opportunity growing at 12% annually," reported our market research director during commercial assessment. "AMT-3471 addresses unmet medical needs that existing therapies cannot resolve while providing therapeutic advantages that justify premium pricing and rapid market penetration."

"What specific market characteristics enable AMT-3471 to achieve blockbuster commercial potential?" I asked.

"Large patient population, significant unmet medical needs, limited competitive alternatives, and therapeutic necessity that enables premium pricing while ensuring rapid physician adoption and patient access."

"And competitive landscape analysis for cardiovascular blockbuster opportunities?"

"Current cardiovascular market dominated by aging therapies with significant limitations while AMT-3471 provides breakthrough therapeutic mechanisms that could establish market leadership through superior clinical outcomes and competitive differentiation."

The therapeutic differentiation strategy required understanding how AMT-3471's novel mechanism could create sustainable competitive advantages while providing clinical benefits that existing cardiovascular treatments could not deliver.

"Therapeutic differentiation includes 78% LDL cholesterol reduction compared to 45% for existing treatments, plus genetic pathway targeting that addresses root causes rather than just managing symptoms," announced Dr. Lisa Chen during differentiation analysis. "Superior therapeutic mechanisms create competitive advantages through clinical outcomes that existing treatments cannot achieve while providing intellectual property protection lasting 15-20 years."

"How does AMT-3471's therapeutic superiority translate into competitive market positioning?" I asked.

"Therapeutic superiority enables premium pricing, rapid physician adoption, and competitive barriers through clinical evidence that demonstrates meaningful therapeutic advancement over existing cardiovascular treatment options."

"And intellectual property protection for AMT-3471's therapeutic mechanisms?"

"Comprehensive patent portfolio including composition of matter, method of treatment, and manufacturing process patents that provide competitive protection while preventing generic competition for extended periods."

The commercial strategy development required understanding how breakthrough therapeutics achieved blockbuster success while building capabilities that could support global market penetration and sustained competitive leadership.

"Commercial strategy includes specialty pharmaceutical positioning, key opinion leader engagement, and value-based pricing that maximizes therapeutic value while ensuring rapid market penetration," announced our commercial director during blockbuster planning. "Blockbuster commercial success requires premium positioning that reflects therapeutic innovation while building physician confidence and patient access that drives sustained market growth."

"What commercial capabilities distinguish blockbuster pharmaceutical products from conventional therapeutic marketing?" I asked.

"Therapeutic value demonstration, clinical evidence communication, and specialty market positioning that build physician confidence while justifying premium pricing through superior patient outcomes and competitive differentiation."

"And global commercial strategy for maximizing AMT-3471's blockbuster potential?"

"Coordinated global launch strategy with regional adaptation that ensures market penetration while maintaining therapeutic positioning and competitive advantages across diverse pharmaceutical markets."

The pricing strategy required understanding how blockbuster therapeutics achieved premium pricing while developing value propositions that could justify costs exceeding $150,000 annually per patient for lifelong treatment.

"Pricing strategy based on therapeutic value and health economic benefits rather than cost competition enables premium pricing that reflects breakthrough innovation while demonstrating economic value through improved patient outcomes," explained our pricing analyst during value strategy development. "Blockbuster pricing requires demonstrating therapeutic superiority and economic benefits that justify premium costs while ensuring patient access and payer acceptance."

"How does blockbuster therapeutic pricing differ from traditional pharmaceutical pricing strategies?" I asked.

"Blockbuster pricing emphasizes therapeutic value and health economic benefits while traditional pharmaceutical pricing focuses on competitive positioning and cost considerations."

"And payer strategy for achieving premium pricing acceptance despite high treatment costs?"

"Health economic evidence demonstrating reduced cardiovascular events, improved patient outcomes, and long-term cost savings that justify premium pricing through therapeutic value rather than cost considerations."

The manufacturing strategy required developing production capabilities that could support global commercial launch while ensuring supply security for blockbuster demand that could exceed our current manufacturing capacity significantly.

"Manufacturing strategy includes global production network, specialized synthetic capabilities, and supply chain security that enables supporting blockbuster commercial success," reported our manufacturing director during capacity planning. "Blockbuster manufacturing requires production scalability and supply reliability that ensure market leadership through consistent product availability and quality standards."

"What manufacturing capabilities enable supporting blockbuster pharmaceutical demand?" I asked.

"Scalable production processes, global manufacturing network, and supply chain redundancy that ensure product availability while maintaining pharmaceutical quality standards for global commercial operations."

"And manufacturing timeline for achieving blockbuster production capability?"

"Manufacturing scalability requires 2-3 years of capacity development and global network establishment before achieving production capability that can support blockbuster commercial success and sustained market leadership."

The partnership opportunities required evaluating collaboration relationships with major pharmaceutical companies that could accelerate global commercialization while providing resources necessary for blockbuster market penetration.

"Partnership opportunities include global licensing agreements, co-development arrangements, and strategic alliances that provide commercialization capabilities while enabling global market access," announced our business development director during partnership evaluation. "Blockbuster partnerships enable accessing development resources and global capabilities while maintaining significant commercial participation and competitive positioning."

"How do blockbuster pharmaceutical partnerships differ from traditional licensing arrangements?" I asked.

"Blockbuster partnerships command premium valuations and extensive commercial support while enabling shared investment in global market development that independent commercialization cannot achieve efficiently."

"And partnership structure that maximizes AMT-3471's blockbuster potential while preserving commercial value?"

"Strategic partnerships with milestone payments, global commercialization support, and significant royalty participation that enable blockbuster market development while maintaining substantial value capture from therapeutic innovation."

The blockbuster compound potential results demonstrated that breakthrough pharmaceutical innovation could create competitive opportunities that transformed companies from regional manufacturers to global pharmaceutical leaders.

"AMT-3471 blockbuster potential positions our company for transformation from mid-sized pharmaceutical manufacturer to global cardiovascular therapy leader capable of sustained competitive advantages through proprietary therapeutic innovation," I announced during our annual strategic review. "Blockbuster success would establish our company among pharmaceutical industry leaders while creating competitive positioning that operational excellence alone could never achieve."

One year after identifying AMT-3471's blockbuster potential, we had developed commercial and manufacturing strategies that could support global market leadership while preparing for competitive transformation that could establish sustained pharmaceutical industry positioning.

"The potential blockbuster compound taught us that pharmaceutical innovation can create competitive opportunities that transform companies beyond operational limitations," I reflected during our blockbuster strategy review.

"The key insight was that blockbuster therapeutic success requires systematic commercial capabilities that transform breakthrough innovation into sustained market leadership and competitive advantages."

The blockbuster compound opportunity had proven that pharmaceutical companies could achieve industry transformation through breakthrough innovation while demonstrating that therapeutic excellence created competitive opportunities that exceeded traditional business limitations.

"The potential blockbuster compound demonstrated that pharmaceutical innovation enables competitive transformation rather than just incremental improvement," I concluded.

The lesson had become fundamental to our strategic vision: blockbuster compound potential enabled creating competitive transformation through therapeutic innovation that established pharmaceutical industry leadership while providing competitive advantages that could sustain market positioning for decades.

PART VI: THE LEGACY CONSTRAINT (2023-2024)

Chapter 27: The Strategic Alliances

Chapter 28: The Market Leadership

Chapter 29: The Succession Planning

Chapter 30: The TIME Recognition

Part VI

The Legacy Constraint (2023-2024)

The legacy constraint revelation struck me during a devastating strategic review meeting in March 2023 when I realized that our company's greatest competitive advantages had slowly transformed into strategic liabilities that were preventing us from adapting to pharmaceutical industry transformation happening at unprecedented speed around us. The cruel irony became painfully obvious as I reviewed performance data showing that every operational strength we had built over two decades - our manufacturing efficiency, our regulatory expertise, our commercial relationships - had calcified into inflexible systems that couldn't pivot fast enough to address emerging market realities.

"We've become victims of our own success," announced Dr. Priya Sharma during her quarterly strategy assessment, projecting competitive analysis that showed nimble biotech companies and digital-native pharmaceutical startups achieving breakthrough innovations while we remained trapped by operational excellence that had become operational inertia. "Our sophisticated manufacturing infrastructure cannot adapt to personalized medicine requirements, our regulatory expertise focuses on traditional approval pathways while competitors pursue breakthrough therapy designations, and our commercial relationships remain concentrated in declining therapeutic areas."

"But we've built sustainable competitive advantages through decades of systematic investment," I protested, though mounting evidence suggested that pharmaceutical industry evolution was rendering traditional competitive advantages obsolete faster than established companies could adapt their operational approaches.

"Sustainable competitive advantages become unsustainable constraints when industry transformation demands capabilities that existing strengths cannot provide," she replied with the analytical precision that had guided our strategic planning for years. "Legacy constraints prevent pharmaceutical companies from participating in industry evolution while newer companies without legacy limitations capture emerging opportunities."

"And our realistic prospects for overcoming legacy constraints while maintaining operational excellence in established business areas?"

"Legacy constraint resolution requires systematic transformation that preserves valuable capabilities while developing new competencies that enable participating in pharmaceutical industry evolution rather than just optimizing traditional approaches."

The legacy constraint had emerged because pharmaceutical industry dynamics were evolving faster than our organizational capabilities, creating fundamental misalignment between internal strengths and external opportunities that threatened our competitive positioning.

Manufacturing Legacy Constraint: Our world-class traditional pharmaceutical manufacturing excellence could not adapt to personalized medicine, cell therapy, and gene therapy production requirements that represented the industry's future while our substantial infrastructure investments prevented pivoting to biological manufacturing approaches.

Regulatory Legacy Constraint: Our sophisticated traditional drug approval expertise remained focused on conventional regulatory pathways while breakthrough therapeutic opportunities required navigating accelerated approval processes, real-world evidence submissions, and adaptive clinical trial designs that our established regulatory capabilities could not support effectively.

Commercial Legacy Constraint: Our extensive relationships with traditional healthcare providers remained concentrated in primary care and cardiology while emerging therapeutic opportunities required accessing specialty physicians, academic medical centers, and digital health platforms that our established commercial approach could not reach efficiently.

Innovation Legacy Constraint: Our systematic small molecule drug development capabilities could not adapt to biologics innovation, platform technologies, and digital therapeutics that required entirely different scientific expertise and development approaches than traditional pharmaceutical R&D could provide.

"The legacy constraint represents our most fundamental strategic challenge since founding the company," I explained to our board during our constraint assessment meeting. "Traditional pharmaceutical success factors have become barriers to participating in industry transformation that defines competitive positioning for the next decade."

"What distinguishes legacy constraints from operational challenges that systematic improvement could address?" asked our lead independent director.

"Operational challenges can be solved through better execution of proven approaches. Legacy constraints require developing new capabilities that may conflict with existing strengths while abandoning approaches that previously generated competitive advantages."

The legacy constraint had created strategic paralysis because transformation requirements exceeded incremental improvement possibilities, forcing consideration of fundamental business model changes that could compromise established competitive advantages while pursuing uncertain emerging opportunities.

Technology Transformation Imperative: Digital therapeutics, artificial intelligence applications, and personalized medicine platforms required technological capabilities that traditional pharmaceutical companies had never developed while digital-native competitors achieved breakthrough innovations through technology-first approaches.

Business Model Evolution Requirement: Outcome-based pricing, subscription healthcare models, and platform-based therapeutic approaches demanded business model innovations that traditional pharmaceutical economics could not support while venture-backed companies experimented with entirely different value creation approaches.

Regulatory Strategy Transformation: Adaptive clinical trials, real-world evidence strategies, and patient-centric drug development required regulatory approaches that exceeded traditional pharmaceutical regulatory expertise while breakthrough companies achieved faster approvals through innovative development strategies.

Competitive Landscape Disruption: Platform biotechnology companies, digital health startups, and technology-enabled pharmaceutical companies were creating competitive dynamics that traditional pharmaceutical competitive strategies could not address through conventional approaches.

"Legacy constraints force pharmaceutical companies to choose between optimizing existing capabilities and developing transformation capabilities that enable future competitiveness," observed Dr. Lisa Chen during our constraint analysis session. "Companies that cannot resolve legacy constraints become gradually irrelevant while companies that successfully navigate transformation maintain competitive positioning."

"How do we balance transformation requirements with protection of existing competitive advantages?" I asked.

"Legacy constraint resolution requires systematic capability development that enables participating in industry evolution while maintaining excellence in traditional areas that continue generating revenue during transformation periods."

The legacy constraint resolution would require unprecedented organizational transformation that challenged every assumption about pharmaceutical success while developing capabilities that could enable competitive positioning in an industry evolving toward personalized medicine, digital therapeutics, and outcome-based healthcare delivery.

Capability Portfolio Transformation: Developing next-generation pharmaceutical capabilities including biological manufacturing, digital therapeutics, and personalized medicine while maintaining excellence in traditional pharmaceutical operations that funded transformation investments.

Business Model Innovation: Experimenting with outcome-based pricing, subscription healthcare models, and platform therapeutic approaches while protecting revenue streams from traditional pharmaceutical pricing and distribution strategies.

Organizational Culture Evolution: Building innovation culture and entrepreneurial capabilities that could enable breakthrough thinking while maintaining operational discipline and quality standards that traditional pharmaceutical success required.

Strategic Partnership Acceleration: Establishing collaboration networks with biotechnology companies, technology firms, and digital health organizations that could provide transformation capabilities while preserving competitive advantages in established pharmaceutical markets.

"Legacy constraint resolution represents the ultimate pharmaceutical strategy challenge," I reflected during our strategic planning retreat. "Success requires transforming everything that made us successful while maintaining performance in areas that continue driving business results."

The following chapters would document our systematic approach to overcoming legacy constraints while maintaining competitive advantages in traditional pharmaceutical markets, demonstrating whether established pharmaceutical companies could successfully navigate industry transformation or would become casualties of their own historical success.

"The legacy constraint taught us that pharmaceutical leadership requires continuous reinvention rather than just operational optimization," I announced during our transformation planning session. "Companies that cannot overcome legacy constraints will discover that yesterday's competitive advantages become tomorrow's strategic liabilities."

The legacy constraint would test whether our pharmaceutical company could achieve the ultimate business challenge: successful transformation that preserved valuable capabilities while developing new competencies required for continued relevance in an industry evolving faster than established players could adapt their operational approaches.

Chapter 27

The Strategic Alliances

When Independence Became Isolation

The strategic alliance awakening came during a crushing rejection from Novartis in February 2024 when their business development director bluntly informed me that while our AMT-3471 compound showed breakthrough potential, our company lacked the global infrastructure, regulatory expertise, and commercial capabilities necessary to maximize blockbuster therapeutic value. The uncomfortable reality crystallized when she mentioned that major pharmaceutical companies preferred partnering with organizations that could contribute strategic value rather than just innovative compounds, forcing me to confront how our independence had become competitive isolation in an industry increasingly dominated by collaborative networks.

"Pharmaceutical success increasingly requires strategic alliances that combine complementary capabilities rather than companies attempting to develop everything independently," explained Dr. Sarah Williams during our post-rejection analysis, reviewing partnership models that showed how biotech innovations achieved commercial success through major pharmaceutical collaborations. "Independent pharmaceutical development creates resource constraints and capability gaps that strategic alliances can eliminate while providing access to global markets that isolated companies cannot reach efficiently."

"But strategic alliances require surrendering control over our therapeutic innovations while sharing commercial returns that we could capture independently," I protested, though mounting evidence suggested that pharmaceutical complexity exceeded any single company's capabilities regardless of resources or expertise.

"Strategic alliances enable accessing capabilities that would require decades to develop internally while providing global market access and commercial expertise that independent development cannot achieve," she replied with the systematic analysis that had guided our business development strategy. "Alliance success requires balancing independence with collaboration that maximizes therapeutic value while creating competitive advantages that isolated companies cannot sustain."

"And our competitive positioning implications from developing strategic alliance capabilities?"

"Strategic alliances enable competitive positioning through enhanced capabilities and global market access while maintaining therapeutic innovation leadership that creates sustained competitive advantages."

This alliance imperative launched our systematic approach to strategic partnership development that would require abandoning our preference for independence while building collaborative capabilities that could amplify our therapeutic innovations through global pharmaceutical networks.

The alliance strategy assessment revealed that pharmaceutical industry success increasingly depended on collaborative networks that combined specialized capabilities while enabling companies to focus on competitive advantages rather than attempting comprehensive pharmaceutical integration.

"Alliance strategy analysis identifies optimal partnership opportunities including global commercialization partnerships, development collaboration agreements, and technology platform alliances," reported our newly hired VP of Strategic Alliances, Dr. Rajesh Khanna, during partnership strategy development. "Strategic alliances enable accessing global capabilities while maintaining innovation leadership that creates competitive advantages through collaborative excellence rather than independent limitations."

"What specific alliance models provide optimal balance between collaboration benefits and independence preservation?" I asked.

"Co-development partnerships, licensing agreements with retained commercial rights, and technology platform collaborations that enable accessing partner capabilities while maintaining strategic control over therapeutic innovation and market positioning."

"And competitive advantages from strategic alliance capabilities compared to independent pharmaceutical development?"

"Alliance capabilities enable faster market access, reduced development costs, and enhanced commercial success while providing competitive advantages that independent development cannot achieve through resource and capability limitations."

The partnership evaluation criteria required developing systematic approaches to assess potential alliance partners while identifying collaboration opportunities that could enhance our therapeutic innovation without compromising strategic positioning.

"Partnership evaluation includes complementary capability assessment, strategic alignment analysis, and competitive positioning evaluation that identifies optimal alliance opportunities," announced our alliance development manager during partner assessment planning. "Partner evaluation enables identifying collaboration opportunities that enhance therapeutic value while maintaining competitive advantages and strategic independence."

"What criteria distinguish attractive strategic alliance partners from potential collaboration risks?" I asked.

"Complementary capabilities, strategic alignment, cultural compatibility, and competitive positioning that enable collaborative success while preserving independence and therapeutic innovation leadership."

"And due diligence requirements for evaluating pharmaceutical alliance opportunities?"

"Comprehensive capability assessment, strategic fit analysis, financial evaluation, and cultural compatibility assessment that ensures alliance success while protecting therapeutic innovation and competitive positioning."

The Roche collaboration opportunity required understanding how major pharmaceutical partnerships could accelerate global market access while providing development resources that independent advancement could not achieve efficiently.

"Roche collaboration includes global commercialization partnership, regulatory development support, and manufacturing capability access that enables worldwide market penetration," explained Dr. Khanna during Roche partnership presentation. "Major pharmaceutical partnerships provide global capabilities while enabling therapeutic innovation advancement that independent development cannot achieve through resource and infrastructure limitations."

"What specific advantages does Roche partnership provide compared to independent global development?" I asked.

"Global regulatory expertise, commercial infrastructure, manufacturing capabilities, and market access relationships that enable worldwide therapeutic launch while reducing development timelines and commercial risks."

"And partnership terms that balance collaboration benefits with strategic independence preservation?"

"Co-development agreements with shared costs and revenues, retained regional commercial rights, and ongoing innovation collaboration that enables accessing Roche capabilities while maintaining strategic positioning and therapeutic leadership."

The biotechnology startup alliance network required establishing collaboration relationships with innovative companies that could provide complementary technologies while creating partnership platforms for accelerated therapeutic development.

"Biotechnology alliance network includes partnerships with twelve innovative companies providing gene therapy, cell therapy, and digital therapeutic capabilities," reported our biotech alliance manager during network development. "Biotech partnerships enable accessing breakthrough technologies while providing collaboration platforms that accelerate therapeutic innovation through shared expertise and development resources."

"How do biotechnology alliances enhance our pharmaceutical innovation capabilities?" I asked.

"Biotech partnerships provide access to specialized technologies, innovative development approaches, and entrepreneurial capabilities that enhance therapeutic innovation while enabling portfolio diversification through collaborative development."

"And biotech alliance management strategies that optimize collaboration benefits?"

"Systematic partnership management, intellectual property coordination, and development collaboration that enables maximizing biotech alliance value while maintaining strategic focus and competitive advantages."

The academic research partnerships required establishing collaboration relationships with leading universities while developing joint research programs that could accelerate therapeutic discovery and development.

"Academic partnerships include collaboration agreements with Harvard, Stanford, and IIT Delhi providing access to cutting-edge research and specialized expertise," announced our academic alliance director during research partnership planning. "Academic alliances enable accessing breakthrough research while providing collaboration platforms that accelerate therapeutic discovery through shared expertise and resources."

"What advantages do academic research partnerships provide for pharmaceutical innovation?" I asked.

"Access to fundamental research, specialized expertise, innovative methodologies, and early-stage discovery that enhances therapeutic innovation while providing collaboration opportunities that commercial partnerships cannot deliver."

"And academic partnership management that balances research collaboration with commercial objectives?"

"Joint research agreements, intellectual property coordination, and publication management that enable accessing academic expertise while protecting commercial interests and competitive advantages."

The technology platform alliances required establishing partnerships that could provide advanced capabilities while enabling therapeutic innovation through collaborative development and shared resources.

"Technology platform alliances include artificial intelligence partnerships, manufacturing collaborations, and digital health integrations that enhance therapeutic development capabilities," reported our technology alliance manager during platform partnership planning. "Technology alliances enable accessing advanced capabilities while providing innovation platforms that accelerate therapeutic development through collaborative excellence."

"How do technology platform alliances enhance pharmaceutical development capabilities?" I asked.

"Technology partnerships provide access to specialized platforms, advanced capabilities, and innovative approaches that enhance therapeutic development while enabling competitive advantages through collaborative innovation."

"And technology alliance coordination that maximizes platform benefits while maintaining strategic independence?"

"Integrated platform management, intellectual property coordination, and development collaboration that enables accessing technology capabilities while preserving therapeutic innovation leadership and competitive positioning."

The alliance portfolio management required developing systematic approaches to coordinate multiple partnerships while ensuring strategic coherence and competitive advantage optimization across collaborative relationships.

"Alliance portfolio management includes partnership coordination, strategic alignment oversight, and value optimization that ensures collaborative success while maintaining strategic focus," announced our alliance portfolio director during management planning. "Portfolio management enables maximizing alliance benefits while ensuring strategic coherence and competitive advantage preservation through systematic partnership coordination."

"What alliance portfolio management capabilities distinguish successful pharmaceutical partnership strategies?" I asked.

"Systematic partnership coordination, strategic alignment management, and value optimization that ensures alliance success while maintaining therapeutic innovation leadership and competitive advantages."

"And alliance portfolio optimization strategies that maximize collaborative benefits?"

"Strategic partnership prioritization, resource allocation coordination, and performance management that enables optimizing alliance value while maintaining strategic focus and competitive positioning."

The strategic alliance results demonstrated that collaborative partnerships could accelerate therapeutic development while providing access to global capabilities that independent development could not achieve efficiently.

"Strategic alliances have accelerated AMT-3471 global development while providing access to commercialization capabilities worth ₹2,340 crores in partnership value," I announced during our annual alliance review. "Alliance success demonstrates that collaborative partnerships create competitive advantages while enabling therapeutic innovation advancement that independent development cannot achieve through resource and capability limitations."

"And competitive positioning improvements from strategic alliance capabilities compared to independent pharmaceutical development?" asked our alliance strategy committee.

"Alliance capabilities have enabled global market access while providing development acceleration and commercial enhancement that create competitive advantages through collaborative excellence rather than independent limitations."

Two years after implementing strategic alliance capabilities, we had achieved collaborative success that accelerated therapeutic innovation while providing global market access that independent development could never achieve efficiently.

"Strategic alliances taught us that pharmaceutical success requires collaborative excellence rather than just independent innovation," I reflected during our alliance strategy review.

"The key insight was that strategic partnerships create competitive advantages through enhanced capabilities while enabling therapeutic innovation advancement that isolation cannot achieve."

The strategic alliance development had proven that pharmaceutical companies could achieve competitive advantages through collaborative partnerships while demonstrating that alliance capabilities enhanced therapeutic innovation and global market success.

"Strategic alliances demonstrated that pharmaceutical success requires building collaborative networks rather than maintaining independent isolation," I concluded.

The lesson had become fundamental to our strategic philosophy: strategic alliances enabled creating competitive advantages through collaborative excellence that enhanced therapeutic innovation while providing global capabilities that independent development could never achieve efficiently.

Partnership with Big Pharma for Co-Development

The big pharma co-development awakening came during a nerve-wracking presentation to Pfizer's executive committee in March 2024 when I realized that our breakthrough compound AMT-3471 represented exactly the type of innovative therapeutic that major pharmaceutical companies desperately needed to replenish aging product pipelines, but our negotiating position was far weaker than I had anticipated. The power dynamics became painfully obvious when Pfizer's head of business development, casually mentioned that they could afford to walk away from any partnership that didn't provide controlling development rights, while we needed their global infrastructure to achieve AMT-3471's blockbuster potential.

"Big pharma co-development requires balancing access to global capabilities against surrendering strategic control over therapeutic innovation," announced Dr. Sarah Williams during our post-Pfizer debrief, reviewing term sheets that showed how major pharmaceutical partnerships typically favored established companies over innovative biotechnology developers. "Successful co-development partnerships enable accessing big pharma resources while preserving meaningful participation in therapeutic value creation rather than becoming a contract research organization for pharmaceutical giants."

"But Pfizer controls global regulatory expertise, manufacturing infrastructure, and commercial capabilities that could accelerate AMT-3471 development by five years," I protested, though partnership terms were forcing me to confront how desperation for resources could undermine negotiating leverage. "How can we achieve global pharmaceutical success without big pharma partnership capabilities?"

"Big pharma partnerships provide essential capabilities while requiring careful negotiation to ensure equitable value sharing and strategic independence preservation," she replied with the diplomatic precision of someone who had negotiated dozens of pharmaceutical partnerships. "Co-development success requires understanding big pharma priorities while maintaining negotiating leverage through therapeutic value and competitive alternatives."

"And our realistic prospects for achieving favorable partnership terms that preserve strategic value while accessing big pharma capabilities?"

"Favorable co-development requires demonstrating therapeutic value while maintaining competitive alternatives that enable negotiating partnerships based on mutual benefit rather than desperation for resources."

This partnership challenge launched our systematic approach to big pharma co-development that would require sophisticated negotiation while balancing access to global capabilities against preservation of strategic control over our therapeutic innovations.

The partnership landscape analysis revealed that big pharma companies were actively seeking innovative compounds to address patent cliff challenges while innovative companies needed access to global capabilities that independent development could not provide efficiently.

"Big pharma partnership landscape includes active business development by Pfizer, Novartis, Roche, and Johnson & Johnson seeking breakthrough compounds to address $180 billion in patent expirations over next five years," reported Dr. Rajesh Khanna during partnership assessment. "Major pharmaceutical companies provide global capabilities while seeking therapeutic innovation that smaller companies can develop more efficiently than internal R&D programs."

"What specific advantages do big pharma partnerships provide compared to independent development?" I asked.

"Global regulatory expertise, commercial infrastructure, manufacturing capabilities, and financial resources that enable worldwide therapeutic launch while reducing development risks and accelerating market access timelines."

"And competitive positioning considerations for big pharma partnership negotiations?"

"Multiple partnership alternatives, demonstrated therapeutic value, and strategic independence preservation that enable negotiating favorable terms while accessing big pharma capabilities through mutual value creation rather than dependency relationships."

The Novartis co-development opportunity required understanding how major pharmaceutical partnerships could accelerate global market access while developing terms that preserved meaningful strategic participation and commercial value sharing.

"Novartis co-development includes shared Phase III development costs, global regulatory coordination, and commercial infrastructure access through partnership terms that preserve 40% commercial participation," explained Dr. Khanna during Novartis partnership presentation. "Novartis partnership provides global capabilities while enabling meaningful value participation through collaborative development rather than licensing arrangement that surrenders strategic control."

"How does Novartis co-development compare to licensing alternatives or independent development?" I asked.

"Co-development enables accessing Novartis capabilities while preserving strategic participation and commercial value sharing that licensing arrangements cannot provide while avoiding resource constraints that prevent independent global development."

"And partnership governance structure that balances collaboration with strategic independence?"

"Joint steering committee oversight, shared decision-making authority, and coordinated development planning that enables accessing Novartis capabilities while maintaining strategic influence over therapeutic development and commercialization strategies."

The Johnson & Johnson strategic alliance required evaluating comprehensive partnership opportunities that could provide access to diverse therapeutic platforms while creating opportunities for expanded collaboration beyond AMT-3471 development.

"Johnson & Johnson alliance includes AMT-3471 co-development plus collaboration on additional therapeutic platforms with shared research capabilities and global commercialization infrastructure," announced our J&J partnership manager during alliance evaluation. "Strategic alliance enables comprehensive partnership that provides access to J&J capabilities while creating platform for expanded collaboration and therapeutic portfolio development."

"What advantages does comprehensive strategic alliance provide compared to single compound partnerships?" I asked.

"Strategic alliance enables accessing broader capabilities, expanded collaboration opportunities, and enhanced partnership value while building long-term relationship that supports continued therapeutic innovation and global market development."

"And strategic alliance terms that preserve independence while maximizing collaboration benefits?"

"Balanced partnership structure with shared governance, collaborative decision-making, and equitable value distribution that enables accessing J&J capabilities while maintaining strategic independence and therapeutic innovation leadership."

The partnership negotiation strategy required developing sophisticated approaches that could balance access to big pharma capabilities against preservation of strategic control and commercial value participation.

"Partnership negotiation strategy includes competitive alternatives development, value proposition optimization, and term structure coordination that enables achieving favorable partnerships while preserving strategic independence," reported our negotiation advisor during partnership planning. "Negotiation success requires demonstrating therapeutic value while maintaining alternatives that enable collaborative partnerships rather than dependency relationships."

"What negotiation approaches optimize partnership terms while ensuring big pharma collaboration success?" I asked.

"Competitive alternatives, demonstrated therapeutic value, strategic independence preservation, and mutual benefit emphasis that enable negotiating favorable terms while building sustainable partnership relationships."

"And partnership term optimization that balances collaboration benefits with strategic value preservation?"

"Shared governance structures, equitable commercial participation, and collaborative development coordination that enables accessing big pharma capabilities while preserving meaningful strategic control and value participation."

The partnership due diligence required comprehensive evaluation of big pharma capabilities while assessing cultural compatibility and strategic alignment that could ensure long-term collaboration success.

"Partnership due diligence includes capability assessment, cultural evaluation, strategic alignment analysis, and competitive positioning review that ensures partnership success," announced our due diligence manager during partner evaluation. "Comprehensive due diligence enables identifying optimal partnership opportunities while ensuring cultural compatibility and strategic alignment that support long-term collaborative success."

"What due diligence criteria distinguish successful big pharma partnerships from problematic collaboration relationships?" I asked.

"Complementary capabilities, cultural compatibility, strategic alignment, and collaborative commitment that enable sustainable partnership success while preserving therapeutic innovation leadership and competitive advantages."

"And due diligence processes that ensure partnership success while protecting strategic interests?"

"Systematic capability evaluation, cultural assessment, strategic alignment verification, and competitive analysis that enables identifying optimal partnership opportunities while protecting therapeutic innovation and strategic independence."

The intellectual property coordination required developing sophisticated approaches to patent management while ensuring collaborative innovation benefits without compromising competitive advantages or strategic control.

"Intellectual property coordination includes patent portfolio management, collaborative innovation agreements, and competitive protection strategies that enable partnership success while preserving strategic advantages," reported our IP manager during partnership planning. "IP coordination enables collaborative innovation while protecting competitive advantages and ensuring equitable value distribution through sophisticated intellectual property management."

"How does IP coordination affect big pharma partnership success and strategic value preservation?" I asked.

"IP coordination enables collaborative innovation while protecting competitive advantages through patent portfolio management and strategic independence preservation that ensures partnership success without compromising therapeutic innovation leadership."

The partnership implementation required developing systematic management approaches that could coordinate collaborative development while maintaining strategic independence and competitive advantage preservation.

"Partnership implementation includes collaborative project management, strategic coordination, and performance optimization that enables partnership success while preserving strategic independence," announced our partnership management director during implementation planning. "Implementation success requires systematic coordination that maximizes collaboration benefits while maintaining therapeutic innovation leadership and competitive positioning."

"What partnership management capabilities distinguish successful big pharma collaborations?" I asked.

"Collaborative project coordination, strategic alignment management, and performance optimization that enable partnership success while preserving therapeutic innovation leadership and strategic independence."

The big pharma co-development results demonstrated that strategic partnerships could accelerate therapeutic development while providing access to global capabilities that independent development could not achieve efficiently.

"Big pharma co-development partnership with Novartis has accelerated AMT-3471 global development while preserving 40% commercial participation and strategic independence through collaborative partnership structure," I announced during our annual partnership review. "Partnership success demonstrates that big pharma collaboration can provide global capabilities while preserving meaningful strategic value and therapeutic innovation leadership."

"And competitive positioning improvements from big pharma partnership compared to independent development?" asked our partnership strategy committee.

"Big pharma partnership has enabled global market access while accelerating development timelines and reducing commercial risks through collaborative excellence that independent development cannot achieve efficiently."

Eighteen months after establishing big pharma co-development partnership, we had achieved global therapeutic advancement while preserving strategic independence and meaningful commercial participation.

"Partnership with big pharma for co-development taught us that collaboration success requires balancing access to global capabilities with strategic independence preservation," I reflected during our partnership strategy review.

"The key insight was that big pharma partnerships enable accessing global capabilities while preserving therapeutic innovation leadership through strategic collaboration rather than dependency relationships."

The big pharma co-development partnership had proven that innovative pharmaceutical companies could achieve global market success through strategic collaboration while preserving meaningful strategic control and commercial value participation.

"Big pharma co-development demonstrated that pharmaceutical success requires collaborative excellence that preserves strategic independence while accessing global capabilities," I concluded.

The lesson had become fundamental to our partnership philosophy: big pharma co-development enabled accessing global capabilities while preserving therapeutic innovation leadership through strategic collaboration that enhanced competitive advantages rather than surrendering strategic control.

Academic Collaborations with IISc and NCBS

The academic collaboration awakening came during a serendipitous conversation at the Indian Science Congress in January 2024 when Professor Raghavan Varadarajan from IISc Bangalore mentioned that his protein engineering laboratory had developed computational platforms that could revolutionize our drug discovery capabilities, but academic research remained trapped in publications while pharmaceutical applications went unexplored. The untapped potential became obvious when he casually described breakthrough technologies that could accelerate our therapeutic development by years while university innovations gathered dust due to lack of industry partnerships.

"Academic institutions generate fundamental discoveries that could transform pharmaceutical development, but the translation gap between academic research and commercial applications prevents breakthrough innovations from reaching patients," explained Professor Varadarajan during our follow-up meeting at the IISc campus, gesturing toward laboratories containing technologies that major pharmaceutical companies would spend billions attempting to develop. "University-industry collaboration enables converting academic discoveries into therapeutic solutions while providing researchers with validation that their work creates meaningful medical impact."

"But academic research focuses on fundamental science rather than commercial applications that pharmaceutical development requires," I protested, though his description of protein engineering capabilities was forcing me to recognize that academic institutions possessed technologies that our internal R&D could never develop independently.

"Academic collaborations require bridging fundamental research with applied development through partnerships that combine university discovery capabilities with pharmaceutical commercialization expertise," he replied with the enthusiasm of someone who had spent years hoping for meaningful industry engagement. "Successful collaboration enables accessing academic innovation while providing researchers with resources and direction that transform basic research into therapeutic applications."

"And our competitive advantages from developing systematic academic collaboration capabilities?"

"Academic partnerships provide access to breakthrough technologies and scientific expertise while creating innovation pipelines that internal R&D cannot generate through collaborative research relationships that enhance therapeutic development capabilities."

This academic partnership opportunity launched our systematic development of university collaboration programs that would require bridging the cultural gap between academic research and commercial pharmaceutical development while accessing innovations that could transform our therapeutic capabilities.

The IISc protein engineering collaboration required understanding how fundamental academic research could accelerate our biologics development while establishing partnership frameworks that respected academic priorities and commercial objectives.

"IISc collaboration includes access to computational protein design platforms, structural biology capabilities, and bioengineering expertise that could accelerate our monoclonal antibody development by 2-3 years," reported Dr. Lisa Chen during our IISc partnership assessment. "Protein engineering collaboration enables accessing breakthrough technologies while providing IISc researchers with pharmaceutical applications that validate academic innovation through therapeutic development."

"What specific IISc capabilities could enhance our pharmaceutical development programs?" I asked.

"Computational protein design, structural optimization, bioengineering platforms, and analytical capabilities that enable developing superior therapeutic proteins while accelerating discovery timelines through academic expertise and technology access."

"And collaboration structure that balances academic research freedom with pharmaceutical development objectives?"

"Joint research agreements with shared intellectual property, collaborative project management, and publication coordination that enables accessing IISc capabilities while preserving academic research priorities and commercial development requirements."

The NCBS cell biology partnership required developing collaboration frameworks that could leverage fundamental cellular research while advancing our biotechnology capabilities through academic expertise in biological systems.

"NCBS collaboration provides access to advanced cell biology platforms, disease mechanism research, and cellular engineering capabilities that enhance our biotechnology development," announced our NCBS partnership coordinator during collaboration planning. "Cell biology partnership enables understanding disease mechanisms while developing therapeutic approaches through academic research that accelerates pharmaceutical innovation."

"How does NCBS cell biology expertise enhance our therapeutic development capabilities?" I asked.

"NCBS research provides fundamental understanding of disease mechanisms, cellular targets, and biological pathways that enable developing more effective therapeutic approaches while accelerating discovery through academic expertise in biological systems."

"And NCBS partnership management that optimizes collaboration benefits while respecting academic research priorities?"

"Collaborative research agreements, shared facility access, and joint project coordination that enables accessing NCBS expertise while providing researchers with pharmaceutical applications and commercialization support."

The joint research program development required creating systematic approaches to academic-industry collaboration while establishing intellectual property frameworks that could protect commercial interests and academic research freedom.

"Joint research programs include collaborative projects, shared resources, and coordinated development that enable combining academic discovery with pharmaceutical applications," reported our academic collaboration manager during program planning. "Research collaboration enables accessing academic innovation while providing universities with commercial validation and resource support that enhances research capabilities."

"What joint research program structures optimize academic-industry collaboration benefits?" I asked.

"Collaborative project design, shared intellectual property agreements, publication coordination, and resource sharing that enable accessing academic capabilities while preserving commercial interests and academic research priorities."

"And intellectual property management for academic-industry research collaborations?"

"Shared IP frameworks, commercial licensing agreements, and publication coordination that protect commercial interests while preserving academic research freedom and collaborative innovation benefits."

The student fellowship and internship programs required developing systematic approaches to academic talent engagement while creating educational opportunities that could build long-term relationships between universities and pharmaceutical industry.

"Student fellowship programs include graduate research support, internship opportunities, and career development that build relationships between academic institutions and pharmaceutical industry," announced our academic talent coordinator during fellowship planning. "Student engagement enables accessing academic talent while building long-term relationships that support continued collaboration and knowledge transfer."

"How do student fellowship programs enhance academic collaboration and pharmaceutical development?" I asked.

"Student programs provide access to academic talent while building relationships that support continued collaboration, knowledge transfer, and innovation development through educational partnerships and career development opportunities."

"And student program management that balances educational objectives with pharmaceutical development benefits?"

"Educational partnership coordination, career development support, and collaborative research engagement that enables accessing academic talent while providing meaningful educational opportunities and industry experience."

The technology transfer and commercialization required developing systematic approaches to converting academic research into pharmaceutical applications while establishing frameworks for intellectual property licensing and collaborative development.

"Technology transfer programs include IP licensing, commercialization support, and collaborative development that enable converting academic research into pharmaceutical applications," reported our technology transfer manager during commercialization planning. "Technology transfer enables accessing academic innovations while providing universities with commercialization support and revenue opportunities."

"What technology transfer approaches optimize academic research commercialization?" I asked.

"IP licensing agreements, commercialization support, collaborative development partnerships, and revenue sharing that enable converting academic research into pharmaceutical applications while providing universities with commercial benefits."

"And technology transfer management that preserves academic research priorities while enabling commercial development?"

"Collaborative commercialization frameworks, IP licensing coordination, and development partnerships that enable accessing academic innovations while preserving research priorities and academic mission alignment."

The collaborative research facility development required establishing shared laboratory spaces while creating infrastructure that could support joint academic-industry research programs and technology development.

"Collaborative research facilities include shared laboratory spaces, joint equipment access, and coordinated research infrastructure that enables academic-industry collaboration," announced our facility development manager during infrastructure planning. "Shared facilities enable accessing academic capabilities while providing infrastructure support that enhances collaborative research and technology development."

"How do collaborative research facilities enhance academic-industry partnership effectiveness?" I asked.

"Shared facilities enable seamless collaboration while providing infrastructure that supports joint research, technology development, and innovation advancement through academic-industry partnership coordination."

"And facility management that optimizes collaboration benefits while respecting academic and commercial requirements?"

"Collaborative facility governance, shared resource management, and coordinated access that enables optimizing academic-industry collaboration while preserving institutional priorities and research requirements."

The academic collaboration results demonstrated that university partnerships could accelerate pharmaceutical innovation while providing access to breakthrough technologies that internal R&D could not develop independently.

"Academic collaborations with IISc and NCBS have accelerated our biotechnology development while providing access to breakthrough technologies worth ₹145 crores in research value," I announced during our annual academic partnership review. "University partnerships demonstrate that academic collaboration creates competitive advantages while enabling therapeutic innovation advancement through research excellence."

"And innovation improvements from academic collaboration compared to internal R&D development?" asked our academic partnership committee.

"Academic collaboration has accelerated innovation timelines while providing access to breakthrough technologies and scientific expertise that internal development cannot achieve through university research excellence and collaborative innovation."

Two years after establishing comprehensive academic collaborations, we had achieved innovation acceleration while accessing breakthrough technologies that enhanced our pharmaceutical development capabilities.

"Academic collaborations with IISc and NCBS taught us that university partnerships provide access to fundamental innovations that commercial research cannot generate independently," I reflected during our academic strategy review.

"The key insight was that academic collaboration enables accessing breakthrough technologies while building innovation capabilities that enhance pharmaceutical development through research excellence."

The academic collaboration programs had proven that pharmaceutical companies could achieve innovation advantages through university partnerships while demonstrating that academic research provided access to breakthrough technologies that internal R&D could never develop efficiently.

"Academic collaborations demonstrated that pharmaceutical innovation requires combining commercial development with fundamental research excellence," I concluded.

The lesson had become fundamental to our innovation philosophy: academic collaborations enabled accessing breakthrough technologies while building innovation capabilities that enhanced pharmaceutical development through university research excellence and collaborative scientific advancement.

Government Partnership for Make in India

The Make in India awakening came during an unexpected summons to the Department of Pharmaceuticals in May 2024 when Secretary Dr. Mansukh Mandaviya presented a classified opportunity to become the anchor pharmaceutical manufacturer for India's strategic autonomy initiative, requiring us to develop domestic production capabilities for critical medications that had previously relied on Chinese imports. The magnitude of this government partnership became clear when he explained that pharmaceutical sovereignty had been elevated to a national priority, backed not by guaranteed procurement contracts, but by performance-linked incentives under the Make in India framework.

Through the Production Linked Incentive (PLI) schemes for pharmaceuticals and bulk drugs, the government has committed a combined outlay of approximately ₹22,000 crore over a six-year period, aimed at strengthening domestic manufacturing of APIs, complex generics, biopharmaceuticals, and high-value formulations.

This marked a decisive shift — transforming Make in India from a policy slogan into a competitive manufacturing and innovation advantage, with the potential to position our company as a strategic contributor to national pharmaceutical resilience and self-reliance, rather than a beneficiary of guaranteed contracts.

"Make in India pharmaceutical initiative requires domestic companies to develop manufacturing capabilities that eliminate foreign dependence while building export competitiveness that positions Indian pharmaceuticals as global alternatives to Chinese production," explained Dr. Mandaviya with the authority of someone implementing policies that could reshape India's pharmaceutical industry. "Government partnership enables accessing guaranteed market demand plus policy support that transforms domestic pharmaceutical companies into globally competitive manufacturers while serving national strategic interests."

"But developing domestic production for complex pharmaceutical ingredients requires massive capital investment and technology development that could strain our resources," I protested, though the guaranteed contract value was forcing me to recognize that government partnership could provide the scale and stability that commercial markets couldn't guarantee.

"Make in India provides policy support, financial incentives, and guaranteed procurement that enable pharmaceutical companies to develop domestic capabilities while building competitive advantages through government partnership," he replied with the systematic confidence that characterized India's industrial policy implementation. "Strategic pharmaceutical manufacturing creates competitive advantages through policy protection plus export opportunities that establish Indian companies as global suppliers."

"And our competitive positioning implications from becoming a Make in India anchor manufacturer?"

"Government partnership enables competitive advantages through policy support, guaranteed demand, and strategic positioning that transforms domestic pharmaceutical companies into national champions with global market opportunities."

This government partnership opportunity launched our systematic development of Make in India capabilities that would require massive infrastructure investment while positioning us as a strategic pharmaceutical manufacturer serving both national security objectives and commercial market opportunities.

The strategic pharmaceutical assessment revealed that Make in India represented unprecedented opportunities to develop domestic manufacturing while accessing government support that could accelerate our transformation into a globally competitive pharmaceutical manufacturer.

"Make in India pharmaceutical strategy includes domestic API manufacturing, critical drug production, and export competitiveness development through government partnership worth ₹22,000 crores over a six-year period," reported our newly hired VP of Government Relations, Dr. Kavya Agarwal, during strategic assessment. "Government partnership provides guaranteed market demand plus policy support that enables developing manufacturing capabilities while building competitive advantages through strategic national positioning."

"What specific Make in India opportunities align with our pharmaceutical capabilities and strategic objectives?" I asked.

"Cardiovascular API manufacturing, diabetes drug production, and biotechnology development that leverage our therapeutic expertise while serving national strategic requirements through domestic manufacturing capabilities."

"And competitive advantages from Make in India partnership compared to purely commercial pharmaceutical development?"

"Government partnership provides guaranteed demand, policy protection, and financial incentives that enable developing competitive capabilities while accessing markets that commercial relationships cannot guarantee."

The domestic API manufacturing initiative required developing sophisticated chemical synthesis capabilities while building supply chains that could eliminate dependence on Chinese pharmaceutical ingredients for critical therapeutic areas.

"Domestic API manufacturing includes establishing synthetic chemistry capabilities for 23 critical pharmaceutical ingredients currently imported from China," announced our API development director during manufacturing planning. "API self-sufficiency enables government partnership while creating competitive advantages through domestic supply security and cost optimization."

"What API manufacturing capabilities enable achieving domestic self-sufficiency while building export competitiveness?" I asked.

"Advanced synthetic chemistry, process optimization, quality control systems, and supply chain integration that enable producing pharmaceutical-grade APIs while meeting international quality standards for export markets."

"And timeline for achieving domestic API manufacturing that satisfies Make in India requirements?"

"API manufacturing capabilities require 24-30 months of facility development and process validation before achieving full domestic production that meets government partnership obligations."

The critical drug production program required establishing manufacturing capabilities for essential medications while developing formulation expertise that could serve both domestic demand and export opportunities.

"Critical drug production includes manufacturing capabilities for cardiovascular, diabetes, and anti-infective medications identified as strategic national requirements," reported our critical drug manufacturing manager during production planning. "Essential drug manufacturing enables government partnership while building capabilities that serve domestic patients and export markets."

"How does critical drug manufacturing align with our existing pharmaceutical capabilities?" I asked.

"Critical drug focus leverages our cardiovascular and diabetes expertise while expanding into anti-infective areas that government partnership requires through manufacturing capability development."

"And production scalability for meeting both domestic demand and export opportunities?"

"Scalable manufacturing platforms enable serving domestic requirements while building export capacity that creates competitive advantages through government-supported market development."

The export competitiveness development required building manufacturing excellence while establishing quality systems that could enable competing in international markets through cost advantages and quality differentiation.

"Export competitiveness includes WHO-GMP certification, international quality standards, and cost optimization that enable competing in global pharmaceutical markets," announced our export development director during competitiveness planning. "Export capabilities enable government partnership while creating competitive advantages through international market access and pharmaceutical excellence."

"What export competitiveness capabilities distinguish Indian pharmaceutical manufacturers in global markets?" I asked.

"Quality excellence, cost competitiveness, regulatory compliance, and supply reliability that enable competing against Chinese manufacturers while building sustainable competitive advantages."

"And export market development strategies that leverage Make in India competitive positioning?"

"International marketing, quality certification, and competitive pricing that position Indian pharmaceuticals as superior alternatives to Chinese production through government-supported market development."

The technology development partnership required establishing collaboration with government research institutions while accessing funding that could accelerate pharmaceutical innovation and manufacturing capabilities.

"Technology development partnership includes collaboration with CSIR, DBT, and other government research institutions plus access to PLI scheme funding worth ₹67 crores," reported our technology partnership manager during development planning. "Government technology partnership enables accessing research capabilities while obtaining funding that accelerates pharmaceutical innovation and manufacturing development."

"How does government technology partnership enhance our pharmaceutical development capabilities?" I asked.

"Government partnership provides access to research institutions, funding opportunities, and policy support that accelerate technology development while building capabilities that serve commercial and strategic objectives."

"And technology partnership coordination that optimizes government collaboration benefits?"

"Collaborative research agreements, funding utilization, and strategic coordination that enable accessing government capabilities while building pharmaceutical excellence through partnership optimization."

The supply chain localization required developing domestic supplier networks while building procurement capabilities that could support pharmaceutical manufacturing independence from foreign supply chains.

"Supply chain localization includes developing domestic suppliers for raw materials, packaging, and equipment plus procurement systems that eliminate foreign dependence," announced our supply chain localization manager during procurement planning. "Domestic supply chains enable government partnership while creating competitive advantages through supply security and cost optimization."

"What supply chain localization capabilities enable achieving pharmaceutical manufacturing independence?" I asked.

"Domestic supplier development, procurement optimization, and supply security that eliminate foreign dependence while building competitive advantages through localized manufacturing and cost effectiveness."

"And supply chain coordination that balances localization with competitive cost structure?"

"Strategic supplier partnerships, procurement optimization, and supply chain efficiency that enable domestic manufacturing while maintaining competitive cost structure through effective localization strategies."

The policy advocacy and regulatory coordination required developing government relationships while participating in pharmaceutical policy development that could enhance industry competitiveness and strategic positioning.

"Policy advocacy includes participation in pharmaceutical policy development, regulatory coordination, and industry representation that influences government strategy while building strategic relationships," reported our policy coordinator during advocacy planning. "Government relationships enable policy influence while building strategic positioning that enhances competitive advantages through regulatory coordination."

"How does policy advocacy enhance our competitive positioning and government partnership effectiveness?" I asked.

"Policy advocacy enables influencing pharmaceutical strategy while building government relationships that create competitive advantages through regulatory coordination and strategic partnership development."

The Make in India partnership results demonstrated that government collaboration could accelerate pharmaceutical development while providing strategic positioning that created competitive advantages through policy support and guaranteed market access.

"Make in India partnership has enabled guaranteed contracts worth ₹47,000 crores while building domestic manufacturing capabilities that position our company as strategic national pharmaceutical manufacturer," I announced during our annual government partnership review. "Government collaboration demonstrates that strategic partnership creates competitive advantages while serving national objectives through pharmaceutical excellence."

"And competitive positioning improvements from Make in India partnership compared to purely commercial pharmaceutical development?" asked our government partnership committee.

"Government partnership has provided guaranteed market access while enabling manufacturing capability development that creates competitive advantages through strategic positioning and policy support."

Two years after establishing Make in India partnership, we had achieved strategic pharmaceutical positioning while developing manufacturing capabilities that served both commercial objectives and national strategic requirements.

"Government partnership for Make in India taught us that pharmaceutical success requires aligning commercial objectives with national strategic priorities," I reflected during our government partnership strategy review.

"The key insight was that government partnership enables accessing guaranteed markets while building competitive capabilities that serve both commercial success and national strategic objectives."

The Make in India partnership had proven that pharmaceutical companies could achieve competitive advantages through government collaboration while demonstrating that strategic partnership enhanced business development and national pharmaceutical capabilities.

"Government partnership for Make in India demonstrated that pharmaceutical success requires building strategic relationships that align commercial objectives with national priorities," I concluded.

The lesson had become fundamental to our strategic philosophy: Make in India partnership enabled creating competitive advantages through government collaboration that provided market access while building pharmaceutical capabilities that served both commercial success and national strategic autonomy objectives.

The Public-Private Partnership Model

The public-private partnership awakening came during a transformative meeting with the National Health Mission in June 2024 when Director Dr. Rajesh Kumar proposed that we pilot a revolutionary healthcare delivery model combining our pharmaceutical innovation with government infrastructure to provide affordable cardiovascular treatments to rural populations that commercial markets had systematically abandoned. The magnitude of this opportunity became clear when he mentioned that successful PPP implementation could scale to serve 127 million patients across 28 states while generating sustainable revenue streams that traditional pharmaceutical business models could never achieve.

"Public-private partnerships enable combining commercial pharmaceutical capabilities with government reach to serve patient populations that neither sector can address effectively independently," explained Dr. Kumar with the strategic vision of someone who had spent decades trying to bridge healthcare access gaps that market forces couldn't solve. "PPP models create sustainable business opportunities while addressing social objectives that pure commercial or government approaches cannot achieve through collaborative value creation."

"But public-private partnerships require navigating government bureaucracy while maintaining commercial viability in markets where patients cannot afford standard pharmaceutical pricing," I protested, though the scale of potential impact was forcing me to consider whether PPP models could create competitive advantages that traditional pharmaceutical approaches couldn't deliver.

"Successful PPP models require innovative business structures that combine social impact with commercial sustainability through partnership frameworks that leverage government infrastructure and private sector efficiency," he replied with the analytical precision that had made him India's leading healthcare policy architect. "PPP success enables accessing vast patient populations while creating revenue models that serve both social objectives and commercial requirements."

"And our competitive positioning implications from developing systematic PPP capabilities?"

"PPP capabilities enable accessing underserved markets while creating competitive advantages through social impact demonstration that enhances stakeholder relationships and regulatory positioning while generating sustainable revenue streams."

This PPP opportunity launched our systematic development of public-private collaboration models that would require innovative business structures while proving that social impact could enhance rather than compromise commercial pharmaceutical success.

The PPP model design required developing innovative frameworks that could combine government infrastructure with pharmaceutical expertise while creating sustainable business models that served both social objectives and commercial requirements.

"PPP model design includes tiered pricing structures, outcome-based payments, and shared infrastructure utilization that enables serving rural populations while maintaining commercial sustainability," reported our newly hired PPP Director, Dr. Meera Sastry, during model development planning. "PPP frameworks create competitive advantages through market access while demonstrating social impact that enhances stakeholder relationships and regulatory positioning."

"What PPP model structures enable balancing social impact with commercial viability?" I asked.

"Tiered pricing based on economic capacity, outcome-based payment models, government infrastructure sharing, and performance-based partnerships that enable serving underserved populations while maintaining business sustainability."

"And competitive advantages from PPP capabilities compared to traditional pharmaceutical business models?"

"PPP capabilities enable accessing vast underserved markets while creating competitive differentiation through social impact demonstration that enhances stakeholder relationships and provides sustainable revenue growth opportunities."

The rural healthcare delivery partnership required establishing systematic approaches to pharmaceutical distribution while leveraging government healthcare infrastructure to reach patient populations that commercial markets had never served effectively.

"Rural healthcare delivery includes integration with Primary Health Centers, Community Health Centers, and ASHA worker networks that provide pharmaceutical access to 89 million rural patients," announced our rural delivery coordinator during distribution planning. "Healthcare delivery partnership enables pharmaceutical access while building government relationships that create competitive advantages through social impact and market expansion."

"How does rural healthcare delivery partnership enhance our pharmaceutical market access?" I asked.

"Rural delivery enables accessing patient populations that commercial pharmaceutical distribution cannot reach while building government relationships that provide competitive advantages through partnership development and social impact demonstration."

"And rural delivery sustainability that balances patient access with commercial viability?"

"Tiered pricing structures, government subsidy coordination, and outcome-based payment models that enable sustainable rural pharmaceutical delivery while maintaining commercial viability through innovative business structures."

The outcome-based contracting required developing sophisticated payment models that could align pharmaceutical performance with patient health outcomes while creating accountability mechanisms that satisfied both government efficiency requirements and commercial sustainability needs.

"Outcome-based contracting includes payment models linked to patient health improvements, medication adherence rates, and clinical outcome achievements rather than traditional volume-based pharmaceutical sales," reported our outcomes contracting manager during payment model development. "Outcome-based models enable demonstrating pharmaceutical value while creating sustainable revenue streams through performance-based partnership agreements."

"What outcome-based contracting models optimize pharmaceutical value demonstration while ensuring commercial sustainability?" I asked.

"Health outcome payments, adherence-based compensation, and clinical improvement incentives that align pharmaceutical success with patient benefits while creating sustainable business models through performance accountability."

"And outcome measurement systems that enable effective performance-based pharmaceutical contracting?"

"Comprehensive health monitoring, adherence tracking, and clinical outcome measurement that enable demonstrating pharmaceutical value while providing accountability mechanisms for outcome-based payment models."

The technology integration platform required developing digital health capabilities while creating systems that could coordinate pharmaceutical delivery with government healthcare programs and patient monitoring requirements.

"Technology integration includes digital health platforms, medication adherence monitoring, and electronic health record integration that enables coordinating pharmaceutical delivery with government healthcare programs," announced our technology integration manager during platform development. "Digital integration enables efficient PPP coordination while providing patient monitoring capabilities that enhance pharmaceutical effectiveness and outcome demonstration."

"How does technology integration enhance PPP effectiveness and pharmaceutical delivery capabilities?" I asked.

"Technology integration enables efficient coordination between pharmaceutical delivery and government healthcare while providing monitoring capabilities that demonstrate pharmaceutical effectiveness and support outcome-based contracting models."

"And technology platform scalability for supporting expanded PPP operations across multiple states?"

"Scalable digital platforms enable coordinating pharmaceutical delivery across diverse government healthcare systems while providing monitoring and reporting capabilities that support PPP expansion and performance optimization."

The government relationship management required developing systematic approaches to bureaucratic coordination while building partnerships that could navigate regulatory complexity and policy changes that affected PPP operations.

"Government relationship management includes partnership coordination, regulatory compliance, and policy advocacy that enables effective PPP operations while building strategic relationships," reported our government relations manager during relationship planning. "Government relationships enable PPP success while creating competitive advantages through partnership development and regulatory positioning."

"What government relationship capabilities distinguish successful PPP operations from problematic public-private collaborations?" I asked.

"Systematic partnership coordination, regulatory compliance excellence, policy alignment, and collaborative problem-solving that enable sustainable PPP operations while building competitive advantages through government relationship development."

"And government relationship sustainability that maintains PPP effectiveness despite political and policy changes?"

"Strategic relationship diversification, policy alignment demonstration, and value creation that maintains PPP effectiveness while building sustainable partnerships that transcend political changes through demonstrated social impact and commercial success."

The social impact measurement required implementing comprehensive systems that could demonstrate pharmaceutical access improvements while providing accountability mechanisms that satisfied government reporting requirements and commercial performance evaluation.

"Social impact measurement includes patient access tracking, health outcome monitoring, and community benefit assessment that demonstrates PPP effectiveness while providing accountability for government partnership and commercial performance," announced our impact measurement coordinator during evaluation planning. "Impact measurement enables demonstrating PPP value while providing optimization insights that enhance partnership effectiveness and competitive positioning."

"How does social impact measurement enhance PPP effectiveness and competitive positioning?" I asked.

"Impact measurement enables demonstrating social value while providing optimization insights that enhance PPP effectiveness and build competitive advantages through social impact validation and partnership accountability."

"And impact reporting systems that satisfy both government accountability requirements and commercial performance evaluation?"

"Comprehensive impact tracking, government reporting compliance, and commercial performance integration that enable demonstrating PPP value while meeting accountability requirements for both partnership objectives and business success."

The PPP model results demonstrated that public-private partnerships could create competitive advantages while generating sustainable revenue streams through innovative business models that served both social objectives and commercial requirements.

"Public-private partnership model has enabled serving 1.2 million rural patients while generating ₹234 crores in sustainable revenue through innovative business structures that combine social impact with commercial viability," I announced during our annual PPP review. "PPP success demonstrates that social impact creates competitive advantages while generating sustainable business opportunities through partnership innovation."

"And competitive positioning improvements from PPP capabilities compared to traditional pharmaceutical business models?" asked our PPP strategy committee.

"PPP capabilities have enabled accessing underserved markets while building competitive differentiation through social impact demonstration that enhances stakeholder relationships and provides sustainable revenue growth through innovative business models."

Two years after implementing public-private partnership models, we had achieved social impact that enhanced competitive positioning while generating sustainable revenue streams that traditional pharmaceutical approaches could never access.

"The public-private partnership model taught us that pharmaceutical success requires combining commercial objectives with social impact through innovative business structures," I reflected during our PPP strategy review.

"The key insight was that PPP models create competitive advantages through social impact demonstration while generating sustainable revenue opportunities that traditional pharmaceutical business models cannot achieve."

The public-private partnership development had proven that pharmaceutical companies could achieve competitive advantages through social impact while demonstrating that PPP models enhanced business sustainability and community health outcomes.

"The public-private partnership model demonstrated that pharmaceutical success requires balancing commercial objectives with social responsibility through innovative collaboration frameworks," I concluded.

The lesson had become fundamental to our strategic philosophy: public-private partnership models enabled creating competitive advantages through social impact while generating sustainable revenue streams that served both commercial success and social objectives through innovative business structure development.

Chapter 28

The Market Leadership

From Challenger to Champion

The market leadership realization struck me during a routine competitive analysis meeting in August 2024 when our market research director casually mentioned that we had achieved 23% market share in Indian cardiovascular pharmaceuticals - surpassing established leaders to become the dominant cardiovascular therapy provider in our home market. The magnitude of this achievement became overwhelming when I realized that what had seemed like gradual progress was actually systematic market conquest that had transformed us from a challenger company into the definitive market champion while our competitors remained focused on traditional approaches that no longer worked.

"We've achieved market leadership through systematic competitive advantages that established pharmaceutical companies cannot replicate," announced Dr. Priya Sharma during her quarterly market assessment, projecting data that showed our cardiovascular portfolio commanding premium pricing while achieving volume growth that defied industry trends. "Market leadership creates self-reinforcing competitive advantages through physician preference, regulatory influence, and supply chain control that make our position increasingly difficult for competitors to challenge."

"But market leadership requires sustaining competitive advantages while defending against responses from well-funded competitors who will attempt to regain market position," I replied, though the data was forcing me to recognize that we had built competitive moats that made our leadership position more defensible than I had anticipated.

"Market leadership enables competitive advantages that challengers cannot overcome through superior resource allocation, relationship building, and strategic positioning," she explained with the analytical confidence that had guided our competitive strategy for years. "Leadership position provides pricing power, regulatory influence, and market access that create barriers to competitive entry while enabling sustained competitive advantages."

"And our prospects for maintaining market leadership while expanding into additional therapeutic areas?"

"Market leadership provides platform for expansion while creating competitive advantages that enable extending dominance into adjacent therapeutic markets through established relationships and competitive positioning."

This market leadership achievement marked our evolution from a company fighting for market recognition to one that defined competitive dynamics in pharmaceutical markets while establishing sustainable advantages that would protect our position for years to come.

The competitive positioning analysis revealed that market leadership had created systematic advantages across every aspect of pharmaceutical competition while establishing barriers that made challenger strategies increasingly ineffective.

"Market leadership analysis shows 23% cardiovascular market share with average selling prices 18% above competitor levels while achieving faster growth than industry averages," reported our competitive intelligence manager during positioning assessment. "Leadership position enables premium pricing and growth acceleration while creating competitive barriers through physician relationships, regulatory influence, and supply chain advantages that challengers cannot replicate easily."

"What specific competitive advantages distinguish market leadership from challenger positioning?" I asked.

"Physician preference through clinical evidence, regulatory influence through compliance excellence, supply chain control through partnership relationships, and pricing power through therapeutic differentiation that create sustained competitive advantages."

"And defensive strategies that protect market leadership against competitive responses from established pharmaceutical companies?"

"Continuous innovation, relationship deepening, regulatory excellence, and competitive intelligence that enable maintaining leadership advantages while preventing successful competitive challenges through systematic advantage reinforcement."

The physician relationship dominance required understanding how market leadership had created prescribing preference while building medical community influence that made competitive displacement increasingly difficult.

"Physician relationship analysis shows 67% of cardiologists preferentially prescribing our cardiovascular portfolio compared to 23% for nearest competitor," announced our medical affairs director during relationship assessment. "Physician preference creates competitive advantages through prescribing loyalty while building medical community influence that prevents competitive displacement through relationship depth and clinical confidence."

"How does physician preference translate into sustainable competitive advantages?" I asked.

"Physician prescribing creates patient volume that enables further clinical evidence development while building medical community relationships that influence therapeutic adoption and competitive positioning through professional recommendation and clinical confidence."

"And physician relationship sustainability against competitive marketing and relationship building efforts?"

"Clinical evidence superiority, educational program excellence, and ongoing medical support that maintain physician confidence while creating relationship depth that competitive marketing cannot easily overcome through systematic medical community engagement."

The regulatory influence development demonstrated how market leadership had created agency relationships while establishing compliance excellence that provided competitive advantages and market access protection.

"Regulatory influence includes priority review consideration, compliance recognition, and agency consultation requests that provide competitive advantages through regulatory relationships," reported Dr. Amanda Richardson during regulatory positioning assessment. "Regulatory influence enables faster approvals and compliance efficiency while creating competitive barriers through agency confidence and systematic excellence that competitors cannot quickly replicate."

"What regulatory advantages result from market leadership positioning?" I asked.

"Priority regulatory consideration, compliance consultation, faster approval processing, and regulatory guidance access that create competitive advantages while enabling market access protection through agency relationships and compliance excellence."

"And regulatory relationship sustainability that protects competitive advantages despite competitor improvement efforts?"

"Systematic compliance excellence, regulatory innovation, and agency collaboration that maintain regulatory influence while creating competitive barriers through demonstrated reliability and regulatory leadership that competitors cannot easily challenge."

The supply chain control analysis revealed how market leadership had created procurement advantages while establishing supplier relationships that provided cost benefits and supply security that competitors could not access.

"Supply chain control includes preferred supplier status, volume pricing advantages, and supply priority that create cost benefits of 12-18% compared to competitor procurement costs," announced our supply chain director during control assessment. "Supply chain advantages enable cost leadership while providing supply security that creates competitive barriers through supplier relationships and volume leverage."

"How does supply chain control enhance competitive positioning and market leadership sustainability?" I asked.

"Supply chain advantages enable cost competitiveness while providing supply reliability that creates competitive differentiation through procurement excellence and supplier relationship development that competitors cannot easily replicate."

"And supply chain defensive strategies that protect advantages against competitor volume building and relationship development?"

"Supplier partnership deepening, contract optimization, and supply chain innovation that maintain procurement advantages while creating competitive barriers through relationship development and supply chain excellence."

The pricing power demonstration showed how market leadership had enabled premium pricing while maintaining volume growth that traditional pharmaceutical competition could not achieve simultaneously.

"Pricing power analysis shows average selling prices 18% above competitor levels while achieving volume growth faster than industry averages," reported our pricing manager during power assessment. "Pricing power enables premium revenue while maintaining growth that creates competitive advantages through therapeutic value demonstration and market positioning excellence."

"What enables maintaining premium pricing while achieving superior volume growth?" I asked.

"Therapeutic differentiation, physician preference, clinical evidence superiority, and market positioning that justify premium pricing while enabling volume growth through competitive advantages and therapeutic value demonstration."

"And pricing sustainability against competitive pricing pressure and market entry attempts?"

"Value-based pricing, therapeutic differentiation, and competitive barrier maintenance that protect pricing power while enabling sustained premium positioning through market leadership and competitive advantage preservation."

The market expansion strategy required leveraging leadership position while developing capabilities that could extend competitive advantages into adjacent therapeutic areas and geographic markets.

"Market expansion includes diabetes market entry, international expansion, and specialty therapeutic development that leverage cardiovascular leadership while extending competitive advantages," announced our expansion manager during growth planning. "Leadership expansion enables accessing adjacent markets while creating competitive advantages through established relationships and market positioning excellence."

"How does market leadership position enable expansion into adjacent therapeutic areas?" I asked.

"Physician relationships, regulatory influence, supply chain advantages, and market positioning that enable extending competitive advantages while accelerating expansion through established competitive infrastructure and market leadership capabilities."

"And expansion strategies that maintain cardiovascular leadership while building adjacent market positions?"

"Resource allocation optimization, capability leveraging, and competitive advantage extension that enable market expansion while preserving leadership position through systematic advantage utilization and strategic development."

The competitive intelligence and response capabilities required developing sophisticated monitoring while creating response systems that could protect market leadership against emerging competitive threats and challenger strategies.

"Competitive intelligence includes systematic competitor monitoring, threat assessment, and response coordination that enables protecting market leadership while anticipating competitive challenges," reported our competitive intelligence director during monitoring planning. "Intelligence capabilities enable proactive response while maintaining competitive advantages through threat anticipation and systematic competitive protection."

"What competitive intelligence capabilities distinguish market leadership defense from challenger strategies?" I asked.

"Systematic competitor monitoring, threat anticipation, response coordination, and competitive advantage protection that enable maintaining leadership position while preventing successful competitive challenges through intelligence excellence and proactive defense."

The market leadership results demonstrated that systematic competitive advantage development had created sustainable positioning while establishing barriers that made competitive displacement increasingly difficult.

"Market leadership achievement includes 23% cardiovascular market share with premium pricing and superior growth while building competitive advantages that create sustainable positioning," I announced during our annual leadership review. "Leadership position demonstrates that systematic competitive development creates sustainable advantages while establishing market dominance that competitors cannot easily challenge."

"And competitive positioning sustainability against responses from established pharmaceutical companies?" asked our market leadership committee.

"Market leadership advantages include physician preference, regulatory influence, supply chain control, and pricing power that create competitive barriers while enabling sustainable positioning through systematic advantage development and competitive excellence."

One year after achieving market leadership, we had established competitive positioning that created sustainable advantages while demonstrating that systematic competitive development could establish market dominance in pharmaceutical markets.

"Market leadership taught us that pharmaceutical success requires building systematic competitive advantages rather than just competing for market share," I reflected during our leadership strategy review.

"The key insight was that market leadership creates self-reinforcing advantages that enable sustainable competitive positioning while making challenger strategies increasingly ineffective."

The market leadership achievement had proven that pharmaceutical companies could establish market dominance through systematic competitive advantage development while demonstrating that leadership position created sustainable barriers against competitive challenges.

"Market leadership demonstrated that pharmaceutical success requires building competitive advantages that create sustainable positioning rather than just achieving temporary market gains," I concluded.

The lesson had become fundamental to our competitive philosophy: market leadership enabled creating sustainable competitive advantages through systematic excellence that established market dominance while providing barriers against competitive challenges that protected long-term positioning and competitive success.

Achieving Top 5 Position Globally in Generics

The global generics breakthrough moment arrived during a stunning conference call with Evaluate Pharma in September 2024 when their senior analyst informed me that our rapid international expansion had catapulted us into the fifth-largest global generics company by revenue, surpassing established giants who had dominated international markets for decades. The magnitude of this achievement became overwhelming when I realized that our systematic global strategy had achieved in seven years what pharmaceutical industry experts had considered impossible for a mid-sized Indian company competing against multinational corporations with century-long market dominance.

"Your global generics portfolio has achieved $4.7 billion annual revenue with presence across 67 countries, establishing market leadership that exceeds companies with ten times your historical resources," announced Dr. Margaret Chen, Evaluate Pharma's lead pharmaceutical analyst, during her global rankings presentation. "Top-five global positioning creates competitive advantages through scale economies, regulatory influence, and market access that enable sustained competitive leadership while establishing barriers that prevent challenger companies from displacing established global players."

"But achieving top-five global status requires sustaining competitive advantages against pharmaceutical giants with unlimited resources and century-long market relationships," I replied, though the revenue data was forcing me to recognize that our global expansion had created competitive moats that made our position more defensible than I had anticipated.

"Global generics leadership enables systematic advantages through manufacturing scale, regulatory portfolio, and market access relationships that create competitive barriers while providing pricing power and growth opportunities that regional companies cannot achieve," she explained with the analytical authority that had made Evaluate Pharma the definitive pharmaceutical industry rankings organization. "Top-five positioning provides platform for continued expansion while creating competitive advantages that enable defending market leadership against larger pharmaceutical corporations."

"And our prospects for maintaining global leadership while pharmaceutical industry consolidation intensifies competitive pressure?"

"Global leadership provides defensive advantages through market diversification, regulatory relationships, and manufacturing scale that enable sustaining competitive positioning while creating barriers against both consolidation threats and emerging market challengers."

This global achievement marked our transformation from an Indian pharmaceutical company with international aspirations to a genuine multinational corporation with competitive capabilities that exceeded established pharmaceutical giants across multiple dimensions of business excellence.

The global market presence analysis revealed that our systematic international expansion had created comprehensive market coverage while establishing competitive advantages that enabled premium positioning in pharmaceutical markets worldwide.

"Global market analysis shows presence across 67 countries with market leadership positions in 23 markets including top-three positioning in cardiovascular generics across North America, Europe, and Asia," reported our global market director during positioning assessment. "International presence enables competitive advantages through market diversification, regulatory influence, and supply chain optimization that create sustained competitive positioning while providing growth opportunities that domestic-focused companies cannot access."

"What specific global capabilities distinguish top-five positioning from regional pharmaceutical companies?" I asked.

"Global regulatory portfolio with 340+ approved products, manufacturing presence across six continents, supply chain relationships spanning 180+ countries, and market access capabilities that enable competing against multinational pharmaceutical corporations through systematic global excellence."

"And competitive sustainability against consolidation attempts from larger pharmaceutical companies seeking to acquire global generics assets?"

"Global scale advantages, integrated operations, and market relationships that create defensive barriers while enabling independent competitive positioning through systematic excellence that makes acquisition less attractive than partnership relationships."

The manufacturing network globalization demonstrated how our continental facility strategy had created production capabilities while establishing supply chain advantages that enabled cost leadership and quality differentiation simultaneously.

"Global manufacturing network includes 12 production facilities across six continents with combined capacity exceeding 45 billion units annually," announced our global manufacturing director during capacity assessment. "Manufacturing globalization enables cost optimization through geographic arbitrage while providing supply security and regulatory compliance that create competitive advantages through operational excellence and market access capabilities."

"How does global manufacturing scale compare to established pharmaceutical giants?" I asked.

"Manufacturing capacity exceeds competitors' levels while achieving superior cost efficiency through facility optimization, process innovation, and supply chain integration that enable cost leadership despite smaller absolute scale."

"And manufacturing scalability for continued global expansion and competitive positioning enhancement?"

"Modular facility design, process standardization, and supply chain integration that enable rapid capacity expansion while maintaining cost efficiency and quality standards through systematic manufacturing excellence and operational optimization."

The regulatory portfolio breadth revealed how our systematic approval strategy had created comprehensive market access while establishing regulatory relationships that provided competitive advantages and defensive barriers.

"Regulatory portfolio includes 2,400+ approved products across major pharmaceutical markets with priority review relationships in 34 countries," reported Dr. Amanda Richardson during regulatory assessment. "Regulatory breadth enables comprehensive market access while creating competitive advantages through approval speed, compliance excellence, and agency relationships that provide sustained competitive positioning."

"What regulatory advantages enable competing against pharmaceutical corporations with decades-long agency relationships?" I asked.

"Regulatory innovation, compliance excellence, and systematic relationship building that enable achieving priority consideration while creating competitive advantages through approval efficiency and regulatory reliability that established companies cannot easily replicate."

"And regulatory defensive strategies that protect global market access against competitive challenges and agency relationship building efforts?"

"Continuous regulatory innovation, compliance leadership, and agency collaboration that maintain regulatory advantages while creating barriers against competitive displacement through systematic excellence and relationship depth."

The commercial excellence globalization showed how our international sales and marketing capabilities had achieved market penetration while building customer relationships that provided competitive advantages across diverse pharmaceutical markets.

"Global commercial excellence includes 4,700+ sales professionals across 67 countries with customer relationships spanning 89,000+ pharmacies and 12,000+ hospitals," announced our global commercial director during market penetration assessment. "Commercial globalization enables market access while creating competitive advantages through customer relationships, brand recognition, and therapeutic expertise that provide sustained market positioning."

"How does global commercial reach compare to established multinational pharmaceutical companies?" I asked.

"Commercial presence approaches top-tier generics companies while achieving superior market penetration efficiency through focused therapeutic positioning and customer relationship excellence that enable competitive advantages despite smaller absolute scale."

"And commercial sustainability against competitive marketing investments and relationship building efforts from larger pharmaceutical corporations?"

"Customer relationship depth, therapeutic expertise, and market positioning excellence that create competitive barriers while enabling sustained commercial advantages through systematic relationship building and market excellence."

The supply chain optimization analysis demonstrated how global operations had created procurement advantages while establishing supplier relationships that provided cost benefits and supply security that regional competitors could not access.

"Global supply chain optimization includes relationships with 2,300+ suppliers across 45 countries with procurement advantages averaging 23% cost reduction compared to regional pharmaceutical companies," announced our global supply chain director during optimization assessment. "Supply chain globalization enables cost leadership while providing supply security through diversification and relationship development that create competitive advantages."

"What supply chain advantages enable achieving cost leadership while maintaining quality standards?" I asked.

"Global procurement leverage, supplier relationship excellence, and supply chain integration that enable cost optimization while ensuring quality and supply reliability through systematic supply chain excellence and relationship development."

"And supply chain defensive capabilities that protect competitive advantages against supplier relationship building by larger pharmaceutical companies?"

"Supplier partnership depth, contract optimization, and supply chain innovation that maintain procurement advantages while creating barriers against competitive supplier relationship development through systematic excellence and partnership strength."

The financial performance validation confirmed that global leadership had generated sustainable competitive advantages while creating shareholder value that exceeded pharmaceutical industry benchmarks across multiple performance metrics.

"Global generics leadership has generated $4.7 billion annual revenue with 18% EBITDA margins while achieving 34% annual growth over past five years," I announced during our annual performance review. "Financial excellence demonstrates that global positioning creates sustainable competitive advantages while generating shareholder value that exceeds pharmaceutical industry performance through systematic operational excellence."

"And financial sustainability against competitive pressure from larger pharmaceutical corporations?" asked our global strategy committee.

"Financial strength enables continued investment in competitive advantages while providing defensive resources that protect market positioning through systematic excellence and competitive advantage reinforcement."

Two years after achieving top-five global positioning, we had established competitive advantages that enabled sustainable market leadership while creating barriers that protected our position against both consolidation threats and emerging competitive challenges.

"Achieving top-five position globally in generics taught us that pharmaceutical success requires building systematic competitive advantages rather than just pursuing market share growth," I reflected during our global leadership strategy review.

"The key insight was that global leadership creates self-reinforcing advantages that enable sustainable competitive positioning while establishing barriers that protect market dominance against larger competitors."

The global generics achievement had proven that mid-sized pharmaceutical companies could establish worldwide market leadership through systematic competitive excellence while demonstrating that focused execution could overcome resource disadvantages against multinational corporations.

"Achieving top-five global position demonstrated that pharmaceutical success requires systematic excellence rather than just scale advantages," I concluded.

The lesson had become fundamental to our global strategy: top-five positioning enabled creating sustainable competitive advantages through systematic excellence that established global market leadership while providing defensive barriers that protected competitive positioning against larger pharmaceutical corporations and emerging market challengers.

Setting Industry Standards for Quality

The quality standard-setting awakening came during an unprecedented FDA inspection in October 2024 when the lead inspector informed me that our manufacturing quality systems had achieved a level of excellence that exceeded not only regulatory requirements but also the performance benchmarks of major pharmaceutical corporations, prompting the agency to request that we share our quality protocols with other manufacturers struggling to meet compliance standards. The magnitude of this recognition became overwhelming when I realized that our systematic pursuit of quality excellence had transformed us from a company meeting regulatory requirements to one defining what pharmaceutical quality could achieve.

"Your quality management systems represent best-in-class pharmaceutical manufacturing that exceeds FDA expectations while demonstrating quality capabilities that establish new benchmarks for the pharmaceutical industry," announced Dr. Patricia Williams, FDA's lead manufacturing inspector, during her closing meeting after the most comprehensive facility evaluation in our company's history. "Quality excellence at this level creates competitive advantages while establishing industry credibility that enables regulatory influence and market leadership through systematic quality superiority."

"But maintaining quality excellence requires continuous investment and operational discipline that could affect cost competitiveness," I protested, though regulatory recognition was forcing me to recognize that quality leadership had become a competitive advantage rather than just a compliance requirement.

"Quality excellence enables competitive advantages through regulatory confidence, customer trust, and operational efficiency that create sustainable positioning while establishing barriers that prevent competitors from achieving equivalent quality standards," she replied with the authority of someone who had inspected hundreds of pharmaceutical facilities worldwide. "Industry-leading quality creates competitive differentiation while enabling premium positioning and regulatory influence that traditional manufacturing approaches cannot achieve."

"And our prospects for leveraging quality leadership to establish industry influence while maintaining competitive advantages?"

"Quality leadership enables industry influence through regulatory relationships, standard-setting participation, and competitive differentiation that create sustainable advantages while establishing market credibility and technical authority."

This quality recognition launched our systematic development of industry leadership capabilities that would enable establishing pharmaceutical quality standards while creating competitive advantages through excellence that competitors could observe but not easily replicate.

The quality system superiority analysis revealed that our systematic approach to pharmaceutical manufacturing had achieved performance levels that exceeded industry benchmarks while creating operational capabilities that enabled sustained competitive advantages.

"Quality system analysis shows 99.7% manufacturing accuracy compared to industry averages of 96.8%, with zero FDA observations during three consecutive inspections spanning five years," reported our Quality Director, Dr. Rajesh Khanna, during excellence assessment. "Quality superiority enables competitive advantages through regulatory confidence, operational efficiency, and customer trust while establishing industry credibility that creates market leadership and technical authority."

"What specific quality capabilities distinguish industry-leading performance from standard pharmaceutical manufacturing?" I asked.

"Predictive quality control, automated monitoring systems, statistical process control, and continuous improvement capabilities that enable achieving quality performance that exceeds regulatory requirements while creating competitive advantages through operational excellence and systematic quality superiority."

"And quality sustainability strategies that maintain excellence while scaling global operations and increasing production complexity?"

"Quality management systems, automated monitoring, continuous improvement culture, and systematic excellence that enable maintaining quality leadership while expanding operations through standardized processes and systematic quality control."

The regulatory influence development demonstrated how quality excellence had created agency relationships while establishing technical credibility that enabled participating in pharmaceutical standard-setting and regulatory guidance development.

"Regulatory influence includes FDA consultation requests, standard-setting participation, and guidance development collaboration that provide competitive advantages through regulatory relationships," announced Dr. Amanda Richardson during regulatory positioning assessment. "Quality-based regulatory influence enables industry leadership while creating competitive advantages through agency relationships and technical authority that competitors cannot easily replicate."

"How does quality-based regulatory influence translate into competitive advantages and market positioning?" I asked.

"Regulatory influence enables priority consideration, guidance access, and standard-setting participation that create competitive advantages while establishing industry credibility and technical authority through quality excellence and regulatory relationship development."

"And regulatory influence sustainability that maintains competitive advantages despite competitor quality improvement efforts?"

"Continuous quality innovation, regulatory collaboration, and technical leadership that maintain regulatory influence while creating competitive barriers through systematic excellence and regulatory relationship depth that competitors cannot quickly achieve."

The industry standard-setting participation required developing technical expertise while establishing collaborative relationships that could influence pharmaceutical quality standards and regulatory guidance development.

"Industry standard-setting includes participation in pharmacopeial committees, regulatory guidance development, and quality standard establishment that create competitive advantages through technical authority," reported our technical standards manager during standard-setting assessment. "Standard-setting participation enables industry influence while creating competitive advantages through technical leadership and regulatory relationship development."

"What standard-setting capabilities enable establishing industry influence while maintaining competitive advantages?" I asked.

"Technical expertise, regulatory relationships, quality innovation, and systematic excellence that enable participating in standard development while creating competitive advantages through technical authority and industry credibility."

"And standard-setting strategy that balances industry collaboration with competitive advantage preservation?"

"Selective expertise sharing, competitive advantage protection, and strategic collaboration that enable industry influence while preserving competitive positioning through systematic standard-setting participation and technical leadership."

The quality innovation development required creating breakthrough manufacturing technologies while establishing quality capabilities that could define next-generation pharmaceutical manufacturing standards.

"Quality innovation includes predictive analytics, artificial intelligence monitoring, and automated quality control that establish next-generation manufacturing capabilities," announced our quality innovation director during technology assessment. "Quality innovation enables competitive advantages while establishing technical authority that creates industry influence and competitive differentiation through systematic excellence and technological leadership."

"How does quality innovation create competitive advantages while establishing industry leadership?" I asked.

"Quality innovation enables superior performance while creating competitive differentiation through technological capabilities that competitors cannot easily replicate while establishing technical authority and industry credibility."

"And quality innovation protection strategies that maintain competitive advantages while contributing to industry advancement?"

"Intellectual property protection, selective technology sharing, and competitive advantage preservation that enable industry contribution while maintaining competitive positioning through innovation excellence and technical leadership."

The customer quality recognition demonstrated how manufacturing excellence had created trust relationships while establishing market credibility that enabled premium positioning and competitive advantages.

"Customer quality recognition includes preferred supplier status with 89% of major pharmaceutical customers plus quality awards from regulatory agencies and industry organizations," announced our customer quality manager during recognition assessment. "Quality recognition enables competitive advantages through customer trust, market credibility, and premium positioning that create sustained competitive differentiation."

"What customer quality recognition provides the greatest competitive advantages and market positioning benefits?" I asked.

"Regulatory agency recognition, industry awards, customer certification, and quality leadership that create competitive advantages through market credibility and technical authority while establishing premium positioning and competitive differentiation."

"And quality recognition sustainability that maintains competitive advantages despite competitor quality improvement efforts?"

"Continuous quality excellence, innovation leadership, and systematic improvement that maintain quality recognition while creating competitive barriers through excellence sustainability and quality innovation."

The quality training and development required establishing educational programs while creating industry expertise that could influence pharmaceutical quality standards and regulatory guidance development.

"Quality training programs include pharmaceutical manufacturing education, regulatory compliance training, and quality system development that establish industry expertise," reported our quality education director during training assessment. "Training capabilities enable industry influence while creating competitive advantages through expertise development and technical authority establishment."

"How does quality training and education enhance competitive positioning and industry influence?" I asked.

"Training capabilities enable expertise sharing while establishing technical authority that creates competitive advantages through industry credibility and regulatory relationship development while contributing to pharmaceutical quality advancement."

"And training program development that balances industry contribution with competitive advantage preservation?"

"Strategic expertise sharing, competitive advantage protection, and selective training that enable industry influence while preserving competitive positioning through systematic training excellence and expertise development."

The quality standard-setting results demonstrated that systematic excellence had created industry influence while establishing competitive advantages that enabled market leadership and technical authority.

"Quality standard-setting leadership has established industry influence through regulatory relationships, technical authority, and competitive excellence that create sustainable advantages while contributing to pharmaceutical quality advancement," I announced during our annual quality review. "Quality leadership demonstrates that systematic excellence creates competitive advantages while establishing industry credibility and technical authority through quality superiority."

"And competitive positioning improvements from quality leadership compared to standard pharmaceutical manufacturing?" asked our quality strategy committee.

"Quality leadership has enabled regulatory influence, customer trust, and competitive differentiation that create sustained competitive advantages while establishing market credibility and technical authority through systematic excellence."

Three years after achieving industry-leading quality standards, we had established technical authority that created competitive advantages while contributing to pharmaceutical industry advancement through quality excellence and systematic innovation.

"Setting industry standards for quality taught us that pharmaceutical success requires excellence that exceeds regulatory requirements while establishing technical authority and competitive differentiation," I reflected during our quality leadership strategy review.

"The key insight was that quality leadership creates competitive advantages through technical authority while establishing industry influence that enhances market positioning and competitive excellence."

The quality standard-setting achievement had proven that pharmaceutical companies could establish industry leadership through systematic excellence while demonstrating that quality superiority created competitive advantages and technical authority.

"Setting industry standards for quality demonstrated that pharmaceutical success requires systematic excellence that establishes technical authority while creating competitive advantages through quality leadership," I concluded.

The lesson had become fundamental to our quality philosophy: industry standard-setting enabled creating competitive advantages through systematic excellence that established technical authority while contributing to pharmaceutical industry advancement through quality innovation and systematic quality superiority.

Thought Leadership in Biotechnology

The biotechnology thought leadership awakening came during an unexpected invitation to deliver the keynote address at the World Biotechnology Congress in November 2024, when the organizing committee informed me that our innovative approach to AI-driven drug discovery and biosimilar development had positioned us as one of the most influential voices in biotechnology innovation globally. The magnitude of this recognition became overwhelming when I realized that our systematic biotechnology advancement had transformed us from a company learning biotechnology to one defining the future direction of biological pharmaceutical development for the entire industry.

"Your biotechnology innovations have established thought leadership that influences industry direction while creating competitive advantages through technical authority and scientific credibility," explained Dr. Sarah Martinez, Congress President and former Genentech VP, during her invitation call. "Biotechnology thought leadership enables industry influence while creating competitive positioning that exceeds traditional pharmaceutical competitive advantages through scientific authority and innovation credibility that established biotech companies acknowledge and respect."

"But biotechnology thought leadership requires sustaining innovation excellence while contributing to industry advancement that could benefit competitors," I protested, though the invitation was forcing me to recognize that our biotechnology capabilities had achieved recognition that exceeded our own assessment of our scientific achievements.

"Thought leadership creates competitive advantages through scientific authority, industry influence, and partnership opportunities that enable sustained competitive positioning while establishing barriers that prevent competitors from achieving equivalent scientific credibility," she replied with the systematic precision that had made her one of biotechnology's most respected leaders. "Scientific leadership enables competitive differentiation while creating industry relationships and regulatory influence that traditional pharmaceutical approaches cannot achieve."

"And our prospects for leveraging biotechnology thought leadership to establish competitive advantages while maintaining scientific innovation excellence?"

"Thought leadership enables accessing partnership opportunities, regulatory influence, and industry relationships that create competitive advantages while establishing scientific authority and technical credibility that enhance market positioning and competitive excellence."

This thought leadership recognition launched our systematic development of biotechnology industry influence that would require balancing scientific contribution with competitive advantage preservation while establishing authority that could shape biotechnology development direction.

The scientific innovation analysis revealed that our systematic biotechnology development had achieved breakthrough capabilities while creating intellectual property and technical expertise that established industry credibility and competitive differentiation.

"Scientific innovation assessment shows 47 breakthrough biotechnology patents, 23 peer-reviewed publications in top-tier journals, and 12 industry awards for biotechnology excellence," reported our Chief Scientific Officer, Dr. Lisa Chen, during innovation evaluation. "Scientific achievements enable thought leadership while creating competitive advantages through intellectual property, technical authority, and industry recognition that establish scientific credibility and competitive differentiation."

"What specific biotechnology innovations distinguish our scientific capabilities from established biotech companies?" I asked.

"AI-driven drug discovery platforms, novel protein engineering approaches, innovative biosimilar development methods, and breakthrough cell therapy technologies that create competitive advantages while establishing scientific authority and technical credibility through systematic innovation excellence."

"And scientific innovation sustainability that maintains thought leadership while protecting competitive advantages from disclosure and competitive replication?"

"Strategic innovation disclosure, intellectual property protection, and competitive advantage preservation that enable thought leadership while maintaining competitive positioning through systematic innovation management and strategic scientific contribution."

The industry conference leadership demonstrated how our biotechnology expertise had created speaking opportunities while establishing scientific authority that influenced industry direction and competitive positioning.

"Industry conference leadership includes keynote presentations at 23 major biotechnology conferences, panel participation in regulatory forums, and scientific advisory roles with industry organizations," announced our scientific communications director during conference assessment. "Conference leadership enables thought leadership while creating competitive advantages through scientific authority, industry relationships, and regulatory influence that establish technical credibility and competitive differentiation."

"How does conference leadership translate into competitive advantages and market positioning benefits?" I asked.

"Conference leadership enables industry influence while creating competitive advantages through scientific authority, partnership opportunities, and regulatory relationships that enhance market positioning and competitive excellence through thought leadership establishment."

"And conference strategy that balances scientific contribution with competitive advantage preservation?"

"Strategic presentation topics, competitive advantage protection, and selective expertise sharing that enable thought leadership while preserving competitive positioning through systematic conference participation and scientific authority development."

The peer-reviewed publication strategy required developing scientific communication capabilities while establishing research credibility that could influence biotechnology development direction and regulatory guidance.

"Peer-reviewed publication strategy includes 23 publications in Nature Biotechnology, Science, and Cell plus editorial board participation with leading biotechnology journals," reported our scientific publications manager during research assessment. "Publication excellence enables thought leadership while creating competitive advantages through scientific credibility, regulatory influence, and industry recognition that establish technical authority and competitive differentiation."

"What publication strategy optimizes thought leadership while protecting competitive advantages and intellectual property?" I asked.

"Strategic research disclosure, intellectual property coordination, and competitive advantage preservation that enable scientific contribution while maintaining competitive positioning through systematic publication management and research excellence."

"And publication impact measurement that demonstrates thought leadership effectiveness and competitive advantage creation?"

"Citation analysis, industry influence assessment, and competitive positioning evaluation that measure thought leadership impact while optimizing scientific contribution and competitive advantage development through systematic publication excellence."

The regulatory guidance participation required establishing technical expertise while contributing to biotechnology regulatory development that could influence industry standards and competitive positioning.

"Regulatory guidance participation includes advisory committee membership with FDA, EMA consultation roles, and biotechnology standard-setting participation," announced Dr. Amanda Richardson during regulatory influence assessment. "Regulatory participation enables thought leadership while creating competitive advantages through regulatory relationships, technical authority, and industry influence that establish scientific credibility and competitive differentiation."

"How does regulatory guidance participation create competitive advantages while contributing to industry advancement?" I asked.

"Regulatory participation enables industry influence while creating competitive advantages through regulatory relationships, technical authority, and standard-setting participation that enhance market positioning and competitive excellence through thought leadership establishment."

"And regulatory participation strategy that balances industry contribution with competitive advantage preservation?"

"Strategic expertise sharing, competitive advantage protection, and selective guidance participation that enable industry influence while maintaining competitive positioning through systematic regulatory participation and technical authority development."

The partnership and collaboration leadership required establishing relationships with academic institutions while creating industry alliances that could enhance biotechnology capabilities and competitive positioning.

"Partnership leadership includes collaboration agreements with Harvard, MIT, Stanford, and IISc plus strategic alliances with leading biotechnology companies," reported our partnership director during collaboration assessment. "Partnership leadership enables thought leadership while creating competitive advantages through scientific relationships, technology access, and collaborative innovation that establish technical authority and competitive differentiation."

"What partnership strategy optimizes thought leadership while enhancing competitive capabilities and market positioning?" I asked.

"Strategic collaboration development, competitive advantage enhancement, and systematic partnership management that enable thought leadership while building competitive capabilities through collaboration excellence and scientific authority establishment."

"And partnership coordination that balances collaborative benefits with competitive advantage preservation?"

"Collaborative innovation management, intellectual property coordination, and competitive advantage protection that enable partnership benefits while maintaining competitive positioning through systematic collaboration excellence and strategic relationship development."

The biotechnology education and training required developing industry expertise while establishing educational programs that could influence biotechnology talent development and industry standards.

"Biotechnology education includes executive education programs, industry training initiatives, and academic collaboration that establish educational leadership," announced our education director during training assessment. "Educational leadership enables thought leadership while creating competitive advantages through talent development, industry relationships, and scientific authority that establish technical credibility and competitive differentiation."

"How does biotechnology education enhance thought leadership while creating competitive advantages?" I asked.

"Educational leadership enables industry influence while creating competitive advantages through talent development, scientific authority, and industry relationships that enhance market positioning and competitive excellence through thought leadership establishment."

The thought leadership results demonstrated that systematic scientific excellence had created industry influence while establishing competitive advantages that enabled market leadership and technical authority in biotechnology development.

"Biotechnology thought leadership has established industry influence through scientific authority, regulatory relationships, and competitive excellence that create sustainable advantages while contributing to biotechnology advancement," I announced during our annual scientific review. "Thought leadership demonstrates that scientific excellence creates competitive advantages while establishing industry credibility and technical authority through systematic innovation and scientific contribution."

"And competitive positioning improvements from thought leadership compared to traditional pharmaceutical market positioning?" asked our scientific strategy committee.

"Thought leadership has enabled scientific authority, industry influence, and competitive differentiation that create sustained competitive advantages while establishing market credibility and technical authority through systematic excellence and innovation leadership."

Three years after establishing biotechnology thought leadership, we had achieved industry influence that created competitive advantages while contributing to biotechnology advancement through scientific excellence and systematic innovation.

"Thought leadership in biotechnology taught us that pharmaceutical success requires scientific excellence that establishes technical authority while creating competitive advantages through innovation credibility," I reflected during our thought leadership strategy review.

"The key insight was that thought leadership creates competitive advantages through scientific authority while establishing industry influence that enhances market positioning and competitive excellence through systematic innovation."

The biotechnology thought leadership achievement had proven that pharmaceutical companies could establish industry influence through scientific excellence while demonstrating that innovation leadership created competitive advantages and technical authority.

"Thought leadership in biotechnology demonstrated that pharmaceutical success requires scientific excellence that establishes industry influence while creating competitive advantages through innovation leadership," I concluded.

The lesson had become fundamental to our scientific philosophy: biotechnology thought leadership enabled creating competitive advantages through scientific excellence that established technical authority while contributing to industry advancement through innovation leadership and systematic scientific contribution.

The Competition Following the Lead

The competition following awakening came during a shocking competitive intelligence briefing in December 2024 when our market analyst informed me that six major pharmaceutical companies, had restructured their R&D strategies to mirror our AI-driven drug discovery approach, while three multinational corporations had announced biotechnology partnerships that replicated our academic collaboration model. The magnitude of our industry influence became overwhelming when I realized that our strategic innovations had become the template that competitors were desperately attempting to copy, transforming us from followers to leaders whose decisions shaped pharmaceutical industry direction.

"Competitive analysis shows systematic adoption of our strategic approaches across the pharmaceutical industry, with 12 companies announcing AI discovery programs and 8 establishing biotechnology partnerships that replicate our innovation models," announced Dr. Kavya Reddy during her quarterly competitive assessment, projecting data that showed our strategies becoming industry standards. "Market leadership has created competitive imitation that validates our strategic direction while forcing competitors to abandon their traditional approaches in favor of methodologies we pioneered and perfected."

"But competitors following our strategies could eliminate competitive advantages while enabling them to achieve similar capabilities using our proven approaches," I protested, though the evidence was forcing me to recognize that our innovations had become so influential that the entire industry was reshaping itself around our strategic breakthroughs.

"Market leadership creates competitive advantages through first-mover benefits, execution excellence, and relationship depth that imitators cannot replicate despite understanding our strategic approaches," she replied with the analytical confidence that had guided our competitive strategy development. "Industry influence demonstrates strategic superiority while creating barriers that prevent successful imitation despite competitive knowledge of our methodologies and approaches."

"And our prospects for maintaining competitive advantages while competitors adopt our strategic innovations and operational approaches?"

"Strategic leadership enables sustained advantages through execution excellence, relationship depth, and continuous innovation that create barriers against competitive imitation while establishing industry influence that enhances market positioning and competitive differentiation."

This competitive following recognition marked our evolution from a company learning from industry leaders to one whose innovations defined competitive best practices while establishing strategic authority that forced established pharmaceutical giants to abandon their traditional approaches.

The strategic imitation analysis revealed that pharmaceutical companies across the industry had begun adopting our approaches while struggling to achieve equivalent results due to execution complexity and relationship requirements that successful implementation demanded.

"Strategic imitation analysis shows 18 pharmaceutical companies implementing AI discovery programs, 12 establishing biotechnology partnerships, and 15 developing specialty pharmaceutical focuses that replicate our strategic framework," reported our competitive intelligence director during imitation assessment. "Competitive following validates our strategic direction while demonstrating execution barriers that prevent successful replication despite strategic knowledge and resource availability."

"What specific strategic elements are competitors attempting to replicate from our business model?" I asked.

"AI-driven drug discovery platforms, academic collaboration networks, biotechnology partnership strategies, specialty pharmaceutical positioning, and global manufacturing approaches that competitors recognize as competitive advantages worth replicating through strategic imitation."

"And competitive barriers that prevent successful imitation despite competitor knowledge of our strategic approaches?"

"Execution complexity, relationship depth, cultural requirements, and systematic excellence that create barriers against competitive replication while enabling sustained advantages through strategic leadership and operational superiority."

The Cipla strategic pivot demonstrated how established pharmaceutical companies were abandoning traditional approaches while attempting to replicate our biotechnology capabilities and partnership strategies.

Cipla has been integrating AI across operations and research, while still maintaining a broad R&D portfolio across generics, complex therapies, and new platforms. Investment in biotechnology capabilities, and academic partnership development that mirrors our innovation strategy," announced our Cipla competitive analyst during company assessment. "Cipla imitation validates our strategic direction while demonstrating the industry recognition of our competitive advantages and strategic superiority."

"How effectively can competition replicate our biotechnology capabilities and competitive advantages?" I asked.

"Cipla faces execution barriers including talent acquisition, relationship development, and cultural transformation that prevent achieving equivalent capabilities despite strategic knowledge and substantial resource investment."

"And timeline for potential competitive threat development through competitors' strategic imitation?"

The strategic transformation requires 3-5 years for meaningful capability development while facing execution barriers that could prevent successful replication despite resource commitment and strategic focus."

Our major competitors' response strategy revealed how international pharmaceutical companies were restructuring global operations while attempting to match our manufacturing network and quality excellence approaches.

Our analysis shows global manufacturing expansion, quality system enhancement, and regulatory relationship development that replicates our international competitive strategy," reported our strategic competitive analyst during response assessment competitors' imitation demonstrates industry recognition of our competitive advantages while highlighting execution requirements that successful replication demands."

"What specific advantages enable maintaining competitive positioning despite our major competitors' strategic imitation efforts?" I asked.

"Relationship depth, execution excellence, quality leadership, and systematic advantages that create barriers against competitive replication while enabling sustained positioning through operational superiority and strategic excellence."

"And competitive response strategies that protect advantages while competitors develop similar capabilities?"

"Continuous innovation, relationship deepening, quality advancement, and strategic evolution that maintain competitive advantages while creating barriers against successful imitation through systematic excellence and competitive leadership."

The multinational corporation partnership strategies showed how global pharmaceutical giants were establishing collaboration networks while attempting to replicate our academic and biotechnology alliance capabilities.

"Multinational corporation analysis shows some of the leading players establishing academic partnerships and biotechnology collaborations that mirror our alliance strategies," announced our multinational competitive analyst during corporation assessment. "Multinational imitation validates our partnership approach while demonstrating execution requirements that successful collaboration demands."

"How do multinational corporations' resource advantages affect their ability to replicate our partnership strategies?" I asked.

"Multinational resources enable partnership investment while facing relationship development and cultural barriers that prevent achieving equivalent collaboration benefits despite financial capabilities and strategic focus."

"And partnership defensive strategies that maintain collaborative advantages despite multinational competitive imitation?"

"Relationship deepening, collaboration innovation, and partnership excellence that create barriers against competitive replication while maintaining collaborative advantages through systematic partnership development and alliance leadership."

The innovation pipeline responses revealed how competitors were attempting to replicate our drug discovery capabilities while struggling to achieve equivalent innovation results and development timelines.

"Innovation pipeline analysis shows 23 pharmaceutical companies implementing AI discovery platforms with limited breakthrough results compared to our systematic innovation success," reported our innovation competitive analyst during pipeline assessment. "Competitive innovation attempts validate our discovery approach while demonstrating execution barriers that prevent equivalent results despite strategic knowledge and technology access."

"What innovation advantages enable maintaining discovery leadership despite competitive imitation of our AI platforms?" I asked.

"Discovery expertise, systematic innovation, talent depth, and execution excellence that create barriers against competitive replication while enabling sustained innovation leadership through systematic discovery capabilities and innovation excellence."

"And innovation protection strategies that maintain competitive advantages while sharing knowledge through thought leadership?"

"Strategic knowledge sharing, competitive advantage preservation, and innovation excellence that enable thought leadership while maintaining competitive positioning through systematic innovation and discovery leadership."

The regulatory influence responses demonstrated how competitors were attempting to build agency relationships while struggling to achieve equivalent regulatory positioning and compliance excellence.

"Regulatory influence analysis shows competitor attempts to develop FDA relationships and compliance excellence with limited success compared to our systematic regulatory leadership," announced Dr. Amanda Richardson during regulatory competitive assessment. "Regulatory imitation attempts validate our compliance approach while demonstrating relationship requirements that competitive replication cannot achieve quickly."

"What regulatory advantages enable maintaining compliance leadership despite competitive attempts to replicate our agency relationships?" I asked.

"Relationship depth, compliance excellence, regulatory innovation, and systematic quality that create barriers against competitive replication while maintaining regulatory advantages through excellence sustainability and relationship development."

The competitive following results demonstrated that industry imitation validated our strategic direction while creating barriers that prevented successful replication despite competitor knowledge and resource investment.

"Competition following our lead demonstrates strategic validation while creating competitive barriers through execution requirements that prevent successful imitation despite industry recognition and resource commitment," I announced during our annual competitive review. "Industry influence establishes strategic authority while maintaining competitive advantages through systematic excellence that competitors cannot replicate easily."

"And competitive positioning sustainability despite widespread industry adoption of our strategic approaches?" asked our competitive strategy committee.

"Strategic leadership enables sustained advantages through execution excellence, relationship depth, and continuous innovation that create barriers against competitive imitation while establishing industry influence and strategic authority."

Two years after recognizing competitive following, we had maintained strategic leadership while establishing industry influence that validated our approaches and created barriers against successful competitive imitation.

"The competition following our lead taught us that market leadership creates industry influence while establishing competitive barriers through execution excellence that prevents successful imitation," I reflected during our strategic leadership review.

"The key insight was that strategic leadership enables sustained advantages through execution requirements that competitors cannot replicate despite strategic knowledge and resource availability."

The competitive following achievement had proven that pharmaceutical innovation could establish industry influence while creating barriers that protected competitive advantages despite widespread strategic imitation attempts.

"Competition following the lead demonstrated that pharmaceutical leadership requires execution excellence that creates barriers against competitive replication despite strategic transparency," I concluded.

The lesson had become fundamental to our competitive philosophy: industry influence enabled creating competitive barriers through execution excellence that prevented successful imitation while establishing strategic authority that enhanced market positioning and competitive differentiation despite widespread competitive following.

Chapter 29

The Succession Planning

Preparing for the Next Generation

The succession planning awakening came during a sobering conversation with our board governance consultant in January 2025 when she bluntly informed me that at sixty-two years old, I had become the primary risk factor threatening our company's continued success, because institutional investors increasingly viewed founder-dependent organizations as unsustainable investments regardless of financial performance. The uncomfortable reality crystallized when she mentioned that pharmaceutical companies with strong succession plans traded at 15-20% premium valuations compared to founder-dependent organizations, forcing me to confront how my leadership had evolved from competitive advantage to strategic liability.

"Succession planning has become investor requirement rather than governance preference, with institutional capital flowing toward companies that demonstrate leadership sustainability beyond founder capabilities," explained Dr. Patricia Williams during her governance assessment, presenting valuation data that showed succession-ready companies commanding premium market multiples. "Pharmaceutical succession requires systematic leadership development that enables organizational continuity while preserving competitive advantages that founder leadership created through systematic capability transfer rather than dependency perpetuation."

"But our company's competitive advantages resulted from strategic decisions and relationships that took decades to develop," I protested, though investor feedback was forcing me to recognize that succession planning represented competitive necessity rather than just governance compliance. "How can systematic leadership transition preserve institutional knowledge while enabling organizational evolution beyond founder capabilities?"

"Successful succession requires transferring strategic capabilities while developing next-generation leadership that can enhance rather than just maintain competitive advantages," she replied with the systematic precision that had guided succession planning for dozens of pharmaceutical companies. "Leadership transition enables organizational evolution while preserving competitive advantages through systematic capability development and strategic knowledge transfer."

"And our prospects for achieving succession that enhances competitive positioning while preserving institutional knowledge and strategic relationships?"

"Succession success requires systematic leadership development, capability transfer, and organizational evolution that enable competitive enhancement while preserving strategic advantages through planned leadership transition and systematic capability preservation."

This succession imperative launched our systematic development of next-generation leadership capabilities that would require balancing institutional knowledge preservation with organizational evolution while proving that leadership transition could enhance rather than compromise competitive advantages.

The leadership assessment revealed the complexity of transferring decades of strategic knowledge while developing next-generation capabilities that could enable organizational advancement beyond founder limitations and dependency relationships.

"Leadership assessment identifies critical capabilities including strategic decision-making, stakeholder relationship management, competitive intelligence, and innovation oversight that require systematic transfer to next-generation leadership," reported our leadership development consultant during succession planning. "Capability transfer enables organizational continuity while developing leadership that can enhance competitive advantages through systematic development and strategic knowledge preservation."

"What specific leadership capabilities require preservation versus evolution during succession transition?" I asked.

"Strategic relationships, competitive intelligence, innovation vision, and stakeholder management require preservation while operational leadership, technology adaptation, and market expansion require evolution through next-generation capabilities and systematic leadership development."

"And succession timeline that balances capability transfer with competitive advantage preservation and organizational evolution?"

"Systematic succession requires 24-36 months of leadership development, capability transfer, and organizational transition that enables preserving competitive advantages while developing enhanced leadership capabilities through planned transition and systematic development."

The internal candidate development required identifying high-potential leaders while providing systematic training and development that could prepare next-generation leadership for strategic responsibilities and competitive challenges.

"Internal candidate development includes Dr. Priya Sharma for CEO succession, Dr. Lisa Chen for Chief Innovation Officer, and Rajesh Khanna for Chief Operating Officer through systematic leadership preparation," announced our succession planning manager during candidate assessment. "Internal development enables organizational continuity while building leadership capabilities that can enhance competitive advantages through systematic preparation and strategic development."

"How do internal candidates compare to external leadership alternatives for succession effectiveness?" I asked.

"Internal candidates provide organizational knowledge and cultural continuity while requiring systematic development for strategic leadership and competitive enhancement through succession preparation and capability building."

"And internal candidate development strategies that prepare leadership for competitive challenges and organizational evolution?"

"Executive education, strategic project leadership, board interaction, and external relationship development that prepare internal candidates for succession responsibilities while building capabilities for competitive enhancement and organizational leadership."

The external advisory development required establishing relationships with industry leaders while creating governance structures that could provide strategic guidance and succession support during leadership transition.

"External advisory development includes board enhancement with pharmaceutical industry leaders, strategic advisory relationships, and governance structures that support succession transition," reported our board development consultant during advisory planning. "External advisory enables strategic guidance while providing succession support through industry expertise and governance excellence that enhance leadership transition effectiveness."

"What external advisory capabilities provide optimal succession support while enhancing competitive positioning?" I asked.

"Industry expertise, strategic guidance, governance excellence, and succession support that enable leadership transition while enhancing competitive advantages through advisory relationships and governance capability development."

"And advisory relationship coordination that balances external guidance with organizational autonomy and strategic independence?"

"Strategic advisory engagement, governance coordination, and independence preservation that enable external guidance while maintaining organizational autonomy through systematic advisory development and governance excellence."

The knowledge transfer systems required developing comprehensive approaches to institutional knowledge preservation while creating documentation and training systems that could enable next-generation leadership access to strategic insights and competitive intelligence.

"Knowledge transfer systems include strategic decision documentation, competitive intelligence databases, stakeholder relationship mapping, and innovation process codification," announced our knowledge management director during transfer planning. "Knowledge preservation enables succession continuity while providing next-generation leadership with strategic insights and competitive intelligence through systematic knowledge management and transfer systems."

"How does systematic knowledge transfer enhance succession effectiveness while preserving competitive advantages?" I asked.

"Knowledge transfer enables organizational continuity while providing next-generation leadership with strategic insights that enhance competitive advantages through systematic knowledge preservation and leadership development."

"And knowledge management systems that balance information sharing with competitive advantage protection and strategic security?"

"Strategic knowledge documentation, competitive intelligence management, and information security that enable knowledge transfer while protecting competitive advantages through systematic knowledge management and strategic information preservation."

The stakeholder relationship transition required developing systematic approaches to relationship transfer while ensuring continuity of strategic partnerships and competitive positioning during leadership change.

"Stakeholder relationship transition includes gradual introduction of next-generation leadership to key partners, regulatory agencies, and industry relationships," reported our stakeholder transition manager during relationship planning. "Relationship transition enables stakeholder continuity while building next-generation leadership credibility through systematic relationship development and strategic partnership preservation."

"What stakeholder relationship strategies optimize transition effectiveness while preserving competitive advantages?" I asked.

"Gradual relationship introduction, stakeholder confidence building, and partnership continuity that enable relationship transition while preserving competitive advantages through systematic stakeholder management and relationship development."

"And relationship transition coordination that maintains stakeholder confidence while enabling next-generation leadership establishment?"

"Systematic relationship introduction, stakeholder engagement, and confidence building that enable relationship transition while maintaining competitive advantages through strategic stakeholder management and relationship preservation."

The competitive advantage preservation required developing strategies that could maintain market positioning while enabling leadership evolution and organizational enhancement during succession transition.

"Competitive advantage preservation includes systematic capability maintenance, strategic relationship continuity, and market positioning protection during succession transition," announced our competitive strategy manager during preservation planning. "Advantage preservation enables succession success while maintaining competitive positioning through systematic capability management and strategic continuity."

"How does competitive advantage preservation enhance succession effectiveness while enabling organizational evolution?" I asked.

"Advantage preservation enables succession continuity while providing foundation for organizational enhancement through systematic capability maintenance and competitive positioning protection during leadership transition."

The succession planning results demonstrated that systematic leadership development could enable organizational evolution while preserving competitive advantages through planned transition and capability enhancement.

"Succession planning has developed next-generation leadership capabilities while preserving competitive advantages through systematic transition planning and capability development," I announced during our annual succession review. "Leadership development demonstrates that succession can enhance organizational capabilities while maintaining competitive positioning through systematic planning and leadership preparation."

"And investor confidence improvements from succession planning compared to founder-dependent organizational structure?" asked our governance committee.

"Succession planning has enhanced investor confidence while improving valuation multiples through demonstrated leadership sustainability and organizational evolution capability that reduces founder dependency risks."

Eighteen months after implementing systematic succession planning, we had developed next-generation leadership capabilities while preserving competitive advantages through planned transition and organizational evolution.

"Succession planning taught us that pharmaceutical leadership requires organizational sustainability rather than founder dependency," I reflected during our succession strategy review.

"The key insight was that succession planning enables competitive enhancement while preserving strategic advantages through systematic leadership development and organizational evolution."

The succession planning development had proven that pharmaceutical companies could achieve leadership transition while enhancing competitive advantages through systematic capability development and strategic knowledge preservation.

"Succession planning demonstrated that pharmaceutical success requires organizational sustainability that enhances competitive advantages through leadership evolution," I concluded.

The lesson had become fundamental to our governance philosophy: succession planning enabled creating competitive enhancement through systematic leadership development while preserving strategic advantages that enabled organizational evolution and competitive sustainability beyond founder capabilities.

Transitioning to Chief Innovation Officer Role

The Chief Innovation Officer transition awakening came during a reflective strategic planning session in February 2025 when I realized that my greatest value to the company had evolved from operational management to innovation leadership, because our transformation from generic manufacturer to biotechnology innovator required systematic innovation capabilities rather than traditional pharmaceutical CEO responsibilities. The magnitude of this transition became clear when our board chairman mentioned that my unique innovation experience could drive breakthrough pharmaceutical development while enabling next-generation operational leadership to manage day-to-day business activities more effectively than founder micromanagement allowed.

"Your innovation expertise represents irreplaceable competitive advantage that Chief Innovation Officer role could optimize while enabling systematic operational leadership through management transition," explained Dr. Patricia Williams during our role transition planning, reviewing organizational structures that showed how innovation leadership could enhance competitive advantages. "CIO transition enables leveraging innovation capabilities while providing operational autonomy that enhances organizational effectiveness through leadership specialization and systematic capability optimization."

"But transitioning from CEO to CIO requires surrendering operational control while maintaining strategic influence over innovation direction and competitive positioning," I protested, though mounting evidence suggested that innovation leadership could create more sustainable competitive advantages than operational micromanagement. "How can innovation focus enhance competitive positioning while ensuring operational excellence and strategic coherence?"

"Innovation leadership enables competitive differentiation while operational leadership provides systematic management that enhances organizational effectiveness," she replied with the governance expertise that had guided leadership transitions for numerous pharmaceutical companies. "Role specialization creates competitive advantages through innovation focus while enabling operational excellence through management expertise and systematic leadership development."

"And our prospects for achieving innovation leadership that enhances competitive advantages while maintaining strategic influence and organizational coherence?"

"Innovation leadership enables competitive enhancement through breakthrough development while providing strategic influence that guides organizational evolution and competitive positioning through systematic innovation and strategic leadership."

This transition opportunity launched our systematic development of innovation leadership capabilities that would require redefining my role while proving that innovation focus could create competitive advantages that operational management could never achieve.

The innovation leadership assessment revealed that Chief Innovation Officer responsibilities could optimize my competitive advantages while enabling next-generation operational leadership to enhance organizational capabilities through management specialization.

"Innovation leadership assessment shows optimal value creation through breakthrough pharmaceutical development, strategic partnership leadership, and competitive intelligence direction," reported our organizational development consultant during transition planning. "Innovation focus enables competitive advantages through systematic breakthrough development while providing strategic guidance that enhances organizational capabilities and competitive positioning."

"What specific innovation leadership capabilities distinguish CIO role from traditional pharmaceutical executive responsibilities?" I asked.

"Breakthrough development oversight, strategic partnership coordination, competitive intelligence management, and innovation strategy direction that enable competitive advantages through systematic innovation leadership and strategic capability development."

"And innovation leadership sustainability that maintains competitive advantages while enabling operational independence and organizational evolution?"

"Innovation leadership enables sustained competitive advantages through breakthrough development while providing strategic guidance that supports operational excellence and organizational enhancement through systematic innovation and leadership coordination."

The operational transition strategy required developing systematic approaches to management handover while ensuring continuity of strategic decision-making and competitive advantage preservation during leadership change.

"Operational transition includes systematic responsibility transfer to Dr. Priya Sharma as CEO while maintaining innovation oversight and strategic guidance coordination," announced our transition planning manager during handover development. "Transition strategy enables operational leadership enhancement while preserving innovation advantages through systematic responsibility allocation and strategic coordination."

"How does operational transition optimize organizational effectiveness while preserving strategic coherence and competitive advantages?" I asked.

"Operational transition enables management specialization while maintaining strategic coordination through innovation leadership and systematic organizational development that enhances competitive advantages."

"And transition timeline that balances operational continuity with leadership specialization and competitive advantage preservation?"

"Systematic transition requires 12-18 months of responsibility transfer and coordination development that enables operational enhancement while preserving innovation advantages through planned leadership specialization."

The innovation portfolio development required establishing systematic approaches to breakthrough pharmaceutical development while creating innovation capabilities that could accelerate competitive advantages and market positioning.

"Innovation portfolio development includes AI discovery advancement, biotechnology platform expansion, and breakthrough therapeutic development that enable competitive advantages," reported Dr. Lisa Chen during innovation planning. "Portfolio innovation enables competitive differentiation while providing sustainable advantages through systematic breakthrough development and innovation excellence."

"What innovation portfolio strategies optimize competitive advantages while enabling sustainable breakthrough development?" I asked.

"Strategic innovation focus, breakthrough development coordination, and competitive advantage optimization that enable innovation excellence while creating sustainable competitive positioning through systematic innovation management."

"And innovation portfolio coordination that balances breakthrough potential with resource allocation and competitive advantage enhancement?"

"Portfolio optimization, resource coordination, and breakthrough development that enable innovation excellence while maximizing competitive advantages through systematic innovation and strategic development coordination."

The strategic partnership leadership required developing systematic approaches to collaboration management while creating partnership capabilities that could accelerate innovation and competitive positioning.

"Strategic partnership leadership includes academic collaboration coordination, biotechnology alliance management, and industry relationship development," announced our partnership director during alliance planning. "Partnership leadership enables innovation acceleration while creating competitive advantages through systematic collaboration and strategic relationship development."

"How does partnership leadership enhance innovation capabilities while creating competitive advantages?" I asked.

"Partnership coordination enables innovation acceleration while creating competitive advantages through collaboration excellence and strategic relationship development that enhance innovation capabilities and competitive positioning."

"And partnership leadership strategies that balance collaboration benefits with competitive advantage preservation and innovation independence?"

"Strategic partnership coordination, competitive advantage protection, and innovation independence that enable collaboration benefits while preserving competitive positioning through systematic partnership management."

The regulatory innovation leadership required establishing systematic approaches to breakthrough therapy development while creating regulatory capabilities that could accelerate approval timelines and competitive advantages.

"Regulatory innovation leadership includes breakthrough therapy coordination, FDA relationship management, and accelerated approval strategy development," announced Dr. Amanda Richardson during regulatory innovation planning. "Regulatory leadership enables innovation acceleration while creating competitive advantages through regulatory excellence and systematic approval optimization."

"What regulatory innovation capabilities optimize breakthrough development while creating competitive advantages?" I asked.

"Breakthrough therapy coordination, regulatory relationship management, and approval acceleration that enable innovation advantages while creating competitive positioning through regulatory excellence and systematic innovation development."

"And regulatory innovation coordination that balances breakthrough development with compliance excellence and competitive advantage creation?"

"Regulatory innovation management, compliance coordination, and competitive advantage optimization that enable breakthrough development while maintaining regulatory excellence through systematic innovation and regulatory leadership."

The thought leadership development required establishing systematic approaches to industry influence while creating innovation credibility that could enhance competitive positioning and market authority.

"Thought leadership development includes industry conference participation, scientific publication coordination, and innovation standard-setting engagement," reported our thought leadership manager during influence planning. "Thought leadership enables competitive advantages while creating industry influence through innovation excellence and systematic credibility development."

"How does thought leadership enhance innovation capabilities while creating competitive advantages?" I asked.

"Thought leadership enables industry influence while creating competitive advantages through innovation credibility and systematic authority development that enhance competitive positioning and market leadership."

"And thought leadership strategies that balance industry contribution with competitive advantage preservation and innovation leadership?"

"Strategic thought leadership, competitive advantage protection, and innovation credibility that enable industry influence while preserving competitive positioning through systematic thought leadership and innovation excellence."

The innovation measurement systems required developing comprehensive approaches to breakthrough assessment while creating accountability mechanisms that could optimize innovation effectiveness and competitive advantage creation.

"Innovation measurement systems include breakthrough development tracking, competitive advantage assessment, and innovation ROI evaluation," announced our innovation metrics manager during measurement planning. "Innovation measurement enables optimization while providing accountability for breakthrough development and competitive advantage creation through systematic evaluation and performance management."

"What innovation measurement capabilities optimize breakthrough development while enhancing competitive advantages?" I asked.

"Innovation tracking, competitive assessment, and performance optimization that enable breakthrough development while creating competitive advantages through systematic innovation measurement and strategic evaluation."

The Chief Innovation Officer transition results demonstrated that innovation leadership could enhance competitive advantages while enabling operational excellence through management specialization and systematic leadership development.

"Chief Innovation Officer transition has optimized innovation capabilities while enabling operational leadership enhancement through systematic role specialization and competitive advantage development," I announced during our annual transition review. "Innovation leadership demonstrates that role optimization creates competitive advantages while enhancing organizational effectiveness through systematic leadership specialization."

"And competitive positioning improvements from innovation leadership compared to traditional CEO operational management?" asked our innovation strategy committee.

"Innovation leadership has enhanced competitive advantages while enabling operational excellence through management specialization that optimizes organizational capabilities and competitive positioning."

Twelve months after transitioning to Chief Innovation Officer role, we had achieved innovation leadership that enhanced competitive advantages while enabling operational excellence through systematic leadership specialization.

"Transitioning to Chief Innovation Officer role taught us that pharmaceutical leadership requires specialization that optimizes competitive advantages rather than operational control," I reflected during our innovation leadership review.

"The key insight was that innovation leadership enables competitive enhancement while providing operational autonomy that enhances organizational effectiveness through systematic leadership specialization."

The CIO transition had proven that pharmaceutical companies could achieve competitive enhancement through leadership specialization while demonstrating that innovation focus created competitive advantages that operational management could never optimize.

"Transitioning to Chief Innovation Officer demonstrated that pharmaceutical success requires leadership optimization that enhances competitive advantages through specialization," I concluded.

The lesson had become fundamental to our leadership philosophy: innovation leadership enabled creating competitive advantages through systematic breakthrough development while providing operational excellence that enhanced organizational effectiveness through leadership specialization and strategic capability optimization.

The New CEO Appointment Process

The new CEO appointment awakening came during a defining board meeting in March 2025 when the independent directors unanimously endorsed Dr. Priya Sharma's elevation to Chief Executive Officer, marking the culmination of our most rigorous executive search process that had evaluated internal candidates against external alternatives from McKinsey, Boston Consulting Group, and former executives from Novartis and Pfizer. The magnitude of this decision became overwhelming when I realized that appointing our first non-founder CEO represented not just leadership transition but organizational evolution that would determine whether our pharmaceutical innovations could achieve sustainable competitive advantages under professional management.

"Dr. Sharma's appointment represents optimal balance between institutional knowledge preservation and strategic evolution capability," announced our lead independent director, Dr. Patricia Williams, during the appointment announcement meeting. "CEO selection required evaluating leadership capabilities that could enhance competitive advantages while maintaining organizational excellence through systematic management and strategic vision that enables pharmaceutical innovation advancement beyond founder capabilities."

"But appointing internal candidate over external alternatives requires confidence that institutional knowledge outweighs fresh perspective and industry best practices," I replied, though the selection process had demonstrated Priya's systematic preparation and strategic capabilities that exceeded external candidate qualifications. "How does internal appointment optimize competitive advantages while ensuring organizational evolution and strategic enhancement?"

"Internal appointment enables organizational continuity while providing strategic evolution through proven leadership capabilities and pharmaceutical expertise," she explained with the governance authority that had guided our selection process for eighteen months. "CEO selection balances institutional knowledge with evolution capability that enables competitive enhancement while preserving strategic advantages through systematic leadership and pharmaceutical excellence."

"And our prospects for achieving CEO transition that enhances competitive positioning while maintaining organizational coherence and strategic innovation?"

"CEO appointment enables competitive enhancement through proven leadership while providing organizational evolution that advances pharmaceutical innovation and strategic positioning through systematic management and strategic capability development."

This CEO appointment process validated our systematic succession planning while proving that internal leadership development could produce executive capabilities that exceeded external alternatives across multiple dimensions of pharmaceutical leadership excellence.

The selection criteria development required establishing comprehensive evaluation frameworks while identifying leadership capabilities that could advance our pharmaceutical innovations and competitive positioning under professional management rather than founder oversight.

"CEO selection criteria include pharmaceutical industry expertise, strategic innovation capability, international expansion experience, and stakeholder relationship management," reported our executive search consultant during criteria development. "Selection framework enables identifying leadership that can enhance competitive advantages while providing organizational evolution through systematic evaluation and strategic capability assessment."

"What specific leadership capabilities distinguish effective pharmaceutical CEO performance from general executive competence?" I asked.

"Pharmaceutical leadership requires scientific credibility, regulatory expertise, innovation vision, and stakeholder management that enable competitive advantages while advancing pharmaceutical development through systematic leadership and strategic excellence."

"And evaluation criteria that balance institutional knowledge preservation with strategic evolution and competitive enhancement capabilities?"

"Leadership assessment includes organizational knowledge, strategic vision, competitive capability, and evolution potential that enable identifying optimal CEO candidates through systematic evaluation and strategic leadership assessment."

The candidate evaluation process required systematic assessment of internal and external alternatives while conducting comprehensive analysis of leadership capabilities and strategic vision that could optimize pharmaceutical performance and competitive positioning.

"Candidate evaluation includes Dr. Priya Sharma's internal assessment plus external candidates from McKinsey, BCG, former Novartis VP, and former Pfizer executive," announced our search committee during evaluation planning. "Comprehensive evaluation enables optimal selection while providing thorough assessment of leadership capabilities and strategic vision through systematic candidate analysis."

"How do internal versus external candidates compare across pharmaceutical leadership requirements and competitive enhancement capabilities?" I asked.

"Internal candidates provide organizational knowledge and pharmaceutical expertise while external candidates offer fresh perspective and industry best practices that require systematic evaluation for optimal CEO selection."

"And evaluation methodology that ensures objective assessment while identifying leadership that can enhance competitive advantages?"

"Systematic interview processes, strategic assessment exercises, board interaction evaluation, and stakeholder relationship assessment that enable objective CEO selection through comprehensive evaluation and strategic capability analysis."

The Dr. Priya Sharma assessment revealed exceptional pharmaceutical leadership capabilities while demonstrating strategic vision and execution excellence that exceeded external candidate qualifications across multiple evaluation dimensions.

"Dr. Sharma assessment shows pharmaceutical expertise through regulatory leadership, strategic vision through innovation development, and execution excellence through operational success," reported our search committee during candidate analysis. "Leadership assessment demonstrates CEO capabilities that exceed external alternatives while providing pharmaceutical expertise and strategic vision that enable competitive enhancement."

"What specific leadership capabilities distinguish Dr. Sharma's qualifications for pharmaceutical CEO responsibilities?" I asked.

"Regulatory expertise, innovation leadership, strategic vision, operational excellence, and stakeholder management that enable pharmaceutical advancement while creating competitive advantages through systematic leadership and strategic capability development."

"And Dr. Sharma's strategic vision for organizational evolution and competitive enhancement under CEO leadership?"

"Strategic pharmaceutical advancement, innovation acceleration, international expansion, and competitive positioning that enable organizational evolution while enhancing competitive advantages through systematic leadership and strategic development."

The external candidate comparison demonstrated that while external alternatives possessed general management expertise, internal pharmaceutical knowledge and strategic vision provided superior qualifications for our specific competitive challenges and organizational requirements.

"External candidate comparison shows strong general management capabilities while lacking pharmaceutical expertise and organizational knowledge that CEO role requires," announced our evaluation committee during comparative assessment. "External alternatives provide industry perspective while internal candidates offer pharmaceutical expertise and strategic vision that enable optimal CEO performance."

"What advantages do external candidates provide compared to internal pharmaceutical expertise and organizational knowledge?" I asked.

"External candidates offer fresh perspective, industry benchmarking, and general management best practices while internal candidates provide pharmaceutical expertise and organizational knowledge that enable superior CEO performance."

"And selection rationale that optimizes CEO appointment for competitive enhancement and organizational evolution?"

"CEO selection balances pharmaceutical expertise with strategic vision that enables competitive enhancement while providing organizational evolution through proven leadership and strategic capability development."

The board approval process required comprehensive governance evaluation while ensuring independent director confidence in CEO selection and strategic vision for pharmaceutical advancement and competitive positioning.

"Board approval includes independent director evaluation, governance committee assessment, and strategic vision review that ensures optimal CEO selection," reported our governance committee during approval planning. "Board evaluation enables CEO appointment while providing governance oversight and strategic assessment that supports pharmaceutical advancement."

"How does board approval process ensure optimal CEO selection while maintaining governance excellence and strategic oversight?" I asked.

"Board evaluation includes independent assessment, strategic vision review, and governance oversight that enables optimal CEO appointment while ensuring pharmaceutical advancement and competitive positioning through systematic governance."

"And board confidence in CEO selection for pharmaceutical leadership and competitive enhancement under professional management?"

"Board confidence in Dr. Sharma's pharmaceutical expertise, strategic vision, and leadership capabilities that enable competitive enhancement while advancing pharmaceutical innovation through systematic management and strategic leadership."

The stakeholder communication strategy required developing systematic approaches to CEO appointment announcement while ensuring stakeholder confidence in leadership transition and strategic vision for continued pharmaceutical advancement.

"Stakeholder communication includes investor presentations, employee announcements, customer notifications, and regulatory communications that ensure stakeholder confidence in CEO appointment," announced our communications director during announcement planning. "Communication strategy enables stakeholder support while providing confidence in leadership transition and strategic vision."

"What stakeholder communication strategies optimize confidence in CEO appointment while ensuring continued pharmaceutical advancement?" I asked.

"Systematic stakeholder engagement, strategic vision communication, and leadership capability demonstration that ensure stakeholder confidence while supporting pharmaceutical advancement through CEO appointment and strategic leadership."

The CEO appointment implementation required systematic transition planning while ensuring operational continuity and strategic advancement during leadership change and organizational evolution.

"CEO appointment implementation includes systematic transition planning, operational continuity coordination, and strategic advancement oversight," reported our transition manager during implementation planning. "Implementation strategy enables CEO success while ensuring pharmaceutical advancement and competitive positioning through systematic leadership transition."

"How does CEO appointment implementation optimize organizational effectiveness while ensuring competitive advantage preservation and strategic enhancement?" I asked.

"Implementation strategy enables operational excellence while preserving competitive advantages through systematic transition and strategic coordination that supports pharmaceutical advancement under CEO leadership."

The new CEO appointment results demonstrated that systematic succession planning could produce internal leadership that exceeded external alternatives while enabling competitive enhancement and organizational evolution under professional management.

"Dr. Priya Sharma's CEO appointment represents optimal pharmaceutical leadership that enables competitive enhancement while providing organizational evolution through proven capabilities and strategic vision," I announced during our annual succession review. "CEO appointment demonstrates that systematic succession planning produces leadership that exceeds external alternatives while advancing pharmaceutical innovation and competitive positioning."

"And organizational confidence in CEO appointment for pharmaceutical advancement and competitive enhancement?" asked our governance committee.

"CEO appointment has generated stakeholder confidence while enabling pharmaceutical advancement through proven leadership and strategic vision that enhance competitive positioning and organizational capabilities."

Six months after CEO appointment, we had achieved leadership transition that enhanced competitive advantages while enabling organizational evolution under professional management that exceeded founder capabilities.

"The new CEO appointment process taught us that pharmaceutical succession requires systematic leadership development that produces capabilities exceeding external alternatives," I reflected during our CEO transition review.

"The key insight was that CEO appointment enables competitive enhancement while providing organizational evolution through proven pharmaceutical leadership and strategic vision."

The CEO appointment process had proven that systematic succession planning could produce internal leadership that enhanced competitive advantages while demonstrating that pharmaceutical expertise and strategic vision created optimal CEO capabilities.

"The new CEO appointment process demonstrated that pharmaceutical success requires leadership that combines pharmaceutical expertise with strategic vision for competitive enhancement," I concluded.

The lesson had become fundamental to our succession philosophy: CEO appointment enabled creating competitive advantages through pharmaceutical leadership that provided organizational evolution while advancing innovation and competitive positioning through systematic management and strategic excellence.

Board Restructuring for Next Phase

The board restructuring awakening came during a decisive governance review meeting in April 2025 when our institutional investors made clear that our current board composition - dominated by longtime associates and industry friends - was fundamentally inadequate for governing a global biotechnology company with $4.7 billion annual revenue and breakthrough pharmaceutical innovations requiring sophisticated oversight. The magnitude of this governance transformation became obvious when BlackRock's representative mentioned that board restructuring had become a prerequisite for continued institutional investment, because modern pharmaceutical governance required expertise that our traditional board relationships simply could not provide.

"Board restructuring represents essential governance evolution that enables institutional investment while providing strategic oversight for biotechnology advancement and global pharmaceutical operations," explained Dr. Margaret Chen, our new board governance consultant, as she presented restructuring plans that would replace seven existing directors with pharmaceutical industry leaders. "Next-phase governance requires board expertise that can guide biotechnology innovation, regulatory strategy, and international expansion through systematic oversight and strategic guidance that traditional board composition cannot deliver effectively."

"But board restructuring eliminates relationships and institutional knowledge that took decades to develop while potentially compromising strategic continuity and organizational culture," I protested, though investor requirements were forcing me to recognize that governance evolution had become competitive necessity rather than optional enhancement.

"Board restructuring preserves strategic value while enhancing governance capabilities through pharmaceutical expertise and international experience that enable competitive advantages," she replied with the systematic precision that had guided governance transformation for dozens of global pharmaceutical companies. "Next-phase governance creates competitive positioning while providing strategic oversight that advances biotechnology innovation and pharmaceutical excellence through board expertise and systematic governance."

"And our prospects for achieving governance restructuring that enhances competitive advantages while preserving organizational coherence and strategic continuity?"

"Board restructuring enables competitive enhancement through governance expertise while preserving strategic advantages through systematic transition and institutional knowledge preservation that supports pharmaceutical advancement and competitive positioning."

This governance imperative launched our comprehensive board restructuring program that would require replacing traditional governance with pharmaceutical industry expertise while proving that board evolution could enhance rather than compromise strategic oversight and competitive advantages.

The governance assessment revealed that our current board composition lacked the specialized expertise required for governing breakthrough biotechnology companies while missing critical capabilities that institutional investors demanded for pharmaceutical governance excellence.

"Governance assessment identifies critical expertise gaps including biotechnology oversight, regulatory strategy, international operations, and digital transformation that current board composition cannot address," reported our governance evaluation consultant during restructuring planning. "Board restructuring enables governance excellence while providing strategic oversight that advances pharmaceutical innovation and competitive positioning through systematic expertise enhancement."

"What specific governance capabilities distinguish next-phase pharmaceutical oversight from traditional board composition?" I asked.

"Biotechnology expertise, regulatory knowledge, international experience, digital transformation understanding, and competitive intelligence that enable governance excellence while providing strategic oversight for pharmaceutical advancement and competitive enhancement."

"And governance restructuring strategies that preserve institutional knowledge while enhancing board capabilities and competitive oversight?"

"Systematic director transition, expertise integration, and institutional knowledge preservation that enable governance enhancement while maintaining strategic continuity through planned restructuring and capability development."

The director recruitment strategy required identifying pharmaceutical industry leaders while establishing board composition that could provide specialized oversight for biotechnology innovation and global pharmaceutical operations.

"Director recruitment includes former FDA Commissioner Dr. Janet Woodcock, former Roche CEO Dr. Severin Schwan, and former Genentech Chief Medical Officer Dr. Sandra Horning," announced our board recruitment consultant during candidate assessment. "Director expertise enables governance excellence while providing strategic oversight that advances pharmaceutical innovation through industry knowledge and regulatory expertise."

"How do pharmaceutical industry directors enhance governance capabilities compared to traditional board composition?" I asked.

"Industry directors provide regulatory expertise, biotechnology knowledge, international experience, and competitive intelligence that enable governance excellence while advancing pharmaceutical innovation through systematic oversight and strategic guidance."

"And director recruitment strategies that balance pharmaceutical expertise with governance independence and strategic oversight?"

"Independent director selection, expertise diversification, and governance excellence that enable board enhancement while maintaining oversight independence through systematic recruitment and capability assessment."

The committee restructuring required developing specialized oversight capabilities while creating governance systems that could address biotechnology complexity and regulatory requirements through expert committee composition.

"Committee restructuring includes Biotechnology Innovation Committee led by Dr. Horning, Regulatory Strategy Committee chaired by Dr. Woodcock, and International Operations Committee directed by Dr. Schwan," reported our governance structure consultant during committee planning. "Committee specialization enables governance excellence while providing expert oversight that advances pharmaceutical innovation and competitive positioning."

"What committee structures optimize pharmaceutical governance while enabling biotechnology oversight and strategic guidance?" I asked.

"Specialized committees with pharmaceutical expertise that enable governance excellence while providing strategic oversight for biotechnology advancement through expert committee composition and systematic governance."

"And committee coordination that balances specialized oversight with comprehensive governance and strategic integration?"

"Committee integration, governance coordination, and strategic oversight that enable comprehensive governance while maintaining specialized expertise through systematic committee management and board coordination."

The governance policy enhancement required developing sophisticated oversight frameworks while creating governance systems that could address pharmaceutical complexity and institutional investor requirements.

"Governance policy enhancement includes biotechnology oversight protocols, regulatory compliance frameworks, and international operation governance that enable systematic oversight," announced our policy development consultant during governance planning. "Policy enhancement enables governance excellence while providing systematic oversight that advances pharmaceutical innovation through governance frameworks and strategic policy development."

"How do enhanced governance policies improve pharmaceutical oversight while ensuring institutional investor compliance?" I asked.

"Enhanced policies provide systematic oversight while ensuring governance excellence through pharmaceutical-specific frameworks and institutional investor compliance that advance competitive positioning and strategic oversight."

"And policy implementation strategies that balance governance enhancement with operational efficiency and strategic flexibility?"

"Policy integration, governance optimization, and operational coordination that enable governance excellence while maintaining strategic flexibility through systematic policy development and governance enhancement."

The stakeholder engagement restructuring required developing systematic approaches to institutional investor communication while creating governance transparency that could satisfy sophisticated pharmaceutical investment requirements.

"Stakeholder engagement restructuring includes institutional investor relations, governance transparency reporting, and strategic communication that enable stakeholder confidence," reported our stakeholder relations manager during engagement planning. "Engagement enhancement enables governance excellence while providing stakeholder confidence through transparency and systematic communication."

"What stakeholder engagement capabilities optimize institutional investor confidence while enhancing governance credibility?" I asked.

"Systematic stakeholder communication, governance transparency, and institutional investor engagement that enable stakeholder confidence while advancing governance excellence through strategic communication and transparency enhancement."

"And stakeholder coordination that balances investor requirements with governance independence and strategic oversight autonomy?"

"Stakeholder engagement, governance independence, and strategic oversight that enable institutional investor confidence while maintaining governance autonomy through systematic stakeholder management and governance excellence."

The transition management required systematic approaches to board restructuring while ensuring governance continuity and strategic oversight during director transition and expertise integration.

"Transition management includes systematic director orientation, governance continuity planning, and expertise integration that enable board restructuring success," announced our transition coordinator during restructuring implementation. "Transition strategy enables governance enhancement while preserving strategic oversight through systematic restructuring and director integration."

"How does transition management optimize board restructuring while ensuring governance continuity and strategic oversight preservation?" I asked.

"Transition coordination enables governance enhancement while preserving strategic oversight through systematic director integration and governance continuity that advance pharmaceutical innovation and competitive positioning."

"And transition timeline that balances restructuring efficiency with governance stability and strategic oversight maintenance?"

"Systematic transition requires 12-18 months of director integration and governance enhancement that enables board restructuring while maintaining strategic oversight through planned transition and expertise development."

The board restructuring results demonstrated that governance evolution could enhance competitive advantages while providing institutional investor confidence and strategic oversight that advanced pharmaceutical innovation and competitive positioning.

"Board restructuring has enhanced governance capabilities while providing institutional investor confidence through pharmaceutical expertise and strategic oversight that advance biotechnology innovation," I announced during our annual governance review. "Governance enhancement demonstrates that board evolution creates competitive advantages while advancing pharmaceutical innovation through systematic oversight and strategic guidance."

"And institutional investor confidence improvements from board restructuring compared to traditional governance composition?" asked our governance assessment committee.

"Board restructuring has generated institutional investor confidence while enhancing governance capabilities through pharmaceutical expertise that advance competitive positioning and strategic oversight excellence."

Twelve months after implementing board restructuring, we had achieved governance excellence that enhanced competitive advantages while providing institutional investor confidence and strategic oversight that supported pharmaceutical advancement.

"Board restructuring for the next phase taught us that pharmaceutical governance requires specialized expertise rather than traditional board relationships," I reflected during our governance evolution review.

"The key insight was that board restructuring enables competitive enhancement while providing strategic oversight that advances pharmaceutical innovation through governance excellence and expert oversight."

The board restructuring had proven that governance evolution could enhance competitive advantages while demonstrating that pharmaceutical expertise created optimal oversight capabilities for biotechnology advancement and competitive positioning.

"Board restructuring demonstrated that pharmaceutical success requires governance that combines industry expertise with strategic oversight for competitive enhancement," I concluded.

The lesson had become fundamental to our governance philosophy: board restructuring enabled creating competitive advantages through pharmaceutical expertise that provided strategic oversight while advancing biotechnology innovation and competitive positioning through systematic governance and expert board composition.

The Family Legacy Preservation

The family legacy preservation awakening came during a deeply personal conversation with my son Rohit in May 2025 when he asked me directly whether our transition to professional management would eliminate the family values and entrepreneurial spirit that had defined our pharmaceutical journey from generic startup to biotechnology innovator. The magnitude of this legacy challenge became overwhelming when I realized that preserving family heritage while enabling professional excellence required sophisticated frameworks that could maintain cultural continuity without compromising competitive advantages that systematic management demanded.

"Family legacy preservation requires balancing family values with professional management excellence while ensuring that entrepreneurial spirit and cultural heritage continue driving pharmaceutical innovation and competitive advantages," explained Dr. Sarah Williams during our family business transition planning, reviewing frameworks that showed how family enterprises could maintain cultural identity while achieving professional management excellence. "Legacy preservation enables competitive advantages through values-based leadership while providing professional capabilities that advance pharmaceutical innovation through systematic management and cultural continuity."

"But family legacy preservation could conflict with professional management requirements while potentially compromising systematic excellence and competitive positioning," I protested, though mounting evidence suggested that family values could enhance rather than constrain professional pharmaceutical management. "How can family heritage preservation optimize competitive advantages while ensuring professional excellence and systematic management capabilities?"

"Family legacy creates competitive advantages through values-driven culture while professional management provides systematic capabilities that enhance competitive positioning," she replied with the family business expertise that had guided transition planning for numerous pharmaceutical family enterprises. "Legacy preservation enables competitive differentiation while providing professional excellence that advances pharmaceutical innovation through values-based leadership and systematic management integration."

"And our prospects for achieving legacy preservation that enhances competitive advantages while enabling professional management excellence and pharmaceutical innovation advancement?"

"Legacy preservation enables competitive enhancement through family values while providing professional capabilities that advance pharmaceutical innovation and competitive positioning through systematic management and cultural heritage integration."

This legacy preservation imperative launched our systematic development of family heritage frameworks that would require balancing cultural continuity with professional excellence while proving that family values could enhance rather than compromise pharmaceutical competitive advantages.

The family values assessment revealed that our entrepreneurial heritage and values-driven culture had created competitive advantages while establishing organizational characteristics that could enhance professional management rather than constraining systematic excellence.

"Family values assessment identifies entrepreneurial innovation, ethical excellence, stakeholder commitment, and long-term vision that create competitive advantages while providing cultural foundation for professional management," reported our family business consultant during values evaluation. "Values-driven culture enables competitive differentiation while providing professional management enhancement through family heritage and systematic excellence integration."

"What specific family values distinguish our competitive advantages from traditional pharmaceutical company cultures?" I asked.

"Entrepreneurial innovation, ethical leadership, stakeholder partnership, and long-term commitment that create competitive advantages while providing cultural differentiation through family values and professional excellence integration."

"And values preservation strategies that enhance professional management while maintaining family heritage and competitive cultural advantages?"

"Values integration, cultural preservation, and professional enhancement that enable family heritage while advancing professional management through systematic values implementation and competitive advantage development."

The governance structure development required creating frameworks that could preserve family ownership while enabling professional management independence and systematic governance excellence that institutional investors demanded.

"Governance structure includes family ownership preservation through holding company framework plus professional management independence through board governance and systematic oversight," announced our governance consultant during structure planning. "Governance balance enables family heritage preservation while providing professional management excellence through systematic governance and cultural integration."

"How does governance structure balance family ownership with professional management requirements and institutional investor expectations?" I asked.

"Governance framework enables family ownership while providing professional management independence through systematic oversight and institutional investor compliance that preserve family heritage while advancing competitive advantages."

"And governance sustainability that maintains family legacy while enabling professional management evolution and competitive enhancement?"

"Governance integration, family heritage preservation, and professional excellence that enable legacy sustainability while advancing competitive positioning through systematic governance and professional management capabilities."

The cultural continuity development required establishing systematic approaches to family values preservation while creating organizational systems that could maintain entrepreneurial spirit under professional management leadership.

"Cultural continuity includes values-based hiring, ethical excellence standards, and entrepreneurial innovation programs that preserve family heritage while enabling professional management," reported our cultural development manager during continuity planning. "Cultural preservation enables competitive advantages while providing professional enhancement through family values and systematic excellence integration."

"What cultural continuity capabilities optimize family heritage preservation while enhancing professional management effectiveness?" I asked.

"Values-driven culture, ethical excellence, entrepreneurial innovation, and stakeholder commitment that enable family heritage while advancing professional management through cultural integration and competitive advantage development."

"And cultural sustainability strategies that preserve family values while enabling organizational evolution and professional management excellence?"

"Cultural integration, values preservation, and professional enhancement that enable family heritage while advancing organizational capabilities through systematic cultural development and professional excellence."

The philanthropy and social impact programs required developing systematic approaches to community engagement while creating social responsibility initiatives that could preserve family commitment to healthcare access and community development.

"Philanthropy programs include healthcare access initiatives, medical education support, and community development programs that preserve family commitment to social impact," announced our philanthropy director during social impact planning. "Social responsibility enables family heritage preservation while creating competitive advantages through stakeholder engagement and community partnership."

"How do philanthropy and social impact programs enhance family legacy while creating competitive advantages?" I asked.

"Social impact programs preserve family values while creating competitive advantages through stakeholder relationships, community partnerships, and regulatory positioning that advance pharmaceutical innovation and competitive enhancement."

"And philanthropy sustainability that maintains family heritage while enabling professional management and competitive advantage optimization?"

"Philanthropy integration, social impact preservation, and competitive enhancement that enable family heritage while advancing professional management through social responsibility and stakeholder engagement."

The next-generation development required creating systematic approaches to family member engagement while providing career development opportunities that could contribute to pharmaceutical advancement without compromising professional management excellence.

"Next-generation development includes career pathway planning, professional development programs, and systematic mentorship that enable family member contribution to pharmaceutical advancement," reported our family development coordinator during generation planning. "Family engagement enables heritage preservation while providing professional contribution through systematic development and career excellence."

"What next-generation development strategies optimize family member contribution while maintaining professional management excellence?" I asked.

"Professional development, merit-based advancement, and systematic contribution that enable family engagement while advancing pharmaceutical innovation through professional excellence and family heritage integration."

"And next-generation coordination that balances family heritage with professional requirements and competitive advantage optimization?"

"Family engagement, professional excellence, and systematic development that enable next-generation contribution while advancing competitive positioning through professional management and family heritage preservation."

The foundation establishment required developing systematic approaches to family legacy institutionalization while creating enduring frameworks that could preserve family values and community commitment beyond individual family member involvement.

"Foundation establishment includes healthcare access foundation, medical education endowment, and community development programs that institutionalize family commitment to social impact," announced our foundation development manager during establishment planning. "Foundation framework enables legacy preservation while providing systematic social impact through enduring family heritage and community commitment."

"How does foundation establishment preserve family legacy while enhancing competitive advantages and professional management capabilities?" I asked.

"Foundation establishment preserves family heritage while creating competitive advantages through social impact, stakeholder engagement, and community partnership that advance pharmaceutical innovation and competitive positioning."

The family legacy preservation results demonstrated that systematic heritage frameworks could enhance competitive advantages while enabling professional management excellence and pharmaceutical innovation advancement through values-driven culture and systematic excellence integration.

"Family legacy preservation has enhanced competitive advantages while enabling professional management excellence through values-driven culture and systematic heritage frameworks," I announced during our annual legacy review. "Heritage preservation demonstrates that family values create competitive differentiation while advancing pharmaceutical innovation through professional excellence and cultural integration."

"And competitive positioning improvements from family legacy preservation compared to traditional pharmaceutical company cultures?" asked our family heritage committee.

"Legacy preservation has created competitive differentiation while enhancing professional management through values-driven culture that advances pharmaceutical innovation and competitive advantages through family heritage and systematic excellence."

Eighteen months after implementing family legacy preservation frameworks, we had achieved cultural continuity that enhanced competitive advantages while enabling professional management excellence and pharmaceutical innovation advancement.

"Family legacy preservation taught us that pharmaceutical success requires values-driven culture that enhances professional management rather than constraining systematic excellence," I reflected during our heritage preservation review.

"The key insight was that family legacy creates competitive advantages through cultural differentiation while enabling professional excellence that advances pharmaceutical innovation and competitive positioning."

The family legacy preservation had proven that family heritage could enhance competitive advantages while demonstrating that values-driven culture created optimal foundations for professional management excellence and pharmaceutical innovation advancement.

"Family legacy preservation demonstrated that pharmaceutical success requires cultural heritage that enhances professional management while creating competitive advantages through values-driven excellence," I concluded.

The lesson had become fundamental to our cultural philosophy: family legacy preservation enabled creating competitive advantages through values-driven culture that enhanced professional management while advancing pharmaceutical innovation and competitive positioning through heritage integration and systematic excellence.

Chapter 30

The TIME Recognition

From Local Success to Global Icon

The TIME recognition awakening came through an unexpected phone call from TIME Magazine's senior editor on June 3, 2025, informing me that I had been selected for their prestigious "100 Most Influential People" list in the healthcare innovation category, joining a distinguished cohort that included breakthrough scientists, policy leaders, and technology pioneers who had transformed global healthcare delivery. The magnitude of this recognition became overwhelming when she mentioned that our pharmaceutical journey from generic manufacturer to biotechnology innovator had captured international attention as a definitive example of how systematic innovation could revolutionize healthcare access while creating sustainable competitive advantages.

"Your pharmaceutical transformation represents the type of healthcare innovation that TIME's editorial board believes can reshape global medicine," explained Dr. Jennifer Walsh, TIME's healthcare correspondent, during our recognition interview. "From developing breakthrough cardiovascular therapeutics to establishing manufacturing excellence that sets industry standards, your company's evolution demonstrates how systematic innovation can create competitive advantages while addressing critical healthcare needs that traditional pharmaceutical approaches have failed to serve effectively."

"But TIME recognition seems premature when our breakthrough compound AMT-3471 remains in clinical development and our global impact, while meaningful, represents just the beginning of our pharmaceutical innovation potential," I protested, though the international attention was forcing me to recognize that our systematic transformation had achieved influence that exceeded my own assessment of our accomplishments.

"TIME recognition reflects demonstrated impact plus innovation potential that could influence pharmaceutical industry direction," she replied with the editorial authority that had made TIME's healthcare coverage definitive industry analysis. "Your systematic approach to pharmaceutical innovation provides a replicable model that other companies and healthcare systems could adopt to address global healthcare challenges that traditional approaches cannot solve effectively."

"And the implications for our competitive positioning when TIME recognition creates international attention and potential competitive scrutiny?"

"International recognition enhances competitive advantages through credibility and market positioning while creating opportunities for partnerships and expansion that local success cannot achieve through global influence and industry authority."

This TIME recognition marked our transformation from a successful Indian pharmaceutical company to a globally influential healthcare innovator whose systematic approach to pharmaceutical development had achieved international credibility and industry authority.

The recognition criteria analysis revealed that TIME's selection had been based on systematic innovation impact rather than just financial success, because our approach to pharmaceutical transformation demonstrated methodologies that could influence industry direction and healthcare improvement globally.

"TIME recognition criteria include innovation impact, industry influence, systematic replicability, and global healthcare contribution that distinguish transformative leaders from successful companies," reported our recognition analysis consultant during criteria assessment. "Recognition reflects systematic innovation that creates industry influence while demonstrating pharmaceutical development approaches that other organizations could adopt for healthcare advancement."

"What specific innovation achievements distinguished our pharmaceutical transformation for TIME recognition consideration?" I asked.

"AI-driven drug discovery breakthrough, biotechnology capability development, manufacturing excellence establishment, global market penetration, and systematic pharmaceutical innovation that create industry influence while demonstrating replicable transformation methodologies."

"And competitive advantages from TIME recognition compared to traditional pharmaceutical industry recognition and awards?"

"TIME recognition provides global credibility and industry authority that enable competitive advantages through international influence, partnership opportunities, and market positioning that traditional industry recognition cannot achieve."

The media coverage expansion demonstrated how TIME recognition had amplified international attention while creating communication opportunities that could enhance our competitive positioning and industry influence beyond pharmaceutical sector boundaries.

"Media coverage expansion includes international news coverage, industry analysis, academic case study development, and speaking opportunity invitations from global healthcare conferences," announced our communications director during media assessment. "Media attention enables competitive advantages while providing industry influence through international credibility and systematic innovation recognition."

"How does international media attention enhance competitive positioning while creating opportunities for pharmaceutical advancement?" I asked.

"Media coverage provides credibility and market positioning that enable competitive advantages while creating partnership opportunities, investment interest, and industry influence through international recognition and systematic innovation validation."

"And media strategy coordination that optimizes recognition benefits while maintaining competitive advantage protection and strategic focus?"

"Strategic media engagement, competitive advantage preservation, and systematic communication that enable recognition benefits while maintaining strategic positioning through international attention and industry influence optimization."

The partnership opportunity acceleration revealed how TIME recognition had created collaboration interest from global pharmaceutical companies, academic institutions, and government organizations that previously had limited engagement with Indian pharmaceutical companies.

"Partnership opportunity acceleration includes collaboration inquiries from Harvard Medical School, partnership discussions with European pharmaceutical companies, and government partnership invitations from developing countries seeking pharmaceutical capability development," reported our partnership director during opportunity assessment. "Recognition enables partnership advancement while creating competitive advantages through international collaboration and systematic innovation sharing."

"What partnership opportunities provide optimal competitive enhancement while leveraging TIME recognition for pharmaceutical advancement?" I asked.

"Strategic partnerships that enhance competitive advantages while providing global market access, technology development, and systematic innovation advancement through international collaboration and recognition-based credibility."

"And partnership strategy that balances recognition opportunities with competitive advantage preservation and strategic independence?"

"Partnership optimization, competitive advantage protection, and strategic independence that enable recognition benefits while maintaining competitive positioning through systematic partnership development and international collaboration."

The speaking engagement proliferation demonstrated how industry conferences and academic institutions worldwide were seeking our systematic innovation expertise while creating platforms for thought leadership and competitive differentiation.

"Speaking engagement proliferation includes keynote invitations from World Economic Forum, pharmaceutical industry conferences, and academic institutions seeking systematic innovation expertise," announced our speaking coordinator during engagement assessment. "Speaking opportunities enable thought leadership while creating competitive advantages through industry influence and systematic innovation sharing."

"How do speaking engagements enhance competitive positioning while creating industry influence and market differentiation?" I asked.

"Speaking opportunities provide thought leadership while creating competitive advantages through industry credibility, market positioning, and systematic innovation influence that enhance pharmaceutical advancement and competitive excellence."

"And speaking strategy that optimizes recognition benefits while protecting competitive advantages and strategic innovation insights?"

"Strategic speaking engagement, competitive advantage protection, and thought leadership development that enable recognition benefits while preserving competitive positioning through systematic speaking excellence and industry influence."

The academic case study development revealed how business schools globally were analyzing our pharmaceutical transformation while creating educational materials that could influence next-generation healthcare leaders and pharmaceutical innovators.

"Academic case study development includes Harvard Business School, Wharton, and INSEAD case study creation plus doctoral research focusing on systematic pharmaceutical innovation and transformation methodologies," reported our academic relations manager during case study assessment. "Academic attention enables thought leadership while creating competitive advantages through educational influence and systematic innovation validation."

"What academic case study development provides optimal competitive enhancement while contributing to pharmaceutical education advancement?" I asked.

"Case study development that enhances competitive advantages while contributing to pharmaceutical education through systematic innovation sharing and transformation methodology documentation that influences healthcare leadership development."

"And academic coordination that balances educational contribution with competitive advantage preservation and strategic insight protection?"

"Academic engagement, competitive advantage protection, and educational contribution that enable case study development while maintaining competitive positioning through systematic academic collaboration and innovation sharing."

The investor interest amplification demonstrated how TIME recognition had enhanced institutional investor confidence while creating capital market opportunities that could accelerate pharmaceutical development and competitive expansion.

"Investor interest amplification includes institutional investor inquiries, venture capital partnership discussions, and public market valuation enhancement that create capital opportunities," announced our investor relations director during interest assessment. "Recognition enables investment advantages while providing capital access that accelerates pharmaceutical development and competitive advancement through enhanced market credibility."

"How does TIME recognition enhance investor attractiveness while creating capital opportunities for pharmaceutical advancement?" I asked.

"Recognition provides investor confidence while creating capital advantages through market credibility, international recognition, and systematic innovation validation that enable pharmaceutical advancement and competitive enhancement."

"And investor strategy that optimizes recognition benefits while maintaining strategic independence and competitive advantage preservation?"

"Investor engagement, strategic independence, and competitive advantage protection that enable recognition benefits while preserving strategic positioning through systematic investor relations and capital optimization."

The TIME recognition results demonstrated that systematic pharmaceutical innovation could achieve international influence while creating competitive advantages that enabled global healthcare impact and industry authority.

"TIME recognition has validated our systematic pharmaceutical innovation while creating international influence that enhances competitive advantages and enables global healthcare contribution," I announced during our annual recognition review. "International recognition demonstrates that pharmaceutical transformation can achieve global impact while creating competitive advantages through systematic innovation and healthcare advancement."

"And competitive positioning improvements from TIME recognition compared to traditional pharmaceutical industry achievements?" asked our recognition strategy committee.

"TIME recognition has enhanced competitive advantages while creating international influence through systematic innovation validation that provides global credibility and market positioning beyond traditional pharmaceutical recognition."

Six months after TIME recognition, we had achieved international influence that enhanced competitive advantages while creating opportunities for global healthcare impact and pharmaceutical industry advancement.

"TIME recognition taught us that pharmaceutical success requires systematic innovation that creates global healthcare impact rather than just commercial advancement," I reflected during our international influence review.

"The key insight was that international recognition validates systematic innovation while creating competitive advantages through global credibility and industry influence."

The TIME recognition had proven that pharmaceutical companies could achieve international influence through systematic innovation while demonstrating that healthcare transformation created global impact and competitive advantages.

"TIME recognition demonstrated that pharmaceutical success requires innovation that creates global healthcare impact while establishing international influence and competitive excellence," I concluded.

The lesson had become fundamental to our innovation philosophy: TIME recognition enabled creating international influence through systematic pharmaceutical innovation that provided global healthcare impact while establishing competitive advantages and industry authority through innovation excellence and healthcare transformation.

Reflection on Thirty-Year Journey

The thirty-year journey reflection began during a solitary evening walk through the IISc campus in June 2025, as I contemplated how our pharmaceutical odyssey had evolved from a desperate attempt to manufacture generic cardiovascular drugs in a cramped Mumbai facility to recognition among TIME's most influential healthcare innovators. The magnitude of this transformation became overwhelming when I realized that every strategic decision, operational failure, and competitive breakthrough had somehow contributed to a systematic evolution that neither I nor any business consultant could have predicted when we began manufacturing generic aspirin tablets in 1995.

"Thirty years of pharmaceutical development reveals that systematic transformation requires embracing uncertainty while building capabilities that enable adapting to industry evolution rather than just optimizing existing approaches," I reflected during my campus contemplation, reviewing mental images of our journey from generic manufacturer to biotechnology innovator. "Pharmaceutical success demanded continuous reinvention while preserving competitive advantages through systematic capability development that enabled participating in industry transformation rather than becoming casualty of technological and market evolution."

The reflection forced me to confront how our company had navigated multiple existential challenges while somehow emerging stronger from each crisis that could have eliminated our pharmaceutical ambitions permanently.

The transformation phases analysis revealed that our thirty-year journey had encompassed five distinct evolutionary periods, each requiring different capabilities while building foundations that enabled subsequent advancement and competitive positioning.

"Journey analysis shows five transformation phases including generic manufacturing establishment (1995-2005), operational excellence development (2005-2012), innovation capability building (2012-2018), biotechnology transformation (2018-2022), and global leadership achievement (2022-2025)," I reflected during my retrospective assessment. "Each phase required different capabilities while building competitive advantages that enabled subsequent evolution through systematic capability development and strategic adaptation."

"What common threads connect seemingly disparate transformation phases across thirty years of pharmaceutical development?" I asked myself.

"Systematic capability building, competitive advantage preservation, strategic adaptation, and stakeholder relationship development that enabled continuous evolution while maintaining competitive positioning through transformation phases and industry evolution."

"And critical decisions that determined transformation success versus potential failure during challenging evolutionary periods?"

"Innovation investment during profitability pressure, international expansion despite resource constraints, biotechnology development without guaranteed returns, and leadership transition while preserving competitive advantages through systematic decision-making and strategic commitment."

The failure and learning integration demonstrated how setbacks and mistakes had provided essential education while building organizational resilience that enabled surviving competitive challenges and industry disruption.

"Failure integration analysis shows critical learning from regulatory rejections, clinical trial failures, competitive defeats, and operational crises that provided education impossible to achieve through success alone," I reflected during my learning assessment. "Failure education enabled competitive advantages through resilience building, strategic adaptation, and systematic improvement that success could not teach while providing capabilities for industry leadership and competitive excellence."

"How did pharmaceutical failures contribute to eventual competitive advantages and industry leadership?" I asked myself.

"Failures provided education about regulatory requirements, clinical development complexity, competitive dynamics, and operational excellence that enabled building capabilities for systematic success while creating competitive advantages through learning and adaptation."

"And organizational culture development that transformed failures into competitive advantages rather than limiting strategic confidence?"

"Learning culture, systematic improvement, resilience building, and strategic adaptation that enabled converting failures into competitive advantages while building organizational capabilities for pharmaceutical excellence and industry leadership."

The relationship evolution assessment revealed how stakeholder relationships had developed from transactional interactions to strategic partnerships that created competitive advantages and industry influence beyond individual company capabilities.

"Relationship evolution shows transformation from vendor relationships to strategic partnerships with suppliers, customers, regulators, and competitors that created competitive advantages through collaboration and mutual value creation," I reflected during my relationship analysis. "Strategic relationships enabled competitive positioning while providing capabilities for pharmaceutical advancement that individual company resources could not achieve through systematic partnership development and stakeholder engagement."

"What relationship development strategies created competitive advantages while building industry influence and strategic positioning?" I asked myself.

"Long-term commitment, mutual value creation, systematic partnership development, and stakeholder engagement that built relationships beyond transactional interactions while creating competitive advantages through collaboration and strategic alliance development."

"And relationship sustainability that maintained competitive advantages while enabling industry evolution and strategic adaptation?"

"Relationship deepening, value creation, strategic partnership, and systematic engagement that enabled relationship sustainability while providing competitive advantages through stakeholder collaboration and industry influence development."

The innovation philosophy evolution demonstrated how our approach to pharmaceutical development had transformed from optimization-focused efficiency to breakthrough-oriented innovation that created competitive advantages through systematic capability development.

"Innovation philosophy evolution shows transformation from generic optimization to breakthrough innovation development that created competitive advantages through systematic capability building and strategic innovation investment," I reflected during my innovation analysis. "Innovation transformation enabled competitive positioning while providing capabilities for pharmaceutical advancement that optimization approaches could not achieve through systematic innovation and breakthrough development."

"How did innovation philosophy changes enable competitive advantages while building capabilities for pharmaceutical leadership?" I asked myself.

"Innovation focus, systematic capability development, breakthrough orientation, and strategic investment that enabled competitive advantages while building pharmaceutical innovation capabilities for industry leadership and competitive excellence."

"And innovation sustainability that maintained competitive advantages while enabling continuous advancement and strategic positioning?"

"Innovation culture, systematic development, breakthrough focus, and strategic investment that enabled innovation sustainability while providing competitive advantages through pharmaceutical advancement and industry leadership."

The competitive advantage development assessment revealed how systematic capability building had created sustainable positioning while establishing barriers that protected market leadership and industry influence.

"Competitive advantage development shows systematic capability building through operational excellence, innovation leadership, relationship development, and strategic positioning that created sustainable advantages," I reflected during my competitive analysis. "Advantage development enabled market leadership while providing barriers against competitive displacement through systematic excellence and strategic capability building."

"What competitive advantage strategies created sustainable positioning while enabling industry leadership and market influence?" I asked myself.

"Systematic excellence, capability development, strategic positioning, and competitive barrier creation that enabled sustainable advantages while building market leadership and industry influence through pharmaceutical excellence."

"And competitive sustainability that maintained advantages while enabling industry evolution and strategic adaptation?"

"Advantage reinforcement, capability enhancement, strategic adaptation, and competitive excellence that enabled sustainability while providing market leadership through systematic advantage development and strategic positioning."

The legacy consideration assessment revealed how our pharmaceutical journey had created impact beyond commercial success while establishing foundations that could influence healthcare advancement and industry development.

"Legacy consideration shows impact beyond commercial success through healthcare access improvement, industry standard establishment, and pharmaceutical innovation advancement that created foundations for continued healthcare impact," I reflected during my legacy analysis. "Legacy development enabled healthcare contribution while providing industry influence that extended beyond individual company success through systematic impact and healthcare advancement."

"How does thirty-year pharmaceutical journey create legacy that extends beyond commercial achievement?" I asked myself.

"Healthcare impact, industry influence, pharmaceutical advancement, and systematic innovation that created legacy through healthcare contribution while establishing foundations for continued industry development and healthcare improvement."

"And legacy sustainability that maintains healthcare impact while enabling continued pharmaceutical advancement and industry influence?"

"Impact preservation, innovation advancement, industry influence, and healthcare contribution that enable legacy sustainability while providing continued pharmaceutical development and healthcare improvement through systematic impact and industry advancement."

The future vision development revealed how thirty years of systematic evolution had created capabilities and positioning that could enable continued pharmaceutical advancement while addressing global healthcare challenges through innovation and systematic excellence.

"Future vision shows capabilities for continued pharmaceutical advancement through biotechnology innovation, global healthcare impact, and systematic excellence that enable addressing healthcare challenges beyond current capabilities," I reflected during my future analysis. "Vision development enables continued advancement while providing capabilities for global healthcare contribution through pharmaceutical innovation and systematic excellence."

The thirty-year journey reflection demonstrated that systematic pharmaceutical transformation required continuous evolution while building capabilities that enabled adapting to industry change and creating competitive advantages through strategic development and innovation excellence.

"Thirty-year pharmaceutical journey reflection reveals that transformation success requires systematic capability building while adapting to industry evolution through strategic development and innovation excellence," I concluded during my retrospective assessment. "Journey demonstrates that pharmaceutical success requires continuous evolution while building competitive advantages through systematic development and strategic adaptation."

The reflection had proven that pharmaceutical companies could achieve sustained success through systematic evolution while demonstrating that transformation required continuous adaptation and capability development for competitive advantage creation and industry leadership.

"Thirty-year journey reflection taught us that pharmaceutical success requires systematic evolution rather than just operational optimization," I concluded.

"The key insight was that transformation success requires building capabilities for continuous adaptation while creating competitive advantages through systematic development and strategic excellence."

The lesson had become fundamental to our strategic philosophy: thirty-year journey reflection enabled understanding pharmaceutical transformation through systematic capability development that created competitive advantages while enabling continuous evolution and industry leadership through strategic development and innovation excellence.

Lessons Learned from Each Constraint

The constraint retrospective awakening came during a reflective analysis session in July 2025 when I realized that each seemingly insurmountable business limitation we had encountered over thirty years had ultimately become a catalyst for breakthrough innovation and competitive advantage development. The profound insight crystallized when I understood that our pharmaceutical transformation had been shaped not by avoiding constraints but by systematically converting limitations into strategic opportunities that created competitive advantages through constraint-driven innovation and systematic problem-solving approaches.

"Constraint analysis reveals that business limitations forced innovation breakthroughs while creating competitive advantages through systematic problem-solving that conventional approaches could never achieve," I reflected during my constraint assessment, reviewing how capital limitations, regulatory barriers, technological gaps, and competitive pressures had each contributed to strategic innovations. "Constraint resolution required developing capabilities that became competitive advantages while establishing organizational systems that enabled sustained excellence through limitation-driven innovation and systematic capability development."

The retrospective forced me to understand how each constraint had provided essential education while building organizational capabilities that enabled subsequent transformation and competitive positioning.

The capital constraint lessons demonstrated how resource limitations had forced operational efficiency while creating systematic approaches to value creation that became fundamental competitive advantages throughout our pharmaceutical development.

"Capital constraint lessons include operational efficiency development, value creation optimization, resource allocation discipline, and systematic investment approaches that created competitive advantages through constraint-driven innovation," I reflected during my capital analysis. "Resource limitations forced efficiency excellence while building capabilities for sustained competitive positioning through systematic value creation and operational excellence that unlimited resources could not teach."

"How did capital constraints create competitive advantages rather than just limiting business development capabilities?" I asked myself.

"Capital limitations forced innovation and efficiency that created competitive advantages through operational excellence, systematic value creation, and resource optimization that enabled sustained competitive positioning beyond resource-rich competitors."

"And capital constraint resolution strategies that preserved efficiency advantages while enabling growth and competitive advancement?"

"Systematic efficiency preservation, operational excellence maintenance, and value creation optimization that enabled growth while preserving competitive advantages through constraint-driven innovation and systematic capability development."

The knowledge constraint lessons revealed how technical limitations had forced systematic learning while creating expertise development approaches that established competitive differentiation and industry authority.

"Knowledge constraint lessons include systematic learning development, expertise building methodologies, capability advancement strategies, and technical authority establishment that created competitive advantages through constraint-driven education," I reflected during my knowledge analysis. "Technical limitations forced systematic learning while building expertise that enabled competitive positioning through knowledge development and technical authority that conventional approaches could not achieve."

"What knowledge constraint resolution strategies created competitive advantages while building technical authority and industry expertise?" I asked myself.

"Systematic learning, expertise development, capability building, and technical authority establishment that enabled competitive advantages through knowledge advancement and industry expertise development."

"And knowledge development sustainability that maintained competitive advantages while enabling continuous learning and technical advancement?"

"Learning culture, expertise advancement, capability development, and systematic education that enabled knowledge sustainability while providing competitive advantages through technical authority and industry expertise."

The scale constraint lessons demonstrated how size limitations had forced focus and specialization while creating competitive advantages through excellence concentration that diversified competitors could not achieve.

"Scale constraint lessons include focus development, specialization excellence, competitive concentration, and systematic capability building that created advantages through constraint-driven specialization," I reflected during my scale analysis. "Size limitations forced focus while building competitive advantages through specialization excellence and systematic capability development that diversified approaches could not achieve."

"How did scale constraints enable competitive advantages through focus and specialization rather than limiting market opportunities?" I asked myself.

"Scale limitations forced focus and specialization that created competitive advantages through excellence concentration and systematic capability development that enabled market leadership despite size constraints."

"And scale constraint resolution that preserved focus advantages while enabling growth and market expansion?"

"Focus preservation, specialization maintenance, excellence concentration, and systematic expansion that enabled growth while maintaining competitive advantages through constraint-driven focus and systematic capability development."

The innovation constraint lessons revealed how traditional approaches had forced breakthrough thinking while creating innovation capabilities that established competitive differentiation and industry leadership.

"Innovation constraint lessons include breakthrough development, systematic innovation, competitive differentiation, and industry leadership establishment that created advantages through constraint-driven innovation excellence," I reflected during my innovation analysis. "Traditional limitations forced breakthrough thinking while building innovation capabilities that enabled competitive positioning through systematic innovation and industry leadership development."

"What innovation constraint resolution strategies created competitive advantages while establishing industry leadership and competitive differentiation?" I asked myself.

"Breakthrough development, systematic innovation, competitive differentiation, and industry leadership that enabled advantages through innovation excellence and systematic capability building."

"And innovation sustainability that maintained competitive advantages while enabling continuous advancement and industry leadership?"

"Innovation culture, systematic development, breakthrough focus, and competitive differentiation that enabled innovation sustainability while providing advantages through industry leadership and systematic excellence."

The legacy constraint lessons demonstrated how founder dependency had forced organizational development while creating systematic capabilities that enabled leadership transition and competitive sustainability.

"Legacy constraint lessons include organizational development, systematic capability building, leadership sustainability, and competitive advantage preservation that created foundations for continued excellence," I reflected during my legacy analysis. "Founder dependency forced organizational development while building systematic capabilities that enabled leadership transition and competitive sustainability through constraint-driven organizational excellence."

"How did legacy constraints create organizational advantages while enabling leadership transition and competitive sustainability?" I asked myself.

"Legacy limitations forced organizational development and systematic capability building that created competitive advantages through leadership sustainability and organizational excellence."

"And legacy resolution strategies that preserved competitive advantages while enabling organizational evolution and leadership development?"

"Organizational development, systematic capability building, leadership sustainability, and competitive advantage preservation that enabled legacy resolution while maintaining excellence through organizational evolution."

The integration constraint synthesis revealed how constraint resolution had created systematic approaches to problem-solving while building organizational capabilities that became competitive advantages through limitation-driven innovation.

"Integration constraint synthesis shows systematic problem-solving development, capability building methodologies, competitive advantage creation, and organizational excellence establishment through constraint-driven innovation," I reflected during my synthesis analysis. "Constraint resolution created systematic approaches while building capabilities that enabled competitive advantages through limitation-driven innovation and organizational development."

"What constraint resolution patterns created sustainable competitive advantages while building systematic problem-solving capabilities?" I asked myself.

"Systematic problem-solving, capability building, competitive advantage creation, and organizational excellence that enabled sustainable advantages through constraint resolution and systematic development."

"And constraint resolution methodologies that created competitive advantages while enabling organizational advancement and strategic positioning?"

"Systematic resolution approaches, capability development, competitive advantage creation, and organizational excellence that enabled advantages through constraint-driven innovation and systematic capability building."

The constraint transformation philosophy demonstrated how limitations had become strategic opportunities while creating innovation approaches that established competitive advantages through systematic constraint resolution and capability development.

"Constraint transformation philosophy shows limitation conversion to strategic opportunities through systematic innovation and capability development that created competitive advantages," I reflected during my philosophy analysis. "Constraint resolution enabled competitive positioning while building organizational capabilities through limitation-driven innovation and systematic problem-solving excellence."

"How does constraint transformation create competitive advantages while building organizational capabilities for sustained excellence?" I asked myself.

"Constraint resolution through systematic innovation and capability development that creates competitive advantages while building organizational excellence through limitation-driven improvement and strategic positioning."

The constraint lessons learned synthesis demonstrated that business limitations could create competitive advantages while building organizational capabilities through systematic constraint resolution and innovation excellence.

"Constraint lessons learned demonstrate that limitations create competitive advantages through systematic resolution and capability development that enable organizational excellence and strategic positioning," I concluded during my constraint assessment. "Limitation resolution requires systematic innovation while building capabilities that create competitive advantages through constraint-driven development and organizational excellence."

The constraint analysis had proven that pharmaceutical companies could achieve competitive advantages through systematic constraint resolution while demonstrating that limitations provided opportunities for innovation excellence and capability development.

"Lessons learned from each constraint taught us that pharmaceutical success requires converting limitations into competitive advantages through systematic resolution and innovation excellence," I concluded.

"The key insight was that constraints enable competitive advantage creation through systematic problem-solving while building organizational capabilities for sustained excellence and strategic positioning."

The lesson had become fundamental to our strategic philosophy: constraint resolution enabled creating competitive advantages through systematic innovation that converted limitations into strategic opportunities while building organizational capabilities for continued excellence and competitive positioning through constraint-driven development and systematic problem-solving excellence.

Advice for Next Generation Entrepreneurs

The next generation entrepreneur guidance awakening came during a heartfelt conversation with my son Rohit and his MBA classmates in August 2025 when they asked me to distill thirty years of pharmaceutical entrepreneurship into actionable wisdom that could help them navigate business challenges I couldn't have imagined when we began manufacturing generic drugs in 1995. The magnitude of this responsibility became overwhelming when I realized that my generation of entrepreneurs had operated in relatively stable industries while today's entrepreneurs face exponential technological change, global competition, and business model disruption that make traditional entrepreneurial advice potentially obsolete.

"Next generation entrepreneurship requires understanding that business constraints will become competitive advantages while technological disruption creates opportunities that conventional approaches cannot capture," I explained during our mentorship session, reflecting on how artificial intelligence, biotechnology convergence, and global connectivity had fundamentally altered entrepreneurial possibilities. "Entrepreneurial success demands systematic capability building while embracing uncertainty that my generation could avoid through predictable industry evolution and stable competitive dynamics."

"But how do we apply lessons from pharmaceutical industry transformation to entrepreneurship in sectors experiencing rapid technological change?" Rohit asked with the analytical precision that had characterized his professional development.

"Entrepreneurial principles transcend industry boundaries while systematic approaches to constraint resolution, capability building, and competitive advantage creation enable success regardless of technological disruption," I replied, recognizing that fundamental entrepreneurship required universal capabilities despite industry-specific implementation differences.

This mentorship opportunity crystallized my understanding that entrepreneurial wisdom required translating specific experiences into universal principles that could guide next-generation entrepreneurs through challenges that would exceed anything my generation had encountered.

The constraint embracement philosophy represented the most fundamental entrepreneurial lesson because business limitations would inevitably force innovation while creating competitive advantages that unlimited resources could never achieve.

"Constraint embracement requires understanding that business limitations force innovation breakthroughs while creating competitive advantages through systematic problem-solving," I advised during our entrepreneurial discussion. "Successful entrepreneurs convert constraints into competitive advantages rather than viewing limitations as obstacles to business development and competitive positioning."

"How do entrepreneurs systematically convert business constraints into competitive advantages?" Rohit inquired.

"Constraint resolution through systematic innovation, capability building, and problem-solving excellence that transforms limitations into strategic opportunities while creating competitive advantages through systematic development and innovation excellence."

"And constraint embracement strategies that optimize competitive advantage creation while building sustainable business foundations?"

"Systematic constraint analysis, innovation development, capability building, and competitive advantage creation that enable entrepreneurial success through limitation resolution and strategic opportunity development."

The systematic capability building approach represented essential entrepreneurial methodology because sustainable competitive advantages required systematic excellence rather than just innovative ideas or market opportunities.

"Systematic capability building requires developing organizational excellence through systematic improvement rather than depending on individual expertise or market opportunities," I explained during our capability discussion. "Entrepreneurial success demands building systematic capabilities that enable competitive advantages through organizational excellence and systematic development rather than just innovative products or market positioning."

"What systematic capability building approaches enable entrepreneurial competitive advantages?" my mentee group asked.

"Operational excellence development, innovation capability building, relationship management systems, and competitive advantage creation through systematic organizational development and excellence establishment."

"And capability sustainability that maintains competitive advantages while enabling business growth and market expansion?"

"Systematic excellence preservation, capability advancement, competitive advantage reinforcement, and organizational development that enable sustainable entrepreneurial success through systematic capability building and competitive excellence."

The relationship investment strategy represented critical entrepreneurial wisdom because stakeholder relationships would ultimately determine business sustainability while creating competitive advantages that individual capabilities could never achieve.

"Relationship investment requires understanding that stakeholder partnerships create competitive advantages while enabling business capabilities that individual entrepreneurship cannot achieve," I advised during our relationship discussion. "Entrepreneurial success depends on systematic relationship building that creates mutual value while establishing competitive positioning through partnership excellence and stakeholder engagement."

"How do entrepreneurs build stakeholder relationships that create competitive advantages?" the group inquired.

"Systematic relationship development, mutual value creation, partnership excellence, and stakeholder engagement that enable competitive advantages through relationship investment and systematic partnership building."

"And relationship sustainability that maintains competitive advantages while enabling business growth and strategic positioning?"

"Relationship deepening, value creation, partnership excellence, and stakeholder engagement that enable sustainable entrepreneurial success through systematic relationship investment and competitive advantage development."

The innovation discipline approach represented essential entrepreneurial methodology because breakthrough innovation required systematic approaches rather than hoping for accidental discoveries or technological breakthroughs.

"Innovation discipline requires systematic approaches to breakthrough development rather than depending on accidental discovery or technological advancement," I explained during our innovation discussion. "Entrepreneurial innovation demands systematic capability building that enables breakthrough development through disciplined approaches to problem-solving and systematic innovation excellence."

"What innovation discipline strategies enable entrepreneurial breakthrough development?" Rohit asked.

"Systematic innovation processes, capability building, breakthrough development methodologies, and competitive advantage creation through disciplined innovation and systematic excellence development."

"And innovation sustainability that maintains competitive advantages while enabling continuous advancement and market positioning?"

"Innovation culture, systematic development, breakthrough focus, and competitive excellence that enable sustainable entrepreneurial innovation through disciplined approaches and systematic capability building."

The competitive intelligence development represented crucial entrepreneurial capability because market understanding would determine strategic positioning while enabling competitive advantages through superior market knowledge and strategic positioning.

"Competitive intelligence development requires systematic market understanding that enables strategic positioning while creating competitive advantages through superior knowledge and market insight," I advised during our competitive discussion. "Entrepreneurial success demands comprehensive competitive analysis that enables strategic positioning through market understanding and competitive advantage development."

"How do entrepreneurs develop competitive intelligence that creates strategic advantages?" the mentee group inquired.

"Systematic market analysis, competitive assessment, strategic positioning, and advantage development through comprehensive intelligence and systematic market understanding."

"And competitive intelligence sustainability that maintains strategic advantages while enabling market adaptation and competitive positioning?"

"Intelligence advancement, market understanding, strategic positioning, and competitive advantage preservation that enable sustainable entrepreneurial success through systematic competitive intelligence and market analysis excellence."

The global perspective adoption represented essential entrepreneurial mindset because domestic market focus would limit opportunities while global thinking enabled competitive advantages through international market access and partnership development.

"Global perspective adoption requires understanding that domestic market limitations prevent competitive advantage development while international thinking enables market opportunities and partnership development," I explained during our globalization discussion. "Entrepreneurial success demands global mindset that enables market expansion while creating competitive advantages through international positioning and systematic global development."

"What global perspective strategies enable entrepreneurial international competitive advantages?" Rohit asked.

"International market analysis, global partnership development, competitive positioning, and advantage creation through systematic globalization and international excellence development."

"And global sustainability that maintains competitive advantages while enabling international expansion and market positioning?"

"Global capability building, international partnership, competitive advantage preservation, and market expansion that enable sustainable entrepreneurial globalization through systematic international development."

The ethical foundation establishment represented fundamental entrepreneurial requirement because sustainable business success required stakeholder trust while creating competitive advantages through ethical excellence and systematic integrity.

"Ethical foundation establishment requires understanding that stakeholder trust creates competitive advantages while enabling business sustainability through ethical excellence and systematic integrity," I advised during our ethics discussion. "Entrepreneurial success demands ethical foundation that enables stakeholder confidence while creating competitive positioning through integrity and systematic ethical excellence."

"How do entrepreneurs build ethical foundations that create competitive advantages?" the group inquired.

"Ethical excellence, stakeholder trust, integrity demonstration, and competitive advantage creation through systematic ethical foundation and stakeholder confidence building."

The next generation entrepreneur advice synthesis demonstrated that entrepreneurial success required systematic approaches to constraint resolution, capability building, and competitive advantage creation rather than just innovative ideas or market opportunities.

"Next generation entrepreneur advice emphasizes systematic capability building, constraint resolution, relationship investment, and competitive advantage creation that enable entrepreneurial success through systematic excellence rather than just innovative opportunities," I concluded during our mentorship session. "Entrepreneurial success requires systematic approaches while building capabilities that create competitive advantages through constraint resolution and systematic development excellence."

The entrepreneurial guidance had proven that systematic approaches could enable next-generation success while demonstrating that fundamental entrepreneurial principles transcended industry boundaries and technological disruption.

"Advice for next generation entrepreneurs taught us that entrepreneurial success requires systematic excellence rather than just innovative ideas," I concluded.

"The key insight was that systematic capability building enables competitive advantages while creating sustainable entrepreneurial success through constraint resolution and systematic development excellence."

The lesson had become fundamental to our mentorship philosophy: next generation entrepreneur guidance enabled sharing systematic approaches that created competitive advantages while building entrepreneurial capabilities for sustained success through systematic excellence and constraint resolution rather than depending on innovative opportunities or market advantages alone.

The Future Vision for Global Healthcare

The global healthcare future vision awakening came during a profound contemplation at the World Health Assembly in Geneva in September 2025 when I realized that our pharmaceutical transformation represented just the beginning of a healthcare revolution that could fundamentally reshape how humanity approaches disease prevention, treatment, and wellness optimization. The magnitude of this future possibility became overwhelming when I understood that convergent technologies including artificial intelligence, personalized medicine, and digital therapeutics could create healthcare capabilities that would make today's medical interventions seem as primitive as medieval treatments appear to contemporary physicians.

"Global healthcare future requires understanding that technological convergence will enable personalized medicine, predictive healthcare, and precision therapeutics that could eliminate most diseases while optimizing human wellness through systematic healthcare advancement," I reflected during my Geneva assessment, contemplating how pharmaceutical innovation represented one component of comprehensive healthcare transformation. "Healthcare revolution demands systematic integration of breakthrough technologies while creating accessible delivery systems that serve global populations rather than just affluent markets through equitable healthcare advancement and systematic wellness optimization."

The vision crystallized around understanding that healthcare transformation required systematic approaches that could address both technological advancement and global accessibility challenges simultaneously.

The personalized medicine revolution represented the most transformative healthcare opportunity because genetic understanding and AI-driven therapeutic development could enable treating diseases at molecular levels while optimizing treatments for individual genetic profiles and lifestyle factors.

"Personalized medicine revolution requires systematic integration of genetic analysis, AI-driven therapeutic development, and precision treatment protocols that enable molecular-level disease intervention," I envisioned during my personalized medicine analysis. "Precision healthcare enables treating diseases before symptoms appear while optimizing therapies for individual genetic profiles through systematic personalized medicine and precision therapeutic development."

"How will personalized medicine transform global healthcare delivery while ensuring accessibility for diverse patient populations?" I contemplated.

"Personalized medicine through systematic genetic analysis, AI therapeutic development, and precision treatment that enables molecular disease intervention while ensuring global accessibility through systematic healthcare advancement and equitable precision medicine delivery."

"And personalized medicine sustainability that maintains accessibility while enabling precision therapeutic advancement and systematic healthcare optimization?"

"Systematic precision medicine, genetic analysis advancement, therapeutic optimization, and accessibility preservation that enable global personalized healthcare through systematic development and equitable precision medicine delivery."

The artificial intelligence integration represented revolutionary healthcare capability because machine learning could enable predictive diagnostics, automated treatment optimization, and systematic healthcare management that exceeded human analytical capabilities.

"Artificial intelligence integration enables predictive diagnostics, treatment optimization, and healthcare management through machine learning that exceeds human analytical capabilities," I envisioned during my AI healthcare analysis. "AI healthcare requires systematic integration of diagnostic algorithms, treatment optimization, and patient management that enable predictive medicine while optimizing therapeutic outcomes through systematic AI advancement and healthcare optimization."

"What AI integration strategies enable healthcare advancement while preserving human-centered care and medical professional expertise?" I reflected.

"AI integration through systematic algorithm development, human-AI collaboration, and healthcare optimization that enables predictive medicine while preserving human-centered care through systematic AI advancement and medical professional enhancement."

"And AI sustainability that maintains healthcare accessibility while enabling predictive medicine advancement and systematic healthcare optimization?"

"Systematic AI development, healthcare optimization, accessibility preservation, and predictive medicine advancement that enable global AI healthcare through systematic integration and equitable technology deployment."

The digital therapeutics expansion represented transformative healthcare delivery because technology-enabled treatments could provide accessible interventions while enabling continuous monitoring and treatment optimization that traditional healthcare could never achieve.

"Digital therapeutics expansion enables accessible treatment delivery, continuous monitoring, and therapeutic optimization through technology-enabled interventions," I envisioned during my digital healthcare analysis. "Digital healthcare requires systematic therapeutic development, technology integration, and accessibility optimization that enable global treatment delivery while advancing therapeutic effectiveness through systematic digital advancement and healthcare optimization."

"How will digital therapeutics transform healthcare accessibility while maintaining treatment effectiveness and patient engagement?" I contemplated.

"Digital therapeutics through systematic technology development, accessibility optimization, and treatment effectiveness that enable global healthcare delivery while maintaining patient engagement through systematic digital advancement and healthcare optimization."

"And digital sustainability that maintains treatment effectiveness while enabling global accessibility and systematic healthcare advancement?"

"Systematic digital development, treatment optimization, accessibility preservation, and healthcare advancement that enable global digital therapeutics through systematic integration and equitable technology deployment."

The preventive healthcare transformation represented fundamental healthcare paradigm shift because early intervention and wellness optimization could eliminate diseases while reducing healthcare costs through systematic prevention and health maintenance.

"Preventive healthcare transformation enables disease elimination through early intervention, wellness optimization, and systematic prevention that reduces healthcare costs," I envisioned during my preventive medicine analysis. "Prevention-focused healthcare requires systematic wellness programs, early intervention, and health optimization that enable disease elimination while reducing healthcare costs through systematic prevention and wellness advancement."

"What preventive healthcare strategies enable disease elimination while optimizing population health and healthcare sustainability?" I reflected.

"Preventive healthcare through systematic wellness programs, early intervention, health optimization, and disease elimination that enable population health while ensuring healthcare sustainability through systematic prevention and wellness advancement."

"And preventive sustainability that maintains healthcare accessibility while enabling wellness optimization and systematic disease prevention?"

"Systematic prevention programs, wellness optimization, accessibility preservation, and healthcare advancement that enable global preventive healthcare through systematic development and equitable prevention delivery."

The global accessibility integration represented essential healthcare imperative because technological advancement required equitable deployment while ensuring that healthcare innovations served global populations rather than just affluent markets.

"Global accessibility integration requires equitable healthcare deployment that ensures technological advancement serves global populations while eliminating healthcare disparities," I envisioned during my accessibility analysis. "Accessible healthcare requires systematic deployment strategies, equitable technology distribution, and global health optimization that enable universal healthcare access through systematic advancement and equitable healthcare delivery."

"How will global healthcare ensure technological advancement benefits reach underserved populations while maintaining innovation incentives?" I contemplated.

"Global accessibility through systematic deployment, equitable distribution, technology optimization, and universal access that enable global healthcare advancement while preserving innovation incentives through systematic accessibility and healthcare equity."

"And accessibility sustainability that maintains innovation advancement while ensuring global healthcare equity and systematic wellness optimization?"

"Systematic accessibility programs, innovation preservation, healthcare equity, and global optimization that enable sustainable global healthcare through systematic advancement and equitable technology deployment."

The collaborative ecosystem development represented transformative healthcare model because integrated partnerships between pharmaceutical companies, technology firms, healthcare providers, and government organizations could accelerate innovation while ensuring global healthcare advancement.

"Collaborative ecosystem development enables accelerated innovation through pharmaceutical-technology-healthcare-government partnerships that advance global healthcare," I envisioned during my collaboration analysis. "Healthcare collaboration requires systematic partnership development, innovation acceleration, and global advancement that enable comprehensive healthcare transformation through systematic ecosystem development and collaborative excellence."

"What collaborative strategies enable healthcare innovation acceleration while ensuring global accessibility and systematic healthcare advancement?" I reflected.

"Healthcare collaboration through systematic partnership development, innovation acceleration, accessibility optimization, and global advancement that enable comprehensive healthcare transformation through collaborative excellence and systematic ecosystem development."

The future vision synthesis represented comprehensive healthcare transformation that could eliminate diseases, optimize wellness, and ensure global accessibility through systematic technological advancement and collaborative healthcare development.

"Global healthcare future vision enables disease elimination, wellness optimization, and universal accessibility through systematic technological advancement and collaborative healthcare development," I concluded during my future analysis. "Healthcare transformation requires systematic integration of personalized medicine, AI advancement, digital therapeutics, preventive care, and global accessibility that enable comprehensive healthcare revolution through systematic development and collaborative excellence."

The future vision had proven that global healthcare transformation could achieve disease elimination while demonstrating that systematic technological advancement could create universal healthcare accessibility and wellness optimization.

"The future vision for global healthcare taught us that healthcare transformation requires systematic technological advancement combined with global accessibility commitment," I concluded.

"The key insight was that healthcare revolution enables disease elimination while ensuring universal access through systematic advancement and collaborative healthcare development that serves global populations."

The lesson had become fundamental to our healthcare philosophy: global healthcare future vision enabled creating comprehensive wellness through systematic technological advancement that provided universal accessibility while eliminating diseases through collaborative healthcare development and systematic wellness optimization for global populations.

Epilogue

The Next Constraint

The Innovation Saturation Paradox

The next constraint revelation struck me during a moment of unexpected clarity at the World Economic Forum in January 2026 when I realized that our pharmaceutical industry's relentless pursuit of innovation had created an overwhelming paradox: we had become so sophisticated at developing breakthrough therapeutics that the sheer volume of medical advances was overwhelming healthcare systems' ability to evaluate, adopt, and deliver these innovations to patients who desperately needed them. The magnitude of this emerging constraint became obvious when I understood that innovation success was creating implementation failure on a scale that threatened to make breakthrough discoveries irrelevant to actual patient care.

"The innovation saturation constraint represents our industry's next existential challenge," I reflected during my Davos contemplation, observing how pharmaceutical companies worldwide were announcing breakthrough discoveries while healthcare systems struggled to implement existing innovations effectively. "We have created more therapeutic possibilities than healthcare infrastructure can absorb, while regulatory systems designed for sequential innovation evaluation cannot process parallel breakthrough development that modern pharmaceutical capabilities enable."

The constraint crystallized around understanding that pharmaceutical innovation velocity had exceeded healthcare system adaptation capacity, creating bottlenecks that could prevent breakthrough therapeutics from reaching patients despite scientific and commercial success.

The regulatory capacity constraint was emerging as regulatory agencies struggled to evaluate breakthrough therapeutics while maintaining safety standards that traditional sequential review processes demanded, creating approval bottlenecks despite scientific merit and patient needs.

"Regulatory capacity constraint shows FDA, EMA, and global agencies overwhelmed by breakthrough therapy submissions that exceed review capabilities while maintaining safety standards," I analyzed during my regulatory assessment. "Agency limitation creates therapeutic access delays despite scientific advancement and patient need, requiring systematic regulatory evolution that can process parallel innovation while preserving safety excellence and systematic therapeutic evaluation."

"How will pharmaceutical companies navigate regulatory capacity limitations while advancing breakthrough therapeutics for patient benefit?" I contemplated.

"Regulatory evolution through systematic review enhancement, agency capacity building, and evaluation optimization that enable breakthrough therapy advancement while preserving safety standards through regulatory innovation and systematic approval enhancement."

"And regulatory sustainability that maintains safety excellence while enabling innovation advancement and systematic therapeutic access?"

"Systematic regulatory advancement, safety preservation, innovation facilitation, and therapeutic access that enable regulatory evolution through capacity enhancement and systematic approval optimization."

The healthcare delivery constraint was developing as medical systems struggled to implement breakthrough therapeutics while maintaining care quality that traditional healthcare approaches had established, creating delivery gaps despite therapeutic availability.

"Healthcare delivery constraint shows medical systems overwhelmed by therapeutic complexity that exceeds implementation capabilities while maintaining care quality standards," I observed during my delivery analysis. "System limitation creates therapeutic implementation delays despite availability and efficacy, requiring systematic healthcare evolution that can deliver breakthrough therapies while preserving care excellence and systematic patient treatment."

"What healthcare delivery evolution enables breakthrough therapeutic implementation while maintaining care quality and patient access?" I reflected.

"Healthcare advancement through systematic delivery enhancement, implementation optimization, and care quality preservation that enable breakthrough therapy delivery while maintaining patient access through systematic healthcare evolution and delivery excellence."

"And delivery sustainability that maintains care quality while enabling therapeutic advancement and systematic patient treatment optimization?"

"Systematic delivery advancement, care quality preservation, therapeutic implementation, and patient access that enable healthcare evolution through delivery enhancement and systematic treatment optimization."

The economic sustainability constraint was emerging as breakthrough therapeutic costs exceeded healthcare system budgets while creating access limitations that prevented innovative treatments from reaching patients despite scientific advancement and therapeutic efficacy.

"Economic sustainability constraint shows breakthrough therapeutic costs exceeding healthcare budgets while creating access limitations despite scientific advancement," I analyzed during my economic assessment. "Cost limitation creates therapeutic access barriers despite innovation success and patient need, requiring systematic economic evolution that enables breakthrough therapy access while maintaining healthcare sustainability and systematic economic optimization."

"How will healthcare systems balance breakthrough therapeutic costs with accessibility requirements while maintaining economic sustainability?" I contemplated.

"Economic evolution through systematic cost optimization, value-based pricing, and accessibility enhancement that enable breakthrough therapy access while preserving healthcare sustainability through economic innovation and systematic cost management."

"And economic sustainability that maintains healthcare accessibility while enabling therapeutic advancement and systematic patient treatment?"

"Systematic economic advancement, accessibility preservation, therapeutic implementation, and healthcare sustainability that enable economic evolution through cost optimization and systematic value creation."

The physician adaptation constraint was developing as medical professionals struggled to implement breakthrough therapeutics while maintaining clinical excellence that traditional medical practice had established, creating implementation gaps despite therapeutic advancement.

"Physician adaptation constraint shows medical professionals overwhelmed by therapeutic complexity that exceeds clinical training while maintaining practice excellence standards," I observed during my clinical analysis. "Professional limitation creates implementation delays despite therapeutic advancement and patient benefit, requiring systematic medical education that enables breakthrough therapy implementation while preserving clinical excellence and systematic patient care."

"What physician adaptation strategies enable breakthrough therapeutic implementation while maintaining clinical excellence and patient care quality?" I reflected.

"Medical advancement through systematic education enhancement, clinical training optimization, and practice excellence preservation that enable breakthrough therapy implementation while maintaining patient care through systematic physician development and clinical excellence."

"And adaptation sustainability that maintains clinical excellence while enabling therapeutic advancement and systematic patient care optimization?"

"Systematic medical advancement, clinical excellence preservation, therapeutic implementation, and patient care optimization that enable physician evolution through education enhancement and systematic clinical development."

The patient engagement constraint was emerging as breakthrough therapeutics required sophisticated patient management while exceeding traditional patient education capabilities, creating engagement gaps despite therapeutic potential and medical advancement.

"Patient engagement constraint shows therapeutic complexity exceeding patient understanding capabilities while requiring sophisticated self-management that traditional education approaches cannot provide," I analyzed during my patient assessment. "Engagement limitation creates therapeutic effectiveness gaps despite scientific advancement and medical implementation, requiring systematic patient education that enables breakthrough therapy management while optimizing therapeutic outcomes and systematic patient engagement."

"How will patient engagement evolution enable breakthrough therapeutic effectiveness while maintaining patient autonomy and treatment compliance?" I contemplated.

"Patient advancement through systematic education enhancement, engagement optimization, and autonomy preservation that enable breakthrough therapy effectiveness while maintaining compliance through systematic patient development and engagement excellence."

The constraint synthesis revealed that innovation saturation represented systematic challenge requiring coordinated evolution across regulatory, healthcare delivery, economic, physician adaptation, and patient engagement dimensions rather than isolated problem-solving approaches.

"Innovation saturation constraint synthesis shows systematic challenge requiring coordinated evolution across multiple healthcare dimensions rather than isolated solutions," I concluded during my constraint analysis. "Saturation resolution requires systematic healthcare transformation that enables innovation implementation while preserving quality, accessibility, and sustainability through coordinated advancement and systematic constraint resolution."

"What systematic approaches enable resolving innovation saturation while preserving healthcare excellence and patient access?" I reflected.

"Systematic healthcare evolution through coordinated advancement, innovation implementation, quality preservation, and accessibility maintenance that enable saturation resolution through systematic transformation and constraint optimization."

The next constraint recognition demonstrated that pharmaceutical success created new challenges requiring systematic solutions that exceeded individual company capabilities while demanding industry-wide collaboration and healthcare system evolution.

"The next constraint teaches us that pharmaceutical innovation success creates implementation challenges requiring systematic solutions beyond individual company capabilities," I concluded during my constraint assessment. "Innovation saturation demands coordinated healthcare evolution that enables breakthrough therapy implementation while preserving excellence and accessibility through systematic transformation and collaborative constraint resolution."

The constraint had proven that pharmaceutical advancement required anticipating implementation challenges while building systematic solutions that could enable innovation benefits to reach patients through coordinated healthcare evolution.

"The next constraint taught us that pharmaceutical success requires systematic solution development that enables innovation implementation rather than just breakthrough discovery," I concluded.

"The key insight was that innovation saturation requires coordinated healthcare evolution that enables breakthrough therapy delivery through systematic transformation and collaborative constraint resolution."

The lesson had become fundamental to our future strategy: next constraint resolution required systematic approaches that enabled innovation implementation while preserving healthcare excellence through coordinated advancement and collaborative solution development that served patient needs through systematic constraint optimization and healthcare evolution.

The Imagination Barrier

As I prepare to handover the CEO role to Priya, my co-founder and longtime partner, I realize that our greatest constraint was never technology, capital, or competition—it was our own ability to imagine what was possible. The profundity of this recognition struck me during our final joint board meeting in December 2025 when I understood that every breakthrough we had achieved, from AI-driven drug discovery to global biotechnology leadership, had required first overcoming the psychological limitation of believing such achievements were impossible for a mid-sized Indian pharmaceutical company competing against century-old multinational corporations.

"The imagination barrier represents the most fundamental constraint that entrepreneurs face," I reflected during my transition contemplation, reviewing how each transformational phase had required abandoning conventional thinking about what our company could accomplish. "We spent years optimizing within perceived limitations rather than questioning whether those limitations actually existed, because imagination constraints prevent seeing possibilities that systematic capability building could enable through strategic vision and systematic advancement."

The realization forced me to understand that business constraints often existed primarily in mental frameworks rather than actual operational limitations, creating self-imposed barriers that prevented breakthrough achievement and competitive advancement.

The perception limitation analysis revealed how traditional pharmaceutical industry thinking had created artificial constraints while preventing companies from pursuing innovation opportunities that systematic approaches could achieve through capability development and strategic vision.

"Perception limitation shows how industry conventional wisdom creates artificial constraints that prevent breakthrough achievement," I analyzed during my imagination assessment. "Traditional thinking limits possibility recognition while systematic capability building enables achievements that conventional approaches consider impossible through strategic vision advancement and systematic innovation development."

"How did imagination constraints prevent recognizing achievable opportunities while limiting strategic vision and competitive advancement?" I contemplated.

"Imagination barriers through conventional thinking, industry limitation acceptance, and possibility restriction that prevented opportunity recognition while limiting strategic advancement through perception constraints and systematic vision limitation."

"And imagination expansion strategies that enable possibility recognition while building capabilities for breakthrough achievement and competitive advancement?"

"Systematic imagination development, possibility expansion, capability building, and strategic vision that enable breakthrough recognition while advancing competitive positioning through imagination enhancement and systematic possibility development."

The conventional wisdom challenge demonstrated how industry accepted limitations had prevented pharmaceutical companies from pursuing transformation opportunities while creating competitive advantages through unconventional strategic approaches and systematic innovation.

"Conventional wisdom challenge shows industry accepted limitations preventing transformation pursuit while competitive advantages result from unconventional approaches," I observed during my wisdom analysis. "Industry conformity creates competitive constraints while unconventional thinking enables breakthrough achievement through systematic innovation and strategic vision that conventional approaches cannot recognize or implement effectively."

"What conventional wisdom limitations prevented pharmaceutical transformation while creating opportunities for unconventional strategic advancement?" I reflected.

"Industry conformity, accepted limitations, conventional approach dependence, and transformation resistance that prevented breakthrough achievement while creating opportunities for unconventional advancement through systematic innovation and strategic vision development."

"And wisdom challenge strategies that enable breakthrough recognition while building capabilities for systematic transformation and competitive advancement?"

"Conventional thinking challenge, limitation questioning, unconventional approach development, and transformation capability building that enable breakthrough achievement through wisdom challenge and systematic innovation advancement."

The possibility expansion framework revealed how systematic questioning of assumed limitations could enable recognizing achievable opportunities while building capabilities that exceeded traditional pharmaceutical competitive positioning and industry expectations.

"Possibility expansion framework enables recognizing achievable opportunities through systematic limitation questioning while building capabilities that exceed traditional expectations," I envisioned during my possibility analysis. "Expansion thinking requires challenging assumed constraints while developing systematic capabilities that enable breakthrough achievement through possibility recognition and strategic advancement that conventional thinking cannot envision or implement."

"How does possibility expansion enable competitive advantage recognition while building systematic capabilities for breakthrough achievement?" I contemplated.

"Possibility thinking through limitation questioning, opportunity recognition, capability building, and strategic advancement that enable competitive advantages while achieving breakthrough results through systematic expansion and possibility development."

"And expansion sustainability that maintains possibility thinking while enabling systematic achievement and competitive advancement?"

"Systematic possibility development, limitation questioning, opportunity recognition, and capability building that enable expansion sustainability while advancing competitive positioning through possibility thinking and systematic achievement."

The mental model transformation demonstrated how changing fundamental assumptions about pharmaceutical possibilities could enable breakthrough strategy development while creating competitive advantages through systematic approach innovation and strategic vision advancement.

"Mental model transformation enables breakthrough strategy development through fundamental assumption change while creating competitive advantages," I reflected during my model analysis. "Transformation thinking requires systematic assumption challenging while building strategic capabilities that enable breakthrough achievement through mental model advancement and systematic innovation that conventional pharmaceutical thinking cannot recognize or implement."

"What mental model transformation strategies enable breakthrough recognition while building systematic capabilities for competitive advancement?" I contemplated.

"Mental model change, assumption challenging, breakthrough recognition, and capability building that enable transformation achievement while advancing competitive positioning through model innovation and systematic advancement."

"And transformation sustainability that maintains breakthrough thinking while enabling systematic achievement and competitive excellence?"

"Systematic transformation development, model advancement, breakthrough thinking, and capability building that enable transformation sustainability while advancing competitive positioning through mental model innovation and systematic achievement."

The strategic vision evolution revealed how expanding imagination beyond traditional pharmaceutical limitations could enable recognizing global opportunities while building systematic capabilities that exceeded industry expectations and competitive positioning.

"Strategic vision evolution enables global opportunity recognition through imagination expansion beyond traditional limitations while building systematic capabilities," I envisioned during my vision analysis. "Vision advancement requires possibility thinking that transcends industry constraints while developing strategic capabilities that enable global achievement through systematic vision development and imagination advancement that conventional approaches cannot envision."

"How does strategic vision evolution enable global opportunity recognition while building systematic capabilities for worldwide competitive advancement?" I reflected.

"Strategic vision through imagination expansion, possibility recognition, global opportunity identification, and capability building that enable worldwide advancement while achieving competitive positioning through vision evolution and systematic development."

"And vision sustainability that maintains strategic imagination while enabling global achievement and systematic competitive advancement?"

"Systematic vision development, imagination advancement, possibility thinking, and capability building that enable vision sustainability while advancing global positioning through strategic imagination and systematic achievement."

The imagination legacy framework demonstrated how expanding possibility thinking could enable future generations of entrepreneurs while creating systematic approaches to constraint resolution and breakthrough achievement that transcended traditional business limitations.

"Imagination legacy framework enables future entrepreneur possibility thinking while creating systematic approaches to constraint resolution," I concluded during my legacy analysis. "Legacy development requires imagination advancement that transcends traditional limitations while building systematic capabilities that enable breakthrough achievement through possibility thinking and strategic vision that future generations can utilize for continued advancement and competitive excellence."

"What imagination legacy strategies enable future breakthrough achievement while building systematic capability frameworks for continued advancement?" I contemplated.

"Imagination development, possibility thinking advancement, systematic capability building, and legacy framework creation that enable future achievement while providing breakthrough methodologies through imagination legacy and systematic advancement."

The imagination constraint resolution synthesis revealed that breakthrough achievement required systematic expansion of possibility thinking while building capabilities that could convert imagination into systematic competitive advantages and strategic positioning.

"Imagination constraint resolution requires systematic possibility thinking expansion while building capabilities that convert imagination into competitive advantages," I concluded during my imagination assessment. "Constraint resolution enables breakthrough achievement through systematic imagination development while creating competitive positioning that exceeds traditional limitations through possibility thinking advancement and systematic capability building."

As I prepare this transition to Priya's leadership, I understand that our greatest gift to future pharmaceutical entrepreneurs lies not in the specific strategies we developed, but in demonstrating that systematic imagination expansion can enable achievements that conventional thinking considers impossible. The companies that will define healthcare's future will be those that refuse to accept current limitations as permanent constraints, choosing instead to build systematic capabilities that can convert ambitious imagination into breakthrough reality.

"The imagination barrier taught us that pharmaceutical transformation requires expanding possibility thinking beyond conventional limitations," I concluded.

"The key insight was that breakthrough achievement demands systematic imagination development that enables recognizing and implementing possibilities that conventional thinking cannot envision."

The lesson had become fundamental to our entrepreneurial philosophy: imagination constraint resolution enabled creating competitive advantages through systematic possibility thinking that converted ambitious vision into breakthrough achievement while building capabilities that exceeded traditional pharmaceutical limitations through strategic imagination and systematic advancement.

APPENDICES

Appendix A

The Theory of Constraints in Pharmaceuticals

The Theory of Constraints application to pharmaceutical development emerged from recognizing that traditional business optimization approaches failed to address the sequential bottlenecks that systematically limited pharmaceutical company performance, requiring specialized constraint identification and resolution methodologies that could enhance competitive advantages through systematic limitation elimination. Pharmaceutical constraints differ fundamentally from manufacturing or service industry limitations because they involve regulatory complexity, scientific uncertainty, and competitive dynamics that create interconnected bottlenecks demanding sophisticated resolution approaches rather than conventional operational optimization.

Pharmaceutical Constraint Categories

Capital Constraints in Pharmaceutical Development Capital constraints represent the most visible pharmaceutical limitations, manifesting through insufficient funding for R&D investment, manufacturing infrastructure, or market expansion that prevents competitive advancement. However, pharmaceutical capital constraints differ from traditional business funding limitations because they involve extended development timelines, regulatory uncertainty, and competitive positioning requirements that create unique capital allocation challenges.

Pharmaceutical companies experiencing capital constraints typically exhibit symptoms including: limited R&D pipeline development, manufacturing capacity restrictions, regulatory submission delays due to resource limitations, competitive positioning weakness, and market expansion constraints that prevent achieving optimal competitive advantages.

Capital constraint resolution requires systematic approaches including: operational efficiency optimization that generates internal cash flow, strategic partnership development that provides external funding, focused resource allocation that maximizes constraint impact, and systematic capability building that enables competitive advantage creation through efficient capital utilization.

Knowledge Constraints in Pharmaceutical Innovation Knowledge constraints emerge when pharmaceutical companies lack scientific expertise, regulatory understanding, or competitive intelligence necessary for breakthrough innovation and market leadership. Knowledge limitations create systematic barriers to pharmaceutical advancement because they prevent recognizing opportunities, developing capabilities, and implementing strategies that could generate competitive advantages.

Knowledge constraint symptoms include: innovation pipeline limitations, regulatory approval delays, competitive positioning weakness, market opportunity misrecognition, and strategic decision-making deficiencies that limit pharmaceutical advancement and competitive excellence.

Knowledge constraint resolution strategies include: systematic expertise development through talent acquisition and training, external partnership establishment that provides complementary knowledge, systematic learning programs that build organizational capabilities, and competitive intelligence development that enables strategic positioning and market advancement.

Scale Constraints in Pharmaceutical Competition Scale constraints limit pharmaceutical companies through insufficient size for competitive positioning, regulatory influence, or market access that prevents achieving optimal performance against larger competitors. Scale limitations create systematic disadvantages because pharmaceutical markets often reward size through economies of scale, regulatory relationships, and market positioning that smaller companies cannot replicate easily.

Scale constraint manifestations include: competitive positioning weakness, regulatory influence limitations, market access restrictions, operational efficiency gaps, and strategic option constraints that prevent optimal pharmaceutical performance and competitive advancement.

Scale constraint resolution approaches include: strategic focus development that optimizes competitive positioning, operational excellence that maximizes efficiency advantages, partnership strategies that provide scale benefits, and systematic capability building that creates competitive advantages independent of absolute size limitations.

Innovation Constraints in Pharmaceutical Development Innovation constraints emerge when pharmaceutical companies cannot develop breakthrough technologies, identify novel therapeutic opportunities, or implement systematic innovation processes that enable competitive differentiation and market leadership. Innovation limitations create fundamental barriers to pharmaceutical advancement because they prevent participating in industry evolution and competitive transformation.

Innovation constraint indicators include: pipeline stagnation, competitive disadvantage acceleration, market positioning deterioration, technological obsolescence, and strategic option limitation that prevent pharmaceutical advancement and competitive excellence.

Innovation constraint resolution requires: systematic innovation capability development, breakthrough technology investment, external collaboration establishment, and organizational culture transformation that enables innovation excellence and competitive advantage creation through systematic innovation advancement.

Legacy Constraints in Pharmaceutical Transformation Legacy constraints develop when pharmaceutical companies become limited by previous success approaches, organizational structures, or competitive strategies that prevent adaptation to industry evolution and transformation requirements. Legacy limitations create systematic barriers because they prevent organizational change necessary for continued competitive advantage and market leadership.

Legacy constraint symptoms include: organizational resistance to change, strategic approach obsolescence, competitive positioning deterioration, market opportunity misrecognition, and transformation capability limitations that prevent pharmaceutical advancement and competitive excellence.

Legacy constraint resolution strategies include: systematic organizational development, strategic approach evolution, competitive positioning advancement, and transformation capability building that enable continued pharmaceutical excellence and competitive advantage preservation through systematic change management.

Constraint Identification Methodologies

Systematic Constraint Analysis Pharmaceutical constraint identification requires systematic analysis that can distinguish between symptoms and root causes while identifying bottlenecks that create the greatest performance limitations. Effective constraint analysis involves comprehensive assessment across operational, strategic, and competitive dimensions that pharmaceutical companies experience.

Constraint identification methodology includes: performance analysis across all pharmaceutical functions, bottleneck identification through systematic evaluation, root cause analysis that distinguishes symptoms from fundamental limitations, and constraint prioritization that focuses resolution efforts on limitations creating greatest performance impact.

Sequential Constraint Recognition Pharmaceutical constraints typically emerge sequentially rather than simultaneously, requiring systematic recognition that constraint resolution will reveal subsequent limitations demanding continued attention and resolution effort. Sequential constraint management enables continued pharmaceutical advancement through systematic limitation elimination.

Sequential constraint management involves: primary constraint identification and resolution, secondary constraint recognition and preparation, systematic constraint sequence planning, and continued constraint resolution that enables sustained pharmaceutical advancement and competitive excellence.

Constraint Resolution Frameworks

Systematic Constraint Resolution Pharmaceutical constraint resolution requires systematic approaches that address root causes rather than symptoms while building capabilities that prevent constraint recurrence and enable continued competitive advancement. Effective resolution involves understanding constraint interactions and developing comprehensive solutions.

Constraint resolution methodology includes: root cause identification and analysis, systematic solution development that addresses fundamental limitations, capability building that prevents constraint recurrence, and continued monitoring that ensures sustained constraint resolution and pharmaceutical advancement.

Competitive Advantage Creation Through Constraint Resolution Pharmaceutical constraint resolution should create competitive advantages rather than just eliminating limitations, because systematic constraint resolution can build capabilities that provide sustained competitive positioning and market leadership opportunities.

Competitive advantage creation involves: constraint resolution that builds superior capabilities, systematic advantage development through limitation elimination, competitive positioning enhancement through constraint resolution, and sustained advantage preservation through continued constraint management and capability advancement.

The Theory of Constraints application to pharmaceutical development demonstrates that systematic constraint identification and resolution can create competitive advantages while enabling sustained pharmaceutical advancement through limitation elimination and capability building that exceeds traditional optimization approaches.

Appendix B

Regulatory Pathway Guide

The regulatory pathway evolution at Malhotra Pharmaceuticals demonstrates how systematic regulatory excellence can transform from compliance burden to competitive advantage while enabling global market access through sophisticated understanding of diverse regulatory frameworks. Regulatory strategy development requires comprehensive knowledge of agency requirements, approval pathways, and compliance optimization that can accelerate market entry while ensuring patient safety and therapeutic efficacy across multiple jurisdictions simultaneously.

Generic Drug Regulatory Pathways

Abbreviated New Drug Application (ANDA) Process - FDA

Pre-Submission Strategy Development ANDA pathway requires systematic preparation including reference listed drug analysis, bioequivalence study design, and manufacturing process development that demonstrates pharmaceutical equivalence to innovator products. Successful ANDA submission demands comprehensive understanding of FDA requirements, comparative dissolution studies, and quality specifications that ensure therapeutic interchangeability.

Key ANDA Requirements:

- Bioequivalence studies demonstrating 90% confidence intervals within 80-125% acceptance criteria
- Pharmaceutical equivalence through identical active ingredient, dosage form, and strength
- Manufacturing site inspection and compliance with current Good Manufacturing Practices
- Labeling consistency with reference listed drug approved prescribing information

- Patent certification addressing intellectual property considerations and market exclusivity

ANDA Submission Components:

- Comprehensive quality data including specifications, analytical methods, and stability studies
- Bioequivalence study reports with statistical analysis and clinical data
- Manufacturing information including batch records, process validation, and facility details
- Environmental assessment for manufacturing processes and pharmaceutical disposal
- Risk evaluation and mitigation strategies if required for safety considerations

Timeline and Approval Process:

- Standard ANDA review: 10 months from submission to approval action
- Priority review consideration: 8 months for competitive generic therapies
- Complete response letter resolution: Additional 6 months for deficiency correction
- First generic exclusivity: 180 days market exclusivity for paragraph IV certification

European Medicines Agency (EMA) Generic Pathway

Marketing Authorization Application (MAA) for Generics EMA generic pathway requires centralized procedure for pan-European approval or national procedures for individual member state authorization. Centralized generic applications provide access to all EU member states through single regulatory submission while maintaining consistent quality standards and therapeutic equivalence requirements.

EMA Generic Requirements:

- Bioequivalence studies following EMA guidelines with appropriate study population
- Quality dossier demonstrating pharmaceutical equivalence and manufacturing compliance

- Reference medicinal product identification and comparative quality assessment
- Environmental risk assessment for pharmaceutical manufacturing and disposal
- Pharmacovigilance system compliance for adverse event monitoring and reporting

Regulatory Submission Process:

- Scientific advice consultations for complex generic development guidance
- Marketing authorization application with comprehensive quality and bioequivalence data
- Committee for Medicinal Products for Human Use (CHMP) scientific evaluation
- European Commission decision and national implementation procedures
- Post-authorization commitments including periodic safety update reports

Health Canada Generic Drug Pathway

Abbreviated New Drug Submission (ANDS) Health Canada requires comprehensive generic drug evaluation including bioequivalence demonstration, quality assessment, and manufacturing compliance that ensures therapeutic interchangeability with Canadian reference product while meeting safety and efficacy standards.

ANDS Submission Requirements:

- Comparative bioavailability studies with appropriate statistical analysis and clinical data
- Chemistry and manufacturing documentation including quality specifications and analytical methods
- Canadian reference product identification and comparative dissolution studies
- Manufacturing site compliance with Good Manufacturing Practices and inspection readiness
- Labeling compliance with Canadian regulatory requirements and safety information

New Drug Application (NDA) Pathways for Innovation

FDA New Drug Application Process

Investigational New Drug (IND) Application IND submission enables clinical investigation initiation while providing FDA oversight of human subject safety and protocol compliance. Successful IND requires comprehensive preclinical data, clinical protocol development, and investigator qualifications that demonstrate readiness for human clinical trials.

IND Application Components:

- Preclinical pharmacology and toxicology studies demonstrating safety profile
- Chemistry, manufacturing, and controls information including drug substance and product specifications
- Clinical protocol and investigator information with institutional review board approval
- Investigator's brochure containing comprehensive preclinical and clinical information
- Annual IND reports and safety updates throughout clinical development period

Phase Development Strategy:

- Phase I studies: Initial human safety evaluation with dose escalation and pharmacokinetic assessment
- Phase II studies: Efficacy evaluation and dose optimization in target patient population
- Phase III studies: Confirmatory efficacy and safety assessment in large patient populations
- Rolling submission strategy: Submit NDA sections as clinical development progresses

New Drug Application Submission NDA represents comprehensive regulatory submission including clinical efficacy data, safety assessment, manufacturing information, and proposed labeling that demonstrates drug safety and effectiveness for intended therapeutic indication.

NDA Submission Requirements:

- Clinical study reports demonstrating efficacy and safety in target patient population
- Integrated summary of efficacy and integrated summary of safety across clinical development
- Chemistry, manufacturing, and controls information with commercial manufacturing validation
- Proposed prescribing information including indications, dosage, and safety warnings
- Risk evaluation and mitigation strategy if required for safety risk management

FDA Review Process:

- Standard review timeline: 10 months for complete application evaluation
- Priority review: 6 months for significant therapeutic advancement evaluation
- Advisory committee meeting: External expert consultation for complex therapeutic evaluation
- Complete response letter: FDA communication of approval requirements or application deficiencies
- Post-marketing requirements: Additional studies or safety monitoring as approval conditions

Breakthrough Therapy Designation and Accelerated Approval

Breakthrough Therapy Pathway Breakthrough therapy designation provides expedited development and review for drugs addressing unmet medical needs with substantial therapeutic advancement over existing treatments. Breakthrough designation enables intensive FDA guidance and accelerated approval consideration.

Breakthrough Therapy Criteria:

- Treatment of serious or life-threatening disease or condition
- Preliminary clinical evidence demonstrating substantial improvement over existing therapy
- Drug development program addressing significant unmet medical need

- Potential for significant therapeutic advancement in target patient population

Breakthrough Therapy Benefits:

- Enhanced FDA communication including meetings and written guidance
- Priority review with 6-month evaluation timeline
- Rolling submission acceptance for expedited regulatory evaluation
- Surrogate endpoint consideration for accelerated approval pathway

Accelerated Approval Pathway Accelerated approval enables market authorization based on surrogate endpoints reasonably likely to predict clinical benefit while requiring post-marketing confirmatory studies to verify therapeutic advantage.

Accelerated Approval Requirements:

- Surrogate endpoint data demonstrating reasonable likelihood of clinical benefit
- Significant unmet medical need in serious or life-threatening condition
- Post-marketing confirmatory study commitment to verify clinical benefit
- Risk evaluation and mitigation strategy for appropriate drug utilization

European Medicines Agency Innovation Pathways

PRIME (PRIority MEdicines) Scheme PRIME provides enhanced regulatory support for medicines addressing unmet medical needs through early dialogue and accelerated assessment that facilitates drug development and regulatory approval.

PRIME Eligibility Criteria:

- Treatment of condition with significant unmet medical need
- Medicine has potential for significant therapeutic innovation
- Preliminary clinical data supporting therapeutic advancement potential
- Development program addressing serious medical condition with limited treatment options

PRIME Benefits:

- Enhanced regulatory guidance through dedicated contact points and scientific advice

- Accelerated assessment with 150-day evaluation timeline
- Protocol assistance for clinical development optimization
- Conditional marketing authorization consideration for early market access

Conditional Marketing Authorization Conditional authorization provides early market access for medicines addressing unmet medical needs while requiring additional data generation to confirm positive benefit-risk balance.

International Regulatory Harmonization

International Council for Harmonisation (ICH) Guidelines ICH provides harmonized regulatory guidance for pharmaceutical development including Good Clinical Practice, quality specifications, and safety evaluation that facilitates global drug development and regulatory submission.

Key ICH Guidelines:

- ICH E6: Good Clinical Practice for clinical trial conduct and data integrity
- ICH Q8: Pharmaceutical Development for systematic product development
- ICH M4: Common Technical Document for global regulatory submission format
- ICH E2E: Pharmacovigilance Planning for safety monitoring and risk management

Global Regulatory Strategy Development International pharmaceutical development requires coordinated regulatory strategy that optimizes approval timelines while meeting diverse agency requirements and cultural considerations across multiple jurisdictions.

Regulatory Strategy Components:

- Reference agency selection for primary regulatory pathway and global coordination
- Regional adaptation strategy for local regulatory requirements and cultural considerations
- Filing sequence optimization for competitive market entry and resource utilization

- Regulatory intelligence for competitive landscape and agency precedent analysis

Specialized Regulatory Pathways

Orphan Drug Designation Orphan drug pathway provides development incentives and market exclusivity for rare disease treatments affecting limited patient populations while addressing significant unmet medical needs.

Orphan Drug Benefits:

- Seven-year market exclusivity from approval date
- Tax credits for clinical development costs
- Expedited regulatory review and FDA guidance
- Waiver of prescription drug user fees

Pediatric Drug Development Pediatric investigation plans require systematic evaluation of drug safety and efficacy in children while providing market exclusivity extensions for completing pediatric development requirements.

Biosimilar Regulatory Pathways Biosimilar approval requires demonstrating similarity to reference biological product through analytical characterization, pharmacokinetic studies, and clinical evaluation that confirms biosimilarity.

Quality by Design (QbD) Implementation QbD approach enables systematic pharmaceutical development through design space establishment and control strategy development that provides manufacturing flexibility while ensuring product quality.

Regulatory Excellence Best Practices

Proactive Regulatory Strategy Successful regulatory strategy requires early agency engagement, systematic planning, and continuous communication that builds regulatory confidence while optimizing approval probability and timeline.

Documentation Excellence Regulatory submission quality determines review efficiency and approval success through comprehensive data presentation, clear scientific rationale, and regulatory compliance demonstration.

Global Regulatory Coordination International pharmaceutical success requires systematic regulatory coordination that optimizes global development while meeting diverse agency requirements and market access considerations.

The regulatory pathway guide demonstrates that systematic regulatory excellence can create competitive advantages while enabling global market access through sophisticated understanding of diverse regulatory frameworks and strategic optimization of approval processes across multiple jurisdictions simultaneously.

Appendix C

Glossary of Pharmaceutical Terms

A

Active Pharmaceutical Ingredient (API) The biologically active component of a pharmaceutical product responsible for therapeutic effect. APIs undergo extensive chemical synthesis, purification, and quality control to ensure pharmaceutical-grade specifications that meet regulatory requirements for safety, efficacy, and quality standards.

Abbreviated New Drug Application (ANDA) FDA regulatory submission pathway for generic drug approval that demonstrates bioequivalence to reference listed drugs without requiring independent clinical efficacy studies. ANDA approval enables generic pharmaceutical marketing with therapeutic interchangeability claims.

Artificial Intelligence (AI) in Drug Discovery Computational approaches utilizing machine learning algorithms and data analytics to accelerate pharmaceutical development through molecular optimization, target identification, and clinical trial design that enhance R&D productivity and success rates.

B

Bioequivalence Demonstration that generic pharmaceutical products deliver equivalent therapeutic effect compared to reference drugs through pharmacokinetic studies showing similar rate and extent of absorption. Bioequivalence enables regulatory approval for generic drug substitution.

Biosimilar Biological therapeutic product demonstrating similarity to FDA-approved reference biological product through analytical characterization, pharmacokinetic evaluation, and clinical assessment that confirms biosimilarity for regulatory approval and market access.

Biotechnology Application of biological systems and living organisms for pharmaceutical development including protein therapeutics, monoclonal antibodies, gene therapy, and cell therapy that enable breakthrough treatment approaches for complex diseases.

Breakthrough Therapy Designation FDA expedited development pathway for drugs addressing unmet medical needs with substantial therapeutic advancement over existing treatments. Breakthrough designation provides enhanced regulatory guidance and accelerated approval consideration.

C

Chemistry, Manufacturing, and Controls (CMC) Comprehensive pharmaceutical documentation including drug substance specifications, manufacturing processes, quality control procedures, and stability data that demonstrate consistent product quality and regulatory compliance.

Clinical Trial Phases Systematic drug development stages including Phase I safety evaluation, Phase II efficacy assessment, and Phase III confirmatory studies that provide regulatory evidence for marketing authorization and therapeutic efficacy claims.

Complete Response Letter (CRL) FDA communication describing regulatory application deficiencies and requirements for approval consideration. CRL provides specific guidance for addressing regulatory concerns and resubmission strategies.

Current Good Manufacturing Practices (cGMP) FDA quality regulations governing pharmaceutical manufacturing including facility design, equipment qualification, process validation, and quality control that ensure consistent product quality and patient safety.

D

Drug Discovery Systematic process of identifying and developing novel therapeutic compounds through target identification, molecular design, optimization, and preclinical evaluation that enables innovative pharmaceutical development and competitive advantages.

Drug Product Finished pharmaceutical formulation containing active pharmaceutical ingredient plus excipients in specific dosage form designed for patient administration. Drug products undergo comprehensive quality testing and regulatory evaluation.

E

European Medicines Agency (EMA) European regulatory authority responsible for pharmaceutical evaluation and approval across European Union member states through centralized and national procedures that ensure therapeutic safety and efficacy.

Excipients Inactive pharmaceutical ingredients including binders, fillers, disintegrants, and coatings that enable drug product formulation while ensuring stability, bioavailability, and manufacturing processability without therapeutic activity.

F

First-in-Human (FIH) Studies Initial clinical trials evaluating novel therapeutic compounds in human subjects to assess safety, tolerability, and pharmacokinetic properties that enable continued clinical development and regulatory advancement.

Food and Drug Administration (FDA) United States regulatory agency responsible for pharmaceutical approval, safety monitoring, and market oversight that ensures therapeutic products meet safety and efficacy standards for patient protection.

G

Generic Drug Pharmaceutical product containing identical active ingredient, dosage form, strength, and route of administration as brand-name reference drug with demonstrated bioequivalence that enables therapeutic substitution and cost savings.

Good Clinical Practice (GCP) International quality standards for clinical trial design, conduct, monitoring, and reporting that ensure patient safety, data integrity, and regulatory compliance during pharmaceutical development.

H

Health Canada Canadian regulatory authority responsible for pharmaceutical evaluation, approval, and post-market surveillance that ensures therapeutic safety and efficacy for Canadian patients through comprehensive regulatory oversight.

I

Investigational New Drug (IND) FDA regulatory submission enabling clinical investigation of experimental pharmaceutical compounds in human subjects while providing regulatory oversight and safety monitoring during clinical development.

Intellectual Property (IP) Legal protection for pharmaceutical innovations including patents for molecular composition, manufacturing processes, therapeutic applications, and formulation technologies that create competitive advantages and market exclusivity.

L

Life Cycle Management Strategic approach to optimizing pharmaceutical product value through formulation improvements, indication expansion, market development, and competitive positioning that extends commercial success and market leadership.

M

Marketing Authorization Application (MAA) European regulatory submission for pharmaceutical approval through EMA centralized procedure or national pathways that demonstrate therapeutic safety and efficacy for market authorization across EU member states.

Monoclonal Antibody (mAb) Engineered protein therapeutic that binds specific biological targets with high specificity and affinity to modulate disease processes. Monoclonal antibodies represent major biotechnology advancement enabling precision medicine approaches.

N

New Drug Application (NDA) Comprehensive FDA regulatory submission including clinical efficacy data, safety assessment, manufacturing information, and proposed labeling that demonstrates drug safety and effectiveness for therapeutic indication approval.

O

Orphan Drug Pharmaceutical product treating rare diseases affecting fewer than 200,000 patients in United States. Orphan designation provides development incentives, market exclusivity, and regulatory support for addressing unmet medical needs.

P

Pharmacovigilance Systematic monitoring and evaluation of adverse drug reactions and medication safety throughout pharmaceutical product lifecycle to ensure patient safety and benefit-risk optimization through post-market surveillance.

Pharmacokinetics (PK) Study of drug absorption, distribution, metabolism, and elimination in human body that determines dosing regimens, therapeutic efficacy, and safety profiles for optimal pharmaceutical utilization and patient outcomes.

Precision Medicine Therapeutic approach tailoring medical treatment to individual patient characteristics including genetic profile, biomarker expression, and disease characteristics that optimize therapeutic outcomes and minimize adverse effects.

Priority Review FDA expedited evaluation pathway reducing standard review timeline from 10 months to 6 months for pharmaceutical applications addressing significant therapeutic advancement or unmet medical need.

Q

Quality by Design (QbD) Systematic pharmaceutical development approach establishing design space and control strategies based on scientific understanding that ensures product quality while providing manufacturing flexibility and regulatory efficiency.

R

Reference Listed Drug (RLD) FDA-approved brand-name pharmaceutical product serving as comparison standard for generic drug development and bioequivalence evaluation. RLD selection determines regulatory requirements for generic approval.

Regulatory Affairs Pharmaceutical function responsible for regulatory strategy development, submission preparation, agency communication, and compliance management that enables market authorization and commercial success through regulatory expertise.

S

Specialized Pharmaceutical Therapeutic products addressing complex medical conditions with limited treatment options that require sophisticated patient management, specialized distribution, and premium pricing through clinical value demonstration.

Supply Chain Management Systematic coordination of pharmaceutical manufacturing, distribution, and logistics including raw material procurement, production planning, inventory optimization, and delivery coordination that ensures product availability and cost efficiency.

T

Target Product Profile (TPP) Comprehensive description of desired pharmaceutical product characteristics including therapeutic indication, efficacy endpoints, safety profile, and commercial positioning that guides development strategy and regulatory planning.

Technology Transfer Systematic process of transferring pharmaceutical manufacturing processes, analytical methods, and quality control procedures between development and commercial facilities while maintaining product quality and regulatory compliance.

Therapeutic Area Medical specialty or disease category including cardiovascular, diabetes, oncology, and neurology that defines pharmaceutical market segments and enables specialized expertise development for competitive positioning.

U

United States Pharmacopeia (USP) Organization establishing pharmaceutical quality standards including monographs, analytical methods, and specifications that ensure drug quality, purity, and identity for regulatory compliance and patient safety.

V

Validation Systematic process of establishing documented evidence that pharmaceutical processes, analytical methods, and manufacturing systems consistently produce results meeting predetermined specifications and quality standards.

W

World Health Organization (WHO) International organization providing pharmaceutical guidance including Good Manufacturing Practices, prequalification programs, and quality standards that facilitate global market access and regulatory harmonization.

Pharmaceutical Industry Acronyms and Abbreviations

ADME - Absorption, Distribution, Metabolism, Excretion

AE - Adverse Event

API - Active Pharmaceutical Ingredient

BLA - Biologics License Application

CMC - Chemistry, Manufacturing, and Controls

CRO - Contract Research Organization

DMF - Drug Master File

EMA - European Medicines Agency

FDA - Food and Drug Administration

GCP - Good Clinical Practice

GLP - Good Laboratory Practice

GMP - Good Manufacturing Practice

ICH - International Council for Harmonisation

IND - Investigational New Drug

MAA - Marketing Authorization Application

NDA - New Drug Application

OTC - Over-the-Counter

PAI - Pre-Approval Inspection

PK/PD - Pharmacokinetics/Pharmacodynamics

QbD - Quality by Design

SAE - Serious Adverse Event

SOP - Standard Operating Procedure

USP - United States Pharmacopeia

Pharmaceutical Development Timeline Terminology

Discovery Phase - 2-5 years: Target identification and lead compound optimization

Preclinical Development - 1-3 years: Safety and efficacy evaluation in laboratory studies

Clinical Development: 5 - 10 years (Human studies demonstrating safety and efficacy)

Regulatory Review: 6 - 18 months (Agency Evaluation and approval decision)

Commercial Launch - Ongoing: Market introduction and lifecycle management

Quality Control and Assurance Terms

Analytical Method Validation - Systematic evaluation of analytical procedures for accuracy, precision, and reliability

Batch Record - Documentation of manufacturing process execution and quality control testing

Certificate of Analysis - Summary of quality control testing results for pharmaceutical batch release

Deviation Investigation - Systematic evaluation of manufacturing or quality control non-conformances

Stability Studies - Long-term evaluation of pharmaceutical product quality under defined storage conditions

Bibliography

Books and Monographs

Christensen, Clayton M. The Innovator's Dilemma: When New Technologies Cause Great Firms to Fail. Boston: Harvard Business Review Press, 2016.

Collins, Jim. Built to Last: Successful Habits of Visionary Companies. New York: HarperBusiness, 2004.

Drucker, Peter F. Innovation and Entrepreneurship: Practice and Principles. New York: Harper & Row, 1985.

Goldratt, Eliyahu M. The Goal: A Process of Ongoing Improvement. Great Barrington: North River Press, 2014.

Grove, Andrew S. Only the Paranoid Survive: How to Exploit the Crisis Points That Challenge Every Company. New York: Currency, 1999.

Kaplan, Robert S., and David P. Norton. The Balanced Scorecard: Translating Strategy into Action. Boston: Harvard Business Review Press, 1996.

Kim, W. Chan, and Renée Mauborgne. Blue Ocean Strategy: How to Create Uncontested Market Space and Make Competition Irrelevant. Boston: Harvard Business Review Press, 2015.

Moore, Geoffrey A. Crossing the Chasm: Marketing and Selling Disruptive Products to Mainstream Customers. New York: HarperBusiness, 2014.

Porter, Michael E. Competitive Strategy: Techniques for Analyzing Industries and Competitors. New York: Free Press, 1980.

Ries, Eric. The Lean Startup: How Today's Entrepreneurs Use Continuous Innovation to Create Radically Successful Businesses. New York: Crown Business, 2011.

Industry Reports and Market Analysis

Evaluate Pharma. *World Preview 2024, Outlook to 2030.* London: Evaluate Ltd., 2024.

EY Global Life Sciences. *Biotechnology Report 2024: Beyond Borders.* Ernst & Young Global Limited, 2024.

IQVIA Institute. *Global Medicine Spending and Usage Trends: Outlook to 2027.* IQVIA Holdings Inc., 2023.

McKinsey & Company. *The Bio Revolution: Innovations Transforming Economies, Societies, and Our Lives.* McKinsey Global Institute, 2020.

PwC. *Pharma 2030: From Evolution to Revolution.* PricewaterhouseCoopers, 2023.

Academic Journal Articles

Chatterjee, Samir, and Asher Hasan. "A Strategic Framework for Artificial Intelligence in Drug Discovery." *Nature Reviews Drug Discovery* 21, no. 3 (2022): 173-188.

Chen, Lisa, et al. "Computational Drug Discovery Platforms: Accelerating Pharmaceutical Innovation Through AI Integration." *Journal of Medicinal Chemistry* 65, no. 12 (2022): 8234-8251.

DiMasi, Joseph A., Henry G. Grabowski, and Ronald W. Hansen. "Innovation in the Pharmaceutical Industry: New Estimates of R&D Costs." *Journal of Health Economics* 47 (2016): 20-33.

Garnier, Jean-Pierre. "Rebuilding the R&D Engine in Big Pharma." *Harvard Business Review* 86, no. 5 (2008): 68-76.

Kumar, Rajesh, and Priya Sharma. "Regulatory Excellence as Competitive Advantage in Emerging Market Pharmaceuticals." *Regulatory Affairs Professionals Society Journal* 28, no. 4 (2023): 312-327.

Scannell, Jack W., et al. "Diagnosing the Decline in Pharmaceutical R&D Efficiency." *Nature Reviews Drug Discovery* 11, no. 3 (2012): 191-200.

Government and Regulatory Publications

Food and Drug Administration. Guidance for Industry: Generic Drug Development and Submission Requirements. Silver Spring: FDA, 2023.

European Medicines Agency. Guideline on Bioequivalence Studies for Generic Medicinal Products. London: EMA, 2023.

Health Canada. Guidance Document: Generic Drug Development Standards. Ottawa: Health Canada, 2022.

Ministry of Health and Family Welfare, Government of India. Pharmaceutical Policy 2023: Strategic Framework for Industry Development. New Delhi: MoHFW, 2023.

World Health Organization. Good Manufacturing Practices for Pharmaceutical Products: Main Principles. Geneva: WHO, 2023.

Industry Conference Proceedings and White Papers

Biotechnology Industry Organization. *Proceedings of the World Biotechnology Congress 2024.* Washington, DC: BIO, 2024.

Drug Information Association. *Global Regulatory Science Strategy Conference Proceedings 2024.* Fort Washington: DIA, 2024.

International Society for Pharmaceutical Engineering. *Pharmaceutical Manufacturing Excellence Summit 2024: Conference Proceedings.* Tampa: ISPE, 2024.

Pharmaceutical Research and Manufacturers of America. *Biopharmaceutical Innovation and Investment Report 2024.* Washington, DC: PhRMA, 2024.

Online Resources and Databases

ClinicalTrials.gov. "Clinical Studies Database." National Library of Medicine. Accessed January 2025. https://clinicaltrials.gov

FDA Orange Book: Approved Drug Products with Therapeutic Equivalence Evaluations. Food and Drug Administration. Accessed January 2025. https://www.fda.gov/drugs/drug-approvals-and-databases/approved-drug-products-therapeutic-equivalence-evaluations-orange-book

GlobalData Pharmaceutical Intelligence Database. "Competitive Landscape Analysis: Generic and Biosimilar Markets 2020-2025." Accessed January 2025.

PharmaCompass Global Pharmaceutical Database. "API and Formulation Manufacturing Intelligence." Accessed January 2025.

Pharmaceutical Industry Analysis Reports

Boston Consulting Group. The Biopharma Innovation Machine: How Small and Mid-Size Companies Are Driving Growth. BCG, 2023.

Deloitte Centre for Health Solutions. Measuring the Return from Pharmaceutical Innovation 2024. Deloitte Insights, 2024.

KPMG. Pharmaceutical Manufacturing: Operational Excellence in the New Era. KPMG International, 2023.

L.E.K. Consulting. Global Pharmaceutical Market Outlook: Trends Shaping the Industry to 2030. L.E.K. Consulting, 2024.

Biography and Leadership Literature

Branson, Richard. Losing My Virginity: How I've Survived, Had Fun, and Made a Fortune Doing Business My Way. New York: Crown Business, 2011.

Buffett, Warren E., and Lawrence A. Cunningham. The Essays of Warren Buffett: Lessons for Corporate America. Durham: Carolina Academic Press, 2015.

Gates, Bill. Business @ the Speed of Thought: Succeeding in the Digital Economy. New York: Warner Books, 2009.

Jobs, Steve, and Walter Isaacson. Steve Jobs. New York: Simon & Schuster, 2011.

Welch, Jack, and Suzy Welch. Winning. New York: HarperBusiness, 2005.

Economic and Strategic Management References

Ghemawat, Pankaj. *Strategy and the Business Landscape.* Boston: Pearson, 2009.

Hamel, Gary, and C.K. Prahalad. *Competing for the Future.* Boston: Harvard Business School Press, 1994.

Henderson, Bruce D. *Henderson on Corporate Strategy.* Cambridge: Abt Books, 1979.

Mintzberg, Henry. *The Rise and Fall of Strategic Planning.* New York: Free Press, 1994.

Rumelt, Richard P. *Good Strategy Bad Strategy: The Difference and Why It Matters.* New York: Crown Business, 2011.

Technical and Scientific References

Kola, Ismail, and John Landis. "Can the Pharmaceutical Industry Reduce Attrition Rates?" *Nature Reviews Drug Discovery* 3, no. 8 (2004): 711-716.

Lipinski, Christopher A. "Lead- and Drug-like Compounds: The Rule-of-Five Revolution." *Drug Discovery Today: Technologies* 1, no. 4 (2004): 337-341.

Munos, Bernard. "Lessons from 60 Years of Pharmaceutical Innovation." *Nature Reviews Drug Discovery* 8, no. 12 (2009): 959-968.

Paul, Steven M., et al. "How to Improve R&D Productivity: The Pharmaceutical Industry's Grand Challenge." *Nature Reviews Drug Discovery* 9, no. 3 (2010): 203-214.

Acknowledgments

The author wishes to acknowledge the invaluable contributions of colleagues, partners, regulatory authorities, and industry experts who provided insights, data, and perspectives that made this comprehensive analysis possible. Special recognition goes to the dedicated team members at Malhotra Pharmaceuticals whose commitment to excellence and innovation created the foundation for this pharmaceutical transformation story.

Note on Sources

This bibliography represents a comprehensive compilation of sources spanning thirty years of pharmaceutical industry analysis, company documentation, and strategic business literature. While some sources reflect actual industry publications and established academic works, others represent the documented experiences and strategic frameworks developed throughout the pharmaceutical transformation journey described in this book.

About the Author

Subba Rao Chaganti

He has a master's in business administration and over fifty-two years of experience in

Pharmaceutical marketing. His experience encompasses all facets of the industry, from sales and sales management to product management and overseeing overall marketing activities. He has experience in both domestic and international marketing, as well as within the Indian and multinational sectors.

He also taught a course on Advertising and Brand Management as an adjunct professor at Gitam Institute of Foreign Trade (now part of Gitam University) in Visakhapatnam for a few years and a course on Marketing as a visiting faculty member at Jawaharlal Nehru Technological University (JNTU) in Hyderabad.

He lives in Farmington, Connecticut, USA, and can be reached at: subbarao.chaganti@gmail.com.

Here is a list of his publications:

1. Pharmaceutical Marketing in India: Concepts, Cases, Strategy
2. Game Plans for Post-GATT Era: Action Agenda of the Indian Pharmaceutical Industry
3. Compete or Forfeit: Strategies for Sustainable Competitive Advantage in the Pharma Product Patents Era
4. Pharmaceutical Marketing in India for Today and Tomorrow - 25th Anniversary Edition
5. Bullseyes and Blunders: Lessons from 100 Cases in Pharma Marketing
6. Digital Pharma Marketing Playbook: Winning With the New Rules of Engagement
7. Cracking the Generics Code: Your Single-Source Success Manual for Winning in Multi-Source Product Markets
8. Reimagine Pharma Marketing: Make It Future-Proof!
9. Brand Positioning in Pharma

10. Transactional to Transformational Marketing in Pharma: The Science of Why and The Art of How
11. A to Z of Pharmaceutical Marketing: World's First and Only Encyclopedia in Two Volumes
12. The Synergy of Minds: Human+AI Orchestrating the Pharma Marketing Revolution
13. Design Thinking for Pharma
14. The Pharma Product Manager: Navigating the Digital Frontier
15. Sentiment Analysis for Pharma Marketers
16. Whispering to AI: Prompt Engineering for Pharma Brand Managers
17. Storytelling in Pharma Marketing
18. Beyond the Molecule: The Art and Science of Metaphors That Matter
19. The Voices Within: Your Body Speaks When Your Organs Tell Their Own Stories
20. Pharma Archetypes: The Science of Meaningful Healthcare Marketing
21. Human Futures: Navigating the AI Revolution with Purpose and Agency

www.ingramcontent.com/pod-product-compliance
Lightning Source LLC
Chambersburg PA
CBHW071402230926
51846CB00001B/4
* 9 7 8 9 3 4 7 3 1 1 4 9 9 *